Acclaim for Ann Hulbert's

RAISING AMERICA

"A rich social history. . . . Hulbert brings a huge amount of social scientific, historical, cultural, and biographical detail to the subject, which makes for a fascinating read. . . . She also brings some real wisdom to the topic."
—*The Washington Post Book World*

"Thought-provoking. . . . Not merely an account of a 'century of advice,' but also a history of the ways in which our ideas about families, women, childhood, and adult responsibility have and have not shifted over the course of a hundred years. . . . Hulbert's achievement is to examine our hopes and fears as they are played out in the lives of our children."
—*Los Angeles Times Book Review*

"Keen and meticulously researched."
—*The New York Review of Books*

"[Hulbert] offers a portrait of a neurotically conflicted nation through its how-to books on children. . . . Well-paced and smartly written, it is also simultaneously respectful and skeptical."
—*Newsday*

"Ann Hulbert's book is that rarest of things—a really intelligent, sophisticated, and knowledgeable book about child rearing."
—Alison Gopnik, coauthor of *The Scientist in the Crib*

"On the surface, her book is a history of twentieth-century child-rearing manuals. Underneath, it is a history of twentieth-century parental anxiety. . . . To every expert in her book Hulbert brings such treatment: nuanced, historical."
—*The New Yorker*

"In her beautifully written and engaging study, Ann Hulbert displays a sense of balance and proportion often lacking in discussions of child rearing. . . . A detailed and masterly history of ideas about parenting."
—*Wilson Quarterly*

ANN HULBERT

RAISING AMERICA

Ann Hulbert is the author of *The Interior Castle: The Art and Life of Jean Stafford*. Her articles and reviews have appeared in many places, including *The New York Times Book Review*, *The New York Review of Books*, and *The New Republic*, where she worked for many years as a senior editor. She graduated from Harvard and spent a year at Cambridge University. She lives with her husband and two children in Washington, D.C.

ALSO BY ANN HULBERT

The Interior Castle: The Art and Life of Jean Stafford

RAISING AMERICA

RAISING AMERICA

Experts, Parents,
and a Century of Advice
About Children

ANN HULBERT

VINTAGE BOOKS

A DIVISION OF RANDOM HOUSE, INC.

NEW YORK

FIRST VINTAGE BOOKS EDITION, APRIL 2004

Copyright © 2003 by Ann Hulbert

All rights reserved under International and Pan-American Copyright Conventions.
Published in the United States by Vintage Books, a division of Random House, Inc.,
New York, and simultaneously in Canada by Random House of Canada Limited,
Toronto. Originally published in hardcover in the United States by Alfred A. Knopf,
a division of Random House, Inc., New York, in 2003.

Vintage and colophon are registered trademarks of Random House, Inc.

Owing to limitations of space, all acknowledgments for permission to reprint
previously published material may be found preceding the index.

The Library of Congress has cataloged the Knopf edition as follows:
Hulbert, Ann.
Raising America: experts, parents, and a century of advice about children /
Ann Hulbert.—1st ed.
p.   cm.
Includes index.
1. Child rearing—United States—History—20th century.
2. Parenting—United States—History—20th century.   I. Title.
HQ769.H825 2003
649'.I'0973—dc21   2002073152

Vintage ISBN: 0-375-70122-2

Book design by Anthea Lingeman

www.vintagebooks.com

Printed in the United States of America

For my children,
and my parents

And, as the saying goes, about this matter of what molds or warps us, if it's not one thing it will be another. At least that was a saying of my elders in those days. Mysterious, uncomforting, unaccusing.

—Alice Munro, "Fathers"

CONTENTS

PREFACE

Like millions of Americans born in the 1950s, I grew up in the long shadow of Dr. Spock. I came of age thinking of him as my generation's ally (though I never carried a "Dr. Spock Delivers Us Again" banner myself). He also seemed to me something of a mystery. Why had he been so popular with mothers, including mine, when I was young, and how had he gotten into so much trouble when I was older? Who were his predecessors, and had they stirred up as much social controversy?

And how had Spock's successors come to be so numerous and contentious? That question joined the list a decade or so later when I became a magazine writer who made American family dilemmas my beat, and then undertook a biography of a fiction writer who made the hidden ordeals of childhood her theme. Less than a decade after that, I became a mother. My own turn had come to confront the flood of child-rearing guides that had by now inundated Spock-marked middle-class parents. The countless popular parenting advisers all saluted the doctor who had told Americans not to be "overawed by what the experts say"—and then, sounding anything but unanimous, went on to tell us just what to do.

A copy of Spock, fatter than my mother's edition, was the one thing I had on hand when my first baby came early. Good Spock student that I was, I dabbled—I didn't delve, or drown—in the many other manuals. And by the time I embarked on *Raising America*, the insecure intensity of the nursery phase was behind me: my second (and last) baby was heading off to kindergarten. Personally and professionally, I was eager to try giving the twentieth century's scientific experts and their books the cool historical scrutiny busy parents rarely have time for.

Whenever my topic came up—at dinner parties and school gatherings, on Little League and soccer sidelines—quirky child-rearing stories came out: about a Skinner-box babyhood, a Mozart-steeped toddler, a toilet-training nightmare (I heard all about it at an elegant State Department banquet), a son's hard-driving girlfriend raised by hippies. And along with the stories came questions from opposite directions. First, had exposing myself to a whole century of advice made me a perfect parent? Second, I was asked (often by the same person) for a more cynical, impersonal assessment: Had a hundred years of child-rearing advice amounted to psychological hokum, male dictums issued in the name of scientific certainty, unnerving mothers who had turned to experts in search of security?

Naturally, I hadn't become a paragon (nobody, I could tell, wanted to hear that I was). And right away I suspected I wasn't on the trail of expert villains, or heroes—or firm science. My first forays beyond the popular advisers' books, into their own lives in the lab and outside it, were enough to suggest that they had stumbled up against their share of contradictions and unintended consequences in their quest to understand children and enlighten parents. What the experts seemed to be offering and mothers eagerly buying (which was not the same as obeying) was indeed something quite different from reassurance. Again and again the advisers' careers and their conflicting counsel reflected American confusions about children's natures and futures, and about mothers' missions, during a disorienting century. Baby boomers assume we're the first to be so obsessed, but I was discovering that for decades the mark of worthy parenthood had been worry.

Dr. Spock once called it a "fascinating and somewhat mysterious phenomenon, this one of the parents of America being this nervous about doing right by their children." The spectacle of experts being so ambitious and contentious about setting parents right has also turned out to be fascinating, and usefully humbling in its way. The irony has not been lost on my children that all the time I've spent probing the experts' lives and lore has sometimes left my own family feeling justifiably impatient. But I'd like to think (and maybe one day they will too) that it's partly thanks to my preoccupation that I've sometimes managed to be uncharacteristically patient. For me, the experts' hidden struggles and escalating expectations and frustrations have served as reminders of how little can ultimately be predicted or controlled, and how often vaunting hopes and acute fears yield surprises.

Two years before he died in 1998, a ninety-three-year-old Dr. Spock heaved a sigh during an interview I had with him over a long lunch. "I don't see that what I've written has made any difference at all," he muttered, sounding like a weary parent. But with a new edition even then in the works, he was not about to let that dampen the curiosity and indefatigable energy that child rearing calls for and, luckily, so often inspires. Leaving the restaurant, his wife, Mary Morgan, told him it was time to rest. "No, Mary, I don't want to take a nap," Dr. Spock whined as he grinned at me. "None of my friends have to take naps."

RAISING AMERICA

Introduction

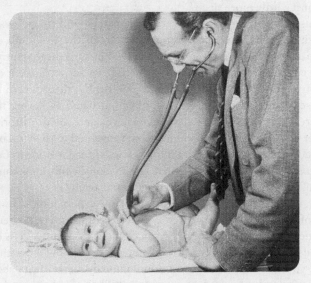

Dr. Spock at work

It is a messy and often impulsive business carried on mostly behind closed doors. We think of it as the source of our deepest happiness and our most intense anxieties. How does our performance measure up? How well, we ask ourselves, do others do it? Do they have any special techniques? Is everyone else as susceptible to seizures of guilt as we are? We want reassurance that our experience is not too far from average, especially in the frustrations, disappointments, and embarrassments we suffer. We also want to feel that our experience, above all in its pleasures, is unique.

Our voyeuristic curiosity, we know, is impossible to satisfy: we can't eavesdrop on the households of others. Instead experts, manuals, magazines, studies, and conferences supply us with ever more informative and normative advice. Public rhetoric is full of exhortations to form deep attachments, to be models of loyal and loving attentiveness—to resist all the corrupting enticements to selfishness and irresponsibility our commercial culture constantly offers. Public rhetoric is also full of warnings about the social, moral, and psychological costs of careless-ness, of casualness. We take the warnings very much to heart, although in private the reality can feel more mundane. There is lots of noise and struggle. There are interruptions, inconveniences, and distractions. Bliss rarely comes as planned. Often what we feel we could use most of all is just a little more sleep.

Raising children has rated very near to sex—and to success—as an American fixation, especially since the start of the twentieth century and particularly among the middle class. "In no other country," one historian noted in the 1950s, "has there been so pervasive a cultural anxiety about the rearing of children." Never has this concern been as intense, as self-conscious, and as publicly debated as during the past hundred years. You don't have to believe (and many historians no longer do) that the idea of childhood was invented in the late sixteenth and seventeenth centuries, as Philippe Ariès argued in 1962 in *Centuries of Childhood*, to be convinced that late in the second millennium the idea of parenthood was reinvented again and again.*

Dr. Benjamin Spock, whose career as an expert took off with the start of the baby boom in 1946, told millions of us and our parents that America had seen "violent changes in child-care teaching." His book—with its reassuring mantra, "Trust yourself. You know more than you think you do"—was the reinvention designed to calm fears about the conflicting scientific wisdom on raising children that by then clamored for attention. The supply of advice was large. Expert prescriptions for parents and descriptions of children had been accumulating ever since the turn of the century, when newly minted psychologists and pediatri-cians had begun founding laboratories and packaging their findings (or, more accurately, their hypotheses) in primers for "modern" mothers.

Over a long life that spanned almost the entire century, Spock dis-covered that his mission was a frustrating (though best-selling) endeavor. Parents were evidently not to be soothed, his fellow experts were not to be stopped. Quite the contrary. The mother's helper who aimed to defuse the debate over "Strictness or Permissiveness?"—as Spock titled a section of *Baby and Child Care*—stirred up more conflict on that core child-rearing subject than any expert before him. Spurred on by the spectacular sales of his book, an already burgeoning advice market grew even more rapidly in the postwar era. "Advice on how to

*Notes appear on pages 371–434, keyed to appropriate words.

be a 'good' parent," a child psychologist sighed in the early 1950s, had become "a big commodity indeed," peddled to mothers and fathers at every opportunity—"in endless books and pamphlets, in every newspaper and magazine . . . dinned into their ears through radio programs, movies and mass advertising." By the time Spock began revising his manual in the mid-1950s, the adviser who had set out to make parental confidence his theme had become obsessed with parental "hesitancy." It was, he worriedly concluded, "the commonest problem in childrearing in America today." He did not change his mind through five more revisions.

Dr. Spock was not the first to offer the diagnosis. In *The Century of the Child*, the best-selling book of 1909 whose title was promptly applied to the dawning era, the Swedish feminist reformer Ellen Key deplored "at present a lax hesitation between all kinds of pedagogical methods and psychological opinions, in which the child is thrown about here and there like a ball, in the hands of grown people." She joined a chorus, louder in America than perhaps anywhere else, calling on science to come to the rescue.

On the brink of the modern age, a contingent of professional men and progressive-minded women led the way in spreading a new gospel that the child's fate could no longer be entrusted to God or mere custom. Only when adults paid more heed to the mysteries of children's growth, and to the miseries they often suffered in a harsh world, would civilization thrive. Yet too many parents were at the mercy of impulse—buffeted between fierceness and fondness as their Victorian parents had been before them—and now they were swayed by motley "opinions" from unreliable sources, too. Children, who faced a future of greater complexity and possibilities than their grandparents had ever dreamed of, could not fulfill their miraculous potential if reared by mothers and fathers so prone to inconsistency. Inspired by Darwin, the doctor's order of the day was to fit a child's nurture more systematically to his nature, which men of science would discover through rigorous study. By the grace of such an "entirely new conception of the vocation of motherhood," in Key's words, human culture would thrive. It was a very tall order.

How tall, the rest of the century would tell. "Let mothers, fathers, nurses, educators, ministers, legislators, and, mightiest of all in its swift, far-reaching influence, the press, make the child the watchword and ward of the day and hour," urged the president of the National Congress of Mothers in 1897 as she welcomed enlightenment from the laboratory. "Let all else be secondary, and those of us who live to see the year

1925 will behold a new world and a new people." The world was indeed different a quarter of a century later, and among the new people in it was a fresh generation of experts. They were still hard at work on the child-rearing problem that she had expected would be solved—and along with it, or so the *New York Times* had dared to hope back when the congress met, "a vast proportion of [the] human ills [on] the face of the earth."

The experts of the interwar era, busier than ever in their better equipped labs, lamented even more loudly the incompetence and inconsistency of mothers, and the social woes they caused. Promoting grander theories and invoking data collected since their turn-of-the-century predecessors had begun their studies, America's scientific advisers more stridently debated the laws that governed a child's nature and should guide his nurture. Some issued harsher calls for more parent-directed strictness. Some urged more comprehensive, child-focused solicitude. Everybody counseled steadiness. "I try to do just what you say," confessed a mother in the mid-1920s who was overwhelmed by all the wisdom, "but I am a nervous wreck just trying to be calm."

Those who lived to see the year 1950 beheld Dr. Spock trying to reassure mothers by the millions, and to make peace among the experts. His efforts succeeded in further stirring everyone up during the 1960s, when the cry went out that children had been "Spocked when they should have been spanked." In his wake, experts sounded more worried and at odds than ever, their audience of women challenging the demands and constrictions of that "vocation of motherhood." America's families, although they had of course never been homogeneous, had never been so diverse—or seemed so precarious. There was hardly time for hesitancy: the harried working parent and "the hurried child" had become the type of the times. Joining in as combatants in the culture wars that closed the century, America's child-rearing advisers branched out from manuals to issue social manifestos. They arrayed themselves in the fight over family values.

America's parenting experts, in short, have fared no better or worse than the rest of us in the quest for calm consistency in child-rearing technique and theory. The story of the popular advisers' search for clarity about children and for authority with mothers is marked by controversies, contradictions, and unintended consequences. Among the most ironic of those consequences has been to leave parents, teachers, policymakers, ministers, and the media—to say nothing of the experts themselves—convinced that expert counsel is precisely what it was not supposed to be: constantly shifting and conflicting, throwing both grown people and children here and there like balls.

That history, from the turn of the twentieth century to the turn of the millennium, is the subject of this book. It is a story with its own unintended, and instructive, consequence. A tour of expertise and the experts who offered it ends up revealing an unexpected continuity in the child-rearing confusions that have accompanied industrial America's surge into secular, urbanized maturity as a technocratic, consumer culture. The advisers' dogmas and data have varied dramatically over the course of four generations of guidance, but the underlying dilemma has remained the same from the start: As children—and just as important, their mothers—prepare to meet the pressures and the allures of an increasingly materialistic and meritocratic mass society, is it more discipline or more bonding that they need at home? The answers to the question have in turn reflected the long-running debate over whether nature or nurture counts most in shaping children's destinies, which parenting experts across the spectrum and the decades have presumed are decisively cast in early childhood.

The popular advisers have regularly lined up at opposite poles with the views they have elaborated in each period, sounding more ambitious and more embattled as the century progressed. But the truth is that both the advocates of more authority for parents and the proponents of greater intimacy with children have betrayed their share of ambivalence about their own theories and advice. That ambivalence, in fact, has been a secret of their appeal.

As Margaret Mead noted (and then sometimes forgot), experts' tenets "throw light on the explicit and changing ideals of the adult culture and only to a very limited degree on the practice to which living children are subjected." This book does not pretend to have discovered how the middle-class American mothers who have constituted the growing clientele for the genre have acted on the advice they have read with ever more avidity as the century advanced; the difficulty of finding out what is happening behind those closed doors, as the experts themselves discovered, is part of what has made their science so slippery. The historians who have probed for mothers' responses—in the records of women's organizations, parent education programs, mothers' clubs—have concluded, as have most of the experts, that even the most reverent of advice-readers have rarely been slavishly obedient.

Each section of this book opens by looking in at one of the much publicized conferences that early on became a trademark of that "new conception of the vocation of motherhood." There lay participants welcomed the latest expert diagnoses of what troubled the nation's parents and children, and learned about the progress of the experts' own child-rearing mission as it marched onward, from one generation to the next. The press, too, flocked to cover the National Congress of Mothers gathering of 1899, the Conference on Modern Parenthood of 1925, the Midcentury White House Conference on Children and Youth in 1950, and two gatherings that bracketed the last period, President Carter's White House Conference on Families of 1980 and the Clintons' White House Conference on Early Childhood Development and Learning in 1997 (known as the "conference on the brain").

The evolving assessments were not objective barometers of prevailing child-rearing practices by any means, but they revealed—and served to broadcast—shifting social concerns and aspirations of science. At the successive meetings, each marking a new generation of parents and of expertise, the verdicts grew more mixed and alarmed: scientific lore was spreading, yet hand in hand with rising expectations of parents' and children's performance went rising apprehensions of failure as the American family, everyone agreed, fought for survival in a society rapidly encroaching on its hallowed terrain. The challenge for "enlightened" mothers at the turn of the twentieth century was to bolster children physically for the new jangly urban world. Their daughters, many more of whom now turned to the experts' books, faced a subtler mission, over which Freud cast a large shadow by midcentury: to assure children's emotional adjustment in a corporate, consumer era. For the baby boom generation, come of age during feminist ferment and embarking on parenthood amid family instability, the Piaget-inspired task was fine-tuning children's recently discovered cognitive capacities. There was no time to waste in readying youth to cope in the fast-paced information age of media overload and more attenuated ties.

As the new millennium approached, "raising a scientifically correct child," which had been a stirring goal a hundred years earlier, risked becoming a "neurotic national pastime," wrote a journalist about the hubbub stirred up by brain research. Meanwhile, the failure to solve the "vast proportion of human ills" was very much on the minds of the late-twentieth-century conferees. Poor children were slipping further behind, teenagers were adrift, mothers had never felt under more stress. Amid rising laments about America's demoralized culture, old-fashioned concern about children's—and parents'—"characters and values" resurfaced, harking back to the Victorian origins from which the scientific mission had sprung. As parenting Web sites spread, so did skepticism about the accumulated psychological wisdom. How solid had the scientists' findings about parents' long-term influence on children turned out to be? Was the ever-rising demand for, and supply of, expert directives for parents helping or hindering America's scrambling families?

They were not new questions. Behind their own closed doors, the experts themselves, almost from the beginning, had been asking them. Well aware that their data was less firm than they hoped, they were at odds among themselves and worried that their public clout was rarely what they expected. This book's real focus lies beyond the scene-setting conferences, in the lives and the labs and the homes, as well as the particular books, of a succession of America's pre-eminent popular child-rearing advisers whose unusual careers helped to shape the genre's course. They emerged from the growing crowd of experts, not just to capture the attention of middle-class American mothers, but to become defining influences on one another. Theirs is the lineage that helps makes sense of the proliferating post-Spock progeny of today.

They were a new breed of men—the mission to elevate child rearing to a high-status science has been male-dominated from the start—who set themselves up as, in essence, the modern mother's new and very modern model of parenthood. And in each generation, much as parents struggle to revise their own parents' ways, a new set of experts wrestled with their predecessors' legacy as they seized their moment to preside. They were also, perhaps not surprisingly, wrestling with more intimate influences. It was their experience as sons growing up when and where and how they did, as much as any timeless experiments as scientists, that shaped their advice. As the best child-rearing experts have appreciated, an ounce of narrative evocation can be worth a pound of abstract prescription, and these men's lives cast an unexpected light on the spirit, and even the letter, of the counsel they have offered over the changing decades.

What unfolds is a peculiar family saga that features an odd couple in each period: one expert a stern father figure of the Lockean nurture-is-what-counts school, the other a gentler Rousseauian proponent of letting nature take its course in childhood. Their allegiance to opposite camps has been essential to their popularity: there is nothing like parental uncertainty to whet an appetite for what sounds like clarity, and nothing like controversy to stir up publicity. The "hard" adviser, extrapolating (often wildly) from data about the power of environmental influences to shape a child's fate, issued the call for parent-directed discipline. His "soft" counterpart, fascinated by the inner developmental forces that guide a child's growth, won attention by urging child-focused bonding as a parent's priority.

Their relations with one another began in harmony at the start of the century, and they envisaged mothers as their able collaborators in a data-gathering enterprise that had just begun. But family feuds lay ahead, and more than a few surprises. To visit the experts in their historical contexts is to discover that they proceeded to hedge their advice, responding to one another and to a market of mothers who, along with children, proved more demanding and multi-dimensional than the scientists' theories allowed: clarity gets you the spotlight, but a degree of ambiguity helps to keep you in it. And their gruff and gentle tones could be somewhat misleading. Over the course of a century, the disciplinarians have often turned out to be unexpected champions of autonomy—for mothers and for children. By the same token, the softer-spoken advocates of loving attachment have had a way of insisting, ever so solicitously, on control and conformity in attentive mothers and responsive children. The choices on offer in the child-rearing advice market, in other words, have rarely been quite what they seem—and what individual parents might find most useful may lie where they are least likely to look for it.

The cast of characters is a curious one, most representatively American in their anxiety about being just that, representative Americans. They were doctors who had grown up with acute cases of a classic middle-class national malady: as the adored sons of imposing mothers often do, they worried about fitting in and dreamed of standing out. As scientists, although a few of them were quite tireless researchers, they were not the most skeptical analysts or circumspect theorizers; popularizers rarely are. Gravitating to psychology and pediatrics, fields eager to win scientific and social prestige, these men brought with them the energy of public and practical crusaders. And though they mostly did their best not to show it, they found the attention of mothers a welcome recompense for the condescension of their colleagues.

The founding great-grandfather generation of experts—G. Stanley Hall, America's first psychology doctorate and the president of Clark University (and the man who brought Freud to America in 1909), and L. Emmett Holt, one of the nation's first and finest pediatricians (the Rockefellers' doctor, no less)—joined the urbanizing wave at the turn of the century, leaving their northeastern farm families behind. As nostalgic and earnestly religious as they were scientific, they united in promising to protect children and mothers from the enervating complexity of city life, and also to prepare them to prosper in it. A similarly ambivalent agenda—one foot in the past, eyes anxiously on the present, mind straining to anticipate the future—has inspired every child-rearing expert since.

"Hard" Holt, as precise in person as in his prose, studied the effect of nutrients on growth, especially in babies; "soft" Hall, given to effusions, probed for the inner currents of growth, especially during puberty. Their books were a study in contrasts. Holt's catechistic *Care and Feeding of Children* of 1894—it was a bible among well-off mothers and cast a far wider influence as the guide that inspired a million and a half *Infant Care* bulletins issued by the federal Children's Bureau between 1914 and 1921—curtly prescribed milk formulas, schedules, and no play with baby. Hall's huge *Adolescence* of 1904 celebrated long and deep communion with the "awkward, often unattractive neophytes." Both Holt and Hall welcomed an audience of eager "scientific" mothers as their accomplices in the fledgling studies of the child, and they endorsed each other. The incongruous harmony, however, proved precarious.

Holt and Hall's heirs, who presided during the interwar era, had ridden the tide of upward mobility in a country that emerged from World War I a more institutionalized, as well as urbanized, society. The behaviorist John Broadus Watson, from the rural South, had become a young star in the Johns Hopkins University psychology department, stirring up the field just before the war with claims that personality was entirely the product of environmental conditioning—and that the process would soon be amenable to control. Arnold Gesell, the son of German immigrants and a former student of Hall's at Clark, aimed for a rigorous, not rhapsodic, vision of growth. He set out at Yale University after the war to record children's maturation on film, promising to discover the underlying laws of development.

Neither succeeded in his grand quest, or ever quite blended into academia: Watson was kicked out of Hopkins after an adulterous affair and became an advertising executive. So when they turned to peddle their wisdom to a public of parents concerned about emotional "adjustment," perhaps it was no surprise that the experts had mixed messages for a middle class as eager and uneasy as they were about fitting in to an increasingly bureaucratic America. In his *Psychological Care of Infant and Child* of 1928, which sold 100,000 copies within a few years, "hard" Watson scoffed at nonsense about how children "develop from within" and made a bow to demure Holt—and then grew strident. He warned against kissing and cuddling children, scolding that mothers were rearing soft citizens ill suited to an impersonal, organized world. Gesell eclipsed Watson in the 1930s, deriding "autocratic" training and emphasizing individuality as essential in a democracy. Yet even as he dispensed his signature "it's just a stage" counsel, he armed mothers with developmental charts and "norms," pioneering what has become the modern milestone mentality. A study in contrasts, Watson's and Gesell's regulated regimens nonetheless both aimed to assure autonomy *and* conformity. It was enough to keep mothers on their toes (and tied in knots) whatever they tried to do, which Watson for one was quite sure would not be what he told them.

Benjamin Spock, born in 1903 to pedigreed gentility and reared with Holtian austerity, was swept into power in the third wave. The first expert to say "Don't be overawed by what the experts say" achieved awesome popularity overnight. His gospel of maternal confidence was greeted as a godsend by the postwar cohort T. S. Eliot once called the "Worried Generation," anxious in an age of rising affluence and possible nuclear apocalypse—and busy having lots of babies. Three quarters of a million copies of Spock's book sold within a year, pushing him to a prominence undreamed of by his predecessors and unmatched by any competitors—and unnerving to him, a man with plenty of insecurities (and more than his share of family troubles).

The only expert to reign alone in the twentieth century, Spock served as, in a sense, his own counterpart. He was, as he put it, the master of "the 'on-the-one-hand, on-the-other-hand' stuff," which was a key to his appeal in a Cold War era preoccupied with security and harmony—and, obviously, with anxiety. Contrary to legend, which casts him as the radical prophet of permissiveness, Spock's distinction lay in succeeding "to an amazing degree in striking a middle ground in his advice," as a review of *Baby and Child Care* marveled. His counsel mixed dilute Freudianism with supervisory solicitude about keeping conflict at bay on the newly democratic home front: children in Spock's warm Oedipal drama were eager admirers, not would-be murderers, of parents who presided like friendly bosses eager to engage their hearts and unobtrusively channel their drives. But it was a delicate balance, and no sooner was Spock's child-friendly first edition out than he worried he had made mothers feel guilty and cowed. He got right back to work on a firmer, "parent-centered" revision—feeling guilty himself, but also growing restless in his role as therapist to mothers.

During the 1960s, America's child-rearing confusions burst from behind closed doors and into the streets, where Dr. Spock the antiwar protester was out marching, never expecting to be caught up in generational and gender wars. His hegemony was over, and when Bruno Bettelheim mounted the political barricades opposite him as the scourge of student radicals, an odd couple was again in the spotlight. An Austrian émigré who made his name in the United States working with severely disturbed children, Bettelheim was an interloper in the American succession who delivered a timely jolt.

Spock's dark Freudian doppelgänger came bearing the "hard" message that children were deeply conflicted creatures in need of limits—and so, Bettelheim surprisingly went on to say, were mothers. Even as Gloria Steinem in 1972 was indicting Spock, the erstwhile savior of mothers, as "a major oppressor of women in the same category as Sigmund Freud," Bettelheim was speaking out against the Spockian vision of emotionally all-consuming maternity; it was suffocating for everyone concerned. Mothers need to be relieved of the total, self-sacrificial responsibility for their children's fate that they had come to bear, he argued, both for their own fulfillment as women and for the sake of an invigorated family. He warned that no prescriptive formulas could guide what was bound to be an arduous process.

Certainly no pre-eminent pair of individual experts staked out the child-rearing terrain in the same way again. Spock's successor Dr. T. Berry Brazelton, joined by the British child development expert Penelope Leach in the late 1970s, introduced the Spock-marked generation to the learning-by-loving-and-listening child-rearing ethos of the cognitive era. But an advice market that surged as baby boomers embarked on parenthood—five times as many parenting books were published in 1997 as in 1975—was ever more cluttered with specialized counsel for a buy-the-books, rather than by-the-book, audience of more and more working mothers. By now feminism had made fealty to a favorite expert seem old-fashioned among a cohort "presumably more worldly and confident and less in need of a guru than their parents were," as the *New York Times* put it in the early 1990s. Or were busy mothers—and fathers—feeling more beleaguered than ever? Brazelton and Leach were not the only generalists to speak out about social pressures. At the same time, as counsel spread to the Web in an increasingly wired world—and brain lore proliferated—a more systematic and less intimate brand of advisory fare set the tone.

Popular experts, in addition to becoming public advocates, sounded more like management consultants to an on-the-go clientele as they peddled programmatic visions of child rearing in a high-tech, hectic era. From "affirmative parenting" to "attachment parenting," trademarked approaches got multimedia promotion. Even Dr. Brazelton had become plugged in. "America's pediatrician," as he was known by the 1990s, signed up with Procter & Gamble as chairman of their Web site, the Pampers Parenting Institute, which helped promote what he called his Touchpoints Model of advisory support for families. (Posthumously, Spock joined in the business whirl, too: with "branding maven Martha Stewart" in mind, a former managing director of a health care venture-capital fund raised $14 million and bought the rights to the doctor's work and promptly launched Drspock.com, the first step toward what he hoped would be a billion-dollar company based on "the power of Spock.")

Yet amid rising alarm about a family-unfriendly America during the 1990s, two camps of experts could again be discerned in the commercial commotion. They gravitated to the familiar poles as they stepped forth to talk, not just about psychology, but about morality and social responsibility—each invoking the spirit of Dr. Spock. With Brazelton and Leach in the lead, joined now by the psychiatrist Stanley Greenspan, the "child-centered" contingent graduated from manuals to manifestos denouncing an impersonal and competitive society as, in Leach's words, "inimical to children." They issued calls for policies to give the nation's overstressed families more time for studiously attentive (not just intuitive) bonding with babies and children—to fine-tune their brains, but even more important, to nurture empathy and thus lay the sturdy foundations for a more compassionate citizenry.

The "child-centered" proselytizers were met by a "parent-centered" corps of self-proclaimed "Judeo-Christian" experts loudly condemning the decadent state of American culture. Dr. James Dobson, a psychologist and the author in 1970 of the popular *Dare to Discipline*, had long been active in the cause. The founder of Focus on the Family, a rightwing Christian radio "ministry" with a following in the millions, he emerged as a prime mover in the conservative family values crusade that crested as the century ended. The "hard" contingent, too, indicted American society as inimical to children and to parents, laying the blame for a sexually permissive, materialistic, morally relativistic culture on "secular humanism in the hands of big government." Parental authority had been undermined, and along with it a core ingredient of morality, as revealed by "the prescriptions of the Creator Himself": self-control.

Dobson was joined by, among other "disciples of discipline," a proponent of "affirmative parenting" named John Rosemond, a bestselling success with a mostly middle American audience. The combative traditionalist took aim at "nouveau parenting" experts who "tried to make a 'science and technology' out of raising children in order to keep it in step with 'progress,'" and had turned child rearing into a thoroughly daunting challenge in the process. The end of the "Age of Parenting Enlightenment" was long overdue, he felt, and it was time "the voice of Grandma" was heard again—at "John Rosemond's Managerial Parent Skillshop." The Century of the Expert was evidently not quite ready to be over, which is all the more reason to find out why it started, how it unfolded, who led the way—and what its perennial two camps may have to say to parents today.

PART I

The Birth of a Science

ONE

The Century of the Child

Our Baby Congress, 1898

I.

Blizzards are famously conducive to conceiving babies. During a huge snowstorm that blanketed the East Coast in mid-February of 1899, a particular group of American women and a few men certainly had babies on the brain. But they were not at home in their beds. The sturdiest among an anticipated gathering of two hundred or so were fighting their way to the third annual convention of the National Congress of Mothers, in Washington, D.C. Headed to the capital for four days of speeches and discussion about the latest enlightened principles of child nurture, the women delegates and the experts who had signed up for the event found the traveling rough. "Nearly all trolley lines had abandoned their trips . . . and livery men refused to send carriages out," it was reported later in the proceedings of the congress. "Hundreds of travelers were compelled to remain from twelve to twenty-four hours in ordinary passenger coaches without food or sleep."

The progressive-spirited mothers, educators, reformers, doctors, and others were the vigorous type, "young enough in years and mind to be affected by new movements," as one attendee put it. Still, some turned back. Those who finally arrived in Washington, full of "strange and wonderful stories . . . of their adventures," encountered a virtual state of nature. The city was threatened by a coal famine, because trains hadn't been running. Gas had given out, leaving many parts of the capital in darkness. "Food was also scarce, and the streets impassable," transformed into mere paths flanked by walls of snow ten to twelve feet high.

The primitive gloom made an ironic setting for a self-consciously modern gathering that aimed "to educate public opinion" about the opportunities that awaited in what was soon to be known as "the century of the child." In the vista of human improvement ahead, as a speaker at an earlier convention had described it, there was no hint of darkness: "It is childhood's teachableness that has enabled man to overcome heredity with history, to lift himself out of the shadowy regions of instinct into the bright realms of insight, to merge the struggle for existence into mutual coordination in the control of the environment. . . . The very meaning and mission of childhood is the continuous progress of humanity." The February storm mocked that faith in control of the environment. Rude nature had dramatically assumed the upper hand.

Yet for that very reason, snowbound Washington also made an ideal backdrop for the conference. Among the participants there was clearly an exhilarated sense that the elements had supplied them with an occasion to display their missionary mettle. In an up-to-date capital that had overnight become a frontier outpost, these respectable pioneers had a chance to prove themselves just the rugged apostles of improvement they aspired to be. The city at a standstill was a vivid reminder of all that they aimed to overcome: the pre-industrial hardships that had made the lives of wives, mothers, and children brutish and, all too often, short, and the efforts of doctors so unavailing. The snowstorm was also a stirring summons to the kind of old-fashioned hardiness that was threatened by the modern age of the city and the machine—a vigor the Congress of Mothers hoped to preserve or revive.

The conferees had strayed from "the fireside" where women belonged, as the upper-class urban leaders of the movement— Mrs. Adlai Stevenson was a vice president and the wealthy Phoebe Hearst, wife of the California senator George Hearst, was the major benefactress—were forever telling their middle-class following of mothers' club members and others. But their mission was domestic, even if they were not at home with their spouses helping to avert the prospect of "race suicide," as females of their sort were urged to do in fin-de-siècle America, when alarm about declining fertility ran high. They prided themselves on not being seduced by the effete "illusion of *self-culture*" that they worried was tempting women out of the house and into careers. They had set their sights on "the sunlight of *service*" to homes throughout the nation, service that required them to be rational and systematic as their Victorian mothers had not been.

They were models for the many nervous women and "precocious" children whose lack of moral and muscular fiber was lamented from the pulpit and in the press as the century ended. And in journeying to the capital, they aimed to speak beyond their club circle to address the needs of struggling immigrants and poor Americans growing up in crowded tenements and laboring in grim factories. The woes of all were to be prevented in the cradle. "In a common cause, the highest welfare of childhood," as their president put it, "we can meet upon a universal platform, regardless of creed, color or condition." Not least, the delegates could look forward to communing at the conference with men who took them and their cause very seriously—perhaps more seriously than did the husbands they had left at home. In Washington, they would confer with the scientists whose "study of the little child" promised to provide the "key to many problems which confront and daunt the race."

"Notwithstanding the difficulties experienced in reaching their destination," the congress secretary reported, "not a single speaker failed to appear." On a program that included addresses by mothers' club leaders, teachers, members of the League for Social Service, and assorted ministers, two scientific and medical authorities on children stood out. Dr. L. Emmett Holt, known as one of America's first and finest pediatricians, and Dr. G. Stanley Hall, who had earned the first psychology doctorate in the country and held the first chair in the discipline, represented contrasting approaches in the turn-of-the-century mission to "[concentrate] national attention on the education and possibilities of parents in the home," as the congress president put it.

Dr. Holt, whose manual, *The Care and Feeding of Children*, had been selling remarkably well since its publication five years before, made his way from New York City to deliver a talk on his specialty, "The Physical Care of Children." (If Holt's name lives on, it is because Dr. Spock was known to invoke, not fondly, his mother's mentor; Mrs. Spock swore by the small book.) With the sober punctiliousness that was his trademark, he informed modern mothers of their duty to become scientific professionals on nutritional matters. They were also to guard their growing children vigilantly against germs and undue stimulation. Dr. Holt prescribed systematic study—of children and of expert wisdom—as the necessary antidote to sentimentality, an old-fashioned impulse all too likely to cloud insight.

Dr. Hall, the president of Clark University and an early supporter of the Congress of Mothers—he sat on its Committee on Education— came all the way from Worcester, Massachusetts. (He has been remembered ever since as the man who invited Sigmund Freud to Clark, where he delivered his "Five Lectures upon Psychoanalysis" in 1909 and won an academic hearing for the first time.) Hall was scheduled to speak twice. His first topic was to be "child study," the popular cause he had helped to spearhead in the 1890s, urging scientists, mothers' clubs, and teachers alike to collect data on every facet of childhood life. Adolescence, about which he was then busy writing a very big book, was his second theme. If his listeners remembered his stirring proclamations at an earlier congress about how "the study of children . . . enriches parenthood, brings the adult and child nearer together," they were perhaps disappointed when he had time to deliver only "Initiations into Adolescence," which didn't begin to live up to its titillating title. This romantic guru was often given to effusions about young people's need for excitement, but that day he spoke in his encyclopedic vein. As Dr. Hall droned on, summarizing mountains of data on puberty rites the world over, even the most attentive in his audience might have been tempted to nap.

But such an urge was to be resisted. For it was a point of pride with the self-consciously modern mothers gathered at the congress, as it was with the self-consciously "expert" men who addressed them, to expect an exhaustive treatment of the many child-related topics that concerned their cause, which was a burgeoning one. Dr. Holt opened his talk by marveling that "at no previous time has there been such a wide general interest in all that concerns childhood, as shown by the numerous books constantly issuing from the press upon these subjects, the periodicals devoted to the different phases of the child problem, and finally, but by no means least, by the organization of such societies as this." His list notably omitted to mention the thriving nineteenth-century genre of women's magazines, where pious portraits of tender youth and devoted maternity had been a staple for decades already. For Holt intended to mark a turning point in a new and demanding direction. The current upsurge of attention was no Victorian crusade on behalf of children, led by soft feminine hearts near the hearth, or by the gentle ministers from the pulpit who by midcentury had joined in promoting the cult of motherhood. The "child problem" now required studious thought for its solution, and scientists fresh from their laboratories proposed to train those maternal minds. To put it differently, the "child problem," which as the congress president noted was inseparable from the "woman question," had grown up—or at least it was ready to.

2.

The turn-of-the century "discovery" of childhood was not the first time adults in the Western world had subjected the family, especially the treatment of its younger members, to reappraisal. Pick any post-medieval century as it turns, and you can find historians proclaiming a notable shift in, and rising concern about, parent-child relations. The classic starting point is the work of the French historian Philippe Ariès. In *Centuries of Childhood*, he located the seeds of a new "child-centered" conception of family life in the late sixteenth century, as education began to acquire new social importance. Over the next century, under the influence of Reformation doctrines, among other things, "the family ceased to be simply an institution for the transmission of a name and an estate—it assumed a moral and spiritual function, it moulded bodies and souls." The "affectionate" family was in the process of being born (the first of many times). "The care expended on children inspired new feelings, a new emotional attitude, to which the iconography of the seventeenth century gave brilliant and insistent expression," Ariès observed. ". . . Parents were no longer content with setting up only a few of their children and neglecting the others."

The turn of the eighteenth century, when Locke published his influential *Some Thoughts Concerning Education* (1693), marked another birth of the child, this time a tabula rasa whose nurture required yet more studious care. "Locke's educational theory redefined the nature of parental authority in very much the way that the Revolution of 1688, which replaced an absolute monarchy with a constitutional one, redefined the rights and duties of the crown," is the way one literary historian has framed the shift. Noncoercive, rational instruction became the parent's newly responsible, rewarding duty. Nurturing "filial reason" rather than breaking fierce infant wills became the goal. Soon after the middle of the eighteenth century, Rousseau's *Emile* (1762) issued the call for more freedom for children's "natural inclinations." The guidance of children must be subtly tailored to their growth, Rousseau urged, which entailed equally intensive (but more unobtrusive) tutorial efforts. Worshipful attentiveness on the part of adults, the Romantic poets concurred, was the least the imaginative child of nature deserved.

The newly self-conscious and solicitous nurturing doctrines found an especially fertile seedbed—to use the gardening imagery the pedagogues loved—in Colonial America during the Revolutionary era, when an upstart generation that had settled down far from home was fiercely debating its relations with the "mother country" and the "father-king," as another historian has put it. The "American revolution against patriarchal authority" was about freeing sons as well as about deposing kings—about preparing ignorant children for independence, rather than exacting slavish obedience from recalcitrant beings. The child-rearing advice that began to appear, much of it aimed at fathers during the eighteenth century, warned against parental tyranny and set store by the taming power of love instead of fear. The message was also conveyed by the best-sellers of that newborn genre, the novel. The family dramas most popular in America—by Defoe, Sterne, Richardson— often turned on children's new claims to freedom and self-control, and parents' new obligations to educate without dominating. (The American abridgment of Richardson's extremely popular novel *Clarissa* altered the rambling subtitle—*The Distresses that may attend the Misconduct Both of Parents and Children, in Relation to Marriage*—omitting any mention of "misconduct of children," emphasizing instead the role of *the Rigours of Parental Authority* in the heroine's downfall.)

The demographic, economic, social, moral, spiritual, literary, and intellectual influences at work creating an increasingly child-preoccupied culture in industrializing America defy neat historical summary. But a familiar refrain brackets the nineteenth century's beginning and its Victorian close: a more affectionate (suffocating, according to some analyses) ideal of family life had arrived, again, this time in newly feminized form. Liberal theologians revised harsh Calvinist tenets, granting children redeemable, docile wills and their parents— increasingly their mothers—more power over the shaping of them.

A religious analogy between God and parent worked in much the same way as the political analogy between king and father did. The Puritans' vengeful and punitive God, appalled at his depraved creation, was replaced by a loving Father, proof of whose goodness lay in his willingness to sacrifice his son to save mankind. In a similar spirit, mothers were gently and patiently to guide their well-meaning children to righteousness, and find proof of their own salvation in the process. As

Ann Douglas has shown, such domestic counsel became a central message of liberal ministers, most prominently the Hartford clergyman Horace Bushnell, who cultivated a softer image themselves as they sermonized in the new vein. No longer did commanding men in the pulpit aim to project a "stern exterior" or to instill "painful . . . awe," as a popular mid-nineteenth-century Unitarian novelist put it. A more insecure pastorate, its prestige in decline in "money-making" America, now projected a "most tender and gentle heart" in forging a sentimental alliance with a mostly female congregation.

Philosophers had reasoned with fathers in the preceding century, urging the wisdom of rationally guiding children and of inculcating, and modeling, restraint. Now ministers, relying less on the "theology of the intellect" and more on the "theology of the feelings," appealed to mothers to rely on their "feminine instinct and sensitivity" in the shaping of innocent, not impulsive or wildly imaginative, souls. With the decline of a subsistence agrarian economy, especially in the minister-saturated Northeast, men's work by midcentury more often took them farther from the hearth, where they toiled, an article in *The Ladies' Companion* noted, "weary with the heat and burden . . . [for] the acquisition of wealth, the advancement of [their] children in worldly honor." Home began to be conceived as the special, "separate sphere" of women, who were no longer partners with men in productive household labor, nor part of the new world of more organized, increasingly mechanized work. Instead they were expected to be soothing presences in an emotional, spiritual "haven" from what Sarah Josepha Hale, the editor of the popular midcentury women's magazine *Godey's Lady's Book*, described as "a society given over without reservation to the pursuit of wealth." A rough and rapacious world lay outside the door.

Tributes to gentle maternal molding power, and tracts about how best to deploy it on sweetly malleable specimens of youth, "as yet untainted by contact with evil . . . like wax beneath the plastic hand of the mother," were the core of the Victorian "cult of True Womanhood." While patriarchal power retreated behind an impressive beard, celebrations of feminine "influence" abounded, glorifying its uncoercive yet pervasive sway. "Like the power of gravitation," exclaimed Hale, female suggestion "works unseen but irresistibly over the hearts and consciences of men." In his *Christian Nurture* of 1842, Bushnell urged a similar sway over children, preaching that gentle rearing at home was more crucial than conversion in instilling a Christian disposition. A mother's influence could guide a child's "emotions and sentiments, and work a character in him by virtue of an organic power."

Even allowing for the conventionally breathless rhetoric in which they were offered, the exaltations of feminine suasion often sounded strained. Certainly the work entrusted to America's delicate hearts was daunting. From within her serene temple, the angelic middle-class mother was single-handedly supposed to solve what have long been the essential child-rearing dilemmas. It was up to her to secure obedience yet foster independence, ideally without rousing undue resistance. And she had to balance the desire to protect her child from a harsh outside world with the need to prepare him (not her: daughters were to be house angels in their turn) to thrive in it—without knowing what that world would be like in the years ahead, or even what it was like right now; she was, after all, in her separate sphere. Charged with such a fraught endeavor, Victorian mothers might be forgiven for wondering whether their vaunted status perhaps left something to be desired.

So what was left to discover at the turn of the twentieth century? That the child had never really been discovered, and that neither the fathers' nor the mothers' solutions to the "child problem" seemed to work satisfactorily—for either fathers or mothers. Nor did they seem to work for the child himself (everyone had a male in mind), whose fate in industrial America seemed more precarious than ever, and his future more mysterious. Only a new quest for the child, the creature of the modern era now dawning, could begin to answer the question of how best to fulfill youthful potential, redefine parental power, and assure social progress. It was time for scientists and children to pick up where philosophers and fathers, and then ministers and mothers, had left off. By the end of the deeply polarized Victorian era, even (or especially) revered mothers and industrious fathers welcomed wisdom from such enlightening sources. And what child complains about being made the center of attention? You might almost say "the century of the child" was born to save a marriage.

Like so much else in the late nineteenth century, the "child problem" was enrolling in school, becoming "professionalized." The women who had once relied on "uncertain instinct" and religious dogma in guiding the growth of their progeny were now to aspire to "unhesitating insight" and to consult empirical data. The science of the child offered an opportunity rise above the dichotomies of abstract "masculine" reason and "feminine" emotion that pervaded Victorian gender lore (according to which men were "great brained" and the salient female characteristic was an expanded "abdominal zone . . . the physical basis of the altruistic sentiments"). Instead, scientists heralded incessant observation—"fine and quick," one of them specified—as the key that would unlock the secrets of growth and guidance.

The old adage that children should be seen but not heard cried out for revision in the century of the child, reform-minded Americans in the Progressive Era agreed. The first impulse, however, was not to encourage or expect a dramatic rise in the infant noise level. The new imperative was, above all, for adults to use their eyes and ears in ways they had never before bothered to—to cultivate a voracious, almost childlike curiosity about children. They had "seen" them, but they had never really looked at them—much less considered making an effort to imagine how the world might look to them, or tried listening to find out. It was time to focus steadily on children and watch them change.

Darwinism gave empirical scrutiny of the human species a new impetus, if not a completely respectable imprimatur in all eyes. But tracing human origins to children rather than to monkeys was an appealing enterprise. The child provided what Darwin's theory needed, an example of evolution in action. One did not have to subscribe to the doctrine that embryonic or human development repeats the evolutionary history of the animal kingdom (the theory of recapitulation)—though many did, foremost among them Dr. Hall—to find the spectacle of adaptive maturation inspiring. At the same time, Darwinism offered what the new devotees of childhood needed, an example of systematic investigation in action. In fact, Darwin, as his American followers eagerly emphasized, paved the way. He kept notebooks about his own offspring, whose first tears, fears, reflexes, rages, noises, and then social and verbal antics he tracked with a naturalist's curiosity and a father's empathy, and ultimately published in 1877.

The fields of American medicine and psychology had long been dominated by, respectively, quackery and philosophy. Now as the century ended, biology promised to bring order and light, and the newly alluring specimen for study was the child. Pediatrics was officially ranked a specialty at a meeting of the American Medical Association in 1880. Its development had been spurred by a drive to discover the cause of a mortality rate among the young so high as to make a mockery of medical claims to curative powers. In America in the 1890s, more than one child in six still died before turning five, half of them before turning one. Almost a third of those infants were killed by diarrhea in the hot months—"summer complaint"—which, like many other diseases of babyhood, was commonly blamed on teething.

But more and more doctors suspected that some kind of germ lurking in unclean surroundings was the source of woe. By the 1890s, most medical men were ready to agree with Dr. Thomas Morgan Rotch of Harvard that the culprit was "an infectious disease caused by a specific organism not yet discovered." The search was on to vanquish this killer and others, and everyone had a part to play. Dr. Holt's dryly descriptive *Diseases of Infancy and Childhood* (1897) served as a landmark for his academic colleagues: an unprecedentedly methodical help in diagnosing and treating the symptoms that often heralded deadly dangers, especially in the early years. His *Care and Feeding of Children* promised to equip nurses and mothers, through exacting dietary prescriptions, to help keep the as yet unidentified germs at bay, since no cures were at hand (except for the diphtheria antitoxin, which was introduced in the mid-1890s).

At exactly the same time, psychology took an empirical, genetic turn, spurred by a conviction that the intricate secrets of the mind were to be found in its unfolding, which could be watched in the infant whose "germ of a human consciousness" grew so rapidly. "Not merely to the perennial baby-worshipper, the mother, and not merely to the poet touched with the mystery of far-off things, but to the grave man of science the infant has become a centre of lively interest," wrote James Sully, a British philosopher of mind and logic, in his *Studies of Childhood* (1896). "Genetic psychology is the psychology of the future," G. Stanley Hall proclaimed from his post at Clark, where he arrived in 1889, determined to establish the discipline on a newly scientific, experimental footing, complete with laboratory resources. The old introspective approach no longer sufficed. "We must carry the work of Darwin into the field of the human soul"—which meant carrying it also into the nurseries of America.

The psychologists stressed the rigorous, unfeminine spirit required for this baby-gazing, which should be "a perfectly cool and impartial process of scientific observation," Dr. Sully emphasized, to which "baby-worship, the sentimental adoration of infant ways, is highly inimical." But Sully, and Hall along with him, also celebrated the role of the "higher gift of sympathetic insight" and "tact or fineness of spiritual touch," both womanly specialties. Hall took the lead in suggesting that mothers, logging long hours with the small specimens, might be useful accomplices—given, that is, some training. The pediatricians, too, emphasized that the new physical regimens called for an exactitude and discipline that had heretofore been lacking in the female precincts of the nursery. But Holt was of the view that a dose of rigor there was just what the doctor ordered. The rather grudging, condescending tone did not deter eager mothers. For increasingly urban and educated American women, the scientific perspective on child rearing presented a welcome challenge. Affection along with religious and family tradition, the nineteenth-century guideposts of parenthood that had made for an often conflicted mélange of fierceness and fondness, could now be supplanted by a modern regimen of investigation. When a group of upper-middle-class New York City mothers formed the Society for the Study of Child Nature in 1888, they were beginning a trend that soon spread.

3.

As Alice Birney, the president of the National Congress of Mothers, observed to the assembled company at the first Washington convention in 1897, they were joining what "is, as every one knows, an age of 'movements' . . . a time of specialized work and of organized effort." The German pedagogue Friedrich Froebel's proselytizing for kindergartens had met with growing success in America since the 1870s, and Birney aspired to unite the nation's mothers' clubs to spread more enlightenment. Although the conferees still employed soaring Christian rhetoric about "the highest and holiest of missions—motherhood," it was science rather than sentiment that inspired the turn-of-the-century ideology of "educated motherhood," as it was called. And what distinguished the occasion was its promotion of an unprecedented relationship in American family life, between parent—mother—and scientific experts. In the contemporaneous domestic science movement (the Home Economics Association was founded in 1899), a similar partnership had formed, but with a notable difference: the experts on household management, like their audience, were themselves women.

The restless women and the ambitious scientists who met in Washington were both embarked on a pioneering quest to establish themselves as prestigious professionals. The bridge between them was the concept of "vocation," which blended spiritual zeal with practical purposes and, above all, with stiff educational demands. In Theodore Roosevelt, whose tenure as head of the congress's advisory council began while he was governor of New York and continued when he arrived in the White House, "scientific motherhood" had the perfect national figurehead. There was no one better suited to ensuring that the cause evoked vistas of thrilling discovery. A buoyant champion of "strenuos-ity," Roosevelt helped to rescue the mission of maternity from Victorian sentimentality.

Roosevelt's preaching did not sound at all sanctimonious, coming as it did from a president who was also a very popular and high-spirited papa. The first family had captured the spotlight as no public figure's ever had before, and the big brood's antics at the White House, eagerly covered by the press, helped give child rearing an aura of adventure. While the younger children slid down banisters and rode horses in the front hall, Roosevelt's eldest daughter, Alice, presided as the first celebrity adolescent, and a wild one. She kept journalists supplied with manic escapades—on rooftops with cigarettes, in red cars without chaperones.

Roosevelt's rhetoric in praise of hardy home life featured the mix of romanticism and rationalized rigor that appealed to reforming matrons like Mrs. Birney, the congress president, and to aspiring scientific researchers, too. It was good PR but also the real TR speaking when he exclaimed in a letter that "it is exceedingly interesting and attractive to be a successful business man, railroad man, or farmer, or a successful lawyer, or doctor; or a writer, or a president, or a ranchman, or the colonel of a fighting regiment, or to kill grizzly bears and lions. But for unflagging interest and enjoyment, a household of children, if things go reasonably well, certainly makes all other forms of success and achievement lose their importance by comparison." He practiced what he preached. He was a father who eagerly found time to be a roughhouser, hike leader, talker, and letter writer. (He admitted, though, that the pubescent Alice could be more than he could manage. Roosevelt, the story went, once told a friend, "Listen, I can be President of the United States—or—I can attend to Alice.")

His image of motherhood was similarly spunky. In a speech about "the American woman as a mother" to his White House Congress on the Welfare of the Child in 1908, he elaborated on the portrait he had painted at an earlier Congress of Mothers gathering. Roosevelt emphasized the nonwomanly virtues required for the role and compared her to a soldier. "Only sentiment and only tenderness of heart" would definitely not do. What he had in mind was the same roster of rugged, altruistic qualities that made the man of science, once a threat to religion, such a revered turn-of-the-century figure. "Sincerity, simplicity, fidelity, and generosity of character, . . . nobility of aims and earnestness of effort": so the president of MIT (himself a general) had itemized the characteristics of the ideal scientist, and Roosevelt's ideal mother was similarly equipped.

He did not put intellect at the top of the list ("if she looks upon her children only with intelligence," Roosevelt warned, "they are not going to care overmuch for her in return"), and he emphasized "the long, slow, patience-trying work of bringing up the children aright." Still, even as he assigned her the "helpmeet" role, he assured her it was better than the "breadwinner role" that nature allotted to men. "The successful mother . . . occupies, if she only would realize it, a more honorable, as well as a more important, position than any successful man." And one that required plenty of schooling. Any woman "should have a right to just as much education, to just as high an education, as any man," Roosevelt declared—plus a little more: see to it, he said, "that with that goes the education that will fit her to do her fundamental work in the world."

Just what that modern mother's education might look like, Progressive reformers were busy helping to spell out, in terms that sounded advanced without sounding too radical, Roosevelt was surely pleased to see. In *The Century of the Child*, Ellen Key invoked "an entirely new conception of the vocation of mother, a tremendous effort of will, continuous inspiration." To appreciate the novelty of the conception, it helps to look back to a vision of motherhood offered half a century earlier in one of the homegrown examples of secular advice literature for American parents, Lydia Sigourney's *Letters to Mothers*, published in 1838. Generally given to gushing exhortations to "write what you will upon the printless tablet [of your infant] with your wand of love," Sigourney framed her notion of feminine influence somewhat more soberly in one passage, heaping on the pedagogical credentials:

> Wise men have said, and the world begins to believe, that it is the province of women to teach. You then, as a mother, are advanced to the head of that profession. I congratulate you. You hold that license which authorizes you to teach always. You have attained that degree in the College of Instruction, by which your pupils are continually in your presence, receiving lessons whether you intend or not, and if the voice of precept be silent, fashioning themselves on the model of your example.

For Sigourney, the college was purely metaphorical, whereas the apostles of scientific motherhood had real degrees in mind, and viewed the educational requirements of motherhood from a different angle.

Teaching was no longer the essence of the mission, invisible and unconscious "influence" no longer the method. On the eve of the modern era,
scientific men were saying, and an audience of women was evidently
avid to believe, that it was the duty of mothers to embark on the even
more absorbing task of learning—from and about their children, and
from the experts who would show them how to study that subject right
under their nose. It was not a demotion, for now self-development was
part of what had previously been billed solely as selfless devotion.
"What, then, would we have?" asked a speaker at the first Congress of
Mothers. She had her answer at the ready: "that women, mothers especially, who are becoming students of everything else under the sun,
become students of childhood and students of every system, scheme,
plan, and practice for the development of the body, mind, and character
of the child; not that the students of to-day shall make good mothers,
but that the mothers of to-day shall make good students."

The notion of parenthood as a vital postgraduate calling offered
a way to deal with important dilemmas facing mothers and experts.
It supplied an answer to the question of what the rising numbers of
college-bound women (85,000 were enrolled by 1900) would do when
they finished their studies, which would, after all, prepare them for so
much more than merely following in their mothers' domestic footsteps.
Impressed by all the "caps and gowns and even all the eye-glasses" yet
concerned to "turn back into the home the tide of femininity, which is
now streaming outward in search of a career," Mrs. Birney and her
followers—none of them radical feminists by any means—had strained
to come up with a solution.

Perturbed though they were about the "universal restlessness among
women of all classes and countries," they were not reactionaries either,
so they extolled college or "national training" for women equivalent to
West Point and Annapolis for men. For the modern mother, it was a
crucial part of "keeping [herself] in a constant process of growth, under
the constant influence of the best things in one's own age," as Key put
it. "No boy of hers will get to that sorrowful age when he feels that he
knows a great deal more than his mother," the congress's magazine
emphasized. "She can be his friend and companion for all time." Without straying far from home (except perhaps to attend a conference or
two or three), she could discover an ample supply of coursework and
casework in that boy of hers, once she recognized that in his sandbox
play with his friends, for example, lay "every question of sociological
ethics with which society is now confronted." The woman who "felt the
drudgery of baby-tending to be incompatible with her attainments"

would continue to discover otherwise on down the years as she scrutinized children's evolving interests and needs.

The experts' role as prophets of health, both physical and psychological, arose out of ambivalent ambitions as well. Holt and Hall had entered academia in the 1880s as it was acquiring newly professionalized prestige in America, eclipsing the clergy in status. The two of them, like their growing cohort of colleagues, were committed to pushing back the frontiers in the most promising and fastest-growing domain, science. Their success represented dramatic upward mobility. Their fathers had been northeastern farmers, and none too prosperous ones at that.

Yet the big-city bustle and godless lab work also needed a higher justification for these earnest sons of the soil. Like so many men during the fin-de-siècle period of rapid urbanization, Dr. Hall and Dr. Holt had left their fathers in the dust, as well as the supremely capable mothers who had been the backbone of their families. Once arrived in the metropolis, they could afford to feel qualms about their escape. Their fathers' rugged sacrifices, too little appreciated then, now merited gratitude. Their devout mothers' admonitions against selfish materialism and vain ambition had left deep marks, too. Dr. Hall and Dr. Holt had the preacher impulse in their blood, and were determined to prove themselves upstanding guides for the future, not impious rebels against the past.

In the closing decades of the century, a new pulpit beckoned. Science was proving itself a morally high and socially helpful pursuit, and a well-funded one, thanks to the support of plutocrats eager to burnish their reputations for posterity—and in need of donnish advisers in the cause. John D. Rockefeller, Jr., was consulting with Dr. Holt on the creation of what was to become the Rockefeller Institute in New York. A decade earlier, Dr. Hall had been recruited by a businessman from Worcester, Massachusetts, named Jonas Clark. With the fortune he had amassed supplying California gold miners with goods, Clark had founded America's first graduate faculty devoted to scientific research and in 1888 had turned to Hall to guide it.

The academics were not just facilitators, and certainly didn't consider themselves hired help. The rich men were their patrons. It mattered to the magnates-turned-philanthropists that the specialists brought with them not merely professional standing, but some public repute as well. In turn, the experts obviously benefited: thanks to the prominent backing, their popular profile rose. No plutocrat could quite hope to become an icon of selfless authority, but his attending doctor or his presiding professor certainly could. Emissaries between the lab and the mother's lap, the experts on children could aspire to help sanctify both realms, bringing rigor into the home and vigor into the halls of knowledge.

What the mission of modern child rearing required, and had created, was a new authority figure for an age in which parental authority had once again come into question. In the speeded-up world that had arrived, mothers and fathers could no longer simply be unreflective models for their children or mere influential forces in the home air. Nor, for the same reason, did it seem possible any longer for parents themselves to rely on mere apprenticeship to their parents as a guide to the new child-rearing challenge. Their children were growing up in settings so different from the ones in which they had passed their youths. It was easy to feel that their own upbringings had not really equipped them for the task of preparing their offspring for a future that would be unimaginably different—and should be greatly improved, if mothers (and, it was to be hoped, fathers, too) only mastered the "hidden mysteries" of development.

Optimism was matched by anxiety. Dr. Hall reflected that while "my father's experiences of life here in his boyhood did not vary very much from mine," such continuity had disappeared. "It is a trite remark," Dr. Holt noted, but perfectly true, "that our American life is every year becoming more complex." And potentially more corrupting. If parents and experts were feeling out of control as they faced the future, they were also feeling nostalgic about the past. Roosevelt had captured the post-agrarian angst when he proclaimed that "it is not a good thing to see cities grow at disproportionate speed relatively to the country," and invoked the "real home" as a bastion against disorder and decadence. To be sure, the brutal battles of rural life were well behind Americans. The grim days when "the most widely read booklets bore the significant title, Crumbs of Comfort for Mothers" stirred no longing in Dr. Hall. "Who can think without tears of the homely monotonous life of our almost forgotten mothers half a dozen generations ago in their inmost struggles with poverty on these Massachusetts farms now often abandoned," he sighed.

Yet with modernity had come a dangerously unmonotonous life, for mothers and children alike. "The conditions which kept child life simple and natural fifty years ago have largely changed since that time; on every side there is more to stimulate the nervous system and less opportunity for muscular development," Dr. Holt lamented. "One of the most important reasons for this is the far greater proportion of children now than formerly who are reared in cities and large towns." Dr. Hall chimed in with concern about the child shut "away from Nature and free movement and play in an unwholesome air, worried and nervous," not just in schools but in factories as well. Victorian gentility, with its soft vision of home life, was no longer the answer. "Feminization" was a name for a new set of fears in the urban America that was emerging. To be "delicate" had become an ailment, not a compliment. The word "nerve" had nothing to do with courage, and everything to do with disease and decadence, especially among women and children, and especially in cities.

The potential appeal for the whole middle-class family of a scientific antidote to sentimentalism is not hard to see. Not only were women more educated, but wives and mothers were less occupied with productive household labors and burdened with fewer children. The fertility rate among white women dropped from 7 children in 1800 to 3.9 in 1890, and to 3.2 by 1920. The black fertility rate was still 6.3 in the early 1890s, but dropped to 3.8 between 1915 and 1919. Adults outnumbered children for the first time, and the "family economy" ceased to be the middle-class norm outside of the South and the West. Between 1890 and 1920 the proportion of Americans living in cities increased from 35 to 51 percent. Women still spent plenty of time on domestic chores (servants became scarce, and the rest of the family pitched in less), but child rearing was obviously the duty most readily upgraded—with the greatest reward, the doctors promised, beginning with the saving of infant life through mothers' preventive solicitude. A vista of attentively supervised development unfolded from there.

Middle-class men were confronting a new economic equation, as they shouldered the role of sole providers in households no longer bustling with industrious members. "Profound must be the depths of affection that will induce a man to save money for others to spend," marveled one hard-working father in 1904 as he planned for the upkeep of a newly dependent entourage. Husbands' helpmeets and fathers' offspring could at least be diligently engaged in developing according to scientific precepts. And if the middle-class model of sheltered childhood smacked of soft privilege, the reformers' zeal to rescue child laborers as well helped to make safeguarded growth seem a basic right of youth, children's true task rather than an effete indulgence. It laid the groundwork for future success.

Finally, the new plight of adolescents, particularly male ones, also helps to explain the appeal of a more systematic vision of guidance. Older boys were joining middle-class girls, who had begun their educational climb decades earlier, in the flight from productive work to school. High school attendance roughly doubled every decade between 1890 and 1920. Almost a third of fourteen- to seventeen-year-olds were enrolled in 1920, up from 7 percent in 1890. The world with "its accumulated mass of cultures and skills, its artifacts, its necessity of longer and severer apprenticeship and specialization," as Dr. Hall put it, demanded more intricate preparation.

To socialize children to thrive under "the powerful influence of modern life, with its extreme and growing complexity," no longer presented itself as a straightforward matter of turning out hardy sons or entrepreneurs who, if they relied on their reason, took risks, and were lucky, might surpass their fathers. Nor were daughters simply to be molded gently in their mothers' selfless image. The utmost parental vigilance was now required to equip children, as Dr. Holt put it, "to grapple successfully with the complex conditions and varied responsibilities which will be their lot." Their futures lay in a world set up increasingly along managerial and professional lines. It stood to reason, then, that middle-class motherhood should become a vocation more akin to professional management, and in an era awed by Frederick Winslow Taylor's efficiency studies, that meant "scientific."

The expert emerged as the missing link: the modern parent's modern parent. He would do more than discover a new model of childhood. He would himself serve as a new model of parenthood for mothers who, like the children they were in charge of, were demanding and receiving more serious attention and stirring more concern than ever before. The experts would be as intently observant of mothers as mothers were to be of their children; as full of ambition for the ever higher development of mothers as mothers were to be for their children's perfection; as torn between the goals of empowering and controlling mothers as mothers were to be when it came to their children; as unsure about how much allegiance to expect from mothers as mothers were about the extent of their influence over their children.

The experts' attitude toward fathers was less clear, not least because they said almost nothing about them. On the one hand, the experts lent a masculine tone to a field that the Victorians had marked off as the special province of women. They set out to make child rearing a more systematic vocation, overseen by male specialists. Thus in theory, at least, they opened it to men as it had not been for more than a century, serving as role models of male interest and lending it rigorous prestige. On the other hand, in making it a vocation, not an avocation, they in practice reduced the father, the wage earner, to newly amateur status on the sidelines while they usurped his place. Ironically, the cure for the "feminization" of the family guaranteed its continuation. The dictates of scientific, "professional" nurture scripted an ever more intensive relationship between mother and child—and expert.

4.

This new authority figure, the child-rearing expert, did not present a single image of enlightened parenthood but, appropriately enough, two basic models—one sterner and more "masculine," the other empathetic and effusive, yet both impressively scientific. At the podium at the Congress of Mothers, Dr. Holt and Dr. Hall made an emblematic pair. Rough contemporaries, Hall at fifty-five and Holt at forty-five performed as complementary public promoters of enlightened scientific wisdom about children. It was a role they had begun to cultivate during the 1890s, Holt with his best-selling little book and Hall with a busy lecture schedule.

Each looked perfectly cast for the part he played. Dr. Holt was the rationalist authority in the physical realm. The pediatrician, who had once described the child as a "delicately constructed piece of machinery," taught that the key to growth and health lay in a carefully regimented diet. He was a study in buttoned-up propriety, almost "immaculately dressed," his hair "parted exactly in the middle," as a devoted—and evidently awed—former student described him. "Not one hair was out of place." Holt's speaking style was just as meticulous. "He spoke in short, crisp sentences, in a voice low and clear. His manner was deadly earnest . . . there was never any digression from the steady progression of facts." (His wife once reported in a letter to her son that a colleague had tried in vain to prod Dr. Holt to more extemporaneous delivery, urging him not to be glued to his text, but "he is demurring on account of stage fright, which seems amusing to me.")

Dr. Hall's completely different appeal, in his biographer's words, "was his special combination of moralism and romanticism." His vast domain was the unplumbed depths of the child psyche, in which he believed lay the "soul of the race," the secrets of growth. He had the full beard, the piercing eyes, and the shining pate of a prophet. His former friend William James once said of Hall, when they had become rivals, that he "hates clearness . . . and mystification of some kind seems never far distant from anything he does." His writing could indeed be Teutonically convoluted, but evidently his rhetorical style at the podium struck his listeners as warm and inspirational. There was nothing crisp about it. Hall cascaded, speaking "with great sincerity and naturalness of manner, gliding easily from simple exposition to lyrical hyperbole."

Dr. Holt and Dr. Hall exemplify contrasting perspectives on the relationships among child, parent, and expert that have coexisted ever since the start of the century and soon enough began to compete. In his speech to the congress, Holt outlined, in Lockean spirit, the all-important power of parental nurture especially during the formative period of infancy. The pioneering "parent-centered" expert, he coolly emphasized rational discipline as the route to self-control in the child and peace for mothers. Hall took a more Rousseauian tack. One of America's first psychological advocates of the "child-centered" perspective, he championed the child's own natural impulses and rich imagination as the best guide to his growth, promising inspiration in the process for mothers as well. It was the spurt of adolescence that Hall felt deserved, and rewarded, the most attention and care.

The two experts' turn-of-the-century urgency about a decadent culture turning children into "miniature men and women" before their time sounds surprisingly current. And their lectures, like the addresses delivered throughout the Congress of Mothers gathering, joined in pointing up two defining features of the experts' child-rearing mission that persist to this day. First of all, on an occasion dedicated to celebrating the promise of childhood and the eradication of "a vast proportion of human ills . . . from the face of the earth," alarm about the perils of parenthood—to say nothing of "The Supreme Peril of Modern Civilization" (the topic tackled by the president of the League for Social Service)—ran notably high. From the very start, an enterprise officially dedicated to understanding and raising children has been as preoccupied, if not more, with criticizing and training parents, mothers in particular. Mrs. Birney's welcoming address in 1899 mentioned children only in passing, in the most blandly general terms. It was their elders who roused her and her expert colleagues' fervor. "I claim, without hesitancy," she announced, "the greatest evil to-day is the incompetency, the ignorance of parents, and it is because of this evil that others exist."

Second, and obviously related, this brand of advice has never engaged in the conventional business of dispensing reassurance. Though nervous adults, and children, had the conferees very worried about the health of the nation, the cure itself—self-conscious, attentive study and care of children—was not designed simply to soothe. Quite the contrary. "No man or woman of even average ability could read some of the admirable books and articles on child study," Mrs. Birney declared, "without becoming painfully conscious of shortcomings in themselves." And though she was sure they would also become "impressed by the wonder, beauty and vastness of the realm of child culture," there was plainly a great deal to master—and for poorer "sisters who are compelled to work," she noted, finding time to pore over the literature would not be easy. In his speech, Holt noted a worrisome problem at the heart of the enterprise: those he judged most in need of enlightenment were "least likely to avail themselves of it."

"The light of science has eliminated the glamor of superstition and the glitter of false theory," a congress report went ahead and announced with excitement. It had also offered a glimpse of reality, suggesting how vast and elusive child study could be, and how extensive a mother's responsibilities might turn out to be. But only a glimpse: this was the beginning of a crusade, and hope outran doubt. And the experts, and children themselves, offered models of indefatigable curiosity to emulate. "Our soul is to be filled by the child, just as the man of science is possessed by his investigations," Ellen Key wrote in *The Century of the Child* as she elaborated her "entirely new conception of the vocation of mother, a tremendous effort of will, continuous inspiration." Then she recast her comparison in homelier terms. Mothers are to "be as entirely and simply taken up with the child as the child himself is absorbed by his life."

At the 1898 meeting of the Congress of Mothers, a speaker had proposed the missing analogy, which closed this circle of avid learners. Mrs. Mary Lowe Dickinson, president of the National Council of Women in New York City, had welcomed the scientific experts and others at the podium as, what else, children: "children [who] have been gathering their pebbles on the shore—new views, profounder convictions, broader theories, more comprehensive plans, deeper truths, more solid facts, daintier dreams, more practical methods—and have brought those pebbles here."

She spoke quite accurately, as well as colorfully. This was the early childhood of the experts' endeavor, and the way ahead seemed wide open. Pioneers in the fledgling field of child study, Dr. Holt and Dr. Hall emerged as partners, not competitors, in improvising roles as popular scientific experts, gurus of a sort for a new age. Different though America's new rational and romantic guides to child rearing were, their labors in and out of the laboratory went hand in hand. Their missionary work among mothers invigorated them as they dipped into their own childhoods for more than a few of their pebbles of child-rearing wisdom. L. Emmett Holt, it may come as no surprise to learn, was a very good and orderly boy. G. Stanley Hall was something of a wild child. They were the first modern experts, but far from the last, whose science had its roots in personal reminiscence.

Two Experts Grow Up

Dr. L. Emmett Holt and Dr. G. Stanley Hall

I.

G Stanley Hall and L. Emmett Holt began life as northeastern farm boys extremely fond, and a little afraid, of their formidable mothers and far from intimate with their farmer fathers. They both left home as soon as they could. Their escapes to the big city were a classic late-nineteenth-century American story—though they were not looking for money or for urban adventure. They had more genteel visions of fame and influence in mind. Both men embarked on an utterly new kind of quest: to promote a gospel of scientific maternity.

In principle, it was a proudly modern, systematic enterprise designed to supersede family tradition, the old-fashioned guide to child rearing. As Dr. Holt had said in his talk at the National Congress of Mothers, it was time to dispense with those "female relatives and friends whose knowledge is very limited, but whose prejudices regarding these matters are very strong, and their conclusions . . . not entirely to be depended on." In principle, it was also an enterprise dedicated to discovering objective truths about children's nature and nurture, which were the prerequisites to producing the balanced specimens of humanity who would thrive in the complex new century. "Arrested development," as Dr. Hall was always saying, was the problem to overcome; the "superior stage of the race," or "superanthropoids," the goal to achieve.

In practice, Holt and Hall based their child-rearing advice for parents at least as much on the drama of their own pasts as on data they amassed as scientists in the big city. Their mothers, who were notably similar types, supplied them with images of the kind of vigilant maternity their work tried to teach modern mothers to approximate and update—just the fealty to "female relatives" they recommended their audiences avoid. The models for their vision of children were quite clearly themselves as youths, which was, again, just the kind of subjective projection that the scientific "discovery" of the child was supposed to discourage. By temperament, the young Emmett and the young Stanley were a study in contrasts. The salient difference in their family environments, back on "the old New England farm" and "the old home at Webster," lay in their fathers. Granville Bascom Hall, who could be fierce, and Horace Holt, who was evidently an aloof presence in the household, were models whom their sons plainly aspired—with mixed success—not to emulate. The different child-rearing visions of America's pioneering "soft" and "hard" scientific advisers to mothers grew out of the way they grew up. To get to the roots of their peculiar, and very influential, books means beginning with biography.

2.

Laura Ingalls Wilder's *Farmer Boy*, the story of her husband Almanzo Wilder's childhood in upstate New York during the 1860s, makes ideal family reading and a perfect introduction to the world from which Dr. Hall and Dr. Holt emerged. Two things in particular about the nine-year-old protagonist are likely to inspire awe in readers of all ages: how hard he worked and how much he ate (huge slices of pie for breakfast!). Working and eating left big impressions on Hall and Holt, too, as they looked back on their own similar youths. Hall focused on the work. He romanticized it as the stimulating adventure woefully lacking in modern, citified America, and he made invigorating exploration a centerpiece of his child-rearing theories. Holt dwelled on the food. In the hardy days of self-sufficient home industry, heaping portions and a hodge-podge diet did no harm to children who productively pitched in, as all were expected to. Bustling mothers took breast-feeding for granted. But for modern children, less firmly moored in a bigger world, the same approach would be indulgence; and for modern mothers, he discovered, nursing could seem an inconvenience. Holt dedicated his pediatric efforts to establishing proper rations.

It is characteristic of the brisk man and of his clinical perspective on childhood that L. Emmett Holt, who was born in the same northern corner of New York State as Almanzo Wilder at almost exactly the same time, had only sketchy memories of his own youth. Of course, a doctor renowned for his professionally impersonal acuity about children's proper care might have wanted to claim objective distance on that stage of life. But Holt was evidently not hiding a rich store of personal reminiscences. When his children were young and he had time to do more than, as he put it guiltily, "simply board in the same house with them and treat their colds when they have them," he discovered that their favorite bedtime stories "always are those rehearsing what I did when I was a little boy." But, he confessed in a letter to his sister, Eliza, he could rarely satisfy their appetite for anecdotes. "I have lived those times over more of late than in many years, as the children are always wanting more details and my memory and my imagination are both severely taxed to meet the demand." He hoped Eliza could supply some more vivid material. She did in a fondly mocking vein that brings to mind Almanzo's feasts, described with comically epicurean gusto in Wilder's book. "I suppose you didn't tell them what you ate," Eliza teased her brother:

> For breakfast crackers and coffee, then, after the long ride, boys could eat everything, and you had chicken pie, pressed chicken, cold baked chicken, and sometimes other kinds of meat; with these went two and three "raised biscuit," pickles, jelly or jam and cheese, then wild blackberry pie (wasn't it good?) and all the other kinds known to that generation; lemonade to drink all through dinner by the children, and coffee for the old folks. . . . after pie came cake—as many pieces as your teacher would pass you—nice, rich cake it was, too; then came the watermelon. . . . and if the

season had been a prosperous one you had candy. And you ate all these things—and still live. Oh, well, they didn't know any better, and had no books on "Care and Feeding"; so they didn't get sick.

Dr. Holt's youthful background was more thoroughly and deferentially preserved in a quasi-official biography that appeared in 1940, with an admiring foreword by a former student (who had gone on to become the chairman of pediatrics at Yale and Johns Hopkins Universities). It was written jointly by an appointed writer, R. L. Duffus, in collaboration with Holt's third son, Luther Emmett Holt, Jr., also a doctor, who found he needed to help the project along. Holt emerges as the paragon—a model of just the sort of eminently manageable, cheerful child of well-ordered habits that he went on to portray in his writings, a youth on the way to an industrious and virtuously ambitious maturity.

Born in 1855 in the town of Webster, the third of four children, Holt was the son of a hard-pressed farmer of New England Puritan stock named Horace and his wife, Sabrah. "For a time the Holt apple . . . enjoyed a considerable reputation," but that is the last we hear of Horace's accomplishments. Sabrah, a devout Baptist and, reading between the lines, a notably bossy figure in the household, dominates the picture. This salubrious influence never let her children forget that there was no reason "why my boys can't do big things as well as others," that nothing was to be done by halves, that failure was not to be countenanced, that knowledge counted for more than wealth, that debt was unthinkable, that usefulness was the key to success—that life, as the biographers summed up, was not a "scramble for power and position . . . [but] a moral issue."

Still, the young Emmett seems to have been full of fun and fond of singing—a fact worth noting, it is implied, because you would never guess it of the sober adult Holt. Otherwise, however, the boy was father to the man. He excelled at school, often outshining his older brother. He proceeded without a hitch through the local little red schoolhouse, then on to Webster Academy, and in 1871, on to nearby Rochester University, a Baptist school headed by a man who condemned Darwin and Huxley as "worms in the pathway of true religion." So impressed was Rochester's Dr. Martin Anderson by the Holt brothers, though, that (Sabrah reported in a letter) he drove by their home one day, just to see "where those boys were raised." Holt dutifully excelled at Rochester, too, apparently acquiring a reputation as a fellow with an enthusiasm for fussily measured potions for various ills. The class historian offered this prophetic squib in the yearbook: "Holt believes in hydropathy and little pills. . . . [He] will present the following for feeding up a patient: 'Hang a small chicken so that its shadow will fall on a hogshead of water; for an adult three teaspoons daily; for a child apply infinitesimal calculus to find the proper dilution.' "

Holt spent a year teaching school before forging ahead on a medical career. A future in business, the head of Rochester University had made clear, was beyond the pale. The dread pathway of science was presumably not much better from his point of view, and Holt may well have felt it was only polite to pause briefly before proceeding on to that bold new frontier. When his parents offered him his "portion" of the family inheritance, he set off for Buffalo Medical College in 1876, one of the better schools in an era when medical education was still poor. Medicine remained essentially an apprentice system, and Holt's real training began in 1878 when he headed for New York, where he worked in the Hospital for the Ruptured and Crippled and at the College of Physicians and Surgeons. He led a strenuously regimented life, at one point even informing his family that he was "sick of this writing-when-you-feel-like-it way of business," and urging a firm correspondence schedule. His mother deluged him with letters, proudly worrying about all the pressure he was under (he needed a new pillow, not "so large and full," to cure his round-shouldered look, she insisted) and warning about "the many, many temptations" in his way. "Don't be in such hot haste to make yourself known and felt in the world as to undermine your health and thereby cripple all your future."

Holt graduated in the top ten of his class, chose surgery at Bellevue, but soon realized he "lacked . . . the exquisite manual dexterity" to excel. So he hung out his shingle in 1881 and decided to specialize, the approved route for rising young doctors. He settled on children out of "practical rather than sentimental considerations," according to his chroniclers. In addition to his practice, he studied diseases at the New York Infant Asylum in Mount Vernon, where lots of small, ailing bodies were available for scrutiny—a "museum of disease," he called it. Holt had made enough money by 1883 to be the beneficent son and send his parents on their first trip ever away from Webster, to Montreal.

The next year Holt himself took a bigger trip, to Europe, which opened his eyes to how much more advanced pediatrics was in Germany than in America. He came home, found a wife, Linda Mairs, in his Bible study group, and continued his steady march to the forefront of the emerging pediatric field. (Holt's sister ribbed him that he had not conducted this romantic transaction with quite the methodical aplomb that he had evidently promised his relatives he would when they pestered the busy bachelor about his prospects. She let him know that she thought it pretty "funny to hear one who has always been so cool and calculating, who has always intended to make his matrimonial venture in the same way in which he would a business one, rave over his beloved like any of the rest of us.")

Dr. Holt went on to work on the newly founded *Archives of Pediatrics*, became an active member of the American Pediatric Society, founded in 1887, and contributed an article on diarrhea to the *Cyclopedia of Diseases of Children*, which was published in 1890 (and which, reflecting a field in rapid flux, his biographers noted, also included an anachronistic article about the effect on children of maternal impressions during pregnancy—a notion of prenatal responsiveness that, with new uterine probing, is now back in circulation). He became an authority on digestive ills and processes in babies. And from among a crowd of white coats hard at work in the lab at the end of the nineteenth century trying to figure out how to make cow's milk an adequate substitute for mother's milk, Dr. Holt emerged as the cook with comparatively manageable formulas to offer.

He peddled a compromise between those who worked out a simple method that did not try to replicate maternal milk and those who had devised extraordinarily complex formulas designed to mimic mother's milk in all its gradations and variations. Pediatricians, never mind mothers, were overwhelmed by the proliferation of recipes, one of them complaining that it "required almost the equivalent of an advanced degree in higher mathematics, employing algebraic equations to compute the food mixture for a baby." A mere college degree would probably do for Holt's method. It was his prescriptions for feeding that were cited by everyone and reprinted in the popular *Infant Care* manuals the Children's Bureau began to publish in 1914. (Europeans dismissed all the American mixing and measuring as far too artificial and arcane.)

In 1889, Holt had taken over the recently founded Babies' Hospital, among the first in the country just for infants, and he presided over it until 1923. As he appreciated, it was an ideal venue for a new specialty in need of proving itself. Pediatricians on the staff provided charitable help to the poor, whose children were the bulk of the hospital's patients, and the doctors had research opportunities and exposure to a wider array of cases than any private practice could supply. Equally important, Holt and his colleagues forged an alliance with "society matrons," women who served on his board and were instrumental in such charity efforts—and, as mothers, were clients themselves for pediatric services. Dr. Holt worked hard on all fronts and, according to his biographers, proved especially gifted in his dealings with the women. He was a diligent educator dedicated to proving how useful he could be to them. At the suggestion of his Board of Lady Managers, he began a school for private nursery maids, which was a great success, producing nannies for the well-off and staffs for infant hospitals, all of them trained in Dr. Holt's specialty: feeding, which he had identified as the key to explaining, preventing, and curing illness.

It was not an unreasonable guess in an era when "wasting diseases," or digestive disorders, accounted for so many infant deaths—and when doctors had no antibiotics to dispense. That the babies under Dr. Holt's care fared much less well than the women in his employ was not for lack of trying. The hospital's mortality rate was about 25 percent during its first decade, in large part because the director turned no infants away, and they often arrived already at death's door. Among the general population, Holt noted in his presidential address to the American Pediatric Society in 1898, the infant mortality rate was at 20 percent, but among the "better class," at most 2 or 3 percent; in his own private practice, he reported, no patient had died before two.

By 1896, Holt had produced four of his own five children (including his namesake, the third of his four sons, in 1895). He had written the catechism for baby nurses training at his hospital, which became a "bible" to American mothers, among whom his antiseptic gospel proved to be in great demand. Sleeping was to be scheduled, too, and Holt frowned on cuddling and playing with babies as unsafe—an invitation to germs, and to nerves. He had also produced *The Diseases of Infancy and Childhood*, which became the best-selling textbook in the field, full of description and free of fanciful speculation. He was president of the American Pediatric Society. As the century turned, he inherited the College of Physicians and Surgeons post of clinical professor of the diseases of children held by Abraham Jacobi, famous as the founding father of pediatrics. The same year, 1901, Babies' Hospital was ensconced and thriving in a new modern building, thanks to successful fundraising among his well-to-do patients and his fellow parishioners at the prestigious First Baptist Church on Fifth Avenue.

One of those parishioners, John D. Rockefeller, Jr., had become a patron on a larger scale as well. With Holt at his right hand advising him, Rockefeller set out in 1901 to fund an institute of medical research with some of his father's fortune. (Rockefeller had not yet had children, but when he did several years later, Dr. Holt was on call.) Among the

Rockefeller Institute's first projects, led by Holt, was an investigation of the abysmal state of the New York City milk supply. It was a public health endeavor that contributed far more to the crusade to vanquish the baby killer "summer complaint" than the formulas for infant milk and the studiously planned child menus of bland mush—potatoes, rice, or macaroni "stewed very soft," certain green vegetables "all thoroughly cooked and mashed," rice pudding "without raisins"—that made Dr. Holt such a hit with a middle-class and well-to-do maternal clientele. He counted on the same dispassionate direction he provided mothers and magnates to work miracles on farmers, too, and even on cows. Harsh laws, he insisted in his report, were not needed to remedy the bacteria-infested system. "Simple instructions given in the right spirit" about the need for "cleanliness, care, and a certain amount of intelligence" inspired a transformation in several filthy farms in the area, whereupon the cows "of their own accord" eagerly returned to their sparkling stalls for milking.

Hectically busy, Dr. Holt himself remained a model of methodical calm—except, perhaps, on the home front, where he was afraid he was failing to measure up to his own standards. "I fear I have not been taking my share of the family burden of late and that you, Dearest, have had too much to carry," he wrote his wife as the family once again headed for the rural respites that he felt were crucial for child health and happiness. The busy doctor was left behind to nurse some qualms about the price he paid for his pace of life. "In the future I am going to try and help you more, especially in the care and discipline of our little boys." He had that last topic very much in mind, for he had had a tough morning with his namesake, who had goaded him to a measure the calm expert only approved of as "a rare treat": "I felt awfully sorry to whip Emmett today but it was that or miss the train. Had I had an hour's time, I am sure I could have managed it, but he was in his most obstinate mood and no ordinary measures would work."

Dr. Holt was acutely aware of the feeling that is all too familiar to hard-pressed parents: he was not the patient, fond presence he believed he should be. And he blamed himself, not just his circumstances. For an aloof fellow, he was surprisingly astute about his emotional limitations. If he owed much of his professional success to his efficient reserve, he evidently suffered a degree of personal distress on account of his famous coolness, too. To his wife, he confided his disappointment in being a man who could not seem to help finding the echo of tiny feet more congenial than their actual pounding. "I realize very much more when I am here alone and the house is so still, how much of a place my dear wife and little children fill in my life here," he wrote her wistfully. "I must confess that when they are here, and I know they are, I don't get nearly as much happiness out of my association with them as I ought, and as I might." Dr. Holt was not too busy to realize how lucky he was to have a wife who did.

3.

When it came to exploring his youthful past, G. Stanley Hall's memory and imagination were, in contrast to Holt's, indefatigable. He enthusiastically followed his own advice that the "impulse to keep on growing through adult years" was best sustained by "introspective meditation" that tapped into one's early and vivid experiences. And true to his theories, he unearthed origins and a development that were notably conflicted and convoluted—and not just by comparison to Holt's streamlined journey to maturity. Hall made a point of emphasizing how protracted his coming of age had been, and devoted considerable space to a psychological analysis of the experience. In his *Life and Confessions of a Psychologist*, the long and revealing memoir he published in 1923 shortly before his death, he unabashedly promoted the persona of the prodigal. ("I know it will seem to you frank," he wrote to his sister as he prepared to send her a copy fresh off the press. "I feel as though, in publishing it, I had been caught out of doors not merely barefoot, but almost nude.") He waited until the end of his life to fully expose the subjective turmoil that so obviously informed his scientific views of childhood, above all his belief in prolonging adolescence. But well before that, he had been perfectly willing to allude to his own pilgrimage. It lent inspirational authority to his more objective findings. Hall's call to discover the adolescent within and the children all around, his audiences could guess, came from the heart.

L. Emmett Holt, the product of a sternly confident evangelical upbringing, made unfiery fastidiousness his style as an expert. Hall arrived at his decidedly more revivalist approach, paradoxically, after a youth in a more agonized Congregational clan. In his *Life and Confessions*, he credited his mother with "one of the first efforts in child-study, to which I have given so much attention." Abigail Beals Hall began keeping a "memorandum" with the arrival in 1844 of Granville Stanley, the eldest of the three children she and Granville Bascom Hall raised on a farm in the hills of western Massachusetts. (Another son, Robert, and a daughter, Julina, soon followed.) As with Sabrah Holt, nothing escaped her notice and her family knew it. In her little book she recorded "not only our cute sayings but many things which were thought to indicate future characteristics, with not infrequent expressions of hopes and fears for our future and notes of our distempers." Years later her eldest son searched for the document, eager to freshen his own memory with her observations and predictions. "This life-and-health book, unfortunately, although it was known to me all through my home-staying life and long after, cannot now be found," Hall reported. "If it could it would surely be of the greatest interest to me now."

Instead he came upon the religious diary kept by his mother, who had been adored and greatly influenced by her pious father, a Congregational deacon. Among the many self-critical meditations of this earnest woman, her son fastened on an entry full of parental anxiety. A surge of remorse about failing to be a vigilant enough mother had overcome her:

I have regarded this matter far too little. I am a mother, and what is my influence on my children on whose young hearts are made ineffaceable impressions which have a bearing on their character through time, and also their future destiny? It is a solemn inquiry and awakens sad reflections. I would this day be stimulated anew to greater watchfulness on this point that in all things my mite of influence may tell for good on my children to the remotest generation.

In response, Hall allowed himself a surge of remorse in his memoir. As if her "excessive domestic duties" and religious woes were not burden enough, he had added to her trials. "Perhaps she felt that she should have prevented all our bickerings if her heart was full enough of love and reproached herself that harmony did not always reign," he worried as he recalled his recalcitrant younger self, the boy who was "almost brutally prone" to "bully my brother and tease my sensitive sister." (Unlike Holt, the speedy student in the family, Hall was often overshadowed by his younger brother in school as a boy, and the underdog found ways to bite back.) Hall went on worrying at greater length:

Perhaps she was so enamored of amity that my then too belligerent disposition seemed to her a standing indictment of herself, because neither the heredity which she transmitted nor the training she had given made me anywhere nearly realize her ideal, so that my nature may have made her feel that the quality of her parenthood or her nurture was defective. If she had borne and reared a more amiable child she might have had less cause for religious discontent.

Hall did not hesitate to emphasize his father's role in her spiritual unhappiness and, by implication, in his own unruliness. Granville Bascom Hall, unlike Horace Holt, was a decidedly obtrusive presence in the household. An impetuous son, Granville Hall at eighteen had "bought his time" from his own father and left home to go to school. He went on to teach (he was "very successful in discipline"), and after that headed west to homestead on government land. He returned before long and married a woman whose "father-image" (which Hall, among Freud's earliest American admirers, believed informed every woman's husbandly desires) this would-be adventurer did not obviously fit. A restless farmer, Granville stood out as a champion of agricultural innovation and an abolitionist; he was a temperance crusader, too. And soon he was the father of an impetuous son who, before he reached adolescence, found Granville an oppressive influence.

That somewhere within the autocrat lurked an empathetic father was a secret the undemonstrative Granville kept with success, certainly as his eldest got older. But a record remains of one occasion when the taskmaster opened up to a child whose gumption, for all the friction it caused between them, could be a source of harmony as well. He wrote a letter to the six-year-old Stanley to thank him for his heroic help on the farm one morning; Granville Hall evidently couldn't bring himself to express his gratitude to his son in person. But his letter was perfectly pitched, with respect and simplicity, to the new reader that Stanley must have been:

My dear son,
    This morning my feet were quite sore, and I was lame and tired. I felt as though I could hardly walk and my cows were above the woods and had not been milked since yesterday morning. Now what to do I did not know. I knew I had a boy who was almost always willing to help me, or do what I asked him. But it was foggy and dark and I knew it would be a great deal for him to get them and I did not know whether a boy but six years old would think himself man enough for so great an undertaking. Once I thought I would not mention it to him lest he should be unwill-

ing. But how happy it made me to find him willing as soon as he was asked. His mother said she did not believe there was another boy six years old in the whole town who would do so much. And I think so too. As I looked out of the window and saw you climbing the steep hill I thought how very bad I should feel if you should be sick and die as many children do, and I hoped God would keep you well and let you live to grow up a good and useful man. Don't you find it hard to drive cows in the morning? The reason is they have not had their breakfast and keep stopping to eat. I was afraid they would trouble you so much you could not get them. But after looking to the woods a while out came the cows.

Your affectionate father,
G. B. Hall

The gruff man's letter recorded a surge of sympathy with his child, and reported his own concern about how best to wield his authority—two feelings an older Stanley was sure were utterly foreign to his father. It was a moment when child and adult met and communed, not as equals but as companions in an arduous endeavor: not just rounding up cows, but forging a tie with each other. The parallel between the two challenges was not lost on Hall's father. The undertaking Granville contemplated—sending a boy out to do a grown man's work, his work, for the first time—was daunting. He was not sure he would be able to drive his son in the darkness of morning.

The son, too, faced a challenge of a magnitude greater than he had ever managed. He confronted hungry cows who might well be recalcitrant. But the father overcame his hesitations, and even as he entertained the worst fear of all—his son's death—he watched his hopes being more than fulfilled. His son not only set out eagerly, but came back successful. The boy swallowed his fears: it was dark and foggy, the hill was steep, the cows were big, woods could be terrifying, his father was intimidating. He had a chance to do the nearly impossible: prove himself to his father. His hopes were more than realized. The cows came home, he came home, and he received this letter.

Far more often, in Hall's memory, what he received were lashes, mostly of tongue but occasionally a flogging, from a dogmatic man he failed to please. He recorded one severe whipping, memorable above all for the weeping it inspired in his mother. With her "morbid dread of conflict of any kind," she suffered greatly at her eldest's "early and especially pubescent antagonisms toward [his] father" (which his brother seems to have shared to a degree). Granville Hall's penchant for the older Calvinist school of "harsh censure" also went against his wife's more solicitously devout grain. Two letters, one written for New Year's delivery in 1853 and the other a year later and both signed St. Nicholas, give the fierce flavor. Gone was the fond empathy. He enunciated six "rules of conduct" for eight-year-old Stanley, each one prescribing perfect obedience to his parents, whose advice must never be rejected "because *you cannot see* it to be wise. . . . Never allow yourself to lean to your own understanding when it conflicts with the experience of your elders." To the nine-year-old boy, he followed up this way the next year:

> Stanley to own the truth . . . I have many fears respecting your future character & end. . . . O, Stanley! do not disappoint the high hopes you have raised in the hearts of your father & mother by forgetfulness & indolence, & worse than all, bring ruin upon yourself. *Struggle with your might to break the chain* which habit has thrown around you & is strengthening every hour, before it is too late. . . .

Half a decade later, a fourteen-year-old Hall memorably lashed back. In the midst of yet another flare-up with his father, who had just impatiently slapped him for accidental clumsiness, Hall "stepped back in anger, partly real and—I distinctly remember—partly feigned for effect, doubled my fists and glared at him as if I were strongly tempted to hit back. I shall never forget his amazed look. I was never hit again." A shift in authority, though evidently no surge of affection ("the very atmosphere of Puritanism chilled almost every manifestation of it"), came with later adolescence. Hall was willing to give his harsh father credit for helping to lay in him "the foundations for a certain independence of authority and impatience of control and an ideal of freedom in thought and action," usefully tempered by an "ambivalent feeling of respect and even awe for him."

Hall had already spent time living away from home on a larger farm during school vacations. Now, in the common antebellum country custom, he intermittently left home to attend school, boarding at other farms, and at sixteen was himself an itinerant teacher. His parents henceforth united in anxiously spurring their children on beyond them. "We children were incessantly exhorted to 'make good' in their place, to succeed as they had fallen by the way," Hall recalled, appreciating both the pathos and the impetus conveyed by the efforts of two who, as he now saw it, "were always oppressed by a sense of failure."

Hall himself was deeply mortified (and even worse, probably deeply relieved) when his father bought him a medical exemption from the Civil War. Actually, the conviction that he was indeed physically—and morally—diseased haunted Hall day and night during these years, he confessed. He even consulted a doctor, in secret, about the source of his panic: nocturnal emissions (and, he strongly implied in *Adolescence*, masturbation). In his complete sexual ignorance, he was sure that he was utterly, irrevocably "corrupt." Writing about his youthful self later, Hall was acutely aware of being a protean creature in a transitional era. Stanley was the dreamy, solitary boy-adventurer in Nature, and the bullying sibling and rebellious son at home. With the "dawn of adolescence," he confessed, "no dread was greater . . . than that of inferiority and mediocrity," which accompanied his deep sexual fears. Yet he was also full of high spiritual hopes and grandiose dreams of escape and fame. "Hard up against the stern realities of life," young Hall felt trapped. At the same time, he experienced the world and himself with an intensity of feeling he never encountered again. He was carried away by books and thinkers, and gloried in "rank lush sentiments and emotions."

Hall polished up his family portrait with filial piety that sounded slightly forced. "If ever parents lived for their children, mine did," he wrote. ". . . My mother always sympathized, encouraged, stimulated; while my father warned, criticized, and sometimes rebuked to the end of his life but nevertheless reinforced, sooner or later, all my mother did and said for our good." Not least, she encouraged her children's desire to get away and be further educated. Granville Hall's arm had to be twisted. He had counted on his sons to stay and help with the farm, and their college plans came as a severe disappointment: Hall and his brother went to Williams College, Julina to Mount Holyoke.

Granville Hall, unlike his own father, did not exact payment for his son's departure before his majority. The era of financial, contractual obligation was past, though the sense of fealty owed was still strong. Hall's escape was condoned as a sign of ambition, but he was not allowed to shake the discomfiting feeling that he was a child who had not lived for his parents. He knew his mother and father recognized his departure as the abandonment, and the possible betrayal, of their Puritan provincial world that it was. Even when seized with nostalgia years later, Hall was honest enough to depict himself as a son whose impatience with hidebound Ashfield, Massachusetts, was in no way hidden from his elders. "As a youth I thought myself most unhappy and this discontent drove me out into the world."

Both of Hall's parents made their growing apprehension clear as they watched their eldest son's subsequent erratic course. They were overjoyed at Hall's "conversion" experience as a sophomore at Williams during a religious awakening that swept across New England campuses, briefly interrupting a secularizing trend. (Hall himself later analyzed his temporary transformation from an earnest Christian into a passionately enthusiastic one as a response to his sexual panic.) His parents were encouraging as he proceeded to the Union Theological Seminary in 1867 with a career in the ministry in mind. It was his mother's dream, although Hall wrote home warning that "I do not think I have got the requirements for a pastor."

While there he explored New York, questioned religious orthodoxy, began to contemplate teaching philosophy, and then, with a loan arranged by Henry Ward Beecher, he set off for Germany in 1869. He read Hegel and studied with an anti-Hegelian, and in pursuing his interest in the process of development, he dabbled in science, too. His parents were soon urging him to come home and get down to honest work. Hall agonized himself: "I am twenty-five and have done nothing for myself, scarcely tried my hand in the world to know where I can do anything." By the comparable stage in his life, Holt was just completing his professional training and was poised to open his private practice.

Hall returned to America in 1870 and graduated from Union Theological Seminary in 1871. While tutoring the sons of a New York banker for two years, he read Darwin and Herbert Spencer in the company of a "little club of Positivists," whose leader published a journal called *Modern Thinker.* The preacher-son his mother had dreamed of was clearly not to be, but Hall set to work trying "to make a good Christian of Hegel," and espousing a developmental vision that reconciled reason and faith. At last he landed an academic job—in literature, not philosophy, but he wasn't picky—at Antioch College, and his fervor for Hegelian idealism fading, began reading Wilhelm Wundt's *Principles of Physiological Psychology.* When Hall's tenure expired at Antioch, and no appointment materialized elsewhere, he headed for Harvard University, where William James had set up the first psychology laboratory in the United States and was offering the only course in the country in physiological psychology. At thirty-two, Hall embarked on yet more graduate training, glimpsing the answer to his spiritual and epistemological dilemmas in the emerging empirical branch of philosophy—the New Psychology—that aimed to submit the mind to the same scientific scrutiny being trained on other physical and biological processes. In 1878, Hall received his pioneering doctorate in psychology.

Even as he seemed to be buffeted this way and that, professional ambition churned in this perpetual student. In 1878, Hall was back in Europe, this time studying with the German eminences Wundt, Hermann von Helmholtz, and other pioneers in physiology, psychology, psychophysics, physics, and psychiatry. In Wundt's newly established laboratory, the American acolyte won praise for "the Geist" he displayed. James, who visited him overseas, felt the dose of natural science left his student "singularly solidified," and Hall himself welcomed the rigor as a needed safeguard against "sentiment or triviality." Hall (whose exposure to German *Mädchen* on his first trip had taught him "what love really meant and could do . . . [and] that I was a man in the full normal sense of that word") also found another heretofore missing ingredient of maturity: a wife. In 1879 in Berlin, he married Cornelia Fisher, a woman he had met back when he was at Antioch, who was herself in Europe studying art.

On their way home, the new husband—now with a child on the way and still without a job prospect—equipped himself with another set of credentials. On the hunch that pedagogy, a field that was beginning to flourish in Germany, might prove to be the New Psychology's ticket to respectability, Hall made a quick sweep, gathering the latest European educational wisdom, which drew on Kantian ideas about the growth of the mind. Liberally cribbing from Francis Parker, the school superintendent in Quincy, Massachusetts, who had gone the Germanic and organic route before him, Hall returned to ride the wave of American interest in "new education." It was to be child-centered and experience-oriented, rather than tied to traditional academic subject matter. The cause was certainly good for Hall's growth. The president of Harvard set him up with a series of lectures in Boston on pedagogy. Hall's recapitulationist version of the new wisdom—parents and teachers should be guided in their efforts by the knowledge that "the stages of a child's mental growth repeat the experience of the race"—was a big sensation.

Then came the real launching of his academic career. In 1881 (the same year that Holt, a decade younger, began to practice medicine), he was invited by Johns Hopkins University—whose president he had been pestering for a job for years—to give a series of lectures; in 1883, John Dewey took his advanced psychology course, and two others the next year. In 1884, Hall was hired full-time to teach pedagogics and psychology and to establish a serious psychology laboratory in America. (William James's setup at Harvard had been more rudimentary.) Meanwhile, he was also engaged in more popular pedagogical pursuits. In a well-publicized scientific paper, "The Contents of Children's Minds on

Entering School" (1883), which was modeled on a survey undertaken a decade and a half earlier by the Pedagogical Society of Berlin, Hall administered questionnaires to a group of six-year-old Bostonians. His purpose was to assess their "general" knowledge, by which he meant rural lore—and was stunned to discover the depth of his urban subjects' ignorance. At the age that he had been out herding cattle, his interviewees were sure a cow was "no bigger than a small mouse": their picture books proved it. A flurry of similar investigations and interest in "child study" among teachers and mothers followed. But Hall now had his academic niche, and began tending it. In 1887 he founded the *American Journal of Psychology*, devoted to promoting the New Psychology. His parents, Hall sighed in relief, were "finally convinced I could 'earn a living without working on a farm.' "

His parents did not live to see that Hall failed to enjoy professorial peace and prosperity ever after. In 1888, Hall was offered the most prestigious of positions in rapidly professionalizing America: the presidency of a new university, Clark. It had been founded in Worcester, Massachusetts, by the retired businessman Jonas Clark, a provincial fellow who was inspired to leave a cultural legacy in his hometown after several trips to Europe (during which he spent time collecting old books, whose covers he liked to stroke). But within a few years, Hall's grand plans for organizing a graduate institution devoted to the natural sciences were foundering. Jonas Clark was threatening to withdraw funds, and the newly founded University of Chicago was plundering his faculty to fill out its own staff of professors—an "act of wreckage," Hall called it. As if he didn't have troubles enough, tragedy struck his family. Recuperating from diphtheria in the spring of 1890, Hall headed west to convalesce in the restorative air and peace of the family homestead in Ashfield, which he had been sorely missing since his parents' deaths several years before. While he was away, his wife and his eight-year-old daughter, Julia, were asphyxiated by a leaking gas pipe in their house. His nine-year-old son, Robert, survived. The bereft father who returned home succumbed to what Hall later called a "Great Fatigue."

"Something of a crisis" was Hall's atypically understated description of his personal and professional trauma, and he later suggested that his ordeals and endeavors in the wake of it felt like a reprise of his adolescent turmoil. Dr. Hall was indeed flailing during the decades around the turn of the century. Desperation and unfulfilled ambition goaded him as he felt his academic status teetering, and he fought against "a certain desiccation of the psyche," a sense "that mere intellectuality had supervened with distinct loss of emotional response to life." Hall rescued himself by returning to child study, which had in the interim become something of a vogue among middle-class American mothers, teachers, and social reformers. He took the lead and, with a proprietary flourish, he announced a public turning point in the mission in 1894. "Unto you is born this day a new Department of Child Study," he told the National Education Association, exulting that "lusty as this infant is, and visible as I believe it to be," great growth lay ahead. It was impossible, he proclaimed, "to overestimate the importance of this event."

To judge by a fictional fragment written by Hall's sister, Julina, and preserved among his papers, he may well have left his own child, Robert, in her care as he took off in quest of the Child. At any rate, the notion of tending the child of the father of child study struck her as worthy of some dry, though fond, humor at his expense. "Professor Harrington . . . was becoming so well known in his scientific work that he was absent from home much of the time," she began her sketch. "There were conventions and congresses and assemblies and association clubs and his responsibilities in connection with these were becoming so heavy that it seemed as if the task of rearing Joe fell more and more completely on my shoulders." Certainly in real life Robert felt abandoned after the tragedy; he told Hall's biographer that his father became a "distant, austere, and authoritarian figure."

To his many lay acolytes, and his many academic critics, Hall became the opposite sort of figure as he fanned the national enthusiasm for probing and reporting on child life. He was permissive with the questionnaires that had become his favorite mode of investigation. He welcomed as his pollsters all kinds of eager amateurs, supplying them with interview materials he churned out on every subject under the sun: "the doll passion," anger, lies, "the different modes of crying and laughing with pleasure and pain," children's games, "their sense of self," fears, "early forms of vocal expression," cloud and moon fancies, moral and religious experiences, and so on and on.

William James soon complained that Hallian questionnaires "ranked among the common pests of life." In an 1897 address to the National Education Association called "Criticisms Wise and Otherwise on Modern Child-Study," John Dewey was withering about the unscientific spirit of the endeavor, with its self-promoting camp followers and its zealous leaders, "lacking in stability." He was just as dismissive of its scientistic pretensions: no one, he said, should expect such a project to "afford a new, certain, positive, and scientific basis for education." Genuine scientific exploration does not provide "on demand usable recipes, ticketed and labeled for all pedagogical emergencies." In any case,

Dewey emphasized, "mere general theories and mere facts *about* children are no substitutes for insight *into* children."

But Hall's enterprise was as popular as it was precisely because it was such a hybrid and lent itself to hype. He defended the methodological muddle as "inevitable at an early stage of such a movement, for it was a new ore and the method of refinement hard to learn." Hall was indeed tackling a kind of naturalistic research, observing children's minds and behavior in everyday social settings, that has stymied many psychologists since—when, that is, they have troubled to try it. Turning to his amateur audience, Hall advertised child study almost as if it were a pep pill, promising that those who participate "are themselves rejuvenated and growing young against the tide of years by finding that life has a new zest." As he recognized, it fit right in with the muckraking and settlement house spirit spreading among a Progressive middle class that felt detached from "real" life. "Best of all, perhaps," he continued his pitch for child study, "it tends to make family life with plenty of children in it more interesting and desirable. Indeed, it is a part of a great culture-movement marked by a new love of the naive, the spontaneous, and the unsophisticated, by a desire to get at what is primitive and original in human nature as it comes fresh from its primary sources." In such moods, he did not at all mind celebrating the rough edges of his "science." "It is a nondescript and, in some sense, an unparalleled movement—partly psychology, partly anthropology, partly medico-hygiene, . . . and it has a distinct ethico-philosophical aspect," he explained, and while he was at it he threw in "a spice of folklore and of religious evolution, sometimes with an alloy of gossip and nursery tradition, but possessing a broad, practical side in the pedagogy of all stages."

At the same time, Hall was given to making prophetic claims for his cause. "I am well aware that this will seem to be enthusiasm," he prefaced one of his more spectacular predictions in the middle of the decade, but "if promises that are now springing up . . . are realized, [the child-study movement] is to be not only an educational renaissance, but a scientific reconstruction that aims at the top and is the salvation and ultimate development and end and aim of creation and of history." Underlying it all was Hall's recapitulation theory, according to which children evolved upward from primitive savagery into civilized humanity at adolescence. His purpose was not so much to confirm the popular theory—he assumed it and clung to the view long after others had jettisoned it—as to spell out an appropriate pedagogical ladder. The "determination of intellectual nascent stages," when children were ripe for particular methods and subjects, beckoned as the ultimate goal of his Rousseauian enterprise, so parents and teachers could "pour into, not onto, them" all they needed to know.

Defensive in the face of doubters like Dewey, and desperate to produce a magnum opus, Hall insisted that his mountains of data would eventually reveal all he needed to know. The chaos of observations would settle "into ultimate unity in such a way that when published in book form the relations between the different parts of the wide and rapidly extending domain of child study might be exhibited in a systematic way," he promised, "and their manifold applications, not hitherto apparent to the public, and often not to the individual investigator, might be set forth."

But Hall's own doubts mounted, and he began complaining about the "soft" Romanticism of his erstwhile allies among the kindergarten movement. Deriding their lack of Darwinian rigor and the fussy activities their program assigned children, the champion of child study was soon embroiled in controversy. "We need less sentimentality and more spanking. We are going child study mad," he finally exploded in 1899 from his well-paid place at the podium. By that time, he had taken a leap—as he said the child himself did—into adolescence, the topic on which he decided he could make his mark. It was a stage his questionnaires had only glancingly touched on, but one into which a man in the midst of a midlife crisis felt he had real insight.

In 1904, Hall published his two-volume treatise, *Adolescence: Its Psychology and Its Relations to Physiology, Anthropology, Sociology, Sex, Crime, Religion, and Education*. Encyclopedic, rhapsodic, full of panic it was; systematic it was not. Lorine Pruette, a protégée of Hall's (who became his first biographer), marveled at its "wide circle of readers among the 'general public,' " a popular success that made it "a triumph and a scientific curiosity." She went further, exclaiming that "anxious mothers . . . hugged its two big volumes to their breasts . . . [finding] . . . within its thousand pages a light to ease their steps and to guide them through the perilous paths of child-rearing." A reviewer (a colleague in psychology) commented that "the book and the ideas it presents [are] plainly in the adolescent stage." In retrospect, Hall implicitly echoed the verdict. "There is a sense in which all my active conscious life has been made up of a series of fads or crazes, some strong, some weak; some lasting long and recurring over and over . . . and others ephemeral," he reflected in his *Life and Confessions*. The prodigal was perhaps not being as humble as he seemed. After all, this was the man who also proclaimed that "the best definition of genius is intensified and prolonged adolescence, to which excessive or premature systematization is fatal."

Certainly Hall's sprawling manifesto about unruly youth, especially paired with Holt's trim manual about orderly infancy, did not cramp parents by providing a lockstep guide to raising children. The "light" these pioneering experts shed on those "perilous paths of child-rearing" showed just how far from straight and narrow they were. Instead the odd pair shared the contradictory hopes and fears of Americans feeling confused, as the century turned, about whether children—and their mothers—needed new stability or new flexibility; more order or more room for spontaneity; greater protection from an urbanized and mechanized world or more careful preparation for it. Should adults be striving for more intimacy or for more authority as they faced new challenges to their parental control? Together Dr. Holt and Dr. Hall in their books supplied the obvious answer to American mothers, and fathers, worrying about the erosion of their power and dreaming about its expansion: everybody needed all of the above.

The advice to be gleaned from Holt's booklet and Hall's volumes does not add up the way you would expect—nor did the experts' own practice at home line up with their preaching. In retrospect, it is easy to cast Dr. Holt as a hidebound advocate of conformity for children and emotional austerity for mothers—the harsh scion, as Dr. Spock portrayed him, of all the disciplinarians ever after who have intimidated mothers into regimenting themselves and their children. Certainly Dr. Holt's "catechism" was not cuddly, yet neither was his gospel of "regularity" designed to turn out dutiful cogs for the machine age, or simply to keep mothers in line. And at home he—thanks to Mrs. Holt—supplied early proof that "parent-centered" experts, beneath their authoritarian manner, are sometimes just as ready to let children be children as their developmentally minded, child-centered colleagues are. Upon closer inspection, there is a standoffish spirit behind this strict rationalist's vision. In his cool way, Holt left room for autonomy and freedom, for mothers and for their offspring—in fact, arguably more than the romantic Dr. Hall himself did.

Open Hall's book, and mixed in with his message of personal liberation and generational communion turns out to lie a conservative vision of social control. Ultimately he was as concerned to preserve stability, in the psyche and in society, as he was to promote vitality. A champion of feminine fecundity and disciplined virility, the conflicted Hall endorsed the virtues of hierarchy, self-control, and industry with a zeal Holt was temperamentally unable to match. And the stirring advocate of "imaginative, emotional" bonding between adult and child turned out to be a stern father with an alienated son. To follow Holt and Hall and their books into the new century is to discover that America's "hard" expert and "soft" expert were, for all the distance they had traveled, in many ways still their fathers' sons.

THREE

Infant Regimens, Adolescent Passions

Lesson in the care of children, c. 1910

I.

Margaret Mead's mother, a new parent at the turn of the century, was the very model of a self-consciously modern, well-educated, progressive-minded, middle-class mother. That did not make Emily Fogg Mead a typical American parent by any means (as she was given to reminding her daughter). She was a perfect example of the exceptional parent who prided herself on her advanced approach to child rearing. "Not satisfied with just getting along," she belonged to the breed of woman praised by the president of her alma mater, Wellesley, for "packing everything they do with brains, . . . studying the best possible way of doing everything small or large." She was, in other words, a kind of ideal reader in a new age of scientific parenting lore, and she showed herself to be not at all literal-minded. Mrs. Mead embraced the wisdom of Holt and Hall, believed deeply in both, and embarked on rearing her children in her own intense and inconsistent way. Her eager eclecticism was just what their work encouraged—in fact, demanded.

Mrs. Mead had made sure to bone up for the arrival of her daughter, who was born in 1901 in the brand-new West Park Hospital in Philadelphia; the usual home birth did not strike this enlightened mother of the new century as desirable. "When I knew baby was coming I was anxious to do the best for it," Mrs. Mead told Margaret later. Awaiting her firstborn, she kept "a little notebook," in step with the child-study teachings of Dr. Hall (including in her journal, "among other things, quotations from William James about developing all of a child's senses"). The minute Mrs. Mead got home with her infant, she turned to Dr. Holt's *Care and Feeding of Children*, as many similar American mothers did.

Margaret Mead emphasized that her mother was hardly an assiduous Holtian, however. "The lack of any contradiction between my mother's ardent support of good principles and her fury at injustice, on the one hand, and her deep personal gentleness, on the other, came out clearly in her response to the advice given mothers in a baby book that was published just about the time I was born," Mead wrote in her memoir, *Blackberry Winter*:

> The author, L. E. Holt, was an advocate of the kind of regimen, such as schedules for bottle-fed babies, that ever since has bedeviled our child-rearing practices. She read the book, but she nursed her babies. She accepted the admonition about never picking up a crying child unless it was in pain. But she said her babies were good babies who would cry only if something was wrong, and so she picked them up. Believing that she was living by the principles of the most modern child-rearing practices, she quite contentedly adapted what she was told about children in the abstract to the living reality of her own children.

What Margaret Mead failed to appreciate was that her mother was in truth quite a good Holtian, because his regimen countenanced—indeed, all but required—a mother's "[working] out her own solution in the light of present knowledge and experience," as he put it, to suit her own situation. And in breast-feeding her babies, Mrs. Mead was in fact obeying the doctor's most medically sound advice to the letter. Dr. Holt made sure at the beginning of his manual to recommend mother's milk as the most wholesome food for the human infant. What no doubt misled Margaret was that he then proceeded to devote the bulk of the book to recipes for mixing artificial formula and schedules for dispensing it. The spirit of his advice was in favor of bottle feeding.

Mrs. Mead also followed the two other injunctions in Dr. Holt's manual that jump out at the contemporary reader: don't play with your baby, and serve only the blandest and softest of food to the child who has graduated to solids. But Margaret credited her mother's ascetic streak to nature, rather than to Holtian nurture. "She had no gift for play and very little for pleasure or comfort. She saw to it that we had wholesome food, but it was always very plain." Finally, Mrs. Mead followed Dr. Holt's injunction to keep meticulous records, which was in step with Dr. Hall's recommendation of the "life book" habit that she had lost no time in establishing. The experts would have marveled at her exhaustive records: thirteen volumes, just on her firstborn.

Yet all of this maternal earnestness did not signify an absence of camaraderie and commotion in the Mead household—thanks to a grandmother, one of those "female presences" the experts warned about, who was actually quite up to date. Martha Ramsay Mead had been an innovative teacher in her youth. She did have the gift for play, or at least for delightful outings and stories, and for confiding in a child, as Hall recommended. And she had no patience for lockstep schooling of a conventional kind. Nor, for that matter, did Emily Mead, who joined her—and both doctors—in firmly believing in country air and freedom; she made sure the family always lived outside the city, and liked to corral local craftsmen to come tutor her brood in carpentry, basketry, and weaving.

Kindergarten passed muster among the pedagogically enlightened women of the family. Margaret attended for two years. But from then until fourth grade, she had no official schooling. When she finally did show up in class it was only for half days, and she went armed with instructions from her parents that she was to be permitted to leave whenever she liked. When nine-year-old Margaret decided to begin a diary, her first entry showed her to be very much the product of her eclectic yet ever so self-conscious rearing: "I'm not sure that I won't miss days some times, For I am not very regalar." At adolescence, she was swept up in a joint project with her mother that would have struck Dr. Hall as the acme of his desires: mother and daughter communed over a child-study investigation. Emily Mead was a sociologist manqué, and the two of them went off to study Italian immigrant children, aiming to find out how language affected IQ scores.

That Margaret Mead grew up to be, if not a "superanthropoid," a super anthropologist who made the culture of child rearing one of her specialties would surely have warmed the hearts of her mother's mentors. Among Dr. Hall's fondest hopes was that conscientious parenting would result in children who themselves had the precepts of enlightened nurturing bred into their bones. (He was not alone in the belief that characteristics acquired before parenthood—especially during puberty, when parents-in-the-making grew so much—could be inherited by offspring. Darwin himself had dabbled in the notion that traits that were not inborn might nonetheless be passed on, and half a century after *On the Origin of Species* appeared there was still plenty of room for speculating about heredity. "We have no glimmer of an idea as to what constitutes the essential process by which the likeness of the parent is transmitted to the offspring," an evolutionist lamented in 1900— and he was speaking of plants, not humans. "The process is as utterly mysterious to us as a flash of lightning is to a savage.")

But Holt and Hall would no doubt have been taken aback to find that Mead proceeded to bite the hands that had fed her. She made it one of her many missions to condemn what she felt had become an American fetish about "regularity" in infancy, arguing that early rigidity undermined a child's sense of security and autonomy—and a mother's as well. Mead also dedicated herself to debunking the notion of adolescent "storm and stress" as romantic rubbish. Teenage turbulence, she was convinced, was the product of American prudery about sex and a source of maladjustment in adulthood, an artifact of a culture that kept youths cut off from adult activity and company too long for their own, or society's, good.

Mead's criticism of infant schedules and of protracted adolescence was an ironic verdict on the two signature ideas of the pioneering experts. For in advancing those ideas, Holt and Hall hoped to cure a version of the very problems that troubled Mead. Read Holt's catechism in context, and it becomes clear that he got his start as a popular expert by doing his best to cater to mothers, not to cow them. The aim of his system, beyond the immediate goal of preventing infant mortality, was to reduce nervousness and promote sturdy independence—in mother and baby alike. Hall's crusade was meant to liberate youths from a prudish culture, and to prepare them to thrive more fully as adults. His hope was to promote communion between adolescents and their elders in the process.

By the end of their careers, both pioneering scientific experts were well aware that their advice had hardly yielded the intended results, but their complaints were not exactly Mead's. In the postwar world they glimpsed before they died, each felt left in the dust in a different way. Hall was dazed to see how fully "flapperdom" had "shattered old conventions." Meanwhile, "the nation's bill for ice-cream and confections in 1921," Holt was appalled to note, "was more than $500,000,000!"—nearly triple what it had been in 1914. He had to wonder whether anyone had been listening to his wholesome dietary strictures at all.

2.

"In the preparation of this catechism," Dr. Holt announced at the outset of the first edition of *The Care and Feeding of Children*, "everything has been sacrificed to clearness and simplicity." He went on to explain that "the style of question and answer has been adopted in order to impress more strongly the facts stated." If he sounded like a schoolmaster talking to students who might face a test, it was because he was—or had been. As Holt explained, his booklet was based on a pamphlet written for use in the Practical Training School for Nursery Maids established in 1889 at his Babies' Hospital, the purpose of which was to educate young women in his employ about "those things which were matters of daily observation in the practical work of the hospital." He was now—"at the request of many friends"—publishing an enlarged primer on "nursery hygiene and infant feeding" for use in other "similar schools for training." And, sounding more tentative, he added that "it is thought it may be of value to mothers in the care of their own children, or a book which they may safely put into the hands of the ordinary (untrained) nurse."

As a manual for nursery maids dealing in hospital wards of poor, "friendless little babies," Holt's sixty-odd-page first edition, with its "simplicity, brevity, and exactness," has an earnestly didactic air. Everything was indeed routinized—from feeding schedules (every two hours during the first month, the intervals lengthening with age) to weighing (before and after meals, without clothes) to toilet training ("easily [done] by the third month if training is begun early") to crying ("necessary for health. It is the baby's exercise" for fifteen to thirty minutes a day). Holt covered the topic of playing, too: "never until four months, and better not until six months. . . . They are made nervous and irritable, sleep badly, and suffer in other respects. . . . [If they are played with at all it should be] in the morning, or after the midday nap. Never just before bedtime."

As regimens for hospital nurses, the terse standardization made sense; that playing was even contemplated—and that the doctor so plainly feared that his prohibition wouldn't hold—actually seems somewhat poignant under institutional circumstances. What was more notable was how studiously scrutinized every detail of daily care was. Both babies and their caretakers, though Holt referred to the former by "it" and addressed the latter in his impersonal catechistic style, were nonetheless being taken very seriously. The infant had a stomach that required fine-tuned tending and cries that needed interpreting—were they of pain, hunger, temper, illness, indulgence, or bad habit?—and the nursery maids were presumed to be very punctilious.

They were veritable scientists, in fact, when it came to preparing milk formulas, which was the focus of the book and the topic to which Holt gave "fuller treatment," at the suggestion of the hospital superintendent, in an 1897 edition that was half again as long. "Some want has also been felt and expressed by mothers," he added. This is a sample of what he supplied, a commentary on the glass jar of milk he had instructed the infant caretaker to set on ice and let stand:

> The upper one fifth (6 ounces from one quart) may be calculated to contain 12% fat. If the milk is very rich, the upper one fourth (8 ounces from one quart) may be used. If milk is used which has been bottled at a dairy the day before, the upper one fourth (8 ounces from one quart) may be calculated to contain 12% fat. This top milk may either be removed by skimming or the bottom layer of milk may be siphoned off, leaving the number of ounces of top milk desired. Should more than 5 ounces of the 12% milk be needed, two quarts of milk should be set.

As Oliver Wendell Holmes, Sr. (the judge's father, a doctor), once remarked, "A pair of substantial mammary glands has the advantage over two hemispheres of the most learned professor's brain in the art of compounding a nutritious fluid for infants."

It was the home economics mentality at work: cooking was equivalent to chemistry. (Fannie Farmer was known as the "Mother of Level Measurements," thanks to her enthusiasm for measuring cups and spoons, tools first introduced in the 1880s.) Simplicity and brevity were not on display, though exactness was. Or it was until Dr. Holt followed up with counsel to the lab cooks to wing it according to the weather, which was, in the business of ensuring safe milk, obviously a crucial variable. During the warm season, he advised, "it is well to make the proportion of cream less than during cold weather. During short periods of excessive heat it should be much less." No measuring spoons here.

Nursery maids needed such information, even if the dietary tinkering to suit the right formula to the right weight and state of the infant often came too late for the malnourished infants who arrived at his hospital; children's nurses in the home did, too. Mothers, however, were not supposed to "want" such information. It was by now well-established medical knowledge—thanks to the efforts of doctors like Holt—that the best thing for a baby in an era of high infant mortality was mother's milk, not formula. (The first question in Holt's catechism was "What is the best infant's food?" and he answered it categorically, "Mother's milk," supplying a stark statistic: babies on formula were three times as likely to die as breast-fed babies.) It was also well-known social knowledge that many a mother did not care to nurse—whether because she was otherwise occupied, class-conscious, physically squeamish, had an envious husband, or the catchall reasons, was "nervous" and found it an "inconvenience"—and that she did not take kindly to being told otherwise. "The running war between the mother, who does not want to nurse, and the philosopher-psychologists, who insist that they [*sic*] must," the psychologist William Kessen once noted, "stretches over two thousand years."

Holt had already learned from his own private practice that "at least three children out of every four born into the homes of well-to-do classes must be fed at some other font than the maternal breast." That "must" was somewhat wryly meant: a tacit recognition of a compact between doctor and non-nurser. She would refuse to breast-feed, and he would countenance her defiance of his best advice and supply her with the alternative nutritional counsel she required. The arrangement served him well. As Holt informed his colleagues, "the man who has mastered [the percentage method of formula mixing] will never lack for patients"—or, he now found, for readers. But Sabrah Holt's son was determined that his services would be of broader benefit to the maternal enterprise as well. The mother who mastered his studiously measured approach would not only have a physically healthy baby; she herself would learn to think like a scientist, or a nurse, which would mean she would be calm and never lack for patience.

Middle- and upper-class mothers were evidently eager to comply; in fact, they sought out the advice with the hospital aura. The underground success of Holt's training manual was a sign of women's interest not just in using bottles but in having schedules and impersonal rules for "nursery hygiene" in general. Holt took the experience of his book as a paradigm for his didactic relationship to his maternal audience, which he proceeded to develop over the next two decades in new and larger editions of his manual, in speeches, and in articles for the "Happy Baby" department of the popular women's magazine *The Delineator*.

It was up to doctors, Holt explained, to dispense "more exact and definite wisdom" as they accumulated it. It was up to a mother to "put herself in relation with the best thought of experts in this field" of nutrition and child care—and to turn a "deaf ear" to "the grandmother . . . [whose] influence is particularly pernicious, as she is supposed by her previous experience to know everything about babies." He admitted that some experts—and too many "manufacturers of the commercial infant foods," busy advertising their wares—could be pernicious themselves; he lamented how "much that is exaggerated, sensational and even false, is given to the public." Still, the vigilant mother should discriminate, and Holt brooked no exceptions to his faith in maternal education. "The greatest obstacle in the way of improving the health of children is not poverty," he believed; "it is ignorance and indifference." Armed with up-to-date information and a "habit of close and accurate observation" of her child, a mother was then to "work out her own solution in the light of present knowledge and experience."

He did not amend his curt nurse-training style for home use, no doubt partly because stiff Dr. Holt would have had a hard time sounding warmer, but also because the clinical coolness was the book's selling point—a rarity in the feminine texts in the field. In the contemporaneous *The Care of Children*, even the superintendent of the Newport Hospital, Elisabeth Robinson Scovil, could not resist decorating her otherwise plainspoken text with tips such as that "deep embroidery is not considered good taste" on baby clothes. "A tiny vine embroidered by hand is admissable." And she, unlike Holt, did not hesitate to make her non-breast-feeding readers squirm. "It is the duty and ought to be the pleasure of every mother to nurse her own baby," she lectured. "All right-thinking women are anxious to do so in spite of the inconvenience to themselves."

The point was not that the dry Dr. Holt was reducing mothers to heartless menials, rearing little automatons by rote. Rather, he was treating them as scientific professionals, or semi-professionals, charged with the care of delicate specimens whose health was under their control, not out of their control, as parents had so long lamented. Mothers could dispense with "the notion of medicine as a mystery" and play their part in what was a "science in which effects regularly follow causes," and for reasons they could figure out, with advice from a doctor. The "laws of health" he laid down sounded reassuringly strict, yet they also left room for maneuvering, for the "conditions affecting nutrition" always varied. As in the case of that container of milk, Holt's imperious dictates could be a curious blend of extremely precise and totally imprecise.

It was up to a mother to steer her way. In a "Happy Baby" column, Holt explicitly told readers that, his many charts notwithstanding, in the end it came down to each mother to chart her course on his key topic: scheduling milk and meals. "The number of feedings in which this is given, and the intervals between the feedings, are matters of secondary importance; these are things which can be arranged to suit the best interests of the mother." On crying, too, as Mrs. Mead appreciated, Holt's advice left a mother to adapt specific dictates (don't respond to every infant wail) and a broad recommendation (allow up to half an hour of crying a day) to the "living reality" of her own baby—and, presumably, to her own tolerance for noise. The important thing, he would have agreed with Mrs. Mead's daughter, was "believing that she was living by the principles of the most modern child-rearing practices," not following them to the letter. Holt even left room for "mothering," or so Mrs. Max West of the U.S. Children's Bureau decided when she appropriated his wisdom for use in the *Infant Care* manual the bureau published to great popularity in 1914, two years after the government office had been founded. After announcing the Holtian "rule that parents should not play with the baby," or rock and jiggle him, she went right on to emphasize that "this is not to say that the baby should be left alone too completely. All babies need 'mothering,' and should have plenty of it."

Suitably careful mothering, of course. Working out her "own solutions" in the same methodical and thoughtful way the doctor did, Holt insisted, helped to keep a mother in control of her feelings—and less inclined to be an intrusive presence in her baby's life, which needed to be calm as well. The goal was to keep "parental affection" and "the natural desire of the young mother to 'enjoy her baby' and please him" from being her "only guide" because emotions were a tyrannical guide, not because Holt aimed to create a maternal tyrant—or to tyrannize her, stern though he could sound about not treating an infant "as a plaything."

Feeding was the model he worked from: he believed "uncontrolled emotions, grief, excitement, fright, passion" were the main source of "the failure of the modern mother as a nurse," causing her milk to dry up or to disagree with the child, leaving him more vulnerable—which stirred yet more anxious passions in her, and the vicious cycle went on. The quest for more "regularity and persistence" was a preventive endeavor, designed to help her escape those emotions, which would in turn permit more methodical oversight of her child. It was crucial to his health—now her "sphere of activity" (and a heavy responsibility)—but also to hers. As Mrs. West emphasized in the *Infant Care* manual more strongly than the teacherly Holt did, the charts and scheduling ought to give her a break. Promising mothers that "the care of a baby is readily reduced to a system," she made the welcome practical promise that such an approach "reduces the work of the mother to the minimum and provides for her certain assured periods of rest and recreation."

Just as Holt did not consider his regimen for mothers coercive or oppressive, he did not view a mother's routines for her child as repressive. Her approach, like the doctor's, was a protective one. According to the preventive view that Holt led his profession in promoting, unpredictable infection from without was best held at bay by maintaining health, which entailed monitoring all signs of vigor. That meant regular feeding and weighing. The extension of that idea, which was widely shared by Americans alarmed about the "nerve-excitation" and "agitation" of modern urban life, was that mother and child needed a habitual steadiness to fortify them against a disorderly—and ever more materialistic, distracting—world.

In demanding outward conformity to schedules, Dr. Holt intended to create room for the growth of sturdy autonomy. As he put it in his Lockean way, his regimen of care was designed not only to save life, but "to secure the early bending of the twig, or, better, to see that the pliable twig is not bent at all in this period." He advised "no forcing, no pressure, no undue stimulation" of infants, on precisely the same grounds that experts now counsel stimulation: the brain grows more during the first two years than over the rest of a child's life, Holt emphasized, warning that "a great deal of harm may be done in this period." But the danger he feared was sensory bombardment, not neglect or boredom—especially "in these days of factory and locomotive whistles, trolley cars and automobiles, music boxes and the numberless mechanical toys in the nursery, door-bells and telephones in the house."

Gone from his pages was the fierce infant and wayward child of Calvinist lore. On the contrary, the subject of Dr. Holt's ministrations was so tractable as to be all but invisible in *The Care and Feeding of Children*, a blank little bundle readily put on a schedule. In the more discursive tone he adopted in articles for the "Happy Baby" department of *The Delineator* magazine, Holt depicted a highly responsive specimen, not naturally given to defiance at all—if, that is, he set off on the right steady track rather than being unduly jostled, from without or within. An "untrained baby or a baby who has been trained to bad habits," Dr. Holt warned, "soon becomes a tyrant in the household, making life a burden to the mother and to all the family"—including himself. It was not that this impressionable creature had an inborn drive to dominate that needed "breaking," though of course "every child likes his own way," he acknowledged. Holt simply wanted to make sure that self-mastery was the lesson the little fellow was learning during a "period of education," Mrs. West emphasized, that is "often of greater consequence than any other two years of life."

"A young baby is very easily molded; in fact, he is about the most plastic living thing in the world," Holt explained. "The disposition to the formation of habit is amazing, and it is just as easy to form good habits as bad ones if one begins aright at the outset and is consistent." William James embraced a similar view that habits were essential to developing individuality, rather than a guarantee of docility. The idea was to "make our nervous system our ally instead of our enemy . . . [and] make automatic and habitual, as early as possible, as many useful actions as we can," James first explained in his *Principles of Psychology*, and again in his *Talks to Teachers*. ". . . The more of the details of our daily life we can hand over to the effortless custody of automatism, the more our higher powers of mind will be set free for their own proper work." It was a mother's duty to herself and to her child, Dr. Holt taught in his much terser way, to provide him a peaceful alternative to an impulsive life.

It was a message for which there was evidently a market, and it was precisely Dr. Holt's aloof manner that made him such a popular messenger. As a writer named Anna A. Rogers lamented in an article called "Why American Mothers Fail" in *The Atlantic Monthly* in 1908, "The whole present tendency in life is to the over-development of emotion among men, women, and especially children." She felt the temperature needed lowering. "What is really needed to precipitate both peace and progress is, not the elimination, but the firm control of emotion and instinct, by cool deliberate feminine wisdom." In fact, she got quite worked up about the situation. "If a mother would but strive to put less heart into it all, and more mind!" Dr. Holt very studiously urged her to do just that.

Another writer, Anna Noyes, celebrated Holt as an ally in the cause, which in her description was hardly the affectless enterprise his own dry style evoked. In a slim account of her success as an American mother, *How I Kept My Baby Well* (1913), this middle-class Holtian in a New York City apartment emphasized what a psychological liberation his approach had been for her—never mind the salutary effects on her son (who did catch some colds and suffer some stomach troubles, despite her claim that he "was kept well for two years by not being allowed to get sick"). "The problem of raising a baby has not only been intellectually stimulating—I know, for instance, I got more out of it than I ever got out of an equal amount of time spent on geometry, though I reveled in geometry, too—but emotionally as well," Noyes reported of her hands-on course in infant digestion. "I find that I have never been more on the qui vive than during these two years." Certainly she needed to be feeling energetic, for Dr. Holt's regimen was not for slouches, and she was not about to pretend it was. But she found all the pre-emptive effort more empowering than unnerving—exactly as the doctor ordered:

> I found it was worthwhile to try to keep the baby well, though it meant constant watch for seemingly trivial indications of indigestion, constant endeavor to prevent their continuance or recurrence, and what some may regard as unnecessary fuss and bother with timing, weighing, measuring, and record taking. But it paid, for it has spared me absolutely from those prolonged sieges of anxious worrying when a little life seems to be ebbing away and one waits and waits through the long, dark night for the tide to turn.

To judge by her report, Holt's regimen certainly did not turn her household into a grim hospital ward. Her book was stuffed with charts of an anal-compulsive variety (nursing times, consistency of stools, quality of cries, etc.), but her tone and the photographs of her chunky son cavorting naked with his parents—all carefully labeled, lab style, of course—told a warmer story. They had plainly been more than data-gathering occasions. "My kind of worrying—if it may be called that," Noyes summed up, "has played its part in giving me a sweet-tempered, rollicking, hearty little lad as my constant companion for these two years, and will, I hope, give to the world later a calm, thoughtful, amiable, dignified spirit."

Closer to home as well, the evidence suggested that Holtian practice could be much less austere than Holtian prose. If Dr. Holt's own wife had any complaint with the nurses that she, unlike Noyes, had the means to hire, it was that they were too aloof or overbearing—not that they were insufficiently chilly for the Holt home. In the notes she kept, she criticized Constance for leaving Emmett Jr. too much alone. (Her third child, the future doctor, saved his mother's files.) "He developed great concentration of mind but was undemonstrative to such a degree that I feared he had no sensibilities or affections." Miss Carroll spooked Mrs. Holt with her command over the child. "He became so docile under her that had I not known him to have a strong will I should have feared the strength of her gentle influence over him."

As for Mrs. Holt herself, her notes convey a mother who applied her husband's regimens as she saw fit, and was less interested in schedules than in her children's emerging characters and their interactions with each other—topics her husband did not touch. She nursed Emmett Jr. only briefly. She was, however, one of the lucky elite able to have it both ways in the safest—and truly old-fashioned—way: she hired a wet nurse for that dangerous interlude, the summer. Her son thrived—"a quiet, happy baby, not boisterous, but good-natured and active physically," she jotted at five months. At eleven months, she indulgently observed, he "stands by the bookshelves and pulls out books by the dozens." Three months later she admitted that "he positively declined to conform to some of the habits in which he has been drilled since he was two months old." This was data, as she was plainly aware, that positively declined to conform to her husband's dictums about bowel and bladder training, but she did not sound terribly worried.

It was considerably more worrisome that, beyond toddlerhood, Emmett became a sickly specimen, hardly a model of the preventive Holtian regime at work. As the junior Holt wrote in an autobiographical sketch he was assigned to do in medical school, "I managed to contract almost every known disease of childhood during the succeeding years, which left me with a tendency toward chronic bronchitis and bronchial asthma." Though his mother's notes don't say, he was presumably adhering to his father's recommended dietary regime for older children, which the elder Dr. Holt systematically elaborated on as he expanded subsequent editions of his booklet. That meant dining at an early hour on mashed, strained, boiled foods, nothing fresh (especially vegetables and fruits—particularly bananas!), nothing colorful, nothing flavorful—again, nothing "unduly stimulating or exciting" for the child in a distracting world. And the carefully measured portions of plain pabulum were intended to check any tendencies toward inconsistent meddling or indulgence in adults as well. Mothers and nurses were to encourage early "self-feeding," and they were not to scold, nag, or coax about cleaning the plate—or to give any treats. "Assuming an attitude of absolute indifference" was the trick, should any trouble arise.

Children were supposed to thrive on the bland mush so dispassionately dished out—above all physically, but also behaviorally. In Dr. Holt's cool, well-aired nursery, compliance without conflict was the rule—or at any rate the goal. "Children who are allowed to have their own way in matters of eating are very likely to be badly trained in other respects," Holt explained, "while those who have been properly trained in their eating can usually be easily trained to do anything else that is important." To judge by his book, he did not have a daunting disciplinary agenda in mind aside from his nutritional regimen and a brusque approach to the other traditional bodily issues. About toilet training, he was terse and overly optimistic—hold babies over the pot very early and often, and it will be done. About thumb-sucking, nail-biting, bed-wetting, and masturbation, he was terse and pessimistic, urging that the bad habits "should be broken up just as early as possible," but warning that restraint and disapproval did not work. "Watch closely" and "keep [the child's] confidence," he advised, adding that "medical advice should at once be sought" if problems continue.

In his career as a self-appointed "middleman" dispensing scientific clarity and calm to mothers, Dr. Holt practiced the persistence he preached, but his patience showed signs of fraying as the "diet problems of childhood" grew apace despite his efforts. As he revised and branched out from his baby domain, it did not escape his notice that mealtime struggles (unheard-of in Almanzo Wilder's day) had become an ever more bothersome child-rearing issue. The truth was that the "accurate, definite knowledge" Holt extolled as the "greatest weapon" in the crusade for child welfare was more debatable than his stark style indicated. (As a speaker on the "Scientific Basis of Reforms in Dietetics" had observed back at a Congress of Mothers gathering, the same bananas Holt judged to be so dangerous had also been rated, along with figs, the only safe fruit for children.) It was no wonder that changing child care habits proved more difficult than he had expected. Even when mothers heeded expert counsel—which Dr. Holt increasingly complained few did often or early enough—the cutting-edge science could leave them anxious and confused, hardly the cool-headed nurses he had hoped to inspire.

3.

"Take good care of yourself, and by that I mean cut out about half of what you wish, in the line of sweets. Father encloses pills for constipation." Dr. Holt's namesake, Emmett Jr., received those instructions from his mother in 1908, the year he became a teenager. ("How does it feel to be 13?" Mrs. Holt had written him a few months earlier, marking the turning point.) His parents, true to form, were worrying about digestion and counting on habits of moderation, self-control, and regularity—the Holtian mantra—to see their son through. At the same time, however, even the Holts were singing a more Hallian tune to their fledgling adolescent, whom they had sent to a tiny boarding school in Lakewood, New Jersey, in search of "a better climate than the big city."

It would be an exaggeration to say that the doctor who had assured parents that "babyhood need not be a time of storm and stress" suddenly advocated adolescent storm and stress. Still, he and his wife were soon urging Emmett to stray from the straight and narrow. Their capable son was ready to head off to college early, and they did their best to deflect him, dispatching him on various experiments in rustic living instead (as in fact they had been doing since childhood). "I am sure from your letters that you appreciate how much it means to live near old Mother Nature," Mrs. Holt rhapsodized to a sixteen-year-old Emmett out west. "We are made for it, surely, or we would not respond to it as we do. It helps the inner life. . . ." To charge ahead academically, they advised, would be "unwise and disadvantageous," and they warned young Emmett, "You will lose everything but the study if you do." It was surprisingly relaxed counsel, coming from the studious, rigorous doctor.

Immoderation, irregularity, irresponsibility: that was the Hallian mantra for youth during adolescence, which he called the "infancy of man's higher nature, when he receives from the great all-mother his last capital of energy and evolutionary momentum." It would be hard to imagine a more radical departure from Dr. Holt's regimen for early life. Yet Hall's outlook was a variation on Holt's preventive ethos: where the rationalist pediatrician aimed to arm children (and mothers) against an unstable world by inoculating them with a hefty dose of regularity, the romantic psychologist gave youths (and the adults who were to dedicate themselves to them) a big shot of flux and fervor to bolster them for routinized modern life. Ideally, the prescriptions went together nicely. Dr. Hall hailed a thrilling "second birth," counting on the earlier Holtian vaccine to keep his "awkward, often unattractive neophytes" from flying off course altogether.

Dr. Hall's two-volume treatise was as unlikely a popular hit as Dr. Holt's catechism, further evidence of the zeal among middle-class American mothers themselves to try to be professional about parenting. He hadn't written with them in mind. As the sweeping subtitle of *Adolescence—Its Psychology and Its Relations to Physiology, Anthropology, Sociology, Sex, Crime, Religion, and Education*—indicated, Hall aimed his tome at academic colleagues, whom he hoped to impress with his synthetic work, and at the pedagogical and social reformers whose numbers were growing in Progressive America. It did create a stir among psychologists, teachers, and helping professionals, but in ranking it "a triumph and a scientific curiosity" thanks to its appeal among the "general public," Hall's protégée Lorine Pruette was right. Criticism of contradictory kinds from fellow experts soon piled up: the work was judged reactionary and scandalous, turgid and exaggerated, overly physiological in approach and culturally skewed, and even before Hall died he knew it was considered dated. But of the "fads or crazes" in his career, it was also clear that with his big book he had helped launch one that was anything but ephemeral. As one of his detractors complained, "we are today under the tyranny of the special cult of adolescence."

And as one of his lay acolytes suggested in a rather breathless review of the book, it made a popular splash because of, not in spite of, the adolescent sprawl that elicited condescension from Hall's peers. What "an immense mass of material . . . a thesaurus of observations, whose diversity at once attracts readers and baffles reviewers," marveled the anonymous critic writing in the general interest magazine *Outlook* about "this really great work . . . the most fruitful work on its subject yet produced." Commenting on the "remarkable book" in her column in *The Delineator*, Mrs. Birney of the National Congress of Mothers agreed that no treatise could be too big, given "the magnitude of such a subject as adolescence." She praised Hall's volumes, and other treatments of the topic, as "more fascinating than any work of fiction could be"—ideal for awakening parental interest in a period that she feared got short shrift. "It is a common sight to see parents and even an entire household lavish time, thought and affection on the dear baby," she chided, "while at the second birth, or advent of adolescence, when tenderness and loving insight are most needed, the boy or girl often experiences real mental anguish through positive neglect, indifference, or misunderstanding."

Hall's idea of adolescence as a sheltered adjunct to childhood, free of the responsibilities of adulthood, was concretely relevant only to a privileged few, of course. Although labor and educational patterns were changing, even by 1920 only one American child in six actually graduated from high school. By then, a decline in farming meant that somewhat fewer children were employed full-time or doing hard labor than at the beginning of the century, but the campaign against child labor had exerted more sway on ideas about children than on their actual activities. (Census figures were highly unreliable, but between a million and a million and a half children ten to fifteen years old were reported "gainfully employed" in 1920.)

In any case, Hall's practical notions of just what the moratorium should amount to for those teenagers who could afford it were less than totally clear. What caught on were his ideas about what the interlude meant for the adults responsible for the age cohort. In focusing obsessively on pubescent youth, Hall encouraged a shift in adult attitudes, making adolescents and their dramas a prime responsibility of parenthood, of adulthood in general. As was his wont, he was riding a wave. Kate Douglas Wiggin's *Rebecca of Sunnybrook Farm* was a best-seller the same year his book came out, in 1904. In the novel about an imaginative ten-year-old sent to grow up in the company of her two spinster aunts in a small village, the drama of the heroine's maturational journey into adolescence was very nearly overshadowed by the spectacle of various of her elders clamoring to be "useful in her development." With proprietary zeal, they called the imaginative Rebecca "our prodigy and pearl."

Dr. Hall made no claim to have discovered adolescence as a "storm and stress period" of life (though ever since he has gotten credit for it). A whole section of his book surveyed "the seething age" in literature, biography, and history. Rousseau had compared the maturing youth to a "tidal wave" and "a lion in heat" a century before him. Hall's Victorian predecessors had noted the "wild desires, restless cravings" of the period, and churned out tracts for pubescent girls on the special perils of youthful stress and for boys about the challenges on the road to success. Hall's signal contribution was to add post-Darwinian biology and proto-Freudian psychology to the mix. And his distinctive appeal lay in making adolescence a developmental turning point in adult life, in parental experience as well: an occasion for "wise mentors and advisers whose character invites the fullest confidence" to discover, through the vicarious projection of hopes and fears onto passionate youths, a newly vigorous connection to life. In Wiggin's novel, adults could not get enough of Rebecca's eyes, "carrying such messages, such suggestions, such hints of sleeping power and insight, that one never tired of looking into their shining depths, nor of fancying that what one saw there was the reflection of one's own thought."

For Hall, immersing himself in adolescence had proved just such a rejuvenating experience. (And, as one critic appreciated, a great deal of projection was indeed at work: "we divine how fully the writer must have lived, not only amid but through much of the experience he describes.") "To rightly draw the lessons of this age," Hall was convinced, "makes maturity saner and more complete" for all concerned—the already grown along with the growing youths who, weathering the storms, successfully arrived at the "highest possible maturity of body and soul." For adolescence, "and not maturity as now defined, is the only point of departure for the superanthropoid that man is to become." Hall's recapitulationist and romantic view had changed the equation. The question was no longer merely what youths were going to do with themselves during an awkward transition. It was how grownups were going to think about youths who were suddenly undergoing a mysterious transformation.

The answer was: adults would think about them with much the same ambivalence and "vague yearnings, ambitions, hopes" that the doctor discovered in the adolescent breast itself, if Hall was their guide. The two hallmarks, so to speak, of *Adolescence* were its "saltatory" science—the view that adolescence marked a developmental leap—and its obsession with sex ("without precedent in English science," remarked the reviewer in *Science*). As a thrilling combination, Dr. Hall could hardly have done better. He intended to be very inspiring on both themes, yet he also managed to be unnerving. As he seems to have appreciated, that only added to the appeal of the work. If American parents were not quite ready to worship adolescents for their hormonal vigor and their higher humanity, they were very ready to worry about them (as, a century later, their descendants still are).

Hall's conviction that adolescence marked a leap in psychological as in physical development, a sudden break with childhood, offered cause for great optimism. As Mrs. Birney eagerly quoted Hall, "adolescence is the age of reconstruction, when new determinants come to the fore, and also the point of departure for new lines of development. It is the age, too, when, if ever, previous tendencies to abnormality may be overcome, both by nature and by treatment." The appeal of the recapitulationist view for Hall was that it allowed for the discontinuities that he saw in development, all without losing "upward, creative, and not de-creative" momentum.

Too honest to pretend that his child studies had revealed a neatly progressive series of nascent stages to steer by, Hall cobbled together a course through childhood not unlike his own—notably wilder than the idyll the proponents of the kindergarten envisaged, more independent than Dewey's collaborative laboratory ideal, and bumpier than anybody's map of growth (though James, too, called attention to "the law of transitoriness governing the ripening of impulses and interests" in children). After a calm infancy, the Hallian child enjoyed the wild freedom of a "healthy little savage" for seven or so years, his active imagination fueled by fantasies and by the mysteries of the "real," adult world. Then came a crash into the "quadrennium," the years of more stable growth from eight to twelve, which Hall considered "preeminently the age of drill. They ought to be sacred to habituation, to discipline, training, obedience to wise authority"—the basics of civilized life—though children still needed room for roaming and self-expression.

As if this alternation between "free and playlike" activity and orderly work wasn't jarring enough, Hall then supplied the biggest bump of all: the "new birth, when higher and more completely human traits are now born." Adolescents, he insisted, needed freedom to fluctuate more wildly than ever before. Thus Hall strongly opposed the "uniformity and inflexibility" of college-focused high school curricula, urging an appeal instead to "the fundamentals of the soul, which are instinct and intuition, and not pure intellect." For the task of "youth [in] . . . this larval stage of candidacy to humanity" was to explore the "whole gamut of feeling, will and thought." The goal was to emerge with altruistic ideals, the strength of which depended on the "ardor and energy of living" that had gone into their making. It was, Dr. Hall emphasized, a chance to cultivate intellectual enthusiasms (rather than Latin skills), and to soar to new heights of morality—more a miraculous metamorphosis than a consolidation of what had come before. "New zests and transforming motives seem to change the very warp and woof of the soul itself," he marveled, noting in a Hegelian vein how "passions and desires" arrived in pairs of "antithetic impulses." Thrilled by the tumult, Hall promised that "no age is so responsive to all the best and wisest adult endeavor."

But the saltatory logic could be unsettling. Troubled children could perhaps be redeemed, yet souls in such flux could also lose their way. And Dr. Hall realistically warned that "parents are often shocked at the lack of respect suddenly shown by the child. They have ceased to be the highest ideals. . . . The passion to realize freedom, to act on personal experience, and to keep a private conscience is in order." Unless it is out of order, which Hall granted was not just a possibility but a tendency. The " 'teens' are emotionally unstable and pathic," was his diagnosis. His prognosis was that "youth must have excitement, and if this be not at hand in the form of moral and intellectual enthusiasms, it is more prone . . . to be sought for in sex or in drink."

And prone to be found in sex: the reader of *Adolescence* was surprised—and surely titillated and rather terrified—to discover its author explaining at some length how thrilling that quest could be. To an audience used to Victorian euphemism ("occult causes, probably of a physical kind," were at work in boys) or to "modern" discretion (the "hygiene of puberty" had supplanted "the curse of Eve" in discussions for girls), Dr. Hall delivered a jolt. Americans were full of "false and . . . morbid modesty," he chided. They erred on the side either of "prudery and painstaking reticence" or of "exaggerated horror, as in the 'scare' and quack literature." Hall believed that more exalted, and more extensive—and more explicit—treatment of the topic was crucial, for this precocious Freudian was convinced that "there is great reason to look to sex for the key to far more of phenomena of both body and soul at this as at other periods of life, than we had hitherto dreamed of in our philosophy." Hall cited Freud on the "psychic strains" caused by sexual drives, and invoked his "talking cure" as a useful concept; "whether as therapeutic theory this be more or less partial," he felt adolescents would benefit from a chance to unburden themselves. Hall himself certainly felt the need to open up.

As the reviewer in *Outlook* had noted, different "classes of readers will fasten on one topic more than another" in the tome, but Dr. Hall's discussion of sex and attendant issues (diseases of body and mind, faults and immoralities) "will draw the attention of all." There comment stopped, and although prudery was probably at work, so no doubt was perplexity. Repression—cold showers, wet girdles at night—was the message of health crusaders such as John Harvey Kellogg, whose *Man, the Masterpiece* (1886; reissued in 1903) was very popular. Sublimation was the gospel of Dr. Hall, who proclaimed that "sex is the most potent and magic open sesame to the deepest mysteries of life, death, religion, and love." According to Hall, passions needed channeling, not subduing: rather than wet girdles, he prescribed alternative pursuits, the wider and wilder the better. But like those passions, Hall's message had a way of escaping control. To read his fervent treatments of masturbation, and also of menstruation, is to watch an empathetic sensualist locked in battle with an old-style moralist—and a sexist.

Thus Hall introduced masturbation as "perhaps . . . the most perfect type of individual vice and sin"—for males: aside from infant rocking and squirming, girls' urges in this direction got short shrift—and echoed the familiar fears that it was fast draining the race of vitality. Before long, however, he was referring to "these forbidden joys of youth" and the "fevered . . . pleasure" they occasioned. And then he added the frisson of confession to his account of youthful penis anxiety. Hall coyly admitted that he was the model for his intimate profile of "anxious urinoscopists," boys spooked by nocturnal emissions and then plunged into what he described as almost manic-depressive cycles, alternately yielding to and struggling against the temptation to masturbate. (He referred to a prominent doctor of philosophy as the sufferer he had in mind—and he included a footnote to an article of his own on fears.) Yet even as he warned against the lures of the flesh, Hall made sexual urges sound irresistible, thrilling, even enlightening—and understandable, given the "ever lengthening probationary period" that youth must endure in a late-marrying society.

Officially, he rated "the act . . . brutal," low "in the phylogenetic scale of animality," but his descriptions evoked a very human experience. "The first orgasm," Hall started out explaining with a scientific air, ". . . consists in a general and diffused glow and exhilaration of the sense of well-being even before emission is possible." Then the poet chimed in. "This gives a heightened sense of the value of life, and a flush of ecstasy and joy that tinges the world with a glory that is far more than sensuous." The psychologist now added a note of alarm, but was still awed by the imaginative drama. "The Nemesis of depression follows hard after these exaltations, and both states arouse thought and fancy in new directions and with a vividness unknown before."

It was a little later that the psychologist returned to the darker dimension. "Abnormal acts impair self-respect," Hall observed, "and tend to a sense of shame and of being an outcast to the better self as well as to society. This, which I nowhere find mentioned in the medical writers, I deem central." But far from making the behavior seem brutish, this symptom only added a tragic luster to it. Emotional introspection, after all, was one of the purposes of the adolescent interlude, according to Hall—a chance for the male to experience, however briefly, the feminine side of his nature. True, the habit tended to leave a "languid appetite for the larger, if less fevered, pleasure of the intellect, of friendship, of high enthusiasms," where Hall felt youth should feel strong hunger. But he also couldn't resist noting the even more fevered pleasure that solitary indulgence could not begin to match—the real thing. Dr. Hall expounded on the delights of leisurely foreplay, with "all the irradiations of touch, sight, gradual approach, the long-circuit stimuli through secondary sex qualities. . . ." Quite worked up himself about the whole business, Hall came down to earth and endorsed a campaign to inform youth that nocturnal emissions were natural—part of the "periodic" rhythm of life and no cause for panic.

Dr. Hall's oddly ennobling account of masturbation was covert (and, it seems, unconscious), but he had no qualms about going against the hygienic grain of the times in glorifying menstruation. He roundly attacked the antiseptic "experts" busy sanitizing the process, in near-complete ignorance of female biology, and also the feminists who went along with them. Hall launched a crusade to publicize and sacralize the deep mysteries of femininity and maternity (he, too, had next to no facts to go on). It was the sister mission to his don't-worry-about-wet-dreams message, and the drama of menstruation that he celebrated had more than a little in common with the travails of masturbation, about which he had been so conflicted.

"Periodicity," according to Hall, was the glory of womanhood, as of adolescence, the stage given over to fertile fluctuations of body and soul. In his organic vision of growth, females merited the somewhat cryptic praise of being "more generic and less specific" in their nature than males—by which he meant, in essence, perpetually adolescent: freer to indulge their "many-sided" natures and fulfill their hereditary potential. Their identities were ever in flux, their individuality never fixed. (That feminists chafed at such a profile puzzled Dr. Hall.) Thus the pubescent girl, plunged into the experience of monthly periods, sent him into raptures. For her was reserved the acme of "changeableness," the chance to become "in the course of the month several different kinds of person" as her moods ebbed and flowed.

Yet if Dr. Hall's portrayal of masturbatory commotion had been more glowing than he was aware, his paean to menstrual instability was more suffocating than he seemed to realize. He outlined what might almost rate as a proto-description of pre-menstrual syndrome. In the course of a month, he wrote, the adolescent girl was "more sensitive, more prone to depression, excitable, moody, feels more fatigued, distracted, suffers pain more or less intense in different parts of the body, especially in the head, is liable to discontent, quarrelsomeness, unstable in appetite and sleep, disappointed, feels oppressed, and can do less work with mind and body." Yet Hall, impatient with invalidism, viewed this as part of a vital adventure. He extolled the freshness with which she emerged from her ordeals and prepared for the next round: "She develops new sentiments, instincts, and insights, is a charm to herself and both a fascination and a study for others." He exulted that "her life is larger and explores all the possibilities of humanity," which he adduced as a reason that she "is less in need of supplementing her own individual limitations by the study of the alien lessons of the schools." Citing results from his questionnaire days, he pronounced that girls "have from six to fifteen times as many ideals as boys" in early adolescence.

That this marvel was also a victim of frustration, trapped by a sense of unfulfilled potential, could not help emerging from the doctor's data and his own observation. "The saddest fact in these studies," he noted, "is that nearly half our American pubescent girls chose male ideals, or would be men." Hall's protean creature did not enjoy such freedom after all, though he did not seem aware of just how poignant the portrait he evoked was. In fact, his verdict on her predicament was bleak. For young women, "the divorce between the life preferred and that demanded by the interests of the race is often absolute." As he noted in a talk shortly before *Adolescence* appeared, the sense of restlessness only mounted as girls drew closer to adulthood.

Dr. Hall was not alone in detecting a hunger for wider horizons in young women further along in life, anxious at eighteen or so about a future limited to motherhood. "To millions, yes, to millions," *The Delineator* worried, the coming of children "is a troublesome question, a question that brings doubts and fears and rebellion and sadness." Hall evoked girls' plight with rare insight, displaying an almost peculiar empathy with a predicament that, as he described it, was indeed one he knew well. They felt, Hall intuited, "a slight sense of aimlessness or lassitude, unrest, uneasiness, as if one were almost unconsciously feeling along the wall for a door to which the key was not at hand . . . [and] slowly lapse to an anxious state of expectancy, or they desire something not within reach." Hall saw what that something was: "They wish to know a good deal more of the world and to perfect their own personalities."

Given such conflicted diagnoses as Hall's, it was perhaps no wonder that he floundered when it came to cures. He was, in short, a prescient pioneer in the quest to rescue Ophelia and raise Cain that has discombobulated experts and parents ever since, and left plenty of adolescents disoriented. His prescriptions were a blend of utterly conventional and thoroughly contradictory wisdom. At his most bromidic, Hall echoed the quacks and prudes he disparaged, recommending that boys' hands be kept very busy and that girls' minds not be kept too busy. Above all, the religious ideals of both must be fed, he insisted, all to maintain "the potency of good heredity."

But Dr. Hall himself betrayed some dissatisfaction with these cautionary clichés. He tied himself in familiar knots trying to overcome the problem that a long limbo, instead of solving, tended to exacerbate: youthful stultification, pent-up energy, anomie. "The one unpardonable thing for the adolescent is dullness, stupidity, lack of life, interest, and enthusiasm in school or teachers, and perhaps above all, too great stringency," he proclaimed. His array of pedagogical recipes for girls and for boys (he opposed coeducation in adolescence) revealed his confusion about whether he aimed to prepare them for the life ahead or to preserve them from it; to challenge them intellectually or to channel their emotional and physical development in vocationally useful and morally uplifting directions; to encourage individual "struggle, effort, and perhaps conflict," as he once put it, or to counsel peer-oriented cooperation, accommodation, ease.

In the various ideas that Hall put forth were confusions that have kept surfacing in different forms ever since. Boys were victims of the "sissifying of the schools," he fumed, even as he urged that they be liberated from the straitjacket of too stringent, masculine standards of specialized achievement. The debate continues in the turn-of-the-millennium battle over boys: a "soft" camp urges that boys get in touch with their emotional and imaginative side, while a "hard" camp complains that a feminist-inspired, therapeutic ethos at home and in school has tamed boys and deprived them of the heroic ideals they crave.

Girls tend to be more competent and hard-working students, Hall appreciated, yet he was also panicked about their vulnerability to the pressures of competitive, coeducational academics. The adolescent girl's crisis of confidence has since spawned an advisory genre full of fears about how girls conform too readily to male-oriented expectations, or underperform out of female fears or scruples. In *In a Different Voice* (1982), Carol Gilligan charted a distinctively female developmental odyssey, mapping the obstacles girls encounter in a world that runs on masculine assumptions about moral and emotional growth. In her wake has come an outpouring of concern about the "silencing" of girls, most notably Mary Pipher's *Reviving Ophelia: Saving the Selves of Adolescent Girls* (1994). And in the general questions that arise beyond the gender debates, Hall's preoccupations still echo. Are peer groups the problem or the solution? Is high school too lax or too long and demanding? Do jobs build confidence and discipline in adolescents, who need exposure to the adult world, or are they a drain on their energy and an invitation to sex and drink? Dr. Hall was far from the last to have it both ways.

It was only fitting that, in the wake of *Adolescence*, Hall got into trouble on the topic that has stirred controversy among parents and pedagogues ever since: sex education. At the height of his enthusiasm for Freud, and feeling marginalized by widespread interest in Dewey among educators, Hall tried to shock his way back into the spotlight in the second decade of the century—only to be shaken by the response. His new agenda was a logical, if somewhat farcical, effort to close the gap between wild adolescent passions and his comparatively tame educational prescriptions: he proposed to make "the pedagogy of sex," as he called it in *Educational Problems* (1911), a centerpiece of education. "It has not yet entered into the heart of man to conceive the amount of genuine scientific knowledge that a deep interest in sex could carry and vitalize," he announced. Dr. Hall hoped to flatter women by turning to them for "the rare combination of scientific and ethical humanistic qualifications" that he considered essential to the enterprise.

The mélange of botany, biology, history, psychology, and morality that Hall had in mind was vast, and quite vague. Nor did he win converts by concluding his abstract discussion with a graphic call for the husbands of the future to become more assiduous students of the practice of sex (though his female readers might well have been quietly grateful). It was time that they became better lovers of their wives, whose "coital experiences are imperfect." Hall lamented that man "never dreams of her passional potentialities and still less of her profound needs which he only tantalizes." (More of that irradiating foreplay!)

The effects, he warned, "are deleterious to the conjugal relations and to offspring alike," for he believed a dearth of orgasms for women explained feminism and race suicide—two of the main child-rearing crises of the era, in his view. Sexually unsatisfied women, according to Hall's psychology, sought to "break away from their proper sphere because man has not done his part to make them happy in it." And, according to his physiology, even if they stayed, they were less fertile and their children more fragile, because the sperm must "put forth abnormal efforts to reach its goal" in the absence of a female climax to speed it along. How could the child born of such a union hope to meet the great challenges of development that lay ahead?

Before long, Dr. Hall was piously backpedaling, rattled to discover that he had shocked his way out of the spotlight. A review in *The Nation* in 1911 ranted that his pages "of sexual detail . . . are not surpassed even by Krafft-Ebing or Mantegazza for quality of nastiness and nudity

of statement." Hall confessed he had never heard "criticism that rankled like this." A few years later, Emma Goldman, feminist and anar-
chist, reported with disappointment on a lecture she heard her fellow
Worcesterite deliver in Denver. Dr. Hall "talked badly and endlessly on
the need of the churches' talking up sex instruction as 'a safeguard for
chastity, morality and religion.' " In his failure to please anybody on
this fraught topic, not even himself, Hall was a baffled father of our
own times, when youths are reared on sexual explicitness and calls to
abstinence.

4.

With the arrival of the second decade of the new century, *Cosmopolitan*
magazine decided it was time to assess the expertise that had accumulated. "What Is to Become of Your Baby?" the editors asked. "Will children reared under the new, scientific methods be superior mentally and
physically to those reared in the old-fashioned way of our mothers?"
They went straight to Dr. Hall for an answer, and found him, like Dr.
Holt, betraying some doubt that all the doctors and "special assistants
and expert knowledge" now available "at every stage of life, even up to
the age of choosing a vocation," had exerted quite the influence the
advisers intended.

It was hard to tell, of course, as the feminist and outspoken rationalist Charlotte Perkins Gilman had pointed out in 1900 in *Concerning
Children*. (Her clear-headed book anticipated Hall's interest in the
"precious ten" years between fifteen and twenty-five, and echoed Holt's
call for "conscientious and rational restraint" of maternal passion—and
failed to catch on, perhaps because Gilman also boldly called for public
nurseries run "by special nurses who knew their business," a notion she
knew would be greeted as "horrific," and still raises hackles.) "Unfortunately, we have almost no exact data from which to compute the value
of different methods of child-training," she had noted. Next to none
had accumulated since.

Dr. Hall was not deterred, but his verdict in *Cosmopolitan* was far
from definite. "Never in the world were there so many and so able and
intelligent men and women devoting their lives to the rising generation
as today," he was certain. But Hall could not decide whether "we are
making sure if slow progress and are improving both in the production

and in the rearing of children," as he asserted at first. Hard though he tried to sound optimistic, rural nostalgia and fears of "race suicide" had him worried that physical and moral "deterioration" might outpace all meliorative efforts. "While we are lavishing immense sums and great energy upon the upbringing of our children," Hall went on to warn, "there is good reason to believe that no nation in the world's history has ever so far lost touch with the real, intimate nature and needs of childhood; and this makes the situation a grave one."

Plenty of "enlightened" parents, to judge by the mother who spoke up for her cohort in a "Letter to the Rising Generation" in *The Atlantic Monthly* in 1911, endorsed the alarmed verdict. She lamented a youthful generation "singularly lacking in force, personality, and the power to endure," and scolded them roundly. "You are markedly inferior to your old grandfather in every way—shallower, feebler, more flippant, less efficient physically and even mentally, though your work is with books, and his was with flocks and herds."

And so are you, youths replied in their turn, unimpressed by the studious parenting they had received. One of their spokesmen, the essayist and radical Randolph Bourne, bemoaned "a complete bewilderment on the part of the modern parent" in a reply to the *Atlantic* scold, which was published as a chapter in his *Youth and Life* of 1913. He diagnosed "timorousness" in his elders, and proclaimed his generation "increasingly doubtful whether you believe in yourselves quite so thoroughly as you would have us think." In fact, she herself had confessed that in the confusion of "not knowing what to teach you," her cohort had "taught you nothing wholeheartedly." Bourne rubbed it in, hard. "What generation but the one to which our critic belongs," he scoffed, "could have conceived of 'mothers' clubs' conducted by the public schools, in order to teach mothers how to bring up their children!"

Behind the scenes, Dr. Hall and Dr. Holt were dealing with the data on their own doorsteps. What was becoming of their babies, who by then had left childhood behind? In touch by mail with sons away from home, the experts were asking themselves—and their sons—just that. Their answers were hardly a scientific indicator of progress or regress, to be sure, but they offer a personal window on the professional and public confusion. In letters Hall wrote to Robert and Holt to Emmett Jr., the doctor-fathers conveyed the ambivalence and the ambition that marked "modern" middle-class nurture. Nostalgic and anxious, the experts echoed grandfatherly edicts from their own youths. But along with their apprehensions went great expectations for sons who were doing just what they themselves had notably not done: following in their fathers' footsteps. Where they might lead, the pioneering experts wisely did not dare predict.

Dr. Hall and his son Robert's correspondence was full of, what else, storm and stress. A chip off the old block, Bob was still adrift in his career at the advanced age of thirty-one, and had sent his father a furious letter in 1912 accusing him of a lack of sympathy. He had finished medical school, but his first year of practice was going badly, and he had asked for financial help so that he could go back to school and study psychology. Hall's harsh rebuff had enraged him. In a long letter, Hall endeavored to calm himself and Robert down—to commune as he, after all, believed fathers and sons should. "It is always hard for father and son to understand each other fully," he opened amicably, regretting deeply their estrangement of many years. ". . . But we must not get apart, for I could not endure that. Let us see therefore if we can not understand each other better."

Dr. Hall was haunted by the fear he had voiced in *Cosmopolitan:* in lavishing sums on his son, perhaps the crucial lesson every child needs and every parent owes him had gotten lost. "My mortal terror," Hall explained, was that "you might lack persistence and pluck to grit your teeth hard and fight your way to success and self-support if need be in a life and death struggle." He acknowledged his own peripatetic career and saluted Robert's interest "in studying my things" as an admirable "sign of growth." But Dr. Hall also let Robert know, at great length, that he was a mere dependent, and a disappointing one who had yet to display either the "strength of character" worthy of his Puritan ancestors or the appreciation of his father that Hall felt he was due.

Eternal adolescence had its limits was the message, and the regimen Hall prescribed was, in essence, an old-style apprenticeship: Robert should read psychology on his own (Hall was happy to recommend reading or supply syllabi—just no more money) while waiting for patients and "wresting a living from your profession." Hall strained to convey some appreciation of his son (lamenting that no mother had been around to provide more), but even Hall's praise had a proprietary air. "When patients begin to come you will be learning precisely those things about children that I have always wanted to know but do not," he emphasized. "I once thought very seriously of studying medicine to practice on children, so you are fulfilling my ideals"—as he noted one of his students at Clark, Arnold Gesell, was already busy doing. "That standpoint too is going to supercede my own psychological study and is the next step." If Robert felt daunted, it was no wonder.

Dr. Holt's correspondence with Emmett Jr. was, of course, a model of regularity—and of an intimacy that escaped poor Dr. Hall. In birthday letters to a son negotiating those "precious ten" years of extended adolescence, he echoed Hall's concerns. But the "hard" doctor also did what his "soft" counterpart could not: conveyed confidence in Emmett, and recognized the limits of his own control. As his son (out west again) turned sixteen in 1911, Holt sent on a classic paternal pat on the back. "Life now has many great opportunities opening up to men of character and ability," he exclaimed, "and our hope and expectation are that you may one day fill an important and influential place."

But Holt could not resist a little nostalgic moralizing to goad Emmett on. With his own youth very much in mind, he recalled for his son's edification that "I was always ambitious and felt that I might do something in the world if I ever could have the chance. To be sure the advantages which my parents could give me were small in comparison with what we have been able to give you and the others. But all through my boyhood and youth I kept before my mind that ambition to do something." He sounded his usual peremptory note: "You *can* if you *will*." But he left it to Emmett, blessed with "natural endowments which in many lines far exceed my own when I was your age," to find his own "path of highest usefulness and longest service to the world."

After a dose of endearments from Mrs. Holt to mark Emmett's seventeenth birthday in 1912—"We miss you. . . . I especially miss kissing your prickly chin. For we think you are a very good boy and we are so glad you came to live with us seventeen years ago"—Dr. Holt was back at it. To an eighteen-year-old now having (as Emmett confessed) lots of fun at Harvard, he could not help sounding more worried and wistful. "To-day is my father's birthday. 94 years ago!" Dr. Holt reflected. "It seems a long time ago. I have been thinking much of my own boyhood today and the old home at Webster, and the discipline and training which the country life of those days—50 years ago—gave. I could wish that you boys also had something that is quite as good." He echoed Dr. Hall's sentiments almost exactly: "My constant fear is that having been reared amid more luxurious surroundings, that these influences may tend to make you less self-reliant, less ambitious and independent in life than those which surrounded my own early life." He had a seven-word solution for a son who he presumed needed no more: "See to it that they do not."

Hailing his namesake's twenty-fifth birthday in 1920, Dr. Holt at last relaxed. He was feeling proud and humble as he thought back on that momentous year in his own life, when he had graduated in medicine—

which was just what Emmett was about to do from Johns Hopkins, having followed his father's course despite paternal counsel to chart his own way. Once again, Dr. Holt made a point of backing off, plainly eager to let his son emerge as a self-made man. It was an old-fashioned, and a very modern, ideal at the same time: Emmett was to be neither a dutiful descendant nor a pampered dependent, but a pathbreaker in his own right. "I often wish I could bequeath you the result of my forty years' experience in medicine, so that you might be able to begin where I shall leave off," Holt wrote him. "But I am afraid it might not prove the blessing that one might imagine, for it is one of the rules of life that it is our own experience which develops us, and not that of others, who would fain give it to us." In any case, his legacy might not be very relevant. "I am impressed with the fact that the medicine of the future is to be very different from the medicine of my time."

Just what lay ahead in the field of parenting advice, though, he could not envisage. It surely would have shocked the demure Dr. Holt that the popular child-rearing expert who would claim to be his heir was a wild psychologist named John Broadus Watson, a prodigal utterly different from the paragon Emmett Jr. (who deftly, and deferentially, updated his father's manual for many years, adding bananas and other medical discoveries). Watson radicalized and extended Holt's nurture position almost beyond recognition in his *Psychological Care of Infant and Child* in 1928. What had begun as a cool invitation to mothers to handle their babies' feedings systematically became in Watson a fierce denunciation of mothers' proclivity to warp their babies' feelings. The stolidly independent character that Holt had elevated as the ideal for an urbanizing era had become a more alienated figure in Watson's pages, and in his person. It was a twist of fate Dr. Holt did not live to see. The overworked doctor died of a heart attack in China in January of 1924.

For Dr. Hall the succession turned out to be smoother. The surrogate son of his dreams, Arnold Gesell, got to work preparing himself to become another popular child-development guide of the interwar generation while Hall was still alive to bask in the role of mentor. Hall had been stung by Gesell's departure for Yale in 1911 (he had aimed to make a place for him at Clark as his "understudy"), all the more so because the biological grandeur of his student's ambitions was right down his alley. At Yale, Gesell wasted no time in getting down to systematic study in the laboratory of those "nascent stages" that unfold naturally in the child. In 1921, three years before his death, a recently retired Hall made sure to claim Gesell as heir, obviously unaware that years hence his protégé would have even more trouble than he had admitting that the "ultimate unity" of growth had eluded him. "The greatest of all pleasures I have is in the great positions and splendid work already accomplished by those who were once here," Hall proudly began a letter to Gesell, and he ended humbly, "I feel certain that in the work that you and others have done and will do, the little I have done will seem crude and obsolete." The pace and the public reach of the scientific mission of child improvement were indeed increasing, but progress did not prove to be quite so steady.

PART II

Psychological Leaps

FOUR

The Era (and Errors) of the Parent

The Better Babies Contest, 1931

I.

The Conference on Modern Parenthood, held in 1925 by the Child Study Association of America at the Waldorf-Astoria Hotel in New York, was all but over when a storm blew in. Wednesday, October 28, "was one of the freakiest days of the season so far as the weather went," the *New York Times* reported. While 1500 delegates from almost every state were enjoying the ceremonial dinner after two days of meetings, a sixty-mile-an-hour gale swept through Manhattan, bringing with it a heavy downpour. By the time the conference-goers emerged, the rain and wind had stopped, but the temperature had plummeted. "Heavy overcoats, furs, thick mufflers and fur-lined gloves will be the order of dress," was the prediction for the following wintry day. The out-of-towners who had come not just for the conference but also for the Child Study Association's six-day "institute" were not the sort who liked to be caught unprepared. They were, however, the type who took pride in their capacity to "adjust," a watchword of their work.

As the *Times* commented, the parents who organized and attended the much-publicized gathering of experts on child rearing were not to be mistaken for flappers out for a gay time. "The modern mother, if we are to believe the popular novel and the scenario writer, is a pleasure-seeking, irresponsible creature who divides her time among bridge and dancing and 'parties' where the conduct is 'advanced'; while the modern father is even less of a father than he used to be," the newspaper's editorial on the event began. "But the Conference on Modern Parenthood," the *Times* continued, "has framed quite a different picture: a renewed sense of parental responsibility and interest which has now reached the proportions of a full-fledged national movement. This modern parenthood . . . is quite unlike the old-fashioned variety, but it has much to recommend it and merits a thorough understanding."

The turn-of-the-century idea of motherhood as a "vocation" was coming of age in America after World War I. Thirty years had passed since Dr. Hall heralded the birth of a "lusty . . . infant," child study, and his most prominent and elite former fan club was celebrating another impressive growth spurt. The Child Study Association (CSA) had begun in 1888 as the Society for the Study of Child Nature, one of the earliest and most earnest organized examples of "educated motherhood." At the Waldorf-Astoria, the leaders of the newly incorporated and now amply funded organization were eager to show off their more mature cause—and eager to establish distance from the doting father whose studies were now considered embarrassingly unscientific. In fact, gazing back on "the primitive parental prairie" of prewar America several years later, one conference participant overlooked Dr. Hall altogether. In the CSA handbook for parents, *Our Children*, the stalwart CSA supporter and popular writer Dorothy Canfield Fisher recalled that "the daunting emptiness" of that "trackless prairie" was "broken by but one small plain blockhouse called Dr. Holt's *Care and Feeding of Children*."

The Conference on Modern Parenthood was evidence of the "civilized town" that had been built since then, "crammed with the latest results of all kinds of research that affect the lives of babies and children," conducted by "distinguished specialists in medicine, psychology, physiology, and education." Gone were the old days of the urbanizing turn of the century, when mothers like Fisher had "hastily and cravenly thrust Dr. Holt's immortal masterpiece under the nearest sofa pillow" to avoid the "relentless sniping from the aborigines" (grandmothers and others) who mocked "book-l'arning applied to babies." In the "organized society" that America was fast becoming in the wake of World War I, the aborigines were in retreat, the scientific mothers were pleased to report. On display at the Waldorf-Astoria event was the vanguard of "the great parental education movement," as one CSA program leader called it elsewhere, ". . . a vast army of fathers and mothers, specialists and educators, all of whom are trying to bring about better ways and better days for parents and children."

Child-rearing information certainly had made notable inroads in America, and the publications of the U.S. Children's Bureau over the previous decade told the story. Between 1914 and 1925 the enterprising women leaders of the bureau had put nearly four and a half million copies of its three Holtian "bulletins" on children's physical care into circulation. The pamphlets addressed to "the average mother of this country" had plainly struck a chord. As many as 125,000 letters from readers arrived at the bureau every year, and the follow-up questions came from would-be book-l'arners in the most remote corners. "I read in one of your leaflet that there was no resin why a Mother could not nurse her baby," wrote a mother from rural Michigan; ". . . we are poor farmers and have 4 children, so I have to over do. All so my milk leakes out." Along with books, "well-baby" care had spread since the enactment of the Sheppard-Towner Act in 1921. Under the legislation, for which the bureau and women's groups had lobbied hard, maternal and infant health stations staffed mostly by public health nurses were set up to supply preventive care and health instruction, especially to poorer women in out-of-the-way places. In 1918 alarm about physically unfit draftees and malnourished schoolchildren had inspired the founding of the Child Health Organization, which expanded and became the American Child Health Association in 1923. Dr. Holt helped spearhead its effort to bring health teaching straight to students themselves, on the theory that they could then take the lessons home to their parents.

By the early 1920s, with infant mortality down by a third, the Children's Bureau had branched out from babies and bodies. Revising its earlier verdict that "the literature of child psychology is so muddled and contains so much twaddle, that the average American mother should be warned against it," the government now supplied her with the latest psychological wisdom in *Child Management*. For where twaddle had been, now there was more data, and to judge by "the great hue and cry about the loss of parental authority in the modern home," as one speaker at the Waldorf-Astoria put it, the average American mother herself was in a muddle—or worse, a state of crisis, which the CSA's president broadcast in a radio address of 1923. "From every home, from city and country, from rich and poor, comes the call," Bird Stein Gans told listeners who could now get parental enlightenment by ear as well as book, " 'What is the matter with our children today? What has come over them? Why are they so different from us? Why is it so difficult for them to do and think as we did and thought as children?' "

"Better Send for This Pamphlet" was the verdict of the press on Dr. D. A. Thom's 1925 revision of *Child Management*, in which the director of the Division of Mental Hygiene in the Massachusetts Department of Mental Diseases informed readers that they had plenty to learn. "A child has a mental life far more delicate and complex than his physical body," he explained, "far more difficult to keep in order and much more easily put out of adjustment." And Dr. Thom was not talking about the mentally "defective," or the deprived, or delinquents, the juvenile specimens who had come under the closest prewar psychological scrutiny. The focus was now on normal—middle-class—children in their tender early years (a growing number of whom were among the clients treated for behavioral trouble at Thom's "habit clinics" in Boston, hailed by the *Times* as the "latest development in child hygiene"). In an expanded section on the "Environment," Dr. Thom closed *Child Management* by warning that "the home is the workshop which, unfortunately, often spoils much good material."

The CSA made sure to send for the author of the pamphlet. As one of the "distinguished specialists" holding forth at the Waldorf-Astoria, Dr. Thom was the speaker in the spotlight. At the key session of the conference, "Parents and the New Psychology," he dealt with the most pressing topic, "The Importance of the Early Years," and he made headlines that encapsulated the expert credo of the day. "Hygienist Decries Indulgent Mother," announced the *New York Times*, followed in smaller type by: "But Dr. D. A. Thom Tells Association a Stern Father Also Has Bad Effect on Child." Needless to say, the doctor did not endorse the spineless "modern father" either, much less those neglectful, bridge-addicted modern mothers about whom the many nonmedical diagnosticians of the 1920s were alarmed (and whom they were given to mocking: "Mother, when you're dummy, will you hear my prayers?" asked a pajamaed waif in a *New Yorker* cartoon).

The family was in need of careful adjustment, which Ernest R. Groves, a prominent sociologist and expert on "the drifting home" (the title of one of his numerous books), had been summoned by the CSA to outline. He joined many others in remarking on how "in our childhood, and particularly in the childhood of our parents, [the family] had almost a monopoly on certain kinds of social experiences that are rapidly being taken from it." (Almost two decades earlier, Dr. Hall had already been worrying over how "home and family life have now shrunken.") But it was all for the best in the fast-paced postwar world, Groves insisted. "The family, like a good administrator, farms out more and more of its functions to school, church and other organizations," he explained. "The specialists who enter the child's life to care for the different sides of his nature are far more efficient in their several fields than any one parent can hope to be in such widely separated kinds of work." And the home, he promised, was still very important—in fact, a more crucial "workshop" than ever. "Relieved of having to carry out all the details of child-care in all their ramifications, the family today can concentrate on the more important responsibilities which no other institution can perform—direction, stimulation and loving friendship." To fulfill their intimate function, however, parents themselves needed direction and stimulation from specialists. "We will realize that the expert can do better than we can do," Groves noted, "but we can at least choose between experts."

In bustling America, more and more partying (and working) mothers, and remote fathers too, according to the *Times*, were awakening to the realization that their services were needed more, not less, on the home front. "By some strange cosmic alchemy the same economic and social forces which have broken up the old-fashioned home and sent women into the world of business and pleasure on much the same terms as men, upsetting the manners and morals of the race, have now distilled a new interest in the business of being a parent." In their classic portrait of Middletown (Muncie, Indiana) in 1925, Helen and Robert Lynd indeed found working-class and business-class mothers alike dying to "lay hold of every available resource for help in training their children"—even a ten-volume set called *Foundation Stones of Success*, peddled by a door-to-door salesman doing a brisk trade in "the great crisis of parenthood," as Dorothy Canfield Fisher called it.

"This modern parenthood" certainly did demand a "thorough understanding," and what was most modern about it was the panoply of experts on hand to guide mothers, and ideally fathers, every step of the way. The "business of being a parent" had become yet more urgent and intricate, and scientific, than prewar "educated motherhood" had been—and more private than the public-spirited approach of the Progressive Era, when lobbying for the Sheppard-Towner Act and visiting tenements had been part of the "vocation." For an interwar generation of parents, as *Children: The Magazine for Parents* put it, "the whole social standard as to what children require is changing, enlarging, refining, becoming more and more stringent in its executions." Middle-class mothers were now supposed to consider themselves emotional specialists in their own homes. There they were charged with a new responsibility: not simply to secure health, or to uplift "the race" in a newly urbanized country, but to keep their own children up to par and "well-adjusted" at every stage—and to consider themselves accountable for any slipup in the process. The bumpy journey from Holtian infancy to the adolescent "reconstruction" that Hall had celebrated looked like an unpaved road in a nation beginning to build highways.

According to contemporary experts' more ambitious agenda, it was parents themselves who needed studying, too, and more steadying now. For the child of the interwar era was not the only one who had become "far more difficult to keep in order, and much more easily put out of adjustment." So had his parents, in particular his mother, just when she was faced with the daunting task of keeping the relational weather in the home "workshop" just right at every turn—not too warm and not too cold, not too calm and not too stormy—so the "good material" wouldn't spoil. The experts had their hands full, but the official word from the Waldorf-Astoria was that in their laboratories a far more comprehensive enterprise was under impressive control.

2.

Of the triumvirate of experts, parents, and children, the scientists had made the most dramatic maturational leap. Certainly the white coats had been multiplying at a rate unmatched by children or parents since before the war. From coast to coast, a second generation of psychology graduates were embarked on clinical and experimental work of many different varieties—behaviorist, psychoanalytic, Gestalt, developmental, and a hybrid approach that went by the name of the "mental hygiene movement." In the rapidly growing field of pediatrics, notable strides had been made in combating disease, and infant feeding was no longer a topic that lent practitioners much prestige. After all, the perfect milk formula had changed embarrassingly often—and a mother did not need an M.D. on call to manage the newer, simpler recipes. (A prominent, and rather caustic, pediatrician noted that once "there was something awesome, something that inspired reverence, about the word 'formula,'" but no more. "The present 'mixture' demands no such obeisance; it is only one of a lot.") Pediatricians were branching out to establish themselves as "family advisers"; the doctor was no longer just "the healer of disease," but "the counselor of health," in behavior as well as body. "Development, quite as much as disease," argued a prominent doctor, "falls within the theory and practice of pediatrics." As a speaker at the Waldorf-Astoria noted, "fundamental issues of personality organization" had risen to the top of the experts' agenda—and it was mothers, as well as their young children, who were now judged to be ripe for diagnoses.

Like so much else in America during the 1920s, an eclectic and growing enterprise was becoming not only more professionalized, but also institutionalized and organized—which had been the hope of Progressive rationalizers from the start. The child welfare reformers and educated women who had presided over an amorphous, still largely amateur realm of concern about childhood before the war were being edged out in its aftermath. By the middle of the decade, credentialed professionals had staked out a broad-based field called child development and were busy buttressing its serious scientific status. The term was first used in 1924–25, when the National Research Council—a consortium of scientists, government officials, and businessmen formed during the First World War—changed the name of its Committee on Child Psychology to Committee on Child Development. By 1930, Arnold Gesell was pleased to announce that "the term *child development* has become a rival, if not a substitute, for that of child psychology. It is a protean term, but useful and surely symptomatic of the current trend of science," about which he was very optimistic, even if the field was "still in its early infancy."

Behind the postwar surge of child science stood philanthropic foundations with a coordinated enterprise in mind. The Laura Spelman Rockefeller Memorial Foundation (LSRM) led the way, joined by the Commonwealth Fund and the Josiah Macy, Jr., Foundation. All were committed to supporting science in the service of social progress, rather than disinterested, "pure" research. War had shown the destructive powers of technology. In peace, science could reveal its utopian promise. The faith was fervent, even if it was expressed in stilted foundationese, a new language in a nation discovering the power of corporate philanthropy. "It was felt," intoned the final report of the Laura Spelman Rockefeller Memorial Foundation, "that through the social sciences might come more intelligent measures of social control that would reduce such irrationalities as are represented by poverty, class conflict, and war between nations."

And, all too often, represented by the family: that addition to the list was the special insight of the LSRM official who played the largest part in the nationwide spread of child development science during the 1920s. His name was Lawrence K. Frank. An economist and progressive education activist by motley training (supplemented by intimate friendship with the economist Wesley C. Mitchell, one of the founders of the New School for Social Research, and his wife, Lucy Sprague Mitchell, the founder of what became the Bank Street College of Education), Frank was full of positivist optimism. It was clear to him that the child-rearing counsel that had so far accumulated was not yet conclusive—was, in fact, somewhat contradictory—but he was convinced that the cure lay in more research, and in its popular dissemination.

A man who preached the need for "systematic and intensive study of child growth and development . . . and for parent education," Frank himself adopted an approach that was more comprehensive and unsystematic, which was the key to his wide influence. "The procreative Johnny Appleseed of the social sciences, a peripatetic horn of plenty, crammed to his lips with everything that's new, budding, possible, and propitious," was the aptly overblown way one of Frank's many beneficiaries described him. This "enlightened, jolly human being" went "from place to place, from symposium to symposium, radiating waves of atmospheric warmth, cheerfulness, and hope, as he spread the seeds for novel, hybrid, research projects to be nurtured, implemented, and actualized by others." (His close friend Margaret Mead once went so far as to say that Frank "more or less invented the behavioral sciences.")

Frank altered the research landscape remarkably quickly. Under the headline "Rearing of Children Becoming a Science," the *Times* in 1925 hailed the "enormous impetus" research had lately received and surveyed the fruits of what were largely Frank's labors. "Laboratories have sprung up, either independently or in connection with institutions of learning, where children of from a few months to several years are studied by scientists—weighed, measured, examined, watched for every sign of development, recorded and indexed with meticulous precision—all in the cause of working out the best methods of care and education." A "psycho-clinic" at Yale opened by Dr. Hall's student Arnold Gesell in 1911 and the Iowa Child Welfare Research Station in 1917 were the models that spurred Frank on.

LSRM grants inaugurated the Institute of Child Welfare Research at Teachers College in New York in 1924. Frank supplied infusions to Yale, which established a guidance nursery where children played and were observed, and to Iowa. In establishing institutes at Berkeley,

Toronto, and Minnesota, he parried academics who feared that children were not a suitably serious intellectual subject, and home economists whose dominance of the field would, he feared, undermine its status. By the mid-1920s, the National Research Council had its Committee on Child Development trying to keep track of all the research that was under way. By the end of the decade, the Institute of Child Welfare at Berkeley had launched two longitudinal studies. In the course of the 1930s, as Yale and Iowa enlarged their operations, the Harvard School of Public Health launched a center, and Antioch College and Columbia Medical School joined the trend. The Society for Research in Child Development, the closest thing to a professional association for the far-flung field, was established in 1933.

And it was a grant from LSRM that supported the Waldorf-Astoria event. Scientific research, Frank insisted, must go hand in hand with scientific outreach. The "orchestrator," as he liked to call himself, made it his priority to see to it that relations between the lab and the public were—what else?—well adjusted. That tended to mean putting some heat on the scientists. Frank could be impatient with the cautious, impartial approach. "Let's have more definite formulations to guide the work," he urged one researcher, at the same time that he told her not to let precise results cloud her conclusions. "A conceptual statement" was what Frank wanted, without "waiting for all . . . [the] clinical data [to be] analyzed, interpreted, and otherwise handled."

Meanwhile, Frank sought out cool-headed lay leaders to spread the latest findings to mothers, which was why he turned to the sober women in charge of the CSA. He counted on them to know how to publicize—yet not vulgarize—the science in which he had such high hopes. They demurred when Frank asked them to oversee the founding of a popular magazine about child rearing in 1926 called *Children: The Magazine for Parents,* preferring to stick with their more elitist *Child Study* instead. But they, along with a phalanx of prominent scientists, agreed to serve as advisory editors. Praised for featuring "scientific findings"—not mere "sugary uplift"—*Children* (soon renamed *Parents' Magazine*) went on to thrive during the 1930s and 1940s, heralded as the most successful educational magazine in the world.

If Frank had any fears (and even he did) that all his synergistic efforts might not save scientific parenthood from lapsing into a faddish enterprise, they were well hidden beneath utopian hopes that he pursued with rare on-the-ground energy. Psychological wisdom straight from the labs would do more than instill in mothers a "habit of intelligent behavior" and equip them with "a carefully worked out technique for meeting the needs of children in the home." Child-rearing science would rescue America from the social and moral drift of the postwar climate, and also from the social and moral rigidity of prewar days. From the conflict-free family would come national harmony. The dreams (and the dread they reflected) were widespread among the experts and their conference-going acolytes. As Dorothy Canfield Fisher proclaimed in her talk at the Waldorf-Astoria, "Every blow that is struck for the essentials of life for children—freedom, individuality, opportunity for creation—may be a blow toward shaping the idea that everybody needs these essentials." So far blows had at least been struck for the scientific experts themselves. They had carved out niches that allowed them to experiment, to explore, and to expound their views on a rapidly expanding array of problems.

3.

The postwar status of children, too, had changed. While the experts were acquiring labs during the 1920s, children were being equipped with labels. One classifying phrase more than any other signaled a transformed set of expectations and apprehensions about childhood. As the *Times* announced, "a new term . . . shows the focus of the movement—the 'preschool child.'" Toddlers, who had previously been referred to more casually and fondly as "runabouts," were now to be honored with serious scrutiny. They had taken the place of babies and adolescents in the experts' pantheon of important specimens. Scientists were moving in to map what had been a " 'no man's land' in the field of social endeavor," as one of them noted, and it was the peculiar behavior of the small natives rather than their physical problems—"discharging ears and deteriorating molars"—that attracted attention. "The child with night terrors, the nail biter, the over-tearful child, the over-silent child, the stammering child, the extremely indifferent child" had become the concern of researchers who now tackled "a whole host of suffering, frustrated and unhealthily constituted growing minds."

For along with a fancy name (which Dr. Arnold Gesell of the Yale Psycho-Clinic was usually credited with coining), preschoolers were graced with a novel attribute: a "personality" in need of assiduously supervised development. The addition of personality to the vocabulary of a newly psychological age conjured up a more social and more self-conscious vision of the self than "character," which it had all but eclipsed by the 1920s. The inspirational writer Orison Marden, who followed up his 1899 reflections on *Character: The Greatest Thing in the World* with *Masterful Personality* in 1921, singled out "the gentle art of pleasing" along with "the strong desire for self-improvement" as two key ingredients of this new wonder of the world. Where character was inseparable from autonomy and self-control and depended on "strenuosity" for its maintenance, personality was "largely developed from mingling with the crowd," and it required and encouraged "poise, serenity, amiability." Personality, as Marden was far from alone in emphasizing, was not considered a product of a child's given nature and his own dogged effort (as character, finally reducible to good and bad, was). It was above all a product of nurture—elaborate nurture that must begin promptly. The budding personality was more malleable than babies' bodies and less elusive than adolescent souls. Ernest Groves explained that "emotional responses," rather than intellect or will or imagination, "make up the nucleus about which the personality forms itself" into a marvelously flexible yet also ominously fragile whole.

Constant vigilance was required to avoid the danger of its "maladjustment," which loomed as a major psychological and social problem of the postwar era, according to the burgeoning mental hygiene movement that played such a large part in making personality a preoccupation in American medicine, education, child guidance, and parenting wisdom beginning in the 1920s. The National Committee for Mental Hygiene, formed in 1909 (the same year Freud came to speak at Clark), was now peddling an amalgam of the New Psychology—a mix of the "psycho-biological" psychiatry championed by Adolf Meyer at Johns Hopkins, the behaviorism pioneered by John Broadus Watson, and the developmental approach pursued by Arnold Gesell, all bathed in dilute psychoanalytic concepts. Mental illness, the movement's prewar promoters maintained, was the result of life stress, rather than any organic disorder of the brain or nervous system. Yet there was a "predisposition" to maladjustment, they believed, arguing that the tendency could be eradicated or avoided much more easily than mental illness itself could be cured. Psychiatric success in dealing with "shell shock" victims confirmed the mental hygienists in their views, and with the end of the war, a preventive crusade was under way. Childhood had become "the golden period for mental hygiene." In the warped personality lay the root of dependency, delinquency, deviancy, crime—all the woes of the world. In childhood adjustment lay the promise of a healthy, happy, harmonious, smoothly functioning, "wholesome" personality—and a serene society.

Dr. Hall's small savage and Dr. Holt's steady little trooper had all but disappeared in the mental hygiene vision of childhood. The preschool child had lost a good deal of his former vitality and sturdy autonomy. (The child the experts had foremost in mind was, as ever, male.) He was not a dreamy or wild fellow left to follow his own rapidly shifting impulses before school routine set it, as Hall prescribed. To secure for him the freedom, individuality, and opportunity for creation that Dorothy Canfield Fisher invoked had become a far more systematized, supervised proposition. For the term "preschooler" was, among the psychological experts who coined and circulated it, ideally supposed to be something of a misnomer. Almost as soon as the under-kindergarten set was classified, classes began being created for it—in the nursery schools that the researchers relied on for their samples and that were touted in the 1920s as a model of home enrichment soon to sweep America.

Despite a surge of interest, the nursery school trend remained a more limited phenomenon before World War II than its proponents had hoped. (In 1928, according to a survey by the National Society for the Study of Education, there were 84 nursery schools in 23 states and the District of Columbia; by 1930, the Office of Education counted 262 nursery schools in the country.) But even if mothers didn't actually send their toddlers, the prescription of the parent educators was that at home they should cultivate a suitably self-conscious, teacherly solicitude themselves. It was a tall order, a representative of one of the leading nursery schools, the Merrill-Palmer School, warned the audience at the Waldorf-Astoria. "To keep a pre-school child legitimately and profitably busy is, for the unaided mother in the home, not at all an easy task." Above all, "it involves more knowledge of stages of development than most mothers possess." Runabouts could not just, well, run about.

But the preschool child was not the readily routinized creature that Dr. Holt described either. He had portrayed a youngster primed to fall into line with comparatively little muss or fuss, his habit training and impulse control a straightforward matter of adult imposition. Basic routines and responses established, the child was considered best left alone. During the important first two years, he was plenty busy just growing, and Dr. Holt emphasized the goal of keeping the twig straight. He did not contemplate the challenge of adjusting the angles at which it should bend. What might be going on in the child's head or heart while he puttered about in the peace Dr. Holt prescribed, the doctor did not presume to say or assume parents wanted to hear from him. (Like Mrs. Holt, they could be trusted to suit themselves as to what, other than pounds and inches, they cared to record.) Changing capacity—meaning how much and what a growing child could consume—interested him more than changing abilities; babies' development went all but unmentioned. Nor was there any indication that the Holt baby or child was eagerly interactive with others. He seemed likely to become a clinger only if a cosseting mother encouraged it. Otherwise, he was evidently a self-contained creature, launched on the journey to independence early and easily, and his social life occasioned next to no comment.

By comparison, the preschool child the experts discovered in the 1920s was a far more complicated, delicate being. He was not yet a full-fledged Freudian handful. In the meliorative version of psychoanalytic theory that many American psychologists had taken away from Freud's 1909 lectures at Clark, the precocious child besieged by Oedipal passions could be, and usually was, conveniently tamed almost beyond recognition. When William Alanson White emphasized children's sexual drives and the natural antagonism between children and their parents (all without mentioning Freud) in his *Mental Hygiene of Childhood* of 1916, he was well aware he was being shocking. The prevailing image of the child portrayed him as less of a riven agent and more of a pliant object in the family drama.

Children were endowed not with libidinal desires, but with a rich emotional life, or in the mental hygienists' terms, "a real mental life, full of hopes, ambitions, doubts, misgivings, joys, sorrows, and strivings that are being gratified or thwarted much the same at three years of age as they will be at thirty," Dr. Thom explained in the government pamphlet *Child Management*. Notably lacking from that list were children's aggressive, conflictual impulses. "Hyper-activity, restlessness, lack of concentration, curiosity": all those energetic, classically "naughty" traits of childhood occasion disproportionate worry, Dr. Thom counseled in his Waldorf-Astoria talk on "The Importance of the Early Years." Interwar experts were on the alert instead for the "shut-in personality," the shy child of the "clinging-vine variety," often with an "inferiority complex." It was a term associated with the Freudian renegade Alfred Adler, whose theory that children were driven by a need to compensate for a sense of social, rather than sexual, inadequacy and frustration enjoyed growing popularity in his native Vienna and in America during the 1920s. At the mercy of an environment of adults prone to foil his efforts both to "[build] up adequate self-reliance and independence," *and* to find his place in the group, this preschooler was ominously, rather than marvelously, plastic. The all-too-impressionable child was the new prototype of "the problem child."

Even more novel was that, thanks to a medical paradigm more entrenched than ever before, the problem child had become the prototype of Everychild. "The problem child has become the problems of the child," proclaimed one expert as he proudly assessed the enlarged domain of child-rearing challenges. The problems certainly had become numerous, one of the speakers at the conference noted, also with more than a little satisfaction: "The hygiene and mental hygiene of the pre-school and school child, an appreciation of the work of the habit clinic, an analysis of the emotional make-up with all the complexity of surrogated affective states and conditioned reflexes—all these have unfolded problems vastly more complex than had even been anticipated." Expressing his gratitude for the many advances in the basic physical care of children, another mental hygienist sounded outright gleeful at the psychological "cases" all the hardy bodies generated for his line of work: "We must first have a live child if we are to have any problem at all."

By definition, rather than by any act of defiance, this emotionally complex, environmentally sensitive child was fated for trouble in the "process of socialization" that interwar child rearing had become. At the same time, he had become the center of unprecedented attention. "We had a little girl at our hospital," a pediatrician wryly reported, ". . . who told any one who came near her and seemed interested, 'I'm a problem.' " The new intricacy of the preschool specimen made him worthy of the experts' interest and earned him new status in the "democratic" family that psychologists, sociologists, anthropologists, and journalists heralded as the successor to the "patriarchal" clan of old.

4.

But the real focus of attention at the Waldorf-Astoria gathering—even more than at the Congress of Mothers before it—was clear in the conference title: modern parenthood. While the experts of the 1920s had graduated into labs and the child had been distinguished by an impressive label, American parents had acquired a host of new liabilities—and responsibilities. This marked an advance for them, too, in a way. Their role in child rearing had become even more formative than the progressive missionaries had proclaimed it to be. And where fathers had been all but invisible, they had now become part of the picture, assigned the role of being solicitous of mothers (not of changing diapers). Yet something else had changed, too. All-powerful parents had in the process become infantilized.

A subsequent editorial in the *New York Times*, which regularly found news of unfit parents very fit to print during the interwar decades, spelled out the new perspective under the headline "Childish Parents." Psychologists who had lately put infants in "the spotlight" (perhaps too much, they now feared) were "turning the beam on the parents" and treating "parents in cases which a few years ago would have been dealt with as child problems only." The diagnosis was dire. "The trouble as the new psychologists now see it is with the parents who are not really quite grown up. They are themselves like children in their dependence on anything or anyone that offers support and security." You might think such deference would please the experts, but it struck them as ominous. "If [parents] feel unable to cope with the hard circumstances of life, they will either try to make home a too sheltering refuge for their own children or will demand unattainable competence from them."

The parent as problem child: it was an image that had seemed to lurk in the back of Dr. Holt's methodical mind, and Dr. Hall had indulged himself in some Wordsworthian visions of the parent as the reborn child. But they had both assumed, with a mixture of regret and respect, that adulthood was where parents were and would stay. For their successors, parental regression posed a real problem—and was also the key to a cure. As Dr. Thom indicated in his talk at the conference, the truly pressing issue was parent management. If preschool children were prone to problems, it was because they so often lacked "an environment in which to live that is not contaminated by the unsatisfied emotional strivings of the parents." The assistant director of the Merrill-Palmer School spelled out the implications in her speech. "We seem to think we have gone a long way toward a solution when we state that parents are to blame," she said. "Let us grant that the parents are at fault. But who are the parents? They are grown-up children. Are we going to make them better parents by just telling them that they are bad parents?" Mere old-fashioned scolding would not do for these sorry specimens, any more than for their progeny.

The enlightened treatment for parents was an interesting variation on the prevailing hygienic view of children. The ideal parents—or to be more accurate, mothers—uncannily resembled well-adjusted preschoolers. They were kept "legitimately and profitably busy" by helpful experts, which saved them from suffocating emotional dependence on their children as well as from undue "bossiness" toward them. The experts provided stage-appropriate advice and knowledge of children, expecting of parents a "willingness to utilize all of the facts in the case to bring about adjustment opportunities." Habits continued to be important for young and old, but the "firmly fixed" kind that Dr. Holt had approved could now be a handicap. "Plasticity" of habit, suited to changing circumstances, had become the goal. This required self-conscious adjustment on the part of the adult, who was "liable to fall victim to his own habits unless he or she revise them constantly in the light of developmental psychology."

The well-adjusted mother who avoided rigidity then had no need or desire to demand excessive docility from her children. (*Children: The Magazine for Parents* ran article after article warning that obedience "is not an end in itself," and that whenever a parent thinks it is, "it is evident that some outworn conception is still active.") Like the well-adjusted preschooler, this model mother betrayed none of those worrisome "shut-in" qualities—"excessive worry, anxiety, and needless fear . . . [that] get in the way of an intelligent approach to many of the problems of childhood." An "objective" approach was her goal, in step with the needs of the "objective-minded, matter-of-fact child" of modernity she aimed to produce.

She was spared subjective stress if she made sure not to get carried away by love, the inevitable source of such buffeting emotions. It was the Holtian recipe, but she could not count on mere "regularity" as the coolant. The overriding goal was to maintain "affection and serenity, the comfort of understanding in the home . . . [which] are infinitely more important than direction and discipline." "Confidence," a word that had come up often in child-rearing literature before, arose constantly now and had acquired a new meaning. The impressive, assertive confidence that parents had once possessed seemed in short supply. In its place, however, "the spirit of mutual confidence and understanding" could flourish. No one need preside if everyone would confide.

And everyone was more likely to confide if everyone had a chance to get outside of the house some. The right calm, detached tone was best maintained if the members of the family were not constant companions but could be "a little more of a treat" to one another. Fathers, obviously, did not have to work on distancing themselves; the worry was that most of them were still too rigid and removed—though articles in *Children* magazine also made a habit of holding the best of them up as models for mothers of how to avoid "too much overhead interference," and still carve out a welcome presence. One dad who felt generally "ostracized" in child-rearing operations at home told of how he surreptitiously

made the most of the minimal "weighing job" he was granted: he transformed it into an opportunity for play, saying "Peep-Peep" if his baby
"said 'yeep' and stretched her mouth until she looked like Wallace
Beery in a grin." For preschoolers, nursery school was touted as the
ideal social respite from home intimacy.

It was the mother who most needed "to have some life of her own,"
to avoid "smother love," a term coined by the director of the Child
Study Association, Sidonie Matsner Gruenberg, to "describe what happens when an intelligent, trained young woman drops all else to devote
herself solely to the demands of her young children." What she should
do with her "greater leisure and freedom" instead of using it "to
impress herself too much upon the child," most experts agreed, was to
nurture her own sexual and emotional adjustment in her marriage, not
just her knowledge of child development. In postwar analyses of the
family, the marital bedroom often occupied the foreground, the nursery a few steps behind. A satisfied couple, the new wisdom went, was
the true secret to a successful "socialization process"—and, of course,
to avoiding divorce, rates of which rose during the 1920s, to widespread alarm. Dr. Hall's quaint physiological concern with the fertiliza-
tion process had been cast aside, though not his basic cure for feminist
frustrations. The gratified woman would not be an overbearing
mother. And what better models for producing a daughter equipped to
be an ideal wife and mother in her turn, and a son primed to be the perfect companionate husband and father?

One of the more liberated participants at the conference, Dorothy
Canfield Fisher, had proposed a daring, but also troubling, variation on
this standard model of adjustment in her best-selling novel of the year
before, *The Home-Maker*. In it a neurotically controlling, housebound
mother found release when she went triumphantly out to work after
her husband was fired from his job as a lackluster accountant at the
local department store—and, on top of that misfortune, injured himself
in a fall. A poetic soul, he thrived once he was wheelchair-bound at
home. He gloried in discovering "the living, miraculous, infinitely fragile fabric of the little human souls" of his children. He was thrilled to
have time "to stalk and catch that exquisitely elusive bird-of-paradise,
their confidence."

A joyless marriage and grim house were transformed. Two wan older
children blossomed, and under his father's attentive but unobtrusive
ministering, a preschooler who had everyone panicked about his devil-
ishness became an angel. There is no one pattern of child-rearing bliss,
Fisher transparently and fervently preached. But her didactic novel also

aimed to show that America had a long way to go. The wonderful father one day discovered that he was no longer paralyzed—and realized that if he could walk, he would have to go to work or face social ostracism. His wife would have to come home and revert to her suffocating ways. For him, the "healthy" choice (in which his doctor colluded) was to act the invalid for the rest of his days.

Fisher's schematic novel underscored the social obstacles to all the high therapeutic hopes for the home. The experts dwelled on the psychological hurdles. The logic that healthy adulthood required a mentally hygienic childhood meant that, in the 1920s, wondrous parents were likely to be rare indeed. Freak accidents had jolted Fisher's characters out of their emotionally warped patterns, but in real life, things could not be left to fate. "Parent education" was the watchword of the period. Yet the central conviction of the era—that the early years were crucial to personality adjustment—meant that the challenge of "reconditioning" grownups looked enormously daunting.

It wasn't merely that parents might consciously resist learning (as Dr. Holt sometimes feared), or that children could be difficult to handle. For unconscious reasons, psychoanalysis had revealed, mothers and fathers might be all but unteachable or require the most extensive treatment. One speaker at the Waldorf-Astoria, the medical director of the Bureau of Children's Guidance in New York City, dourly summed up the dilemma: "The fact that the problems of parents are so often deep seated and that the genesis of their attitudes is found far back in their own experience at the hands of their parents or in their phases of the authority-dependency relationship indicates the scope and the ramifications of the solution processes."

Thus the problem parent had become Everyparent. Where a Freudian influence first made itself felt most in child-rearing expertise in the 1920s was in the portraiture of motherhood rather than of childhood. The "maladjusted" mother, still waging infantile struggles if not facing marital troubles, bore a disconcerting resemblance to a voraciously dependent baby. It was not the family "democracy" the experts had in mind. Unable to wean herself from her attachment to her child, presumably as a result of her own "hidden conflicts and emotional turmoils," she guaranteed that he carried "an affliction throughout his life." Her burden was "emotional servitude." For her child, the danger was "emotional bondage," which was routinely accompanied by the adjective "crippling."

As perturbed about the state of the family as it was optimistic about the power of science to rescue it, the Conference on Modern Parenthood at the Waldorf-Astoria was a barometer of interwar child-rearing tensions. To sum up the mixed message: The home had been declared absolutely crucial amid worries that it was breaking apart. Emotion had become the sole specialty of this newly narrowed domestic sphere. Yet coolish "affection" was as high as the temperature in the bosom of the family was supposed to go. Parents were hopeless, lacking self-control and control over their children. Yet parents were the only hope, given the proper education in how to nurture—a challenging endeavor, since these big students were so hard to size up. Fathers were too aloof. Yet fathers were intrusively stern disciplinarians. Women, with their new freedom and status, were taking an unprecedentedly mature interest in child-rearing science. Yet mothers were distracted as never before by immature conflicts and confusions.

Children were just as hard to add up. Prolonged dependence was required to subtly mold the modern personality equipped to face a complex, shifting world. Yet extended dependence was the greatest danger to the health of that personality. Postwar adults were transfixed by adolescents and their Jazz Age antics with peers. Yet soft-skinned toddlers usurped most of the scientific attention. Social adjustment was the trait most important to a "wholesome" individual, but a child's course was presumed to be all but set by the sixth year of life—and the preschool period loomed especially large. Creativity, individuality, and autonomy were highly (or at any rate nominally) prized in children. Yet the nonconforming "shut-in" aroused alarm, and the "normal" pre-school student, able to fit in and function in groups, was the model. The child was expected to be more intensively, self-consciously shaped at home than he had ever been before. Yet the home was seen to resemble the world for which the child was being prepared less than ever before. And soon enough, though no one suspected it, the world would cease to resemble the one Americans enjoyed in the mid-1920s.

5.

"It would be interesting to read the thoughts of an intelligent, common-sense mother on her way home from such a meeting, to take up again the humdrum burden of the conflicts, annoyances, and irritations of the home," reflected an intelligent, commonsense—and, some would have said, curmudgeonly—Chicago pediatrician named Dr. Joseph Brennemann, who by 1932 had his doubts about the "wholesale education of the laity in all that pertains to child study, guidance and training; in parent education; in child psychology, psychiatry, behaviorism, and even in psychoanalysis of different brands." Was Waldorf-Astoria–style wisdom as wholesome as educators, editorialists, and, of course, experts themselves claimed? In post-Crash America, the supply of it certainly showed no signs of abating. A much larger phalanx of experts dominated President Hoover's White House Conference on Child Health and Protection in 1930, testimony to the guiding assumption that "it is beyond the capacity of the individual parent to train her child to fit into the intricate, interwoven and interdependent social and economic system we have developed." The event generated thirty-two volumes of findings. Yet was a genuine demand being served in the popularization and avid dissemination of as yet indeterminate science? The head of pediatrics at Children's Memorial Hospital in Chicago dared to wonder in his 1932 address to the Philadelphia Psychiatric Society (as he had at the New England Pediatric Society the year before).

Indulging in a bit of mind-reading, Dr. Brennemann imagined that his earnest middle-class mother, though she "would hardly dare to express her doubts," might well arrive at her doorstep asking herself "whether it is really helpful, except to the speakers and the promoters, for her to be schooled" so vigorously in the scientific psychosocial hygiene of the family. She had set out with high hopes, of course, that the "great child study, child guidance, and mental hygiene movement [would] help her keep, or make, her child normally adjusted in, and to, a rather complicated world." But with clamoring kids awaiting her inside (and a tight budget, and no maid), she might be forgiven for suspecting that what her runabouts needed most was more running and a mother who got more rest—or who could bring in some income.

Brennemann urged his audience to read the "heartrending" account of the cramped "Business of Parenthood" on a "modest income" by an anonymous, exhausted mother who had already discovered Betty Friedan's "problem that has no name" in *Harper's* in 1931. As for mothers in even more straitened circumstances, the coordinator of the Child Study Association's Harlem outreach effort had tacitly acknowledged the limited appeal of the kind of scientific parental self-scrutiny they specialized in. Study groups, she indicated, were at best a much-needed break, but not a very useful boost, to mothers "well-nigh overcome with the practical details incidental to running a home on a meager income, bringing up a family of children in limited quarters, and living in a crowded neighborhood—the very conditions that create many serious problems."

Other experts had been having their own doubts about the parent education "movement," and the problem of supply and demand. Only days before the Conference on Modern Parenthood gathering in 1925, the Committee on Child Development of the National Research Council had met in an upbeat mood. Research was booming, even if firm results were nowhere in sight. But two years later, the forthright report of the executive secretary of the same committee was sounding more apprehensive. "The century of the child" was thriving, the report observed, surveying a far more extensive network of national, state, and municipal services, agencies, and programs than had existed before the war, as well as "increasingly frequent large sectional and national conferences"—not to mention "a swelling tide of literature on the child." The trouble was, science could hardly keep up.

"The fruits of present research, it is to be feared," the report confessed, "are not sufficient to maintain in scientific health the rapidly growing movement. In the very success of the childward movement is the grave danger that the demand from various quarters—legislative, humanitarian, educational, journalistic—will so far exceed the supply provided by the slow processes of research that the movement will escape the bounds of fact and wander off into the alluring jungle of easy generalization and over-confident dogmatism. Science is asked to point the way where as yet there is no way—but the movement proceeds nonetheless." The risks, the report went on, were particularly high in that realm of research "in which popular interest is now so strong and popular demand so insistent": studies of "some phase of personality or behavior in other than their intellectual aspects." Data, though piling up, did not yet add up, certainly not to verifiable prescriptions for parents. "Notwithstanding the volume of research activity in this field, our plotting of childhood personality is still merely a crude impressionistic sketching of a few dominant, distorted outlines."

The trouble showed little sign of abating, the National Research Council secretary and Dr. Brennemann concurred. After all, as the pediatrician knew from his clientele, the modern mother "loves science, and she likes it raw," no matter that the wisdom from the lab often failed to line up very well with her life. (The beleaguered mother writing about "The Business of Parenthood" in *Harper's* reported wryly that she boned up on "Child Psychology between confinements, measles, whooping cough, and mumps.") And the modern psychologist, the National Research Council official was well aware, loved the lab and the clinic, and he liked to inspire public awe. A report on psychology and psychiatry in pediatrics issued by a committee of the

White House Conference on Child Health and Protection sounded wistful about the problem, too. "The technique of propaganda and instruction is decidedly faulty," the report agreed, urging that it "be studied with prayerful eagerness." But the only cure in view plainly did not inspire much faith: "We trust that restraint, a peculiarly difficult attitude for the pioneer, will become a routine virtue as the science of psychiatry grows to maturity."

As of yet, however, restraint was still a virtue of great rarity. The two experts who seized the spotlight during the interwar decades were notably lacking in just that quality—which was, to the consternation of skeptics like Dr. Brennemann (and to the pleasure of promoters like Lawrence Frank), precisely the reason for their popularity. Neither Dr. John B. Watson nor Dr. Arnold Gesell had been at the Waldorf-Astoria event, although in 1925 their reputations as experts at opposite poles of the child development spectrum were already rising. Watson, the strident founder of behaviorism, was very much in the public eye and continued to be through the end of the 1920s. By then Gesell, who had been observing children's maturation for a decade, was about to move into a fancy new facility at Yale (helped by Laura Spelman Rockefeller Memorial Foundation money), and to begin spreading his name as the man who made movies of infants' and children's growth. Each boasted lab credentials and eye-catching methods few others in the "childward movement" could match. More dramatic experiments than Dr. Watson's and more exhaustive observations than Dr. Gesell's were hard to find, and they had graphs and, even better, photographs to show for their efforts.

They were businesslike experts for an age that greeted Herbert Hoover's inauguration in March 1929, a journalist wrote, "in a mood for magic. . . . We had summoned a great engineer to solve our problems for us; now we sat back comfortably and confidently to watch the problems being solved." In his prewar "Behaviorist's Manifesto" in 1913, and in a succession of books over the next decade and a half, Watson had helped to usher in the mood by insisting that "it is the business of behavioristic psychology to be able to predict and to control human activity," a mantra he never tired of repeating. "Prediction and control—these are rather ambitious concepts in light of our meager knowledge of the laws of human behavior," Gesell more modestly admitted, only to go on, "but they are permissible scientific goals." He set his sights on a "system of developmental diagnostics" to meet them.

It helped that both men were talented popularizers, with a gift for clear prose, and that they were polarizers. The old days when Dr. Holt and Dr. Hall reigned as an odd but not incompatible couple with a northeastern-minister aura were over. The newly vast expectations of the science of child development meant that competition for the most comprehensive theory, the most systematic techniques, was on: like parents, experts of the interwar years were feeling more ambitious—and more embattled—than their predecessors had. In a country where the old elites were eroding, Watson, a southerner, and Gesell, the son of German immigrants who had settled in the Midwest, were a pair of outsiders. And Watson certainly expected to scramble—and to squabble—for attention.

Neither expert was quite what you would expect, given the "father" each claimed for himself. Dr. Watson, the self-anointed heir of Dr. Holt, had none of his demure style except in his impeccable wardrobe, perfect hair, and mastery of the staccato sentence. (And, *The New Yorker* noted in a profile in 1928, the dapper fellow "watches his weight on the scales twice a week.") Otherwise, he was wild: "an 'enfant terrible,' " as Brennemann was not the only one to call him, "in the psychologico-psychiatric fold such as are found in all such large aggregations of workers in a new and progressive field of endeavor." Dr. Holt had explored stomachs, held the most prestigious academic post in his field, and studiously guided John D. Rockefeller's scientific philanthropy. Dr. Watson did away with consciousness, was kicked out of Johns Hopkins University after a personal scandal, and ended up in the advertising business, "the chief show piece of the J. Walter Thompson" agency, *The New Yorker* noted. His specialty was strident claims based on a sweeping theory that all behavior was the result of environmental conditioning.

In 1925, Dr. Watson had established himself as a public figure with a brazen boast in his first popular book, *Behaviorism.* "Give me a dozen healthy infants, well-formed, and my own specified world to bring them up in," he proclaimed, "and I'll guarantee to take any one at random and train him to become any type of specialist I might select—a doctor, lawyer, artist, merchant-chief and, yes, even into beggar-man and thief, regardless of his talents, penchants, tendencies, abilities, vocations and race of his ancestors." In 1928, amid a flurry of excerpts and articles in *McCall's* and *Harper's,* his *Psychological Care of Infant and Child* caused a stir. With its photographs of Watson conditioning a baby to fear fur, its fierce warnings about "The Dangers of Too Much Mother Love," and its call not to kiss children, just to "shake hands with them in the morning," his manual delivered a frisson no mental hygienist—eager for "poise, serenity, and amiability"—could match.

"For the first time—a book on child psychology becomes a bestseller," W. W. Norton's advertisement in the *New York Times* proclaimed.

Dr. Gesell, who credited his career to his mentor Hall's fascination with the mysteries of developmental stages, prided himself on having none of his predecessor's faddish approach to them. In a tribute to his old Clark patron, Gesell made sure to suggest that the sobriety and regularity Hall lacked were the stereotypically German traits he himself brought to the ongoing enterprise. (Hall, who had years before complimented his psychology student's "clear level-head"—and the persistence he showed in pursuing a medical degree as well—would have put up no argument.) "What if he could not verify his prolific suggestive thrusts," Gesell wrote of Hall, "what if he seemed unsystematic and self-contradictory, what if he exaggerated the doctrine of recapitulation—he nevertheless was a naturalist Darwin of the mind, whose outlook embraced the total phylum, and lifted psychology above the sterilities of excessive analysis and pedantry." Gesell joined Hall in extolling the child as "an individual, after all, who has his own desires and his own propensities," about which Gesell, too, could be quite lyrical. Yet in his Psycho-Clinic at Yale University, he was intent on demonstrating that "growth *is* lawful and in no sense whimsical, fortuitous." There was to be no "saltatory" stuff for this believer in continuity.

Gesell made his mark in 1925 with *The Mental Growth of the Pre-School Child.* Although not aimed at a popular audience, the book won praise for its "delightful freshness and simplicity of style." A former colleague of Gesell's, the psychometrician Lewis Terman, predicted its "wide distribution not only among physicians and psychologists, but among parents and teachers." For Gesell's book contained something almost as exciting as Watson's boasts in *Behaviorism* about the malleability of blank slates: claims about the measurability of growing minds. In what he announced to be "the *first* systematic piece of work in the developmental psychology and developmental diagnosis of infancy," Gesell supplied "developmental schedules" and "developmental age scores." Preschoolers' "personal-social behavior," like their physical growth, he proposed, could be assessed and compared on the basis of norms.

In 1928, Gesell followed up with *Infancy and Human Growth*, in which he lovingly described his photographic survey of growth, babies "basking in the light of a bright, airy, though windowless, room," quietly observed as they performed fascinating tasks (no scary fur here). When *Parents' Magazine* awarded its prize for "outstanding scientific contribution to child development published during 1928," it was his book, not Watson's bombshell, that won it. "Infants," Brennemann wistfully noted by 1931, were "already being matched with Gesell, with resulting gloom or elation" in their mothers. And Gesell's reign had hardly begun; his debut in the manual market, *Infant and Child in the Culture of Today*, was more than a decade away.

America during the interwar decades had a new "hard" and "soft" duo presiding *in loco parentis*—and a new prodigal and paragon. It was an irony that Dr. Holt's self-proclaimed heir, whose fierce treat-kids-like-adults dictates made him sound old-fashioned, was in his peculiar way a social and psychological upstart. The same Dr. Watson who endorsed systematic "efficiency" also derided what he saw as the suffocating conformity demanded by the modern age. The technocrat with his anti-maternal tirades and attacks on the sanctity of the home was clearly as drawn by a vision of radical equality and independence as he was afraid of it. A bullying expert, he never really imagined he would be obeyed—and his reign was indeed tempestuous and brief.

Dr. Hall's successor was the gentler advocate of family "democracy" and the man who gave us "it's-just-a-stage" leniency. Yet it was Dr. Gesell whose work could subtly encourage not only conformity but also that competitive anxiety Brennemann said he saw in his office. And with his solicitous advisory style, Gesell aspired to exert a sway with parents that Watson never dreamed of. When Dr. Spock captured mothers' hearts in 1946, he was hailed as a savior come to dispel the Watsonian dark ages at long last. The real story, as a look into the lives and the overreaching science of America's second-generation experts will show, was rather different.

FIVE

The Misbehaviorist

Dr. John B. Watson

I.

"Never rock the baby" was Dr. John Broadus Watson's Holtian motto. Always rock the boat was his un-Holtian habit. He was an expert for a decade frequently described as giddy, a star act in what one critic at the time characterized as "a strange orgy of flagellation" that seemed to have become a form of national entertainment during the 1920s. As a popular child-rearing authority, Watson catered to the "appetite of Americans for hearing themselves abused"—and, like his fellow performers H. L. Mencken and Sinclair Lewis, he appreciated the desire of Americans to be disabused of prevailing pieties in the process, and perhaps to be somewhat amused. At any rate, a scolding should be suitably scandalizing.

How else to understand a child-rearing expert who pronounced that "parents today are incompetent. Most of them should be indicted for psychological murder"? Or who, as the *New York Times* reported, urged a "rotary plan for training children," shuttling them among different adults every three weeks? Or who, rather than join the chorus of concern about "flaming youth," regularly derided the bourgeois home front, as *The Independent Woman: A Magazine for Business and Professional Women* recounted in 1928? "Instead of leveling criticism at youth because of their petting and necking parties," the expert-provocateur proposed (with "a genial look in [his] eyes," the interviewer noted), "why not go further back than that and launch our tirades against homes that pet too much?"

That was, as readers of the *New York Times* or *The Independent Woman* (or plenty of other popular magazines in America) knew by then, precisely what Dr. Watson had just done in *Psychological Care of Infant and Child*, the book published by W. W. Norton in 1928 that capped more than a half decade of journalistic exposure; Watson was prolific, and often profiled. To be sure, his "small hand book" was not packaged as a tirade. It was marketed as the work of one of America's best-known scientists. The reporter in *The Independent Woman*—quite dazzled by Dr. Watson's "fine well-modeled face, sensitive mouth and deep penetrating eyes"—praised him as a renowned empiricist, who had carried out "certain experiments with more than a thousand infants." The manual's cover touted his academic credentials ("Ph.D., formerly Professor of Psychology, The Johns Hopkins University"). The acknowledgments, which cited "scientific material" as the basis of his "convictions," included an impressive list of "Drs." And Watson's introduction began by invoking that embodiment of calm, Dr. Holt, as his inspiration.

No one would have guessed from W. W. Norton's publicity that this scientist-turned-popular-expert was anything but family-friendly, either. The advertisements hailed the manual as "a common sense work," "long awaited and badly needed," in fact "indispensable." Illustrating the ad copy were snapshots of the doctor's own adorable boys, beaming "Behavioristic Children," held up as "children adults like to be around. They lose themselves in work or play. They sleep and rest when put to bed for sleep and rest—they eat what is put before them. They are free from fears and temper tantrums—they are happy children." His wife, Rosalie Rayner Watson, joined in dispensing the "safe and wholesome" advice. She got title-page billing as her husband's assistant. And Dr. Holt's name made it into the ad campaign as well.

"Parents write," or so the copy claimed, "that not since Dr. Holt's 'Care and Feeding of Children' has a book appeared so immediately helpful to parents."

But to flip only a few pages into the book was to discover that the scientist was a polemicist eager to ridicule and to shock—not only "mawkish" mothers and the American fetish for the family, but also his fellow experts. They were denounced as full of Deweyite nonsense about how children "develop from within" (a "doctrine of mystery"). Dr. Watson himself was not exactly a model of lucidity. Even "the behaviorist does not know enough today to do a thoroly [sic] satisfactory job" raising children, he granted, and complained that "prejudice against lab work" with children was to blame for "almost a bankruptcy of facts." But that did not stop him from invoking his own lab work as ample proof for the dictates he presumed to dispense with dogmatic assurance anyway—or from berating parents who balked at the advice, as he predicted just about all of them would.

He dismissed the run-of-the-mill mother as not only "unquestionably unfitted to bring up her child" but impervious to counsel. To hear him, the notion that she would welcome his manual as "immediately helpful" was laughable. "Even in the homes of 'advanced' mothers—mothers who are listening eagerly for words of wisdom about the care of their children you find the complaint—'The behaviorists are on the right track but they go too far.' " To which Dr. Watson's response was to go yet further. Not content with shaping children's fates, the behaviorist also burdened mothers with guilt. "Won't you then remember when you are tempted to pet your child that mother love is a dangerous instrument?" he asked. "An instrument which may inflict a never healing wound, a wound which may make infancy unhappy, adolescence a nightmare, an instrument which may wreck your adult son or daughter's vocational future and their chances for marital happiness."

Dr. Holt's self-anointed heir was not one for filial piety. Watson's manual was as inflammatory as Holt's booklet had been chilly. With impersonal sobriety, Holt had lectured an audience of mothers who he presumed could, if they were as careful as he, bring health, not harm, to their children as well as calm to their own lives. And Holt already had a real heir to carry on his advisory tradition, Dr. L. Emmett Holt, Jr., who had received his medical degree from Johns Hopkins in 1920 and then stayed on, hard at work in the family business of pediatric research on digestion. Rickets, fats, vitamins, amino acids: he studied each in turn, and updated his father's classic with notable circumspection, careful not to jolt readers and to maintain the trademark Holtian aplomb in pursuit of the latest science. (The spirit of gradualism was clear in the minor family fuss he stirred up in daring to approve bananas in his first, 1926 revision. "I am sorry Calvert does not approve of the statement about bananas in the little book," he wrote his mother after his brother had complained about the swerve from paternal fiat. "I think I really should have come out stronger for them, but it seemed a little better not to jump from condemnation to out and out praise at one fell swoop.")

Such deference—to his predecessor, to his audience, much less to science—was not Dr. Watson's radical way. He felt, and the prominent social historian Arthur Wallace Calhoun agreed in an essay in *The New Generation: The Intimate Problems of Modern Parents and Children* in 1930, that parents and children—and experts, too—needed something tougher to chew on than the pabulum they were used to. "The civilized world is only just beginning to learn the lesson of roughage, vitamins, and mineral salts, and to undo some of the damage done by preposterous bourgeois standards of softness, whiteness, and niceness in nutriment," Calhoun announced. He hoped that "a similar lesson will be learned in the mental realm." Or in the realm of human "guts," the term favored by Dr. Watson, who did not mean mere intestines but emotions. Watson presented himself as the upstart teacher, and his extreme brand of behaviorism, which banished heredity and consciousness and accorded the environment total formative power, made a sweeping promise: that emotions could be conditioned, with complete predictability, to produce a personality that was neither soft nor nice, but tough as nails—ready to withstand any adversity, and to seize any opportunity, in an ever more impersonal, organizationally intricate society.

"Dr. Watson's Book on Child-Nurture Called as Epoch-Making as Darwin's Findings" read the headline of a review by his fellow popularizing behaviorist, Dr. George A. Dorsey (whose Watson-approved *Why We Behave Like Human Beings* was on the best-seller lists the next year). Or had Watson "Become the Billy Sunday of His Own Evangelical Religion"? Reviewing Watson's companion volume of 1928, a collection of *Harper's* articles called *The Ways of Behaviorism*, the young Columbia University professor Mortimer Adler denounced him for preaching his creed "with all of the dogmatic zest and vulgarity of Billy Sunday." What is more, Adler was convinced, he had already converted the nation. "Watsonism has become gospel and catechism in the nurseries and drawing rooms of America."

Dr. Watson was more dubious, of course, convinced that mothers were too soft-headed and -hearted to be avid disciples. *Life* magazine was similarly skeptical about the purported power of the Reverend Sunday's "coarse, rude, vulgar way": "What makes you believe that it works, and what exactly is the condition of those upon whom it has worked? How does a 'convert' differ from an ordinary person? Is he better? Is he worse? When you say it 'works,' maybe you mean that Billy Sunday draws a crowd." Riding on the coattails of Dr. Holt, a pioneer from the days before the swarms of experts, the fifty-year-old Watson certainly aimed to stand out from the crowd—and succeeded. His manual, which sold some 50,000 copies within roughly a year, inspired controversy if not conversion. He was the loud, "hard" voice in the chorus of counselors calling for "adjustment," and high on his agenda was a desire to make Americans squirm. As he pursued a crusade that exposed the contradictions of the national preoccupation with social control, Dr. Watson the scientist became, not altogether unwittingly, a social satirist. In the process, he emerged as a parody of that interwar icon, the all-knowing expert. By nature an embittered man and by nurture an embattled one (or perhaps it was the other way around), Watson had been born and reared for the role.

2.

According to the basic tenets of Watsonian behaviorism, "the main emotional habits are set" in infancy and toddlerhood, by "two years or younger." For it was then that "the unverbalized"—by which Watson meant the bedrock of conditioned fear, love, and rage responses, his substitute for the "psychoanalyst's unconscious"—was forming. Further emotional responses (which he reduced to vascular changes in erogenous tissue) built atop them throughout life, producing the personality, which he defined as "but the totality or sum of my habit systems, my conditionings." Watson was highly inconsistent as to just how much that early habit-shaping could be modified or overcome later. In his own case, he did his best to avoid self-scrutiny, but his background plainly helped to produce a man defiantly, and defensively, eager to portray himself as a self-made phenomenon. Where his predecessors Holt and Hall dutifully claimed to have their devout mothers and their undistinguished fathers always in mind, Watson was eager to banish them. The only nostalgia detectable in his rare excursion into memoir, a terse account produced on request for the prestigious multi-volume

History of Psychology in Autobiography in 1936, was for the stretches of childhood when he felt the freest from adult interference.

Born in 1878 in a small town outside of Greenville, South Carolina, Watson had something more important than neat clothes and perfect hair in common with his expert predecessor Dr. Holt: a zealous Baptist mother. Emma Watson evidently set her sights on him, the fourth of her six children, as the vessel of all her devout hopes. To judge by her actions, she believed what her son would later preach: that the choice of a child's vocation lies in his parents' hands, and that career-shaping efforts cannot begin too soon. Christening was the first step. She named him after the ascendant Southern Baptist theologian of the time, John Broadus. Be careful of what you wish for, that well-known warning to parents, has rarely been more apt: her son became a virulent atheist, but a fervent evangelist for a science that scoffed at the notion of a soul.

Watson's lineage, as one of his biographers has remarked, was straight out of American folklore. To go along with a fervent and beleaguered mother, he had a ne'er-do-well for a father. Dr. Hall's fierce sire and Dr. Holt's weak one were nothing compared to the man whom Watson, years later, sent a new suit of clothes but refused to see. At sixteen Pickens Butler Watson had run away from home, which was a prosperous farm near Greenville, and joined the Confederate Army, where he quickly became known for great recklessness. Drinking and raging were habits he evidently acquired early and kept. His marriage to Emma, whom his parents considered a socially unworthy match, made his break with his family final, and the bond he formed with his new family was not exactly stable. In a non-slaveholding region of hardscrabble farming, he couldn't stick with the labor and started wandering.

His wife held the rest of the family together, refreshed in her struggles by the religious revivals she faithfully attended (presumably dragging her children along with her). In his account, Watson emphasized a pre-pubescent idyll of busy independence and precocious competence, no parent anywhere in sight. (At nine, he was adeptly "handling tools, half-soling shoes, and milking cows," by twelve he was doing carpentry.) But Emma Watson was determined that her offspring get an education as well as religion. In 1890, when Watson was twelve, she moved the family to Greenville, where grammar schools were divided into grades and there was a high school. Legend had it that Pickens Watson ended up living with Cherokees in the backwoods.

John Watson did not respond to his opportunities with anything like the alacrity shown by the Holt boys to theirs, though (or perhaps because) his mother had to work doubly hard to arrange them, given how isolated much of the still rural South was at the time. No sooner did Emma and her children arrive in Greenville than her favorite son went wild. A lazy and insubordinate student, he dedicated himself to brawling. "Twice I was arrested," was Watson's only comment on his eruption of adolescent rage, "once for 'nigger' fighting, and the second time for shooting off firearms inside the city limits." So much for his mother's dreams of schooling. He was doing just what his mother must have dreaded, though he himself made no note of it: following in his father's footsteps.

Except that he then proceeded on to Furman University, the local Baptist school—thanks, one presumes, to his mother's pressure. Watson did not cotton to that either. "Those years made me bitter, made me feel that college only weakens the vocational slants and leads to softness and laziness and a prolongation of infancy with a killing of all vocational bents." Still, there he underwent a fortuitous tussle with a father figure—Professor Gordon Moore, who introduced him to philosophy and psychology, and by flunking him in a course, Watson said, goaded him to excel at research. Then Emma died. This plainly marked the moment when Watson felt his adulthood began. To hear him tell it, he at last made his escape and undertook the "behaviorist self-correcting" he later prescribed as the key to personal success and social progress. In 1900, Watson wrote the president of the University of Chicago, explaining his need for "better preparation" at a "real university." The pitch worked, and the graduate student set off (working as an assistant janitor and waiter to make ends meet).

Here Watson's story acquired the contours of a Sinclair Lewis saga. The small-town southern boy had arrived in a rapidly modernizing city and at America's most businesslike university. With John D. Rockefeller's money, its president, William Rainey Harper, had dedicated himself to building a "useful" institution designed to supply systematic, specialized "training" (and had availed himself of some of Dr. Hall's disgruntled Clark faculty in the process). "I felt at once that I had come to the right place," Watson recalled in his memoir. But there were tensions between the lines of his brisk report of three "frightfully busy years" during which he thrived under the guidance of the head of the psychology division within the department of philosophy, James Rowland Angell. Following the lead of his colleague John Dewey, Angell presided over a "functionalist" turn away from the "structuralist" interest in measuring mental states. The new Darwinian project was to explore the mental activity of organisms adapting to their environment, or situation—"Dewey's favorite word," William James noted in 1904, excitedly announcing that "Chicago has a School of Thought!"

In the ambitious young Watson, as Angell could see, he had found a protégé who stood out as a model of adaptive activity. Less immediately evident was that the frenetic researcher was also a bundle of social and professional anxiety. Watson's account of becoming the man who made the University of Chicago the capital of white rat experimentation betrayed someone who felt caught in a rat race himself. For Watson, "the spark was not there" in his studies in philosophy. He flunked a course on Kant, and about Dewey, under whom he studied, he wrote dismissively, "I never knew what he was talking about then, and, unfortunately for me, I still don't know," a swipe at a man who had in fact been an ally then—and at least an indirect influence: from the notion that consciousness is inextricable from activity and that the total organism is inseparable from its environment, Watson in essence removed the dialectical drama to arrive at his stark brand of behaviorism that posited a "stream of activity" totally channeled by the environment.

The formative German influence on Watson was a controversial physiologist named Jacques Loeb. He had emigrated to escape German idealism, but his zealous vision of biology as an engineering enterprise aimed at controlling and modifying, rather than merely understanding, nature soon made him impatient with Dewey's Hegelian evolutionism, too. Along with the neurologist H. H. Donaldson, Loeb helped steer Watson onto the new terrain of animal research, where he proceeded to undertake a project more prodigious—and laborious—than anyone had yet tried on rats (new to American labs in 1892). For his dissertation, Watson set out to discover the relation between a rat's learning behavior and the growth of its nervous system. Functionalism, in Watson's enterprise, was put through mazes and onto the dissecting table: he concluded that rats' problem-solving activity got more complex faster than their nerve fibers matured.

Watson was certainly working at a pace that overtaxed his nerves. "I worked night and day and established work habits that have persisted the rest of my life," he reported, but the year before he graduated, Watson collapsed. "I had a breakdown—sleepless nights for weeks—a typical Angst," he said with characteristic brusqueness. "A month there during which, for three weeks, I went to sleep only with a light on. A sudden recovery and back to work." He proclaimed it "one of my best experiences in my university course," saying it "in a way prepared me to accept a large part of Freud," or rather his own idiosyncratic dose of

Freud. The insomniac had discovered the power of what he later called "infantile carry-overs," which he judged "one of the most tragic things in our make-up." This frantic man, in flight from his past, had grown up with the fear that "there was something in the dark that would get me," he would admit in his popular talks, usually blaming it on child-hood conditioning by "negro nurses"—and lamenting that "I carry that inferiority with me all my days." But during his breakdown, he perhaps glimpsed a deeper Oedipal drama, which eventually led him to become such a fierce critic of the nuclear family: on the brink of academic suc-cess and under great stress, he may well have halted in his tracks, haunted by the schoolmarmish Emma and the scofflaw Pickens, eager to flout both yet follow neither.

The Watsonian response to this double bind was to redouble his labors, emphasizing that only exhaustive studies—and ever more spe-cialized expert training to do them—could establish psychology as a real science. Spurred on by a feeling of "deep-seated inferiority," he hurried onward, castigating himself for not getting a summa cum laude (as he noted a woman, Helen Woolley Thompson, had two years ear-lier) and for not pursuing a medical degree—"to save me from a little of the insolence of the youthful and inferior members of that profession." But the prickly Ph.D. prospered, parlaying counteroffers into an assist-antship and then in 1903 an instructorship at the University of Chicago. He also married one of his students, Mary Ickes, over the fierce protests of her brother Harold Ickes (the future secretary of the interior under President Franklin Roosevelt), who derided Watson as an unreliable southerner and a social climber.

For another four years at Chicago, Watson devoted himself to his "menagerie" and to the elaborate apparatuses he constructed for their performances. He was driven by ambition—the experimental approach, Angell noted in petitioning for more laboratory funds for Watson, "is enjoying a great 'boom' just at present among the universities"—but also by ambivalence about working with human subjects. With people, "I was always uncomfortable and acted unnaturally" was the revealing admission of a man who was soon to denounce the "subjective" meth-ods that were the mainstay of his psychological profession. "With ani-mals I was at home."

Industrious as ever, Dr. Watson prepared to unsettle the older gen-eration of philosopher-psychologists whose experimental approach still relied on introspection. Summoned in 1908, at the age of thirty, by James Mark Baldwin to head the psychology lab at Johns Hopkins Uni-versity, he "began to perfect [his] point of view about behaviorism." For a few years, Watson enjoyed an idyll of productive independence without pressure—reminiscent of his pre-teen puttering. Baldwin's ignominious dismissal in 1909, after he was caught at a black bordello, left Watson in charge of the department and editor of the *Psychological Review*. "The whole tenor of my life was changed. I tasted freedom in work without supervision. I was lost in and happy in my work." Home he avoided. "Two kids are enough, Teddy [Roosevelt] to the contrary," he said after the birth of his second, a son, in 1907, by which time his womanizing reputation had ensured a rocky relationship with his wife. Absorbed with his animals, he was developing a methodology that focused on observable behavior.

Watson was riding "a rising tide of discontent with subjectivism," as functionalists and others brought an increasingly biological perspective to psychology, a confused new discipline eager to establish itself as a "hard" science. The sense of drift was conceptual and institutional. The still academically insecure field needed, as Watson put it, "an objective standard of determination," which he felt consciousness would forever elude. And if psychology, like physics or biology, could also boast some practical applications, this admirer of the engineering-minded Loeb appreciated, its social and scientific status would be assured.

Avid tinkerer and worker that he was, Watson ran experiments with an energy few in the field could match. And ever the enterprising outsider determined to make his mark, he orchestrated a well-timed campaign to redefine the empirical ground on which psychology should rest. In a lecture at Columbia University in 1913 called "Psychology as the Behaviorist Views It," which became known as his "manifesto," he proclaimed that "psychology as the behaviorist views it is a purely objective experimental branch of natural science. Its theoretical goal is the prediction and control of behavior. Introspection forms no essential part of its methods." He announced the goal of describing a "unitary scheme of animal response," which assumed "no dividing line between man and brute." Watson followed up with *Behavior: An Introduction to Comparative Psychology* (1914), a textbook that was bold without being too belligerent in its criticism of introspective techniques and results, and in its claims for animal behavior as a legitimate field of inquiry.

What Watson obviously needed, having consigned introspection to the dustbin, was a method for working on humans, not just animals. By 1915, he felt he had found an answer in the conditioned reflex, though he had only murky reports of Pavlov's work and no evidence of his own to offer. So when his colleague, the psychiatrist and mental hygienist Dr. Adolf Meyer, invited him to turn from rats to infants at the Phipps

Clinic in Baltimore in the fall of 1916, he was eager—and started out sounding humble. His efforts to study reflexes and instincts in babies, funded by the American Association for the Advancement of Science, prompted him to write to another colleague that "it is a far more difficult field than I had anticipated. It is no wonder good work has never been done in it before. At the present moment I am not at all cockey [*sic*] about my own attempts in that direction."

But soon enough Watson revealed a zeal for dogmatic theory that outstripped his passion for empirical methods. The moment was ripe—in psychology, in American society, in his personal and professional trajectory (he was a man in his thirties, and in a hurry)—for a scientific controversy. Some reservations among colleagues about applying the reductively materialist methods he used with animals to humans sufficed to rouse Dr. Watson to an all-out assault on the study of consciousness. Alert to the insecurities of a fractious field, he denounced psychology for dithering over ephemera while true sciences dealt in testable phenomena.

World War I, though he complained in his memoir that it "played havoc with my work," was just the boost his crusade needed. The formation of the National Research Council in 1916 brought scientists, businesses, and government officials together and inaugurated a new technocratic approach to social and organizational problems. For applied psychology in particular, the wartime enterprise of testing mental efficiency brought the field cachet it had lacked. Watson was caustic about his own contributions as an expert in uniform: he helped devise aviation examining boards, only to see an unfit supervisor installed; studied homing pigeons just as the radio took over; twiddled his thumbs overseas and made trouble for his superiors.

But with victory, and the sense of social decay and drift that accompanied it, Watson now had plenty of company in the quest to predict and control behavior—which meant he had no time to waste. A more ambitious behaviorist and a less scrupulous researcher got back down to work, on more babies and on a new book. In *Psychology from the Standpoint of a Behaviorist* (1919), Watson appropriated the Pavlovian idea of the conditioned reflex—still with no experimental foundation for it—as the centerpiece of what had become a reductive system in which heredity played absolutely no role. At the Harriet Lane Hospital for Invalid Children in Baltimore, where he was welcomed by the physician-in-chief, Dr. John Howland (who at roughly the same time recruited young L. Emmett Holt, Jr., to study digestive chemistry in the basement of the building), Watson was determined to come up with the "objective facts" that, after all, were supposed to be behaviorism's claim to fame.

This time, he was completely cocky about his efforts. The only extended, published studies of children ever conducted by Watson himself took place during little more than a year there. He wisely left an indeterminate trail, but a close look suggests that a sample reputed, years later, to be in the hundreds and then thousands in fact amounted to "several" babies, all of whose mothers were wet nurses at the hospital. Of the group, it was tests on only two of them that Watson reported in any detail. In *Psychology from the Standpoint of a Behaviorist* he recounted the stoic reactions of five-and-a-half-month-old Thorne to being exposed to a variety of potentially fearful stimuli—a black cat, a fluttering pigeon, a rabbit, a rat, a dog, a burning newspaper, all of them presented to her in the light, and then in darkness. (Although elsewhere, and in a later revision of the book, Watson also invoked the "almost daily observation of several hundred infants from birth through the first thirty days of infancy and of a smaller number through the first years of childhood," he credited the scrutiny to someone else, a woman named Mrs. Margaret Gray Blanton, whose developmental descriptions he simply appropriated.) These observations served as further confirmation of the theory he had advanced before the war that the child's "unlearned equipment," and the "nucleus out of which all future emotional reactions arise," consisted of a trio of responses (he was inconsistent as to whether they rated as instincts), each evoked by a particular stimulus: fear, caused by loud noises or sudden loss of support; rage, provoked by physical constraint; and love, elicited by stroking in erogenous places.

It was the other baby, "Little Albert," who became famous and who changed the future of Dr. Watson the academic, in not quite the way he expected. At nine months old, Albert was subjected to Thorne's ordeals, and two months later, this "wonderfully 'good' baby" was chosen as the ideal "stolid and phlegmatic" specimen for an experiment in conditioning a fear reflex. (The same extreme environmentalism that made controlled testing seem so fruitful, of course, could not help also making it seem fraught. Watson found himself in the awkward position of claiming, in almost the same breath, that babies were phenomenally—dangerously—malleable and, in defense of his own work, that "infants are really very hardy—not at all the hot house plants they are supposed to be.") Enlisting his other favorite lab specimen, the white rat, Dr. Watson set out to condition the little boy to fear the rodent by clanging a steel bar whenever it scuttled into view. He also aimed to find out whether his fear would be transferred to other animals and furry objects, and to discover how long the child's apprehensions would last. The point was to establish that, as Watson's theory claimed, all emotional responses were the product of environmental forces—and, in the process, to demonstrate the power to control those reactions.

In the February 1920 issue of the *Journal of Experimental Psychology*, Dr. Watson published what proved to be the last article of his academic career, "Conditioned Emotional Reactions," co-authored with a graduate student named Rosalie Rayner, from a prominent Baltimore family. They duly began it by acknowledging that "experimental work has been done so far on only one child," but closed it by claiming to have proved that conditioned emotional reflexes instilled early on "persist and modify personality throughout life." In between, they presented laboratory notes documenting an experiment that was anything but "objective," much less conclusive—except, perhaps, as evidence that even a "phlegmatic" baby subjected to abusive enough treatment will react by fretting, crying, toppling over, crawling away, and recoiling from his tormentor.

To read the account is to agree that Watson had indeed found a remarkable specimen—and to see why the experiment proved unreplicable. What other baby (or mother) would have put up with it? The most striking revelation of the study was how much trouble the experimenters had getting more than a transient rise out of Albert—and how much trouble they surely would have had getting a more "unstable" subject to sit calmly enough even to administer the tests. Over ten days, Albert endured three sessions of unpleasant stimuli. First he was jolted by the sight of a rat accompanied by clanging, seven bouts of which succeeded in making him crawl frantically away upon being presented with a rat in quiet. Five days later, Albert was exposed to a rat, a rabbit, a dog, and a fur coat, all of which did rouse signs of aversion in him without any clanging. Finally, five days after that, Watson staged another round, when Albert gave the experimenters a harder time, and vice versa. This time they had to "freshen the reaction" of the unflappable little fellow with more clanging—and then moved him to a bigger, brighter room for more of the same, only to have the uncontrolled drama culminate in a complete upset of protocol. "When only about six inches from the baby's face," the dog barked, producing "a marked fear response in the adult observers!" Albert wailed.

A month later, Albert returned on his last day at the hospital for a final test of the longer-term effects of conditioning. The experimenters, to judge from their account, were certainly feeling under pressure. Albert was not just confronted with the furry objects, but with very pushy psychologists—provocateurs, not observers. They took his hand and forced him to touch a Santa Claus mask, put the rat on his arm and then on his chest, plopped the rabbit right into his lap and "took hold of his left hand and laid it on the rabbit's back," shoved the dog closer and closer. (All along, they revealed in their discussion, they had been yanking Albert's thumb out of his mouth to get him to react.)

The poor baby's response was to cover his face with his hands, a poignant display of human distress, never mind fear of fur. The experimenters proceeded to declare total success, and to extrapolate—quite wildly, they confessed in passing. "Our own view, which is possibly not very well grounded," Watson and Rayner breezily concluded, "is that these responses in the home environment are likely to persist indefinitely, unless an accidental method for removing them is hit upon." Based on Albert's far from consistent response to their hectoring, Watson proclaimed his theory of the molding of the personality all but proved.

He and Rayner were deprived of (or spared) any occasion to pursue what had been more than a professionally exciting endeavor. "All of this work came abruptly to a close with my divorce in 1920. I was asked to resign," was Dr. Watson's clipped version in his official account. ". . . I went to New York, stranded economically and to some extent emotionally." He left out the lurid details of his affair with Rosalie Rayner, twenty-one years his junior, mentioning only that he was "front-page news in Baltimore." The reason was a much publicized scandal stirred up by his wife. (Mary Ickes supplied journalists with purloined love letters, featuring behaviorist endearments such as "My total reactions are positive and towards you. So likewise each and every heart reaction.") Watson was stunned to discover that at Johns Hopkins total reactions were negative (though he should have known better of an institution that had recently given the boot to James Mark Baldwin for his sexual exploits, and that had once fired a philosopher, Charles Peirce, for cohabiting with a woman who was not yet his wife).

But to hear Watson tell it, he took it like a man—or rather, like a businessman. He depicted his downfall as the kind of "reconditioning" shake-up that he later recommended complacent Americans undertake in midcareer. It was the hardening he needed to "rub off the academic." With the aid of a friend, the sociologist W. I. Thomas, he was steered into advertising in New York City. Expressing deep gratitude for Thomas's "understanding counsel and . . . helpfulness," Watson portrayed himself as humbly ready to start from the bottom and work, as always, doggedly. His retraining quite literally put him through new paces. He tramped the Mississippi valley "studying the rubber boot market" and getting a feel for "the great advertising god, the consumer" in preparation for his rise to vice president of the J. Walter Thompson agency in 1924. The "growth of a sales curve of a new product," he insisted, proved "just as thrilling to watch . . . as . . . the learning curve of animals or men."

It was a phenomenal rebound, which left Watson as defiant and defensive—and demanding—as before, or more. (Though behaviorists are reluctant to admit it, it can be hard to teach an old dog new tricks: Watson himself, despite claims about how "personalities . . . can be changed as easily as the shape of the nose," also acknowledged what a struggle it was and scoffed that few have the "guts to stick to the long arduous routine one should have to follow." Elsewhere he concluded that "the zebra can as easily change his stripes as the adult his personality.") Hosting a guest who clearly got on his nerves, W. I. Thomas wrote to a friend in exasperation that Watson is "more childish than I imagined." His diagnosis depicted the ex-professor as just the sort of infantile, emotionally needy specimen that Watson derided. Watson has "the mother complex that the Freudians glorify, and he has it for fair," Thomas had decided, and went on to elaborate.

Watson's "fault is that he expects instant appreciation and help from all who are allied with him and has no consciousness at all of reciprocity. He is like a child who expects petting and indulgence, but has no return. . . . He thinks people have and must have a perpetual good opinion of him without regard to his behavior." Or at any rate, he was remarkably impervious to the animus he inspired. Thomas gave Watson low marks for perspective on himself. "He has scales on his eyes, and becomes quickly a pest or a comedy to all men who know him intimately," he complained, grudgingly noting that "his efficiency depends on these things." Women who knew him intimately felt otherwise, or so the rumors went. Rosalie Rayner promptly married him, and a son, Billy, was born in 1921.

Watson the advertising man was as adversarial as ever, above all in his crusade not just to moonlight as a psychological expert now that he was out of the academy, but to hog the limelight as a popular expert. In defensive mode, he claimed later that W. W. Norton—and the magazines, from *Harper's* to *Cosmopolitan*—had come clamoring, which indeed they had. He subsequently professed regret over *Behaviorism* as a "rush job," and over *Psychological Care of Infant and Child* "because I did not know enough to write the book I wanted to write." But he could not refrain from bristling that any down-and-out ex-academic would "have sold himself to the public," too. Watson had made one more stab at real lab work in 1923, though only as a consultant on a study in unconditioning a child, funded by the Laura Spelman Rockefeller Memorial Foundation. Mary Cover Jones, a graduate student at Columbia University, did all the work of trying to cure Peter, a ready-made Albert afraid of furry animals, and she wrote up her results cautiously. Jones found that associating good food with the bad rabbit helped, and so did peer pressure, but wisely warned against easy generalizing to other fears. (And the practical applications were not immediately obvious: as a sensible mother in a study group noted, it is "impossible to put a grandmother in a cage at the end of a forty-foot room during the child's lunch, as Watson suggests with the rabbit.") Dr. Watson, however, did not hesitate to broadcast great success.

The real trademark, not surprisingly, of Watson's post-academic proselytizing was his almost perverse defiance. He did not need the money he earned from the importunate publishers. By the time he wrote those books, he was a well-paid employee of J. Walter Thompson, not a foundering ex-academic. He was eager to be famous, but also to flagellate—himself, among others. It was as though Watson were bent on revenge, not just against his former colleagues but also against the credulous public that had become his audience instead— and against himself, for joining the ranks of the "medicine men" he had always scorned as the antithesis of the modern scientist, mere manipulators who peddled superstitious fears (and hopes) to dupe and control the masses.

Watson became more of an extremist. That is generally what scientific popularizers do, and even as an academic, Watson had never shied from grandiose claims that were "possibly not very well grounded." But he went further, and became a walking collection of the tensions of the time: a conservative businessman espousing self-determination and egalitarianism, and a social iconoclast urging social control and determinism. Behaviorism, a peculiarly American creed, inspired visions of open-ended freedom, and of studiously engineered order. Watson was an adviser of mothers calling for the abolition of homes. And Watson was a scientist insistent on "observable facts," preaching a behaviorist doctrine that he took every opportunity to admit was a "terrific superstructure of theory [erected] upon a foundation of very meager experimental results."

To be sure, the modesty of that last claim was a rhetorical strategy: Watson went right on to add that the behaviorist's "position, however, is the only one that has even meager experimental support." (In the same vein, he accompanied his famous boast about creating merchant-chiefs or thieves with a caveat: "I am going beyond my facts and I admit it, but so have the advocates of the contrary and they have been doing it for many thousands of years.") In dispensing wisdom to the public, laboratory researchers in the twentieth century discovered early on that admissions of fallibility boost, rather than erode, the authority of science.

Still, the final paradox of Dr. Watson was that the expert who seemed to have the most definitive of answers for parents was in fact a relativist, at least about child rearing. "There is no ideal system of civi-lization—there are only actual civilizations, hence the child must be brought up along practical lines to fit a given civilization," he said. And, acknowledging the dilemma faced by any dispenser of "scientific" dogma to parents, he noted that a civilization that seems "given" today can be gone tomorrow—and would be, he wagered. "I believe that the internal structure of our American civilization is changing from top to bottom more rapidly and more fundamentally than most of us dream of," he pronounced, aware of how events had a way of overtaking advice. Watson made that prescient admission in, of all places, his own child-rearing manual in 1928. But it came at the end, in a "Behaviorist's Apologia," by which time—or so he hoped—he had roused Americans' attention with a hefty dose of hysteria.

3.

Dr. Holt was the official inspiration behind *Psychological Care of Infant and Child*, but the man who seems to have served as the more immedi-ate catalyst was someone very different. He was probably, of all people, H. L. Mencken, the "iconoclast from Baltimore," whom Dr. Watson got to know when he arrived at Johns Hopkins University. That year, 1908, Mencken had beaten him to it in becoming an upstart successor to Holt. In one of the more peculiar escapades of his youthful journalis-tic career, Mencken was commissioned by Theodore Dreiser, then edi-tor of the women's magazine *The Delineator*, to try his hand as a popular medical writer. With facts supplied by a Baltimore doctor named Leonard Hirshberg (who lifted them from Dr. Holt), Mencken pro-ceeded to ghostwrite a series of articles on baby care (about which he knew nothing, either from reading or from real life).

In 1920 the articles were published as a book, *What You Ought to Know About Your Baby*, which bore Dr. Hirshberg's name but Mencken's acerbic imprint. "The Slaughter of the Innocents," he titled the first chapter, which began by accusing a doting mother, observed fussing with her baby on a train ride, "of no less than seven separate and distinct crimes . . . against her innocent youngster, and, indirectly, against posterity, her country and long-suffering humanity." (She was benighted enough to bounce the child on her lap, and in chattering to a fellow passenger revealed an array of other pre-Holtian, unhygienic habits as well—from pacifiers to taking tips from Grandmother.) Mencken heaped on the insults with comic verve, becoming especially apoplectic about "overcoddling" as a source of "infantile ills" and a sign of maternal evil. "She loves [her child], and so, after it has had its fill, she coddles it, bounces it and plays with it—and it vomits," he wrote. "Kissing the baby after it has been fed," he warned, ". . . is very likely to cause it to vomit, and vomiting is even more exhausting to a child than to an adult." And then after more of the same, turning sober, he dared his audience to laugh. "Is the picture overdrawn? Is it a farce? Not at all."

Distributed for free by the Butterick Company, a producer of dress patterns as well as of various publications (*The Delineator* among them), the booklet went through several printings—not nearly the hit that Dr. Holt's "bible" still was, but a hint that mothers had perhaps acquired a taste for training that was much more lively, if also a lot more derogatory of their talents. It was issued until 1923, when Leonard Hirshberg, who was sent to jail by Learned Hand on charges of financial swindling that year, took over the copyright from Butterick. (Hirshberg went on to confirm his status as a quack: as an ex-con, he worked for a fake outfit called the National Health Service, dispensing panaceas and proclaiming himself "the world's greatest specialist . . . recognized as one of the few great medical geniuses of the present century.") Word was soon to leak out that Mencken was the true author, but his psychologist friend Watson—to whom Mencken was constantly pitching lucrative popular-science hack work—had no doubt been in on the joke for years. It was a gag, and an advisory gig, of a sort that must have appealed to the adman: frustrated in his efforts to sustain any real research and ready for a chance to give Americans a comeuppance, Watson was ready to get writing several years later.

Like Mencken, Watson dared his audience to dismiss his book as a farce, which had the desired effect of getting allies and enemies alike to hail *Psychological Care of Infant and Child* instead as a major influence. In fact, after a brisk lesson in behaviorist principles, Watson proceeded to dispense a perverse blend of pernicious nonsense, above all about mothers, and prevailing "common" sense about children. The rhetorical flair that was original with Watson (inspired by Mencken) and that garnered it so much press also served to marginalize the book within only a few years of its appearance. The joke, Watson was bitterly aware, was on him, the behaviorist-propagandist who would never be able to sell mothers on his idea of "infant farms" and rotating caretakers instead of intimate families, and thus could never hope truly to test and prove his extreme theory (which in the 1930s was, in any case, losing the radical cachet it had had in an era of prosperity).

It was clear from the opening page that the purpose of Dr. Watson's manual was only secondarily to train those fear, rage, and love responses of children. The primary goal was to intimidate, infuriate, and titillate mothers. His book was an experiment in conditioning adults: the trick was to play on maternal fear in the cause of drastically weakening maternal love, and he was ready to risk some maternal fury to rouse attention. The standard advertising bromides—"Never make an audience feel inferior" and "Never be angry at the audience, only with them," as H. A. Overstreet had advised in his best-seller, *Influencing Human Behavior* (1925)—were not for Watson. His experience of mankind (reinforced by reading Mencken) had taught him an alternative that had helped speed him on his way at J. Walter Thompson: "tell [the consumer] something that will tie him up with fear, something that will stir up a mild rage, that will call out an affectionate or love response, or strike at a deep psychological or habit need." The first two tactics came most naturally to Watson.

In its basic substance, *Psychological Care of Infant and Child* offered notably little in the way of new practical advice about the daily handling of children. The sensationalist novelty of the primer lay in the anti-maternal diatribe begun in the introduction and brought to a crescendo in a chapter called "The Dangers of Too Much Mother Love." The topic of the last chapter—"What Shall I Tell My Child About Sex?"—also had obvious allure.

What set Watson apart was not his suspicion of maternal sentiment per se. As the Conference on Modern Parenthood had made abundantly clear, the experts were all scratching their heads over just how cozy American hearths should be. The defense of the "affectionate" family, the cause that united the many advisers and parent leaders at the Waldorf-Astoria in 1925, was not without its awkwardness for

champions of "adjustment." The very reason that intimacy was considered so crucial—because it cushioned children for a cold and complicated world—was also a reason it could be counterproductive,
incapacitating even. Hence there was much fiddling with the thermo-
stat to avoid excess warmth. Watson just blew the house down. He
gleefully called for the collapse of the fragile family. What good could
such a cosseting, and also constraining, environment possibly be for
preparing a child to live in an ever more impersonal and unpredictable
world? Watson raised the question that went right to the heart of confused thinking about socialization.

He was well aware that home-wrecking was hardly a natural sell in
America, and it rankled. "The home we have with us—inevitably and
inexorably with us," he wrote, highly annoyed that "the behaviorist has
to accept the home and make the best of it." It brought out the satirist
in the scientist, and Watson adopted the mode of the Swiftian modest
proposer. Echoing Mencken, he opened his chapter ("The Slaughter-
ers of the Innocents," he could have called it) with a scene of a car
(rather than a train) ride that was rife with coddling behavior. At the
sight of two children, obviously his own, being smothered with tenderness, he outdid himself in indignation. Watson tabulated the kisses he
witnessed, each a crime in itself: 32 kisses in all, 4 from Mother, 8 from
the nurse, 20 from Grandmother! Don't fool yourself that this is an
exaggeration or an exception, he wrote, ridiculing any notion that
"mothers are getting modern" and less mushy. "Kissing the baby to
death is just about as popular a sport as it ever was."

Don't mistake it for an innocent pastime either, Watson warned. All
that fondling, he was pleased to shock his sentimental audience by
announcing, was "at bottom a sex-seeking response" on the part of
frustrated females. Again, what distinguished Watson was his zeal, not
his suggestion that lack of wifely "fulfillment" spelled trouble with and
for children; that was a standard theme among the marital experts who
proliferated in the 1920s. But where they fidgeted and fudged in an
effort to assure family harmony, Watson took a hard-core approach
that zeroed in on biology. Love, he said, consists merely of "stroking
and touching its skin, lips, sex organs and the like." Infant gurgles can
be elicited by any caresser. "Hard to believe? But true," he told his
readers.

"All affection, be it parental, child for parent or love between the
sexes," Watson emphasized, is built up of (and comes down to) physical, self-centered indulgence. No wonder, in a way, that his prohibition

against any displays of it sounded like a parody of Victorian scare-mongering about masturbation. "Mothers just don't know, when they kiss their children and pick them up and rock them, caress them and jiggle them upon their knee, that they are slowly building up a human being totally unable to cope with the world it must later live in," Watson wrote. He didn't quite threaten insanity, but severe debility was assured. A "child gets honeycombed with love responses" for parents and nurses, and succumbs to "invalidism" and "nest habits," disarmed of any power to "conquer the difficulties it must meet in its environment," or to succeed in marriage. Watson's proposed cure was a flight of wicked fancy: if only, he mused, children could be tended by a different nurse every week—and why not go even further than that? "Somehow I can't help wishing that it were possible to rotate the mothers occasionally too!"

No one could complain that this diatribe against mother love was "dull as dishwater": Watson the adviser heeded Watson the adman's call to stir up some "news" in order to sell one's wares. But the rest of Watson's book, on the more practical subject of handling children's fears and rages and routine care, was quite standard. The training methods he recommended for use with children were altogether different from the merciless mocking he resorted to with mothers. And they were not, despite his reputation for exerting a formative influence on the advice of the decade, trend-setting techniques at all. Watson's book—with its accompanying media blitz—came out years after the 1921 *Infant Care* and 1925 *Child Management* booklets issued by the Children's Bureau that urged "habit training," regularity, by-the-clock feedings, and let-them-cry attitudes; the 1929 edition of *Infant Care* did not list him in its index. It was Watson who followed their Holtian-inflected approach, rather than the other way around. In fact, he lagged behind them, for in the interwar Children's Bureau material the mellower mental hygiene mood of the times had left its mark. Those manuals, in addition to condoning "[a] few minutes of gentle play now and then," mentioned "developmental" variations and reminded parents that they were "dealing with a sensitive being endowed with all the desires, inclinations, and tendencies that they themselves have." It was not behaviorist gospel, Watson style.

In any case, Watson's own practical advice was not nearly as fierce as his bullying style with parents, or his claims about molding children's personalities, would lead you to believe. And the spirit behind his recommendations was, in its way, less controlling than his "softer" colleagues' attitude. In the confines of his manual, Watson sounded almost more resigned than pleased about parental molding power, sighing that "parents *slant* their children in age-old ways that reflect the way their own parents brought them up." The "method of handling" he urged was more detached, not more manipulative. In *Behaviorism* he went so far as to urge that the child be left to "shape itself properly," and above all independently. The same expert who was so emotionally abusive to mothers, in other words, was otherwise not particularly fierce at all—and had no tips for creating lawyers or merchant-chiefs in the cradle.

Thus on the subject of fears, Watson invoked his Albert experiment to warn parents that "home-made" terrors turn bold newborns into quivering adults ("thousands of . . . things," he despaired, "literally torture us even in this modern, supposedly secure life we lead"). How to avoid it? Right in step with typical interwar advice (to say nothing of turn-of-the-millennium wisdom) against demanding old-style obedience, Watson urged a "positive method of training": fewer "don'ts," ample distractions in a childproof environment full of activity, and briskly "rapping the fingers" when necessary—not as punishment but as a deterrent designed to condition "appropriate commonsense negative reactions." Realistically, Watson did not promise easy success. "Fears do get built in no matter how careful we are." (So much for the poor mother who confessed to her mother's group, "I swallow Watson whole because I want to believe I can do something about fears, not because I am convinced that he is sound.") Watson's approach to rage was just as uncoercive. Having identified physical constraint as the stimulus that evoked rage, he urged parents to dress children gently, in loose clothes, and let them take over the job themselves as soon as possible; in general, more independence was his cure for balky resistance.

Basically nonconfrontational—and highly impersonal—tact also informed Watson's treatment of day and nighttime care. He prescribed calm routine and lots of "uncensored play" alone, without adults—and no thumb-sucking, though he admitted he had no magical cures. In favor of flannel mitts, he ruled out hospital arm braces as a "cruel" impediment to movement, and surely would have scoffed at the uselessness of products such as the "Baby Alice Thumb Guard" or "Bite-X" solution advertised in *Parents' Magazine*. Aside from germs, Watson's main objection to the habit, which he diagnosed as an auto-erotic response that blocked out "*all other stimuli,*" was that it interfered with the child's "manipulation of his universe," and he recognized that most kids were enterprising enough to wriggle out of a guard, ignore a bad taste.

In much the same brisk spirit, Watson cast his stern views on early toilet training as a matter of instilling autonomy in a child, not demanding obedience to an adult. (His account made perfectly clear that despite his counsel to start at three to five weeks, toddlers would still be untrained.) Cool detachment, and no punishment, was key on the part of the parent; "dependent behavior" was the problem on the part of the child, whose penchant for "dawdling, loud conversation," and general stalling to get adult attention during the process was not to be tolerated. Solitary exile in the bathroom did not rate as punishment with Watson: he was all for it.

Far from tending to "steam roller the child" into abject conformity, Watson insisted that his routinized, depersonalized approach was the secret to creating the "person in life who is effectively original." In *The Ways of Behaviorism* he worried in a similar vein that the behaviorist's "rough pattern of a new weapon for controlling the individual" might well be misused by society. "Will it use this weapon when perfected as a steam roller to flatten all that is different in human personalities . . . ?" he wondered. "Or will it use this method wisely?" Watson extolled the "*happy child free as air . . . a child that meets and plays with other children* frankly, openly, untroubled by shyness and inferiority." That this ideal child was also, he added later, one who was as "free as possible of sensitivities to people and one who, almost from birth, [was] relatively independent of the family situation" put something of a chill into the air. Still, from the opening lines of the passage often quoted as the Watsonian child-rearing creed, you could easily take him for a proponent of the "democratic" family. "There is a sensible way of treating children. Treat them as though they were young adults. Dress them, bathe them with care and circumspection. Let your behavior always be objective and kindly firm," he proposed in the reasonable enough spirit of his practical advice, invoking a vision of mutually considerate equals.

But then the other Watson burst in, adding big "don'ts" for mothers, and suddenly a call for respectful sympathy turned into a harsh ban on intimacy. The better known part of his incantation delivered a frigid jolt. "Never hug and kiss them. Never let them sit on your lap. If you must, kiss them once on the forehead when they say good night. Shake hands with them in the morning. Give them a pat on the head if they have made an extraordinary job of a difficult task," Dr. Watson instructed. "Try it out. In a week's time you will find how easy it is to be perfectly objective with your child and at the same time kindly. You will be utterly ashamed of the mawkish, sentimental way you have been handling it."

The caricatured Holtianism was heartless, and Dr. Watson dared his readers to dismiss it as overdrawn. In fact, it fit with the anti-maternalist style of the Jazz Age (when skirts like sheaths made it awkward for a stylish mother to crouch down, much less offer a capacious lap). Frostiness signaled efficiency, which mothers and children should welcome as a sign of being advanced, or at any rate not old-fashioned. (Complaining in the *Ladies' Home Journal* that "the home is not so much insufficient as it is oversufficient. It is cloying," F. Scott Fitzgerald went on to praise the "charming woman" whose "children were always treated as though they were grown": it was her independence and verve that he admired.) Yet as Watson proceeded to tackle that other "advanced" topic of the day in his closing chapter, "What Shall I Tell My Child About Sex?," he unexpectedly invoked some Hallian wisdom that helped to melt the glacial gap between parent and child.

Watson's endorsement of sexual honesty starting early was echoed by family experts who had decided that ignorance was fatal to marital bliss. But few made as big and explicit a deal about it as he did—except perhaps Dr. Hall (whose *Adolescence* Watson elsewhere praised, scoffing at criticisms of Hall as "a little bit queer" because he dared to be graphic). One reviewer judged Watson's "an astonishingly frank chapter, which few publishers would have dared to print a few years ago." Even more notable, certainly compared to the preceding pages of his book, it was a friendly chapter.

Watson recommended a "talk it out club" as "a safeguard to health and sanity," and more than that, a "golden opportunity to establish *rapport*" between the generations. (Who would have guessed that the bullying behaviorist was a forefather of scheduled "floor time" and the "communication" vogue?) Parents were to set aside several times a week to converse openly with their child from the age of two onward. The idea was to answer his many questions (Watson always assumed a boy), "not just along sex lines but along every line." Avoid moralism at all costs, he instructed, and be as interesting as possible, or your children won't come to you as their "clearing house"; they'll rely on their peers. Watson urged parents to ask questions, too. Rounding out his surprisingly familiar-sounding wisdom, he encouraged the effort "to get [a child] *to formulate in words* the things that have happened to him during the day."

In passing, Watson noted "the danger of too strong fixation by the child upon the father or mother" developing from these tête-à-têtes, but he kept uncharacteristically calm. There was not a word about the catastrophes that might ensue from such intimacy (constant quivering, stalled careers, ruined marriages, etc.). On the contrary, Watson hailed this communing, especially about sex, as the prerequisite to a healthy love and marital life in the future. To be sure, Watson the sexologist was more mechanical than emotional. He urged parents to discourage masturbation as a "kiddish trick" that takes away "time and energy *for doing and learning . . . other things*," and emphasized that one of those other things to learn—for males—was to be a "successful and skillful sex companion for his wife." But in the end, Watson warmed up and talked, if indirectly, about trust. "To achieve skill in this art," wrote the man you assume would reduce sex to a chilly science, "requires time, patience, willingness to learn from each other, frankness in discussion."

And in their coda, "The Behaviorist's Apologia," Dr. Watson and Rosalie Rayner Watson spoke up together, sounding almost Dewey-eyed as they declared that "above all, we have tried to create a problem-solving child." Here, tucked at the back of the book, was the real "news": even more of a shock than Watson's skewering of mawkish mothers was his warning to beware of dogmatic experts with dictates for raising an "ideal" child. The message came as a surprise, not least because it was delivered by one of America's most overweening experts, and one renowned for urging vocational training in the cradle. Here was Dr. Watson arguing against "the fixed molds that our parents imposed upon us," on the grounds that no one could know what the future would hold—except that whatever lay ahead would not be "fixed" for long.

For readers who stuck with him to the close, Watson ended by endorsing a more minimalist goal than Americans might expect from the author of *Behaviorism:* train children to be resourceful, resilient, persistent (and frenetic, it seemed, for the workaholic Watson singled out "boundless absorption in activity" as a prize feature of his problem solver). Give me a dozen children, he was in essence saying (and in a jumble of inconsistent popular articles did say), and I'll train any one so that he can end up choosing to be either (or both) a rebel or a con-formist, a maverick or a company man, a psychologist or a business executive, a sexual radical or a political conservative. In the bargain, Watson guaranteed that such a child would be happy under the regi-men. He was, as child-rearing experts usually are, his own best proof of how precarious such promises can be. Watson, writing in 1928, was prescient about the unpredictability of America's future—and about his own tenuous popularity.

4.

Even more than preachers' children, child-rearing experts' children invite scrutiny; so do their wives, who are well aware that they can't win, no matter how model a household they manage to present. Leave it to Dr. Watson to use his family for publicity designed to prove just that: a degree of misbehaviorism on the home front. From the chipper book ads in 1928, Watson had graduated two years later to a campaign for his gospel designed, as he might have put it, to "freshen the reaction" of Americans coping after the Crash. In its December 1930 issue, *Parents' Magazine* ran an article by Rosalie Rayner Watson called "I Am the Mother of a Behaviorist's Sons." The editors heralded the piece in tones that hinted at a subversive exposé: "The whole world has heard from Dr. John B. Watson, author of 'Behaviorism,' " they announced, "but this is the first time his wife has ventured to tell how these theories work at home." Looking like a sophisticated former flapper in her photograph— with bobbed hair, arched eyebrows, eyes and lips barely suppressing a smile—the striking Mrs. Watson, it seemed, might air some dirty linen. It was quite titillating, and not at all intimidating or infuriating.

Which was exactly the idea. Obtuse though Dr. Watson could be, the adman had not failed to notice that Americans in the midst of what was now plainly a depression had lost some of their zest for flagellating experts, especially ones who mocked their "nest habits" and lampooned maternal love. Back in a spring issue of *Parents' Magazine*, Bertrand Russell (a fan who had reviewed Watson's manual favorably and boasted of being a behaviorist dad himself) had spoken up in favor of motherly cuddling. "I deprecate the onslaught of modern theorists on maternal affection," he felt it was time to emphasize. "The fact is, that not enough is known about this whole matter to justify our removing it from the sphere of common sense to that of science." The hard-boiled philosopher's softening elicited a wry plaudit from the *New York Times* ("the surprise is as great as though . . . Dr. Watson were to favor kissing the children goodnight"), and the piece went on to attack "behaviorist theories and Watson's extreme application of them," hailing what it hoped was a trend toward "a more common-sense view" and less deterministic science.

With the economic system in collapse, the family whose fragility had been a constant refrain now looked more like a pillar of stability. The cult of the expert, meanwhile, ceased to inspire quite the old awe. Specialists draped in science, though by now omnipresent, could no longer claim omniscience. (The same month that Rosalie Watson's piece appeared, Harold Laski was writing in *Harper's* about "The Limitations of the Expert.") At the White House Conference on Child Health and Protection in the fall of 1930, President Hoover cautioned the throngs of professionals that "our function should be to help parents, not replace them" (even as he edged out the female-led Children's Bureau, urging an expanded role for the Public Health Service, dominated by men and doctors, instead).

Nor should experts unnerve parents. In a time of austerity, their tendency to do so began to trouble the same parent educators who, back in an era of prosperity, had furrowed their brows about how to rouse mothers out of their complacency. "If bewilderment, confusion, insecurity, and self-consciousness follow upon the writings based on research," a popular manual proclaimed, "parent education has failed signally of its purpose. Knowledge of child development and child behavior should produce not shocks but shock absorbers." Parents should not have to panic that "any contact which they have with their children may have serious effects in one way or another." Emotional stinginess and environmental determinism can lose their allure when the going gets as tough as it had in the Depression.

And the tough, Dr. Watson the relativist was savvy enough to appreciate, better tone it down. The enfant terrible made a point of sobering up as he revised *Behaviorism* in 1930. He was "taking out all tricks of trade by means of which a lecturer tries to keep his audience awake," he wrote in his introduction. "I have tried to take out most of the overstatements and exaggerations common to all lectures." That was itself an overstatement, not surprisingly, but Dr. Watson did modulate his presentation some. His manual posed more of a problem, since its strident tone was its trademark; take it out, and what would be left?

But Rosalie Watson—surely with his support, though she pretended otherwise—waged a crusade to humanize the harsh booklet. Although it was a transparent public relations ploy, she told the truth as she did her best to save him from his own worst instincts: his tenets did have some liberating implications for mothers, and for children, too. Her inspiration was to admit, in the widely read pages of *Parents' Magazine*, that she was anything but a heartless mother, and to twit readers for taking her blustery husband too seriously themselves. Certainly she didn't, as her article was there to testify.

Sounding cheeky, she revealed lapses from the behaviorist faith and confessed to less than perfect results in her boys—to the accompaniment of photos of her menfolk that evoked energetic individuals, not by-the-book specimens. Eight-year-old Billy Watson had an alert gaze and an expectant smile, and six-year-old Jimmy was clearly an imp. Their handsome father looked far from fierce. The caption struck a light note with its jaunty boast that "Dr. John B. Watson has two young sons who can swim, skate, box, hang from trapezes, stand on their hands and get along with people." Outside the lab, the little monkeys were thriving.

To judge by the memories that a septuagenarian James Watson thoughtfully dredged up in an interview, Rosalie Watson was perhaps wishfully exaggerating a bit in the portrait of fond and child-focused parenting that she proceeded to paint. (With a psychological caution he did not inherit from his father, James admitted that his own version of events was surely blurred, too.) But Rosalie herself made a point of disarming her readers with an admission that she did indeed yearn for a more "homey" household—and had needed to fight for what conviviality she had brought to their family life. "Many personal resentments have grown up within me in respect to strict behaviorism being practiced in our home, chief among these the exclusion of the children from our quarters (now a modified rule)," she boldly complained. But she also reminded her readers that a hectic world could cast as much of a chill over the hearth as any particular child-rearing techniques did—and that behaviorists were not the only scientists whose shadows darkened the doorstep.

My regrets are perhaps more for the sophisticated life we urbans lead than anything else. I wonder how many parents eat their evening meal at a reasonable hour with the children, light the fire afterwards and have at least a social hour or half-hour together? In our family we do this on birthdays and holidays. The result is that the occasion so excites the children that the whole family becomes emotionally exhausted and very grateful when bedtime arrives. I hope I am not being sentimental, but I feel this is rather an unfortunate situation. I would like to feel that our sons are a little more part and parcel of the home. Although I hold no intellectual brief for the values of the "home," emotionally the idea pleases me. I think lots of people are forgetting in this epoch of scientific rationalization what fun a home can be.

Her case for the home as a warmer refuge was right in step with times in which most Americans, although not suffering from the Watsons' brand of sophisticated bustle, were scrambling to make ends meet.

"My most earnest wish for my boys," Rosalie Watson announced, "is that throughout life they will continue to be as adaptable to all situations as they appear to be now." She spoke in the spirit of the manual's "Apologia," and her portrait avoided all suggestion of grim determinism or dour firmness. Instead, she evoked a liberated woman raising liberated children, everybody self-sufficient, confident, and resilient—the antithesis of an intimidated mother anxiously trying to dictate her offspring's careers beginning in their tender years, panicked by any slipup. She played up a rebellious style. In truth, she was hardly departing from the calmer advice of her husband's manual, but what sounded like an austere regimen in his pages became more of a rough-and-tumble adventure as she told it.

Rosalie Watson did not pretend the process was smooth. She had weathered plenty of wails when she first bustled off and left her babies behind, but she felt the results were well worth it all around. "Now both my boys accept the fact that I go when and where I please, and their lives are organized so independently that they don't care." Habit training, too, could be rocky, but even if a behaviorist approach brought no miracles, she could detect no psychological traumas either. They had failed to cure Billy of nail-biting by threatening to deprive him of a weekend trip—in part because her adaptable child was perfectly happy to putter at home. Their close-the-door-and-let-him-manage strategy for toilet training seemed to work fine with Jimmy—until they discovered that he had blithely been lying when he reported success. (The pediatrician reassured her that it was all right "to go through life independent and well-adjusted, if a bit constipated.")

Rosalie Watson did not miss the other obvious humanizing opportunity: she made a point of talking up the "talk-it-out-club" dimension of her husband's advice, which was the last thing that Dr. Watson's critics associated with him, deafened to it by his own ranting. The Hallian spirit of communing came completely naturally to her as it did not to Watson himself. Never mind enlightening her boys about sex (though she did, she reported, even before they asked); they enlightened her in the ways of play and affection. In a comic blend of romanticism and behaviorism, she effused over how much the little tabulae rasae had to teach, and how much fun it was to learn from them. Once "youngsters have learned certain of the conventions they are really diminutive adults and very good company, for they have a newer and fresher philosophy of the world in which we live than the generation which is temporarily making a bold effort to guide their behavior, and we pompous sophisticates have a lot to learn from them."

She did not at all mind admitting that "I hang on to my adolescence with a vengeance," defying the behaviorist reputation for premature maturity and sobriety. (She encouraged her kids' taste for practical jokes at their father's expense, sharing in their hilarity, even though "the behaviorists think giggling is a sign of maladjustment.") Most important of all, Rosalie Watson defended unruly emotion. "I cannot restrain my affection for the children completely; I secretly wish that on the score of their affections they will be a little weak when they grow up, that they will enjoy a little coddling once in a while, that they will have a tear in their eyes for the poetry and drama of life and a throb for all romance." No stolid businessmen for her. She closed her revisionist account with a rousing tribute to resilience in the face of the unpredictable unknown. "They will know that life is a stunning drama and, no matter what happens, around the corner lies a new adventure," she told an audience eager to hope for better times ahead. "They will find love because they can give it and, above all, they will keep a sense of humor about this rollicking universe and laugh up their sleeves once in a while—especially at themselves. This is my fondest dream for my two small pieces of protoplasm."

Instead, Billy and Jimmy faced something of a nightmare in their personal lives—and the universe confronting Americans during the 1930s as totalitarianism menaced Europe was not exactly rollicking. An expert who spoke up for collective nurseries and talked about social conditioning was a hard sell, no matter how he modulated the message. (*Brave New World* appeared in 1932.) And with the unexpected death of his wife from pneumonia in 1935, Dr. Watson lost whatever softer touch he might possibly have gleaned from her—certainly with his sons, and with the public, from which he began to retreat. Twelve when she died, James Watson was eager late in life to ruminate on a past that veered into darkness in the second half of the 1930s. His memories, even of early childhood, featured governesses—his parents spent lots of time away—and major feeding problems (Jimmy's finicky eating infuriated Dr. Watson) that never made it into his mother's article. Nor did Rosalie mention the experiment in which Watson staged a mock physical fight with her to see how their sons reacted—traumatic testing that left "many a reader . . . upset," the *New Yorker* profile of Watson reported. Excessively homey their household had never been. Still, the father James described after his mother's death was a man who imposed an extremist regimen of emotional austerity less out of zealous behaviorist principle, it seemed, than out of personal desperation.

A devastated Dr. Watson gave his sons their only (and fleeting) hug, never mentioned their mother again, and shipped them off to boarding school. When James ran away from school and came home, he was dispatched to a neighbor. Watson retreated to a more rustic part of Connecticut to commune with his animals (and, who knows, perhaps with the memory of Pickens Watson). What contact he had with his children was coolly corporate in spirit. James Watson recalled feeling judged on "bottom line performance" in everything. His memories of the "talk it out club" consisted of intimidating dictates about sexual technique: you must be able to "go a hundred strokes before climax," his father told two barely teenage boys, and expressed irritation that training time could not be arranged! Nearly seventy years later, James Watson was still dazed to think back on it.

Of all things, his sons followed in his footsteps—with Billy fulfilling Dr. Watson's old dream of going to medical school, where he suffered a serious depression, as his father had at the University of Chicago. In the psychoanalysis he underwent, Billy rebelled against behaviorism and became very angry with his father. James followed a more circuitous route, but ended up pursuing the "practical applications of general and industrial psychology"; he worked on labor-management relations in a large food corporation for many years. Yet after Watson's death in 1958, the story took a grim swerve, just what his many detractors warned was bound to follow from love-starved childhoods. In 1962, Billy Watson committed suicide. His brother had a breakdown around the same time and battled against suicidal impulses for several years. But even then, and more since then, James Watson hesitated (unlike his brother) to trace their troubles straight to their "spartan" emotional relations with their father.

To be sure, Watson's youngest son had dredged up plenty of grievances in years of analysis and therapy, more than enough to know that he had no desire to subject his children to the emotional austerity his father, though not his mother, had tried on him. James broke that "fixed mold" and did plenty of hugging and kissing of his children. Still, he also emerged convinced that, for good or ill, he could not understand himself as the mere product of his behaviorist training. The suicide of his own much loved daughter in middle age, after years of struggle with manic-depressive illness, left James Watson with one more reason for asking the question his father considered closed, a question that had never disappeared from the American debate about rearing children: How much about the way they turn out might be a matter of nature rather than nurture?

SIX

The Anatomist of Normalcy

Dr. Arnold Gesell

I.

on't watch the clock, watch the child" became Dr. Arnold Gesell's Hallian motto. Aim to make life and work go like clockwork was his un-Hallian way. He was a model of sobriety who had been patiently hatching a theory of growth when a grim era arrived. His vision of maturation promised that change in children would be orderly and well regulated, and that families were the "cultural workshop for transmitting the social inheritance" of democracy. He proclaimed that his "developmental philosophy" was a guarantee of social security and social mobility. It was a message well timed for an America chastened by the Crash and then confronted by another world war. Dr. Gesell, with a firm, bespectacled face that conveyed gravity and empathy, even looked somewhat like Franklin Delano Roosevelt.

"There was this handsome Gesell, with his crib and his dome" was how the psychologist Myrtle McGraw remembered the aura of the director of the Yale Clinic of Child Development when she was a young researcher at Columbia University's Child Development Institute as the 1930s began. At the turn of the decade Gesell had graduated into an elaborate new clinic in a Georgian building, equipped with a photographic dome specially designed for his celebrated examination project. He was filming normal infants and preschoolers at different ages as they performed assorted behavioral tasks, and he was deriving a "normative schedule" of children's physical and mental growth from his observations. "Everybody was either using Gesell's tests or some tests, or they were making their own," McGraw recalled, looking back years later for an oral history of the child development movement in America.

Under the intriguing headline "Tom Thumb Yale Bowl," a "Talk of the Town" item in *The New Yorker* in January 1931 offered readers a peek at just what was going on in his dome, a sort of igloo-like enclosure. "Yale, it seems, has taken to studying babies, to try and discover whether or not people are the way they are because of being born that way," the piece announced. "Dr. Arnold Gesell, head of the psychology clinic, thinks they pretty much are. We went to his movie last week at the New York Academy of Medicine, and observed the infants doing the little hereditary things that their characters dictate. The babies, or 'subjects,' are photographed while in a bowl-shaped world of their own, the cameras recording the scene through peep-holes. Into this miniature Yale Bowl the child is put naked, strapped in a baby armchair."

The spectacle of the little collegians hard at work struck the "Talk of the Town" reporter as quite fascinating, especially when he dropped in on another site of Gesell-inspired study at Columbia University, where the babies were behaving like . . . *New Yorker* writers. Given pencil and paper at seven months old, the subject could be counted on to respond with crumpling activity. By one year, "the poor sprite, if normal, will make marks on the paper, try to write, and in the baby brow will appear little wrinkles looking strangely like pain." Dr. Gesell, busily taking notes as he peered through his camera at Yale, betrayed no such signs of frustration himself. On the contrary, his quest to "delineate what the generic individual is in the ascending stages of maturity," as he put it elsewhere, was off to an impressive start. Data, *The New Yorker* noted, was piling up. "Thousands of records have been made, Dr. Gesell explained in the talkie, to set up the developmental sequences that are comparable to our adult intelligence tests—and they seem to show that children are born with definite characteristics."

On screen in *The Study of Infant Behavior at the Yale Psycho-Clinic,* Dr. Gesell presided as a calm contrast to the bullying Watson with his blurry photos of babies frightened by furry animals. Yet America's most meticulous maturationist was easily a match for the behaviorist in his aspirations to predict and control. As his film made clear, Gesell was not a fatalistic hereditarian by any means, or a go-with-the-flow kind of fellow. Conducting a tour of his domain, he conveyed the "remarkable equanimity" and dignity his contemporaries always noted, along with an air of quiet command. There was just a hint of a German accent in his cadences as he led the viewer through a streamlined facility that, like its boss, embodied the spirit of systematic development that he and his associates were sure they were seeing emerge in their pictures and charts.

An enlightened mother—"she knows what is happening" and is "happy to cooperate" with the eminent doctor's studies—was shown entering the clinic, bundle in arms, escorted by a social worker and greeted by a psychiatrist. After witnessing her baby's reaction to being undressed, she was ushered behind a one-way vision screen. This innovative tool of Gesell's was transparent from one side and opaque from the other, allowing her to "watch in a sense of security," all-seeing yet unseen herself. Her baby was meanwhile whisked off into the dome, which had been constructed to solve the photographic problem of glaring illumination and noisy generators. Greeted by "a mild and suffused light which is steady, noiseless, and cool," the child was placed in a crib and belted into a canvas chair, with a tabletop set across the crib rails as a desk.

No experimenters poked or prodded. There was no clanging of steel, and no animal surprises were in store. This white-coated researcher was not manipulating his subject's emotions, he was watching the baby girl's every move as she manipulated the (inanimate) objects with which she was presented. And even the watching was discreet; the camera was hidden and the examiner, Gesell emphasized, "must not peer with piercing eyes," for fear of discomfiting the performer. The small star herself supplied the action, displaying her steadily advancing capabilities. At sixteen weeks she slumped and fumbled with her various testing materials. By forty-four weeks, Gesell called attention to her "fine pincerlike prehension" as she easily picked up a sugar pellet, and "exploited" various cubes. She was right on schedule in a process of growth that Gesell argued was "organized by inherent inner mechanics" that propelled development in a patterned way toward behavioral integration. Elsewhere, the camera captured older children bustling industriously in his guidance nursery, a teacher glimpsed briefly in the background.

All of the adults were behind-the-scenes figures, as absorbed in their work as the children were in their purposeful activities. Gesell's devoted staff of female collaborators were shown looking intently through cameras and then analyzing the results frame by frame at slower speed, tracing the pictures, drawing on the "infallible memory" of film to capture behavior for "systematic study and comparison." Mothers gazed at their children through the one-way screen, while the narrating doctor advised that "much child guidance is parent guidance," which meant counseling mothers to be constantly attentive to their child's growth trajectory.

It is not enough, Dr. Gesell intoned in closing, "to safeguard physical growth alone"; medical supervision and protection must extend to mental growth as well, and must begin in infancy. For as he had just emphasized in his latest book, *The Guidance of Mental Growth in Infant and Child* of 1930, he did not subscribe to the "quasi-primitive" notion that "growth is predetermined, that it is so natural that it takes care of itself, and that there is little to be done about it." Those inner maturational forces, he noted, inevitably worked in tandem with environmental influences. Thus although children did not need molding, their development required the closest monitoring. According to Gesell, "plasticity . . . is a positive 'function of growth,' " not a matter of mere malleability or a sign of passivity. "Science"—he gave the word somber emphasis—"is exploring the laws which control this," with the goal of preventing undue, or dangerous, deviations along the path to maturity.

Dr. Gesell's film was both a promotional vehicle—this was the era when getting grants first became a priority on the scientist's agenda—and a novel piece of parent education material, especially valuable because it worked by showing rather than telling. Photographs have a "simplicity and beauty which arise out of authenticity rather than didactic propaganda," Gesell appreciated. With their descriptive power, he felt they helped to "build up attitudes as well as knowledge" about children as no "prescriptive, rule-of-thumb procedures" for parents could hope to do.

Pictures were thus the ideal medium for what Gesell presented as a welcome, anti-Watsonian message: that "making over the child in terms of a preconceived pattern" was not the task of parents. Instead they, like those rapt scientists on the screen and the mothers behind the screens, were to study "the natural patterns of his own growth in a sympathetic and constructive way." And in a comparative way: aware of the "normative standards" of behavior at every stage, parents could better ensure that their child was on the path of "optimal growth"—and could better appreciate his distinctive qualities. For what every parent needed, Gesell hastened to add, were "wholesome attitudes of tentativeness, a philosophical readiness to rear the child in terms of his unique growth needs."

Soon enough, you did not have to be a *New Yorker* writer haunting the halls of the New York Academy of Medicine to catch one of Gesell's productions. Some department stores showed his movies—"in the most dignified, sincere manner possible," or so urged the "promotional aids" circulated to Abraham and Straus and Marshall Field & Co. Sponsorship by local child development groups was considered the ideal arrangement, readily secured "due to the reputation of Dr. Gesell and the Yale University Clinic of Child Development and the scientific, authoritative nature of the films." Due to the commercial nature of the venue, however, tie-in potential could not be overlooked. "Although no particular kind of garment or accessory is emphasized in the picture"— the stars were generally naked!—"almost any sort of infant merchandise may be featured." A baby contest might also appeal—perhaps "The Best-Developed One-Year Old" or "The Youngest Walker"—but "care should be taken not to let the contest over-shadow the importance and value of the films."

Gesell's message was as ambitious, and almost as ambivalent, as Watson's. He promised an "inborn tendency toward optimum development," reassuring parents that a child "suffers less than he logically should from our unenlightenment." At the same time he heralded "almost inexhaustible opportunities for guidance of growth," and urged that the "growing mind, like the body . . . come under systematic health supervision." He invoked standardized norms of behavior, yet set store by a child's "unique" individuality. In his own way he ratcheted up parental responsibility, and he, too, emphasized the predictability of children's growth from the early years onward. In other words, Gesell faced and hoped to finesse many of the same child-rearing dilemmas that confronted the behaviorist whose popular pulpit he was now poised to fill: the heightened hopes, and the fears, about fitting in, standing firm, keeping up, and standing out that interwar parents harbored, for themselves as well as for their children—or at any rate that the edgy experts harbored on behalf of a growing middle-class audience that had experienced the promise, and the perils, of social mobility.

Yet Gesell's descriptive, child-centered approach was a striking contrast to the hard Watsonian perspective, which put parents—and experts—emphatically in charge, armed with curt prescriptions to keep their audience (whether mothers or children) in line. Gesell offered a package that sounded much softer. He joined his mentor Dr. Hall in promising rejuvenation if "parents will attune and adjust their own growth to that of the child," billing it as a promotion and far less pressure. Where Watson had scoffed that mothers were balky babies who couldn't possibly handle the job and who "resent . . . strenuously any advice or instructions on how to care psychologically for their children," Gesell envisaged an audience of eager students responding "very spontaneously to the developmental approach itself because it releases so many tensions and because they see that there is a certain relativity about things, which gets them away from an overly moralistic point of view." Watson had delivered a harsh conditioning jolt to the whole family, mothers in particular. Gesell invoked a vista of development for all involved. "Even parents should not consider themselves grownups in the presence of their problems of child training, but preserve a faith in their own growth potentialities."

Arnold Gesell himself, the eldest son of a German immigrant, had been a model of developmental continuity, and of upward mobility. He fell right into the responsible role that firstborns of foreigners often fill: the future specialist on maturation displayed uncanny maturity almost from the word go, and his growth never swerved from "an optimum course." He was the ultimate big brother, keeping an eye out for (and on) everybody in his family. He knew in turn that he was the cynosure of all eyes in a clan that considered America the land of opportunity— not for crass advancement, but for model sons who had always been the best developed in (and of) their class. Given the seeds from which it grew, it should perhaps not come as a surprise that Dr. Gesell's child-rearing gospel was not as relaxing as he advertised.

2.

Unlike John Watson the southerner, whose backwoods origins helped make him a belligerent upstart, Arnold Gesell the German-American proceeded methodically and confidently on his way from the provinces to the genteel pinnacle of power in the Northeast. He was born in 1880 in the "two-street village" of Alma, Wisconsin, on the upper Mississippi, the first of five children who arrived at two-year intervals in the lives of Gerhard Gesell and Christine Giesen. The pair, who had married in 1879, fit the by now familiar profile of progenitors of child-rearing experts: an intensely devoted mother, only this time a woman without any religious zealotry to impose on her scientific son, and an idiosyncratic father, only this time a man whose course had been heroic in its way (if also rather hapless). Arnold Gesell had little need to rebel, and all the more reason to excel.

Gerhard Gesell, born in 1844 in Floersheim, Germany, had lost his parents early on and was soon scrounging a river rat's dismal existence on the banks of the Rhine. At nineteen he somehow managed to book passage to America, where he enlisted in the Union Army in 1863 in Minnesota, fighting Indians on the frontier. (The Guards of the Frontier were unfairly "sneered at," his obituary in the *Buffalo County Journal* complained, for the largely immigrant band endured brutal winters, to say nothing of ambushes by Indians.) Mustered out in 1866, he became a bartender in Minnesota and Wisconsin, where he opened a saloon of his own. (This interlude went unmentioned by his *Buffalo County Journal* memorialist.)

It was in 1870 that Gerhard, "a lover of the beauties of nature and endowed with the soul of an artist," found a higher calling: he learned photography, and in 1876 moved to Alma and set up shop as a "photographer and proprietor of the Art, Book, and Stationery Store" (with letterhead that, prophetically, featured a naked cherub in front of a camera). He married a renowned teacher in the town. Christine Giesen, to judge by the fluent English of the letters she showered on her children whenever they were away, was a second-generation German settler and the calmly regulating force in the close-knit family. In that role, she relied on the aid of her accommodating eldest. It wasn't that her husband was a Teutonic tyrant at all; the friend who delivered Gerhard Gesell's funeral oration in 1906 praised him for "making his sons and daughters his companions, treating them as his equals." But this outspoken agnostic with "pronounced views"—among them "that Americans were becoming subservient to those in authority"—was a brusque and moody fellow who suffered bouts of rheumatism (the result, he felt, of those harsh winters). Given to gloominess, he could be a source of "Donnerwetter," or thunderstorms, as his wife noted in a letter after a squall had evidently passed through the household.

She, and the rest of the brood, could count on Arnold—"so admirably poised," she once marveled—to help keep everything running smoothly in their lives and in his own. Writing to her son's betrothed, Beatrice Chandler, in 1909, Mrs. Gesell gushed more than was her usual levelheaded way, but she was not embellishing. "Arnold comes to you pure—with noble aspirations—his whole life has been a model one—an inspiration to many. . . . Someday perhaps—if you should visit his old home you will find there stored away hundreds of letters—which will tell you better than I can what a dutiful loving son he has always been." His correspondence was indeed quite remarkable, although not as remarkable as his parents' mail to him, he effused in his typically devoted vein. "I have never received a bad letter yet from home. Every one has some sweet kisses in it, and a great deal of love. What more can you wish for?" (Arnold was fifteen.)

He in turn sent only good letters home. From his tenderest years onward, Gesell made sure to let his parents know that he was being helpful and, above all, careful—and to let his siblings know that they should be, too. The boy who, as one chronicler put it, adopted "the state's motto, which was one word: Forward," was vigilant about any untoward forces that might derail progress, or any false steps that might be taken. And looking back on his village life, Dr. Gesell could not help being struck by how many lurking dangers there were. For all "the tranquil beauties of Nature" he treasured in memory, what left the most significant "deposit of impressions" were "the dark . . . facets of our microcosm . . . death, funerals, devastating sickness, ominous quarantines, accidents and drownings at close range." Like all children, Gesell reflected, he was "forever looking, scanning, watching," but unlike many children, he was already worrying, warning, and reassuring.

"We made six loads hay," a very young scrawl reported, his bilingual upbringing showing through in his report of a visit with Montana relatives. "We picked strawberries. Everyday I help to watch the cows." At fourteen, he was more fluent, and swift with reassurances about a swimming trip he took on off-hours from his summer job at *The Photographic Recorder: A Monthly Record of Photographic Progress and Events in Minnesota* (evidently where his father had gotten his start). "I had to be perfectly assured that there was no danger before I went into the lake," he told his parents. "The bath was fine. I am getting to be a regular duck in the water. You ought to see me," he proclaimed, only to close with further promises that he would always take precautions. "I will not go in any water unless I am sure that there is no danger. You need not be afraid that I will be reckless." Indeed they needn't, for their eldest was diligent in all he did; not least, he swam like a very competent fish in school. Full of "young seriousness," he even attended the teachers' institutes that came to town. On graduating from high school in 1896, he impressed the commencement audience with a display of "the wonders of the new electrical era," igniting a tube of hydrogen (doubtless with great care).

His siblings, too, were accustomed to Arnold's extraordinary attentiveness, even from afar. That same Minnesota summer, he checked in with them and clucked like a mother hen, or like an attending doctor. "I'm glad that you're all enjoying good health; and that you are getting along nicely," he wrote his brothers and sisters in 1894, again at the ripe old age of fourteen. "Keep up the many good things you stated in your last letters and I'll be satisfied. What more can I wish than to have you get along nicely?" He could worry about their getting along safely, and he did. Gesell ended his letter with warnings that they must not be reckless near water. "Somehow or other I have to feel a little uneasy about the boys. You can't be too careful, Gerhard and Rob. Don't go along the shore that's toward Henrich's and the Post Office for it is deep there."

Three years later, enrolled in Stevens Point Normal School and studying for a career as a high school teacher (following his mother's footsteps and his own schoolmarmish proclivities), Gesell was more self-conscious about his advisory intrusions into his siblings' lives, but that didn't stop him from nudging his favorite and youngest sister, Bertha. "I like to see you get so many stars and get along so nicely in school," he told her, "but you want to get outside and have a good time as much as you can. Don't study too much. Get fresh air and exercise. Rob and Gerhard, and Wilma, I guess, get enough of that, but Gerhard must look out for his stomach. You will probably say: 'There the old preacher is preaching again.' Maybe I am, because it's much easier to preach than to practice what you preach; but as far as I can see I am keeping pretty well, and you don't know how anxious I am for you all."

He was indeed keeping very well, though soon his father was sick with digestive troubles. It was Arnold's siblings who stepped in to keep the business going, while he forged ahead. During the decade and a half after graduating from Stevens Point in 1899, he alternated between teaching and pursuing higher education for himself. A stint spent instructing Wisconsin teenagers in everything from accounting to ancient history (he coached football, too) was followed by two years at the University of Wisconsin, where Gesell studied with Frederick Turner and with psychology professor Joseph Jastrow (a student of Hall's at Johns Hopkins) and earned his undergraduate degree in 1903. He then spent a year as a precociously young principal at a large Wisconsin high school, which won him praise and spurred him to move on. "He is ambitious and throws his whole self into his work," the board of education observed, praising his "originality and thoroughness" and his "strong, forceful character." Urged on by Jastrow, Gesell attended Clark University for two years, pursuing "child study" under the "ardent, exuberant" Hall, and writing his thesis on jealousy at different ages in animals and humans, though evidently not sharing his mentor's interest in Freud.

He got his doctorate in psychology in 1906, the year his father died, and he plowed onward. Gesell set off to teach at the Los Angeles State Normal School, lured by his Clark colleague Lewis Terman, whose study in Worcester of "Genius and Stupidity" had blossomed out west into work on an American adaptation of the intelligence testing methods pioneered by Alfred Binet in France. (The Stanford-Binet test, available in 1916, was his handiwork.) There Gesell met and married Beatrice Chandler, a fellow faculty member and graduate of the University of Chicago interested in progressive pedagogy. Instead of settling down in their bungalow, they were a couple with broader ambitions. He set off during the summer of 1908 to explore clinical work with mentally defective children, and the two of them began gestating a brainchild or two. First they began collaborating on a book, *The Normal Child and Primary Education* (1912). And while they were at it, Gesell embarked on the medical training they agreed he needed for a longer-term venture: "to make a thoroughgoing study of the developmental stages of childhood." His wife's own professional career lapsed as she, active in the suffrage movement and child welfare work, became the behind-the-scenes promoter of the grand endeavor. Inspired by the quest for "g," or general intelligence, the psychologists in the emerging testing movement were busy measuring IQ. Dr. Hall's protégé was inspired to come up with a way to measure growth, mental and physical.

After spending 1910–11 at the University of Wisconsin studying anatomy and histology, he was invited to join the faculty of the newly formed education department at Yale University—and to continue his medical studies. But Gesell was not about to wait for a degree to begin that "thoroughgoing study," which was bound to go slowly, not least because children are harder to come by than white rats—even if, unlike Watson, you merely want to observe them, not condition them. In 1911, thanks to the dean of the medical school, Gesell was given a room at the New Haven Dispensary and trained his attention on "the problem of exceptional school children" as an assortment of students with difficulties passed through his door. He gave himself a title, "director," and the Yale Psycho-Clinic was born—a year after the birth of his son,

Gerhard. In 1915, Gesell received his M.D., and by then had a daughter, Katherine, too. The year before he had been made a full professor of child hygiene, and he was also "State Director of Child Hygiene, summer school director, psycho-neurologist, contributor to magazines, contributor to Childhood and Youth series, commencement speaker," as he crowed in a note to his wife, which ended: "Position-Income-Joy."

Over the next decade and a half, Dr. Gesell's work on his great project was hardly systematic, but it was unceasing. A whirlwind of social welfare work all over Connecticut—he was, among other things, the first school psychologist in the country—involved him in studying and providing services for a wide range of children, most of them deemed abnormal in some way. School troubles, Gesell concluded, could often be traced to developmental immaturities, which stirred his interest in the preschool period. He became active in the mental hygiene cause, and with the end of the war made it one of his missions to urge that kindergarten be reconceived as the moment for comprehensive assessment, from children's teeth to their habits; among his main goals was to avoid hurrying students onward in school before they were ready.

Back in his little room, Gesell was still examining children of various ages and kinds—from a cretin to a pair of gifted twins—and in 1919 he began bringing in normal infants for observational study. With the help of a staff of graduate students and clinical assistants, he enlarged his normal sample by consulting local birth records for specimens of the right age, and then knocking on doors in hopes of finding cooperative parents. He soon counted on the help of cameras in his labors as well, his father would have been proud to know (although Gesell cited the management specialist Frank Gilbreth, who relied on film for his time-and-motion studies, as his inspiration). By 1925, Gesell had rounded up what he considered enough data points to write *The Mental Growth of the Pre-School Child*, which in a "personal bit of braggadocio" in a letter to his wife he declared "is now on the map and will remain there as the *first* systematic piece of work in the developmental psychology and developmental diagnosis of infancy."

It was a landmark, in which Gesell introduced his clinical and comparative method—including action photographs—and outlined his "system of developmental diagnosis," based on normative summaries and schedules of behavior at successive stages. Having set forth in the exploratory spirit of his mentor Dr. Hall to amass a "vast amount of descriptive material" about children's growth, Gesell was determined to analyze it, not merely rhapsodize about it. As he freely acknowledged, that entailed imposing "orderly systematization" on it, which meant first of all relying on age—very precisely defined by lunar months—as his organizing principle. From his mass of observations, he proceeded to deduce "specific behavior items both characteristic and distinctive of the various age levels," which he lumped under four "clinically service-able" categories—"motor characteristics," language, "adaptive behav-ior," and "personal-social behavior."

Gesell then devised a series of exercises to measure a child's perfor-mance on those "normative items"—cubes to put in cups, blocks to stack, imitations to perform, shoes to put on, objects to name—with a view to ascertaining his "developmental status." That was not, Gesell emphasized, the same as "so-called general intelligence." But such assessments, when refined, should "enable us to estimate more pre-cisely the maturity of a child in terms of personality adequacy and of character formation." He added that "however sublime the fatuity of such an undertaking may seem to the pure psychologist, it represents a basic clinical task in the mental diagnosis of children"—and in the "broader and . . . continuous type of developmental supervision" that he felt pediatricians and parents should make their preventive, mental hygienic mission.

As pioneering efforts can afford to, Gesell's book mixed great ambi-tion with notable modesty about the difficulty of finding "solid ground for generalization," and about the "danger of over-simplification in theorizing about the personality aspects of the child's behavior . . . [given] how ramified and complicated the child's mental structure is." He acknowledged the subjectivity of examiners, who required "a judi-cious amount of flexibility" in conducting their assessments of wriggly specimens and whose "ratings" of infant performance were inevitably impressionistic. He admitted the unavoidable selectivity of his samples. (His data base of infants and children from the New Haven area— all from roughly similar middle-class backgrounds—was indeed too homogeneous to be representative. At the same time, it was too hetero-geneous to be easily controlled. Some children were brought to the clinic for diagnosis, some simply for appraisal by their conscientious mothers; some stayed with it, others dropped out. Policies in his Guid-ance Nursery were similarly inconsistent, with some preschoolers there simply for observational purposes, others for treatment.)

Gesell noted the "confessedly preliminary and approximate charac-ter of the normative data." He stressed the artificiality of his behavior categories, remarking that even "the term motor development is so sweeping and general as to be almost metaphorical in character." He emphasized the importance, and the complexity, of estimating the child not only "as a detached individual but . . . in terms of his natural dependence on his mother." And he kept coming back to the intricacies of the "development of personality make-up." It was "infinitely more complicated and baffling than the development of intelligence," he emphasized. It was "profoundly conditioned by metabolic and physiological factors and by racial and temperamental elements which are hereditary," but Gesell was just as struck by its being "so dynamic, so reactive to all stimuli within its exploitation, so impressionable to stimuli beyond its control, that its structure and its overt actions reflect at every turn the influence of its social environment." Finally, he warned that norms "are readily misused if too much absolutist status is ascribed to them," as he knew from having arrived at them by observing countless deviations. That was why he favored normative summaries, too, "diffuse and prolix" though he acknowledged they could be. He judged maternal interviews helpful as well, despite their "sketchy state." In his review of *The Mental Growth of the Pre-School Child*, Gesell's colleague Lewis Terman, at the forefront of the testing movement, indeed complained that Gesell made "no attempt . . . to establish the reliability of the various tests or their exact diagnostic significance (validity). Statistical results are not given."

But Dr. Gesell was undaunted. And thanks to his book, which had just what the "organized" era admired—a diagnostic system—he found himself amply funded as never before. Money began to flow from the Laura Spelman Rockefeller Memorial Foundation, his photographic program took off, and in 1930 his dome and enlarged facilities were in operation. A grant supported the construction of "a homelike studio unit" on the premises, too, where babies and mothers could be filmed together in their daily rounds. Acutely aware of the limitations of experimental situations, Gesell was especially eager for a "naturalistic" survey to supplement the normative records derived from the laboratory setup in the dome. Perhaps even more important for Gesell's greater outreach to parents in the course of the decade was the arrival in 1933 of two young women who became his indispensable collaborators.

Louise Bates Ames, hired as Gesell's personal assistant, was a diminutive twenty-five-year-old newly equipped with a master's degree in psychology, which she had earned with a thesis that offered a behavioral analysis of her infant daughter, complete with cinematic documentation. Frances Ilg, six feet tall, was a pediatrician finished with her residency and eager for postgraduate work. "She thought there were two ways of doing research," Ames later recalled: "Louise's way (that's the scientific) and her way which was just intuitive."

The Gemeinschaft that emerged in the Gesellschaft was not exactly cozy. "He was a very firm man," Ames stressed; "he was of German background, and there was no informality." But the arrangement served everyone's interest. With Gesell's support, Ames and Ilg boosted their academic credentials. In 1936, Ames had a doctorate and a post as a Yale instructor; Ilg, who had become the single mother of an adopted baby, had been appointed assistant professor of child development. (Ames was soon divorced, and her mother stepped in to help with her granddaughter.) With adulatory support, and pressure, from his researchers, who were also struggling mothers, Gesell gradually culti-vated his popular credentials.

Where Watson had become a more radical and rhetorical behavior-ist during his psychological exile of the 1920s, Gesell in his sober way became a more grandiose developmentalist as he closed ranks with his accomplices and presided in his dome during the 1930s. "He had an idea and he was going to follow it through come Hell or high water," explained another, more senior colleague, Helen Woolley Thompson, who had become a clinical psychologist since rousing Watson's envy by graduating summa cum laude from the University of Chicago. Gesell's initial admission that obstacles and obscurities lay ahead for his project only fueled greater aspirations to discover a unifying symmetry in men-tal growth—a vast quest that, as Watson had found with his crusade, served Gesell better with the public than with fellow academics, who were skeptical of his presumption and of his growing popularity.

The mission the master of the dome was embarked on had become ever more herculean and hereditarian, inviting the criticism from col-leagues that it verged on arid, old-fashioned cataloguing. Influenced by the morphological patterns charted by the contemporary embryologist G. E. Coghill, Gesell identified no fewer than fifty-eight stages of "pel-let behavior," fifty-three stages of "rattle behavior," and kept it up for forty other behavioral patterns! He was convinced that the balanced forces he saw at work propelling, and then stabilizing, development in the physical realm—"reciprocal interweaving" was his phrase for the regulated process—governed growth in general. Glued to his "cine-matograph" (Gesell's preferred term long after the rest of the country said "movie camera"), he pursued his formal patterns and paid scant attention to ferment in the field.

He resisted Lawrence Frank's efforts to get him to fraternize with the adjoining, Freudian-inclined Institute of Human Relations at Yale.

Nor did Gesell show much interest in the longitudinal studies begun in the late 1920s at various child welfare institutes, which were not producing particularly tidy data; an interim report in 1933 from the Berkeley Growth Study, begun with 74 babies in 1928, found mental growth to be far more intricate, irregular, and unpredictable than expected. And Gesell declined to be any more responsive to his colleagues' reservations about his own work than he was to the discoveries emerging from theirs. "Don't worry so much about what those people say," Louise Ames recalled her magisterial boss telling her. "If we're right, they'll know it one day."

Gesell continued to sprinkle caveats about his enterprise here and there in the academic work he turned out through the decade. "It might be contended that social and personality characteristics cannot be adequately explored by normative methods, that these characteristics are too closely identified with emotional and individual motivational factors to yield to the same treatment that we apply to impersonal phenomena like posture and prehension," he and his co-author, Thompson, granted in *Infant Behavior: Its Genesis and Growth* (1934). "The contention is sound to a degree, for we shall never truly know the inner, personal life of the infant until we can get out of our own subjectivity into his."

Yet he was not about to give up, and his photographs rolled forth as proof that, in the physical realm at least, Gesell was indeed discovering that "in spite of its inexhaustible complexity and variability, the developmental stream of early human behavior assumes ordered pattern." And the pictures, he was aware, were worth a thousand words. In the fall of 1934, *Time* magazine devoted a two-page spread to his two-volume *Atlas of Infant Behavior*, with Dr. Gesell recommending his compendium of 3200 action photos—107 cherubs in his lab striking a "vast array of postural attitudes" in predictable sequence (volume 1), and six mother-child pairs cuddling in distinctive yet familiar ways in his homelike studio (volume 2)—as the ultimate coffee-table book. It might "be put to uses for which it was not planned," he suggested, thanks to its "charm from the standpoint of sculpture and the graphic arts." This encyclopedic work (unlike Hall's *Adolescence*) was adorable, as *Time*'s sampling of the frame-by-frame baby data showed.

Dr. Gesell was less pleased when his other trademark research effort—what he called "co-twin control" experimentation—inspired a public spectacle of a sort that he very definitely had not planned. In 1928, he and Helen Woolley Thompson had set out to test behaviorist claims about the efficacy of training, using a pair of genetically identical infant girls (whose growth they continued to follow and film all the way through puberty). Just as the babies were turning a year old, the scientists provided one of them with special practice in stair-climbing and "cube handling" over a ten-week period, to determine whether trained twin "T" would master the skills more quickly than "control" twin "C" did. The cube-handling part proved too hard to judge, but their verdict on the stair performance was that "maturation plays the primary role," with learning having only a transient effect.

Unlike Gesell's vast observational records of growth—which no one in the child development field could really begin to replicate, or refine, or refute, and which magazines like *Time* reported on with awe—his twin experiment invited follow-up, and roused a media controversy. In 1930, a young Myrtle McGraw, working under Dr. Frederick Tilney at the Normal Child Development Clinic of the Neurological Institute in New York, embarked on an analogous, more extensive study with twins named Johnny and Jimmy Woods. When her initial results appeared in 1933, stirring up great press excitement about "the twins of Amsterdam Avenue" and the amazing feats of the trained member of the pair, Gesell deplored the exploitative sensationalism—bad for the boys, he emphasized, but he plainly did not appreciate the challenge to his own position either. In fact, Gesell needn't have worried. The decade-long media fascination with McGraw's "incredible twins" that ensued, although the actual science at stake was hopelessly distorted, turned out to be evidence of a receding behaviorist tide in public opinion, well-timed for Gesell's own maturation as a popular expert.

As Americans soon learned from unusually avid newspaper and magazine coverage, the Woods twins were sons of a former ballplayer turned groundskeeper at Yankee Stadium and a telephone operator, an English-Irish couple with a big brood who were happy to farm two children out every day to the sunny lab on the fourth floor of the Babies' Hospital for two whole years. McGraw provided Johnny (at birth the more "flaccid" of the twins) with exercise in various motor skills the moment she saw them emerging, and then stimulated him with assorted physical challenges—walking up and sliding down inclines, jumping, climbing to reach objects, swimming, roller-skating. Jimmy was left alone, his opportunities for exercise limited, until he was almost two, when he got a dose of intensive training. Over the next four years, follow-up visits were made to see how the boys were faring.

At first, the media spin portrayed a Watsonian victory over the Gesellian position. " 'Conditioned' Infant Excels Twin Brother" read one of the many headlines that hailed McGraw's initial results.

Newsweek's 1933 account pronounced that "Experiments Prove Value of Child Training," and extolled Johnny's precocious ability to "shoot the chutes, climb off blocks, and roller skate." Confronted with the same challenges, a lumpish Jimmy cried or avoided them. It was little wonder that Dr. Gesell deplored all the peering at the boys, and he evidently blamed McGraw for her presumption and lack of discretion ever after—though in her 1935 book about the project, *Growth: A Study of Johnny and Jimmy*, she agreed that the press accounts and verdicts were skewed. Her study had not "negated Gesell's famous maturational theory," she wrote; ". . . it merely modified it." A careful experimenter with no axe to grind, her interest from the start had been in how, rather than when, a trait first develops and whether there might be a moment when the maturing nervous system was "ripe" for improving skills by practice. Her conclusion was that although Johnny had responded with alacrity to his training, Jimmy had managed to do lots of catching up. In the end, the difference between their performances was far less than Johnny's early feats of roller-skating—and swimming—suggested. As for the boys' contrasting personalities, McGraw emphasized that there was no proof whatsoever that their lab experiences were the cause.

In fact, even the simplified press accounts betrayed a shift in a Gesellian direction by mid-decade. An article in *Parents' Magazine*, though still marveling at trained Johnny's exploits, sounded more perturbed about how restrained poor Jimmy had been. He had become an example of "all the thwarted children who are prevented from doing the things their growing bodies cry out to do"; steady encouragement, rather than strict conditioning, now seemed to be the secret of Johnny's success. And Jimmy got credit for putting his physically abler brother to work for him. "Whatever inferiority feelings he may have he seems to be converting into executive powers. He will doubtless be The Big Boss, some day."

By the end of the decade, the harshest—and near unanimous—press verdict was reserved for hubristic scientists who were now accused of having presumed to predict a dramatic contrast between the two that had not panned out. (Actually, McGraw had warned against just such extrapolations.) If there was any difference—and conclusions varied among the journalists, who were basing their verdicts on the briefest of school vignettes, circus visits, and other sightings of the boys—it was " 'Just Plain' Jimmy" who was judged to have it all over " 'Scientific' Johnny." The contest now turned on the boys' personalities rather than their physical abilities, and the "Zest of One Who 'Just Growed' " made for spirited populist headlines. Johnny had taken Jimmy's place as the "thwarted" child, whose early conditioning may have equipped him to excel in the "rarefied atmosphere of the clinic," but had disarmed him for life in the real, democratic world. Jimmy had taken Johnny's place as the model—and now less firmly molded—child. He displayed more sociability, garrulity, flexibility, and spontaneity than his aloof brother. And he was top dog, too. Johnny was merely "a Little Above Average in Studies," but Jimmy "Gets All-Perfect Marks."

The publicity that Gesell had disdained in the early 1930s turned out to serve his cause. When he made a public splash with an unusual manual a decade later, he was the popular expert who dispensed his science in a humanistic, impressionistic spirit—and who urged that children be brought up more "naturally." By that, Dr. Gesell did not mean casually. Between hard covers he sang the praises of individuality and democracy more loudly than he had a decade earlier on screen—joining the chorus of journalists, along with just about everybody else in wartime America. But he was also worried about ensuring national harmony, social mobility, and conformity, right in step with a middle-class audience on edge in an era of instability. In fact, according to Gesell's big new book, seeing to the adjustment of " 'Just Plain' Jimmys" was no less a feat of engineering than Watson had envisaged.

3.

In 1943, Dr. Gesell's workshop published a new kind of primer for parents—and for teachers, social workers, and guidance counselors, too—called *Infant and Child in the Culture of Today*. He listed Frances Ilg as his co-author; his collaborators were Louise Ames, along with Janet Learned, the principal of the Guidance Nursery. This was no mere child-rearing manual, but it didn't have the clinical chill of a psychology textbook or the technical air of a laboratory investigation either. The filmmakers had emerged from their dome to provide the American home, the "cultural workshop" of democracy, with an unusual learning tool: a screenplay for a dramatic child-rearing epic. They had massaged their unwieldy data—with all its "bewildering pageantry of behavior"—to create dramatic scenes in the life of the growing child, with stage directions for parents.

And they supplied a stirring message. To embrace a "developmental philosophy," Dr. Gesell intoned in his accompanying narration, was to "learn to think of growth as a living reality" that manifested itself in a "marvellous series of patterned events." What might look like "aimless variability" in the behavior of babies and children was in fact a self-regulating process of three phases, "innovation—integration—equilibrium." The instability "so often associated with 'naughty' behavior" heralded a "forward thrust" on a journey more thrilling than any "straight and narrow path" could ever provide. "The growing organism does not advance in an undeviating line, but oscillates along a spiral course toward maturity." Gesell and his colleagues billed it as a story to inspire faith in the "spirit of liberty" and respect for the "unique individuality" of every child. The theme music called for was Aaron Copland, not marching bands.

One radio program peddled the book with the unusual promise that it "does not contain a single 'Do' or 'Don't' for parents." Dr. Gesell and his colleagues had indeed departed from the usual prescriptive format of the genre. The "rising generation," they felt, needed and would "readily absorb" a science of child development that was not merely "instrumental, even technological," but also "humanistic . . . [with] an esthetic integrity of its own. It would in itself be a value and a creator of values"—a "necessary counterbalance to the prodigious physical technologies which threaten to split our culture." Just what those values officially were, Gesell had helped to articulate as a prominent participant at the White House Conference on Children in a Democracy of 1940. The "democratic" child-rearing goal of a country at war with authoritarianism, the conference report had announced, was "to produce persons with vitality, initiative, competence, and sufficient vigor to enable them to give expression to their unique qualities of personality": Jimmys, in other words.

The alternative, according to the highly rhetorical report, was "to make of [children] good soldiers, good breeders, and efficient units in a state geared to production": Johnnys, who had become emblems of outmoded behaviorism, which Gesell now denounced as an "authoritarian" view, "foreign to the idea of democracy and the genius of liberty." You would never have guessed that back in 1930 the *New York Times* had called behaviorism "fundamentally hopeful and democratic," more American than any view that emphasized the "blind forces of heredity." Watson had been demoted to cold conditioner of mindless automatons, of whom America—and the world—certainly needed no more; even the aloof "problem solvers" that Watson had actually envisaged seemed too dogged a breed for the times. To sustain democracy in a world of uncertainty, the nation now needed "unique" individuals eager to join in creative solidarity. "Unity Without Uniformity" was the slogan of the 1939 World's Fair. For the mantra on the occasion of the White House conference, Dr. Gesell was ready with a patriotic riposte to the Watsonian scolds who had taunted parents in 1931 that "clarity does not begin at home." He told the assembled organizers that "democracy, like charity, begins at home and with the parents."

Three years later, he had produced a book to guide parents on the new mission. "In some way parents have to catch the idea not that children must be made good, or merely that they must be made mature," Gesell had explained in White House conference discussions, "but that there is a complicated, tedious, long, gradual process of maturity, or growing, which introduces a principle of relativity into all the problems of home life, and which is not too philosophical for them to grasp." Complicated, tedious, long, gradual: that parents might well not perk up at such news had already occurred to him. With prodding from his accomplices in the dome, he saw to it that their "outreach" films had a tempo and interest that their documentary reels lacked. Gesell's "intuitive" collaborator, Frances Ilg, was particularly eager to add drama to the data. Working on *The First Five Years of Life*, a guide to developmental study produced by the Gesell workshop in 1940, Ilg had urged an expanded chapter on personal-social development that went well beyond their testing. And she continued to lobby the director to pursue the "homey" topics, and to portray successive ages as each having "a special and different personality" that developed in a patterned way. *Infant and Child in the Culture of Today* was the result. In it Gesell and his team banished all suggestion that growing might be a frustrating enterprise, for parent or child (or expert). The cinematographers, more daunted than they liked to admit by miles of footage that refused to reveal the ubiquitous symmetries they sought, had gone ahead and spliced together a fascinating adventure.

Dr. Gesell and Dr. Ilg's saga of self-regulated growth was most definitely not a high-spirited precursor of *Home Alone*, however. A developmental philosophy "does not mean license or indulgence. It means guidance," the authors emphasized, and their book proceeded to reveal how subtly directive an expert, and a parent, could be without ever issuing a Do or a Don't. Beneath the endorsement of the "spirit of liberty" and of "unique individuality" there was a quiet but steady drumbeat of concern about conformity and security. In replacing behavioral demands with behavioral norms, Dr. Gesell and his colleagues promised parents relief, but also supplied them with new cause for alarm. Freed from "an overly moralistic point of view," they were now to take a comparative point of view. Liberated from imposing "regularity," they were charged with the gentler task of "regulation." It was a bargain with burdens of its own: the same developmental approach that "releases so many tensions" required an unprecedented level of attention. The key to the Gesellian ethos was constant supervision, and the doctor quite literally meant "super" vision.

The medium was the message for the filmmakers from Yale. Mature eyes must be trained more obsessively, yet less obtrusively, on children than even the most assiduous child-study snoopers had managed. The problem, Gesell agreed with Watson (and with every other expert before and since), was parents' tendency to see the child's "behavior in a false emotional light," and to "project their own personalities into the interpretation of the young child." But he had a practical solution (unlike Watson with his modest proposal of infant farms), and it was also a metaphor for his ideal parent-child relation: the one-way vision screen, behind which adults noiselessly took notes. Children should be seen and heard, but not be aware of it. Mothers would be constantly seen (at home, after all, there were no screens), but heard hardly at all.

Like Dr. Gesell and his partners, mothers should walk—and speak— ever so softly, and carry a big chart. On it, they would monitor their child's pace and place on the oscillating journey through successive phases. "Instead of striving for executive efficiency," Gesell and his associates wrote of the ideal mother, "she aims first of all to be perceptive of and sensitive to the child's behavior. Thus she becomes a true complement to him; alertly responsive to his needs. The child is more than a detached individual who must be taken care of at stated clock intervals. And he is more than a treasured possession. He is a living, growing organism, an individual in his own right to whom the culture must attune itself if his potentialities are to be fully realized." Feeding, as it had been for Dr. Holt, was the paradigm. An early promoter of the "self-demand schedule policy," Dr. Gesell touted it as a model of the synchrony he had in mind. Instead of "looking at the clock on the wall," the mother directed her "interest to the total behavior day of the baby as it records itself on the daily chart." Thus she made "the baby (with all his inborn wisdom) a working partner," helping her to arrive at "an optimal and a flexible schedule suited to his changing needs." For mother and child, Gesell emphasized, the alliance promised an "organic sense of secureness."

Mothers were, in short, glorified stagehands to the stars, and in return for requiring them to be very busy but never bossy, Dr. Gesell gave mothers a screenplay that portrayed children's growth as never boring or bewildering—or burdensome. The heart of *Infant and Child in the Culture of Today* was the middle section called "The Growing Child," which featured close-up scenes of birth through age four, closing with a panoramic survey of "five and the years after" (a period on which the clinic's preschool studies had shed no light at all). "Words alone will not reshape attitudes, but images may," Gesell had said in urging cinematic parent education. Now he transported the nonprescriptive portraiture into prose, pioneering a new form of anecdotal lore that has typified the child-centered branch of advice literature ever since.

Cautionary and exemplary stories, of course, were staples of the ministers' and mothers' child-rearing literature of the nineteenth century, but such descriptive "life" narrative had been a casualty of the laboratory era. Dr. Gesell restored illustrative fare, but substituted a scenic touch for the sermonic tone. The point of his tales was that they had no morals—for child or parent. His device was the "Behavioral Profile," written as if it were an evocation of a particular child at a particular age. Basing his composite on clinical records, Gesell offered what was in essence a popularized version of his normative summaries, as Frances Ilg had urged. Instead of a dry inventory of "developmental items," he sketched with the verve of an artist *en plein air*: a two-year-old, for instance, "loves to romp, flee and pursue."

Gesell then amplified with the "Behavior Day," narrating the little fellow's typical antics from dawn to dusk. Here he was adapting the naturalistic observations gleaned from the "homelike" setup in his dome. (In their zeal for the generic, Dr. Gesell and his associates simply never mentioned girls, other than when they described a nursery school group. Their "he," though, was a genderless creature: the few sketches in the book—photographs, the Gesellian specialty, appeared only as a collage on the book's front and back endpapers—showed babies without penises, right above prose that referred to "he.") Instead of a stilted case study, the authors supplied a script written to fit a phenomenal performer whose role, quite literally, was to define the stage. The child's behavior was never erratic, it was always symptomatic—of a phase, rather than of a disease. "By nature," Gesell said, the modern child "is a creative artist of sorts. Remembering that the infant is, culturally speaking, a novice, we may well be amazed at his resourcefulness, his extraordinary capacity for original activity, inventions, and discovery."

Dr. Gesell and Dr. Ilg's verbal camera captured competent vigor—and comprehensive order. "There is much promise," they glowed in their profile of a four-month-old, "in the cooing, the expectant inspection, the excited breathing, the mutual fingering, and the coverlet clutching of the socially smiling just sixteen [week] baby." Pausing at many points on the way to two, they admired the baby's "burgeoning neuro-muscular system," and his efforts to figure out "the difference between himself and others." Signs of frustration, bound to arise on "bad" days, were often really "thrustration," Gesell proclaimed in one of his exuberant coinages. So was the "fluctuation" that, as the authors explained in describing the two-and-a-half-year-old, is "Nature's favorite method of growth—the method of reciprocal interweaving by means of which she brings flexors and extensors, yes and no, come and go, grasp and release, push and pull into balanced equilibrium."

Growth proceeded in an upward spiral, from periods of transition to stages of equilibrium, and Gesell brought his own buoyant balance to summing up stable three. "There is something 'threeish' about the scope of his attention and insight," he and Ilg announced, catchily extrapolating from lab data about three-year-olds. "He can repeat three digits, he is beginning to count to three; he enumerates three objects in a picture; he is familiar with the three basic forms, circle, square and triangle; he can combine three blocks to build a bridge. Many of his sentences and questions consist of three units. He likes to compare two objects and this requires a three-step logic."

Gesell and Ilg, like the child, were on a roll. "Five is in focus; four is fluid," they announced with a lilt after lingering on "delightful" three. It was another cycle of "lability" followed by "stability." And with the portrait of five-year-old perfection, the "bewildering and almost kaleidoscopic eventfulness" of early childhood development had fallen into beautifully symmetrical form. "All told," the authors summed up in Gesell's characteristically euphonious style, the five-year-old

> presents a remarkable equilibrium of qualities and patterns, of self-sufficiency and sociality; of self-reliance and cultural conformance; of serenity and seriousness; of carefulness and conclusiveness; of politeness and insouciance; of friendliness and self-containedness. If not a super-man he is at least a super infant! He is an advanced version of delightful three year oldness.

In fact, way back when Dr. Gesell's main piece of data had been his own son, Gerhard, he was already singing the praises of five-year-old equipoise—and mocking himself a little as he did so. To read a comic birthday letter he sent to his firstborn in 1915 is to be struck that all the years of study and photography in a sense amounted to a quest to confirm a developmental philosophy Gesell had been all but born with. "My dear son, Today is your birthday, and it is fitting that I should take this solemn occasion and address you in Polonian terms," he wrote, and the Shakespearian parody that followed was reminiscent of young Arnold clucking over his siblings, and prescient of Dr. Gesell preaching to the public in a humanistic vein.

Today you are a half decade old. You have attained five years, yes, my son, this is your chronological age. Your sister has not even entered upon the second quarter of a decade. It behooves you to deport yourself with circumspection in her presence. Lift not your voice to unseemly pitch; let not your lachrymal glands gush with infantile freedom. In all things be circumspect. Be mindful of the responsibilities which your seniority over your tender sister demands of you. Remember you are the eldest of our children. Finally to thine own self be true, and it must follow as the night the day, thou canst not be false to any man. . . .

As the drama of growth unfolded in *Infant and Child in the Culture of Today*, there were no numbers, no schedules, no monotony, and plenty of momentum. Adults were unobtrusive as well. And instead of advice, readers were greeted with an admonition not to expect any, which Gesell frequently repeated. "The behavior day is illustrative and is not set up as a model," he warned. "It is intended to give suggestive orientation." In small type, after the descriptions, he and his collaborators supplied "further child care details," but they studiously avoided a how-to style. The child's activities were merely redescribed under more user-friendly headings (sleep, feeding, elimination, bath and dressing, self-activity, sociality), with an implicit nod to the presence of a big person in the background—but only implicit. Rarely was a mother (much less a father) actually mentioned; instead she was an unseen force at work. On the eighteen-month-old's agenda, for example, "the nap follows the noon meal. . . . Occasionally he awakes crying and then responds best to a motor workout of running about before being toileted."

In brackets, after the small print, Gesell and his colleagues occasionally included "specific guidance suggestions" for sticky situations, but they were brief and often somewhat obscure. Their counsel on handling the fussy but obviously well-fed baby typified the cryptic style. "The mother is well advised not to over-stimulate the child in response to this type of crying, but inasmuch as it is symptomatic of psychological growth needs, it deserves discriminating consideration." A parent would have to consult the index to locate comments on toilet training or thumb-sucking, which were scattered and elusive: let nature take its course was the implication, yet children well under two were being "toileted" in his profiles, and thumb-sucking could be "worrisome."

When the authors arrived at toddlerhood, they did offer teachers "nursery techniques," also adaptable for home. Invoking the drama metaphor themselves, they characterized the child's caretakers as, in essence, the prop crew. "It is very essential to set up his room as though it were a stage, with the planned beginnings of spheres of interest—a doll corner here, fitting toys over there, a magazine on the bed and a tray of plasticene on the table." The book's own oblique style emphasized that mothers, like teachers, should make sure to remain peripheral—crucial though their contributions were. "The culture must plan, foresee, direct, restrict, prod, and channelize to bring about mutual accommodation between the individual and his environment," was the way Gesell put it, having explained at the outset that by "culture," he generally meant mother.

With the knack that experts (like parents) seem to have, Dr. Gesell and his colleagues had embraced an approach ripe with potential to encourage just what they claimed to want to cure: standardized expectations of children, and anxious exhaustion in mothers. Nor was that the only irony of their enterprise. Poles apart in theory, in practice Gesell and Watson converged to a surprising degree. The harmony that Gesell insisted on in his smoothly scripted drama did not in fact feel very cozy. His wriggly baby and protean preschooler, though full of energy, often seemed strangely lacking in agency; they were developing dynamos driven by nature, molded by forces beyond their control.

As for Gesell's ideal mother, she was an agile facilitator who was not supposed to be briskly "efficient" but was certainly not supposed to be effusive either. He emphasized the nursery-school-teacher traits of "a pleasing voice . . . nimbleness and manual facility . . . leisureliness of tempo combined with quickness of reaction," and, of course, she needed "a fundamental knowledge of the theory and principles of child development." She was a keeper of charts, and though he granted that she would also be guided by her heart, he evidently meant a demurely solicitous organ, never out of control, as he indicated in a remarkable aside: "It is also well known that among the colored race there are many women who are supremely endowed with an almost unique emotional equipment which makes their services ideal for infants and young children." Watching from the wings, Dr. Gesell's model mother found her "most important function" in "the planning of the environmental apparatus": Dr. Watson's dream.

An air of impersonal determinism hung over the Gesellian "cultural workshop," and the democratic spirit of cooperation he celebrated could seem somewhat strained. "The child is now both more responsive to and more demanding of the adult," Gesell noted of the twenty-one-month-old, but he did not proceed to encourage the sociable interaction. Back in 1925 he had urged that "not only from the breast must the child be weaned. Slowly but progressively he must attain befitting fortitude and detachment." Two decades later, Gesell stressed the importance of "self-activity," recommending tactics more intricate than Watson's dictates: the behaviorist's little "problem solver" was simply shooed into the backyard and expected to keep busy. Gesell's child needed to be equipped with the right array of age-appropriate, non-people props to play with behind his closed bedroom door (which might be tied shut if necessary, the small print indicated). For Watson, conformity to externally imposed routine instilled autonomy in a child. Gesell envisaged the more daunting task of bolstering a child's sense of security by arranging a world that responded to his rhythms, without indulging his whims.

Not far from the surface of Gesell's scenarios ran a current of uneasy competition: Who was really running the show, and was the performance—of mother and of child—up to par? Naturally, he waved away such worries. Gesell the organicist was fond of incanting, "Everything in season!" "Growth has its seasons and sequences," and of reminding his readers not to get perturbed, for "development is a little like the weather. It should be accepted at least within reason." He wisely counseled "a sense of proportion" during those trying "transitional" stages. "Things are not as bad as they seem," for equilibrium is around the corner. Dr. Gesell, whose considerate attentiveness toward his little subjects was well known, was forever emphasizing that "the constant task of teacher and parent is to notice how the growing child achieves his adjustments. Only in this way can we understand his individuality." No two children were alike.

Yet at the same time, Gesell had been saying since the White House conference of 1930, and before, that "mental health does not take care of itself." His own vision fed an expectation of constantly temperate weather—of development that rarely strayed far from the "trend toward an optimum." He urged constant in-home monitoring, and he never passed up a chance to call for a "democratically conceived system of developmental supervision," from infancy onward, to back up the home—avoiding, he hastened to add, "the dangers of regimentation" by incorporating "a rigorous recognition of the factor of individuality." Yet what mother, equipped with his chronologically based norms, could resist the temptation to match up her child with his agemates at least as often as she marveled over his uniqueness?

And even the mother who could resist, wisely recognizing that "the child himself is the norm of last resort," had to be on constant alert for deviations. Was he proceeding through each stage according to Dr. Gesell's map, and if not, was the overarching pattern sure to get out of whack? The stakes were high, even if Gesell had absolved mothers of Watsonian blame for every slipup, reassuring them of a child's inborn resilience. For he had also impressed parents with a child's amazing inheritance, the fulfillment of which depended on their vigilance. The super-infant, and the mother with super-vision: his was a message for middle-class Americans on the go, yet also on their guard, in an emerging meritocracy.

4.

When *Infant and Child in the Culture of Today* appeared, Dr. Gesell's thirty-three-year-old son, Gerhard, was the father of an infant and a child, and was on the fast track in the culture of the day: then a lawyer at the Securities and Exchange Commission in the nation's capital, he went on to become United States District Court judge of the District of Columbia, a well-known figure in the Watergate and Oliver North trials. One would never have guessed that this rising star had nearly been expelled from prestigious Phillips Andover Academy for abysmal grades in 1928—a "disequilibrium" that he, and his parents, had weathered like developmental philosophers. Sent an SOS by the prep school that "your boy . . . needs pressure put on him to prevent disaster," Dr. Gesell and his wife were told by their son not to worry, it was just a phase. "I am going to keep my head up and I know everything is going to come out all right," Gerhard wrote home, sounding surprisingly jaunty. ". . . Well there is no use crying over spilt milk and I am putting myself doggedly to work with even more intensity if such is possible." When his parents evidently decided some prodding was in order, their young dynamo let them know they could leave the optimum course adjustments to him. "The way you write it seems that you think I still need a nurse maid,"

Gerhard bristled. "This is not the case. I know just what to do in this case."

In Washington in 1943, he was equally confident on behalf of his father, whose book came out amid late-career struggles with Yale, on top of other funding troubles. Dr. Gesell's "one-man show" at the clinic had begun to grate on the university, and with psychoanalytic breezes blowing in the foundation world—"the long, strong Freudian period," his collaborator Louise Ames called it—grants were not coming Gesell's way. He was feeling uncertain about the fate of his primer, too, despite promising signs that he had a popular success on his hands. "Parents are constantly in search of 'a book' on bringing up children," a review in the *New York Times* announced. "This is the book." All his friends agreed, Gerhard Gesell wrote home in a reassuring tone reminiscent of his father's youthful correspondence with his parents. "I keep telling you that Dad's book *is* selling," he told his mother. ". . . The stores here have been sold out for weeks—there is a long waiting list. Our friends constantly tell us how much they like the book or how hard they are trying to get a copy. One mother tried all over New York without success. The book appeals to young fathers and mothers of over-average intelligence. A real sales campaign would sell many copies here—Congratulations!"

To judge by more detailed comments from Gerhard's wife, Peggy, the appeal was indeed to a hard-driving elite—or rather, to their wives. Still in the manual-mania stage of early motherhood herself, with a daughter recently born, she was an ideal reader to whom Gesell had shipped pages of *Infant and Child* before it was published. Like popular experts before and since, he made the most of the very select sample closest to home—in this case, his son and his daughter-in-law and their two children: Peter, born in 1940, and Patsy, who arrived two years later. He welcomed Peggy's reactions, though he perhaps did not expect that his daughter-in-law would be quite as confident a "working partner," and as independent-minded a mother, as she showed herself to be.

Addressing her father-in-law in a comically arch "Dear Sir" vein (at other times she saluted her in-laws as "Dear Kiddies"), she did not hesitate to inform him that the Gesellian regimen, however solicitous it might be of growing children, could be quite a headache for their guides. It wasn't that she failed to find the drama of growth fascinating; she was suitably awed. Still, she saw something obviously missing in the pages she perused: "the Mother's Point of View." Thus Peggy Gesell joined the growing ranks of the experts' in-house critics, from Linda

Holt and Julina Hall to Rosalie Rayner Watson, whose on-the-ground toil muddied the experts' pie-in-the-sky theories. Her comments suggested that the Gesellian exhortation to let growth take its course was hardly the laid-back message it seemed. Like Rosalie Watson, she wrote in a lighthearted, impudent spirit about maternal burdens the "Director" failed to take into account—and indeed the demands she faced were a match for any personality-molding regimen a behaviorist might impose.

Peggy Gesell confessed that she bridled a little at the way her father-in-law the doctor simply assumed that "self-demand routine and breastfeeding" were the wise mother's course. "Assert quite definitely (or even in that scientific language that can so happily embrace both pro and con!) that you so recommend," she wrote him; be more prescriptive, and then a mother can choose, rather than feel subtly coerced. And the choice, she intimated, might well be against. Certainly that was her view on the related policy of "rooming-in" with a newborn—allowing babies to remain with their mothers, rather than being whisked back to the hospital nursery after feeding, a change Gesell actively promoted (and helped to make an option in maternity wards). "I have enjoyed the period of solitude, undisturbed by any responsibility whatever," Peggy Gesell admitted of her own hospital experience, her infants off squalling down the hall where she couldn't hear it. (She also worried that nurses would be overburdened by trying to help new mothers get breast-feeding under way.) "Your pro carries far more essential goodness than such an expression of personal preference contra," she granted, just a little sheepish about being selfish. But she was not about to pretend that having a newborn roommate would be her idea of bliss.

"Then," she continued with humorous sigh, "we come to the charts. I am having a veritable field day with my 5 colors. Really, a field day." Gesell's daughter-in-law somewhat impertinently let it be known that she was feeling like a child too immature to complete one of his lab tasks. (That was, of course, just how Watson envisaged his readers, and just what Gesell hoped his readers would not feel.) For by the time she had received his special charts, Patsy was already six weeks old, which meant her poor mother had to play catch-up: no stage-skipping allowed! "My memory was too feeble to fill in anything except occasional crying spells of the week or 2 previous. Of course I can record little if anything of the hospital stay." Peggy Gesell had irresponsibly been sleeping, not observing her baby or learning from a methodical nurse how to master "a very simple device, namely the behavior chart."

Even keeping pace day to day was hard (and, Peggy Gesell implied, a little ludicrous). If adhering to Watsonian dictates was taxing, simply filling in Gesellian charts was next to impossible. It had evidently not occurred to the doctor whose lab associates had been tirelessly keeping developmental records for decades that it might strike a weary mother as a chore rather than a fascinating challenge. "One symbol I must of necessity ignore, because of my ignorance, that is—urination. The space is not large enough for UR at 20+ or – min. intervals so I have not entered some at all." Less elemental activities were hard to fit onto the grid, too. "When I change her pants, I do not count the episode as social (yellow) because usually time is too brief to show up much." And as Patsy's periods of play lengthened, they could be hard to categorize, often "embrac[ing] moments of fussing which have the elements of both happiness and unhappiness." (Anna Noyes, the Holtian disciple who had written *How I Kept My Baby Well* back in 1913, found the paperwork problematic, too. Having run a nursery school during the intervening years, the erstwhile nurture zealot had been impressed by Dr. Gesell's emphasis on children's natures, but less so by his chart-keeping methods. She boldly wrote to tell him so and—evidently angling for a job in the dome—boasted that she had a better way of "recording all that is pertinent as to changes evolving . . . [and] how these changes were brought about.")

Peggy Gesell went ahead and sent back some charts for the data bank of "Dear Sir," making no effort to pretend that her records revealed a model of maternal responsiveness at work. "You will note a wide variation here and there in her feeding schedule. That is not due to Self-Demand," she informed him, "but to my incapacity to catch up with Father Time and my housework or sleep." Nor did she measure avidly. "There are feedings in the early a.m. when I have omitted the weight-readings," she pointed out, and plainly felt the doctor would be amused by the prosaic reason why. "That is because the scales make quite a distinctive loud noise and Pete at that hour is easily wakened by it. And frankly, Science is as nothing to me when compared to a few minutes more sleep." And then, dutiful daughter-in-law and up-to-date mother that she was, she asked him to send off "a new batch" of charts right away.

Gesell himself proceeded to stray further and further from science in his popular efforts, while sticking as avidly as ever to his neat charts. The very funding troubles that hampered his research had the effect of hastening his second primer for parents. Given the cold shoulder by Yale, the éminence grise needed an aggressive strategy: "Popularize your literature about the future work of the clinic etc.," Gerhard wrote him. "You are an old hand at this with years of experience, and there are no angles you and mother will miss in your councils of war." His even better advice was to get Dr. Spock "of the old New Haven family . . . in pronto for a look see." The pediatrician was just out of the navy and instead of private practice was evidently "considering something more academic."

Instead, Gesell got back to work on another popular book (unaware that Dr. Spock was working on one of his own). In 1946, a mere three years after acknowledging in *Infant and Child in the Culture of Today* that "too little is scientifically established as to the developmental morphology of the child's mind in the important years after five," all the data gathering seemed miraculously to have been done. He and his loyal collaborators Frances Ilg and Louise Bates Ames, along with Glenna Bullis, came out with *The Child from Five to Ten*. In it they freely admitted that "in spirit and technique our methods were clinical, rather than statistical, or rigorously experimental." Their sample was even less representative than before, consisting of some fifty children "of high average or superior intelligence . . . from homes of good or high socioeconomic status."

The same harmony characterized the process of growth in this book as in its predecessor, as stage followed stage in symmetrical fashion. Four was "expansive," five "focal" and a "nodal age" that marks the end of one "growth epoch" and the beginning of another, he reminded his readers. Six was "dispersive," seven "pensive," and eight again "expansive, but on a higher level of maturity." Nine, "a business-like, fair-minded, responsible individual," and ten, "a golden period for planting liberalizing ideas," sounded very grown up. But Gesell and his co-authors also incorporated more amusing realism, as they were forced to acknowledge that the post-nursery show unfolding at home did not always go without a hitch by any means.

The style became more honestly anecdotal—about children's obstreperousness, about mothers' dilemmas. Contradict a five-year-old, they warned with a smile, and don't be surprised when you get called "a 'naughty girl,' 'dirty rat,' etc." Deflect conflict with humor, the most "tolerant," democratic of emotions. That was Gesell's recurrent advice, even as he indicated that moods on the home front were a serious matter indeed. "What the mother does for the child is as important as it was earlier," he wrote, "but more important is what she thinks and feels about him." Dr. Gesell was resolutely un-Freudian in his view of children, but he did not mind urging mothers to monitor their own psyches as well as their children's activities.

Peggy Gesell, his fond critic, couldn't wait to get her hands on the new primer, which was perfectly timed for her, with Pete an all too typically "dispersive" (a.k.a. "explosive") six-year-old when it came out. In her usual self-mocking style, she once again did not hesitate to let the doctor know by letter just how far she was from measuring up to a model of maternity that expected her to be fondly tolerant, rather subservient, and constantly vigilant. She fell right in with his comic portrayal of tumultuous six-year-olds, describing herself as "convulsed, it was so true to life." ("For a while," she confessed, "it was with trepidation that I asked [Pete] to do anything at all lest the roof blow off to the accompaniment of 'Mean' 'Unfair' 'Stupid' and 'Stink.' ") But she was daunted, too, by the distance between Gesell's amusing scene and the scenes in her house. "On a page this hideous period is terribly funny—in actuality it calls, on the parents' part at least, for an unheard of mixture of the patience of Job and Milton's spirit of laughter. I am not equal to it." Her fallback was to count on, what else, fluctuation. "However I am hoping the crisis has been passed. The moments of wild and passionate conflict seem perhaps a hair less often though not much less wild."

Meanwhile, on the school front, she was "wallowing" in worries about Pete and norms, she informed Gesell. Behind in reading, her son faced the prospect of "being with the less-rapid group—the non-leaders, or . . . possibly not being promoted to third grade." Thanks in part to the supervisory ethos that Gesell and the mental hygienists had helped promote among educators, she was besieged with professional advice. (Gesell's School Readiness Test is still widely administered to kids on their way to kindergarten.) But should she meddle, or let time take its course? "I am lost in this business," she confessed. As well she might be, given that Gesell in *The Child from Five to Ten* urged a less academic focus, going so far as to declare that "the school system places excessive emphasis on the importance of the printed word." And yet Gesell had made keeping up with one's age-mates seem all-important. Meanwhile Gerhard, it seemed, favored patience with Pete (perhaps remembering his travails at Andover). But what counsel he had to offer was clouded by his impatience with the experts. "Gerry grows belligerent," Peggy reported in distress, "dismisses the Remedial Reading School as a group of childless psychopaths and is really not much help."

A year and a half later, however, Dr. Gesell's theory and his descen-

dants were in good, calm shape. Equilibrium had returned, as he predicted it always would at some point. His daughter-in-law was still tirelessly keeping records, and his grandchildren were, if not setting
records, evidently keeping up just fine. "I wish to acknowledge receipt
of the excellent reports concerning Peter Gesell (case 9209) and Patricia Gesell," he wrote their mother in his self-mocking guru vein. "I
congratulate you on the excellence of these reports, which is doubtless
based on the excellence of the children." Which, in turn, was doubtless
based on genes—but also, Gerhard wrote his parents some years later,
thanks to all the guidance that he and Peggy, too, had received. "You
have both been far more than parental in your kindness and unceasing
affection—It has left me speechless but proud and grateful—what fun
to be able to show you the concrete results in that fine crop of grandchildren."

Dr. Gesell himself was at the brink of retirement, on the eve of the
baby boom. He presided over an audience of parents like his own children, with at least a college degree, and he described himself as a
spokesman for "democratic" values. He profiled a crop of children conceived in and destined for similar "superior" surroundings, and he proclaimed his behavioral norms to be universal. He pored over his films,
and he paid no attention to Freud. The expert who had overtaken Watson was, in other words, shortly to be overtaken by postwar events.

And yet he plowed steadily ahead, much as he said children would
and could. Into the 1950s he kept on writing for lay readers from his
more peripheral position at the unaffiliated Gesell Institute of Child
Development set up in New Haven by his unflagging collaborators Ilg
and Ames, who became a prolific pair themselves. *Youth: The Years from
Ten to Sixteen* appeared in 1956. "The children," Peggy Gesell reported
of her teens, "find it a bestseller," and one eighth grader whose class
was assigned the book offered this verdict: "I think Dr. Gesell made one
glaring mistake which in my eyes degrades his book. That is the fact
that he only studied 200 children and all in one area. But I still have to
admit that it is amazingly accurate." Academic critics were not so forgiving, but by then the seventy-six-year-old Gesell had long since been
swept off his pedestal by the psychoanalytic current; his dome had been
dismantled, and he had bequeathed no experimental agenda to eager
acolytes. It was a popular audience that he and his loyal associates
counted on for support (Ilg and Ames's advice column was syndicated
in sixty-five newspapers), and American parents to this day have
remained a strong market for Gesell's "anatomy of normalcy."

Its accuracy has never been the point, exactly. *Youth* is "curiously non-sexy. Or perhaps I should say a-sexy," a reviewer wrote of the book, putting her finger on the distinctive appeal of his vision as a whole: in all their nakedness, Gesell's babies were adorably unique yet also reassuringly uniform, chubby embodiments of innocent energy. No Oedipal shadows darkened his pictures. (When Erik Erikson briefly worked with him—relations soon soured—he ventured to include note of erectile behavior in the records, and met with disapproval from the master of the dome, who deemed it abnormal, unworthy of mention.) Little demons of upward mobility, his infants—and children, too—were also models of stability and continuity.

Gesell's growth trends seemed stolidly untrendy—and ever more so, for with every passing year his patterns looked more schematic (imposing symmetry on puberty seemed a particularly artificial feat), his norms narrower and more culture-bound, his data more limited and dated. (Already in his 1946 film, *Infants Are Individuals*, he noted that he was using material that was twenty years old.) Gesell did not, as critics pointed out, try to probe for either the "how" or the "why" of development; he stuck with the "when." His timetables, in short, had a timeless quality. They beckoned with the promise that even if American culture was, as Watson had warned, "changing from top to bottom more rapidly and fundamentally than most of us dream of," at least the way children changed was the same as ever. To be sure, few kids actually fit his perfect patterns. And with his "glacial public surface," Dr. Gesell was a model of aloof serenity few mothers could match. But unwieldy children and unnerved parents were problems he bequeathed to his successor, the super-expert of midcentury, Dr. Benjamin Spock, who was a bundle of insecurities himself.

PART III

Identity Crisis

SEVEN

The Awkward Age of the Expert

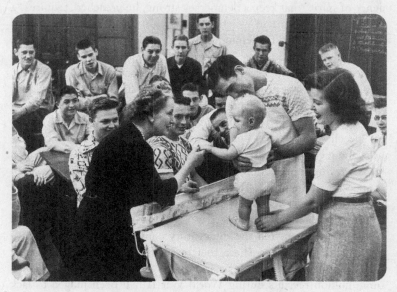

High school class in family living, 1950

I.

The official subject of the Midcentury White House Conference on Children and Youth, which opened in Washington on December 5, 1950, was "the healthy personality," or "personality in the making," the titles of two reports that emerged from the event. The real subject of the gathering was anxiety. So it was fitting—and disconcerting—that the conference opened just as the United States found itself facing a major crisis. The Chinese had routed General Douglas MacArthur's U.N. forces in Korea the week before, and President Truman was about to declare a national emergency. In what the *New York Times* judged to be "perhaps the president's most nerve-shattering week since those grim days when he first stepped into the White House as President in 1945," Truman briefly turned his attention from the war to address the nearly five thousand conference delegates in the National Guard Armory, the only space in the capital that could accommodate a meeting so large.

"We cannot insulate our children from the uncertainties of the world in which we live or from the impact of the problems which confront us," the president told the conferees, welcoming their aid in fortifying the nation's youth to face the "moral and spiritual dangers that flow from communism." To foster the "individual self-reliance and independence of spirit" that keep a democracy strong, he preached, requires "a good home—a home in which [children] are loved and understood," and a commitment to helping "young people. . . . better understand our democratic institutions." (Truman's own practice left something to be desired, the media gleefully leaked later that week, exposing the president as an overprotective stage father. He fired off a furious letter to the newspaper critic who panned his beloved twenty-six-year-old Margaret's singing performance in Constitution Hall the same day as his speech: if I ever meet you, Truman warned him, "you'll need a new nose and plenty of beefsteak and perhaps a supporter below." So much for conveying appreciation of "our democratic institutions" of freedom of speech and the press—though the president's daughter calmly commented that the reviewer had a right to his opinion.)

"I do not claim to be an expert in . . . the moral and mental health of children," Truman told the midcentury conference delegates, whose long-planned arrival to share their expertise now seemed especially well timed. Wars often fuel alarm about the caliber of youth (some three million recruits during World War II had been judged to lack "the ability to face life, live with others, think for themselves and stand on their own two feet," as the consultant to the surgeon general of the army and navy summed up their deficiencies). And the setbacks in Korea, which soon occasioned public worry about "coddled" soldiers, only confirmed rising Cold War concern that even, or especially, those "good homes" of more doting postwar parents were due for scrutiny: Were the personalities more gently reared in them turning out to be adequately prepared for the challenges and perils ahead?

If the busy president hoped he was ceding the floor to child development experts armed with definitive scientific directives on how to "build up those inner resources of character which are the main strength of the American people," however, he was disappointed—as were the experts themselves. "This White House Conference," its planners had proclaimed several years earlier, "could make its greatest contribution by bringing together, systematizing, and integrating the accumulated knowledge of the behavior of children and young people and by seeing how social institutions and individuals concerned with children were making use of this knowledge." An interdisciplinary Fact Finding Committee of eminent professionals—from the psychoanalyst Erik Erikson to the anthropologist Margaret Mead to the now world-famous Dr. Benjamin Spock, whose manual had come out in 1946—had been appointed. Their goal was to "synthesize the relevant findings of psychiatry, anthropology, physiology, and so forth, into a statement concerning the development of a healthy personality in children" for the enlightenment of the large lay audience invited to what was billed as a "broad-scale citizens'" gathering. Yet arriving at a scientific consensus, which was supposed to be "the major strength of the conference," turned out to "present one of its major problems."

In fact, with furrowed brows, the multi-professional committee confessed to something of a crisis of confidence. Their theme—"How can we rear an emotionally healthy generation?"—had caused the specialists considerable emotional and intellectual stress over the two preceding years of preparation and meetings, and they had evidently decided it would be unhealthy to repress it. They had set out to find coherence in a field "artificially fragmented by the isolation of the several scientific disciplines and specialties." Instead they had discovered "great chasms of ignorance" in their science, they announced in their report. "Our nation at midcentury has within it many unknowns—processes and patterns—operating beyond our control or in undetermined ways." As advisers to the public, the experts thus felt burdened by a "very difficult problem." Given that "the best now known is still known so tentatively," they lamented, how could they live up to what they saw as their newly pressing duty to parents, which was "to build their self-confidence rather than to destroy it"?

On the Fact Finding Committee, of course, was the doctor who had made that his mission, to the evident gratitude of millions. Yet "Dr. Spock's gift" for reassurance was hailed by his colleagues in a spirit of some nervousness, too. After all, the phenomenal popularity of his *Common Sense Book of Baby and Child Care*—which had sold three quarters of a million copies its first year out—could itself be taken as a worrisome sign of parental insecurity. Who would have guessed that so many American mothers and fathers were in such need of soothing advice? True to their professional bent, the assembled academic authorities were inclined to spot an alarming symptom in their colleague's success, rather than to hail a cure. And the book's author himself was awash in ambivalence about his purported influence. In fact, the midcentury conference coincided not just with a public crisis, but with private crises—personal and professional—in the life of Dr. Spock. It was in keeping with the mood of the hour that the man with the message "Trust yourself, you know more than you think you do" was suffering self-doubt.

Though officially a vice chairman of the conference, Dr. Spock did not spend much time in the spotlight. From the moment he set out on his trip to the capital, he had felt on edge—and edged out. He had taken the train all the way from Minnesota, where his position on the Mayo Clinic faculty was in jeopardy, because his unhappy wife phobically begged him not to fly. (She never forgave him for failing to stop en route to visit their elder son, Michael, who was a miserable freshman at Antioch College.) Though warmly received in Washington, Spock was promptly upstaged. He and Margaret Mead were the celebrities chosen to preside at a press conference, except that Mead stole the show. She blithely fielded questions that were directed to her colleague. "I was too polite to object," Spock ruefully recalled years later.

And he had already been overshadowed by the émigré child analyst Erik Erikson, whose ambitious eight-stage theory of personality development had set the tone and perspective of the midcentury conference from its planning onward. Like the rest of the conferees, Erikson graciously praised Dr. Spock's "remarkable ease and matter-of-factness" and repeatedly cited his book. But the prevailing spirit of the event was not the confident optimism that was considered the Spockian trademark, as Spock observed in a talk that was itself far from upbeat. After so many "reports on the complexity of personality growth" in a changing culture, he noted, there was a risk that healthy development might sound "so hazardous" that American parents would just give up hope—or at least give up on their experts. The lay delegates, to judge by a minister who spoke up for the assembled company, were indeed feeling dazed. "In such a world it is strange that any child survives," the bemused cleric remarked. "There must be a special providence watching over fools and children."

The contrast between the Conference on Modern Parenthood a quarter of a century earlier and the 1950 gathering was notable. At the Waldorf-Astoria in 1925, the demands of "educated motherhood" had become more specialized than the expectations proclaimed at the Congress of Mothers in 1899. On the agenda by the 1920s had been, in essence, a taxing program of businesslike studies with a far longer reading list of expertise—and with lots of remedial coursework piled on for good measure. And two experts who projected overweening assurance during the interwar period, Dr. Watson and Dr. Gesell, had staked their claim to popularity with vows that their science held the secrets of "prediction and control," which suitably serious mothers could master, too. At midcentury, however, the professionalizing pressure in the child-rearing arena had let up. No post-doc program was unveiled at this White House conference. Instead, the experts struck the note of an earnest therapy session, where all parties could feel free to examine their identities and confess their insecurities in neo-Freudian style.

The star of the proceedings, Erikson, evoked the ethos in the anthropological vein he favored: the conference should aspire to convey that "precious inheritance from the past, the town-hall spirit." To be avoided, he counseled at the pre-conference meeting, was a crusading spirit of scientific indoctrination, which only encouraged polarized views and exaggerated claims. A more communal ambience of give-and-take was the ideal, for it "quickly subdues the noisy onslaught of sensationalism, tolerantly lends an ear to honest presentation, and in permitting the discussion of extreme pros and cons helps each individual to absorb what he, as well as the group, is ready for." (It takes a village to raise an expert, not to speak of parents.)

Erikson's presentation to the Fact Finding Committee became the conceptual centerpiece of the conference. ("His paper relieves me of tremendous responsibility," sighed the committee director, who had not been finding that the heaps of facts were falling into place as hoped.) What he delivered was a version of "Eight Ages of Man," the core chapter of his book *Childhood and Society*, which also appeared in 1950 and established him as America's most popular postwar proponent of ego psychology. Erikson's chart of successive stages in the life cycle of the ego as it develops within the family and in society is by now well known. From the all-important first phase of infant conflict between "trust" and "mistrust," psychological growth proceeded through a series of struggles as the self forged relations with the world of others: "autonomy vs. shame," "initiative vs. guilt," and "industry vs. inferiority," culminating in the pivotal conflict of adolescence between "identity" and "diffusion," or role confusion. In adulthood, the continuing quest for socially fulfilled selfhood unfolded in three further conflicts: "intimacy vs. isolation," "generativity vs. stagnation," and "integrity vs. despair." With this suggestive map, Erikson gave the conference just what it needed in dealing with a topic as amorphous as "the healthy personality": a rubric that was neat and ambitious without being too abstruse. His Freudian focus was cultural and historical rather than obsessively sexual. It proved culturally and historically very congenial.

Perhaps just as important, Erikson set a self-critical, questioning tone for the event. He was a chart-making expert who cautioned that "charts, to paraphrase Lincoln, are the kind of thing which help the kind of people who are helped by that kind of thing." (His own map, it pained him to have to point out again and again, was meant to suggest flow among the stages, not a lockstep journey from one to the next—never mind that it looked just like a ladder.) Erikson's paper conveyed newly probing concerns not just about experts, but also about parents and children, concerns that Watson would have scoffed at and that Gesell skated over. As they explored their own scientific uncertainties, the midcentury experts had grown ever more anxious about the level of insecurity they detected in young and old alike.

2.

In his prefatory remarks to the Fact Finding Committee, which he called "On the 'Expert,' " Erikson captured the less doctrinaire self-image the advisers aimed to convey. The quotation marks around "expert" signaled the shift in perspective. The professionals at the 1925 Conference on Modern Parenthood had felt their scientific status depended on promising that a comprehensive description of children, along with predictions about them, would emerge from their labs before long; eagerly applying research to practice, they began dispensing clear-cut prescriptions to parents in an authoritative style.

By contrast, their postwar successors felt under some pressure to acknowledge that they had outgrown such facile faith. The boom in child development studies of all different kinds during the 1920s and 1930s had been interrupted by World War II, and the researchers who resumed work in its aftermath faced the challenge of coordinating and consolidating—and trying to corroborate—lots of disparate theories, data, and methodologies. Not least, they were struggling with the legacy of Freud, whose influence surged in academia and among the public in the wake of his death in 1939.

In a speech at Clark University in 1949, which marked the fortieth anniversary of Freud's lectures there, Anna Freud confirmed her status as her father's emissary in America, and she surveyed the scene with the undogmatic clarity that was her specialty. Psychoanalytic hunches, hypotheses, and theories, she reported, had lately proved fertile in many branches of the behavioral sciences. Indeed the ego psychology she had helped to promote, which played up the ego's strength in its struggles with the outer world rather than its vulnerability in the face of unconscious drives, found an especially receptive audience in the United States. But Freudian ideas had also stirred up controversy and confusion, she pointed out. She went on to warn against simplistic edicts for parents and to welcome the efforts of academic psychologists to test psychoanalytic principles. She called for subtler observations of children and more modest predictions, aware of how much patience both required.

In passing, she took a swipe at Lawrence Frank, the interwar "catalyzer" of child developmentalists, who had since moved on from the Laura Spelman Rockefeller Memorial Foundation to the Josiah Macy, Jr., Foundation, and then to the Institute of Personality Development in New York. He had become among the most zealous American promoters of the neo-Freudian cause, and his utopian extrapolations from ego psychology went too far for Anna Freud. It was rosy promises like his that children reared with ample "gentleness and reassurance" would learn "the required conduct without a feeling of resistance, resentment, hostility, or aggression" that she cautioned against at Clark.

But even Frank, impatient with the Oedipal ordeal of subduing impulses and internalizing parental ideals, by now acknowledged that healing a "sick" society by rearing unconflicted young citizens amounted to a daunting cultural challenge. It certainly posed a scientific challenge, as the child development researchers whose work Frank had done so much to launch before the war were discovering. It was left to them to find proof for the proposition that "the process of socialization creates . . . warped, twisted, and distorted individuals and that this process of personality development can and will be changed," as Frank put his meliorative vision in an essay called "Freud's Influence on Western Thinking and Culture" in 1940. Over the following decade, behavioral scientists of different stripes stepped up efforts to bring greater rigor to their accounts of children's personality growth and of parents' part in it. The task presented more hurdles than the behaviorists or maturationists had faced, now that unconscious drives were involved.

As Watson had enjoyed taunting Freudians back in the 1920s, the psychoanalytic couch generated plenty of childhood memories, but they were fuzzy findings—certainly compared to the graphic evidence that he gleaned from his stimulus-response tests, or that could be seen in Gesell's films. Freud himself had emphasized that his only case study of a child, five-year-old Hans with a horse phobia, was "not, strictly speaking, derived from my own observation"; the little boy's father had relayed the account of his son's Oedipal drama. And in the 1909 case, Freud had confessed that "what [a child's] upbringing is to aim at and at what point it is to be brought to bear seem at present to be very doubtful questions." Since the 1920s his daughter, along with Melanie Klein and others, had pursued analytic work with children. But as Anna Freud had acknowledged back in 1928 in her four lectures collected as *Psychoanalysis for Teachers and Parents*, and reasserted twenty years later at Clark, all kinds of questions remained as to how children's developing egos were shaped by the particular circumstances of their lives, to say nothing of what the "right proportion of instinct-gratification and instinct-restriction" might be.

If the ego's quest for mastery seemed a less elusive theme for study than the mysteries of the id, it was still an unwieldy one. The normal as well as the neurotic now needed observing. Aggressive drives, in addition to libidinal urges, had to be taken into account in explaining that potentially warping process of socialization. Anxiety was no longer considered a telltale symptom of repression, but was recognized to be a complex source of repression itself. Explorations of growth must encompass more than the intrapsychic processes of personality development, Anna Freud urged and her student Erikson agreed, and so did Margaret Mead and fellow Freudian-minded anthropologists of the "culture and personality" school. The postwar cross-disciplinary aspiration, as daunting as it was exciting, was to map the larger social and cultural forces—and the deeper psychological pressures—that played a part in children's adaptation to the world, and in their parents' approaches to raising them.

As Dr. Spock later remarked, "Freud was much too smart to get involved with child rearing himself." Meanwhile, of course, interwar psychologists in America had gotten very involved with child rearing, bequeathing a legacy of conflicting advice for parents and accounts of children that only further complicated their midcentury successors' predicament. Back in the early, halcyon days when Dr. Hall and Dr. Holt had coexisted without competing, they could pride themselves on being pioneers, laying the scientific groundwork and winning the allegiance of middle-class mothers. Vying for pre-eminence, Dr. Watson and Dr. Gesell had made a more polarized pair, each in his own way demanding more parental obedience—and making more vaunting claims for his science. By 1950, child development professionals could not help being sobered by the inconsistent, often quickly obsolescent, counsel peddled to the public so far.

And they had reason to fear that ordinary Americans were themselves more dubious about "scientific" methods and predictions—even as parents continued to clamor for more expert child-rearing counsel. (A psychoanalyst quoted one midcentury mother's plaintive query to the *Encyclopaedia Britannica:* "What is the cause and the cure of child psychology?" The same doctor noted that the demand for advice was nonetheless unceasing: there is "this powerful tendency of 'wanting to be told an exact answer'—and probably nobody in our culture is completely free of it.") In 1950, *Life* magazine testily noted that "the average citizen, inclined to accept 'scientific discoveries' at face value" might be pardoned for skepticism, given the latest revolutionary swerve in expert advice. "If Watson was right in 1920–30, why not in 1950? The answer would seem to be that he never was right but was the enthusiastic victim of his own mistakes, from which he leaped to very large and totally unwarranted generalizations." Nor should "the latest theory" be presumed to rest on more "solid, demonstrable fact."

Postwar pediatric advisers were acutely aware of navigating an awkward transition, at odds among themselves but also caught off balance with their patients—or rather with their patients' mothers. The stress level was high in the profession, as Milton J. E. Senn, Dr. Gesell's successor at Yale, revealed in a brief memoir, "The Peregrinations of a Pediatrician" (part of his oral history of the child development movement). "Conflict arose," Senn recalled of the late 1930s, "between those who recommended strict, regular feedings of accurately measured food and those who believed flexibility and individualized handling were more physiological and certainly more practical and less anxiety producing in mothers." And then the doctors had to deal with their contentious clientele, too, riled up by all the confusion. By the 1940s, Senn reported, "pediatricians were confounded and annoyed by the large number of distraught, angry and frazzled mothers in their practices, private and hospital clinics." Dr. Spock's 1946 success was but a brief moment of calm consensus that "common sense" might reign. By 1950, overdependence on advice, the very problem he had hoped to cure, had become a topic of concern among advisers. No wonder Erikson had put those quotation marks around "expert."

Erikson's semi-apologetic preamble "On the 'Expert' " touched all the nerves. First, he cautioned that if he limited himself to what was "*known* about the 'healthy personality,' " in the sense of being provable by accepted scientific techniques, his discussion would be marked by "honorable but very uninspiring austerity." Next he emphasized that he himself was not drawing on as "consistent theory" as might be expected from an expert. The Freudian school of psychoanalysis that informed his ideas about the healthy personality, he noted, was actually derived from the study of disturbed personalities—hardly an ideal model. Thus Erikson had to roam into cultural anthropology for clues as to what kind of men and women "educational and cultural systems at their best are striving, each in its own way, to create, to support, and to maintain."

What he had come up with, he concluded, was best called "*insight*, a term both modest and vain." It gave him the latitude to admit that his "knowledge, his theory, and his skills [would] change and develop." It also gave him license to "aspire to state what I consider to be the universal elements of a healthy personality under any and all cultural conditions." But he didn't want that ambition misconstrued and schematized, which as he warned in closing had become almost a reflex in America. "I am concerned about the fact that any statement in this field falls prey to sloganlike generalization and overstatement, as if insight, to be of interest, had to be *new* and *against* something," Erikson lamented. "The publicists of expertness ride on a wave of sensationalism which quickly withdraws, only to return as something brand-new with the next wave, or the wave after the next."

The tone of ambition mixed with self-deprecation was struck repeatedly by the experts as they prepared for the White House conference. The final report, published under the title *Personality in the Making*, joined Erikson in remarking how "much of this knowledge [about the healthy personality] . . . is still tentative." The authors emphasized the "great need for tested knowledge in the social and psychological sciences," calling attention to how "much more research remains to be done before practice can be said to rest upon a firm scientific foundation." By 1950, when the flurry of child-rearing studies that followed the end of the war had picked up speed, it was becoming more obvious how difficult to design, and to conduct and interpret, such research was bound to be. Problem children often had problem parents, but how to figure out which came first? Successful children often had good environments in their early years, but did they continue to thrive because they continued to enjoy favorable surroundings, or because they had developed sturdy personalities? "Probably," the report judiciously proposed, "there will be no single answer."

Indeed, results from one of the best-known longitudinal projects, the Berkeley Growth Study launched in 1928, had begun emerging at the end of the 1930s, and they had been confounding tidy predictions ever since. Children often coped well in stressful family situations; troubles had a way of cropping up where least expected, and then disappearing. As the mass of motley data on "normal run-of-the-mill" families continued to accumulate, the study's directors were led to marvel at how the child "threads his way to some measure of stable and characteristic patterning." They humbly added that "when we look at the hazards of the course, we are not sure that we have begun to understand how or why." Nor did the study ever answer the question that had originally motivated it: it proved impossible to say whether the "mental hygiene sensitized group" of parents, who had been treated to six years of professional child-rearing guidance, experienced fewer problems than the control group of families who muddled along.

Few solid answers were forthcoming from a grand research agenda that got its start before the war in interdisciplinary work at the Yale Institute of Human Relations, spearheaded by Clark Hull. The aim was to subject psychoanalytically inspired hypotheses to behaviorist methods of study, a hybrid approach that went under the name of "social learning" theories. Could Freudian ideas about infantile sexuality, about ego and superego struggles, about repression and resulting frustration (all derived from adult analyses) be observed in the actual behavior of infants and children under different conditions? Prominent in the group of promising young scientists who tackled the task were the psychologists Robert R. Sears (who went on to direct the Iowa Child Welfare Research Station) and his wife, Pauline Sears, joined by the anthropologists John and Beatrice Whiting.

Of the many questions posed by Freud's theory they might have set out to explore, they seized on a very American one: during an era haunted by economic depression and by war, it was perhaps no surprise that the uses of sublimation held less allure as a topic than the dangerous, potentially violent, effects of repression. The basic psychological model that informed the "social learning" project was laid out in 1939 in *Frustration and Aggression*, by the Yale sociologist John Dollard and colleagues, among them Robert Sears. The slim book (Lawrence Frank's bible) encapsulated a conflict-averse vision of human relations that quickly proved popular. Coercive and inconsistent child-rearing methods in America, the authors hypothesized, intensified the inevitable frustrations entailed in socializing impulsive young children, who vented their feelings in aggression toward others. Tensions crested again during adolescence, when sexually mature and assertive youths chafed at social demands for continued dependence. A presumed remedy, or at least part of one, lay in easing the "forbidding atmosphere of our patriarchal family"—and indeed the Gesellian "self-demand" approach to feeding was already in the air then.

But a decade later, research had not exactly clinched the paradigm. An article in the *Psychological Bulletin* in 1949, "Infant Care and Personality," by the Yale anthropologist Harold Orlansky, made news well beyond the academic orbit; *Life* magazine even cited it. Orlansky scrounged up all the evidence he could for the widespread claim that a cuddly infancy, free of repression, makes for unneurotic adulthood. What he found were meager, indeterminate, conflicting, uncontrolled, misrepresented studies that did not begin to prove that flexible feeding, gradual weaning, lenient toilet training, and empathetic "mothering" had measurable benefits. Nor was there much evidence, he noted in his blunt inventory, to suggest that harsher handling or swaddling had indelibly destructive results. Parental attitudes, cultural situations, varieties of temperament, the longer-term malleability of personality: such complexities, Orlansky sighed, got ignored in most of the empirical work that had been done.

More elaborately designed studies under way in the 1950s, fascinating though they were, did little to clarify matters. *Personality in the Making* soberly noted that "the problem of tracing personality formation in a relatively simple and static culture is great; infinitely more so to attack a complex, multicultural setting such as exists in the United States." Along with several colleagues, Robert Sears embarked on a study of nearly four hundred American families. But as one of his collaborators, Eleanor E. Maccoby, reported years later, "few connections were found between parental child-rearing practices . . . and independent assessments of children's personality characteristics—so few, indeed, that virtually nothing was published relating the two sets of data." And as Margaret Mead herself had concluded in the wake of her interwar studies in Samoa and New Guinea, cross-cultural comparisons were hard to use, given the pervasive variations among cultures. A vogue in "overeager interpretations" linking adult personality (or even national, or tribal, character) to early child-care techniques gave rise to a dismissive term: "diaperology."

A longer-pants version of the enterprise, pursued by another group of researchers in the Midwest, was generating widespread interest. A longitudinal study at the Fels Research Institute for the Study of Human Development at Antioch College explored, among other things, the different effects of "democratic" and "authoritarian" parental styles, inspired by the "field theory" of the émigré child psychologist Kurt Lewin. Convinced that understanding group dynamics, not simply individual psychic dramas, was essential to accounting for children's behavior, Lewin and several colleagues had done experiments at the University of Iowa during the 1930s that became classics when he and colleagues refined and wrote them up in 1939. Lewin compared clubs of ten-year-old boys under democratic, authoritarian, and laissez-faire leadership, and the democratically run group got the highest marks for healthy peer interactions and adult-child harmony.

But probing family leadership styles, or "atmospheres," for their long-term influence on personality proved a trickier enterprise. Some studies did seem to suggest that more independent, better socialized, friendlier, more curious—but also, at least as Alfred Baldwin of the Fels Institute noted, more aggressive—children emerged from more "democratic" homes. Yet simply finding clear-cut extremes in child-rearing styles to use as a basis of comparison turned out to be difficult, several other researchers acknowledged. Even in "upper-middle-class Westchester . . . [where] 'mental hygiene' was looked upon as favorably as Divine Grace had once been," truly indulgent hearths seemed hard to find. And parental approaches had a way of changing as kids grew, another investigator noted; she found parents got stricter. In any case, "a correlational study cannot satisfactorily answer questions of causation," one researcher rightly cautioned. Not that such caveats kept Theodor Adorno and his co-authors from leaping beyond what they admitted was "no more than a schematic outline of prevalent group trends" to draw just that kind of conclusion in *The Authoritarian Personality* of 1950. Their verdict was that authoritarian homes, where parents were undemonstrative and stern and where status anxiety was high, bred "prejudiced" people.

The lurking question of class, and race, had the midcentury experts discomfited as well. "The social and economic situation plays a large role," they emphasized in *Personality in the Making*, vaguely urging meliorative policies of a structural sort, noting that all too often "low family income and inadequacy in personality development" went hand in hand. Just what that meant was, however, hard to say. Scattered efforts to branch out from the usual middle-class samples to assess American families according to the new typology of "democratic" and "authoritarian" child-rearing styles suggested widespread flux. Surveys back in 1930 had already undermined the conventional assumption that looser methods were rampant—and unfortunate—among poorer Americans, while the "better" classes embraced schedules with zeal. Data seemed to reveal greater rigidity among rural families, while affluent urbanites were easing up and becoming more intimate—findings that seemed to be confirmed in the 1940s when African-American and lower-class families were rated as "traditional" in their views, compared to the "developmental" approach increasingly favored by parents higher on the income and occupational scale. But by midcentury, the situation was admittedly murky. A Chicago study discussed at the White House conference showed poorer babies getting a more "gratifying" start—lots of nursing, later weaning, leisurely toilet training—but losing out later, lacking lessons in "middle class foresight and moderation."

Meanwhile, other psychologists and psychiatrists were focusing more on bonding than on discipline, and by 1950 concern and controversy about the topic had reached new heights. What could be said about the influence of maternal attitudes, understood in emotional terms? During the Freudian 1940s, the quest was on to probe the formative early relationship between mother and child, and to show the Oedipal drama's crucial role in helping the immature ego distinguish reality from fantasy and achieve a sense of security. Maternal overprotection had promptly become the diagnostic slogan of the hour, as Erikson noted in *Childhood and Society* in his discussion of "Momism," the term popularized in 1942 by Philip Wylie in his pop-sociology screed against feminized America, *Generation of Vipers*. In *Maternal Overprotection* in 1943, the psychiatrist David Levy had medicalized the syndrome in what purported to be a scientific study of twenty "pure" cases of the affliction, which he identified as a displaced form of maternal aggression and hostility.

But soon enough absent mothers vied with overbearing ones for expert attention, as wartime crises and family disruptions supplied disturbing evidence of "maternal deprivation" to explore: What was the fate of young children who had endured the trauma of separation and experienced institutional care? With Dorothy Burlingham, Anna Freud wrote about the babies and toddlers they tended in nurseries set up during the Blitz, stressing children's emotional need for intimate relationships to specific adults, which no ties with peers could replace. In 1947, an émigré psychoanalyst named René Spitz made a wrenching film called *Grief: A Peril in Infancy*. His footage of babies languishing in a foundling home lent even more emotional urgency to debates about children's need for warm nurture.

By 1950, expert and public concern about "attachment" was about to escalate yet further. The year the Midcentury White House Conference was taking shape, the British psychologist John Bowlby embarked on a survey for the World Health Organization of a decade's worth of expert thinking about the plight of homeless children. Continuous "mother-love . . . is as important for mental health as are vitamins and proteins for physical health," he declared a year later in *Maternal Care and Mental Health*—granting, as he closed his report, that the evidence "is at many points faulty." Bowlby was not deterred, however, from extrapolating to ordinary homes, warning of the high costs of "partial" deprivation there, too—by which he seemed to mean anything less than "constant attention day and night, seven days a week and 365 in the year," from a mother or other "warm, intimate, and continuous" caretaker during the early years. The consequences were dire: a lack of love "brings in its train acute anxiety, excessive need for love, powerful feelings of revenge, and, arising from these last, guilt and depression."

As an editorial in *Parents' Magazine* at the start of 1950 sighed, "There is much too much talk of rejection these days; everyone is busy either rejecting or being rejected." The midcentury conference report was inclined to agree. While devoting many pages to the topic, the authors took note that "studies of the effects of these various kinds of parental attitudes on children's personality development have been largely limited to clinical investigation." The view that children invariably suffer "has not been subjected to rigorous scientific examination." Anna Freud soon registered her doubts about "The Concept of the Rejecting Mother," as she called an article in which she complained that "the idea of rejection in its present form is imprecise, vague, and through overuse has become almost meaningless."

For experts to admit that they were not on very solid scientific ground was, of course, not entirely new. (Remember Dr. John Watson's cagey caveats: "possibly not very well grounded" was his comment on the sweeping conclusions he drew from Little Albert's ordeals.) Still, to air their perplexity, as the midcentury conferees did, marked a retreat from past pretensions. It was also a sign of new assurance, however. Helping professionals were no longer battling to carve out a niche for themselves. They had clients and public clout aplenty, and were "here to stay in spite of not yet fulfilling the wonderful promise of better mental health through better psychological child care," as Hilde Bruch, a psychoanalyst later famous for her work on anorexia, put it in her hard-boiled *Don't Be Afraid of Your Child* (1952). Modesty was an ingratiating gambit in a crowded market, designed to disarm skepticism. What is more, in shrugging off some of their commanding scientific aura, child-rearing advisers were drifting toward a potentially more encompassing role. One of the central themes of the 1950 conference, as of Spock's already phenomenal career, was that child-rearing experts had outgrown their arrogantly dogmatic ways—or should have. With his folksy tone and down-to-earth book, Dr. Spock had emerged as a novel and powerful figure with great appeal to the American imagination: the amateur expert.

This less grandiose style of popular guru was not primarily a missionary of science. He was an inspirational figure, whose postwar arrival was well timed, as the careers of Dale Carnegie and Norman Vincent Peale demonstrated. (Carnegie's *How to Stop Worrying and Start Living* and Peale's *Guide to Confident Living* were both best-sellers in 1948.) In pediatric form, this figure presided as a spokesperson for warm common sense and for youthful promise—and, like his nonmedical companions on the public podium, for confidence. In step with the power-of-positive-thinking spirit, the child-rearing expert in his new incarnation did not claim to be dispensing transcendent truths. He or she strove to be a beacon for fast-changing times, whose precepts were expressly intended to mutate in tandem with larger historical changes—as indeed child-rearing tenets clearly had so far. For that was the other revelation of the clear-eyed research undertaken in the late 1940s and early 1950s. A wave of surveys appeared of child-rearing advice trends over the century, as revealed in Children's Bureau publications and popular magazines. Their authors were led to relativist conclusions as they charted a shift from stricter to more flexible approaches. It wasn't firm data that drove child-rearing expertise, but changing social concerns that seemed to dictate its swerves and emphases.

Watson and Gesell had acknowledged the socially conditioned nature of their prescriptions. But they did not dwell on how the theories from which those prescriptions sprang were also perhaps influenced by concerns of the day, or what vista of constantly evolving counsel that implied. Now, as the conference report showed, experts made a veritable cause of proclaiming just how historically and culturally contingent child-rearing expertise had to be—especially in a country like America, in a century like the twentieth.

Erikson was out in front of the pack. The aim of socialization is to provide a child "with a conscience which will guide him without crushing him and which is firm and flexible enough to fit the vicissitudes of his historical era," he announced in *Childhood and Society*. And for vicissitudes, contemporary America could not be beat. "This dynamic country subjects its inhabitants to more extreme contrasts and abrupt changes during a lifetime or a generation than is normally the case with other great nations." Margaret Mead chimed in, proclaiming at the conference that "American children are growing up within the most rapidly changing culture of which we have any record in the world, within a culture where for several generations, each generation's experience has differed sharply from the last."

Differed except in one obvious and important way: every generation shared the awareness of change. Mead herself noted the continuity. "So longstanding and so rapid have been these processes of change that expectation of change and anxiety about change have been built into our character as a people," she announced. From the start of the century, child-rearing experts had been ambivalently addressing this restlessness in an ever more socially and geographically mobile audience, calling for calm even as they issued shifting dictates. By midcentury, their mission had undergone a subtle metamorphosis: they would keep parents company in an anxiety about social change that they now acknowledged was endemic and all too susceptible to escalating.

As *Personality in the Making* portrayed it, the new identity marked a mature step forward for experts, who had once been content merely to "tell parents what to do and how to do it" but who had become self-conscious about wielding their authority more solicitously. Given that "the prestige of the specialist is a well-recognized aspect of present-day society," it was no wonder that "parents sometimes feel threatened" by the sense that the "scientists and technicians . . . [were] about to take over." Instead, the experts' new goal was "to help parents resolve the feelings reflected in their problems, rather than merely answer their questions." As the conference report put it, "mutual study began to replace authoritative 'telling' " and what had too often gone along with that, harsh blaming. "Parent-education activities began to develop means for relieving parental anxiety," on the new understanding that "therapeutic help"—not just "instructing, imparting to parents, textbook fashion"—"has a place among services to parents."

The parallel with parental authority was all but explicit. The popular experts had become less scientific and more sympathetic models of the responsive support that mothers and fathers, in turn, were now supposed to provide their children. The paternal adviser, who had become a more demanding figure between Drs. Hall and Holt and Drs. Watson and Gesell, had given way to the attentive partner of parents. It was a role that invited more intimate relations but, as experts and mothers alike were already discovering, it did not spell liberation or ease by any means.

3.

The mother, as she emerged from Erikson's talk and from the reports of the conference, merited therapeutic commiseration—a gentler touch than the condescension and exacting expectations that had greeted her back at the Conference on Modern Parenthood. The "problem parents" of the mid-1920s, according to expert lore, had been the maladjusted product of an old-fashioned, unscientific upbringing (and of unfulfilling marital relations). Their troubles were "deep-seated," as one speaker at the Waldorf-Astoria had emphasized, since they dated back to early childhood. Especially mothers, but fathers as well, were all but doomed to repeat the worst of their parents' old-style ways, which were either overly sentimental or tyrannical. The much derided, and not easily cured, result was the overbearing mother in need of close expert supervision.

That diagnosis had been given a boost, but also a twist, during the postwar years. A loud and wide array of advertisers now joined child-rearing advisers in telling Americans that the home, threatened with marginality during the 1920s, reigned supreme in a burgeoning consumer economy. The term "nuclear family" was introduced in 1949 by the anthropologist George Murdock, who noted that in America it was "the type of family recognized to the exclusion of all others." The interwar alarm that the stifled middle-class housewife might be chafing to barge into the world of business (as the mother in Dorothy Canfield Fisher's *The Home-Maker* had been), or else to escape into bridge-playing indolence, had given way to a different mood. Amid postwar fecundity, even film stars—Joan Crawford, for example—were portrayed eagerly giving up glamour to be mothers. The American woman had been out in the working world during the war, filling in for absent men. She had not returned home to prove her skills as a cool molder or demure monitor of growth, as her interwar predecessor was supposed to do. What awaited her was billed as a subtler and more enriching endeavor. She was to be a "source of emotional security." It was her function to provide children with the "valuation [that] is essential for health of personality," as *Personality in the Making* put it. For the home, the conference report explained, was "one of the few places in which an individual can count on being valued for himself rather than for his ability."

But it was not, the conference report sympathized, an easy role to fill, precisely because in "middle-class U.S.A." young mothers could not help sensing that "it is not sufficient that they merely 'be.' " Where the problem mother of the 1920s had been portrayed as resembling a needy baby, overly dependent on her offspring, the midcentury mother who elicited professional concern was more like an unstable adolescent. There was the extreme Mom of wartime semi-popular lore, "vain in her appearance, egotistical in her demands, and infantile in her emotions," as Erikson sketched the "historical phenomenon." But behind the repressive, and emotionally repressed, specimen the experts spotted a more representative emerging type of "middle-class American married women . . . more or less dissatisfied and unsure of themselves, not certain that what they are doing is of real worth, fearful of failure in a job that is ill defined." And where her predecessor was prone to lapse into the ways of her own pre-scientific upbringing, the postwar mother felt more on her own. For this product of the Freudian 1940s was presumed to have absorbed the experts' injunction not to be cowed by her parents' child-rearing wisdom. To find fault with her elders' approach, "in one form or another," was now considered "part of the process of growing up, of becoming independent and self-reliant."

In short, although suffocating mothers had by no means disappeared from expert analyses, they had been joined by uncertain, overwhelmed mothers, usually in the same weary bodies. The birthrate had unexpectedly skyrocketed by the mid-1940s, as Americans of all classes began marrying younger and quickly producing an average of three children before they were out of their twenties; the January 1950 issue of *Parents' Magazine* hailed the start of a "Children's Decade" no one had foreseen, after a dearth of Depression-era births. The postwar mother, according to her up-to-date profilers, played a more pivotal role than ever—and one with more pitfalls than ever. In the neo-Freudian family, her dilemma went beyond arrested development: she faced an identity crisis. Meanwhile, the paternal authority crisis had come back to haunt the experts who had helped to edge Dad out of the picture in the first place. They now worried that American husbands, returned from valorous combat to feel anonymous in large corporations, often felt marginal on the home front as well, despite proddings from places like *Parents' Magazine* that "being a real father is not 'sissy' business."

The "third-generation American" was Margaret Mead's term for the midcentury middle-class specimen of uneasy parental ambition—

"always moving on, always, in his hopes, moving up, leaving behind him all that was his past." For mothers wondering how their "worried version of life compares with the average, with the normal, with those who are 'really' happy," and for fathers awaiting their moment to be "outdistanced and outmoded," Mead wrote, parenthood had "become a very special thing." It was no longer (if it ever had been) a straightforward matter of giving "their children final status and place, mooring them firmly for life in a dependable social structure," for there was no such thing. Instead, parents confronted an elusive quest to keep up with fellow Americans on "an unknown chart called 'happiness.' " Progress depended on their child's "achievements, upon the way in which he shows up against other children and against their idea of other children"—which in turn depended on their efforts to "foster and sustain [his] developing sense of individuality and worth," as *Personality in the Making* framed the maternal mission.

It guaranteed insecurity all around, which was of course just what parents and children alike needed to avoid. And as the midcentury conferees emphasized, experts were ready to acknowledge that they, too, were implicated in the anxiety—an ingratiating (if also self-aggrandizing) admission. Back at President Hoover's 1930 White House conference, there had been the first hint of alarm (aimed at Watson) about dogmatic experts intimidating parents. By 1950, advisers diagnosed themselves as perhaps a mother's number one problem. As Erikson put it, "Conflicts between mother's ways and one's own self-made ways, conflicts between the expert's advice and mother's ways, and conflicts between the expert's authority and one's own self-willed ways may disturb a mother's trust in herself," especially, he added, since she was probably already in a dither. "All the mass transformations in American life (immigration, migration and Americanization; industrialization, urbanization, mechanization, and others)," Erikson had concluded, "are apt to disturb young mothers in those tasks which are so simple yet so far-reaching."

What this self-conscious, disoriented postwar mother was judged to require was expert empathy to help her overcome the insecurity that the experts had helped create. Instead of thinking that motherhood was "a sort of final examination—and that maybe without cramming she couldn't pass," as Dr. Spock once put it in a speech, she appeared to need a course she could ace. That meant guidance targeted at mothers' hearts rather than at their heads—"an antidote to the critical, restraining influences now acting on them," as a participant in the midcentury conference put it. An approach to parenthood rooted in " 'naturalism' in acting upon one's best impulses" would surely appeal more than the "artificial, 'scientific' methods of a generation ago, which called for rigid routines and the smothering of native desire to be solicitous." Since "the absolute answers and sure directives that parents seek are nowhere available," as the conference report admitted, mothers and fathers could now be liberated by the presumably less intimidating wisdom that "children's sound development does not require specific formulas and sure directives . . . that healthy personality development is not dependent upon any particular know-how but rather, and to a far greater extent, upon parental love."

Yet it was an approach with troubles of its own, the midcentury conferees had to admit. As *Personality in the Making* acknowledged, "for a generation or more, parents have stumbled along, dissatisfied with the old ways and somewhat guilty and dubious about the new." Why should they suddenly follow the latest psychoanalytic wisdom, warm though it might sound, especially when, as the experts had noted, there was as yet no "firm scientific foundation" for the love approach, either? For that matter, who could think that answering a call to relax and be "natural" would come easily to mothers who were bundles of tension?

Certainly some of the vague formulas of a Freudian kind for mothers could be unnerving, in particular the first on the list, the importance of love in raising an emotionally healthy child. "It has been discovered that it is useless to exhort parents to be loving," the White House conference report noted, "that, moreover, such advice can be destructive to parents' self-confidence and hence harmful to children." The whole point, after all, was that the loving must be spontaneous; faked or forced affection was likely to be worse than coldness. Now that the unconscious had entered the equation, and mothers had been warned of the warring desires that lurked there, who could ever be sure what passed muster as "natural, intuitive"?

Peggy Gesell's headache as she tried to chart all those exact measurements was minor compared to the heartache that could await the mother enjoined to make sure she found authentic enjoyment, fulfillment, "profound satisfaction" in every feeding, burping, and moment of babbling. The Gesellian "household engineer," though she might chafe as a mere handmaiden to "growth," could at least sit back as a spectator of some of the swerves in her dynamo's development. The "libidinal" mother had to wonder whether her every early move might, somewhere down the road, be revealed to have been a traumatic event with indelible consequences.

"There is some danger that the new ideas will be misunderstood and misused," the authors of the conference report worried, "for they are neither easily communicated nor easily put into practice"—which did not stop some version of them from being more widely disseminated than expert ideas had ever been before. "As for parents," W. H. Auden wrote in 1952 of the Freudian generation, "not only the few who have read up on the Oedipus Complex and Erogenous Zones, but also the newspaper-reading mass, the poor things, are today scared out of their wits that they will make some terrible mistake." Yet as one mother in a workshop at the conference in 1950 made clear, the poor things were also readier to complain about their plight. "Mothers are not ready for all the psychology and psychiatry they're expected to practice on their children," she announced. "There's no stability in us. We jump from one feeling to another and end up feeling completely inadequate." If she sounded disoriented, it was possible to detect a note of defiance, or at any rate impatience, too.

In a scene in her novel *The Group* (1954), Mary McCarthy captured the peculiar conjunction of over-dependence on experts and restless erosion of deference toward them that she already sensed a decade earlier among the most precociously enlightened maternal set. Two Vassar-educated mothers sat on a Central Park bench in 1939, swapping child-rearing expertise. And what a confusing catalogue of wisdom they invoked, all of it supposedly cutting edge! Priss Crockett, the wife of an up-and-coming pediatrician, had been buffeted by conflicting advice ever since two-year-old Stephen's birth. Her confidence in herself, and in the experts, was shaken. Still, she eagerly invoked Gesell. "When he publishes his findings in p-p-popular form," she informed her classmate Norine Schmittlapp, her nervous stammer emerging, "every mother will have a y-yardstick." But Norine was not impressed. With her infant sunning naked and sucking lustily on a pacifier in his carriage, she looked to be, and sounded, a decade ahead of her time. "I know Gesell's work," Norine yawned. "He's a fossil relic of behaviorism."

Norine was already well on her way to relegating the founder of psychoanalysis to the dustbin, too. "Most of Freud's out of date," she told Priss (who had been meaning to read him, and was relieved to think perhaps she could cross that off her list). "Not that I don't owe a lot to Freud," Norine duly added, but she currently subscribed to the anthropological approach. Invoking a cross-cultural perspective, she scoffed at Priss's toilet-training panic. Why get upset that Stephen (admirably "regular" in every other way, Priss proudly reported) refused to cooperate on the "toidey-seat"? The American emphasis on early cleanliness was unknown among primitive peoples. Her son Ichabod would "give up his anal pleasures" under peer pressure in nursery school, Norine announced. "Have you read Margaret Mead?" she asked. "A great woman, that."

Educated mothers, as McCarthy depicted them, were running through child-rearing dictums the way their babies ran through diapers. A potentially problematic type seemed to characterize "advanced" midcentury motherhood: the expert amateur, fervent but fickle in her allegiance to child-rearing advisers, and therefore prone to getting frustrated and confused. Certainly the expert-approved mission of motherhood had become murkier than ever before. Mothers were supposed to be the emotional bulwark in a complex family relationship that was the key to a healthy society, not just a healthy personality. The many tensions that Watson and Gesell had skimmed over had become an earnest topic of discussion, for the challenge of meeting contradictory demands was now considered the essence of "the American identity," as Erikson titled a chapter in *Childhood and Society*. "The functioning American, as the heir of a history of extreme contrasts and abrupt changes," he wrote, "bases his final ego identity on some tentative combination of dynamic polarities such as migratory and sedentary, individualistic and standardized, competitive and co-operative, pious and freethinking, responsible and cynical, etc."

To help give a child such an identity, a mother must strike a balance herself—"be a genuine person in a genuine milieu" was the delphic way Erikson put it at the conference. "This, today, is difficult because rapid changes in the milieu," he explained, are so disorienting and because "psychiatric thinking," he acknowledged, "sees the world so full of dangers that it is hard to relax one's caution at every step." A writer in *Parents' Magazine* in 1950 was more impatient, convinced that dithering was just what neither mother nor child needed. The spectacle of parents "unable to take the responsibility for being grown-up and making decisions" was bad enough, and it was compounded by adults then feeling "despairing and frustrated because the child won't do what the parent never told him to do in the first place—never told him and meant it, that is." It was hardly a way to build the trust all the experts talked about so much. "Why should a child have to go mining around in the caverns of your mind to discover what you expect of him?"

The difficulty, of course, was that the American mother was not sure what she was supposed to expect of him—or of herself. As Erikson went on at the conference, it is "hard to know whether one must be genuine *against* a changing milieu or whether one may hope for a chance to do one's bit in the way of bettering or stabilizing conditions." A vision of a smooth fit between home and world beckoned more strongly than ever, yet "suddenly and for no plain reason the women of the United States [were] seized with an eerie restlessness," according to a 1949 issue of *Life* magazine. The very "stampede to the suburbs" and the incessant trumpeting of the split-level ideal of family togetherness—all those articles in the women's magazines whose titles Betty Friedan later cited in *The Feminine Mystique*, from "Femininity Begins at Home" to "Are You Training Your Daughter to Be a Wife?"—suggested strains in the postwar vision of all-consuming motherhood and domesticity. And the experts, it was quite clear from the discussions of the voguish field of socialization research at the White House conference, were on edge and ambivalent themselves about what goals were to guide American mothers.

"Social adjustment," that watchword of the interwar period, now failed to convey an adequate sense of dynamism and interaction; it sounded staid. One of the women living in Park Forest, Illinois, the midcentury suburb William Whyte studied in *The Organization Man*, explained that "the best adjusted people are the ones who are constantly adjusting." The term of the day was "adaptability," the key attribute of the "healthy personality" primed not only to keep up in a world "geared to change" but also to fit into "increasingly complex and centralized systems of economic and political organization," without losing "autonomy in the form of independence and initiative in the form of enterprise," as Erikson put it. For in the more bureaucratic America of the consumerist era, "an increasing number of social and economic activities calls for team play rather than individual competition," *Personality in the Making* emphasized. "There is a trend toward managing people rather than managing things."

The rules for readying children for the newly group-oriented game were in flux, raising questions as to "whether the kind of people the country most needs are the kind" produced by "traditional" mothers still enamored of the old American virtue of "self-sufficiency," or by more "psychological" mothers concerned with adaptability and "fitting in." "On this point no one can be certain," the midcentury conference report decided, although in *The Lonely Crowd*, published in 1950, David Riesman suggested that the question was moot. He ruefully argued that a new kind of people had already begun to appear: the "inner-directed" individual was being eclipsed by the "outer-directed" type, whose compass in life was set—and constantly reset—to conform to the attitudes and desires of his contemporaries.

No wonder *Cheaper by the Dozen*, the memoir of one large clan's well-oiled interwar upbringing as told by a now grown son and daughter, was a best-selling book in 1949 and a hit on screen in 1950. The filial tribute to family efficiency blended the old-style by-the-chart mentality and methods with more up-to-date togetherness—and was funny. The industrial management experts Frank and Lillian Gilbreth, a gruff and a gentle duo, and their brood of twelve seemed to have had the best of both worlds: paternal fiat and family councils, individuality and group solidarity, rationality and plenty of room for rascality—"a document of American life at its best," exclaimed the Hollywood director in an article in *Parents' Magazine*. Precisely what Frank Gilbreth, Jr., and Ernestine Gilbreth Carey nostalgically evoked—a secure harmony between autonomy and conformity, between authority and equality—beckoned as the goal that eluded the American home. And Lillian Gilbreth managed the feat of being a fun-loving mother, an adored wife, and—as the movie announced in closing—an industrial engineer who was voted America's woman of the year in 1948.

No such vision coalesced in *Personality in the Making*, which struggled to formulate the amorphous mission of postwar parenthood. "All in all, then, what the predominant type of American family seems most to need in order to promote the well-being of children (and seems to be in the process of securing) is a revised conception of American values, a conception that is in line with current social realities rather than with past American history." Parents, like experts, had to keep up with change, or as Erikson put it in his book, always be "reflecting changing cultural prototypes and institutions." And the report went on in the most abstract vein: "This new conception would stress cooperation and mutual appreciation, consideration for the emotional as well as the rational aspects of life, respect for weakness as well as for strength." It was intended as a recipe for that all-important midcentury American virtue, security. For this conception "would provide a firmer basis for trust, would make of American autonomy and initiative a less selfish thing, and would introduce into American life that sense of intimacy which is at present so rare a personal possession."

Personality in the Making did not use the term that had entered the child-rearing lexicon with the baby boom of 1946, but the psychoanalyst Hilde Bruch supplied it as she summed up the ethos of the day, according to which parents "plan the education of their child from the well-balanced diet to the equally well-balanced ratio between discipline and giving in to the child, now called in psychological lingo,

'permissiveness.' " Freshly minted, the term evoked vistas of new harmony, which was certainly what the report did its best to hold out to
mothers. Farewell to the old complaints about " 'boredom' . . . with
household tasks, the perplexities of child rearing, the lack of appreciation on the part of husbands, the sexual dissatisfaction, the ingratitude
of children," *Personality in the Making* promised. "These new attitudes
toward and about children and the new ways of rearing them make the
mother's job a more rewarding one." Insight, in the dryly intellectual
sense it had been taken during the heyday of educated motherhood,
was no longer the goal she should strive for. Nor could she rely on
mere instinct. Child rearing was advertised as an exciting "challenge to
her ingenuity."

Indeed it was. She was no longer supposed to be instilling habits in
her child, behaviorist style. Nor could she simply be guided by the child
and by tidy norms. She was, whether she liked it or not, a role model, a
guiding presence in her child's conscious and unconscious life, Freud
taught, and the key was to preside gently and without incurring (or
feeling) too much guilt. Furthermore, she was supposed to do that
without expecting detailed guidance from the experts. Instead, "the
rules of the new child-rearing scheme are few and not very explicit."

Except for one all-important rule, which was not to be anxious. The
call to calm, although hardly a new message, had become the ironic
centerpiece of prescriptive lore. Don't be anxious, the experts anxiously
insisted. The irony was not lost on Erikson. He noted that the directive
was as futile as it was popular—and he suggested that might in fact be
why it was so popular. He didn't mean that experts were cynically feeding maternal fears that kept child-rearing advisers in business (though
some surely were: there were ever more "demi-professionals . . . ,
starry-eyed disciples and uncritical crusaders and new converts . . .
plain charlatans and fakes," as Hilde Bruch lamented). The experts, as
Erikson saw it, were reflecting a widespread uneasiness.

After all, parents were not simply dupes of specialists; they were the
market that determined their success. Intimidated though mothers
might be by experts, *Personality in the Making* pointed out, "they have
always been the ones to determine when they should seek help and what
they should do with the advice given to them." And family advice, to say
nothing of "intuitive, nonverbal knowledge gained through life itself,"
was not so easily supplanted by "outside" sources. An expert's popularity depended on a palatable message, one that was responsive to his
audience's desires. American parents, Erikson astutely judged, in some

sense wanted to feel anxious—and to have their experts confirm them in that mood, not necessarily cure them of it.

"At present there is a tendency to try to talk people out of their anxiety," he observed, yet it was an uphill task. "Saying now that science has shown that you don't have to be anxious will not change the tendency of people to develop anxiety or to interpret it; in certain cases and at certain times whatever you say will be interpreted in such a way that a sense of guilt is produced in order to gratify a need to feel guilty." Erikson proposed a broad analysis of this self-punishing impulse. "It seems quite obvious that the kind of anxiety which parents feel about the way they handle their children has sources outside of their immediate relation to the child."

More than personal psychology and conniving experts were at work making American parents feel so unsettled about child rearing. "It has to do with their own past," Erikson thought; "it has to do with work conditions and with social changes such as, let us say, the lessened reassurance gained from religious doctrines, for it is partially from religious doctrines that people have transferred their wish to have things stated clearly, to be made to feel guilt, and then be reassured in that very guilt—or be punished." Another member of the Fact Finding Committee of the midcentury conference, the psychologist Sibylle Escalona, pursued the same analysis in historical rather than spiritual terms, suggesting that the masochistic worry about child rearing was best understood as expiation and remedy for Americans' chastened sense of the destructive power of human irrationality. Two world wars, among other things, had eroded adult confidence that "technical mastery" could assure a stable future.

Yet "to make many of the recommended child-rearing practices the vehicle of our group anxieties and collective guilt," Escalona pointed out, was likely to backfire. In worriedly striving to eliminate frustration and aggression—the irrational behavior that had blighted the century—adults could not help "burden[ing] children with our historically and socially understandable terrors and uncertainties." And given the new vision of the child, that was a heavy burden indeed. For where Watson's child was at least theoretically retrainable and Gesell's would have gone on with his growing, the postwar conception of the child suggested that he would nurse profound feelings of mistrust for a very long time, very deep down.

4.

The image of the "problem child" had dominated discussions among experts and parents during the 1920s and 1930s. Every child was one, at least potentially, and every parent was a problem child, too. Since then, a notable change had taken place. To be an adult was, almost by definition in the age of anxiety, to be a problem. Or at any rate, it was an arduous challenge—the challenge of being engaged in an ongoing Eriksonian struggle of ego development within a complex society. What was perhaps even more striking was that every child was now envisaged as a problem adult, too—a problem adult with less experience than actual adults, but with the potential to negotiate the many struggles along the way more smoothly than big people had so far managed.

This shift was an ironic one, happening as it did in an era that specially prided itself on abandoning a traditional "adult-centered" view of child rearing for a "child-focused" approach to family life. *Personality in the Making* lauded "those who have come to recognize that childhood is not just adulthood in miniature." But then, in the very same breath, the report declared that the enlightened way to look at children was to see them as small humans on a purposeful quest, one that sounded very similar to their elders' endeavors. It was time to move beyond the description of mere motor skills and basic behavior, the Gesellian emphasis on "what." Now the goal was to plumb motives, the "why." At every stage of a child's life, "one is purblind if one sees, and so takes into account, only what the child now characteristically does. It is essential also to understand from this what he now characteristically seeks."

As it turned out, "the strivings characteristic of each successive level of development" were ageless. For the most that could be said of adults was that they "have, to some greater extent, brought these strivings closer to resolution, for better or for worse." What is more, children were prone to stumble for the same reason. The worry was, what else, worry—just as it was for adults. By the early 1940s, even the un-Freudian Gesell had stressed children's need for a sense of security. In postwar expertise, helping children deal with anxiety had become the overriding goal. "Human childhood is long," Erikson observed. ". . . This long childhood exposes the child to grave anxieties and to a lasting sense of insecurity which, if unduly and senselessly intensified, persists in the adult in the form of vague anxiety—anxiety which, in turn, contributes specifically to the tension of personal, political, and even international life."

Thus contrary to conventional wisdom, the century-long quest to deal with children "in their own right"—to give them their due and their full dignity—has meant closing the gap between them and grownups. An infantilizing view of adults abetted the convergence at first, but by midcentury the emphasis had shifted to crediting children with the (newly malleable) contours of maturity. The psychoanalyst Hilde Bruch was among the few to note the irony. "The reproach raised against past ages is that children were looked upon as little adults and their specific needs were not fulfilled," she wrote. "Yet much of what goes on now under the name of 'psychological insight' is nothing more but a reading-in of some theoretical notions or adult feelings and passions into the child's behavior."

Freud was obviously the most important force at work. By the 1940s, when psychoanalytic lore was rapidly spreading on the popular level, it left its mark on ideas about normal children, not just neurotic mothers. Endow preschoolers with sexual and aggressive drives, Oedipal struggles, and anxiety, and suddenly they acquire a more sophisticated aura. Add to that the emerging neo-Freudian focus on the role of culture, not simply the family drama, in shaping personality, and children start to resemble little anthropologists, mini "participant-observers" busy making sense of their intricate milieu.

For understandable reasons, the socially precocious portrait of childhood proved more palatable than the sexually precocious one. Freudian libidinal drives tended to take a back seat to psychosocial urges of the ego. Thus *Personality in the Making* explained that the child "began to be conceived no longer as a self-contained entity or even as the clean slate of an earlier day . . . but rather as a social being, the product of interchange between himself and his environment." A lyrical description followed of small explorers at work the world over, each "interacting with a different cultural environment." The child is constantly "experiencing, learning, acquiring new meanings and new ways of reacting to situations because of the new meanings," especially in America, thanks to its distinctively "diverse and complex" culture.

The emphasis on interpersonal, rather than sexual, development was even more pronounced in *A Healthy Personality for Your Child*, an illustrated pamphlet for parents derived from conference wisdom, which was published by the Children's Bureau. The process was also simplified. In the booklet, "your youngster" was portrayed as having "one big hunger" at every stage, and having sex with Mother or Father was not noted as one of them. Instead, the child was pictured working methodically to achieve "a feeling that his world is O.K." (the "trust" stage), and then a "good, strong, firm feeling of I-I-I" (the autonomy phase), followed by Erikson's other stages of initiative, industry, and finally identity formation. These drives were portrayed as manageable, moderate, and very pro-social, given the right handling by parents.

Proper handling, the rather circular logic went, entailed viewing those drives as manageable, moderate, and sociable—and not, by implication, as dangerous (sexual) urges in need of repressing. "He is the one who has the wants and urges inside of him. You side with him. You believe in him. You back him up in what he is after—or else those wants and urges are likely to go awry." The *Infant Care* manuals from the early 1940s to the early 1950s echoed this message. Treat masturbation as a mere expression of babies' desire "to handle and investigate everything that they can see and reach"—the infant researcher, in other words—and all is well. So with thumb-sucking; children are easily distracted by "other interests" from indulging their oral drives. (And remember, *Parents' Magazine* missed no opportunity to counsel its readers—in articles with titles like "Don't Be Afraid of Strong Feelings" and "What Every Baby Needs"—"even we grownups have our ways of getting mouth-satisfaction." The baby who, upon seeing her uncle puffing away on his pipe, cried out "baba" for bottle had it all figured out.) Bowel training was an opportunity to teach cooperation and to encourage autonomy, not a locus of competition or coercion.

With her usual astuteness, Mary McCarthy conveyed the midcentury mother's apprehensions about the newly mature image of the child, especially her eagerness to block out the leering little Freudian as much as possible. Priss's Stephen, exposed to the "advanced" environment of Norine's apartment, was simultaneously confronted with Ichabod's buxom nurse and a big piece of "chocolate cake, from a Jewish bakery"—two pleasures heretofore unknown in his narrowly wholesome life. He responded with alacrity, particularly to the breasts. As for choosing between the temptations, the flustered Priss hurriedly opted for broadening his cultural horizons and deflecting his sexual curiosity. She shoved the exotic cake into the hand that had a moment before "plunged . . . into the neck of [the nurse's] dress."

Norine's heroine, Margaret Mead, was herself rearing a daughter during the 1940s according to cutting-edge wisdom, and for her, too, psychosocial drives took precedence over psychosexual ones. Unlike Priss, she was supremely confident as she adopted methods designed to raise a culturally flexible child, who would at the same time be free of sexual conflicts. Through the all-important trust-building stage of the first two years, Mead prided herself on being a pioneer in pursuing the infant-driven synchrony deemed crucial to ensuring a sense of security—even if, as some of her associates noted with amusement, the anthropologist-mother was not always quite as assiduous in accommodating baby Mary Catherine's rhythms as she liked to claim. The story of her daughter's birth, under spotlights, made the rounds. Mead arranged to have the event filmed by the psychologist Myrtle McGraw, one of a crowd of expert onlookers that included Dr. Spock, whom she had lined up as her pediatrician. That a newborn specialist in the entourage, on hand to diagnose the baby's inborn temperament, judged it "on the quiet side" and advised "as little occasion as possible to cry" did not save the infant from being "poked and tickled, bent and dangled, howling and finally exhausted." As for Mead's insistence on "adjust[ing] the feeding schedule to the baby instead of the clock," she could sometimes be readier with her boasts than with her breasts, McGraw recollected. Mead once agreed to attend a neuroscience conference, stipulating one condition: a limo to bring her eight-month-old daughter along for her demand feedings. Mead then schmoozed late into the night, never pausing to dispense milk, and finally sent car, child, and nurse back to the city without her.

With her father, Gregory Bateson, away during much of the war and Mead traveling constantly, Mary Catherine was soon ensconced in "a complex household with much coming and going" in Greenwich Village. In arranging a home for herself and her daughter in an extended family presided over by her friend Lawrence Frank, Mead aimed to kill at least two birds with one stone. The author of the famous *Coming of Age in Samoa* (1928) had come away from her study of purportedly storm-and-stress-free South Sea island maturation eager to "avoid the tightness of bonding to a single caretaker that so often provides the ground of an entire neurotic system," as her daughter explained it in her memoir. But Mead had an even higher priority than sparing her child the Oedipal jealousies she felt were rife in nuclear families. Growing up in an arrangement more like the "great households" of Samoa, Mead believed, was ideal for spurring her child to develop that "most important characteristic . . . —adaptability to different kinds of people and situations." In addition, of course, the setup also freed Mead to pursue her often far-flung work.

Far from mainstream though many of her practices were, Mead nonetheless exemplified the interpersonal and neo-Freudian vision of

personality development in children that went on to be widely
espoused in midcentury expertise. And Cathy was the perfect specimen
of confidently acculturating youth, or at least she was presented that
way by her mother—and presented herself that way to the experts and
cameras that had been ubiquitous in her life from the start. She was
indeed the poised little participant-observer among the luminaries who
gathered at the Franks' New Hampshire house in the course of the
1940s. In that voluble village—regularly visited by the Eriksons and the
Lynds (of Middletown fame), among many others—Cathy maneuvered
unerringly among the manpower available. When she cut her foot one
day, and had a choice of first-aid assistance, the six-year-old anthropologist knew just which elder to turn to: "Daddy is good with nature, but
Uncle Larry is better with wounds."

Cathy's healthy display of autonomy, initiative, and industry was presumably proof that she had successfully negotiated that formative first
struggle between trust and mistrust. But Mead herself admitted that it
was not as easy to assess progress through these Freudian-based phases
of childhood as it was to demonstrate Watsonian reflexes, or to trace
the journey through, say, Gesell's stages. And she knew because she had
tried. Mead set out several times to capture on film the new core of the
child's personality, trust, using her resident exemplar of the quality. It
was a difficult feat, she acknowledged. "Fear and rage are easy to photograph, but trust is not." In her final effort, the scene was a pediatric
exam, with her three-year-old daughter as the patient and star.

> Cathy was chosen to portray the child because she was so unfright-
> ened and so accustomed to photography. But no one considered
> the response of the pediatrician. The film turned into a sequence
> in which Cathy, smiling and nude, put the pediatrician, who was
> shaking with stage fright, at his ease. But the film was never used.

For in truth, no film could really capture the postwar portrait of childhood, which had not only become a longer interlude than ever before
but had also acquired a new depth. Gesell had doggedly tracked the
forces of growth at work in frame after straightforward frame, making
the emerging motor skills of the early years the emblem of all development. ("Behavior grows. Mind manifests itself," was his motto.) Examiners and parents were skimmed over by his camera, their role and the
child's response to them played down.

But the light had changed. The child's relationships to "persons
strategic in his emotional life," as the midcentury conference report put

it, were now considered crucial to personality making, and the intimate drama that unfolded was one that eluded the lens. For the most revolutionary Freudian suggestion was that it was children's own vantage on those relationships that mattered most of all, and that they felt more than they could, or would, say or than those strategic persons, particularly parents, could readily imagine. As Hilde Bruch noted, "children always impress me as uncanny in their ability to respond not to the overt act but to the underlying emotional attitudes."

Margaret Mead, undaunted though she was in her child-rearing experiments (as in her anthropological exploits, too), expressed humility in the face of this multi-dimensioned understanding of childhood. She admitted that she could not adequately account for her sturdy daughter. "How much was temperament? How much was felicitous accident? How much could be attributed to upbringing? We may never know. Certainly all a mother and father can claim credit for is that they have not marred a child in any recognizable way." And she closed by acknowledging in passing what cold comfort that might be: after all, parents may always be left wondering whether they have perhaps done unrecognized harm. "For the total adult-child situation could be fully understood," she observed, "only if one also had the child's own interpretation of the parts that adults played in its life."

That Mead was not unnerved but instead trusted that she had tried her best, her daughter later mused, distinguished her from the anxious specimens of postwar maternity whom the anthropologist, along with the other midcentury conferees, feared were proliferating all around them. And her confidence probably helped ensure that Mary Catherine weathered the vagaries of her rearing as well as she did. For, as Erikson warned, "you cannot fool children." They would pick up on false feelings, and were particularly astute in sensing when anxiety lurked behind a show of assurance.

To build trust, you must be trustworthy. If you are not—or even if you are just honestly uneasy—your all-seeing (mistrustful) child can make you feel even guiltier. And so can even the most comforting and forgiving of experts, Dr. Spock was discovering from mothers as the 1950s began. Erikson spoke too soon when he suggested at the Fact Finding Committee meeting of the White House conference that the expert "does not have the time to become the father-confessor for all the doubts and fears, angers and arguments which can fill the minds of lonely young parents." That was the long-running role that, in the wake of the first edition of his book, Dr. Spock was preparing to play.

Or perhaps surrogate husband–confessor was more like it. For Dr.

Spock had discovered that the down-to-earth intimacy of his book had not only won him a huge audience, but emboldened readers to talk back—about their own difficulties, and also about what they did and didn't like about his advice. He couldn't just listen, aloof behind the screen of his fame and expertise. He would make it his business to try to respond to those maternal doubts and fears, angers and arguments more forthrightly and more flexibly than any adviser ever had.

What Dr. Spock offered was what no expert before him had aspired to, and what parents were to supply to their children as well: a "friendly but firm" bond that would last but ideally not bind too tightly. The bond was based on at least the pretense of equality, and its main claim to authority was empathy. Dr. Spock had just what it took. For the man revered as an icon of reassurance actually thought of himself as an emblem of American insecurity. The most famous child-rearing adviser of all time still wasn't entirely sure of his identity. And in 1950 he was on the brink of a series of symptomatic crises that shaped his work over the next several decades in ever more public ways. Never mind reliable experiments, this expert had the experience that equipped him perfectly to play the paradoxical role of anti-expert. He made it look easy, but he and his book were both in fact full of anxiety, and this was the secret of their ongoing success.

EIGHT

The Therapist

Dr. Benjamin Spock with his son Michael

I.

A child born in the middle of the baby boom might be forgiven for getting Dr. Spock and Dr. Seuss mixed up. It seemed somehow possible that the cat with a striped stovepipe who bossed the kids in the beloved beginner book also inhabited the well-thumbed paperback that told parents what to do. America's lanky, legendary pediatric expert as the Cat in the Hat: the image links two upstart heroes in the postwar generation's pantheon. The mothers of baby boomers learned to rear us with one, while we learned to read from the other—and both lessons were billed as a liberation from the old, dull methods. When Dr. Benjamin Spock's book arrived on the scene in 1946, mothers could throw their daily charts away. Thanks to the cat a decade later, children could escape the monotony of "See Spot run."

Here were two mother's helpers with bags of tricks that promised to blur work and fun, freedom and responsibility, for housebound Americans big and small.

Millions of middle-class parents in the late 1940s and 1950s—and lots of less well-off ones, too—fell head over heels for their Dr. S. Some were so attached to *Baby and Child Care* that they kept copies all over the house—and even in the glove compartment. No other child-rearing guru could compare, much less compete, with him. For the first time in a century, American parenting expertise did not feature polarized advisers striving for popular and scientific stature. One expert monopolized mothers, and it was his relaxed manner, rather than any rigorous data, that was his selling point. Dr. Spock had an amazing gift for juggling the many demands of life with children, and for sounding jaunty and gentle as he did it. An infatuated follower spoke for millions when she exclaimed, "He's as sympathetic and understanding as a woman, that wonderful man!"

Dr. Spock was the confiding companion whom suburbanizing mothers yearned for, living as they did miles away from their parents and a well-manicured lawn away from everyone else. And unlike an in-law or a nosy neighbor, America's first truly pop Freudian urged mothers to loosen up and get in touch with their feelings and their children's. Meanwhile, the other Dr. S was conjuring up a thrilling (and terrifying) babysitter who swept in when Mom slipped out for a moment. The Cat in the Hat, hardly your ordinary nanny, defied adults and joined Spock in introducing us—and our parents—to our libidinal urges. (Scan the classic with a Freudian eye, and you might think twice about what Mother may be up to and why "Sally and I" are so anxious about playing with Thing One and Thing Two.)

These doctors, or men, or cats (they were protean, and they purred) so quickly made themselves at home that Americans, young and old, felt that we had invited them in. They spoke intimately, right into mothers' and children's ears and to their deepest desires and fears. The Dr. S's understood the illicit and fantastic forces that lurked beneath the prosaic surface of domestic relations. They were familiar with cold, cold wet days, and with the worries about being trapped and about being abandoned that gathered in the damp for children and for mothers. Their whiskered voices conveyed an awareness that the fathers who came and went, newspapers under their arms, seemed to lack. The counselors-on-call implicitly acknowledged the boredom, loneliness, frustration, potential chaos of life at home. And they explicitly encouraged dreams of fulfilling fun and confident control—of words, of kids.

By the turn of the millennium, when Seuss-spawned fabulists and Spock-inspired parenting books and Web sites abounded, the Dr. S's had acquired the status of stalwarts rather than upstarts. But even at the outset, they were not as subversive or revolutionary as they seemed. Wildly popular figures rarely are. Dr. Spock was riding a wave, not boldly bucking a behaviorist tide, with the book that sold phenomenally well its first year, without any advertising. As the *American Journal of Public Health* put it, *Baby and Child Care* was seen to "typify the present-day departure from rigidity in schedules and training." Its author, the review marveled, "has succeeded to an amazing degree in striking a middle ground in his advice." Where Watson and Gesell had veered to extremes, Spock headed straight for the vital center.

Dr. Spock, like Dr. Seuss, was immediately appealing because he was a spokesman not simply for emotional and imaginative spontaneity, but also for the anxiety such invitations to freedom stirred up, in children and in the grownups raising them. Dr. Spock joined Dr. Seuss in making room for fantasy—often frightening—in the psyches of the young, and of their parents. ("Sally and I," eyes popping and mouths gaping while the cat creates mayhem, are portraits of panic.) Yet they also insisted that everybody come to terms with reality—and, more than that, develop a sense of mastery and of social morality. (The cat leaves everything very tidy.) These solicitous doctors, chatty and funny though they could be, were very serious.

In fact, they were models of a new kind of grownup authority: they were wonderfully friendly instead of cool or harsh, their signature warmth nonetheless shot through with more worry than ever. Dr. Spock was not quite the calming—or calm—figure suggested by his opening mantra, "Trust yourself. You know more than you think you do." His real métier, as was becoming clear by midcentury, was ministering to parental uneasiness. And that turned out to mean sharing rather than curing it.

The confidence that Dr. Spock prescribed in 1946 in a tone of such "remarkable ease and matter-of-factness" was not the whole story. Within the famously anodyne manual, Erik Erikson pointed out at the Midcentury White House Conference, lurked a Freudian drama of family insecurity. "There is an indication of the sinister forces which are leashed and unleashed, especially in the guerrilla warfare of unequal wills," he noted, "for the child is often unequal to his own violent drives, and parent and child unequal to each other." As if that weren't unsettling enough, the runaway success of the book soon suggested that parents were unequal to experts as well: mothers clung to the very adviser who told them, "Don't be overawed by what the experts say"—only to be left feeling, if anything, guiltier than ever that they weren't measuring up.

It was enough to make an ingratiating expert like Dr. Spock feel guilty along with them. He was conscience-stricken, he confessed, by an aggrieved letter from one of his myriad disciples in the early 1950s. "Don't you realize that when you always emphasize that a child basically wants to behave well, and will behave well if he is handled wisely, you make the parent feel responsible for everything that goes wrong?" a mother in Texas wrote in distress. "Perhaps some people wouldn't get that feeling. But I do; and it is more burdensome and discouraging and oppressive than I can ever express. Can't you see that a parent is a human being, too?" Closer to home, Spock's wife was on the verge of a breakdown, feeling discouraged and oppressed herself—and she was expressing it. Meanwhile, the warm academic welcome that had been extended to the popular superstar was cooling. Behind closed doors, America's adored adviser was in crisis.

By 1957, when Dr. Spock's revised primer appeared amid Sputnik panic, an optimistic manual about children naturally achieving self-control had become a warier, well-timed book for grownups fearful of losing control—by a grownup who knew the feeling well. The "soft," child-centered Dr. Spock emerged as his own "hard," parent-centered counterpart: an odd couple all by himself. It had been his personal coming-of-age saga, rather than batches of lab data, that had guided him from the start of work on his original edition. "I never looked at my records," Spock once admitted—a fitting approach for a man whose motto was "Trust yourself. You know more than you think you do." Nor did he bother with "a lot of looking into things and how other books have been written in the past," he maintained. "It really all came out of my head." And it continued to come out of his head, and his anxious gut, as America's peerless expert met an intimidating challenge: coming up with a second act.

What Dr. Spock found within were doubts that growing up could be the idyll he had yearned for as a boy, or that parents could be the naturally confident role models he had promised in his buoyant *Common Sense Book of Baby and Child Care* in 1946. In fact, the seeds of doubt had already been there in that first edition, beneath a pastoral scene of boyhood bliss conjured up by a man straining to exorcise the ghosts of a childhood he felt had been fraught with tensions. But the doubts had blossomed by the time Spock produced his 1957 revision, after a decade of turmoil that he kept hidden behind a classic postwar facade of "permissive" ease and stability at home and at work. He now tried to reckon more realistically with maternal (and, in passing, paternal) anxiety and family disharmony—and with mounting ambivalence about his own expert authority. The son of Mildred Spock had been reared for the role.

2.

Benjamin McLane Spock was born in 1903 in New Haven, Connecticut, into a socially and professionally successful family. By the standards of his expert predecessors—a pair of farm boys bent on the big city, followed by a southerner and a German-American forging their way into the mainstream—the respectable urban northeasterner had already arrived before he had begun. Young Spock, the first of six children—three sisters, a brother, and another sister followed—had a sense of privilege pressed upon him early. His mother, Mildred Stoughton Spock, made much of her high-toned Yankee lineage, which featured Puritan moralists, military heroes, and prosperous bankers, lawyers, and businessmen. (Secular fervor had replaced spiritual zeal early on.) His father, Benjamin Ives Spock, had risen from modest middle-class origins to excel at Yale, and had since worked his way up to general counsel for the New York and New Haven Railroad. A diligent lawyer, Mr. Spock was a pillar of the community, a member of various boards of directors. He was an opera buff, too.

But being born to privilege, of course, has its own pressures; the insider's fear of falling can be as unnerving as the outsider's scramble to make it. In fact, Spock's parents were acutely aware of the precariousness of their position, and although they did their post-Victorian best to repress it, a spirit of insecurity prevailed within their drafty household. His mother's snobbery concealed a trauma. Her father, Charles Bradley Stoughton, had been a drunken rake who brought ignominy to the family. After indulging his infidelities and disappearances for years, his wife, Ada, retreated into bitterness when he finally abandoned her. Her children, whom she raised with ample help from her well-off Bostonian kin, bore the brunt of her fierce rages and icy distance.

Ada's moralistic daughter Mildred felt especially shamed—and confirmed in her moralism. Determined to avoid her mother's fate, she sacrificed pedigree for stolidity and married Benjamin I. Spock (whose relatives she refused to visit). He in turn understood the price he paid for his well-bred, strong-willed wife: he never strayed from the line of duty, which was to be dogged at work and docile at home. And so the past, with a twist, repeated itself. Mildred ruled the roost as fiercely as Ada had—but far more intrusively—and she daunted her six children, especially her favorite firstborn, Benny, with dire warnings about sex.

Thanks to psychoanalytic training, temperament, and the temper of the times in which he made his uneasy way to maturity, Benjamin Spock spent a great deal of energy probing the symptoms of what should by now sound like a veritable occupational malady among America's most popular child-rearing experts: the mother's boy syndrome (or the fear of it). His forerunners (with the exception of his precocious fellow Freudian Dr. Hall) had politely, and self-protectively, kept any insecurity inspired by their mothers mostly under wraps. Spock the earnest analysand made diffidence the key to his character and his career, and his mother the key to his diffidence.

His first analyst, Bertram Lewin in 1932, had prodded him to confront the shadowy presence of his father, who had recently died of a heart attack. For Dr. Spock, it was a revelation to discover how much he had felt betrayed by the meek man. The same father remembered by his daughters as "cozy" had been remote with his namesake, conveying silent disapproval and rarely praise. Perhaps worse than his failure to shore up his unassuming son, that son decided, was his failure to shield him from his mother. Yet the analysis had an abstract, intellectual quality for Spock. Won over by the idea of Oedipal struggle, Spock had never dared wage it against his undemonstrative father—and still didn't. On the couch, he was as unable as ever either to defy or to identify with the remote figure. The obvious similarities between them brought clarity but no catharsis: father and son were both Mildred Spock's cowed factotums, obeying and never rebelling and always feeling that they didn't quite measure up.

It was Mildred Spock who dominated her adult son's psychoanalysis, because she had dominated his childhood and also because she perfectly fit the maternal profile that fascinated Spock's second analyst, a Hungarian émigré named Sandor Rado. Spock always said he chose Rado in 1937 out of a need for a forceful father figure who could help him overcome a sense of uncertainty about who he was and what he believed. "Sandor Rado gave the impression of being an unusually assertive person," he recalled later. "I hoped to acquire assertiveness by going to an assertive psychoanalyst." In fact, what he found was a Freudian revisionist who assigned the mother, rather than the father, the crucial role in the creation of the child's conscience—a shift of emphasis tailor-made for America, a nation renowned not for Viennese-style patriarchs but for attentive mothers.

Well ahead of the curve on the maternal "overprotection" craze, Rado had written an essay called "An Anxious Mother" in 1927 in which he discovered aggression and narcissism at work in super "conscientious" mothering. Dr. Spock was relieved to feel that at last he had found a diagnosis that fit his predicament—that helped explain his domineering mother and, just as important, rescued him from the great fear that his was a uniquely peculiar plight. In the essay, Rado portrayed a mother whose blend of intense devotion and fierce discipline echoed Mildred Spock's style, and his interpretation helped make sense of contradictions that had bewildered Ben Spock. "She tormented the child in spite of, or rather precisely with, her infatuated love," Rado commented on his case study, arguing that the mother's harsh vigilance allowed her "ego [to wallow] in its hyper-morality," even as she gratified "her secret pleasure in aggression." Meanwhile, the child of such a mother raged and cringed within. He was riven by guilt and desires for revenge, Rado diagnosed, desperate to please and dying to escape.

Spock was too cowed a son—or too genial an American—to subscribe wholeheartedly to the dark Rado version. As he told his story, at least up through the 1950s, he was an intimidated soul who nonetheless squirmed his way to unexpected success. Baby Benny had basked in Mildred Spock's adoration only briefly before he was subjected to her high expectations and sexual admonitions. She began by worshiping her infants, and he came in for even more than the typical firstborn's special dose of devotion (perhaps in part because he was not really her firstborn: a brother before him had died soon after birth). But with the first sign of self-assertion, and the arrival of another bundle, Mildred Spock set about being the "conscientious" mother the erratic Ada had failed to be. Relegating other household tasks to an array of servants, she claimed child rearing as her consuming mission. As a gauge of her devotion, she "refused to play bridge until all her children were grown up, in spite of the fact that she was very crafty at the game and loved victory," her son recalled.

Rather like Margaret Mead's mother, a proud specimen of advanced turn-of-the-century maternity, Mrs. Spock consulted the "modern" experts as she saw fit. In good Holtian fashion, she considered feedings—not feelings—to be the main arena for training, which meant, as Spock remembered it, serving up meatless mush very early in the evening and packing the children off to bed, in as chilly quarters as possible. Eager to cool the blood at all costs, Mildred Spock was also a fresh air fanatic, as advisers of the time almost all recommended in a rustic spirit. In fourth grade, she dispatched Ben and his favorite sister, Hiddy, on a progressive pedagogical experiment: school outside in a tent, led by a teacher who called herself "South Wind." The "hot-air kids" came in for gleeful taunting by local public school students, who found their folk dancing—to warm up—especially hilarious; the spindliest boy in the class, sure he would stick out, chose freezing over dancing.

Big brother Benny, slow to develop (except in height), duly ate his food and did what he was told, whether it was to help mind his siblings or to learn his lessons huddled in a thick felt bag. When a friend's mother offered a snack of bananas, which were on Dr. Holt's list of forbidden foods, he remembered being terrified—and mortified to be the only boy who declined. During rugged summers in Maine as he got older, Spock the mother's helper enjoyed rare moments of being man of the house: with his father absent (hard at work in New Haven), and Mildred in her element (that bracing sea air!), their eldest felt happily independent, chopping wood, trekking miles to the store, and never worrying what his peers might think about the Spocks' spartan ways and superior attitudes.

There at least he enjoyed a brief respite from the guilty conscience and the sense of difference that burdened him back home, eroding his confidence more with every year. "We would have just loved to be ordinary people," Spock once reminisced about himself and his siblings. "We were always made to feel that we had to disapprove of other people who were slacker in their morals in any way. . . . There's always this feeling of being an outsider, being special, having to disapprove of other people but know that other people didn't accept our disapproval. . . . Children don't like somebody who's at all different from themselves." Needless to say, Mrs. Spock's idea of "special" did not involve boosts to self-esteem; her own children were always made to feel disapproved of themselves.

The judgmental Mildred interrogated her brood about their deeds, thoughts, and friends, and her fury at any suspected lapse from purity made for terrifying scenes—and often draconian penalties. Her children were convinced that she was all-seeing (the telltale symptom, according to Rado, of maternal oppression). Her inner Ada raged ever more unreasonably as her eldest's adolescence approached. If Mildred Spock had gotten wind of G. Stanley Hall, he had only fanned her panic that within every pubescent male lurked a sexual predator who must be repressed at all costs. And Spock, ever more convinced that he was a chinless coward in thrall to his mother, perversely invited her vengeful vigilance. Liberated at last in 1919 to spend two years at Phillips Academy in Andover, and anxiously awaiting the chance to prove himself on paternal turf at Yale, he could not resist a confession guaranteed to rouse her wrath and sabotage his plans for independence.

In the weekly letter home that she required (without fail), the Andover senior reported a rare get-together with some girls, one of whom had told the gangly teenager that he was "very attractive"—just what his mother always assured him he was not. ("You just have a pleasant smile," was her verdict.) Spock even elaborated on a near kiss, and then concluded with a coy parenthesis: "By the way, this is very private, don't read it to the girls." By return mail, Mildred Spock informed her son that "when you come back to New Haven to go to Yale next fall, you should live at home to try to recover your ideals." It was not a suggestion. It was an order, which her son obeyed.

Thus his debut as his own man on campus at Yale, where he enrolled in the fall of 1921, was delayed. Perhaps the son who was worrying about how to surpass his father's record there had not really been ready to rush into the college scene. In any case, waiting turned out to serve Spock well. By now, "my immaturity, my lack of initiative, and my lack of assertiveness" were his theme; yet his very tendency to hang back kept landing him in the right place at the right time. The diffidence that the mama's boy so despised in himself served him better than the "regular guy" confidence that he yearned for would have. For without ever really bucking his mother's authority, Spock backed his way into the social conformity he craved and knew she, with her Puritan principles and scruples, scorned.

In fact, Spock achieved just what she took pleasure in telling him he would, and should, never enjoy: popularity. (And it was to be some time before he found out that popularity also spelled trouble, which was just what his mother had warned him almost from the cradle.) By unlikely luck, at Yale it was sports—hardly his forte, or his father's—that launched the sophomore on the classic collegiate quest to fit in while also standing out. Looking back, the self-deprecating Spock saw his route to athletic stardom as following a typically circuitous pattern. Timing was all, and his timidity helped. He was belatedly inspired to sign up for crew by the sight of a classmate who had the poise he envied—and prowess at rowing. It just happened to be the moment when the Yale crew was switching its technique, so being a beginner was no disadvantage. Even better, being tall was an asset. Spock practiced tirelessly, and the team showed great promise.

Academics suffered, for he was also distracted from schoolwork by his first serious girlfriend, a high-spirited and beautiful seventeen-year-old named Jane Cheney, who was on her way to Bryn Mawr. From a wealthy silk manufacturing family in Connecticut, she had a pedigree that pleased Spock's mother (and a father reminiscent of Mildred's own, though Jane kept it a secret from everyone but Ben: John Davenport Cheney had died several years earlier, and horribly, of syphilis). Jane also had flapper airs that thrilled Mildred's son, and she fueled his growing confidence. ("The inferiority complex is now a thing of the past," she assured him during his junior year crew triumphs, "and you have the honor you deserve.") Spock barely averaged a C at college, but he was the star of the Yale boat that rowed to victory in the 1924 Olympics in Paris. It was a boost to his ego that still made him glow at ninety-three.

Spock entered Yale Medical School in the fall of 1925 with the goal of becoming a pediatrician, a choice that finessed his family dilemmas. He sidestepped his lawyer father, while emulating him: like Spock, Sr., he aimed to prove himself professionally worthy of a woman above his class. He made a bow to his mother—her devotion to children, he said, inspired him—while also standing up to her: even she, her son had not failed to notice, had deferred to men in white coats. It was a career decision that also seemed to suit him and Jane Cheney, given the pressures they felt and the plans they nursed as a privileged couple of the 1920s anxious to prove themselves on their own terms rather than their parents'.

For Jane Cheney, who prided herself on her cultural sophistication yet also harbored a sense of inadequacy, a man in pediatric medicine promised stability and sensitivity (though she presciently worried about jealousy, too: "Think of all the creatures you will be comforting, counseling them and holding their hands," she wrote to him during his first year in medical school). Her great-grandfather had been none other than Horace Bushnell, the mid-nineteenth-century minister who advocated anti-Calvinist gentleness with children. At Bryn Mawr, she had pursued her own interest in psychology and child development; a determinedly modern woman, she looked forward to being a catalyst, not a mere sidekick for her medical man. And that was what Ben Spock was convinced he needed for success, as he had told her throughout their courtship: not just her sympathetic support, though he relied on that to help him bear down and believe in himself, but also her liberating spark, which just might make him bolder. "In the stern family in which I grew up, there was no allowance made for psychological or human explanation of naughty or unwise behavior," as he put it years later. The Cheneys had enjoyed social prominence with no such austerity.

After they married in 1927 (supported by allowances from both families), Dr. Spock very cautiously began to stray from the straight and narrow pediatric path. He always resisted describing his career as a case either of outright revolt against home or of revolution in the pediatric field. Indeed, though he played this down later, too, he was a man following both his wife's lead and something of a crowd. His turn toward psychology came after he left Yale with his new wife, eager to launch their life in New York. Spock transferred to the Columbia University College of Physicians and Surgeons, where he graduated at the head of his class. (He credited Jane with making him stick to his books.) He lined up two internships, first a two-year stint at Columbia's Presbyterian Hospital and then a year at Cornell's New York Nursery and Child's Hospital.

Thus instead of gravitating to Dr. Gesell, who was eagerly drawing up plans for his dome when Spock left Yale, Spock found himself drifting on the outskirts of the psychoanalytic orbit in the early 1930s. Jane forged the way. To help make ends meet, she had taken a job as a research assistant to one of Spock's internist friends who was exploring the link between psychology and physical ailments at Presbyterian Hospital. She found the interviewing of patients fascinating, and readily took Dr. George Draper up on his suggestion that psychoanalysis would help make her a subtler recorder of personal histories.

She and her husband were oddly undaunted when her weekly sessions left her in emotional distress; Spock betrayed some doubts, but Jane dismissed them and he deferred. Nor did they take it amiss when Draper fired her, deciding that therapy had made his assistant "too sensitive." So much for her hopes for a semi-career in psychology, or for personal stability. Jane, who went to work at Macy's, continued treatment: she was a fervent convert to Freud, and a proselytizer, too. When she soon embarked on motherhood (and quit the Macy's job), she not only took up part-time crusading against Prohibition but evidently stepped up a campaign at home to interest her husband in Freud.

A series of personal and professional disappointments helped her cause. Their premature baby died, and shortly after that, so did Spock's father. The Depression arrived. A shaken Spock, seeing that prospects for private pediatric practice were dim, started a one-year psychiatric residency at Payne Whitney in 1932. Looking back late in life, he couldn't quite say why he took that turn—perhaps because he was not ready to acknowledge how much Jane's influence swayed him. His caution (and disinclination: not so long before, he had dismissed child psychology as "nonsense") hardly made it an obvious course for him to pursue.

Spock was feeling his way in a field that was in flux, and his own rigid rearing left him more confused than Jane about what to make of the new signs of flexibility. The stringent handling of children he had watched at the New York Nursery and Child's Hospital did not obviously "work"; the memory of babies crying for their thumbs, their arms in preventive braces, stayed with him. Then again, the children on the psychiatric ward at Payne Whitney didn't fare very well either, and he found that the psychoanalysts' "negative kind of knowledge"—beware of harsh toilet training, say—did not translate into the "positive, practical advice" he needed. His own sessions with Lewin convinced him he "lacked the strength of character" to deal with severe neurotics.

But for Spock the doctor (as for Spock the rower), insecurity and dogged industry eventually made him look like more of a leader and innovator than he felt himself to be, or in fact was. By 1933, with the birth of a son, Michael, Dr. Spock had to bring in a paycheck. He opened a private pediatric practice in the depths of the Depression, not advertising any psychological bent, although he continued training at the New York Psychoanalytic Institute during the evenings for five more years. Patients were few. The uneasy new doctor did not dare ask for much money, and felt driven to offer lots of time, just the comforting, counseling, and hand-holding that Jane had predicted—and abetted. The psychological education she had urged on him, though he wasn't really drawing on it in his standard physical treatment of children, had already left a mark on his dealings with their mothers; he was paying unusually solicitous attention to their worries. Meanwhile, Jane Spock took her troubles, which were substantial (when Mike was six months old, her mother died and she became severely depressed) to her own shrink.

Spock's constant absence from home, and his meager income, stirred up tension between him and Jane, which only kept him away more—a pattern his analysis with Rado helped him to see. He was Mildred's son, eager to be loved rather than judged by the mothers who came to him with their children, yet also eager to provoke the strong-willed wife who reminded him of his mother. Meanwhile, with the colleagues who condescended to his "soft" psychological credentials, Spock was the passive-aggressive son of his father. As he saw it later, he was typically unassertive about challenging traditional pediatrics. It was a combination of "rebelliousness and uneasiness about conventional competition that [made him] go around, in football terms," bypassing the usual professional demands to write articles and keep abreast of all the latest journals. "Instead of going through the line I go around the end and say I'll fool them all by developing a new aspect of pediatrics."

Actually, as Jane Spock noted later in life with a debunking edge in her tone, his psychological approach was not all that pathbreaking. By the late 1930s, "there was a great movement toward permissiveness which had nothing to do with Ben, but with the interpreting of Freud that was going on." (Even Dr. Sloan Crockett, Priss's stodgy pediatrician husband in Mary McCarthy's *The Group*, got impatient with rigid bottle regimens.) Spock himself was forthright that he was hardly a crusader. He hung back, and made no radical breakthroughs behind the scenes in his cramped New York office. When an astute Doubleday editor eager to commission a primer by a psychoanalytically oriented pediatrician found his way to Spock in 1938, the thirty-five-year-old doctor demurred. He was "a very tense person in all respects . . . at that time," he recollected (a state he shared with plenty of his fellow Americans as war arrived with the end of the Depression). "My picture of myself in the office," he remembered later, "is somebody sweating along with a sweating mother about what can we do to make that child more happy."

It was half a decade before Spock dared to speak up. In 1941 he signed a contract with Pocket Books, and in 1943 he began work in earnest on the book. Then war, on top of his own wariness, delayed the manual further. And once again, he who hesitated was not lost at all. What emboldened Spock over those years were not revelations about how to make children happier. He had been trying to figure out ways to apply Freudian ideas of underlying drives—rather than the usual notions of mere bad habits—as he experimented with down-to-earth advice about thumb-sucking, weaning, toilet training, separation anxiety. But neither his methods nor his findings amounted to much. "I worried a lot," he admitted decades later about his years of practice, "gave the safest middle-of-the-road advice I could conceive of and anxiously assessed the results."

At home with Mike, Spock was struggling, too, as a once sunny baby developed various difficulties, which a worried and resentful Jane traced in part to paternal neglect. Thanks to a diagnosis of dyslexia (friends in progressive education circles were precociously alert to the problem), Mike was enrolled in the flexible program at Fieldston School. But he still had a hard time, and Spock's Freudian insights did not prevent him from conveying harsh disapproval to an insecure little fellow who reminded him all too much of himself as a cringing boy. "Though I knew I was wrong," Dr. Spock later confessed in one of his magazine columns, "I used to get so mad at my son when I thought he was being a crybaby at three and four that he still remembered it 20 years later."

What Spock did find out during those years, which greatly boosted his confidence, was first, that he could get along wonderfully with mothers and second, that he was not as out of step with his fellow experts as he had feared he might be. Anecdotes abound about his rapport with the women who brought him their children. "The man with the gentle face and eyes," was the way a colleague heard Spock extolled at the time. While their sons and daughters sat on his examining table (having climbed up on their own, using the little ladder Spock supplied: less scary, he thought, than being scooped up by a big doctor), mothers got what no previous expert had thought to provide: a little couch time. The "very concerned, overly conscientious and overly intellectual, psychologically oriented parents" who tended to consult him, he found, were desperate to air what they apologetically called their "silly" concerns.

Spock realized that all that nervous sweating in his office could grease a therapeutic doctor-patient relationship that was new for pediatrics. He had learned a crucial skill at his mother's knee: "Don't let yourself be *seen* worrying about yourself" was her Puritan injunction about dealing with physical ills—and by extension with psychological discomfort, too. Spock's successful effort to transform his own anxiety, which mirrored the unease of parents, into sympathy was a key accomplishment of his years as a fledgling doctor. His gift was not for "the fancy job . . . [of] treating a neurosis," he readily admitted, but for "such things as getting along with mothers and making them feel comfortable," above all, by listening patiently.

Spock was listening carefully, too, to another woman, Caroline Zachry, a "pillar of strength and wisdom in the Progressive Education Association," he called her. She was a psychologist at Columbia's Teachers College whom he met in the mid-1930s when they were both in psychoanalytic training. Where Jane had galvanized him, Zachry now guided him into a thriving network of reform-minded behavioral scientists and educators in New York City. There he encountered disciples of John Dewey. He was also exposed to an array of Lawrence Frank's beneficiaries and friends. Finding support for their meliorative social vision in Freud—*The Ego and the Id* (1923) and *Inhibitions, Symp-*

toms, and Anxiety (1926) were key texts for hopeful Americans—they championed greater public awareness of psychoanalytic ideas; it was a cause abetted by, among other things, the appearance of the Modern Library edition of *The Basic Writings of Sigmund Freud* in 1938.

From the circle of social scientists, anthropologists, teachers, psychologists, and other students of child development whom Zachry drew into the seminars sponsored by her Institute for the Study of Personality Development, Spock got what a wobbly doctor needed: ideas to build on and, even more important for him, company to lean on. He readily admitted that he was "a person who's learned by sort of latching on to people and acquiring second-hand whatever I'm able to comprehend." And he emphasized that he gravitated to the concrete rather than the abstract. "My whole bias," he once explained, "is to find the usable . . . in anything that I hear about and anything that I've studied . . . and by transmuting it a little, working on it, by rephrasing it, to make it useful to people."

By the early 1940s, Spock had discovered just what a man of his temperament needed to be sure of: that he would not be sticking his neck out too much if he wrote a manual with psychoanalytic underpinnings and more "permissive" advice. Dr. Gesell had been laying a non-Freudian groundwork for more flexible handling of children for almost a decade, of course. Though he was out of favor with Frank, the publication of his *Infant and Child in the Culture of Today* in 1943 clearly spurred Spock on. Lower-brow counsel had relaxed noticeably. The 1942 and 1945 editions of the Children's Bureau *Infant Care* manuals endorsed gentle handling of baby urges, from thumb-sucking and masturbation to weaning and toilet training. *The Woman's Home Companion* endorsed indulgence with "the child who has strong drives . . . for in them lies the secret of courage, scientific curiosity and boundless energy," and disparaged the ideal of rearing children "who are subservient to the arbitrary personal command of an adult."

The hesitant Spock also got some pushes from headstrong women closer to home. In his East Side office, he had an expert/mother as a new client who was busy exposing him to the kind of bracing certainty about cutting-edge wisdom that he lacked: a pregnant Margaret Mead signed up for his pediatric services in 1939. Hardly one of his typically timid young mothers, she made him uneasy. But she also made his life easy in a way, by issuing the doctor the most up-to-date orders on tending mothers and babies. (In her memoir, Mead's daughter, Mary Catherine Bateson, chided Spock for not crediting her mother with enlightening him about "self-demand feeding"—perhaps the doctor's unconscious revenge on the patient who pushed him around, to his benefit but also discomfort.) And not least, Dr. Spock had his wife, Jane, urging him to undertake a book and offering help, the way she had during their courtship and early years, except that now there was an edge to her encouragement.

Beleaguered and lonely at home with Mike, Jane Spock had concluded after several miscarriages that no second child was in the offing. Work on a book evidently beckoned as the proxy baby that could save the marriage: it would keep her husband home, and restore some semblance of the collaborative relationship that she and he had once so enjoyed. Indeed, the project unfolded as a honeymoon of great industry, as she sat and typed while her husband talked. In the bargain, it was good for fertility. In 1943, after a blissful Adirondack summer of book work, Jane found herself pregnant, and a son, John, was born in the spring of 1944.

The birth of the book involved more protracted, interrupted labor. The war disrupted the harmonious home workshop, as Spock was sent first to Maryland and then to California as a doctor in the navy. The unfinished manual kept the two of them in almost nightly contact, with Jane Spock serving as intermediary with editors and publishers and also as amanuensis for her perfectionist husband, doggedly revising and indexing over the phone. But his tireless assistant was feeling the strain. Spock was once again the long-distance daddy and overworked doctor busy prescribing the very intimacy that his own family lacked. Jane Spock was hardly the relaxed wife and confident mother portrayed in the pages she so diligently worked on with him. By her presence (and, as he later publicly acknowledged, with her practical touch), she helped to give his book its truly distinctive mark: the warmly conversational style of a mother's confidant. Yet in his absence, she was drained of faith in herself and flooded with fears that, as she had written him during their courtship, she would be a "tremendous disappointment" to him.

When she headed west to be with her husband during the homestretch of book work in the summer of 1945, it was a drama fraught with tension, not full of togetherness. In what she later confessed was jealous fear of the pert nurses at the hospital where he was posted, she hurriedly arranged to leave baby John behind with Ben's favorite sister, Hiddy. But as Jane's absence stretched to six months, a nurse was hired to tend a toddler who grew paler and more miserable, suffering from celiac disease, a chronic intestinal ailment. Concerns about the trauma of early separation had yet to crest in America: Bowlby and others had only just begun to explore the subject. Still, the Freudian mother who finally fetched John was consumed with guilt.

Shortly after the Spock family returned to Manhattan, John's troubles were tended to and at last the manual came out, in May of 1946. Once again, repeated delays made Spock's timing perfect. The baby boom had just begun, and unprecedented fertility and mobility meant a vast market for a doctor delivering precisely the kind of advice that Americans were said to be awaiting. That very month, at a pediatric meeting of the Medical Society for the State of New York, a keynote speaker announced that "it is well for doctors to remember the same things in handling the parents that they are trying to get across to parents in their handling of children. Don't scold. Don't blame. Don't shame or frighten. Be patient, be responsive, give encouragement. Seek the causes, don't stop with the symptoms." It could have been a blurb for Dr. Spock's book.

The twenty-five-cent paperback—accessible, portable, and practical where Gesell's textbook had been heavy and often pontifical—took off. (It helped that it was so affordable; the genteelly unmercenary doctor also made sure that his royalties were unusually meager.) "All parents do their best job when they have a natural, easy confidence in themselves," Spock assured his readers, not when they're trying to "do everything letter-perfect out of a feeling of worry." Anyway, he pointed out, there is no such thing as "letter-perfect" in the upbringing of a child. "Our ideas about how to treat a child have changed a lot in the past and will certainly change in the future," he wrote. "This book only tries to give you sensible present-day ideas of the care of a child, taking into account his physical and emotional needs. It's not infallible." The book was irresistible. "I feel as if you were talking just to me," one of his early followers wrote him. "You make me feel as if you thought I was a sensible person."

By the end of the year, Spock had arranged what he and Jane agreed would be best for a celebrity expert who aimed to keep up his academic credentials, and for a family who wanted him at hand: a professor's life, rather than a doctor's arduous rounds. He set off to teach at the Mayo Clinic in Minnesota and work on the Rochester Child Health Project there, directed by Dr. C. Anderson Aldrich, an early proponent of a more relaxed approach to feeding and handling. The author of *Babies Are Human Beings* (1938) had written of Spock's manual in *Parents' Magazine* that he could "go along pleasantly with almost everything that is said . . . one is everywhere struck by his calm judicial attitude." When Mildred Spock reported that she found the book "quite sensible" herself, it seemed that all of Benjamin Spock's pains had paid off. He had peacefully surmounted his own past and won popularity with a book that promised his fellow Americans that they, too, could escape their childhood insecurities and find comfort in "free, warm, life-loving" families unruffled by conflict.

But behind the breezy prose was a father and a husband—and, as ever, an uneasy son—who already knew the feat was not as simple as the friendly doctor made it sound, and who learned over the next decade just how hard it could be. Sales were spectacular, but the royalties were not, and though the glow of fame felt great, Minnesota proved to be a cold interlude in more ways than one. By the early 1950s, the family strains already evident during the 1940s had intensified in a nightmarish way. Life at home with the Spocks was nothing like the easygoing idyll the primer officially promised. Dr. Aldrich's death late in 1949 left Dr. Spock without allies at the Mayo Clinic, where he soon found himself disparaged as an unrigorous popularizer by his academic colleagues. Meanwhile, he was denounced as mercilessly stringent by his wife, who was mixing the anti-depressant Miltown with far too many martinis and making scenes reminiscent of Mildred Spock's outbursts.

The misery that a marginalized Jane Spock felt in Minnesota escalated in 1951 when the family moved to Pittsburgh, where Dr. Spock got a job at the university. There she lashed out, desperate to expose America's beloved doctor as a demanding man who refused to face her problems and who could be fierce. "He just gives this [impression of being a] lovely, sweet, easy going, natural kind of person," she would rant at parties, but "this isn't the way he is at all." While Dr. Spock, a fabulous dancer, glided off with soberer partners, out would come details of his "highly critical," hard-driving ways with himself, his children, and her.

It was true enough that her husband was in a knot, struggling at work in his efforts to coax his pediatric and psychiatric colleagues into harmonious collaboration on child development and public health projects. ("First I seem too easily manipulated and too ingenuous, and then by the time I'm ready to assert myself it's a hell of a job," was his harsh self-rebuke about a four-year stint in Pittsburgh that he rated a failure.) He could maintain his imperturbability in the face of Jane Spock's public tirades only so long. In the car or at home he would proceed to live up to her dark billing, and worse, his son John later remembered. Spock would upbraid her for behavior that he failed to see had slipped way beyond her control—often with a scared boy in the back seat, or in his bedroom, listening.

In 1954, Dr. Spock had no choice but to confront psychological disaster—and to cover it up, for the formerly modest celebrity now felt pressure to promote the famous facade: he was desperate for money to pay his wife's medical bills. (Though the manual was selling at a record-breaking rate of a million copies a year, his proceeds by the mid-1960s amounted to only $25,000 to $30,000 annually.) During the winter Jane Spock had a nervous breakdown and was diagnosed with paranoid schizophrenia compounded by alcoholism. She spent six months in New York Hospital's Westchester asylum, and returned a fragile creature. John, ten when trauma hit and already intimidated by a father he found undemonstrative (despite the progressive touch of letting his sons call him "Ben"), had nowhere to turn. His big brother was away at college, foundering himself and seeing a psychiatrist. And the giant man who so often made John feel, as he later put it, "judged, criticized, scared, beaten down" was profoundly distracted.

Spock breathed nothing to his colleagues or friends. He plunged into lucrative public speaking and popular magazine writing for the *Ladies' Home Journal,* where he rejected the headline "Dr. Spock Says" as too "pontifical." He proved to be a great showman, somewhat (but not totally) to his chagrin. (An anti-expert, after all, should not be encouraging a cult following.) He could make Vassar girls squeal as he acted out "baby, mother, father—the works" in their child care course, though "he turned absolutely scarlet" at his fans' response. And he could make PTA mothers melt. "It's a revelation to see audience reaction to him," a friend marveled. "The women strain toward him, they're happy, they seem to be saying, 'Tell me more! Tell me again that I'm not so bad!' " He even hosted a television show, and was taken aback when producers and participants clamored for "authoritative preachment." That was, after all, what he was determined to avoid dispensing. At home and on the road, however, the confident maternal ease that Dr. Spock had promised in his postwar manual was evidently not spreading. There seemed to be every sign that it was eroding, and America's super-expert was feeling on the spot.

3.

Beneath the surface of Dr. Spock's friendly first edition, as Erikson had seen, lurked a darker vision of nuclear family life beset by escalating tensions. In the Cold War edition of 1957, it belatedly emerged—

another case of perfect timing. The doctor who had blessed mothers with buoyant children and urged everyone to relax and feel confident now acknowledged that an expectation of constant sunniness at home could itself be a strain. Peace was in fact precarious, children could be imperious, and "getting into trouble with permissiveness [rather] than with strictness," as he put it on page one of the second edition, had become the danger of the day.

Dr. Spock was right in step with the consensus, already emerging during the Korean War and confirmed by Sputnik, that a cure for coddling and squabbling on the American home front had taken on "new and strategic significance" during an era when "democracy is facing acid tests for survival." So proclaimed the sponsors of Parenthood in a Free Nation, a parent education project that boasted Spock on its "panel of scholars." From little devils refusing to go to bed and big "delinquents" painting the town red (two symptomatic youth problems of the 1950s), alarmed Americans feared it was a slippery slope to reds under every bed. An "intelligent middle-of-the-road viewpoint" for parents, the project was far from alone in urging, had never been more important.

What that meant was that friendly Dr. Spock had to become a firmer Dr. Spock, for unlike his predecessors Hall and Gesell, he lacked a Watson or a Holt to help hold the line. To be sure, there was a competitive crowd of professional colleagues (which could make Spock feel defensive, as he did at the midcentury conference and in Pittsburgh). Still, he had no real popular competition. Where a behaviorist might have barked a stern challenge, B. F. Skinner with his baby boxes amounted to a special taste, not a trend. (After the *Ladies' Home Journal* ran his article on "Baby in a Box" in 1945, Skinner spent a decade vainly trying to find a manufacturer to produce and popularize the self-cleaning, temperature-controlled bin that he touted as the hands-off environment infants required for optimum growth. One shyster turned out a couple of shoddy models under the name "Heir Conditioner," and the Aircrib Corporation that finally went into business in 1957 sold at most a thousand cribs in the next decade.)

And few of Spock's own Freudian ilk could match his skill (though many tried) at dispensing psychoanalytic concepts "camouflaged in such palatable form that they slide like soda pop down the most distrustful gullet," an admirer marveled. (Erikson's appeal had a decidedly more academic flavor; Spock confessed that he himself often found the "fascinating, stimulating" Erikson hard to digest.) At a time when the " 'child psychiatrist' instead of being a help has become for many a threat, a sort of modern bogey man," as Hilde Bruch put it in her *Don't Be Afraid of Your Child* of 1952, Spock reigned supreme as the trustworthy exception—one of the ten "unknockables" in American life, Russell Baker rated him in *Esquire*. "I Want to Spark with Dr. Spock," went a song in a revue. For the course correction that seemed so crucial, Dr. Spock was the anti-expert expert at the wheel.

The time was right for him, personally and professionally, to toughen up his gentle original. For the son of harsh Mildred Spock, the daunted husband of Jane Spock, and the far from cozy father of Michael and John Spock, it was a load off his conscience to acknowledge that harmony on the home front was harder to come by than he had perhaps admitted. Spock claimed, in his chipper way, that he "was not too shaken in my own attitude toward life and my career and things like that" by the family nightmare of the mid-1950s, but his body betrayed him with a terribly painful symptom. He felt as though something was caught in his throat and refused to go down, making "the eyes water and the mouth water," creating "enormous amounts of saliva" and a desperate need to spit, he recalled in an interview in the 1960s. (Talk about a man who was choking as he chatted about family bliss to adoring millions!)

For the cautious expert who had hung back with his book until "the need for greater understanding of children and flexibility in their care had been made clear by educators, psychoanalysts, and pediatricians," it was also a relief to correct any misimpression that he had ever been a crusader "foolish enough to say that a child does not need control . . . [as] some people imagine we have said." Well before the Cold War clamor for firmness, Spock had been grumbling behind the scenes: this was the doctor who in 1948 was already writing to his publishers that he foresaw the "need to monkey around with the topic of *spoiling* which I am afraid is going to become more important as over-enthusiastic parents take over the idea of flexibility, hook, line and sinker." In fact, he got right to work, out on the lecture circuit and in magazine columns over the next half decade, drawing crowds with his message that "there is a big difference between not forcing a child to do something that's unnatural for his age and letting him get away with murder." Dr. Spock made a point of voicing concern that parents were being unnerved by psychoanalytic principles. By 1952, the *New York Times Magazine* was not alone in running articles with titles like "How Far Permissive Attitudes?"

Ensconced as a celebrity professor at Western Reserve Medical School in Cleveland, where he had been hired on the rebound from

Pittsburgh in 1955, Dr. Spock began revisions of his book. The "soft" expert imported basic tenets from the "hard" experts' camp as he monkeyed with passages throughout his primer, "especially about discipline, spoiling, and the parents' part." Thus a postwar manual that he now said had been " 'child centered,' like America generally," became a more parent-focused second edition. (The shift in perspective was spelled out in the titles of his two collections of *Ladies' Home Journal* columns from the same period—*Dr. Spock Talks with Mothers* and *Problems of Parents*.) The romantic summons to bond with a child and let his own wise nature guide his growth was still there. But the Rousseauian Spock had always had Lockean inclinations, too. Exposing a more rationalist bent, Spock the realist now emphasized the need for adult-directed nurture to keep a potentially unstable, willful creature in line—and a parent from losing control, of herself and her child.

In short, the popular expert who had floated the dream that little Bennys could be free and that Mildreds (and Janes) would always be calm and fair revealed to his readers what he had known all along but hoped to suppress: boys (and girls) and mothers (and fathers) had fears and could be fierce. Dr. Spock said he "tried to give a more balanced view" in his second edition. He could more accurately have said that he succeeded in conveying the ambivalent view of parents and children—and of experts, too—that had been there from the start. For the truth was, Dr. Spock had never really been as "soft" as he sounded. And what was perhaps most striking about the new, harder Dr. Spock was how gently he managed to deliver his more ominous version of life on the home front.

The man who had become a household name as America's cheerful champion of children made sure not to become a dour guide for grownups. Dr. Spock eschewed one habit of the no-nonsense "nurture" camp—the accusatory Watsonian way that by midcentury had become, if anything, a more insidious specialty among his own Freudian fold. The chilly, chiding style with mothers that *Parents' Magazine* in 1950 felt amounted to "a sort of Get-Even-with-Mothers movement"—an "overemphasis at present on making parents, and especially mothers, the scapegoats for anything that goes wrong with children"—was definitely not for him. After all, Dr. Spock's public trademark was his warmly confiding tone about children. (He hopped right into the toddler's head, for example, as the eighteen-month-old paused to respond to a "No!" from across the room: "He says to himself, 'Shall I be a mouse and do as she says, or shall I be a man and grab the lamp cord?' ") And Spock had carved out his anti-expert niche by being the "non-critical, sympathetic listener" type with their parents, rather than a lecturer or one of those "scolders of parents" he once described as "taking the general attitude toward the reader, 'Look out, stupid, you'll kill the child if you don't do exactly what I say.'"

Now "Mother's Big Helper," as the *New York Times* hailed him, made it semi-official: he was mothers' therapist. Of course you feel anxious and furious, was his revised message to readers on whom he had once urged breezy confidence, and so will your children without firmer guidance from you. Don't repress your feelings, panicked that they will harm your child; harness them to help keep everyone on an even keel. "It's almost a form of group therapy," a spectator reported of his public appearances, where Spock was swarmed with pleas to "reassure me that it won't be awful if I get angry with my child!" And "Spockism," a profile in the *New York Times Magazine* was pleased to report, did just that.

The sympathetic doctor, the staff writer Martha Weinman wrote, was a godsend to the "modern mother . . . paddling frantically about in a dark pool of Freudian implications, torn between the embattled forces of Discipline and Permissiveness, dazed by the potential perils of rejection, affection, early weaning, late toilet training and chronic thumb-sucking, traumatized by the fear of causing a trauma and helplessly stuck with the suspicion that a little psychiatric orientation is a burdensome thing." Spock bestowed "blessed assurance that the sun will rise tomorrow even if she should bow to her instincts and say tonight: 'Beat it, you brat, you'll eat when I'm ready.'" An article in the *Saturday Review* welcoming the 1957 edition was equally grateful that the doctor was now so willing to acknowledge mothers' plight. "It might well be entitled, 'Baby, Child, and Mother Care,'" the reviewer (plainly a mother herself) applauded. She gave Spock lots of credit for sending "a weepy and anxious mother out to a movie or to buy a new hat. Mother will be reassured to know that the doctor cares as much for her bonnet as baby's." It was right up there with permission to blow her top.

Only rarely did Spock betray the urge to let off steam himself—for example, in a *Ladies' Home Journal* column where he sputtered in passing that "I can hardly bear to be around rude children. I have the impulse to spank them, and to give a lecture to their parents." (In private, his former censoriousness was also in check; Spock's style had become protectively paternal with Jane, whose struggles with drink and depression were far from behind her.) Instead Spock offered parents what he called "anticipatory guidance" to help them keep children, and themselves, in line. Apologizing for the "stuffy" term, he explained that it meant alerting parents to troubles ahead; "more specifically," he said bluntly in a speech, they should know "how unattractive and irritating children can be at many stages of their development." It also meant alerting parents to tensions in their own pasts, for "we all learn to be parents by having been children," however avid we are to incorporate by-the-book counsel.

The revised "gospel according to Spock," as *Parents' Magazine* and *Reader's Digest* hailed it, sounded just as friendly as the old, and more comforting in its way, with the new sections up front telling readers like the beleaguered mother from Texas what they wanted to hear: "Parents are Human," "Parental Doubts Are Normal." But it also sounded a lot less carefree. "Different parents seem to find in the book quite different meanings," Dr. Spock once astutely observed of a manual that had already been full of, as he put it, "on-the-one-hand, on-the-other-hand stuff" before he got to tinkering in 1957. What the changes exposed was how deeply mixed the doctor's message really was, and how demanding the mother's mission—and her child's impulses—could be. The spirit of "natural" spontaneity Spock had become famous for urging on mothers, it became clearer in his second edition, was in fact part of a management strategy that called for emotional subtlety.

The firmer Spock was a less wishful Freudian, and more of an "organization man," the title of the best-seller of 1956 by William Whyte about a new "social ethic" of group loyalty emerging in America in the era of the big corporation. Dr. Spock's 1946 primer had featured children eagerly "wanting to be like [their parents] . . . what the psychologists call 'identifying,' " with rarely a thought of defying them. In fact, the "reasonable, friendly" fellow—Spock hoped "parents of girls will understand and forgive" the hes and hims—"wants to do the right-thing, the grown-up thing, most of the time," from very early on. Thus it was smooth sailing through the oral, anal, and Oedipal phases (none of which Spock named, and none of which were nearly the fraught psychic dramas that Freud had in mind). With "self-demand" feeding, a new "back to nature" approach that Spock saluted, he assumed an infant would settle into a rhythm. His first-edition advice was to "leave bowel training almost entirely up to your baby," for "a child will completely train himself sooner or later if no struggle has taken place."

In the same upbeat spirit, the Oedipal drama between three and six was all about parental emulation, not dark frustrations: "a nice age," Spock called it. He steered clear of rivalrous, incestuous sexual currents with sweet anecdotes about anatomical fears ("I heard of a little girl who complained to her mother, 'But he's so fancy and I'm so plain' ") and with folksy tips to fathers, who had at last acquired a crucial job on the home front. In the wake of a war that had sent women to work and men away, the all-important paternal mission was to guide children toward their appointed gender identities. Spock made it sound simple for Dad to drop in and do his part in directing sex-role differentiation. With a son, be more palsy than pushy, and "give him the feeling he's a chip off the old block." With a daughter, "little things like approving of her dress, or hair-do, or the cookies she's made" did the trick. "Latency," between six and adolescence, followed without a hitch, a sunny interlude during which the rule-loving child was puttering with his rock collection and eagerly fitting in with his peers, getting ready to "take his place as a responsible citizen of the outside world."

All in all, "discipline, good behavior, and pleasant manners" were "part of the unfolding of his nature." Yet precisely because that nature was so sociable (the sort of solitary "behavior day" that Gesell narrated in his book would rate as a bad day for a Spockian child), its unfolding depended on "natural . . . comfortable, affectionate" nurture from parents doing "what . . . they instinctively feel like doing for their babies" and children. It was an improvisational drama without a script, except a cautionary reminder did keep cropping up. Should a problem arise, "if the cause and the cure are not easy to see, a children's psychiatrist will be able to help." In Dr. Spock's manual, as a reviewer in 1946 remarked, referrals were a constant (and less than confidence-inspiring) refrain: "When in doubt, consult your own doctor."

It was hardly surprising that Dr. Spock himself had harbored doubts that "pleasant" (a favorite word) peace between two such remarkably mature and "agreeable" (another favorite word) personalities would quite so readily prevail. (Experts are human, too.) In his professional articles, he went ahead and let the squalling cats out of the bag. "At its worst," he was warning specialists in 1947, "the second year is an all-day-long, 12-month-long struggle between two grim immature personalities. Both child and mother get badly mauled. But the effect is longer lasting on the child." Indeed, the manual let slip some pretty drastic effects of mealtime struggles: "a balky, suspicious attitude toward life and toward people," feeding issues that "may last for years" and cause "other behavior problems, too." By the mid-1950s, Dr. Spock forthrightly told overflow crowds of parents the same thing—with a new emphasis: the effect on the mother, he had decided, was longer lasting. Children "are resilient. Their peskiness in childhood is harder on the parents than on the child."

But that only made peacefulness on the home front more elusive and essential, for how could children identify with parents so lacking in stability? Parents' "anxious deference," Spock now emphasized as he revised, goaded a child into defiance as readily as old-style dominance ever had: "the more they submit to his orders, the more demanding he becomes. (A human being of any age finds himself imposing on a person who is too submissive.)" The organic Dr. Spock who had promised freedom from tension and confrontation began to sound more concerned about pre-empting conflict. "Don't be afraid to love [your baby] and respond to his needs," he had urged in earth-father tones back when he had thought parental bossiness was the problem. "Don't be afraid to love him and enjoy him. . . . Don't be afraid to respond to other desires of his as long as they seem sensible to you and as long as you don't become a slave to him," he spelled out more carefully now that he worried baby bossiness had become the issue.

And it was a subtler mediating style, rather than instinctual bliss, that Dr. Spock endorsed more explicitly by 1957—a nonchalant yet no-nonsense mode of operation that avoided either giving children too much choice or subjecting them to overt force, yet allowed them to feel part of the decision-making process. Being a gentle role model and companion was very important, but what Dr. Spock was also proposing, and had been from the start, was that mothers be genial social facilitators who encouraged conformity without causing discomfort or confrontations. The ethos that surfaced in his manual, and that suffused his magazine columns, had more in common with a midcentury American corporate mentality that enshrined a new therapeutic value—group harmony—alongside old-style efficiency.

It would be hard to say whether a postwar trend in industrial relations became a postwar theme of family relations or the other way around, for both drew on a common idea. It was not simply coincidence that in 1946 Peter Drucker, a political scientist hired to study General Motors, popularized the notion that workers would be more productive if they were not treated as mere children—the same year that Dr. Spock offered the century's most compelling version of the message that children should not be viewed as little workers to be kept busy in their own carefully regulated realm. (The Watsonian, and even the Gesellian, child still had a dutifully independent air about him; playfully sociable urges hardly predominated.) What Spock's manual did for mothers and the baby business, Drucker's best-selling *The Concept of the Corporation* did for men and big business: put "social relations," as the sociologist Talcott Parsons called the new department he set up at Harvard in 1950, in the spotlight. Both Spock and Drucker were graceful writers who did it in a warmly accessible, and empirical, way that eluded the academics who were busy blending Freud with Emile Durkheim to formulate theories of "small group solidarity," which they promised would bring unity to a world threatened by instability. In 1954, when *McCall's* magazine launched a "togetherness" campaign in its pages, a popular slogan was born: it was "the word that has captured America," the editors were pleased to report, ". . . a new word for a new pattern of living."

By the late 1950s, William Whyte was not alone in pointing out that the "quest for a utopian equilibrium" among personalities permeated thinking about work and home (and school, too, where "development as a co-operative social person" had become an ever more insistent refrain). And, as he noted, the new "social ethic" was as arduous in its own way as the pursuit of the Protestant ethic of individualism and hard work had ever been. Cozy and decentralized though the group ethos could sound (especially in the conversational prose of the popularizers) and was of course supposed to feel, it in fact required intensive control from the top and intimate oversight all the time, to promote and steadily direct the cooperative spirit. "The concepts of the responsible worker and self-governing plant community," Drucker felt the need to insist, "must not be confused with permissivism," in the sense of laissez-faire. "Strong leadership . . . uncompromising goals and standards, and very high self-discipline" in the enlightened manager were the sine qua non of success.

With his friendly-and-flexible-but-firm formula of the late 1950s, Dr. Spock was trying to clarify a similar message for his readers. Watsonian regularity and Gesellian self-regulation were straightforward principles compared to the on-the-scene mediation and the deft manipulation—of their own feelings and their children's—that Spockian mothers were expected to perform. In fact, they were feats that called for more than spontaneity and naturalness, which was just as well, since those were virtues that plenty of mothers evidently failed to feel welling up from within.

It was hesitancy that came all too naturally, the "commonest problem in child rearing in America today," Spock judged, blaming it in part on "child-care experts [who] have imposed unnatural patience and submissiveness on her." A chipper, take-charge "air of cheerful certainty," an "air of self-confidence"—never mind the real thing—was all the more crucial; a baby "can be quite impressed by a mother's tone of voice," the doctor assured the mother primed by Freudian lore to fear that her infant could sniff out a phony and might suffer a loss of trust. A child was happier and more secure if "steered . . . in a friendly, automatic way through the routines of the day." He was glad "to feel that his mother and father, however agreeable, have their own rights, know how to be firm, won't let him be unreasonable or rude. He likes them better that way. It trains him from the beginning to get along reasonably with other people." But almost more to the point was the "firming effect on the mother" of the brisk, but not too brusque, "I mean business" style. Spock observed that a "reasonable amount of consistency" was less important for children—they were adaptable—than for parents. It helps a mother "really feel like a responsible person in charge," and conceive of herself as "a leader" in control.

It was a sense she needed, since those routines of the day, and of the passing years, did not unfold quite so smoothly as Spock's first edition had suggested. Maternal "judgment and decisiveness" were called upon constantly in "steering, stopping, and starting the average small child," who was not, it turned out, quite as steady a specimen as advertised. The doctor who had hoped that "self-demand" could lead naturally to synchrony now worried that parents were letting babies be "demanding" and were becoming "as fanatical in their devotion to self-regulation and self-expression" as they had ever been with four-hour regimens; coax your infant steadily toward a schedule, he advised. And don't get carried away by the concept, which Spock felt had spilled beyond food with exhausting results. A baby may know how much milk he needs, but on most other matters, "he doesn't know what's good for him." Sleeping problems, on the rise, were Spock's emblem of trouble that called for the supportive yet assertive remedy to convince her baby, and herself, that limits would hold.

Similarly, with toilet training parents could no longer skirt struggle by simply following the toddler's lead. They had been "bullied into a jam" by experts (including himself) who made them panic about a misstep, Spock felt, and were as "balky" as their children—which only made their children, who sensed it, balkier. Leery of overt negotiations, Spock recommended more of that "tactful" (another favorite word) parental navigation. Let the child help determine the timing but leave it to the parent to establish the terms—and to be matter-of-fact about expecting them to be met. A top-down, not a drawn-out, procedure was what he had in mind. Spock's advice on sibling rivalry, a big issue in the fecund postwar decade, captured the pre-emptive-strike spirit. When a mother saw her child "advancing on the baby with a grim look on his face and a weapon in his hand, she must jump and grab him," he wrote. "But she can occasionally turn the grab into a hug."

The latency period, too, required noncoercive but constant vigilance, Dr. Spock admitted in his magazine columns, where he stressed a "continuing need for parental control" as peer allure entered the picture, and the child struggled none too "graciously" for independence. The starring figure here was the father, now a shaper of ideals and not just of gender identities, and thus the man to help ease this transition. In the family he was the "instrumental" conveyer of cultural values, complementing the mother, the "expressive" relayer of emotional support, the Parsonian sociologists explained—"chairman of the board" to her "personnel manager" were terms Talcott Parsons's followers used. In his columns especially, Spock acknowledged that tensions had a way of mounting. But "the grittiness which comes between him and his school-age child," the doctor diagnosed, "is not a sign that the parent has lost his touch or that his child is in trouble." Don't be "excessively understanding and patient," or too critical of "the craving to be in the swim." The key was enforcing a few rules "firmly but cordially."

Yet the calm authority that was called for, Dr. Spock had to admit, could be as hard to come by as spontaneity. Corporate managers needed "uncompromising goals and standards" to guide them in the quest for cooperation, Drucker emphasized, and workers would not be won over by mere feel-good propaganda. Group harmony had to encourage efficiency and productivity, and would be oppressive if it amounted to merely a semblance of affability. By contrast, Freudian child managers, faced with a "relaxation of standards in this half-century," Spock noted, lacked any such clarity or bottom line. As he had pointed out back at the White House conference in 1950, "it's difficult to bring up a child when you don't know yourself what you are bringing him up for. To bring him up to be what an expert calls well-adjusted is not really enough"—especially when the experts' ideas of "adjustment," and the world itself, kept changing.

"We are uncertain about how we want our children to behave because we are vague about our ultimate aims for them," Dr. Spock wrote later in the decade in one of his columns, and by "we" he meant not just American parents, but American experts, too. Like some of his professional colleagues, Spock uneasily envied the Russians' "strong sense of common purpose," which apparently made their nurseries havens of group serenity and personal security—no wobbly adults, no squabbling children—all without any discernible evidence of severity. (A report on a visit to the Soviet Union by Dr. Milton Senn had impressed him.) To be sure, "Russian moral superiority and the scene of conformity" were offensive to Americans and yet, to judge by Sputnik, scientific ingenuity was hardly being squelched by the Soviets' approach to socialization.

Moreover, it seemed to be the vaunted American ideals of individuality, progress, and success, Spock worried, that were making parents, like children, so "balky"—by which he didn't mean stubborn so much as fickle and lacking in commitment to more communal goals (the spirit of "belongingness" that William Whyte, by contrast, feared was on the rise). Spock hastened to emphasize that the national values were not "unworthy, they just don't serve to unite us." In a country with a "tradition against traditions," during a century of great mobility, it was "hard to settle on a philosophy of life which would give us all a firm sense of direction in rearing our children." Thus Americans were especially prey to "the flood of unsettling new concepts which came from the professions concerned with child development," and which inspired conflicting advice. No wonder parents were adrift, Spock told them, lacking "the self-assurance and firmness which they've needed more than ever, perhaps, to guide their children through these unstable times."

Dr. Spock, of course, was not about to recommend that Americans listen instead to a dictator with a monolithic theory, Soviet style. Drawing on his own experience with the martinet Mildred, he suggested parents try what he hoped might be the best alternative: listen to their own parents, for they were the true source of the "basic convictions that parents have about child care" in any case. "Most of any mother's knowledge of child rearing, in the sense of how she manages the thousand minor crises that arise everyday, comes from inside herself," Dr. Trust Yourself had already said before, but now he went on: "And it comes from her own childhood, of course. The same applies to fathers." Experts who try to steer parents too far afield, and parents who try to stray, run into trouble. A "theory of child rearing" can't be made to "work by will power alone (ignoring the deeper feelings of parent and child)," as experts once thought. "This is nothing to be ashamed of," he assured readers of his 1957 manual who might figure they should have graduated from go-by-grandma gospel. "This is the way Nature expects human beings to learn child care—from their own childhood."

In its way, it was a more disconcerting new concept than American mothers and fathers had heard from an expert in many decades. After all, for gurus before Spock, Grandmother had been the nemesis, and scientific progress had been the promise. ("I would suggest as a heading for a chapter, 'The elimination of the grandmother,' " one pediatric adviser had half joked at a meeting in 1917, calling her "the great trial of my life. She probably has had eight children and I have not had any.") For that matter, American mothers themselves had long been more famous, abroad and at home, for flouting their mothers' child-rearing wisdom than for following it. That was why the experts had so readily horned in. In *Problems of Parents*, Spock remarked on the habit of upstart parenting in this country and century, as daughters vied to raise their children their own way—or at any rate, the "new" way, whatever that happened to be.

Dr. Spock had a hard sell on his hands, and he knew it and said it. Almost as soon as his revised manual appeared, Spock the columnist offered his most withering assessment yet of expert complicity in parental anxiety, betraying impatience with the limitations of his therapeutic genre. "In summary," he wrote in what amounted to a blunt self-indictment in *Problems of Parents*, "I am making the point that the popular American philosophy of child rearing can be very hard on parents and confusing to children unless the parents themselves happen to have had an unusually stable and purposeful upbringing to rely on. It is based too largely on the negative fear of maladjusting the child. Its positive aims are vague and do not closely gear the parent or the child to the positive aims of the family, country, religion. It leaves parents too much on their own." Clearly the philosophy was proving hard on its popular promoter, too. Dr. Spock was still feeling guilty about widespread parental insecurity, but murmuring "Don't worry" no longer seemed to work very well—for them, or for him. He sounded like a man who was getting frustrated.

Dr. Spock did blow his top within a decade. The baby doctor went out and put on a completely new hat: he became an antiwar activist. As the son of Mildred and Benjamin I. Spock saw it, he had taken his own advice and gotten in touch with the parental voices within—with the most unsettling results of all. America's soothing therapist emerged a zealous moralist and embattled father figure.

NINE

The Moralists

Dr. Benjamin Spock and Dr. Bruno Bettelheim

I.

"Will you still need me, will you still feed me, when I'm sixty-four?" The Beatles posed the question on their *Sgt. Pepper's Lonely Hearts Club Band* album in 1967, the year Dr. Spock actually turned sixty-four and decided he was not going to worry about the answer. "Mother's Big Helper" was tired of feeling indispensable. He was "officially retiring to a boat in the Virgin Islands," the Western Reserve University Medical School professor and avid sailor announced in a profile in the *New York Times Magazine* called "Peace, Man, Says Baby Doctor Spock." Unofficially, after two decades as the most solicitous care-and-feeding expert Americans had ever known, Dr. Spock was embarking on a new career, one that meant getting used "to not being loved by everyone, to being hated a little"—or, as it turned out, a lot.

He seized the spotlight as an antiwar activist. Dr. Spock, of all people, was rocking the boat. In fact, he soon found himself facing a near mutiny, as he encountered battles at home—over women's rights and hopes—that he had not even realized were under way. And Spock confronted a rival expert for the first time, too. Bruno Bettelheim, himself on the brink of retirement from the directorship of a school renowned for its success with autistic children, took up a position on the opposite side of the police barricades as campus unrest spread. Few would have guessed that both Freudians, out preaching to a changing world with a passion unmatched by popular child-rearing authorities before them (or since), had lately been disappointed by psychological work they had hoped would cap their careers. Instead, they had discovered the limits of their expert wisdom. Smooth sailing did not lie ahead for either of them—or for their ever less deferential audience of mothers.

"I guess I've said all I can say about babies," Dr. Spock explained as he hung up his white coat and stethoscope. "From now on I will try to talk to youth about their problems," and to those in power about their lack of humanity and credibility in waging the Vietnam War. "Some people say I'm preaching politics. I prefer to call it morality." In his three-piece Brooks Brothers suit, complete with watch fob, Spock took to the streets. He was arrested for civil disobedience during a demonstration in December at the Whitehall Street Induction Center in New York City. In January 1968 he was indicted, along with the Reverend William Sloane Coffin, Jr., Marcus Raskin, Mitchell Goodman, and Michael Ferber, on charges of conspiring to aid and abet draft resisters.

The trial of the "Boston Five," held in June (in Boston), notably failed to become the moral referendum on the war that the defendants and their supporters had hoped. It was "a fizzle," Jane Spock said, "a spectacle of nit-picking and legal logic," as Coffin dispiritedly described the tedium that led to their conviction. Dr. Spock even nodded off now and then. Still, the verdict galvanized a man who had spent his whole life feeling guilty without being charged. He created a stir at his sentencing (two years in prison, but he was free on $1000 bond, pending an appeal, which he ultimately won). The guru famous for advising mothers to calm down righteously cried out, "I say to the American people, *Wake up! Get out there and do something before it's too late!*"

The weaning of America was under way. Despite what the books say, the process rarely happens smoothly, even when the separation drama seems overdue on both sides—as it did by the late 1960s for mothers and the expert they had long clung to. Five years earlier, in *The Feminine*

Mystique, Betty Friedan had already detected the doctor's restlessness. "It is clearly a terrible burden on Dr. Spock to have 13,500,000 mothers so unsure of themselves that they bring up their children literally according to his book—and call piteously to him for help when the book does not work." By 1968, Spock's plaintive hangers-on—"dependent on the latest word from the experts," Friedan had sighed—were ready to throw the book at him. The unthinkable was happening to the "unknockable": a "Spocklash," as one magazine called it, had begun.

"Many people expected that the arrest, on such a basis, of a man who had been doctor, teacher, and adviser to millions of American mothers would cause a torrent of protest," Philip Slater wrote in *The Pursuit of Loneliness: American Culture at the Breaking Point* in 1970. "Instead it was met with a profound and malicious silence." More accurately, Dr. Spock's prominence on the barricades prompted questions and accusations from all sides, as Americans tried to make sense of the generational tumult. "Is It All Dr. Spock's Fault?" was the title of an article by Christopher Jencks, a sociologist at Harvard, in March 1968, probing for reasons why "respect for authority, for the school, for the family has broken down." Six months later, in a five-page spread, *Newsweek* wondered, "Is Dr. Spock to Blame?"

By that time, the magazine could quote a crowd of diagnosticians who had no doubt about the answer. From his pulpit, the Reverend Norman Vincent Peale had denounced the youthful generation that was demonstrating in the streets and on campuses as "the most undisciplined in history." The student rabble, he complained, "thinks it can get what it yells for," thanks to the soft-headed advice dispensed by Dr. Spock, which he summed up this way: "Feed 'em whatever they want, don't let them cry, instant gratification of needs." Stewart Alsop, the conservative columnist, scolded that youths had been "Spocked when they should have been spanked."

Lady Bird Johnson's press secretary, Liz Carpenter, derided the demonstrators during the chaotic 1968 Democratic National Convention as a "charming group of little children who never made it through the toilet-training chapter of Dr. Spock." Spiro Agnew made the sins of "Spockmanship" a campaign theme. The vice-presidential candidate rarely missed a chance to call activists "spoiled brats who never had a good spanking," selectively quoting from the baby bible. Richard Nixon denounced the "fog of permissiveness" that had settled on the country. (When Mrs. Nixon later spoke up in *McCall's* about how she and "Dick . . . never said a harsh word to the girls" and "didn't try to dominate" but "always stressed that they should be themselves and not try to change their natural instincts in any way," she was evidently unaware that she was not toeing the party line.)

"Permissiveness," a term that had once applied to the nursery, had become, as Barbara Ehrenreich has put it, "a catchall code for moral breakdown" in American society. Toward the end of the year, the *New York Times* stood back to review the case against the doctor, who was depicted as the carrier of a childhood disease that, rather than going away, got progressively worse. Spock had "turned out a generation of infants who developed into demanding little tyrants," according to his detractors. "And now the world is reaping a whirlwind, they say. The small monsters have grown up to be unkempt, irresponsible, destructive, anarchical, drug-oriented, hedonistic non-members of society." (The absence of "Spock-marked" baby boomers among the vanguard of radicals and musicians did not deter Spock's critics: Abbie Hoffman was born in 1936, Jerry Rubin in 1938, Tom Hayden in 1939, John Lennon in 1940, Bob Dylan in 1941—all well out of diapers when *Baby and Child Care* caught on.)

This trial of Dr. Spock, which took place outside the courtroom, was anything but boring. It did get bewildering, however, when another balding, big-eared, bespectacled child development expert, an exact contemporary of Spock's, brought his Freudian credentials to the fray: Dr. Bruno Bettelheim, a professor of psychology and education at the University of Chicago and director of the Sonia Shankman Orthogenic School for severely troubled children. A Viennese émigré who had arrived in the United States in 1939 after being released from Buchenwald, he made headlines in 1969 as a scourge of student protesters. Bettelheim took to the barricades to compare them to Hitler Youth in their incendiary and paranoid zeal (of which he himself displayed more than a hint) and to diagnose their "psychosocial" Oedipal problems. Summoned by Congress for a house call, he analyzed the "emotionally disturbed" specimens—and took a swipe at the "parents who failed to give them direction and set them against the world by exposing their immature minds to criticism of all that could have given meaning to their lives."

"Although often very bright, some of [the radicals] remained fixated at the age of the temper tantrum," Bettelheim testified before a House subcommittee investigating student unrest. ". . . Nor should the symbolic meaning of students invading the dean's or president's office, whether violently or nonviolently, be overlooked; big in age and size, they inwardly feel like little boys, and hence they need to play big by sitting in papa's big chair. They want to have a say in how things are run, want to sit in the driver's seat, not because they feel competent to do so, but because they cannot bear to feel incompetent." Forget the decades of fear lest children develop overly harsh superegos, this fierce Freudian now insisted. As Bettelheim summed up his verdict elsewhere, American youths born amid postwar affluence "suffer from both an ego that is weakened by the onslaught of over-aroused or unsatisfied instinctual desires, and a poorly established superego." They had been deprived of "strong-father-figures with strong convictions," whom children need to "bring order into their inner chaos."

"In an age of confrontation politics," a cover article about Bettelheim in the *New York Times Magazine* pronounced, "Bettelheim is counter-Spock, the Dr. No of child-care authorities." After a long era of one-man rule, polarized experts again presided in America, more dramatically at odds with each other than their predecessors had been. At least it looked that way, to judge by Spock's and Bettelheim's positions at opposite ends of the political and generational spectrum.

The towering Spock, with his patrician Yankee accent, was the renegade father who sided with youth, defying rulers and fanning the rebel fires. "Dr. Spock Delivers Us Again" proclaimed the placards of young picketers in Boston, while Spiro Agnew led the charge against him as the proselytizer of permissiveness. By contrast, Bettelheim fit the profile of the avenging father. A small man "with an accent not unlike Dr. Strangelove's," a reporter noted, he stood out as a defender of the "system," in league with adult oppressors—and aligned with President Nixon. Students at the University of Chicago and elsewhere demonized a doctor who had forfeited his former politically liberal credentials. "Dr. Brutalheim" was a popular nickname on his own campus.

But if protesters and politicians readily identified the expert-provocateurs with opposing camps, Dr. Spock's once adoring audience of mothers and Dr. Bettelheim's colleagues could be forgiven for wondering just what to make of child development specialists who had become angry upstarts along with everyone else. Their late 1960s metamorphosis, on the verge of retirement, was disorienting. As recently as 1960, a firmed-up manual under his belt, Dr. Spock had clinched his status as the iconic expert, the child-rearing authority who had fulfilled the promise made by all the preceding advisers: if Americans, especially mothers, minded the medical men who were busy examining children, then social change could happen smoothly—

without undue strife between youths and their elders, or between husbands and wives—even in a century as dizzying as the twentieth. Enlisted in a campaign ad for John F. Kennedy, Spock had presided as the grandfatherly family adviser, giving his blessing to a new generation. A TV spot showed Mrs. Kennedy, obviously pregnant, sitting with the proud doctor—a tableau of national stability, charged with Jackie's innocent seductiveness and Spock's gallantry. "Dr. Spock is for my husband," she confided, "and I am for Dr. Spock."

By then, Dr. Bettelheim had joined him as a warm voice of humanistic optimism amid Cold War hysteria. The same Bettelheim who hailed Kennedy's election for inspiring "an upsurge of purpose" in drifting youths and in their anxious elders had acquired renown, certainly among the intellectual elite, as a stirring liberator himself. His early writings about concentration camps had introduced him in America as a witness-bearing survivor; in 1943 when he published his article "Individual and Mass Behavior in Extreme Situations," an analysis of prisoners' "personality disintegration" based on his Dachau and Buchenwald experiences, he was a rare reporter from a realm of horror. His school, and the two eloquent books he had written about it in 1950 and 1955, made him famous as a doctor dedicated to rescuing the most powerless of victims, emotionally disturbed children.

And with his *Dialogues with Mothers*, which appeared in 1962 (shortly after *Dr. Spock Talks with Mothers*), Bettelheim reached out to a more popular audience—"intelligent and fairly cultured" was how he described the "by no means select group" of mothers whose discussions with him made up the book. He joined Spock in aiming to shore up American mothers who he felt had been "swamped with literature in which they are sometimes made out to be saints, sometimes vipers, but always persons bearing vast responsibility" and bowing to expert authority. His goal, he explained, was to show them how their own powers of empathy, and more respect for their children's autonomy, could be their best guide.

In 1967, only two years before lashing out at students, Bettelheim had been anointed a savior of youth, an expert with a halo to match Spock's aura as supreme mothers' helper. Reviews of *The Empty Fortress: Infantile Autism and the Birth of the Self* heralded "The Holy Work of Bruno Bettelheim" and called the man himself "A Hero of Our Time," saluting his "spectacular successes" with the most difficult of cases. He sounded tough on mothers, diagnosing "the precipitating factor" in schizophrenia and autism to be "the parent's wish that his child should not exist," but he did not stand out from the crowd. His was a widespread view, in line with the assessment of Leo Kanner, the doctor who a decade earlier supplied the first clinical definition of autism and coined the term "refrigerator mother" to go along with it. And Bettelheim's approach with the troubled children at his school was renowned for its gentleness. In *Time* magazine that year he was called "Chicago's 'Dr. Yes,'" whose "principal prescription is almost total positivism. Whatever his patients ask, he usually says yes. . . . Dismissed as ultra-permissive by some psychiatrists, his approach has been impressively successful." By contrast, in the *New York Times* "Dr. Spock as a Father" was being christened "No Mollycoddler," and the review of the 1968 edition of his book—the third—ran under the headline "The Less Permissive Dr. Spock."

By which time, of course, all the promises of generational peace had exploded. In *The War Between the Tates*, Alison Lurie's dark comedy of domestic and campus upheaval set in 1968, Erica Tate was stunned as her psychologically correct dreams of family unity and equality were dashed. "This whole house is a broken home now, she thinks—as if some stupid teenage giant walking over the world had picked it up and then, losing interest, flung it aside." The power relations and the emotions, so carefully managed in the Tates' middle-class idyll in Corinth (Lurie's hometown of Ithaca, New York, site of Cornell University), were exposed as a sham. "The Children" whom Erica and her husband had "worshiped [as] gods" had become pubescent ingrates. "You always give us this bullshit about fairness and democracy," their daughter ranted, "but you don't mean it . . . phony . . . mean. . . ." Erica's "rather old-fashioned marriage" lay revealed as a fraud, too. Her husband, a professor, had "secretly abandoned the adult side and gone over to the adolescent enemy" to have an affair with one of his students. In this uncivil war, none of the old ties seemed to bind anymore, and Erica groped for some explanation. "How has it all come about?"

Although you would not have known it from their belligerence on the barricades, the experts had been taken by surprise, too. They were ultimately forced to admit that they had no simple answers—no tidy causes or cures to be found in child-rearing theories. Each in his own way, Spock and Bettelheim arrived at a similar conclusion: their influence as experts had been far less than they had hoped (and, at times, feared). Or at any rate, it had not been at all what they had anticipated. And their fate, as it unfolded in the 1970s, continued to confound the advisers themselves, to say nothing of the Erica Tates of America, whose faith in the old Freudian father-confessor figures was fading fast.

In the midst of feminist revolt, both experts were on the defensive, yet it was Bettelheim who, beneath his bluster, proved unexpectedly prescient about women's demands and the family's dilemmas.

2.

When the diffident Dr. Spock stepped forth as the defiant Dr. Spock, he told anyone who would listen that he had not turned out to be very different from Mildred Spock after all. "I have come smack back into what my stern, moralistic mother brought me up to do," he announced in a newspaper profile in 1968. "What I'm really being is a moralist," he said in *Esquire*. ". . . I'm my mother's and my father's moralistic child, having found something very important to be moralistic about." He would often follow up with an Oedipal analysis. In finding a fierce father figure—Lyndon Johnson—whom he finally dared to defy, he was able to embrace his true "stern, puritanical" identity, which he had too long tried to deny. At last he could exert his authority and get angry without feeling guilty. When the professed "peace candidate" LBJ (who had personally solicited Spock's support) revealed himself "to be a war-monger," Spock sputtered to the press, "then my moral indignation is really . . . it is fierce."

Dr. Spock, whose advice had always come out of his own head, revised his manual in 1968 with the aim of recommending just such a moral awakening to adolescents and, even more important, to parents. In doing so, he departed from the trademark Spockian manner of kindly maternal confidant that he had maintained even as he firmed up his 1957 edition. His additions were made this time in more forceful, paternal tones. Where Spock the therapist had been eager to soothe and build confidence, Spock the moralist aimed to rouse consciences. Gone were his apprehensions about intimidating readers, for he had learned to his surprise that mothers were perhaps not the cowed acolytes that he had once anxiously—and rather patronizingly—assumed they were.

Research (a rarity for Spock), on top of experience, had brought home this timely lesson. By the early 1960s, results were emerging from a project he had launched upon arriving at Western Reserve University in 1955. Backed by ample funding and a staff of fellow pediatricians, psychiatrists, and child therapists, Spock's Child Rearing Study was, among other things, a popularizer's bid for scientific respectability.

The ambitious, long-term survey signaled a doctor who was ready and eager to deal in psychological data, not mere anecdote. His sample was a representative group of twenty-two middle-class, mostly college-educated mothers. They came to University Hospitals in Cleveland for biweekly and then bimonthly visits with their children, beginning in their last trimester of pregnancy and continuing through the fifth year of the firstborn children's lives. The overarching goal of the study was to see how ordinary parents responded to expertise of the Spockian psychoanalytic variety, with a view to helping advisers better anticipate and handle their problems.

The Child Rearing Study turned out to be hopelessly lacking in scientific rigor (no control groups, little consensus on standards, few consistent records), and all the more revealing for that. Unmethodical but open-minded, Spock and his colleagues managed to gain unusual insight into the way parents actually used advice like his in the midst of normal family bustle—just the sort of day-to-day muddling that clinical evidence drawn from families seeking professional help in a crisis could not really illuminate. The Spock-led investigators were taken aback to discover how often expert counsel was blithely ignored. The professionals' predictions about parental dependence on them, the refrain of the early 1950s, failed to pan out.

Hovering specialists were more marginal, and mothers considerably more resourceful, than Spock had ever imagined. No synthesis of the study's results was published. Instead assorted scholarly articles appeared, on such classic topics as childhood aggression, weaning, and toilet training, as well as on the cutting-edge issues of bonding and separation anxiety. Yet Spock did step back to comment on the project in 1964 in a letter to Anna Freud, the original inspiration behind the innovative family-centered curriculum and clinics at Western Reserve University that Spock zealously promoted. "Despite the fact that we counselors considered ourselves mature, impressive, comfortable people," he wrote her, "we were amazed at how resistant these young mothers were to following much of our advice, especially when it came to matters with an emotional charge." The counselors were struck by, among other things, the abruptness with which many mothers took the big separation step—whether it was weaning, leaving their babies more often, or going back to work—despite expert advice to be cautious, and make the transition gradual. Nor did the mothers suffer from the excess of anxiety that Spock had been so anxious about. If anything, they were overly sanguine when confronted with serious problems, as several were after difficult births.

As for pre-emptive counseling, or "anticipatory guidance," it did not begin to live up to the experts' hopes. "Though we consider that we were helpful in many ways," Spock went on to Freud, "we were clearly incapable of preventing many problems (e.g., toilet training problems) and distortions of personality, most of them minor, two quite serious." Meanwhile, parents themselves proved to be surprisingly good at rising to challenges as they occurred. "Professional counselors too often expect parents to meet children's needs in rather stereotyped ways," Spock's main collaborator, Mary Bergen, observed. "Actually, these parents were astute in establishing the balance between their own needs and the child's that best promoted growth."

It was a blow to the experts' egos, a study that "shattered . . . a little fantasy," in the words of Bergen, who concluded that mothers "were no more interested in letting us interfere than they would be interested in letting their mothers interfere or their husbands." (Spousal collaboration, evidently, was not an ideal mothers or counselors set much store by.) At the same time, of course, "it was a healthy phenomenon," she gamely recognized, a sign of just the self-reliance *Baby and Child Care* preached.

In fact, the rebuff came as something of a relief to Spock. His guilty concern about "robbing educated parents of their self-confidence (by convincing them that we know best and that they must follow our precepts)" had crested in the late 1950s when he also began worrying that "it's only a matter of time before we also confuse the less educated layers," as he wrote to the developmental psychologist Urie Bronfenbrenner at Cornell University. But on that score, Spock discovered from his work in the medical school's family clinic, his fears were evidently even more unfounded. The poorer and predominantly African-American clientele, Spock reported, "silently but firmly refuse to take advice which is pressed on them month after month by my students, who have been made anxious by their teaching in pediatrics and psychiatry." Mothers fed their children as they always had, shared rooms and beds with them, toilet trained them early, and went "back to work in a few months" (as though they could have afforded to follow the doctors' orders on that last point had they been inclined to).

"I keep saying to the students that it's wonderful that there are parents with complete confidence in their own beliefs and traditions," Spock told Bronfenbrenner, admitting wryly, "I must say that it leaves a physician who has gotten his gratification from rescuing anxious parents feeling out of work and unwanted." And by the mid-1960s, it seemed to him that his calls for more parental assertion—in his 1957 edition and ever since—were falling on deaf ears as well. The solicitous Dr. Spock was feeling superfluous all around. Switching over from the *Ladies' Home Journal* to *Redbook* in 1963, he sighed in his first column, "I sometimes think I've been sounding like an old crank these past ten years. But I don't see that I'm making much of an impression—at least, not on those parents who are inclined to be overpermissive."

He had warned that "slavish" accommodation to children risked creating not just infant and toddler tyrants but aimless adolescents, prey to the trio of maladies that had social critics alarmed by the late 1950s: conformity, apathy, and delinquency, symptoms of youths whose need for emotional security had been catered to, the experts had begun to fear, at the expense of any larger sense of social allegiance. In his magazine columns, where he branched out from babies to bigger children, Spock had kept on promising that with the right psychological tactics, applied early and more firmly, trouble could be skirted and harmony sustained. Or when all else fails, he continually urged, consult a psychiatrist, a child guidance clinic, a social welfare agency.

But that fallback refrain had become more insistent than ever, as the radical Paul Goodman observed in a review of *Problems of Parents* in 1962, complaining about Spock's constant "recourse to clinics or psychologizing about a secure structure no matter what the structure"—and noting that the doctor himself seemed to be getting restless with his own therapeutic fare. Goodman sensed that Spock, for all his "monstrous middle-classness," shared some of the disillusionment with Cold War American culture that he himself had lately aired in *Growing Up Absurd: Problems of Youth in the Organized System* (1960). Spock had indeed just joined the National Committee for a Sane Nuclear Policy (SANE), and startled Americans by appearing in an ad that violated the trademark calm and optimism so recently on display in the Kennedy campaign spot. There was the nation's icon of reassurance, his brow furrowed, frowning down on an adorable child, with an ominous message in bold type: "Dr. Spock is worried."

And half a decade later, in 1968, his revised manual had toughened up yet more and branched out—though in a way to confound the likes of both Paul Goodman and Norman Vincent Peale. As the reviewer in the *New York Times* noted, the "sturdy New England grandfather" was dispensing stodgier counsel to parents than ever before. He was anything but the Pied Piper of permissiveness portrayed in the media. In fact, Spock beat the reverend himself to the punch in preaching against the morally and socially corrosive effects of "today's child-centered viewpoint." In the opening pages of the latest revision of his bible, he chided parents for fussing too much about what their child "needs from them and from the community, instead of thinking about what the world, the neighborhood, the family will be needing from the child and then making sure that he will grow up to meet such obligations." The echo of the Kennedy-era call to civic duty—"Ask not what your country can do for you but what you can do for your country"—was unmistakable.

Mothers' empathetic mentor had incorporated the style of an emphatic minister into his manual. What ailed Americans, he now worried openly, was not so much personal insecurity as a lack of social solidarity and idealism. Spock fattened his primer with calls to parents to exert moral leadership. "Fortunate are the parents with a strong religious faith," a more hortatory doctor wrote. "They are supported by a sense of conviction and serenity in all their activities." The next-best guide "in a disenchanted, disillusioned age," he proposed, was for parents to embrace a conviction that "the most important and the most fulfilling thing that human beings can do is to serve humanity in some fashion and to live by their ideals."

Wearing his stiffer clerical collar, Spock warned with new vigor against undue reliance on the very helping professionals whose involvement in family life he had so often urged. Guided by "basic principles" drawn from their own consciences and experience, parents need never be in thrall to shifting "psychological concepts . . . [which have] been helpful in solving many of the smaller problems but . . . are of little use in answering the major questions." It was a rather radical bit of revisionism he had slipped in. In a new section entitled "What Are Your Aims in Raising a Child?" Spock rendered a verdict that the Reverend Peale, had he ever cracked the book that he was shortly to indict, would have endorsed with zeal. "We've lost a lot of our old-fashioned convictions about what kinds of morals and ambitions and characters we want [our children] to have."

And the counsel Spock offered in his other main additions, which dealt with teenagers and their troubles, was, if anything, too spiritually correct and behind the materialistic times for the likes of the enterprising Peale, "God's Salesman" in an era of prosperity. For the doctor urged the loftiest of ideals, ambitions, and characters on America's youths, fearful they might lack the selfless drive to improve on the world of their parents that he felt was the hallmark of every up-and-coming generation. "Progress in human relations, in spiritual serenity or in world security," Spock preached, depended on restoring dignity to a culture sliding into hedonism.

He left in his famous emphasis on friendly equality with children. But in revising, Spock was clearer about the need for strong parental authority, especially beyond the nursery (though, concerned about what seemed to have become a tempest over potty training, he also urged more spine with preschoolers: start at eighteen months, he said in the no-nonsense tone he recommended parents use). Spock's more pressing concern, however, was that among college-educated Americans, "parental hesitancy has been more marked in relation to adolescent children than to any other age group."

The doctor, now that he was an activist, had gotten used to talking to an audience beyond the nursery: he plainly hoped that his revised commentary on parental authority would make its way to paternal ears. For if gender adjustment had once been fathers' special province, the character building he now emphasized required some Oedipal resistance. It was easier to rebel, which teenagers needed to do in some form, if youths knew where their parents stood, so adults should hold their ground—and the higher the ground, the better. "The parent's experience should be presumed to count for a lot" in arguments with adolescents. "In the end, the parent should confidently express his judgment, his request and, if appropriate, his order." And Spock expected youth to respond with respect: "adolescents, like adults," should "be civil to people generally and definitely cordial to their parents, family friends, teachers and the people who serve them." In turn, Spock prescribed, they should have "serious obligations in helping their families," and more. For youths who "cultivate dishevelment" or lapse into disillusionment, the doctor who had once urged visits to the guidance clinic now recommended an uplifting dose of social commitment.

When the manual appeared in 1968, Dr. Spock's call to public activism sounded rather redundant—and his opponents' attacks on his indulgent Freudian child rearing sounded irrelevant. His book out-Pealed Peale, showing more old-fashioned moral stringency than many of Spock's foes mustered. At the same time, "the most socially conscious youth America has ever known," as Philip Slater put it, outstripped Spock's expectations, for he had predicted that parental hesitancy would breed apathy in the next generation. That was why he had revised as he did, to wake up the whole family.

If Spock deserved blame—or credit—for the outbreak of activism, it was a case of entirely unintended consequences, as he acknowledged in an article in *Redbook* in 1968 called "The Fuss over 'Baby and Child Care.'" "I'd be proud to be responsible for producing them," Spock wrote rather wistfully, hailing hippies and radicals as "thoughtful, conscientious, self-disciplined . . . workers for peace and social justice" (whose "eccentricities" and "provocativeness"—that "dishevelment" he didn't care for—would surely soon be outgrown). But, he went on, "I don't think there is evidence that *Baby and Child Care* has played more than a very small part."

And soon enough, Spock faced yet more unanticipated fallout from his counsel. Drafted in 1971 to be the radical People's Party candidate for president, he found himself denounced as a sexist dinosaur by his most important constituency, women. "Dr. Spock," Gloria Steinem "thundered in the tones of Jehovah" at a meeting of the National Women's Political Caucus the following year, "I hope you realize you have been a major oppressor of women in the same category as Sigmund Freud!" Suddenly he was identified as a counterrevolutionary influence, and by critics within his own camp. His book was implicated in the unrest, they charged—but not because it played any special role in inciting youthful rebellion; children's freedom from authority was a trend that had been progressing apace long before *Baby and Child Care* appeared, as Spock often pointed out. His revisions, in fact, aimed to curb its excesses. The real problem with his primer, he now learned, was that it encouraged women's oppression.

Female domesticity was indeed the distinctive postwar trend that Spock's famous manual had furthered with unparalleled success. The way it did so, reader after reader discovered, was by ever so gently and ingratiatingly intensifying a mother's responsibility for tending to the subtle emotional and social unfolding of her wonderfully responsive infant. And Spock championed the cause of maternal devotion more vigorously than ever in his 1968 edition—just when economic, and cultural, pressures were pushing the opposite way, undermining expectations that women in developed Western societies should any longer be destined for homebound lives.

Even compared to Spock's stodgy views on generational relations (that parents should be models of virtuous duty, and so on), his ideas about gender relations were old-fashioned. And in his second revision, he made no effort to hide or to update them. Quite the contrary. In 1967, looking ahead not just to his new edition but also to the two other books he had in the works—*A Teenager's Guide to Life and Love* and *Decent and Indecent: Our Personal and Political Behavior*, his meditations on the "nature of man," both published in 1970—Spock promised to startle his readers with his "opinions about other areas than peace and babies and civil rights." Be prepared, he said, for "a person who by reputation seems to have become an extreme radical" to show himself "an extreme conservative when it comes to relations between the sexes and so on." His was a position, he predicted with pride, that would "be timely, timely by being ahead of its time," though he quickly admitted, "I'm counting my chickens before they're hatched."

Indeed he was. The doctor's oeuvre as the 1970s arrived was singularly deaf to the stirrings of feminism that promised, two sociologists pointed out in *McCall's* (where recipes made way for a taste of social analysis), to "have more serious consequences for the character of society and the nature of man than any other current dilemma confronting us," even the war and perhaps the civil rights struggle. The doctor, so alert to international nuclear tensions, failed to pick up on the domestic ones. As Philip Slater noted, "from the very beginning Spock's book has tended both to encourage Pygmalionesque fantasies in mothers and to stress the complexity of the task of creating a person out of an infant." And in her book *The Magic Years*, which was a big success upon its publication in 1959, his fellow Freudian Selma Fraiberg made the task seem even more all-absorbing. "It was motherhood," Betty Friedan wrote of the ethos, enshrined as "a full-time job and career if not a religious cult." The less "child-centered" vision Spock advanced in his 1968 edition, and the more father-directed wisdom he hoped to be imparting in *Decent and Indecent*, did not offer any letup.

In the newly arduous civilizing process that Spock now scripted, children were expected to identify even more fully (although less readily, he admitted) with the appropriate parent. The Oedipal drama did double developmental duty, shaping spiritual aspirations and ideals along with sexual identities. In *Decent and Indecent* Spock dispensed his Freudianism like a wholesome moral tonic, no longer like therapeutic "soda pop," as an early fan had written. The psychoanalytic concept he clung to most fervently was sublimation: keep hedonism in check, and idealism will flourish; deny feminism, and the community-minded family can triumph. Dr. Spock's prudishness about sex must have struck his youthful allies as bizarrely quaint; his manual discouraged even dating before seventeen. But his broader vision could be construed to have a certain countercultural appeal. Success, according to Spock, was almost as suspect as sex. (Money was dirty, Mildred's son had learned early.) And he put great emphasis on curbing aggression. Mankind's animal drives needed inhibiting, so that cooperation could thrive and transform a culture riven by competition and mired in materialism.

But Spock's gender-specific recommendations in *Decent and Indecent* had an outright reactionary ring. This anti-establishment upstart was awash in nostalgia for an era of pre-modern harmony. He sounded like a Hallian throwback as he praised the social and spiritual virtues of sub-limation for females. A girl's Oedipal drama and "inborn temperament" left her "not as apt as a boy to become fascinated with such particularly abstract subjects as mathematics and, later, physics and law." Instead, she was filled with "a strong urge to satisfy human needs." In the same Victorian vein, he worried that "when women are encouraged to be competitive too many of them become disagreeable."

Spock praised them for their selfless emotional strengths, and for their greater patience "in working at unexciting, repetitive tasks," both of which made them "indispensable as wives, mothers, nurses, secre-taries." Especially mothers: "My prime concern is that, back at the childhood stage, parents and schools not encourage girls to be compet-itive with males if that is going to make them dissatisfied with raising children, their most creative job in adulthood." Thanks to their sacrifi-cial natures and duties, women devoted to the home were the beacons who could lead the way toward a more "idealistic, spiritual, and cre-ative" world, in which "loving service" would "dominate over greed and power craving." Timely such gospel was not.

Steinem's attack in 1972 while he was out on the presidential cam-paign trail took Dr. Spock completely by surprise, but he did not strike back, as he had at Peale. He stood speechless at the podium at the National Women's Political Caucus, stunned at the jeers that greeted the "very reasonable and charming . . . polite, even chivalrous" apolo-gies he had just offered for anything that might be considered sexist in his classic or his latest books. A Freudian who had always prided himself on being "a friend of women," Spock had no precedent for such a wholesale indictment of his motives and morals—except, as he later pointed out, Mildred Spock. She was the female scourge he could never forget, even when he had become defiant himself, lashing out at power-ful men and bristling at male challenges to his ever more radical politics. "I always listen to criticism," he said about his efforts to accommodate feminists, "not because I am noble, but because I was criticized all through my childhood and I had to adapt one way or another to my mother's constant criticalness toward her children in general."

In truth, he had not always listened to female criticism. Jane Spock's complaints, the first to be lodged about the kindly doctor's oppressive expectations of women, had gone largely untended since her crisis of the 1950s. "Well, I'm just back of him and don't object to many things he wants to do, and make life as comfortable for him as possible," she once told a reporter who bothered to ask about the plight of an itiner-ant activist's helpmeet. What she had longed for in Spock's "retirement" had been a quieter idyll together, but instead she often found herself stranded alone in New York, waiting. "My role. Regular women's role," she had sighed. As Spock proceeded to show his usual resilience in adapting his books to the reality of working mothers and the quest for gender equality, there was one woman with whom he could not come to an accommodation: his wife.

Dr. Spock brought out his third revision in 1976, scrubbed clean of sexism. "What's most interesting about this change of mind," observed the author (a mother), of a *New York Times* "Parent and Child" column about the doctor's new wisdom, "is that it's a case of 'expertise' taking its cue from social change, rather than the other way around. Very gradually parents are beginning to call a few of the shots." Critics of feminism were furious at just that, and accused Spock of caving in. The doctor, unfazed, readily admitted that his updating, though partly a matter of principle, was also inspired by—what else?—common sense. "I'm a writer of books for young women," he explained, "and obviously more and more young women are going to be for women's liberation. Just from a practical point of view, I can't be twenty years behind them." The fourth edition of *Baby and Child Care* was testimony to how many feminist demands had made their mark on middle-class American consciousness—if also to how little experts (or anyone) had to offer when it came to handling the real dilemmas in store for reconfigured families.

Spock solved the "he"-child problem by using "they," and shifted the mother focus by referring to "parents." With the arrival of plurals, the cozy "you" receded, and the Spockian child, so deftly and fondly drawn, lost a little vividness. The old tone of conversational intimacy was not gone, but it had faded. He downplayed boys' and girls' sex roles and the drama of gender identity formation, emphasized fathers' domestic responsibilities, and supported equal opportunity for women. Just how dual-career couples or divorced parents would cope, he skimmed over, sometimes supplementing "parents" with a parenthetical "(or care-givers)," without dwelling at any length on the child care challenges or psychological conundrums posed by working motherhood. Instead Spock waxed utopian as he discoursed on how "The Family Is Chang-ing," invoking a "more humane society" in which men and women could both "feel that the care of children and home is at least as impor-tant and soul-satisfying as any other activity."

But his own changing family betrayed the strains of shifting power relations at home in America. Though the children were, of course, long gone (Michael was directing the Boston Children's Museum, John drifting after a stint as an architecture graduate student at Harvard), peace did not prevail. After the fizzle of her husband's presidential campaign, Jane Spock felt that she had paid her dues as the tagalong, or left-behind, wife. Still drinking much too much, she was often bitterly demanding, sabotaging her own efforts to get the septuagenarian Spock to slow down and go sailing with her. The tensions, and outright battles, between them became impossible to ignore by the early 1970s. Upset at Jane's state and at Ben's obtuseness—and impatient with what had now been decades of friction between them—their sons (and a daughter-in-law, Michael's wife, Judy) corralled them all into family therapy. It brought some clarity but still no harmony.

And the revising of the manual, long ago a unifying mission in their lives, only stirred up old resentments for Jane Spock. Instead of getting credit for her work on the book, she had been eclipsed by a super-famous doctor who, she complained with newfound feminist vehemence, could only see her as a lowly housewife, not the true co-author she felt she was. "I might have been more of a somebody," she tearfully told an interviewer in 1976 when the new edition came out. "But I don't think he could stand it, sharing the spotlight."

It was a poignant cry from a woman who was thanked more profusely than ever before in a new dedication. Yet she saw that she had in fact stepped into the shadows. After a trial separation in 1975, hoping for some new perspective on their differences and on her drinking, Dr. Spock had filed for divorce, ending nearly a half century of marriage. Jane knew he had "[taken] up with a 38-year-old girlfriend." More accurately, the spirited Mary Morgan—a divorcée with a daughter—had swept him off his feet. The doctor was still making audiences swoon after all these years, and she had been one of many women smitten when he came through Little Rock, Arkansas, on a lecture tour—the one with the gumption to go after him.

Dr. Spock never really settled down again. With Morgan (a conference coordinator, and now his wife) at his side, he became the guru-on-the-go, updating his home wisdom for a mobile century from, first, a sailboat docked in the Virgin Islands and then, when the deck got too slippery for even an agile octogenarian, from a twenty-two-foot Winnebago called the Tortoise. Perhaps it was no wonder that his revisions sometimes sounded written on the run, as he duly made sure every edition of his comprehensive classic (1985, 1992, 1998) covered all the new bases. From "Divorce, Single Parents, and Stepparents," issues he knew firsthand, he branched out to teenage pregnancy, homosexuality, and "superkids"—aware that every topic now had its specialists, whose books crowded the bookstore shelves.

The homey tone that had once distinguished his book was still in there, but Spock's new trademark became the earnest homily. He made a point of showcasing the social concern about macro-issues—from "the deterioration of the environment and international relations" to "the influence of giant corporate interests that care little for human individuals"—that he urged on middle-class parents. (He also found a macro-issue closer to home: Spock made it his mission to push macro-biotic food, inspired by Mary Morgan's zeal in devoting hours of her days to procuring, and preparing, the exotic—and bland and mushy—diet for him as his health declined. The son of a Holtian fanatic about wholesome food had come full circle.) Spock's last edition, which came out just after he died in March 1998, opened as its predecessor had with a sermon on "Raising Children in a Troubled Society" and closed with "A Better World for Our Children." The "I" was still there, but the voice in those sections had acquired the oddly bland urgency heard at countless conferences on the crisis of the American family.

3.

The other doctor in high dudgeon in 1969, Dr. Bruno Bettelheim, had vowed upon arriving in America thirty years earlier that he "would make a new life for myself very different from the old one." Yet watching students attack the citadel where he had re-created himself, he panicked that he had not escaped after all. "I see exactly the same thing happening here from the so-called left as happened in Germany from the right," Bettelheim seized the microphone to say during a siege on the main administration building at the University of Chicago. He went on, there and elsewhere, to diagnose a dangerous yearning in youth for absolute authority. But what seems to have had Bettelheim just as unnerved was the protesters' demand for "authenticity," the rallying cry of a generation that accused its parents, and American culture, of betraying the very values they claimed to support. For never had an expert been more aware of the limits of his own credibility than Bruno Bettelheim.

Twenty years later, after he committed suicide in 1990, the true novelty of that "new life" of his was revealed. Bettelheim's renown turned out to have rested on a series of fabrications about his Austrian past and about his exploits at his Orthogenic School. In *The Uses of Enchantment: The Meaning and Importance of Fairy Tales*, his idiosyncratic child-rearing classic of 1976, he celebrated the power of fairy tales to help children "achieve a unified personality able to meet successfully, with inner security, the difficulties of living." As he put it elsewhere, "We must live by fictions—not just to find meaning in life but to make it bearable." Just how extensively Bettelheim had practiced what he preached, two biographers revealed in the decade after he died.

One, Richard Pollak, produced a bitter exposé of an egregious self-promoter and a school director who was violent with his charges and virulent in blaming their mothers. The other, Nina Sutton, sympathetically evoked a Holocaust survivor driven to fulfill a very big fantasy: that he could salve his own guilt at having been saved by proving himself a larger-than-life rescuer of children at the Sonia Shankman School he led for almost thirty years, starting in 1944. Neither quite captured Bettelheim the ex-director of the 1970s, who emerged in retirement as an embattled child-rearing expert with a discomfiting message about America's changing families. The same doctor who urged a tougher line with radical youth, and had taken one himself with the mothers of his patients, also spoke out for more autonomy for women and children in the American family—warning as he did so that plenty of struggle was in store.

Bettelheim's ambition was undeniably of grandiose proportions. It also seems clear that by the mid-1960s he was a man who was feeling increasingly ambivalent about his own inventions. At first, his dream of being a savior seems to have justified in his mind the various fictions that helped to launch his career in America during the 1940s and to win him fame during the 1950s. His version of his ordeals in Dachau and Buchenwald endowed him with more heroism, and his fellow prisoners with more passivity, than he or they evidently deserved. He claimed to have a psychology degree from the University of Vienna and to have known Freud, neither of which was true. His report of having been the guardian of two autistic girls during the 1930s was false, too; there was only one girl, who was not autistic, and his first wife did the tending.

The morally and intellectually lustrous credentials were concocted, yet Bettelheim had the gifts and the energy to make them credible. His experience in the camps and his exposure to the Viennese psychoanalytic milieu, though they failed to conform to his own accounts, nonetheless served to inspire a one-of-a-kind crusade: to help "children nobody else did." And his conviction that he could succeed seems to have excused his continuing deceptions, not just about his European past but now about the healing "therapeutic milieu" of his school during its early "magical years" as well.

Thus in *Love Is Not Enough: The Treatment of Emotionally Disturbed Children* (1950) and five years later in *Truants from Life: The Rehabilitation of Emotionally Disturbed Children*, Bettelheim featured inspiring odysseys. In vivid prose, he portrayed children making dramatic progress under the patient, permissive care of a staff of young and untrained yet empathetic counselors. Most of them young women, they became his acolytes and quasi-patients, their own emotional self-discovery bound up with their efforts to reach the students. The school's accomplishments were indeed remarkable. But "Dr. B," as the domineering director was called, airbrushed out the firm discipline he also resorted to, acting as the "superego" to the children's "id" and the counselors' "ego." He was playing to a public he felt would not appreciate the need to instill order, and some fear, to help troubled children learn to control their destructive impulses: his Big Bad Wolf role, bound to be misunderstood, was not good PR.

Bettelheim was not burnishing with a view simply to resting on his laurels, however. He was also—no doubt unconsciously—courting failure. He craved the adulation he received, but it also drove him to raise the stakes for himself ever higher. The revered doctor took in more severely disturbed children all the time—which in turn meant that Dr. B showed his fierce face more often, for they were hard to handle.

By the mid-1960s—just as Dr. Spock's "little fantasy" of expert power was being shattered by his Child Rearing Study—Bettelheim's much grander fantasy of benevolent salvation was under severe strain. For in 1956 he had tackled the biggest challenge of all: he got a grant from the Ford Foundation to study and treat autistic children, whose prospects for complete recovery most experts judged then (as now) to be dim—and whose diagnosis was still ill defined. Bettelheim proposed to prove that his "total therapeutic environment" could cure them, and to shed light on the parental inadequacies that he felt lay at the source of the illness. Success with autism would, "more than anything else, establish the merit of the school's philosophy and of its methods."

Yet by the early 1960s, he could see that the children's progress was not living up to his boasts and to the expectations he had built with his previous books. Nor had he emerged with any proof of parents' catalytic role. And to judge by the reminiscences of counselors and patients, Bettelheim was becoming an even more fearful master of his frustrating realm as he struggled with his difficult students and with setbacks. Pollak dug up accounts that had him slapping, punching, and shaming students—and fondling some of the girls. The memories of abuse are hard to corroborate and evaluate, but Bettelheim's "philosophy" and "methods" plainly did not fit the "Dr. Yes" image he cultivated in public. Nor, by the end, was he the steadying "superego" either, it seems. As Bettelheim's tenure as director drew toward a close—retirement loomed in view by the mid-1960s—punitive impulses seemed to get the better of a deeply uneasy man faced with the collapse of his heroic dream.

On the eve of America's public crisis of authority, he was facing his own crisis of authority and legitimacy. And a visit to a kibbutz in Israel in 1964 failed to boost a demoralized Bettelheim. Finding it impossible to write his Ford Foundation report, he had set off eager to challenge recent critics of the kibbutz, and to pronounce its communal approach to child rearing a triumph of personal and social integration—and an indirect endorsement of his own nonparental milieu. He also hoped to find a useful corrective for an America that he (unlike Spock) diagnosed on the brink of nuclear family trouble, from the suburbs to the slums. Drugs and delinquency seemed to be rare among kibbutz children, and he wondered if there might be a model for dealing with the troubles of poor urban youth.

In articles in *Daedalus, Harper's, The New Republic,* and elsewhere during the early 1960s, Bettelheim had been subjecting the American family in the consumer era to a withering analysis, mixing Oedipal and social interpretations of the rising tensions. The quests for "self-identity" and "a place in society" seemed to stymie not just "culturally deprived" youths, but more and more middle-class adolescents, too, he argued. Weak fathers felt trapped in the corporate "rat race," toiling to afford consumer luxuries rather than the necessities the entrepreneurs and producers of old had worked for. In their own eyes, they were spineless and superfluous, a view that was not lost on their children, because these beleaguered dads "did a good job of showing the young how hollow a life they had built."

Mothers and daughters were in, if anything, a greater bind. "Growing Up Female," Bettelheim lamented in an essay whose title echoed the radical Paul Goodman's *Growing Up Absurd,* entailed facing an even more "absurd" set of "strangely—and often painfully—contradictory expectations." American girls were raised and educated, like boys, to expect "the kind of work that gives meaning to their lives," not to be "(of necessity) a drudge" whose "psychosocial identity resides in child-bearing and homemaking," he wrote in "The Problem of Generations" in 1962. Yet they came of age only to be confronted with the dull round of modern, mechanized domestic life. Even—or especially—the challenges of psychologically correct child rearing, Bettelheim insisted in "Women: Emancipation Is Still to Come" in 1964, could not make "being a full-time wife and mother . . . in and by itself absorbing or rewarding enough to fill out 30 or more years of a woman's life." Instead Freudian fears left her more hobbled, fretting "overly about her infant" and then feeling "she must always be available to her child, to protect him from overstimulation, and to lovingly take care of him at all moments." Bettelheim took aim at his hidebound colleagues. "Some of our psychologists and psychiatrists—and those social scientists whom they unduly influence—will have to stop viewing the Victorian woman as the ideal female type, as the only mother who does not cheat her children out of motherlove."

At Ramat Yohanan, among the oldest collective farms in Israel, Bettelheim intended to find cures for domestic and social strains. Yet here, too, his high expectations were dashed. He came home from his six-week stay (that was as much as he could take of group life, and enough for the usual Bettelheimian brand of impressionistic rather than systematic research) with yet more findings that failed to add up the way he had hoped. The kibbutz founders had indeed devised solutions to the problems that he singled out: mothers trapped in domesticity, and teenagers kept in dependent limbo far too long. Kibbutz women, working alongside men, had autonomy and little maternal guilt. Adolescents, working productively alongside adults, were free of anomie; their egos were strong. Yet those solutions came at a price, Bettelheim worried: a loss of intimacy and of individual complexity—"an emotional flatness" of character that he thought even the kibbutz founders had not expected and might discover was a problem in the future. In any case, such a streamlined method of socializing children, so consistently applied and so closely allied with the values of a homogeneous society, was hardly a workable model for a pluralistic, open country like America.

Bettelheim was as blocked in his efforts to produce a report or a book about this "experiment" as he was with his much bigger Ford Foundation endeavor, the project that was supposed to cap his career at the Sonia Shankman School. He stewed over his mixed feelings as he watched the spreading "restless dissatisfaction of youth" and of women during the mid-1960s. When he at last turned to deal with his own dissatisfying autism work, Bettelheim—this time more than ever—could see no uses in disenchantment: he needed his heroic dream intact. And so in the book he sat down to write, *The Empty Fortress*, he went ahead and exaggerated his success more egregiously than ever before and once again hid the violence that had become more pronounced. "Scientific rigor," as the Ford Foundation had noted in doling out the funds in the first place, was not Bettelheim's strong suit. An evocative case history approach like his allowed for fudging of samples, methods, and final results, and Bettelheim did so quite brazenly.

In the group of children he included in his study were boys and girls for whom the label autistic was a stretch, elusive though diagnoses were then (and still can be); certainly it didn't fit "Joey the Mechanical Boy," one of the three case studies that became the heart of *The Empty Fortress*. Bettelheim claimed "good" results with 42 percent of the children in his project, "average" outcomes with 37 percent, and failure in only 20 percent of the cases—outstripping by miles any other achievements with autistic children before or since. Bettelheim offered no evidence for his assessments. And he breathed not a word about the terror he could instill behind the school walls.

But it was as though Bettelheim could not help betraying his image as the liberator of lost innocents. This fiction seemed to be one he could not quite forgive himself, though he could never confess the lie either. Instead, in 1969 he burst forth on the barricades as the Big Bad Wolf for all the world to see. The erstwhile savior of children shocked his liberal worshipers, and shook up the hallowed image he knew he did not deserve. The doctor whose own rescue efforts had not nearly lived up to his hopes, or claims, castigated Americans—parents and youths alike—for their failures. And they were now ready to indict him in return: evidence for the biological basis of autism had begun to accumulate by the late 1960s, and Bettelheim was soon under attack as the ur-mother-blamer.

He was an expert in need of coming to terms with his compromised authority, and also with reality—hardly an enterprise that came easily to Bettelheim. Yet as the 1970s unfolded, he did the best he could by carving out a curious niche as America's disenchanted parenting expert. Disappointed in his ambitions for his "Home for the Heart," as he called the school in his last book about it in 1974, Bettelheim the director had hidden the dark side of his endeavor and his many difficulties. Bettelheim the child-rearing adviser turned around and made the ambivalence at the heart of family life his theme as he spoke out to "normal" America, where he saw plenty of souls struggling with conflicting demands and desires.

Bettelheim the former miracle worker became a troublemaker, now priding himself on being the brave bearer of a disillusioning message:

that, as he put it in, of all places, *Playboy* magazine in 1971, the postwar ideals of "leisure, the absence of struggle, order . . . the principle of harmony at all costs," whether embraced by hippies or by company men or by conscientious mothers, were not the solution to what ailed America but the problem. "The affluent middle-class American wants life to run smoothly, doesn't want any difficulties. He wants the mountain to be level and the pool to be tepid. And then he wonders why his children reject him," Bettelheim complained.

He continued the denunciation of the meretricious culture fostered by a bureaucratic society and a consumer economy that he had begun in the early 1960s. No wonder youths, as they neared the end of the long educational ladder they had to climb to please credential-obsessed parents intent on vicarious success, looked around and lashed out at "the system" and its conflicting values. Raised on the middle-class virtues of "soft" self-expression and hard-driving achievement, they had been endlessly "understood" and subtly pushed. Yet they had never had a chance "to stand up on [their] own two feet," as Bettelheim liked to put it. They had "nothing to push against because everything gives way." They lacked a role in society, any firm parental authority to challenge, and thus any chance to discover their autonomy or define their identity.

And their parents were equally confused about their role as adults in relation to their children. "What I would really like to do," Bettelheim wrote a friend in 1971 as he left Chicago for a first stab at retirement at the Center for Advanced Study in the Behavioral Sciences at Stanford, is "a book that sees the kid in contact (or, if you want, emotional back and forth) with the parent." He worried that it would be "impossibly difficult to bring off" what he had in mind: an effort to understand why "today . . . parents are so dumbfounded by their kids though they understand them so much better than other generations. So there is a problem: We know so much better what makes them tick, and are so much less able to live with them." It was 1987 when Bettelheim finally produced the book, *A Good Enough Parent*, but in the meantime he had already set himself up as a disconcerting expert who refused to dispense neat prescriptions, but instead aimed to shake up American expectations about family dynamics.

By the 1970s, dire verdicts on the embattled American family had become a national specialty, and soothing messages about togetherness were a relic of the past. Managing power struggles, rather than assuring peace, was the mission of child-rearing expertise as the decade unfolded. The statistics that regularly made headlines told the story of domestic instability. The birthrate dropped to the lowest it had been since the 1930s, half what it was during the 1950s, and the divorce rate had been steadily rising. In 1976 the *Times* announced a banner year of breakups: more than a million (double the number in 1965). Mothers were working in greater numbers than ever before. At mid-decade, 46 percent of children under eighteen had mothers employed outside the house. In case anyone was in doubt about the anti-domestic zeitgeist, Hollywood projected it in a bumper crop of horror movies of the home-is-hell and children-are-demons variety during the decade: after *Rosemary's Baby*, a hit in 1968, came *The Exorcist, It's Alive!, The Omen*, and *Carrie*.

Now that Dr. Spock's sway had been challenged, any pretense to expert consensus had also vanished, except that the calm "trust yourself" ethos and reliance on motherly intuition were passé. On increasingly crowded bookshelves ("there are many more books and many more readers of them than ever before," noted a *New York Times* "Parents and Child" columnist in 1976), the style was fiercer and more formulaic, on the "parent-centered" right as on the "child-centered" left. Dr. James Dobson's *Dare to Discipline* of 1971 sternly advised taming little hellions with a hard squeeze of the trapezius muscle ("lying snugly against the base of the neck"). Dr. Fitzhugh Dodson's bestselling *How to Parent* (the book that coined the verb in 1970) sounded just as peremptory about not being peremptory: "Thou shalt NOT ignore the crying of a baby." "Thou shalt NOT try to toilet train a baby." "Thou shalt NOT worry about spoiling a baby." "Thou shalt NOT let father ignore the baby." But thou shall, he also preached, attend to "the intellectual development of children in the first five years." Chiding Spock for being "particularly deficient in discussing the importance of . . . intellectual stimulation during those crucial early years," Dodson joined researchers and policymakers in sounding a cognitive theme.

And there was another "Dr. D," as Rudolf Dreikurs, a follower of the Freudian renegade Alfred Adler and the author of *Children: The Challenge* (1964), was known. An émigré from Vienna (of roughly Dr. B's vintage), Dreikurs made the Adlerian concept of "the inferiority complex" the centerpiece of child-rearing advice that was at once gruff and egalitarian. As goal-driven children struggled for social status and a sense of their place in the family, Dreikurs instructed, parents must encourage them to discover their own competence and independence—and to cooperate, for "unrestricted freedom has made tyrants of children and slaves of the parents." He was ready with techniques to help parents and children assume "ownership" of their problems in a post-authoritarian era. Dreikurs's signature "democratic" methods were the family council and a disciplinary approach he called "logical consequences": children were to learn "the principles and restrictions necessary for group living" not from power-wielding or wheedling parents, but from facing up to the results of their own actions—with support from adults, whose role was to help clarify and codify the many choices on the road to maturity. ("Homework not done brings the teacher's wrath. Toys destroyed are gone—not replaced." Logical conditions are coolly laid out, and stuck to: no toothbrushing in the morning, no ice cream with the other kids after school.)

Haim Ginott, an Israeli-born psychologist also of an Adlerian bent, concurred that "insight is insufficient," and supplied the other crucial tool to quell the "raging storm" in too many American homes. His *Between Parent and Child* (1965) was a guide to nonconfrontational dialogue, the purpose of which was to replace heavy-handed authority with skillful empathy. It had sold a million and a half copies by the end of the decade, and it spawned a vogue in communication techniques as the key to noncoercive control. "Empathic," or "active," listening was the first step ("Sounds as if it really hurts!" rather than "Come on, don't make such a fuss"). Avoiding judgmental "you" messages was the accompanying principle ("Skates belong in the closet," or "I don't like tripping over skates" instead of "Why don't you ever remember to put your skates away?"). A California psychologist named Dr. Thomas Gordon peddled his own systematized version in his Parent Effectiveness Training program, which despite its "forbidding sound" had the makings of a "movement," the *Times* judged as the 1970s began.

A severely un-Spockian spirit united the disparate experts of the decade: "The raising of a child is a complex and difficult proposition," as Dr. Dodson put it, certainly not an invitation to warm fun. But Bettelheim emerged as the most daunting expert of all. For where Dr. Dobson urged an old-fashioned approach, and the other Dr. Ds and Dr. Gs dispensed formulas for orderly "democratic" family life, Dr. B refused to do either. And he resisted the early cognitive push prescribed by, among others, Dr. Burton L. White of Harvard, who assigned mothers the job of cribside educational consultants in his popular *The First Three Years of Life* (1975). As if to make up for glossing over the battles and obstacles in his school, Bettelheim now wrote as a grim realist rather than a romantic about the difficulty of achieving empathy, about the inevitable inequality between adults and children, and about the dilemmas facing women in their quest for fulfillment beyond motherhood.

While Bettelheim the reluctant retiree struggled to separate from the school where he had forged (in both senses) his professional reputation, he was scrambling for popular sway as a columnist in the *Ladies' Home Journal*. "Very frightening," Dr. Spock once commented in passing about his successor in the slot—"scared the hell out of people." Bettelheim was indeed an alarming presence in the glossy pages, offering anything but predictable nostrums in his "Dialogues with Mothers," which appeared for three years starting in 1970. Barely half a year into his stint as resident guru writing in a dogmatic/Socratic vein, he began his campaign to challenge the ladies-at-home assumptions of his venue with "Why Working Mothers Have Happier Children." Here was a Freudian to flummox Steinem, and everybody else, too. Was this doctor eager to get meddling mothers out of the way and to whip children into line, or to give women a chance to work and children more freedom to find themselves?

Bettelheim was far from a conventional advocate of women's liberation. He derided the gender-blind goals of the feminist movement. In his own household, he had left it to his wife, Trude, to be the superparent who tended without complaint to his workaholic needs and to their three children—and to her own career as a pediatric social worker. He had been a paternalistic, intimidating guide to the restless young counselors at his school, and a merciless judge of his patients' mothers. But Bettelheim greeted feminism as the social crisis that would perhaps spur the postwar family to face its contradictions.

At stake for women, in his view, was not a fight against an authoritarian patriarchy, the power of which had in fact been eroding for decades in industrial and post-industrial America. Bettelheim instead saw women waging a subtler struggle to escape what had become a permissive matriarchy at home. Now, in their quest for control over their own lives, women had to confront the question of just how much control, of what kind, they could or should exert over their children's lives. The doctor who worried about maternal rejection also worried about maternal projection: Were mothers foisting their thwarted ambitions onto their children, depriving them of their own struggle for "inner integration"?

In his bullying way, Bettelheim goaded his readers to such questions. He portrayed at-home mothers not as mere oppressed victims, but as deeply conflicted accomplices in a fate that history had now made intolerable for many of them. They were not eager to overthrow the family, he felt, and not even all that eager to join the "rat race." Yet many an American mother was dying to escape her "unsatisfying existence" as the "one family member . . . [who] exists simply to serve the needs of all the others"—and, worst of all, who is expected to feel that all her "needs and aspirations are fulfilled through service to her family." Bettelheim did not mince words in "What's Happening to the Family." It was "a life of bondage. . . . If one person, the mother, gives the other family members all options and denies herself any, she puts herself in a self-made jail. And if she does not do so, but feels guilty because she doesn't, then she puts herself in a psychological jail."

He rejected the usual expert salves for female discontentment. To prescribe more psychologically (and sexually) satisfying relations with her husband was merely to gild the bars of her prison. And to promise a more "rewarding" vision of her child-rearing mission, raising expectations of fulfillment through others, only guaranteed the "subtle enslavement" of the whole family. In *The Children of the Dream: Communal Child-Rearing and American Education*, the book based on his kibbutz visit that Bettelheim finally wrote in 1969, he described how "resentment that her life should be swept up entirely in her wifely and motherly roles" drove "many a middle-class American mother," abetted by experts, to a self-sabotaging "solution" for her guilty drive to derive more satisfaction from her days: "She works doubly hard at being a good mother, with the result that she pushes her child, often beyond his endurance. He must perform well, and thus prove her a good mother, though she worries that she is not."

Compared to Spock—though he, too, peddled a more bracing Oedipal formula in his 1968 edition—Bettelheim dispensed bitter Freudian medicine, certainly for the postwar American palate. He focused more on children's aggressive drives than on their sexual desires, and pushed parents to grow up and grapple with their role as powerful rather than merely lovable figures in their children's lives. It was a "hard" line that got Bettelheim lumped in with the parent-centered camp and cast—as Holt and Watson had been, too—as a pro-punishment expert, scolding mothers and especially fathers not to give in to their kids.

And he did indeed sound like a fierce crusader against children's freedom as he lectured parents on their "adult responsibility" to help their sons and daughters erect "in their minds an institution—we call it the conscience or super-ego—that will tell them what to do and what not to do." He warned that the process entailed strenuous labor, not peace or pleasure, for Bettelheim's baby was no Spockian Buddha who needed merely to be kept in natural equilibrium. Complaining that "psychoanalysis tends to see the infant as passive," he portrayed him instead as an "immensely active" self-in-the-making, flailing amid "raw emotions" and fearful fantasies to deal with his abject dependence—and then, as he grew, to claim his independence and the "inner control" required to "act on the basis of long-range goals." His "efforts are monumental," and his parents in turn had better be prepared, Bettelheim warned, for their confrontational part in the drama. "What was wrong with old-fashioned, authoritarian education was not that it was based on fear," he argued in an article with the intimidating title "Children Must Learn to Fear" in the *New York Times Magazine* in 1969. "That is what was right with it."

At the same time Bettelheim could sound like a champion of children's interests and a merciless critic of parental narcissism and middle-class hypocrisy. Preaching in a gentler vein (which he evidently failed to practice), he emphasized that by fear he did not mean old-style terror of punishment, "the debilitating fear of damnation that haunted our grandfathers, nor the unconscionable fear of being beaten black and blue." He was well aware of "the crippling price of inhibition and rigidity [such fear] exacts," and his goal was to empower children with a sense of their own resources. "What was wrong with [old-fashioned, authoritarian education]," he went on to explain in the *Times Magazine*, "was that it disregarded the need to modify the fear in a continuous process so that irrational anxiety would steadily give way to more rational motivation." But that was the flaw, too, in what "we call 'permissive' training," which Bettelheim denounced as, if anything, more effective at instilling insecurity deep in children—and in their parents, too.

Children needed a chance to "accept themselves as imperfect beings," full of anger and forbidden desires and thoughts, Bettelheim insisted. In addition, every child required "much greater autonomy and a chance to develop true mastery of his body. . . . He also needs much greater intimacy, which is the opposite of popularity." Middle-class parents, he felt, sent deeply mixed messages about children's "instinctual experience," basing their "decisions on what to repress and what to discharge . . . not on the interests of the child but on the convenience of adults." He was among the first to protest the plight of "the hurried child," labeled and much lamented in the 1980s and ever since. What looked like indulgence, Bettelheim wrote, was in fact part of a subtle negotiation the child could never win, leaving him at the mercy of his parents' often confused aspirations—and of a technocratic consumer society's contradictions and pressures. "Didn't I let you hang onto your bottle?" his parents in essence told him. "Now go and be a whiz at school." What looked like "a desire that our children become independent, form their own judgments and make their own decisions," Bettelheim chided his readers, only held up so long as "the result of their 'independence' jibes with what we want them to do." He accused parents of in fact demanding the utmost conformity, all in the name of harmony and equality, thereby depriving their child of "the most important thing of all: the right to form his own inner opinions, influenced not by their authoritative preachments, but only by his own direct experience with life."

Yet even as Bettelheim emphasized again and again what an embattled, unbalanced institution the nuclear family had become in the post-industrial era, he refused to panic over its fragility. The big mistake postwar Americans had made, he declared in the fiftieth anniversary issue of *Parents' Magazine* in 1976 as he had in *Playboy* half a decade earlier, was to expect that the modern family should be "free of serious difficulties, and should run like a smoothly-working machine," that children and parents should discover peaceful unity, that worries should fly out the window. On the contrary, "the prime task of psycho-analytic education," as he put it elsewhere, lay in "transforming this force of anxiety from one that shrivels us into a force that expands us and our lives."

This Freudian had never imagined a family that was not fraught, and his pessimism, oddly, gave him hope. Bettelheim looked back to a pre-psychological era when an economic compact and a sense of reciprocal obligation—parental support in return for child labor—had bound young and old, not in bliss and peace or equality, but in busyness and a sense of solidarity, especially in the face of adversity. In the vision that emerged from his popular writings, freeing women to work was a step on the road to reviving the sturdy spirit of loyalty, without which there could be no true "feeling of belonging," the crucial experience that only a family can give. "If the correct view prevailed—that when people live together this, in itself, creates problems," Bettelheim the realist wrote, "then it could be seen that the good family isn't one in which problems don't occur, but one in which the members work together to solve problems as they happen."

Work together: that was Bettelheim's prescription for frustrated women, and for festering families. It was time Americans acknowledged that current family and job arrangements were not "God-given . . . but . . . can be readjusted to new conditions," and that it was up to "everybody [to] make adjustments"—by which he meant that mothers must not, yet again, be expected to make all the sacrifices in what was bound to be a difficult transition. Ahead of his time, Bettelheim appreciated the inseparable structural and psychological dimensions of the task. "So long as the working mother feels that no matter how good working may be for her it is still bad for her child," Bettelheim observed, "little good will come of it for either of them." She required allies close to home. "Another change in inner attitude will also be necessary," Bettelheim emphasized, "namely men must become convinced that they and their children will be better off with a fully satisfied wife and mother than with one who reluctantly tries to fit herself into an unnatural role because she feels she has to."

All these shifts of perspective teetered on a Catch-22. Everyone had to feel confident that children would thrive if they spent at least part of a day tended by people other than their mothers, in good child-care arrangements—though such arrangements, Bettelheim acknowledged, would come into being only once this "conviction becomes commonplace." Who better to proselytize for group care than the author of one of the few treatments of the subject then available, *The Children of the Dream*? Yet in that book Bettelheim revealed how deeply conflicted he felt about nonparental, peer-directed rearing—and how dubious he was that such a homogeneous approach to child care could ever suit motley America, not least because coping with contradiction and conflict was a skill its citizens needed to start learning early. Instead, he invoked a vague vision, à la Spock. "Let me suggest that working arrangements should be much more flexible than family arrangements—although the opposite now prevails," he wrote, again sounding ahead of his time. Unlike the Spockian haven of high communal ideals, Bettelheim envisaged an idyll of—what else?—dogged industry. "Children must not be isolated from their parents' work world," he proclaimed, urging that it "once again become possible for boys and girls to work alongside their parents." Just what he had in mind, he never made clear, but he certainly sounded behind the times.

In 1976, Bettelheim came the closest he ever did to a how-to book, and in it he retreated from society to the psyche—and to a literary remedy. In *The Uses of Enchantment: The Meaning and Importance of Fairy Tales* (which made it onto the New York Public Library's list of the 159 most influential "Books of the Century" in 1995), he defied the schoolmarmish and therapeutic emphasis on exposing children "only to the sunny side of things" in their reading. Instead he championed the long suspect genre of fairy tales (the fiercer the better) as just the bracing lessons the young need in their struggles for selfhood. Bettelheim did not, however, have in mind cuddling by the hearth. Parents should read the tales (and Bettelheim's "deep" Freudian reading of the tales) in order to understand them as "a magic mirror which reflects some aspects of our inner world, and of the steps required by our evolution from immaturity to maturity." But adults should not " 'explain' to the child the meanings of fairy tales," which breaks their spell. Only an enchanted listener can experience the stories in a way that ministers to his or her "nameless anxieties" and "chaotic, angry, and even violent fantasies."

It was not exactly toiling in the fields or the office together, but Bettelheim had parallel labors in mind. Adults would remind themselves of what mysteries they, the giants, are to children and also of what miseries there are in being powerless. At their side, children would work toward "self-mastery." If readers of his magazine columns had been at something of a loss as to how to stage the superego-forming drama he recommended, here was an answer—complete with a script. "As the stories unfold," Bettelheim explained in his introduction, "they give conscious credence and body to id pressures and show ways to satisfy these that are in line with ego and superego requirements." He promised that a child dealing on his own with fairy tales about being abandoned, devoured, or married off to beasts would be helped "a great deal to overcome his oedipal anguish." Fairy tales, which Bettelheim celebrated as repositories of the narcissistic fears and desires of childhood, had the power to deliver a "moral education which subtly, and by implication only, conveys to [a child] the advantages of moral behavior, not through abstract ethical concepts but through that which seems tangibly right and therefore meaningful to him."

Bettelheim's book gave a boost to his battered humanistic credentials. (It was only after his death that his heavy borrowing from a clinical psychologist named Julius Heuscher, who had written *A Psychiatric Study of Fairy Tales: Their Origin, Meaning and Usefulness* in 1963, became widely known.) In the *New York Times*, John Updike praised the "warmth, humane and urgent, with which Bettelheim expounds fairy tales as aids to the child's growth." The interpretive challenges he set small readers meshed with rising interest in honing children's cognitive capacities, even if Bettelheim offered far from typical brain-boosting fare and warned parents not to be pushy or intensive co-readers. The books-every-day-keep-the-doctor-away credo had caught on as Piaget ousted Freud as the psychologist of the hour, and *The Uses of Enchantment* had an intellectual cachet lacking in an ever more commercialized how-to market.

Yet the balance, as always with Bettelheim, was uneasy. There were readers, and there were scholars—more of them as time went on—who were put off by the reductive Freudian parsings and the overly moralizing tone, and by Bettelheim's presumption to know just how children, of all classes, unconsciously respond to their reading. Meanwhile Bettelheim himself, as Updike had pointed out, was plainly uncomfortable with the prospect that "the struggle of growing up" might not lead inexorably to the goal he so prized, "a unified personality able to meet successfully, with inner security, the difficulties of living." One story in particular—hugely popular among nineteenth- and twentieth-century readers—"vexed" him by refusing to fit his patterns, Updike noted. "At its end there is neither recovery nor consolation," Bettelheim wrote testily of "Goldilocks and the Three Bears"; "there is no resolution of conflict, and thus no happy ending."

Bettelheim was too astute not to see that this quest without closure had become a modern favorite precisely because its lesson is that there is no comforting lesson. "The story's ambiguity, which is so much in line with the temper of the times, may also account for its popularity," he reflected, "while the clear-cut solutions of the traditional fairy tale seem to point to a happier age when things were believed to permit definite solutions." But it unnerved him that this tale might suggest that "running away from a problem" was the only solution if no triumphant end was in sight. For he knew firsthand how alluring it could be to choose denial rather than indefiniteness. Bettelheim, after all, had fled from reality rather than face up to his many failures to be as heroic as he had hoped.

If ever a man knew the driving need to "live by fictions—not just to find meaning in life but to make it bearable," it was the survivor Bettelheim, whose vast ambitions were supposed to absolve him of guilt but instead left him still grasping for that "feeling of belonging." Did Goldilocks's story rattle him because in the "unsolvable predicament" of that intruder, ultimately cast out, he saw his own fate? It had been, as he saw, a story that spoke to a turn-of-the-century era when "more and more persons came to feel like outsiders." And as the end of the century approached, an increasingly depressed and ailing Bettelheim, whose beloved wife had died in 1984, was feeling there was no home that would take him in. Living with his eldest daughter, Ruth, proved impossible, and they became bitterly estranged.

So much for being *A Good Enough Parent*. That was the title (inspired by the British psychoanalyst and pediatrician D. W. Winnicott) of the parenting book he finally published in 1987, after struggling mightily with himself—and with his editor—to produce the ultimate non-primer: a dense book without an index, telling parents there was no simple "how-to" in child rearing, there was only an unending "why," as mothers and fathers probed their own pasts in search of the empathy that might help them comprehend their children's ordeals. Bettelheim's Freudian insight into parenthood was that "as much as [children] identify with us, we identify with them, usually much more and in more various ways than we consciously realize"—and in far more ambivalent ways than we are usually ready to admit, or than any expert can ever do more than begin to help us figure out. But struggle we must, Bettelheim urged, to fathom our feelings on our own as we work through the intimate dilemmas of family life that fit no "norm" in any book or chart. The struggle itself conveys "the depth of our commitment" to our children, which is "often the most important ingredient in reaching them, and with it gaining our goal: a satisfying and hence successful parent-child relationship." If only, Bettelheim had wistfully told a BBC interviewer several years earlier, he had conveyed more empathy for mothers facing this challenge—or, though he didn't say this, had seen what can happen to a father who feels he has failed to face it fully.

Experts, as far as this disenchanted one could see, had no useful seat at the table: Goldilocks's plight spoke to the dilemma of advisers on the family, too. In the aftermath of 1960s upheaval, the experts had lost their old certainty about Mama's and Papa's and baby's places, and they had been run out of the house. While Dr. Spock jauntily took to the seas and the road, jotting in his book along the way, Dr. Bettelheim ultimately found nowhere to flee but into dark woods alone.

PART IV

Psychological Limits

TEN

All in the Family

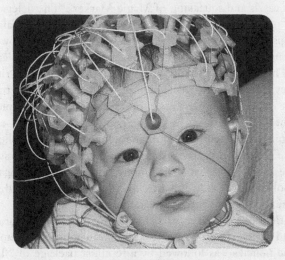

Studying the infant brain

I.

At the Baltimore meeting of President Jimmy Carter's White House Conference on Families in June of 1980, the quietest spot in the gleaming new convention center was the "family room," set up for children of the 671 delegates from nineteen eastern and southern states. One white baby doll, one black baby doll, and two small girls had the place to themselves. The dolls were sitting in what was labeled the "housekeeping area," having tea at a knee-high table in a miniature kitchen. A sign in another corner marked it out as the "creative area." There was an easel, equipped with paper, and stacked on a nearby shelf were paints and thick Magic Markers in many colors. Puzzles and games had been laid out on a low table in the "manipulative area." The girls were standing in the middle of the room, considering their options, with notable poise. These were children who plainly knew how to take new situations and separations from their parents in stride. They were intent on the work that had been laid out for them, which was play, "the learning of childhood," as "the new Dr. Spock," Dr. T. Berry Brazelton, liked to say.

Outside the door, where "a unique process of listening to American families" was taking place, the adult scene was much less orderly. In room after room, there was lots of chatter and rustling of large sheets of paper on easels and squeaking of Magic Markers. The delegates, heralded as "ordinary" Americans (a representative mix of "racial and ethnic groups, men and women, handicapped individuals, low income families, and diverse family forms"), had been divided into twenty work groups. They were busy sharing ideas about the state of American families under the guidance of a "facilitator," whose role was to turn every comment into a recommendation for a president who had pledged to "reach out to all Americans so that we could listen to them—and learn from them," with a view to formulating a "national family policy." (Two months of "speak-outs" across the nation had already generated more than nine thousand pages of testimony. Two more meetings, one in Minneapolis and the other in Los Angeles, were scheduled for later during the summer of Carter's reelection campaign.)

Up at their easels the facilitators, nodding constant encouragement, wrote and wrote. A proposal to add "family impact statements" to workplace policies was followed by a feminist package of "flashpoint issues"—ratification of the Equal Rights Amendment, approval of "diversity of family life," and abortion rights. That was in turn followed by a call to recognize the status of the homemaker, which was followed by demands for better-quality child care, and so forth. At the final plenary session, hundreds of recommendations scribbled on all those easels eventually emerged, after more facilitating, as fifty-seven disparate proposals—or rather, wishful avowals. The government should not interfere in family life; the government should do all it could to help families cope. The economy should be better. ("Jobless Rate Soars, Stirring Forecasts of a Deep Recession" was the major headline that June weekend.) So should television.

The "flashpoint issues" made it onto the list, just barely—because, true to the stormy tradition of American conferences on family issues, the feminists' proposals had prompted a walkout by right-wing delegates, who otherwise would have been there to vote them down. Phyllis Schlafly's staunchly conservative, anti-feminist Eagle Forum and their sympathizers, many of them on the newly energized Christian right, pronounced the event "contaminated by the liberal Carter machine."

Despite the show of open dialogue, they charged, the event had been stacked against "pro-family" Americans who believed in traditional domestic arrangements—no feminism, no abortions, no homosexual or unmarried parents, no government meddling in family affairs. Their dramatic departure became the story of the conference, of course, and guaranteed that the message that went forth, loud and clear, was precisely the one they opposed. As the American Family Services Association (on Mrs. Schlafly's list of liberal suspects) put it, "there are no neat norms or standards for family life." Nor was there, quite obviously, anything like a consensus for the national family policy that Carter had called an "urgent priority."

This conference was as much an emblematic product of the post-Spock era as the Midcentury White House Conference on Children and Youth and its predecessors had been of their historical moments. President Carter's gathering conveyed the embattled spirit of the postmodern family, which since the upheavals of the 1960s and 1970s had become more diverse, vulnerable, and volatile than ever before—and more voluble about the public dilemmas of raising children than about the private emotional dramas. America's child-rearing discussion, of course, had never been calm, as the Carnegie Corporation's Council on Children noted in its much publicized report of 1977, *All Our Children*, a catalyst for Carter's conference. "What *is* new and very American," wrote Kenneth Keniston, the sociologist who headed the council, "is the intensity of the malaise, the sense of having no guidelines or supports for raising children, the feeling of not being in control as parents." And what was newer still was that parents, rather than being diagnosed with pathologies and told how to nurture "healthy personalities" in nuclear families, were being urged to "speak out on what they think is right and wrong with the public and private policies that affect their lives." It was their turn to point the finger. Carter's conference planners invited them "to articulate their needs and strengths" and to diagnose the problems and pressures posed by the nation's "major institutions": Just how "responsive and sensitive" to the "changing realities of family life" were businesses, governments, schools, the media?

The realities of family life had indeed changed, outstripping even the dire predictions voiced at each preceding conference during "the century of the child." Back at the National Congress of Mothers convention, Mrs. Alice Birney had worried about the middle-class "tide of femininity . . . now streaming outward in search of a career," along with the poor "sisters who are compelled to work." By 1980, a tidal wave of working women had swept the country. For the first time, more than half (54 percent) of married women with children under eighteen worked outside the home, up from about a quarter in 1948, and the rise in employment among mothers with preschool children was even more dramatic, up to 45 percent from 12 percent. "The Superwoman Squeeze," as *Newsweek* called it in May of 1980, was on. (By 1999, slightly more than 60 percent of children under six had working mothers, compared to slightly less than 40 percent twenty years earlier. For infants, the increase between 1980 and the end of the century was more than double, from 24 to 54 percent.)

At the Conference on Modern Parenthood in 1925, alarm had escalated about the "drifting home," as the sociologist Ernest Groves had labeled America's problem. Two new symptoms, along with women's restlessness, had stirred interwar concern: marriages had become precarious and parental influence all too tenuous, as "organized" urban society usurped functions once performed by the family and children's peer groups claimed more of their time and attention. Middletown mothers in 1925, struggling in vain "to make home as much a center as possible," sighed that "children of twelve or fourteen nowadays act just like grown-ups." By 1980, the "breakdown of the family" was the far more unnerving specter. Forty percent of American marriages ended in divorce, and unmarried motherhood had increased as well. In 1980 one American child in six lived in a single-parent family, and one in eight was born outside of marriage, more than double the percentage in 1950. (By 1997, the proportion of children living in single-parent families had risen to almost a third, and three quarters of that cohort had mothers who had never been married. The racial differences were striking: only 35 percent of black kids lived with two parents, compared with 63 percent of Hispanic and 79 percent of white kids.)

And while the family had been eroding, the external world had continued to encroach. Earlier and earlier in their children's lives, parents shared their rearing with more and more nonfamily influences: not just with peers, teachers, doctors, and ever more professional specialists, but with TV producers and advertisers, too. By eighteen, the average American youth of 1980 had spent more time in front of the television screen than in school or with parents. (The computer era had arrived, but PCs had only begun to spread.) Without ever leaving home, children were exposed to a commercialized, sexualized, violent media culture, and they were diagnosed with an acute case of the "early sophistication" that had disturbed the Middletown matrons. Dire turn-of-the-decade titles—David Elkind's *The Hurried Child* in 1981, *The Disappearance of Childhood* by Neil Postman the next year, followed by Marie Winn's

Children Without Childhood in 1983—sounded the alarm about the
" 'adultification' of children." The prematurely wise specimen was
expected to cope in an "increasingly complex and uncontrollable world"
that left her "childified" elders feeling overwhelmed themselves, caught
"in a pressure-cooker of competing demands, transitions, role changes,
personal and professional uncertainties."

It was little wonder that by 1980 the doubts about the experts' therapeutic role that had surfaced at the Midcentury White House Conference had intensified, too. Back in 1950, Erikson was not the only
Freudian to fret that delving into emotional drives might exacerbate the
maternal crisis of confidence the advisers aimed to cure—and by the
1960s a frustrated Spock had taken to the streets to stir up social consciences instead. In 1980 the watchword among the psychologists swept
up by the so-called cognitive revolution during the 1960s and 1970s was
"competence." The new goal was to focus positively on the American
family's "capacity to interact effectively with its environment"—as the
scientists studying mental processes and learning defined the term—
rather than rush to diagnose maternal neurosis as the cause of widespread child-rearing worries and woes.

The question to ask was no longer why parents were failing, the
White House conference's National Research Forum of scholars and
experts had agreed in the spring of 1980, but how society might help in
an era when so many families—dual-career couples with kids and needy
and non-nuclear households alike—struggled daily with external
"stresses" (the word that had edged out "anxiety") "that sap their self-
esteem and power." The time had come to apply some pressure in
return. "In addition to being in charge of the private facts of inner family life, parents now have little choice but to concern themselves as well
with the public facts of the society that impinge on their families," the
Carnegie Corporation's *All Our Children* urged in 1977. "In addition to
being private nurturers, responsible parents and all who care about
children growing up must become public advocates for the children's
interests, and that cause must be interpreted far more broadly than it
has ever been before." Just how broadly, and divisively, all those "speak-
outs" and Baltimore buzz groups now revealed.

The parents-as-public-advocates leaving the convention center
had hardly enjoyed a stress-free experience. The "creative area" of the
conference—the easels full of proposals—had turned into a "manipulative" arena as the cause of "children's interests" turned into a cacophony
of special interests, with feminist and fundamentalist extremists polar-
izing the age-old American debate about federal involvement in the

affairs of the hearth. And nothing was going to happen in the "house-keeping area," it was clear. The congressional calendar of the 1970s was already littered with child care–related proposals that failed to pass; the economy was grim; controversy was guaranteed. "We don't think the Federal Government has the competence to deal with the family," Phyllis Schlafly the public advocate announced; "it aggravates problems rather than solves them" was her uncompromising verdict. The many conference recommendations—a "laundry list of hopes and inten-tions," one observer called them—would not be "[translated] . . . into reality," even if Carter was reelected, which five months later he was not. As a member of the president's own conference advisory board had predicted from the start, the reams of verbiage were just "another study to gather dust." But the debate over what would come to be called "fam-ily values" had begun, and would stir up dust until the turn of the mil-lennium—and beyond.

2.

While the family had been undergoing a metamorphosis, so had the child, rediscovered for the last time in the twentieth century by scien-tists who heralded a new specimen "beautifully prepared for the role of learning about him or herself and the world all around"—more beauti-fully prepared, in fact, than his or her bewildered, overburdened elders. So promised Dr. T. Berry Brazelton, celebrating an "interactive" infant whose "competence will call up competence from parents," as he put it in his 1983 revision of his 1969 classic, *Infants and Mothers: Differences in Development*, the book that had launched his career as the child-centered neo-Spock of the Spock-marked generation, while the famous doctor himself was pursuing his itinerant activist career. "In nurturing a small baby," Brazelton told readers embarking on parenthood in the era of the Swiss cognitive psychologist Jean Piaget's ascendancy, "adults learn as much about themselves as they do about the infant"—not least that theirs, too, is an interactive role. "We used to see the parents shap-ing the child, but now we see the child also helping to shape the parents," was the message of the doctor who in turn called himself "an 'interactive pediatrician'—interactive with both the infant and the parents."

Born in 1918, a decade and a half after the popular American expert he called his hero, Brazelton was, like Spock, the son of a formidable mother (the first woman elder in the Presbyterian Church and founder of the first abortion clinic in Texas in 1940). He had come north and followed a Spockian path through pediatric and psychiatric training, and then on to private practice, in his case in Cambridge, Massachusetts. He had even carried on the tradition of service to the Mead family. Ever since the start of the century, mothers of the clan had made a point of consulting only the latest, best wisdom in the child development field, and Mary Catherine Bateson, Margaret Mead's daughter, was no exception. When she brought her baby to Brazelton in 1969, she had chosen a doctor embarked on cutting-edge research, which had shifted from children's emotional drives to those hard drives that Piaget, among others, had discovered between their ears: Dr. Brazelton was the pediatrician on call at the birth of the new field of infant cognition.

He had signed on in the mid-1960s to work with the psychologist Jerome S. Bruner—"the most widely quoted American educational theorist," according to *Harper's* in 1964—whose recently founded Center for Cognitive Studies at Harvard was a pre-eminent site of the Piaget-inspired work that swept child psychology in post-Sputnik America. "Accumulated evidence did not permit continued loyalty to either psychoanalytic or behavioristic theory, both of which had provided direction to experimentation for close to half a century," as Bruner's Harvard colleague Jerome Kagan later put it. Piaget's theory of children's stage-by-stage intellectual development pointed in a fruitful new direction. Piaget's own startling observations—from his baby daughter Lucienne discovering that Papa's watch had not ceased to exist just because she couldn't see it inside the matchbox (the dawning of "object permanence") to seven-year-olds suddenly understanding that a round ball of clay pounded flat was the same amount of clay (the mastery of the principle of conservation)—energized American psychologists after the empirical drought of the Freudian era. The promise of early educational enrichment as the route to social and racial equality in turn galvanized policymakers, whose funding helped spur the ferment—and the founding of Head Start. Bruner led the way in probing the paradigm of the child as an explorer, busy constructing more and more complex conceptions of the world out of the adaptive interplay between her mind and her environment. Soon realizing he needed to start back in the nursery, Bruner welcomed the premier Cambridge pediatrician as the ideal guide to acquaint him with his new subjects.

In the mid-1960s, Bruner and Brazelton went every week to play with babies at Children's Hospital in Boston, where Brazelton was affiliated, and the pediatrician showed off how much alert attention neonates could summon to respond to their surroundings. "It just turned Jerry on like a beacon," Brazelton reminisced for an oral history of the child development movement. "He got more and more excited," and so did his guide. "It was a new world and here I was in my forties," Brazelton recalled, "and I felt, good lord, I should know everything, but I could see that their rigor was a window into recording and looking at things that I cared about that I had just never been exposed to."

What became known by 1980 (the year Piaget died) as the "Golden Age" of infant research was under way. The almost faddish excitement recalled the era when Dr. Hall's questionnaires had blanketed the country, and child-study zeal swept through labs and the public alike. ("Possibly the first conscious communication takes place," Hall had ventured in his "Notes on the Study of Infants" of 1891, "when the mother first catches and holds her infant's eye by smiles, nods, chirps, and chucks its chin till it grins in its first ridiculously awkward way and writhes all over with joy.") As Gesell had before them, the new generation of investigators relied heavily on cameras, lucky to have ones much less cumbersome than his dome apparatus. Along with video cameras, they soon had computers, too, which supplied a powerful analogy—the mind as information processor—as well as new means with which to experiment. The tools allowed fine-tuned monitoring of infants' eye movements, sucking rates, heartbeats, vocalizing tones—the signals the scientists read to determine their pre-verbal specimens' discriminating responses to their environments. (Researchers made use of the phenomenon known as "habituation": presented with the same stimulus, babies will quickly get "bored"—averting their eyes, their nervous system tuning it out—and then perk up when presented with a new or, to them, more salient event.)

The idea of the interactive, "constructivist" child helped to jolt developmentalists of every stripe to new and active construction themselves. Piaget focused on the child as an independent experimenter investigating a world of objects, solving the classical epistemological problems of space, time, causality, and categorizing. Others—most notably the Russian psychologist Lev Vygotsky, the British psychoanalyst and pediatrician D. W. Winnicott, and John Bowlby, the British psychiatrist busy formulating his "attachment theory" during the 1950s and 1960s—portrayed a more sociable collaborator who counted on emotional and cultural communication with adults to manage his feats of meaning-making and psychological growth. Research on the mother-infant tie flourished thanks to the Strange Situation procedure, a twenty-minute series of staged separations and reunions between toddler and parent designed by Bowlby's American colleague Mary Ainsworth to gauge how "securely" or "anxiously" attached children were to their "sensitive" or "insensitive" caretakers.

Meanwhile, the New York psychiatrists Stella Chess and Alexander Thomas were looking at the "two-way circuit between parent and child" from another perspective. The husband-wife pair, along with the pediatrician Herbert Birch, embarked on a longitudinal study of children's inborn temperaments. They discovered wide variations in an array of behavioral qualities, from "activity level" to "attention level and persistence," and showed how different dispositions can mesh well, or poorly, with different parental temperaments and tactics—the "goodness of fit" helping to smooth children's course (and ease their parents' days). Urie Bronfenbrenner of Cornell University took a more encompassing interactive view in *The Ecology of Human Development* in 1979. Seeing how parent-child relations fit—or failed to—into the "complex of nesting, interconnected" environments in which they unfolded, he argued, was crucial to understanding children's "growing capacity to discover, sustain, or alter" their adaptive ways in the world.

Brazelton, who liked to say that a friend described him as "the tallest two-year-old he's ever known!," brought plenty of eclectic vigor to the rigor of research, which he plunged into at his Child Development Unit at Children's Hospital in Boston during the 1970s and 1980s. Infant communication, temperament, parent-infant attachment, and the ecological as well as the cross-cultural dimensions of development: Brazelton and various collaborators made forays down all the major avenues of interest. (The curiosity was contagious: not long after the birth of her own baby, the much-filmed Mary Catherine Bateson seized her chance to be on the other side of the camera, working on a project about "Mother-Infant Exchanges" at MIT. She snatched moments between breast feedings to analyze frame after frame of "proto-conversations," her attentiveness to the interplay heightened, she felt, by new motherhood.)

"What Do Babies Know?" a *Time* cover story asked in 1983, reporting on the booming industry of infant studies that had radically revised William James's famous notion of the baby mind full of "great blooming, buzzing confusion." The magazine was ready with an answer: "Much more than many realize, and much earlier, according to new research." Actually, the latest from the labs had already become popular lore, thanks to a busy parenting magazine sector as well as eager coverage by the newsweeklies, which had spotted a market for a new mission: *Newsweek* became especially assiduous about keeping baby boomer parents up to date on the latest child development data—and the advice avidly extrapolated from it. Even the teenage mothers yet to graduate from their small-town New Hampshire high school in Joyce Maynard's novel *Baby Love* (1981) were suitably awed by what babies knew, or were supposed to know. One mother, viewing her bundle as a small pupil, "began cutting out pictures of babies for him (she calls them his study boards) when he was just four weeks old." In her satiric updating (and classing-down) of McCarthy's *The Group,* Maynard gave her struggling young mother a dose of attachment wisdom to go with the cognitive enlightenment. "Most of the pictures show mothers and babies, but she's always on the lookout for pictures of fathers and babies because she believes this will help Mark Junior in his bonding. When she was pregnant Sandy read a great deal about infants, and one of the big things they talked about was bonding."

Brazelton's signature popular contribution, in *Infants and Mothers,* was his portraiture of three different kinds of babies—quiet Laura, average Louis, active Daniel—as they changed and, just as important, changed their families over the course of the first year. Adopting the Gesellian descriptive (as opposed to prescriptive) advisory style, Brazelton, too, worked from composites and identified "types," but his mission was to evoke unique dramas, rather than to establish norms. From his interactive vantage, "types" of temperament did not dictate anything like typical development. The goal of his vivid narratives was to promote learning by looking (he supplied photos), but also by listening to the intimate dialogues unfolding in different families as parents, siblings, and baby discovered from and with one another how to cope with the frustrations of dependency and the challenges of autonomy. The "deepest principle is mutuality," Bruner wrote in the foreword he supplied to *Infants and Mothers,* marveling over "the first time the child sustains his look into his mother's eyes and begins on a career of social exchange of such complexity that no grammar has yet been devised to explicate it." Where Gesell had parked mothers in the corner with charts to measure an inner-driven process of maturation, and Spock had encouraged them to brim with spontaneous emotion and be models for emulation, Brazelton invited them to partake in a fascinating conversation, which supplied enriching stimulation for all involved.

Brazelton's signature clinical innovation in 1973 was the Brazelton Neonatal Behavioral Assessment Scale, known as "the Brazelton," a test widely performed on newborns to, as he put it in lay terms, "tell whether a baby is neurologically normal, how alert he is, and something about what kind of baby he will be to live with, at first." Ideally performed in the presence of parents, its function was also to show them that their baby was "not only normal but wonderfully capable," his nervous system primed to engage with a post-womb world of complex stimuli. In the process, Brazelton revealed what would become clearer and clearer in the course of the 1980s: the doctor who designed it saw infant, and parent, development as not simply wonderful, but also quite stressful for all concerned.

The roughly half-hour exam featured a Gesell-style list of twenty reflexes and twenty-eight "behavioral items," more than a few of which had a rather Watsonian quality: bells were rung, rattles shaken, pins were pricked into a little foot, cloths dropped onto a face—all done to a baby who had started out the ordeal asleep. The test also assessed responses to common soothing and stimulating caretaking tactics—a voice, an expressive face, rocking, holding—as the baby passed through "his or her repertoire of states" of consciousness, from sleep to gradual wakefulness and on to fussiness and fierce crying. The idea was to watch how a "newborn, even under stress, would make massive attempts to control interfering motor activity" (flailing of limbs) "and cardio-respiratory demands" (crying) and use "a series of maneuvers to maintain an alert 'state' of consciousness"—to listen and look, be an "active, eager interactant with the world around him." Just as important was a baby's protective ability to tune out disturbances that threatened to be overwhelming.

Unlike Watson and Gesell, Brazelton was not listening and looking for some static and universal response, nor did he conceive of the examiner as a detached, "objective" presence. On the contrary, the tester was trained to perform as a collaborator, eliciting and observing the baby's unique "adaptive and coping strategies and capacities" as a "caring mother and father" might—or should. By demonstrating and describing the baby's behavior to the parents, Brazelton could also use the test as a "window into the baby's performance, and by their reactions to it, uncover a window into the parents' feelings." It was a first step in gauging the interactive "fit" between them for the drama that would unfold as the baby proceeded "from each new level of achievement to the next." There was a competitive undercurrent to this cooperative adventure— not the Gesellian fear that baby might be below average, but that Mother might be behind on the learning curve. "Babies are competent to withstand 'mistakes' that their inexperienced parents might make and even to let the parents know when they are on the wrong track," Brazelton assured his readers—but it was up to parents to listen to and learn from their baby's distinctive language of social exchange.

"Don't frighten parents!" Jerome Kagan understandably cautioned in the *Time* article of 1983 about the awesome intricacies of development revealed by all the infant research. "The baby is a friendly computer." And an ever more phenomenal computer, with each passing year of work by post-Piagetian investigators, whose disparate studies shared a common thrust in the course of the 1980s. Piaget had emphasized how alien were the ways that children thought about the world, and how uniformly children progressed from "egocentric" animism toward the "logico-mathematical" understanding that he saw as the universal mark of mature, "sociocentric" thinking. It was a Swiss-style journey, with trains running punctually and climbing steadily to peaks and clear air, predictable scenery passing by on a well-mapped itinerary of four stages—the sensori-motor period of infancy (when babies discovered "object permanence"); the pre-operational phase from eighteen months through five (when children mastered language); the concrete operational period until eleven (when they arrived at the principle of conservation, the concept of classes, the idea of number relations); and finally the adolescent stage of formal, or propositional, operations when powers of abstraction emerged. Post-Piagetian experimenters, by contrast, found something more like American sprawl, with different aspects of cognitive development happening at different paces, and with babies much more precocious from the start and much more gregarious as time went on. The revisionists' child was born an innately capable specimen, with "rich and abstract representations of some aspects of the world," and a keen alertness to novelty and discrepancy. Not least, as psychologists at work in the thriving field of attachment research concurred, she was primed to tune into the human company she encountered.

Babies' interactive feats were impressive, and scientists found ingenious ways to showcase them. One rather comic experiment became a widely cited classic: newborns could imitate adults sticking their tongues out, indicating an innate awareness of being "like" another face that Piaget had thought dawned far later. (When a doctoral candidate first found that seven-week-old babies would copy an experimenter's antics, she hurried to ask the master himself what he thought of it. Piaget reportedly paused, pipe in mouth, before replying, "I think that's very rude.") Brazelton and his colleagues devised a cognitive twist on the "gold standard in attachment research," the Strange Situation procedure. They filmed infants and mothers in a "still-face situation" that showed, in a six-minute interaction, just how responsive and resourceful even small babies are: after three minutes of back-and-forth between them, the mother was instructed to withdraw and then return and be impassive. Her baby worked hard at reengaging her, with wiggles, sounds, and eye contact, before turning somber, giving up, and finally withdrawing; it was a poignant drama that often left mothers unsettled to see all the communication conveyed—both ways—in mere cuddling. Dissecting and assessing a subtly choreographed entwinement of baby and caretaker had become an academic industry, as psychologists from different camps probed in their own ways for the sources of a child's sense of competence in her early experiences of interconnectedness.

By the 1990s, some of the most interesting cognitive research explored what Bruner called "the wizard act of 'intersubjective' sharing," or the ways in which children's awareness of the mental states of others propelled their learning. Eight-month-old babies point at objects early on and look for recognition in the eyes of others, an investigative strategy performed by no other primate. By eighteen months, toddlers have begun to comprehend that others have desires different from theirs, and are busy exploring the implications. (The terrible twos have an epistemological agenda.) In fact, an influential group of post-Piagetian researchers proposed that young children were a version of those most curious and creative of adults, scientists. According to the "theory theory"—"the idea that cognitive development is the result of the same mechanisms that lead to theory change in science," as Alison Gopnik, a cognitive psychologist at Berkeley, summed it up—infants and toddlers were socially attuned, self-revising, bumbling but brave hypothesizers busy making predictions and constantly testing their theories with empirical zeal.

Already in the 1980s, the new insights of the cognitive era were exciting, but they were also disorienting—for scientists, as well as for parents. Discovering how much energy and agency children bring to their own development and to their relations with adults, researchers who had been hard at work exploring personality and social development had to acknowledge their failure to account for "child-driven" effects. Investigations of temperament, too, made reams of work, including attachment studies, seem too simple. Surely the jolly baby helped to shape the engaged parenting style, and the irritable infant could trigger insensitive mothering; it wasn't just the other way around. The result was to raise questions about decades' worth of socialization research. As Eleanor E. Maccoby of Stanford University pointed out, study after study was based on "top-down conceptions in which parents were seen as trainers or transmitters of culture and children as empty vessels"—compliant (or noncompliant) objects, rather than the competent and communicative subjects they really were, primed to "socialize adults or anybody else who came near them, probably more effectively than the reverse," Urie Bronfenbrenner once commented.

As the capacities and varieties of babies came into focus, what had once been in the foreground grew fuzzier than ever: the long-term effect of mothers' and fathers' actions and attitudes, or "parental styles," on the personalities of these responsive creatures, who soon clambered out of their cribs to interact with a wider world. The malleable Freudian child, decisively shaped by a family drama starring all-powerful parents as role models, had been eclipsed by a more elusive specimen. The young child of the cognitive era was a whirring laptop, linked by a fast modem to parents who, though programming his future was beyond them, should spare no input or effort to ensure that his own self-programming capacities were up to speed—crucial in a world of flux. What direction he was headed in, or how much stimulation really helped, was disconcertingly unclear.

The work of behavioral geneticists, begun in the mid-1970s, introduced more questions. Their studies of twins and adopted children did what more than half a century of socialization research had failed to do: they distinguished between conscious parental influence—the "home environment"—and a child's genetic inheritance. The unsettling discovery was that the former could not actually be shown to count for much in determining the personalities that emerged. Adopted children did not resemble their adoptive parents or siblings, even when they had shared a home since birth; identical twins reared apart turned out to have a great deal in common—and those reared together were quite different. Their "shared environment" appeared, if anything, to be making them less, rather than more, similar. In the opening chapter of the volume on "Socialization, Personality, and Social Development" in the *Handbook of Child Psychology* of 1983, Maccoby and a colleague raised doubts that were to spread. They rendered a startling verdict on recent studies that had at last begun trying to take account of heredity and interactivity, overlooked in so much socialization research of the past. "Indeed, the implications are either that parental behaviors have no effect, or that the only effective aspects of parenting must vary greatly from one child to another within the same family."

The second of the alternatives was, of course, the message with which Dr. Brazelton had made his name, and he was not about to change his mind. But as the 1980s progressed, he began to worry that too many parents were finding their sense of competence frayed, facing as they now did the challenges of "working and caring" and feeling caught between "crisis and caring." Those Brazelton titles of the decade conveyed his mounting alarm. "America's pediatrician," as he was often called, joined the continuing post–Carter era chorus of concern that it was parents, more than children, who risked being overwhelmed by disorienting transitions and stressful distractions—poor and single mothers, and his middle-class, increasingly two-income family readership alike. In *Working and Caring* (1985), he lamented that the "social pressure to be a child development expert as well as a loving parent requires a kind of 'supermom' or 'superdad,'" which hardly helped matters. A "cocksure 'cog sci' baby-as-computer-to-be-programmed" ethos, as Bruner put it, found a receptive audience in mothers and fathers anxious to be sure their children were not losing out as their parents hurried off to work. Without explicitly acknowledging that his own guidance on self-conscious, intensive "attunement" had inadvertently added to the pressure, Brazelton set out to try to alleviate it. He stepped forth as a public advocate, and a specialist now on parent development.

"Parents need as much care, as much 'mothering,' as their baby," Brazelton announced—or perhaps more, since what overburdened adult can be expected to match "the great energy that fuels the child for learning"? Like infant, like mother: the long-running parallel implicit in child-rearing counsel over the century had surfaced again. Brazelton had started out counting on the "inner" sense of mastery derived from achieving "synchrony" with their baby to give mothers "powerful confirmation of well-being and of competence in the development of the parents-infant relationship"—which was just what babies, too, derived from the relationship. Brazelton still counted on it. And in his books— and on his cable television show called *What Every Baby Knows*—he continued to promise that by "understanding their babies' responses better, parents can feel more and more sure of themselves and not feel quite so guilty when they find themselves in conflict with their new and precious, but not-so-helpless infant"—or later on, locked in combat with a toddler, who needed parents confident enough to set limits.

But babies were energized by more than inner excitement, and Brazelton concluded parents needed a double boost, too—and in America, mothers and fathers were rarely getting it. Infants were spurred onward in their learning by responsive reinforcement from their environment as well: that "Oooh, aren't you amazing!" that they were programmed to elicit from their caretakers with their captivating ways of signaling "Wow! I've done it." Dr. Brazelton felt it was high time for more appreciative nurturing for beleaguered parents, in whom he felt he sensed a growing "hunger for professional support" of just the kind he had in mind: "interactive" specialists like him, who would do more than briskly weigh and measure or merely reassure. They would prod and praise parents every step of the way as they confronted the domestic challenges that his books of the 1980s now made sure to include. The vignettes were still almost all middle class, but now it was the variation in family predicaments rather than in child temperaments that took center stage—divorces, job pressures, adoptions, blended families. And Brazelton himself had become a co-star in every drama, "an active part of each family system, as it interacts and readjusts to stress or to each new level of learning in any one of its members." He was on hand to warn parents of the regressions that preceded any surge in a child's cognitive, motor, or emotional development—and to help them work through their own tendency to regress at the same time.

Yet parents themselves, like babies, had to do some signaling for the support their expert diagnosed them as needing and wanting: in America, it is ordinary citizens, not doctors, who have to help write the prescriptions for the social policies they prefer. Brazelton was out in front, hoping to further their development as public advocates in their own cause. He was a more up-to-date model of activism during the 1980s than Dr. Spock, who was still intermittently getting arrested as he demonstrated against, among other things, housing cuts, missile defense, and nuclear power. Brazelton was busy lobbying the government for a health care system that would make his kind of developmental guidance widely available, especially to the neediest parents of all; for parental leave; and for better child care. And in 1989 he took to the road lobbying for parents' support for the lobbying.

With Representative Patricia Schroeder and Gary David Goldberg, the producer of a hit television sit-com of the 1980s, *Family Ties*, he went cross-country on his own talkathon—but found no greater consensus among parents than Carter's conference had a decade earlier. Brazelton's campaign for a national movement, Parent Action, left many "touched and excited," he reported. But the urge to organize that roused the liberal experts failed to unite the constituents themselves— perhaps because they feared that "public family support might lead to invading family privacy," he speculated. Or perhaps it was simply that parents were "too tired." Not the seventy-year-old Dr. Brazelton. Playing with Goldberg's preschooler on a stopover in the Atlanta airport, the "man who really likes children," as *Newsweek* called him, did a somersault for the cause.

3.

The indefatigable Dr. Brazelton was on hand for the public brainstorming about child rearing that began a decade later, which certainly woke parents up—and further jolted child development scientists, too, who were soon embarked on a stressful, but useful, reevaluation of their own competence. As the turn of the millennium approached, a Hollywood sit-com celebrity set in motion a multi-media extravaganza that made President Carter's populist roadshow look like a quaint relic of the early information age (and that dwarfed the Goldberg-Schroeder-Brazelton tour). It was Rob Reiner who helped inspire President and Mrs. Clinton's Conference on Early Childhood Development and Learning, otherwise known as the "conference on the brain," in 1997. A quarter of a century after starring as Mike Stivic, Archie Bunker's son-in-law on *All in the Family*, Reiner the movie director had become not just a parent but a super–public advocate, and what Erik Erikson had called a "publicist of expertise."

Reiner had acquired a cause. A one-man Parent Action movement, he launched his "I Am Your Child" campaign to enlighten American mothers and fathers about the latest "breakthroughs in brain research," which *Newsweek* touted as having the "potential to revolutionize child-rearing theory and practice"—and, Reiner hoped, social policy as well. When the former Meathead phoned the baby boomer White House to enlist their participation, his call went right through. And when Hillary Clinton rounded up "the leading experts in the field of early childhood development, the scientists and pediatricians, the researchers and all of the others . . . to explain their discoveries and to put this invaluable body of knowledge at the service of America's families," Brazelton was naturally on her list, though it was neuroscientists who were in the spotlight.

As at the Carter event two decades earlier, a much-publicized Carnegie Corporation report served as a catalyst for the Clintons' occasion. Called *Starting Points*, it appeared in 1994 and sounded the by now familiar alarm about how "powerful institutions of society such as business and government have done little to strengthen families in the rapidly changing circumstances of the late 20th century." And its set of liberal recommendations, though less ambitious than the economic agenda Kenneth Keniston had laid out in its Carnegie Corporation predecessor, *All Our Children*, was familiar, too: promote responsible parenthood, guarantee quality child-care choices, provide better health services, mobilize communities to support young children and their families. (Only two years earlier, in 1992, roughly the same "New American Agenda for Children and Families" had been endorsed by Senator Jay Rockefeller's National Commission on Children, on which the tireless Brazelton had also served; that report had been wishfully called *Beyond Rhetoric*.)

Yet *Starting Points* did have one novelty: roughly three pages of what were presented as the latest discoveries in neurobiology. It turned out to be news perfectly pitched to make Americans, "habituated" by now to outcries about imperiled children, sit up and take notice, as Reiner, Hillary Clinton, and the media indeed did. The formation of neural synapses in the brain happened more rapidly after birth and was more environmentally sensitive than scientists had realized, the Carnegie task force reported. The way brain cells were pruned and wired in the long run, the account went on, depended heavily on what sort of sensory experience guided the process during the crucial first few years. Moreover, severe neglect threatened young brains with irremediable damage, for stress-activated hormones left learning and memory capacities impaired. It was time, the president of the Carnegie Corporation urged, to close "the wide gap between scientific research and public knowledge, between what is known and what we do about that knowledge, what we do to meet the essential requirements for healthy child development in the earliest years."

Closing the gap was precisely what Reiner—teaming up with his wife, Michele Singer Reiner, and the Families and Work Institute, a New York nonprofit advocacy research group—and the Clintons set out to do. Their "Early Childhood Public Engagement" campaign crested in the spring of 1997 in a burst of high-energy stimulation that they rightly judged could not fail to make an impression. The Families and Work Institute issued *Rethinking the Brain: New Insights into Early Development*, an illustrated guide to the state of brain research and of work in the attachment field, just in time for the Clinton conference, which was beamed by satellite to audiences around the country. A spring/summer special issue of *Newsweek* called "Your Child: From Birth to Three," planned with input from Reiner and the White House, arrived on the newsstands—and flew off them. (Roughly a million copies were sold, setting a record for the magazine.) Reiner's "I Am

Your Child" Web site went up, and ABC promptly aired a prime-time special by the same name, which he directed. Reiner had summoned his famous Hollywood friends (Roseanne Barr, Mel Brooks, Billy Crystal, Tom Hanks, Charlton Heston, Rosie O'Donnell, Robin Williams), supplied them with his version of the latest from the neurobiology labs, told them to cram—and then to ham it up.

There was only one problem with the "hard" and dire brain data that child advocates seized on as far more compelling for their cause than the softer social science and psychology that had been the staples of foundation reports—and conference agendas—for years now. Along with most of the media, Reiner failed to note the fact that no such radically new evidence of neural vulnerability actually existed. It was an admission that the Carnegie report made in passing: "Researchers say that neurobiologists using brain scan technologies are on the verge of confirming these findings." In truth, they were nowhere near demonstrating that the "cognitive deficits" measured in toddlers growing up in poverty reflected irreversible neurological damage caused by understimulation and stress during the first three years. Nor had their studies proved that "enriched" environments in babyhood are responsible for the long-term social, emotional, and cognitive success of many who have the luck to start out in them.

Moreover, what neurobiologists did know was not brand-new, and owed little to the latest technologies, at least when it came to babies. As one neuroscientist noted, the "new techniques in brain imaging that allow us to see brain processes as they are happening are not very baby-friendly." Functional magnetic resonance imaging (fMRI), which tracks oxygen use by active brain cells, requires absolute stillness; positron-emission tomography (PET) involves injecting the brain with radioactive glucose, the burning of which produces a traceable glow. Even Dr. Watson would have balked, to say nothing of parents—and babies themselves. PET scans of children were rare, done for diagnostic reasons (epilepsy, for example). During the late 1970s and 1980s, brain researchers had indeed been busy discovering what Dr. Holt had simply asserted almost a century earlier: that synapses between nerve cells in the brain are soldering at a fantastic rate between birth and three. The period of "exuberance," they found, is followed by a plateau, and then a gradual decrease in synaptic density to roughly adult levels in adolescence. Investigators relied mostly on an old, and arduous, method: counting the connections in slices of dead brain, more of them from animals than from humans.

But neuroscientists had not proved that the rapid early synapse formation is initiated by environmental stimuli. Nor had they showed that there are well-defined "critical periods" when particular influences must be available if particular capacities are to develop, or that enrichment during the exuberant first three years of neural growth is the last chance to ensure a more densely wired brain before the pruning begins—all the supposed findings that were touted by Reiner and his fellow publicists as the "revolutionary" scientific support for their build-a-better-brain message. In fact, the neurobiologists of the 1980s and 1990s had been busy discovering an organ (much like the cognitive child herself) remarkable for its interactive, resilient "plasticity," rather than for its age-specific impressionability or its vulnerability.

The two active scientific researchers at the Clintons' conference— only one of them a neuroscientist, the other a leading psychologist at work on children's language development—did their best, in their brief turns at the podium, to convey the more complex interplay at work. Dr. Carla Shatz, a neurobiologist at Berkeley, described the brain after birth actively continuing its own wiring, building on the main "trunk lines" that linked eyes and ears, et cetera, to the appropriate parts of the brain and that had been laid down by genes. It was the brain itself that was genetically programmed to initiate a process of constant neural firing in response to the "expected" experience available in any human environment, even the most primitive. The result was the dense web of connections that accounted for the "species-typical" strides in development that babies make the world over. No unusual interventions were required, and only the grossest neglect seemed to impede the process in normal babies.

Dr. Patricia Kuhl of the University of Washington, too, portrayed the infant as a resourceful little communicator primed to get busy "cracking the language code," in need of no special "input" at the start—or particular supplements along the way. The feat was driven by infant powers of attention, more than by adult stimulation—crucial though that was, too. Equipped at birth with a phenomenal ability to "discriminate all of the sound contrasts used in any language of the world," she explained, infants quickly begin a process of fine-tuning. They form a sound map of the tongue they will end up speaking, and they do it by—what else?—listening to those around them (and losing the capacity to discern other sounds). "Motherese," the higher-pitched nattering that seems to come naturally to adults in the presence of infants, seemed to be what babies like and learn from best.

Critical periods, insofar as they exist for the development of species-wide capacities and behavior—vision and language, basic memory, basic social interaction, hearing, movement—had not proved to be clear-cut. From what was known, it appeared to be the pattern of neural activity over various phases, not simply the amount of it during a discrete period, that mattered, as John T. Bruer explained in his clear-eyed guide through the brain mania, *The Myth of the First Three Years.* And for most other kinds of "experience-dependent," as opposed to "experience-expectant" learning—of culturally acquired skills like vocabulary, literacy, or music—there was no evidence that critical periods as such existed. Learning that begins earlier is better in large part because that usually means the exposure lasts longer, studies suggested, not because zero-to-three enrichment itself can assure subsequent success or because its absence guarantees failure; young and old brains continue to benefit from educational environments.

What happens to brains under conditions of severe neglect, nobody really knew. Experiments, of course, were impossible. What is going on during the synaptic pruning on the way to adulthood? How does the experience that precedes it affect the process? Are adults who emerge having preserved greater synaptic density smarter? All were questions yet to be answered. The real neurobiological news of the 1990s was that neural change seems itself continually to change the way the brain processes new experience. Moreover, the transformations continue far later—well into adolescence, and beyond—than had been supposed.

The brain campaign had not exactly closed the "wide gap between scientific research and public knowledge, between what is known and what we do about that knowledge," as the president of the Carnegie Corporation lamented. In fact, the unintended revelation of the "Early Childhood Public Engagement" blitz was how hard, perhaps impossible, that was to do. It was not just that scientific findings were almost bound to be distorted on the way from the lab to the public: "The question of how to rear the better baby is so glamorous, so attractive to Americans and so fraught with emotionalism," as Jerome Kagan had written in 1980, "that it invites precipitous judgments and ungrounded speculations," and had for a century. It was also that in the gap between what is known and what we do about that knowledge lie personal, social, political, and moral preferences, trade-offs, and uncertainties that data can rarely settle. The firmest scientific findings rarely translate clearly or uncontroversially into policy decisions. That was true "either at the small scale of the parent grappling with the terrible twos or at the grand scale of the White House," as Dr. Patricia Kuhl and two co-authors, Alison Gopnik and Andrew Meltzoff, put it in their book, *The Scientist in the Crib: Minds, Brains, and How Children Learn.* If the turn-of-the-millennium brain mania did anything to "revolutionize" child rearing, it was by planting doubt about whether it was within the power—or the purview—of science to do just that.

"Babies understand more than we have understood about them," was the frequently quoted conclusion President Clinton drew from his conference. Certainly the lessons for mothers and fathers that emerged from the brain crusade were confusing, in a completely familiar way. The event had dispensed a classic version of the mixed message that Brazelton had helped make a staple of post-Spock expertise, a message in which the conflicting child-rearing counsel of an entire century converged: trust your instincts and train your insight, follow your baby's nature and spare no effort on her nurture—relax and enjoy those first years and don't forget for a minute that your child's future is at stake.

In short, feel very important—and find yourself worrying more often than you would like that perhaps you are not quite competent. Thus Mrs. Clinton had opened her remarks by hailing the news from the lab as a reassuring endorsement of middle-class common sense. "Science, as we will hear from the experts today," she announced, "has now confirmed what many parents have instinctively known," that children thrive on "the activities that are the easiest, cheapest, and most fun to do . . . singing, playing games, reading, story-telling, just talking and listening" with their nearest and dearest. But she had felt the need to close by hastening to add that the purpose of the conference, and the science, was not to make mothers and fathers "anxious or imprison them in a set of rules." For over the course of the Public Engagement campaign, Americans had also been warned—by Brazelton and his younger colleague, the Washington, D.C.-based psychiatrist Stanley I. Greenspan, among others—that the requisite interactive intimacy was a fine-tuned feat, on which their child's and the nation's fate hung. "Only 20 to 30 percent of parents," Greenspan judged, "know how to do this instinctively."

In fact, as Dr. Kuhl emphasized in her talk, "research can't tell us yet how much communicative interaction it takes to allow this kind of development to occur," nor tell us that if the intimate exchanges aren't ideally pitched to a child's capacities from the start, trouble is bound to follow. The same Brazelton who boasted in *Newsweek* that he "could tell by a child's behavior when I test him at eight months of age whether he expects to succeed or fail in the future" acknowledged, in his academic work, that predictions were in fact shaky. (Nor had research proved, as readers of the newspapers were shortly to be informed, that exposure to Mozart at birth "affects the spatial-temporal reasoning that underlies math, engineering and chess," despite the claims of Georgia governor Zell Miller, who had made it hospital policy in his state to send new mothers home with classical CDs.) Kuhl stuck to her guns when President Clinton prodded her for "some minimum threshold of vocal interplay," or some proof that simply having the TV on isn't enough. "There's just no answer to that question," she insisted, "and we can only guess whether or not language would develop if you hung a tape recorder on the child's crib and said, well, this is going to do it." But since babies are extremely sociable—it's part of what helps them be "very, very clever"—Dr. Kuhl was willing to bet that a disembodied voice would not work.

Neurobiology, as the president had implicitly acknowledged, was still in its own infancy. Laboratory explorations failed to produce the kind of clear-cut direction for parents, and long-term predictions about children, that the public advocates claimed, and that policymakers expected. *Rethinking the Brain*, the Families and Work Institute's primer, closed by admitting that "new insights into early development confront policymakers and practitioners with thorny questions and difficult choices"—all too familiar ones, in fact. How does the interaction between nature and nurture work, and can it be tweaked? "Just how critical are critical periods?" Is a focus on the first three years, as opposed to subsequent years, really sensible—and if so, what should it amount to? Even Rob Reiner, who had declared that "the policy implications are absolutely clear," had to admit there might be debate. A crusader for higher-quality nonparental child care between zero and three, he was taken aback to discover that the same research could also be invoked in support of an alternative agenda: an at-home parent as the best brain-tender during those crucial first years. "I hadn't thought of that," he confessed.

Right after the pronouncement that "the ramifications of these findings clearly have the potential to revolutionize child-rearing theory and practice," the *Newsweek* writers added a caveat: "But to an uncertain end." In fact, the reading of the data that Reiner and others hoped would inspire a liberal social agenda could just as readily be invoked in the service of a deeply pessimistic position that was not at all what they intended. If young brains subjected to deprived conditions, and to the inadequate parenting that often goes along with them, are irrevocably damaged—pickled in stress hormones, stripped of synapses—there is no time to waste, that is true. Yet such alarm, though it conveys urgency, can all too easily fuel defeatism. If children become neurologically unresilient at an early age, then only intrusive and intensive

remedial efforts seem equal to the job. And if—or, let's face it, when—
such intervention fails to materialize, the case for subsequent help is
bound to seem weaker.

It was an analysis that assigned parents the blame for any subsequent
trouble their child encountered, even though brain studies had not
begun to trace the long-term effects of the earliest, most intimate communication and stimulation. (Nor had attachment research proved that
the first bonds a parent forges with a baby serve as a template for a
child's relationships, and the key determinant of his competence, ever
after.) It consigned the child, as much as genetic determinism ever had,
to a fate shaped decisively by her parentage, thus depriving her of more
than baby talk. She was denied a resourceful role in helping to shape a
future that was still unfolding long past the age of three, influenced by
forces well beyond simply her parents' ministrations—even though all
kinds of research, on the brain and in almost every domain of child
development work, had lately begun to suggest how much a child's own
actions, and social circumstances, counted. The real scientific breakthroughs of the closing decades of the century had converged on an
unsettling recognition: there was far more complexity, and indetermi-
nacy, in children's trajectories than scientists in the child development
field had ever expected to discover—or had yet figured out how to
handle.

4.

"Goodnight mush," General Colin Powell murmured to his toddler
grandson in the cozy closing scene of family reading in Reiner's "I Am
Your Child" television special. ". . . Goodnight noises everywhere." In
fact, almost as soon as the brain crusade had quieted down, a "fragile,
elfin grandmother," as a profile in *The New Yorker* described her, occasioned another public furor that put child development scientists in the
spotlight and on the spot. Judith Rich Harris was the antithesis of a
Hollywood celebrity, but she was full of impertinence grise. "Kicked out
of Harvard's Department of Psychology with only a master's degree . . .
[and] stuck at home for many years due to chronic health problems,"
she was a former freelance writer of college psychology textbooks—
and a woman with a cause, which was the opposite of Reiner's. Where
he embraced the latest laboratory findings as parenting dogma, she

denounced piles of child development data as just that—hoary American child-rearing gospel, a "cherished cultural myth."

In *The Nurture Assumption: Why Children Turn Out the Way They Do* (1998), Harris set out to show that decades of weak research had assumed, rather than proved, the "notion that parents are the most important part of the child's environment and can determine, to a large extent, how the child turns out." Meant to reassure and inspire, it was a myth that had turned out to be anxiety-inducing for all concerned. She went on to proclaim her own theory instead: kids' peers (especially during their middle childhood years), rather than their parents, determine how the genetic predispositions with which children are born develop into the socialized personalities they are blessed, or burdened, with in adulthood. Harris's book—equipped with a foreword by the well-known linguistic psychologist at MIT Steven Pinker, who predicted it "would come to be seen as a turning point in the history of psychology"—immediately stirred up controversy.

Within a month of its publication, *Newsweek* was, as ever, ready with a cover story, "Do Parents Matter? A New Heated Debate About How Kids Develop." Columnists saluted Harris for calming "some nerves in this age of high-anxiety parenting"—and columnists denounced her for exonerating "self-absorbed parents with a track record of putting their own desires ahead of their children's needs." Radio interviewers and TV talk shows clamored for Harris. Few school-sponsored gatherings ended without principals or teachers citing "that new book about how parents don't matter" (usually with raised eyebrows) and parents conferring about "that book about how much peers really do matter" (usually with furrowed brows).

But perhaps most interesting of all was Harris's reception among scientists. The iconoclastic debunker plainly expected her exposé of dubious methodology and data to rile the child development establishment. Her combative irreverence and rigor did get academic backs up, but her challenge also served to push research dilemmas and doubts out into the open, where they belong. As the turn of the millennium approached, a field that had been born amid grandiose hopes of delivering predictive certainty and control to parents, and policymakers, was ready with more mature humility about its own less than steady progress over a century.

Harris flung open the door on decades of indeterminate research that had indeed failed to clinch the case that some pure extract of parental power, untainted by genetic factors or by "child-driven" effects, exerted a decisive effect on children's personalities over the long term. Having rigorously exposed the frailty of findings that ignored heredity and interactivity (among other flaws), she declared that she had thereby proved that parents have no influence—other than what can be explained by genes. And she went on to propose that her own peer principle could take over as the omnipotent—and scientific—explanation of why children turn out the way they do. The scientists themselves were much less categorical. They took the occasion to go public with skepticism concerning overly deterministic theories about children's development in general, theirs and hers. They sounded unexpectedly modest about the power of their measurements to capture the many influences that children encounter inside, and outside, the home as they grow up—or to predict what children will make of the inextricable blend of genetic and environmental forces at work in their lives.

Much of the case that Harris built for the scientific shakiness of the nurture assumption had in fact been quietly anticipated by academic specialists themselves over the years, behind the walls of what the 1998 edition of the *Handbook of Child Psychology* charitably described as an "English garden" of child development research, "a bit unruly but often glorious in its profusion." Already back in 1927, remember, the Child Development Committee of the National Research Council had fretted that the "very success of the childward movement" meant that "science is asked to point the way where as yet there is no way." And the "illimitable research" that lay ahead, the committee secretary had presciently warned, was bound to be difficult to design. The inadequacies of the "artificial experimental set-up" must be overcome through work in "the normal child environment." It was a daunting task. So much time was required for home investigations, and so many mundane variables had to be accounted for—"the slamming of a door, the sudden thunder shower, one angry temper display of a parent." And few investigators had even begun to factor in such far more germane variables as children's temperaments and busy minds.

The research had indeed gone on and on, doggedly, awkwardly, ingeniously, inadequately attempting to overcome the obstacles posed by specimens who are, alas, neither as quiet nor as manipulable as mice. In the seventy years since the Child Development Committee's meeting—and during the closing two decades of the century in particular—academic researchers had become only more aware of how often the mysteries of child rearing and personality and social development eluded the mastery of science. How do you create a control group of squirmy children and parents? Can you really rely on the observations and the memories of family members? Who on earth has a consistent "parenting style," the same for all children or even for one child all the time? How can studies be designed that take account, not just of parent-child interactions, but of sibling effects on those interactions? Can you trust personality studies, given the notorious problem of context—the inconvenient fact that tests of the same person yield very different results depending on the setting, among other things? Can you conclude, as Harris did, that because "parents have no predictable effects on their children," they do not have unpredictable effects? Is "the hypothesis that children's within-family micro-environments play a causal role in the shaping of their personalities" disproved, as she decided, simply because it is so resistant to good testing? Finally, what can you really say about results when, as Harris said, "correlations come with no built-in arrows to distinguish causes from effects"?

"It is indeed true," Howard Gardner, the well-known cognitive psychologist at Harvard (and author of the popular *Frames of Mind: A Theory of Multiple Intelligences* of 1983), wrote in his review of Harris's book, "that the research on parent-child socialization is not what we would hope for." Readily acknowledging the sorry "state of psychological research, particularly with reference to 'softer variables' such as affection and ambition," he emphasized that "we do not really know what to look for or how to measure human personality traits, individual emotions, and motivations, let alone character." And behavioral genetics presented its own set of difficulties, he reminded Harris, not least the puzzle of accounting for the ways in which genes help to shape environments. When small genetic differences between children (one sibling's beauty, say) trigger larger environmental differences for them (parental pride and popularity with peers), do you then chalk up the divergence in their paths to nature or to nurture? The complexities posed just as much of a problem for testing Harris's peer hypothesis, evidence for which was, she acknowledged, as yet sparse. She was surely right to focus on children's out-of-home lives, especially in contemporary America, where the sway of the youthful pack can hardly be underrated even if it, too, cannot be neatly calibrated. And it was high time to give middle schoolers their turn in the spotlight, elbowing babies and teenagers out of the way. Still, Harris's extreme case for peer clout as the universal, all-determining engine of socialization and personality formation invited her own brand of skeptical scrutiny.

In a slim book called *Three Seductive Ideas* that coincided with Harris's, Jerome Kagan wagered that "no present concept in personality will survive the next half century." And he proceeded to challenge another central tenet of the nurture assumption that went hand in hand with parent power: "the allure of infant determinism," or the idea that the die is cast by age three or so, during the years of intensive parental care in most societies. Peddled as gospel for decades by behaviorists, psychoanalysts, and maturationists alike, it had rarely been championed more zealously than by neuroscientists—or rather by their publicists. Kagan made the point that in an "immature" field such as psychology that often rests on "weak evidence"—think of the difficulties in getting "robust" measurements of any trait over the long journey from infancy to adulthood—such an idea can thrive even though it is not readily demonstrable, because (pace Harris) it is not readily deniable either. Meanwhile, it conforms to the Western faith in personal responsibility and in an unbroken continuity between past and present. Kagan also noted another source of its popularity: telling mothers to kiss or not to kiss their babies—or how to babble to them—is cheaper, and less controversial, than overhauling social policies.

With the arrival of the millennium, the National Research Council again addressed the role of science in what it had once called the "childward movement." The convening of the somberly named Committee on Integrating the Science of Early Childhood Development was well timed, coming as it did in the wake of the brain crusade that had dramatized the tendency of "well-meaning advocates to overstate the science or 'oversell' its conclusions." A field that had evolved for a century now "under the anxious and eager eyes of millions of families, policy makers and service providers" was due for a public and thorough assessment. The mission of *From Neurons to Neighborhoods*, as the 588-page report was called, was "to review what is known about the nature of early development and the influence of early experiences on children's health and well-being, to disentangle established knowledge from erroneous popular beliefs or misunderstandings, and to examine the implications of the science base for policy, practice, professional development, and research." Could science, to echo the NRC memorandum of three quarters of a century earlier, yet "point the way"?

The committee's evaluation, two and a half years in the works, was as sober as Harris's book was acerbic—yet it was surprisingly skeptical. *From Neurons to Neighborhoods* was comprehensive, surveying roughly twenty-five years' worth of multi-disciplinary research and clinical work in developmental science and canvassing a wide variety of intervention efforts, all focused on the years between birth and five. Predictably devoid of the prosecutorial verve that inspired Harris (its authors were eminent academics, after all, not gadflies), the report was also studiously lacking in "false self-reassurance" and "we're sure we're right" arrogance. So noted a reviewer, a member of the premier early childhood research/advocacy group, Zero to Three, just a little wistfully. "Faint praise! Thin gruel!" had been her first reaction to parts of *From Neurons to Neighborhoods,* she admitted.

The committee was forthright in acknowledging the frailty of a great deal of work in a field in which truly controlled studies are practically, and ethically, all but impossible to come by. Moreover, the number of variables to conjure with had multiplied as the "core concepts of development" became much less reductive: research that respected the complex interplay between biology and experience, the continuities and discontinuities of growth, the countless variations among children, the subtleties in human relationships, and the disparities among cultures inevitably posed ever greater challenges. The report also noted the limitations imposed by "science . . . based largely on studies of typical development in white, middle-class samples and developmental vulnerability in samples that do not disentangle race, ethnicity, or socioeconomic status." Much of what "guides responsible policy, service delivery, and parenting practices at any given point in time," *From Neurons to Neighborhoods* admitted, falls in the domain of "reasonable hypotheses," not "established knowledge." But those hypotheses were becoming ever more reasonable, which meant, as is often the case in science, more cautious and complicated.

Thus the report emphasized that "the recent focus on 'zero to three' as a critical or particularly sensitive period is highly problematic," not because the early years aren't important for the brain, and for the rest of development, but because growth is more intricate than the mantra suggests—cumulative but also discontinuous, vulnerable but also resilient. The committee agreed with Harris that identifying parents' long-term (nongenetic) contribution to their children's personality traits and fates is next to impossible. But that did not mean that parents, or caregivers, were negligible influences on the "growth of self-regulation [that] is a cornerstone of early childhood," involving the intertwined emotional, social, cognitive, and moral development of very sociable creatures. Ferreting out parents' specific—and rarely static—contributions to a process, never mind a final product, had "become a very complex endeavor."

Tracing the long-term effects of early experiences in general, the seventeen members found again and again, was a problematic enterprise, whether it was maternal attachment, or cognitive enrichment, or quality of child care that was at issue. Yet in the short term, children clearly thrived on all three, though even there, good measurements were harder to achieve than many had imagined. Plenty of attachment research had failed to pay enough attention to children's temperaments and experiences. Evaluating early cognitive development, researchers had concluded, was not simply a matter of measuring IQ and mastery of skills; a child's "self-regulatory" capacities—her social and emotional control and powers of attention—had to be taken into account. And day care research was famously fraught. Higher-quality child care appeared to make a statistically significant (although not very dramatic) contribution to children's early cognitive and linguistic progress, but effects on behavior and on emotional development were open to debate. Surprisingly, the influence of maternal employment on low-income, rather than middle-class, children had hardly been explored.

Given that "one of the most consistent associations in developmental science is between economic hardship and compromised child development," it was striking how far research still had to go in elucidating the pressures at work. How much family structure, genetic factors, maternal education levels, a diminished "home literacy environment," neighborhoods, and parent-child interactions contributed to the notable gaps between poor and middle-class children's school readiness at age five proved difficult to sort out. And data from intervention efforts with at-risk families were rarely solid enough to shed definitive light. In general, program evaluations were too motley to be readily compared, but *From Neurons to Neighborhoods* emphasized that no ready formulas for success stood out. (Grand promises, psychologists had learned back when Head Start's power to boost IQs had been oversold, were risky.)

Efforts aimed at the "enhancement of parenting skills" were often disappointing. "Shifting parental behavior in ways that shift the odds of favorable outcomes for children is often remarkably difficult," the committee acknowledged. The report's review of results from "child-focused" programs for at-risk preschoolers was humble, too. The best designed and most intensive of them produced developmental gains that were impressive—higher IQs and better school performance when the kids arrived in kindergarten—but there was little evidence for the early-intervention-as-vaccination view perennially popular in America; the gains tended to decline with time, and maternal IQ often accounted for more of the improvement than the program did. Empirical evidence about how well "family-centered, community-based, coordinated orientations" worked was, the committee remarked, still "thin," though it seemed promising.

The chairman's verdict on the evidence about "promoting healthy development through intervention" was notably cautious. "Children's early pathways clearly can be shifted by efforts to change the contexts of their lives. Less is known, however, about what it really takes to shift the odds, and very little is known about the factors that keep children moving along adaptive pathways once they leave the early childhood years behind." That was no reason to give up or fail to act, he urged, especially in a society that had become less "family-friendly" than ever before in the nation's history. "The key," the chairman emphasized, "is to blend skeptical scientific thinking with passionate and determined advocacy." Once more the call went out for "a new national dialogue focused on rethinking the meaning of both individual and shared responsibility for children, as well as underscoring the importance of strategic investment in their future." But the committee did not delude itself that calm conversation lay ahead—or promise that child development research could readily cut through disputes. Theirs was, it was clear by now, a science "typically viewed through highly personalized and sharply politicized lenses."

In fact, as *From Neurons to Neighborhoods* tacitly acknowledged, this familiar public child-rearing debate would inevitably be driven as much by appeals to conscience (and, as ever, by ideological allegiances) as by definitive data derived from science. For what the evidence had revealed was that the quest to "nurture, protect, and ensure the health and well-being of all young children" was going to have to be embraced "as an important objective in its own right, regardless of whether measurable returns can be documented in the future," because all too often they could not—or at least not the kind of dramatic returns that clinch a policy debate, or can dictate one "right" course for all parents to take. The choices ahead posed a challenge to the nation's "ethical and moral values," the report emphasized. America's, as well as children's, "well-being and 'well-becoming'" depended on rising to it.

The scientists did not say "family values," the phrase that had become a popular rallying cry on the rightward end of what had indeed become a "highly personalized and politicized" discussion about children and parents during the 1990s—in fact, more publicly polarized than ever. Two decades of cultural and cognitive ferment had unfolded since the days of the Carter conference. In the wired world where yet more women worked and "diverse family forms" had become the norm, the crisis of competence that had stirred up child-rearing confusion was far from over. The familiar "parent-centered" and "child-centered" tensions in popular advisory fare carried a new ideological charge. But across the spectrum, the tenor of the fin-de-siècle parenting enterprise had acquired a novel ring, and it was old-fashioned: amid the clamor to build better brains, the call had also gone out to shore up children's characters. In a culture that seemed adrift, the stirring task was to lay "the foundation of morality, a person's sense of right and wrong," as an octogenarian Brazelton declared in a "special 2000 issue" of *Newsweek,* which cited poll data that showed raising "a moral person" had by now edged out rearing a happy or a smart child at the top of the list of parental goals. Yet advice in that endeavor, a tall one in high-tech consumerist America, sounded as divisive as ever.

The century had begun with popular scientific experts elbowing out the ministers who had presided over the Victorian hearth (in whose clerical footsteps the devout mothers of Drs. Hall and Holt had hoped their sons would follow). It was ending with the return of parenting preachers eager to hold forth as the nation's arbiters of conscience and ready with sermonic and systematic child-rearing guidance in the cause. "America's pediatrician" had collaborated with Stanley Greenspan, a popular parenting adviser himself, on a new book called *The Irreducible Needs of Children: What Every Child Must Have to Grow, Learn, and Flourish.* It was a turn-of-the-millennium exhortation in a very different key from Brazelton's vivid developmental vignettes of old, but in tune with an increasingly urgent and less intimate tenor of expertise in the post-Spock marketplace of the 1990s. Amid a surfeit of specialized counsel, advisers had arrived with social manifestos and with manuals urging programmatic child-rearing creeds on busy parents dizzied, and disillusioned, by shifting lore from the labs. Yet there were, as ever, doctrinal battles. Dr. Brazelton and his allies faced opponents speaking out from their own pulpits, and they had proved to be very popular—and eager to be provocative.

ELEVEN

Ministers, Mentors, and Managers

Dr. T. Berry Brazelton and a young patient

I.

"It shall be the glorious crusade of this closing century and at the opening of the next, not the rescue of a tomb from the grasp of infidels who hold it, but the rescue of the cradle of childhood from the evil influences which have encompassed it," the chaplain of the United States Senate had promised in his opening prayer at the National Congress of Mothers meeting in Washington in 1897. A hundred years later such missionary zeal, far from sounding quaint, once again infused discussions of children's fates and parents' duties. Some of America's most prolific, high-profile child-rearing advisers—figures whose names were associated with a general approach, not simply a specialized niche—spoke up during another closing century as more than scientific experts or even public advocates. Striving to be heard above the din of child-raising counsel of every kind, they abandoned all pretense to being voices of reassurance. They warned with the utmost moral urgency that a materialistic, competitive, and spiritually corrosive culture threatened the values at the core of America's families, the very fiber of the nation.

And they held forth with fervor from opposing pulpits. In the 1990s a contingent of what the *New York Times* called "disciples of discipline," busy marshalling their forces for more than a decade, challenged the ascendancy of the well-ensconced " 'helping' professionals" in the child-rearing advice industry. It was high time, according to the conservative "Judeo-Christian" camp of self-proclaimed "parent-centered" popular experts, to rescue the cause of children from the grasp of infidels—"Eastern establishment, liberal, secular humanists"—whose "child-centered" views and psychological research had dominated, and distorted, parenting counsel for too long. At stake was the preservation of adult authority and family integrity, "the last defense against an 'overweening state' " and a decadent society, they declared in the style of righteous ministers.

Their "child-centered" opponents, whose conversational counsel had long been their trademark, had meanwhile become more sermonic themselves. In the tone of earnest mentors, they voiced their concerns about the fragility of the family and the erosion of intimacy in a country that put more and more of a premium on "competitive mastery," and less and less on "nurturing care." And they worried about unenlightened intruders into the nursery. In an anti-family society already demoralized by impersonal values and marketplace pressures, Dr. Brazelton and Dr. Stanley Greenspan judged it an ominous sign that "professionals and parents are embracing a back-to-discipline ethic that flies in the face of what we know about infants and young children."

America's child-rearing debate had not sounded quite so polarized, or so politicized, since Dr. Spock was pilloried by the Reverend Norman Vincent Peale. In fact, the long-running opposition between "hard" and "soft" views had taken more than just an ideological, partisan turn. The fin-de-siècle confrontation harked back much further than the 1960s, to the very start of the "century of the child," when scientists had challenged the power of religion and tradition to show parents the way to bring up children in a fast-changing, modern world. Back then, Victorian ministers and their grandmotherly allies had been dismissed as the outmoded voice of soft dogma and "uncertain instinct." Science, by contrast, promised to deliver the firm data and "unhesitating insight" required to prepare youth for the future. A century later, the "disciples of discipline" turned the tables, echoing none other than Dr. Spock himself. Uncertain science, the conservative school of minister-style experts charged, had eroded parents' instincts. Worse, it had armed them with hesitating insight, hardly what they needed to raise "children of character in an indulgent age," as one book title summed up the theme sounded more loudly in popular child-rearing expertise across the spectrum by the time the new millennium arrived.

At the close of a century during which scientific explorations of children's bodies, personalities, and, finally, minds and brains had left their mark on parenting advice and public debate, concern had resurfaced about children's—and parents'—moral behavior and values as well. And Dr. Spock's "liberal, secular" successors were aware that psychology's track record on the topic left something to be desired, certainly in the average parent's mind. The fraught Freudian drama of superego formation had hardly given the conscience a good reputation; the engine of guilt and fear, it loomed as a likely source of neurosis, never mind of virtue. Behaviorists had reduced morality to a bundle of trained reflexes. And Piaget's work on the growth of moral reasoning—which inspired an influential American follower, Lawrence Kohlberg, to more elaborate theorizing—had downplayed the parents' part in the process; the focus shifted to children's interactions with peers as they worked toward a mature sense of justice based on equality and autonomy, rather than on mere obedience to authority.

Eager to supply guidance to a public evidently now convinced that "conscience is as important a focus of education as cognition," child development professionals had gotten to work urging the relevance of their science. Morality had become "one of developmental psychology's hottest topics," William Damon, then of Clark University, broadcast in *The Moral Child: Nurturing Children's Natural Moral Growth* (1988). And one of the pre-eminent conservative analysts of America's social crises, the social scientist James Q. Wilson, chimed in to say in *The Moral Sense* (1993) that "however much the scientific method is thought to be the enemy of morality, scientific findings provide substantial support for its existence and power."

The only trouble was that, as Wilson went on to acknowledge in musing about different aspects (and defects) of moral conduct in *On Character* (1995), "surprisingly, we do not know how character is formed in any rigorously scientific sense"—though a consensus on the core qualities of "what anyone can reasonably mean by 'character' " seemed clear: self-control and empathy. Even as busy researchers were discovering that both were budding earlier than had been supposed—in a child's second and third year—they were also finding it harder to say for certain how experiences with parents served as "catalysts for the growth of prosocial behavior and the rudiments of conscience," as *From Neurons to Neighborhoods* put it. On the pressing matter of engendering virtue, however, the Judeo-Christian newcomers had a head start and no such doubts. Impatient with the "wobbly-legged insights" from the lab, they knew what source of authority to invoke—the Bible, and "the voice of Grandma." And the "parent-centered" forces were eager for a fight. Divisiveness, after all, had always been good for the popular experts' business.

The minister-experts, unmatched in their zeal for the moral mission, cast it as a quest to direct children's "hearts and minds" and mold (not break) wills. For the mentor-experts, the challenge was to guide the well-integrated growth of children's naturally emerging "sociocentric" emotional and cognitive capacities. The "hard" and "soft" contrast was as striking as ever. Yet, different as the ministers and the mentors were, what emerged from their high-pitched and high-minded battle in the closing decade of the century was an unexpected affinity between their gospels. The two kinds of experts, it turned out, were not cut from entirely dissimilar cloth. Their kinship emerged in the social and moral alarm they displayed, but also even in the style of advisory fare some of them dispensed. Ministers and mentors alike revealed themselves to be management experts armed with systematic principles and tools for engineering a home culture of structured commitment, cooperation, and communication. And "parent-centered" traditionalists and "child-centered" psychologists embraced much the same mixed aim: to prepare children for, and protect them against, an overstimulating, alienating culture of competitive achievement and unbridled consumerism.

They were no longer intimate Spockian counselors of spontaneity: What mothers, or fathers, had time for companionable role-modeling all day long, or the inclination for an unscripted struggle for insight, Bettelheim style? In the hectic era of dual-income and diverse households, experts had become more like family consultants specializing in systems analysis and motivational uplift. The diagram-drawing, mantra-intoning advisers were reminiscent of the organizational gurus whose parallel fin-de-siècle mission was urging CEOs to ensure quality by cultivating a highly self-conscious culture of shared values in American companies. It should come as no surprise that the experts envisaged plenty of work for the engineers of excellent character that parents were to become. What may be more startling is that the mentors' softer brand of empathetic home management could be just as stringent for parents, and for children, as the ministers' regimens for inculcating self-control—if not more so.

2.

The experts themselves now ran organized enterprises. The founding father of the parent-centered camp was Dr. James Dobson, the author of *Dare to Discipline*, which had sold more than three million copies since 1971, as well as of numerous spin-off manuals that invoked the Bible far more often than the laboratory. The son and grandson of preachers in the evangelical Church of the Nazarene, he had started his career as a psychologist teaching pediatrics at the University of Southern California School of Medicine and working at Children's Hospital of Los Angeles. But in the late 1970s, he had felt called to a pulpit of his own devising: Dobson launched and assumed leadership of Focus on the Family, a non-profit conservative Christian radio-based parenting "ministry" in Colorado Springs that eventually claimed a core audience of almost four million and a mailing list of two million (and a budget five times larger than the Christian Coalition's). Five years later, in 1982, he created a lobbying arm in Washington as well.

In 1990, Dobson declared war in a dire manifesto, *Children at Risk: The Battle for the Hearts and Minds of Our Kids*, co-authored with Gary Bauer, the president of his Washington advocacy group, called the Family Research Council. "Nothing short of a great Civil War of Values rages today throughout North America," they announced. "Two sides with vastly different and incompatible worldviews are locked in a bitter conflict that permeates every level of society. Bloody battles are being fought on a thousand fronts." Up in arms about day care, they proclaimed no front more important than "the issue of child care," warning that the national future hinged on the preservation of parental power: American child-rearing choices "will determine, to a large extent, what philosophy of living, loving, begetting, and getting through life will prevail in . . . the twenty-first century."

By mid-decade, more recruits for the "parent-centered" side had lined up. Gary Ezzo, not trained as a preacher either, was the founder of a little-known for-profit evangelical Christian parenting "ministry" in Chatsworth, California, called Growing Families International.

With the church-based "Growing Kids God's Way" (GKGW) program of "biblical ethics for parenting" he developed in the 1980s with his wife, Anne Marie, Ezzo had joined the quest to rout the "ideological humanists" and "capture the hearts and minds of the next genera-tion"—and enjoyed notable success: by one estimate in 1999, the GKGW classes, tapes, and a workbook by that title had reached as many as a million parents. Eager to educate more "minds of today's parents" in "rightly applying God's principles in parenting," Ezzo began revising his routinized child-rearing approach for the main-stream parenting market. Between 1995 and 2000, he repackaged his program as a more secular series, unified by a suffix: two popular books of advice On Becoming Babywise were followed by On Becoming Child-wise, On Becoming Preteen Wise, and On Becoming Teenwise, along with a supplementary guide on communication, On Reaching the Heart of Your Teen.

Outside the fold of the Christian right, the traditionalist parent-centered warriors found a somewhat incongruous ally in the self-described "loose cannon, a maker of much mischief, an excitable boy," John Rosemond. He was a family therapist from North Carolina who had made his name in Middle America during the 1980s as an icono-clastic "tough-love" advocate—the "antipsychologist's psychologist," U.S. News & World Report called him. In the syndicated columns and two manuals that launched his career, Parent Power! (1981) and John Rosemond's Six-Point Plan for Raising Happy, Healthy Children (1989), he derided his psychological colleagues as soft-headed, pseudo-scientific saboteurs of parental gumption and held forth in an old-fashioned yet upstart vein himself—the "voice of Grandma, of common sense," with a smart-aleck style.

In A Family of Value (1995), his midcareer manifesto, Rosemond the renegade signed on to the crusade. Now a right-wing convert (he called himself a "recovering liberal" as of the mid-1980s), he pronounced it no longer "possible to separate child rearing from politics." Echoing Dobson's alarm about "social engineers" encroaching on the family—promoting sex education, homosexuality, no-fault divorce, anti-spanking laws, and children's rights, among other things—Rosemond denounced "ultraliberals, leftists, socialists" and their plot to make "big government . . . a de facto member of the family." And he worked some Scripture into the books and talks he churned out through the 1990s. (Book sales hit one million by 1999.) Now the director of his own Cen-ter for Affirmative Parenting—the term he had made his trademark—he hosted a Web site, peddled audiovisual wares, published a monthly

Traditional Parenting magazine, and had a packed speaking schedule (more than 250 talks and workshops a year, as well as a cruise).

The "Eastern establishment, liberal, secular" old guard lacked the evangelical enterprise of the minister camp. Still, the genteel experts who had made their name dispensing nonprescriptive, intuitive guidance displayed a zeal for outreach and hortatory rhetoric, too, as the energetic Dr. Brazelton had proved. He was joined on the stump in the mid-1990s by Penelope Leach, the British psychologist whose *Your Baby and Child* of 1977 had long shared shelf space as the other by-the-baby-not-the-book classic of the child-centered camp in the post-Spock era. (Her book had sold one and a half million copies by the middle of the 1990s, Brazelton's *Infants and Mothers* one million.) Leach swerved from manual to manifesto with *Children First: What Our Society Must Do—and Is Not Doing—for Our Children Today* in 1994. A twenty-year career of relaying the discoveries of child development research to parents had left her frustrated by the limits of "good parenting" counsel alone to ensure healthy nurturing in a high-pressured world where work, not home, came first for mothers now, too.

"What is needed now," Leach declared, "is something that cannot be produced by further scientific advance or a new technical fix": a shift in fundamental, and financial, priorities to give parents a more realistic chance to provide children the intimate, interactive, intensive home care she insisted they needed well past infancy—needed with special urgency, given "an adult world whose values are centered in the marketplace and disseminated by powerful media." Somewhat surprised to discover that she was, as she put it, "one hell of a pamphleteer," Leach urged a public agenda that featured government-mandated paid leaves and part-time work options for parents as an alternative to the day care she opposed for babies and young children. A co-founder of End Physical Punishment of Children (EPOCH), a movement to outlaw spanking, she included recognition of children's civil rights, above all protection from corporal punishment, on her roster of other recommendations, including neighborhood family centers.

Meanwhile, Dr. Brazelton was busy proselytizing for his Touchpoints Model of a "more caring, seamless system" of "anticipatory guidance" for parents, his cure for what ailed "the least child-oriented society in the world—10 years behind every other civilized country in backing up our families." The goal was to "give them back what we've lost in our culture—the feeling of being surrounded by a protective extended family" as overstressed mothers and fathers weathered rocky developmental stretches from the pre-natal period onward. The multi-disciplinary

entourage of white coats whom Brazelton envisaged as surrogate relatives were trained to "dialogue," not just to diagnose: the specialists
were on hand to mediate and encourage, he insisted, not to meddle or
encroach on families' private ways and views. Much of the pilot work on
his sweeping vision of intervention was funded and disseminated by
Procter & Gamble, on whose Web site, the Pampers Parenting Institute
(PPI), Brazelton now presided as chairman. It was "cause-related" public relations designed to spread the committed, caring image and message of both doctor and corporate sponsor.

And as the millennium turned, Brazelton, too, issued a manifesto,
teaming up with Stanley Greenspan, who had carved out his place on
the child-centered shelves during the late 1980s by prescribing what his
discursive fellow promoters of intensive child-focused advice did not: a
child-rearing technique, which he called "floor time," a daily thirty-
minute dose of one-on-one interplay between parent and child. The
prescriptive spirit pervaded their joint effort, *The Irreducible Needs of
Children: What Every Child Must Have to Grow, Learn, and Flourish*,
which supplied, in essence, the child-centered camp's doctrinal creed
for enlightened parenthood. Here were the tenets, as well as the techniques, deemed crucial to promoting healthy emotional and cognitive
development and laying the "foundation for any lasting sense of discipline and morality"—for "any child, in any society." From broad needs,
they descended to details about "what specific types of experiences are
most important and how much of each of them is necessary" to fulfill
those needs—going so far as to outline the "optimal structure for a
child's day," which included hefty doses of child-driven interaction.

In their social diatribes and in their practical child-rearing rituals,
the ministers and the mentors faced off as a century of conflicting
advice to parents drew to a close. Ideology led back to the nursery,
much as it had when Spock was being spanked in the late 1960s, and
newspaper headlines called attention to dissension in the expert ranks
over the child care basics, and beyond them. "Two Experts Do Battle
over Potty Training," announced a front-page story in the *New York
Times* in 1999, pitting Rosemond's train-them-by-two message against
Brazelton's let-them-take-their-time approach (in which, Rosemond
charged, the doctor had a vested interest: Brazelton had also begun
appearing in ads for Pampers, now available in super sizes). Barely a
month later, the *Washington Post* announced "A Tough Plan for Raising
Children Draws Fire." The stern "parent-directed" system championed by Gary Ezzo and his wife, Anne Marie Ezzo, in their briskly selling "Babywise" books had stirred up enough concern to elicit a warning

from the American Pediatric Association that overly rigid feeding schedules can lead to "failure to thrive."

The Ezzos' insistence on through-the-night sleeping and their endorsement of "swats" were also grist for age-old arguments on two other classic Western child-rearing themes, which had become more value-laden than they had been in years. Especially on the Web (where weary parents increasingly surfed for advice), the familiar skirmishes between the let-them-cry-it-out and the rock-and-coax-them schools of bedtime routine were as frequent as ever. Meanwhile, child-centered advocates of "co-sleeping" gave parents yet another option to toss and turn over: proponents of the "family bed" challenged the all-American insistence on solitary slumber as the bedrock, so to speak, of personal autonomy. And "no debate is more contentious—or longer running— than the dispute over spanking," noted the *Times* in an article reporting that science was not about to settle it. A hard look at weak data found no ill effects traceable to its "normative" use, a discovery sure to feed the rancor between an increasingly "impassioned anti-spanking" movement championing children's rights and defenders of the timely whack (Dobson, Rosemond, and the Ezzos), who saw an assault on parents' rights.

Beyond the nursery, experts (or advocates who invoked them) fought over sex education and gender issues in dire and confrontational terms. Proponents of an "abstinence-only" message had multiplied and mobilized. They lobbied legislators and educators, and parents, with much the same zeal they denounced in their opponents, longtime promoters of comprehensive sexuality curricula and reproductive health services for teenagers. The fervor on both sides was fueled by the long-running battle over abortion. And in a new genre of save-their-souls-and-self-esteem counsel for parents and teachers, a crusade to rescue adolescent girls in crisis was matched by a divisive movement to come to the aid of boys. By the late 1990s, they were the gender judged to be in special distress, although the boy-savers were at odds over diagnoses and cures. Let boys be more like "emotional" girls was the message of a "soft" contingent of psychologists concerned about the straitjacket of traditional masculinity. A conservative backlash of worry about sissification ensued, as Dr. Dobson and others rallied around the let-boys-be-boys flag. At the heart of the debate lay the continuing controversy over feminism and its legacy.

Even as they fanned the sense of moral and social crisis, the experts also vied over who could convey more concern about all the child-rearing commotion, every one of them lamenting the pressure and the polarization of advice—and its profusion. Five times as many parenting books were published in 1997 as in 1975, and books were now merely one corner of a multi-media market. Ministers and mentors alike diagnosed middle-class parents as driven to distraction by all the conflicting counsel, addicted to it yet hardly calmed by its competing directives—prone to be too demanding or too indulgent with their children, or worse, both.

Concern about "out-of-control parents," high in 1980, had evolved into alarm about over-controlling parents, and the hovered-over child had joined the "hurried child" as a victim of "counsel, if not outright insistence, often offered in the name of science or medicine," that Americans should "raise our children in an amazingly intense and competitive manner." So wrote Dr. Robert Coles (recent chronicler of *The Moral Intelligence of Children*, *The Moral Life of Children*, and *The Spiritual Life of Children*) in an introduction to a how-not-to meta-manual of 2000 called *Hyper-Parenting: Are You Hurting Your Child by Trying Too Hard?* The question posed by the authors—Dr. Alvin Rosenfeld, a psychiatrist who had collaborated with Bettelheim decades earlier, and a freelance journalist and mother named Nicole Wise—was echoed on both sides of the spectrum by experts trying awfully hard themselves to be heard and heeded.

3.

The classic Norman Rockwell *Saturday Evening Post* cover of 1933—mother with child over her knee and "child psychology" book in hand, scrutinizing the spanking instructions—had long since been superseded by a less composed caricature of expert-attuned motherhood, and now often fatherhood, too. The fin-de-siècle specimen, with "puffy eyes and disheveled appearance," was having a meltdown in the midst of the "answer mecca of the universe . . . the parenting section of a trendy bookstore," as Gary Ezzo archly put it in one of the five books he had churned out for that mecca in half a decade. Yet on the scale of hyperactivity in the child-rearing marketplace, it was the prolific experts themselves, increasingly fraught in tone, who deserved a place near the top. And on closer inspection, what was particularly disorienting about the array of variously credentialed doctors was an underlying similarity between the two competing camps.

Though you would never have guessed it from their press, much less from their opposition to each other, the parent-centered ministers and the child-centered mentors professed allegiance to the same cause: "authoritative parenting," an approach that struck a balance between love and control, which was the consensus position in the child development field. Both schools toed the conventional line in distinguishing it from "authoritarian parenting" on the one hand, which they all agreed was overbearing, and "permissive parenting" on the other, which they concurred was indulgent.

The tough experts were particularly concerned not to be mistaken for tyrants. Introducing his *New Dare to Discipline* in 1992, Dr. Dobson took pains to reaffirm the kindly family-doctor style that had long leavened his trademark gruffness. "Disciplinary activity must take place within the framework of love and affection," he had always emphasized, and did so again—and again. ". . . One must *dare to discipline* in an environment of unmitigated love." And for any reader who still needed convincing, "May all doubts be dispelled. *I don't believe in parental harshness.* Period!" Nor was his aim to inculcate submissiveness. "The principles in this book are not designed to produce perfect little robots who can sit with their hands folded in the parlor thinking patriotic or noble thoughts!" Dobson wrote. "Even if we *could* pull that off, it would not be wise to try." Worried about an "epidemic of inferiority," especially among teens, he had even devoted a book to the trendy theme of self-esteem, writing in his most psychological vein—though he also availed himself of more biblical terms: the goal was gently to nurture the fragile "spirit," reserving tougher treatment for shaping the steely "will."

On the evangelical right, Gary Ezzo, too, made sure to criticize not just laissez-faire parents, but also the "authoritarian household" for its insistence on "outward conformity [rather] than helping the child internalize the guiding principles for interpersonal relationships" (precisely the criticism the mentors themselves leveled against the "hard" camp). The result, Ezzo and his wife warned, is endless "power struggles" and a "child who is bitter and full of resentment." Even the blunt John Rosemond, who did not hesitate to call the home regime he had in mind a "benevolent dictatorship," stressed that he did not mean "rigidly . . . authoritarian." His "authoritative" parental rulers, careful not to give kids undue attention, nonetheless "encourage discussion (as opposed to argument), but they make the final decisions." And Rosemond was emphatic that the "goal is not to make the child passively subservient, but to make the child autonomous." Both he and Ezzo took swipes at the self-esteem vogue for turning parents into guilty appeasers of their children: feeling good is not the precursor to doing good, they lectured, but the other way around.

Meanwhile, the mentor school of experts took care to protect themselves against accusations of laxness. Brazelton denounced "permissiveness" as "a nightmare" and an "abdication of parental responsibility," bound to result in children "frightened of themselves . . . anxiously looking for limits." Building self-esteem was not, he stressed, about removing all obstacles from a child's path and lavishing him with praise; it was crucial to appreciate "the enormous power of frustration" in fueling a child's quest for "mastery and a sense of his own competence." In a similar spirit, Stanley Greenspan emphasized that "limit-setting" was a linchpin of his approach. He warned parents that it "won't be easy," but urged them not to let their own "fear of the child's discomfort and anger" deter them from a task he considered developmentally critical to establishing a sense of security and self-control. "Understand," he told his readers with hard-boiled realism of the sort the tough advisers faulted the gentle ones for lacking, "that your children will certainly challenge whatever limits you set. Isn't that what children are for?" Every one of the experts, on both sides, invoked Dr. Spock with approval, as the sturdy icon confirming that expert's own "authoritative" stance.

And they all echoed Spock's late-career reminder to parents that more than the psychological task of promoting healthy personalities and cognitive capacities was at stake. The quest at the turn of the millennium, as the minister-experts exhorted very explicitly, was above all to rear a "morally responsible child who will grow up to be a morally responsible adult" (Ezzo), raise "respectful, responsible young citizens" who would bring back "honesty, truthfulness, and unselfishness" to America (Dobson). Brazelton and Greenspan invoked an ethic of solicitude, and proclaimed the goal of bringing up "human beings . . . able to work cooperatively, compassionately, and empathetically with others in a group, in all aspects of life." But where Spock, pragmatic and companionable to the core, had done his best to buck up mothers—and fathers—with assurances that their children would forge their ideals in eager emulation of their elders, his successors were ready with much more programmatic wisdom for a clientele that presumably stuck with Spock for his practical tips, not his outdated Freudianism.

Parents were still exhorted to be moral examples, of course, and all the experts deplored materialist excess. But the firm-yet-friendly-and-flexible formula was deemed in need of updating. The minister school, and the mentors in their subtler way along with them, reconceived the family as, in essence, a firm in need of more formal guidelines. It was an organization whose priority lay in cultivating consciences and souls—or "healthy minds," in Greenspan's phrase—rather than making sales, in creating values rather than generating revenues. Consuming revenues was more like it, Dr. Dobson noted: "Oh yes, *children are expensive, but they're worth the price*"—and worth an investment in managerial enlightenment.

For the "hard" and the "soft" generalists urging moral earnestness in an ever more specialized market, the task during an era of family flux and dual-career pressures was to supply parents with structures, techniques, and a coherent nurturing "vision." To be sure, the unique interactions between children's distinctive temperaments and parental treatment eluded one-size-fits-all scripting. Even the parent-centered advisers duly noted a variety of types and the different tactics they required. And the Brazelton camp had been busy profiling an ever wider array of brain wirings (culminating in the pediatrician Mel Levine's best-selling guide of 2002, *A Mind at a Time*). But prominent popularizers on both sides of the spectrum were not about to leave parents to mere improvisational customizing. To assure the healthy emergence of productive, morally purposeful children—and parents—called for, as Dobson put it, a "well-designed model or 'game plan.' "

In prescribing systematic planning and codified methods, the advisers had a common goal: the creation of a self-conscious family culture of regular communication, scheduled personal interactions, clear-cut methods of conflict resolution, and planned occasions to promote a spirit of enriching collaboration—all remarkably lacking in Spockian informality. The enterprise was in fact more reminiscent of life in an enlightened, late-twentieth-century corporation. For in the strategies of the ministers and mentors there was a curious convergence with the so-called total quality management (TQM) movement heralded as the salvation for companies foundering during the transition to a global economy in the information age.

In the quest to revive American industry, the most influential wave of organizational theorists by the late 1980s focused on a "strong culture" of shared values as a cure for corporate drift and decline. And as one of those business gurus, Stephen R. Covey—rated the "world's most influential management thinker" by *The Economist*—explained, the family served as a model in the endeavor. In the participatory rituals and cooperative values of (highly idealized) hearthside life watched over by fair and far-seeing parents, management consultants of the closing decades of the century found expressions of the moral, communal ethos they urged CEOs to engineer at work. The goal was a " 'motherly' work culture . . . that incorporated the best aspects of home," as the sociologist Arlie Russell Hochschild observed in her portrait of a "total quality" workplace. In a company that showed itself to be not "a cold, economic machine," but a "moral world" united by a "mission statement" that laid out a set of carefully "managed values" and a "common vision," managers and workers alike could find personal motivation, emotional dedication, and even spiritual fulfillment—all of which was good for business, of course, not just for employee happiness.

Turning the process around and applying the enlightened management principles to ever more harried unhomey families was "an absolute natural. It fits," proclaimed Covey as he branched out into the child-rearing market in 1997 with *The 7 Habits of Highly Effective Families*, a spin-off of his spectacularly successful *The 7 Habits of Highly Effective People* of 1989. (The original book had sold twelve million copies in North America by 2000, and helped make the Franklin Covey Company in Utah a thriving business seminar enterprise, with clients in two thirds of the Fortune 500, as well as countless smaller organizations.) After all, the large Covey family—his Mormon household of nine children practically constituted a firm—was where his "7 Habits material . . . was really learned" in the first place. In Covey, America had its purest incarnation of an ethos that had crept into more and more turn-of-the-millennium child-rearing counsel: "total quality management for the character, re-engineering for the soul," as two historians of management theory summed up "Coveyism."

The mingling of management theory and child-rearing expertise was not new. The mission to professionalize parenthood had been launched at the turn of the century alongside efforts to systematize and humanize industry. Since then, expert scrutiny of the family and of the factory had often shifted focus in tandem. Thus an industrial ethos of regularity had left its mark on Drs. Holt and Watson (with the Gilbreths, of *Cheaper by the Dozen* fame, showcasing their own modified brand of Taylorite "scientific management," family style). Dr. Spock offered a home version of the modern managerial approach envisaged by Peter Drucker, the cold claims of hierarchy and efficiency making room for rising demands for equality and group harmony.

After Spock and Bettelheim took to the barricades and Piaget caught on, "democratic parenting" in the cognitive era focused on promoting a sense of "competence" and honing communication skills, even as employee self-respect and creative collaboration became priorities in management lore. Piagetian and attachment wisdom blended in Brazelton's descriptive brand of advice; the prescriptive camp drew on techniques derived from the Adlerians Rudolf Dreikurs and Haim Ginott, two of whose mother-acolytes, Adele Faber and Elaine Mazlish, scored a huge success in 1980 with the cheery workbook-style primer, *How to Talk So Kids Will Listen & Listen So Kids Will Talk*, which had sold two million copies by the millennium. All of them specialized in fine-tuning interactions in the "learning organization" that the family—like American companies—was now conceived to be.

The "total-quality" enclave that beckoned to experts on home and work at the century's end entailed a more systematic—and reverent—"transformational" approach for a learning team now deemed in need of a culture of values. Covey, a guru worshiped by Newt Gingrich and President Clinton alike, had the gift of crossover appeal. He soared above the parent-centered and child-centered combatants with his "family flight plan," as he called his repackaged seven-step guide for building the "principles of mutual respect, understanding, and creative cooperation into the very structures, systems, and processes of the family." With the serene air of a consultant on call, Covey turned from the boardroom to the family room to unveil a credo based on familiar rituals: Dreikurian family councils and disciplinary reliance on "logical consequences," one-on-one bonding time, mission statements. Each of those programmed exercises in harmony in turn required a set of communication skills for its success, above all Ginottian "empathic listening."

In Covey's homiletic/how-to pages a "hard," parent-centered mood blurred into "soft," child-centered methods. With his celebration of the inward-looking "interdependent family" united against a "turbulent world" and anchored by the husband-wife relationship, Covey signaled a traditionalist stance. He echoed the minister-experts in emphasizing "spiritual renewal" and "worshiping together," and in summoning fathers to help guide the agenda. The Covey clan that had moved "from 'me' to 'we' " was the morale- and moral-building alternative to the "independent," child-dominated family that he, like Dobson et al., saw as the sorry American norm—a household of "me's" focused outward, all too vulnerable to "intrusive values" and prone to divorce.

But Covey also gently intoned, "You are your children's first mentor." Invoking his wife's child development degree, he urged respect for children's "competency" and their need for stage-appropriate challenges and choices every step of the way. Like the child-centered camp, he placed great emphasis on letting children know "you care about them—deeply, sincerely, personally, unconditionally." And "punishment" was a concept that had no place in his system. In fact, Covey could often rather sound like the relativist "secular humanists" whom Dobson and company loved to hate. His constant refrain was that moral harmony depends on a nonjudgmental stance: to avoid a critical "mind-set" and listen to children "without any moral evaluation or judgment" were his highest priorities.

What Covey always sounded like, however, was an organizational consultant who constantly talked about home as where the heart is, but thought about home as where the chart is. (The Franklin Covey Company produced a lucrative line of personal organizers, weekly planners, worksheets, software, tapes, and lots of other 7 Habits "effectiveness" paraphernalia, including *Loving Reminders for Kids: 60 Nurturing Notes and 60 Stickers*, with endearments and ego boosts pre-printed on them for the parent too busy to grab a pen and a Post-it.) The key to an "effective"—synonymous for him with "beautiful"—family culture ("the feeling, the 'vibes,' the chemistry, the climate or atmosphere in the home") was the Emotional Bank Account. It was not just a figure of speech, but an actual box to be decorated by the kids, into which family feelings, on index cards, were to be dropped and from which they could be withdrawn. "Every family problem," Covey declared, "can be turned into an opportunity for a deposit."

He blended the aura of a prophet with the language of profits—and of highly structured process. It required an elaborate planner indeed to keep track of all those mission statement meetings, family times, one-on-one bonding times, and family councils that Covey prescribed as the secret to cleansing the home of "four 'cancers' that are deadly to family life: criticizing, complaining, comparing, competing"—and to assuring "empathic" communication and a common mission. Parents arrived at the "vision" required to be "quality" leaders of such a family culture when those seven habits of his (among them, be "proactive," think "win-win," and "synergize") had become rote, and when the four human "gifts"—self-awareness, conscience, imagination, independent will—had become, quite literally, reflexive. Cultivating them, according to Covey, was "like developing a muscle," but possession of them liberated his ideal mother or father from any need, or desire, to display any muscle.

On the Coveyite family plan, a fifth and sixth cancer were also kept at bay: overt conflict and heavy-handed control. The managerial guru who portrayed the parent as a transformational "creative force"—"an agent of change"—all but whisked the potentially recalcitrant child off the page. In Covey's vision, children were a valuable part of the "team," and vulnerable, too, given the wider "turbulent, family-unfriendly environment" around them. But with a well-managed emotional investment plan—and enough "nurturing notes and stickers" ("Run, share, jump, play, Have a ball today!")—those family assets need not be too volatile, and they would become "morally accountable." Covey's credo exposed an ironic consequence of the moral managers' quest. A calculating mentality—not very "motherly"—seeped into the expert schemes to revive values and vital human connections in American families, hardly the spirit they intended. Theirs was a mission, after all, quite fervently dedicated to countering the impersonal, hyper-scheduled ethos of a crass and competitive marketplace.

4.

Covey's "family flight plan" did not take off as his original book had (sales of *The 7 Habits of Highly Effective Families*, in print and audio, reached 350,000 by late 2002), but one of his sons sold two million copies of *The 7 Habits of Highly Effective Teens* (1998). And back on the ground among the battling child-rearing advisers, a systematic spirit akin to Covey's helped to propel two experts to attention in their respective camps as the century ended. While Dr. Dobson, the father figure among the minister-experts, was caught up in Washington culture-war politics during the mid-1990s, Gary Ezzo of Growing Families International emerged as a controversial new child-rearing voice on the parent-centered side. His glossily packaged *On Becoming Babywise* series prospered, sales of the volumes on infancy soon passing the quarter-million mark. On the child-centered side, the torch was being passed from Dr. Brazelton to the prolific Dr. Greenspan, whose *The Growth of the Mind and the Endangered Origins of Intelligence* (1997) and *Building Healthy Minds* (1999) were the blueprint for their joint millennial manifesto, *The Irreducible Needs of Children*.

Greenspan and Ezzo each set out to supply a comprehensive, schematic vision of what Ezzo did not hesitate to call "moral training." Greenspan, sounding Gesellian, framed the task as promoting "healthy intellectual, moral, and social growth actively and in an *integrated* way." Poles apart in the philosophies they aimed to impart and in their advisory styles and clientele, they nonetheless joined in envisaging parents as programmatic managers who should waste no time in turning to the job of "enabling all the members of a child's mental 'team' to work together," as Greenspan put it. In Ezzo's blunter Watsonian formulation, you "can't sit back and hope good character emerges naturally. It won't." As second-generation proselytizers of ideological creeds often are, they were both more zealous systematizers than the elders in whose footsteps they followed. In fact, they ended up disconcerting—and in Ezzo's case, alienating—their own constituencies.

It was not Gary Ezzo's conservative Christian ardor that was his undoing, surprisingly enough, so much as the pseudo-scientific rigor and the managerial fervor he counted on to win him a conservative following beyond his church circle. His gambit was to market his wares as the sensible corrective to an extreme, in this case "child-centered" indulgence. That meant toning down his own extremism, dispensing with almost all of the Scriptural exegesis and some of the cultural animus that had pervaded his original Growing Kids God's Way material on "biblical ethics for parenting."

There he and his wife had been preaching to the converted, and they had inveighed against "secular theorists" (Gesell was a particular target) who assigned parents the spineless job of "facilitating a child's nature rather than actively directing the child's moral conscience." Displaying a passion for biblical citation that made Dr. Dobson look like a mere dabbler, the Ezzos had chimed in on the theme of taming "willful defiance," but their tone and techniques were more doctrinaire than his. Toddlers and teens needn't stir up trouble, they insisted, and compared to Dobson's no-nonsense Dad style in endorsing the squeeze of the neck to get speedy compliance, they sounded lawyerly, citing chapter and verse on the fine points of when to use "chastisement" (the "biblical term for spanking") and how.

In forgoing his Scriptural texts as he joined the secular theorists on their own ground, Gary Ezzo updated but did not abandon his canonical spirit. On the covers of his handy-sized paperbacks were photos of multi-cultural cuties, and the deity had been edged out by a new collaborator, this one with a medical degree: Dr. Robert Bucknam, a pediatrician from Denver. (Anne Marie Ezzo was no longer a co-author.) In the first Babywise book, the word "biblical" had even been replaced by "natural" in the subtitle: *How 100,000 New Parents Learned to Put Their Children to Sleep the Natural Way*. Ezzo had not failed to notice that sleep was a best-selling issue among weary, overworked baby boomers: Dr. Richard Ferber's hit of 1985, *Solve Your Child's Sleep Problems*, had inspired a thriving genre.

But to open the book was to discover Dr. Holt, and Frederick Taylor, making a centenary reappearance. In the prescriptive style long familiar in the "hard" child-rearing literature, Ezzo offered no fine prose or portraiture, and the homiletic vignettes sprinkled throughout suggested the readership he had in mind (as anecdotes in the how-to genre often do): at-home moms (among them his wife) in the middle of the middle class, on blandly middle American terrain, with two or three kids and hands-on husbands (among them Ezzo himself). He had picked up on what made for a good pitch in the oversaturated market: he peddled "an infant-management strategy" to those who "desire to achieve excellence in parenting."

His had the ring of a familiar old-fashioned regimen, yet could be packaged as a full-service program, complete with an acronym: the "parent-directed feeding system," or PDF. Ezzo began by billing his regularized three- to four-hour feeding schedule—which in turn led to routinized infant sleep- and wake-time cycles to suit family rhythms—as a Spockian brand of "structure mixed with flexibility," a middle way between the ideological extremes of "demand feeding" and "clock feeding." Attend to a baby's "hunger cues," but guide her toward regularity, always making sure to show plenty of "love, caring, concern" and never being "legalistic" about the timing.

Yet even as Ezzo entered his caveats, he struck a legalistic—and pseudo-medical and doctrinaire—tone himself, adding punctilious instructions and making sweeping claims. PDF was the foundation for harmonious "we-ism" in the "interdependent" family he championed; it was, he promised in managementese, a win-win formula to consolidate parental leadership and confirm, right from the start, the child's "role in the family as a team member—where giving is as important as receiving." Bucknam's name on the cover also licensed him to claim, in medicalese, that PDF was essential to avoiding the "metabolic confusion" caused by irregularity, which jeopardized "healthy learning patterns." Sleep deprivation might "negatively impact an infant's developing central nervous system," he suggested in a similar vein as he promoted early through-the-night sleeping. The result could be learning disabilities later.

Here were edicts with more power than Scriptural tenets to intimidate the credulous—and to rile some doctors, who stepped forth to confront Ezzo the interloper, concerned that he had proved so popular. They direly invoked the danger of overly regimented feeding: failure to thrive. And they challenged him to show data, refusing to be appeased by his insistence in his primer that he did not intend an old-style let-them-cry-until-the-clock-strikes regimen. And they were further incensed by Ezzo's bristly (Watsonian) response, in which he turned the tables and charged them with dogmatism: on his Web site he mocked those who "religiously insist on child-led feedings exclusively," and went on the medical defensive. Ezzo posted charts with citations to prove that his book included every one of the American Pediatric Association's infant feeding guidelines.

It was a furor to confirm Spock's fear, voiced half a century earlier, that infant feeding philosophies elicit "fanatical" responses in Americans, or at any rate in their experts—though Dr. Dobson, for one, managed to keep his head as Ezzo's former Christian allies joined in denouncing him, in a display of the sort of internecine organizational feuding with which the founder of Focus on the Family was familiar. "I've never attacked it, but I don't endorse it," was Dobson's equivocal comment on a baby care approach that was, after all, hardly alone in failing to meet high scientific standards. "I'm not out campaigning against the Ezzos; I'm just not their greatest fan."

In truth, the PDF schedules that caused such a stir sounded decidedly cozy compared to the strictures in the follow-up *Babywise II* book. Covering pre-toddlerhood between five and fifteen months, it revealed the daunting next step in Ezzo's "moral model of child development," as he called his alternative to the usual "psychological model" that he criticized for putting either a child's emotional ease or his cognitive prowess first. During the period when Dr. Dobson urged parents to be warm encouragers of their more mobile baby's explorations, Ezzo had sterner stuff on the agenda. For according to his overarching "philosophy," top-down "self-control training" came first and interactive guidance in empathy began later, in a graduated sequence that ultimately "delivers the whole package," he promised: "emotionally balanced, intellectually assertive, morally sensible children, raised to the applause of a grateful society."

"Highchair manners" was the tough course that came next on the PDF pre-toddler curriculum, as Ezzo seized on another "opportunity for learning" during feeding. There was to be none of the food dropping and mashing that some Piaget-inspired experts had hailed as creative experimentation, although Ezzo touted his own tactics in unexpectedly cognitive terms. Babies were to be clearly told (it builds vocabulary) as well as shown where to keep their hands (out of the way, except with finger food), and then given "light swats" or isolation for failure to follow the instructions—or for arching defiantly in the chair. To banish whining, they should be taught simple sign language. This was all-important practice, Ezzo explained, in a trio of essential virtues that were not "stage-acquired activities" that parents could simply encourage, but "moral developmental skills" that parents must instill, the earlier the better: "sitting, focusing, concentrating"—to which he had now added another, choosing "a better way to communicate."

The rest of his pre-toddler's life was no picnic, either, and though Ezzo advertised the daily routine as a respite for mother (much as Holtians had done decades earlier), it sounded like she would need a personal organizer to keep it straight. There was "structured playtime alone," which consisted of "playpen time" (a "structured learning center," where "mental focusing skills . . . sustained attention span . . . creativity . . . self-play adeptness . . . orderliness" are developed), and assigned "roomtime." There was also some "free playtime." And then there was interactive playtime with family members. Reading while "nestling" was at the top of a list that also included the usual babbling and "flirting with your baby, smiling, talking, and gently moving his or her arms and legs," though Ezzo felt the need to stress that "your baby does not need to be entertained by you all day long." Perhaps fifteen minutes of "full attention" from Mother, beyond the daily (and friendly, he urged) routines of feeding, changing, and bathing, would do.

Yet from *On Becoming Childwise* (age three to seven) in 1999 onward, Ezzo's tone lightened, and Taylorite dictates gave way to total-quality tactics. Where Holt's spirit had reigned, echoes of Dr. Hall were to be heard in Ezzo's fervent emphasis on "reaching the heart of your teen," as all too many Americans, he lamented, failed to do. It was the Growing Families International moral philosophy at work: firm parents were to grant progressively more freedom, with friendship or partnership the ultimate "relational goal"—*not* the starting point, Ezzo emphasized in denouncing what he saw as the prevailing pal-parent style that encouraged adolescent drift and rebellion.

But the softening of strict Ezzo was also a commercial strategy at work (unsuccessful, it turned out several years later, when Multnomah Publishers succumbed to pressure to drop their embattled author, who promptly went into business publishing himself). Parents have the "ultimate responsibility to research the parenting philosophies available today and make an informed decision as to what is best for their family," he now took care to tell readers, sounding more pragmatic than dogmatic. What seemed best for Ezzo, eager to hold an audience, was to ease up.

The remainder of his series blended into Coveyite counsel on creating a caring family culture in which "heart training," as Ezzo called discipline, entailed more encouraging and communicating "the moral reason why" and less correcting. For the time had arrived to begin cultivating empathy, or "otherness appreciation." And the time had also come for Ezzo to skirt the charged issue of spanking, leaving it to Dobson to preside as its unapologetic advocate "when willful defiance is involved." Ezzo instead supplied this advisory: "*Childwise* will not address spanking as a disciplinary method. This decision should not be construed as a recommendation to spank or not to spank. It is simply a recognition of the complexity associated with the method." He appended a footnote counseling "those seeking more guidance on the proper use of spanking" to take one of the Ezzos' church-based Growing Kids God's Way courses. It was the dodge of a consultant who knew he was not preaching to converts.

By their children's late pre-teen years, mothers and very engaged fathers were beginning to shift "from authority to influence" as they worked to be sure their child was "pre-loaded" for "moral processing" and showed no "willful desire to overthrow family leadership . . . [or] willingness to walk away from relational accountability." And it was time to promote "family think" to counterbalance the growing "power of groupthink"—that is, of peers. The identity-forging enterprise especially required Dad as an "active part of the management team"; the "encourager of the family," Ezzo once called him, also urging him to be a hugger and to slip notes into lunch boxes.

The crucial tool was—what else?—"healthy, proactive communication," even as Ezzo cautioned that "communication has become a catchword" and that "communication skills are not a substitute for common or shared values." In his biblical program, he had criticized the contemporary credo of learning to "talk so your kids will listen, and listen so your kids will talk" as a legacy of the "democratic parenting" he disapproved of. But his tight-knit clan now hinged on an intensive, scheduled version of it. On the roster were Mother talk times, Father talk times, Mother-Father talk times, and family talk times. Above all, there was "couch time," which Ezzo had made his parent-centered trademark: ten to fifteen minutes of husband-wife talk in the presence of quiet children, who bask in the security of a strong marriage.

The secret in all this talk was lots of "empathic" listening for the real message, and learning the "primary love languages of every family member." And "the sex talk," Ezzo joined the chorus of experts in saying, was a parent's responsibility, and must be warm and intimate—and better not come too late. (He left the fight against "aggressive sex-ed [and] safe-sex programs" at school to Dobson.) Ezzo, like Dobson, made a point of telling fathers in particular not to "keep your son's sexuality at arm's length." Whatever level of detail dads chose (whether it extended to "the awkward stiffness," etc.), they should convey a message of "self-control with purpose."

The reward was teenage years free of rebellion, Ezzo promised, and free of the parental coercion that turmoil inevitably brought with it. "Adolescence *is* a time of self-discovery," he granted. "But discovery doesn't have to mean defiance," never mind what all the psychologists said—including, as it happened, Dr. Dobson, who wrote of the "heartburn and indigestion known as adolescence" and worried about "Christian parents [having] a harder time letting adolescents go." Ezzo had no such qualms, instead celebrating religion as a potent source of the "family identity"—and the "moral community"—that was central to his cure for teenage alienation.

Teens craved allegiance to a group united by shared values, and if they found it at home, they also tended to choose "like-minded" peers. (And spouses, if Ezzo had his way, though he was well aware that most parents, to say nothing of teens, would dismiss as too "radical" his parent-managed "courtship" concept—complete with pledges of sexual purity, sealed by rings or necklaces exchanged with Mom or Dad.) Ezzo called on market metaphors in portraying adolescence as the time for consolidating a family firm that, for all the talk of fondness, at times sounded like a fortress against the world. "Bounding" rather than "bridging" was the psychologist William Damon's term for the inward-turning tendency, which he warned could limit a child's range of empathy. But Ezzo celebrated the bonding as crucial to the family business. Teenagers who feel they have "invested in the stock" of the family, he promised, will "consult the state of their relational portfolio," and moral management will prosper.

5.

At the other end of the child-rearing spectrum, Dr. Stanley Greenspan was tending to "the essential partnership," the title of the second of his more than half dozen popular books. He did not mean the "husband-wife team" that the parent-centered champions of the "interdependent" family believed was the key to successful child rearing, and that Ezzo's "couch time" was designed to strengthen. Greenspan meant the parent-child team, which was the focus of his signature concept, "floor time." The starting point in raising a child—not the "relational goal," as Ezzo had it—was engaged intimacy on the child's level. Every parent, Greenspan instructed, should strive to be "a good play partner, a fellow debater, opinion seeker, and collaborator with [his or her] child," and the companionable alliance could not be forged too soon. ("A playful exchange of meows" might be just the thing.) The engagement was more than developmentally desirable. It was a moral imperative. The early experience of "rich, ongoing interaction" amid "loving compassion and caring" nurtured not only powers of complex thinking, but of empathy, which for Greenspan was the original, and crucial, source of a "child's sense of morality, or eventual ability to make good choices and to want to do what's 'right' rather than what's 'wrong.' "

Proceeding on a far more sophisticated level, invoking assorted research as he went along, Greenspan joined Ezzo in conceiving the first year and a half of a child's life as very serious business indeed for parents—far from an idyll of unreflective cuddling. It was also more than an interlude when phenomenal brain building went on and a baby's "intellectual, social, and emotional functioning [improved] enormously," though Greenspan emphasized all that. It marked "the beginning of character formation," and parents could not afford to stand back. Greenspan, like Ezzo, lamented that the deeper significance of the period was too often overlooked by experts and parents busy bathing babies in emotional comfort or barraging them with cognitive stimulation. Striking an explicitly didactic note, Greenspan proclaimed it his weightier mission to show parents how to "help your child learn his or her emotional ABCs." His course in engineering empathy was no less arduous than—and in a curious way analogous to—Ezzo's regimen, which began with that other crucial ingredient of moral behavior, self-control. Not least, Greenspan armed parents with charts and a managerial outlook, hastening to assure them even as he did so that his approach wasn't "meant to be a rigid agenda but a philosophy of what children need."

Greenspan had embarked on his academic career in psychiatry during the 1960s as the Piagetian wave swept psychology. In the 1970s he emerged with his own ambitiously synthetic vision of how Freudian psychosexual drives might relate to the development of intelligence. He proposed that cognition unfolded in response to internal emotional stimuli, not simply to the external environment. It was "theory-building" that awaited "controlled studies . . . designed to test . . . the model," he acknowledged in his "partially speculative" (and highly abstract) *Intelligence and Adaptation: An Integration of Psychoanalytic and Piagetian Developmental Psychology* of 1979. Busy doing clinical work with multi-risk families at the National Institute of Mental Health through the mid-1980s, Greenspan then quit to devote more time to private patients and to write for a popular audience.

In *First Feelings: Milestones in the Emotional Development of Your Baby and Child* (1985) and *The Essential Partnership: How Parents and Children Can Meet the Emotional Challenges of Infancy and Childhood* (1989), Greenspan turned his theory into a "road map" of children's development through six milestones on the way to, by age three or four, what he called "emotional thinking." By that Greenspan meant the capacity to "reason about feelings, not just feel them and act them out," and to "build bridges between ideas on an emotional level." In this "ability to reflect on ideas and understand consequences," he explained, "your child is developing a true moral consciousness."

Greenspan extended the map into middle childhood in *Playground Politics: Understanding the Emotional Life of Your School-Age Child* (1993), and explored differences in personality patterns in *The Challenging Child: Understanding, Raising, and Enjoying Five "Difficult" Types of Children* (1995). He repackaged and elaborated his approach with a tone of greater social and moral urgency in the two books he turned out at the end of the decade. In Brazeltonian style, Greenspan supplied narrative description, and the dual-career professional families featured in his pages reflected his Washington, D.C.–area clients. This was the educated, affluent elite—the acme of the "independent family" lamented by Ezzo and Covey—that he plainly presumed to be the main audience for his readable but not exactly breezy prose: couples more focused on their work than on their marriages, the husbands often especially distracted. They were used to providing the best for their children—and to talking to therapists. In a schematic prescriptive style unusual among the mentor set, Greenspan also equipped parents with "five principles of healthy parenting."

It was here that he turned to the formulas that lent the experts' vision of family life the feel of an organizational culture—which was precisely the structured, subtly pressured, "managed" ethos that Greenspan and Brazelton in their manifesto made a point of warning was all too widespread in a country where institutionalized care was becoming the norm. Four of Greenspan's principles—"problem-solving time," empathizing, breaking a challenge into small pieces, and limit-setting—were familiar versions of the negotiation and communication techniques first popularized in the mid-1960s and by now available in many variations. (Covey's habits were, in fact, not very different: be proactive; seek first to understand, then to be understood; put first things first.) And with his other, trademark principle—floor time—Greenspan had beaten everyone to the punch: the concept, which he began to popularize in the 1980s, was echoed in Covey as "one-on-one bonding time," and in Ezzo's father-son, father-daughter, mother-son, and so on, "talk times."

Except that what Greenspan had in mind was far more fine-tuned relational engineering than any of the rest of them dreamed of. When Ezzo, in his GKGW material, derided the "secular therapists" for telling parents their job lay in merely "facilitating a child's nature" rather than taking charge of his moral conscience, he was perhaps unaware of just how demanding such a facilitator could be. Wimpy noninterventionism was definitely not Greenspan's approach to optimizing a child's growing capacity to "regulate her impulses, stabilize her moods, integrate her feelings and actions, focus her concentration, and plan." That was his high-toned version of Ezzo's trio of enabling virtues, "sitting, focusing, concentrating," which Greenspan concurred must begin being practiced in very early childhood, or else it is too late.

He supplied parents with what he called a "Functional Developmental Growth Chart," which graphed much more than the usual basics of emerging motor skills, and a questionnaire to go with it. The material served to guide assessments of those six "interactive milestones" and gauge "how well a child puts together and uses all his intellectual and emotional capacities to meet his needs and solve problems. It reveals whether his 'team' of mental abilities is working together in an integrated fashion, as well as how the specific contributive components are developing." And Greenspan studiously outlined the parental role in rallying that "team" to its highest performance at each stage, culminating in "emotional thinking."

For babies, the six tasks in store sounded challenging—a word that cropped up a lot. In the first three months, they were supposed to master the "ability to look, listen." Between four and six months, they learned to relate to others, smiling and "falling in love" with parents. During the next three months they became a "two-way communicator," using and reading gestural signals or "nonverbal cues." By four-teen to eighteen months, they should be at work "solving problems and forming a sense of self," showing their needs and wants in the course of more complex and purposeful interactions. Between two and three, toddlers ought to be able to form and use ideas, words, and symbols to convey intentions or feelings. Finally, they were ready to build those logical, emotional bridges.

For parents, the enterprise was, if anything, more demanding than for babies. It could not help seeming like a complex managerial feat of quality monitoring when every interactive moment was scrutinized for its contribution to the long-term program. "She is not just sitting in your lap, cuddling and hugging," Greenspan wrote of an instance of floor time, as though such unreflective fun might not be up to snuff. "She is having a great time: practicing and coordinating her fine and gross motor skills, receiving information through language, experienc-ing closeness and relatedness, experiencing positive self-esteem. All of this and being assertive, too." Even as he emphasized that in floor time, "your job is to let your child set the emotional tone of your plan and then to follow his lead," he also instructed—in boxes bearing the peremptory heading "Dos and Don'ts as You Raise the Bar"—that "play sessions" were also about nudging the child onward to more "complicated social, emotional, and language-related behaviors" than the child would master on his own.

Greenspan's child did not have to offer up a "yes, Mommy" when-ever addressed, as Ezzo's did. But Mother had to see to it that any given "circle of communication" was closed—no tuning out allowed for either party. The diligent interaction not only put her small partner on the road to "being a creative and logical thinker," but helped him "become empathic and eventually distinguish between right and wrong." Ezzo's mother could just use her "command voice" (as op-posed to her "praise voice") and expect prompt obedience. Greenspan's parent was instructed "to think of yourself as an authority figure along the lines of a Smokey the Bear," but to make sure not to be menacing, conveying instead the nuanced message that "you must reluctantly, but definitely, steer her toward self-control."

By the time Greenspan arrived at the sixth milestone in *Building Healthy Minds* and was about to inform parents that now they were to become an all-important "collaborator in exploring the world," he himself paused to note the rather forced spirit of camaraderie at the heart of the "play partnership" he prescribed: "This may seem like a tall order, and you're probably saying to yourself, 'Hold up just a minute here; my head can only hold so many hats! It's difficult enough being a nurturer, reading my baby's facial expressions, and responding back in an animated way. As far as pretend play goes, I never thought I'd have to do that again! Now you're asking me to be a debater, negotiator, and structural engineer. That sure wasn't in the job description!' " Nor did child and parent get any breathing room as the years progressed. Moving up through pre-adolescence as "your child . . . gradually takes all that she has absorbed from peers and parents and organizes it into her own set of standards and values," parents were to be at the ready, alert to any detours or bottlenecks in progress on that "road map," which did not end with preschool.

In the "independent" family that Greenspan presumed, parents could not rely on being mainly team leaders, building "family identity" and doling out greater freedoms, as in the self-consciously "interdependent" clan. They were soul adjusters. To be sure, the softer post-baby Ezzo also emphasized (for dads especially) that to "find out what is going on with your middle-years child, you need access to her private world." But his pat counsel did not presume to go much beyond advising parents to seize the "open-window moments" that a trusting child will reveal and to "strive for meaningful conversations." Greenspan outlined much more probing scripts for his floor and problem-solving times. For as children negotiated the all-important—and intricate—world of peers beyond the family, a parent needed to make sure they had indeed mastered and integrated those milestones. More than that, was the child honing those capacities of self-regulation, attention, and subtle interaction? There on the floor, having fun, parents were adding to the file. They were assessing subtle progress in the creation of "a stable sense of self" with which to navigate the "turbulent seas ahead" in adolescence, and eventually to engage in a world more complicated than the "like-minded" enclave that Ezzo envisaged for his child. "*Give more, and expect more,*" was Greenspan's less than relaxing motto.

It was a time-consuming enterprise for all concerned, and group child care in the early years could not hope to rise to its intensive demands. Greenspan urged parents to embrace flexibility and adopt what he called the "four-thirds solution"—both parents working two-thirds time—hardly a cure, he recognized, for hard-pressed and single parents. Nor was it exactly what his high-powered dual-career family clientele necessarily wanted to hear. Flexibility, however, was notably absent from his and Brazelton's manifesto. In *The Irreducible Needs of Children*, the two of them spelled out a surprisingly one-size-fits-all (and very middle-class and mentor-ish) vision of the optimal child-rearing approach—not quite what one would expect from experts who prided themselves on their cultural sensitivity and chided the "hard" school for rigidity. They had in mind another regimen that cried out for a Covey planner—and that, ironically, warned against too much independence for children.

In fact, Brazelton betrayed some uneasiness as they hammered out their calibrated caretaking scheme. "If parents try to use this as a yard-stick," he wondered aloud in one of the book's recurring dialogues, "will they get nervous or run away from it?" (As Dr. Spock had observed thirty years earlier in a characteristically down-to-earth column, "the fact is that setting aside a chunk of time to be devoted exclu-sively to companionship with children is a somewhat boring prospect to a lot of good parents," and he was not about to hound them. "There is no basis," he wrote, "for saying that every parent should play with his child in certain ways.") But Brazelton's coauthor had no such qualms, and the directives multiplied. Where Ezzo's daily agenda aimed at max-imizing self-entertainment, theirs did the opposite.

Thus for preschoolers, Greenspan and Brazelton prescribed "at a minimum . . . four 20-minute or longer opportunities for direct interac-tion," with "breaks for facilitating a child's interaction with his environ-ment," working toward a goal of making "the completely independent time . . . less than one-third" of his waking time. For kindergartners through fourth graders, the formula was three hours of "family time," divided into independent time, time for facilitating, and time for direct interaction (floor time)—ideally, they said, in a "seamless back-and-forth manner." The rule of thumb was that for half of a child's non-school hours, a loving adult should be "available" to provide this "key interaction and attention."

Beware, they kept warning, of "too much time in the independent mode" for a child, stressing that the solo stretches during a day should each last no more than fifteen minutes for children under three and a half. After all, they might daydream or drift, and there was so much to do to nurture "the capabilities necessary for reasoned, considerate, moral thinking and behavior." Greenspan's list of the requirements was long: "the feeling of connectedness with humanity, a well-developed sense of empathy, the ability to express and evaluate abstract concepts, the individual sense of her place in relation to the larger community, an understanding of consequences, a capacity to weigh alternative values and to place her own wishes in the context of others' wishes and needs, the ability to recognize legitimate authority and limits."

6.

In their prescriptive zeal and their vision of intensive developmental management, Ezzo and Greenspan (joined by Brazelton) converged from opposing directions on a daunting message for families. It presumed parents and children to be in need of step-by-step guidance in an endeavor that, given the vigilance it demanded, could not help sounding fraught with danger. Relations between a child and her mother and father required constant monitoring and recalibrating, whether it was to make sure that she was suitably responsive to the adults or the other way around. At stake was not merely growth, or social adjustment, or emotional health, but anxiously calculated moral worth—as much the parent's as the child's, the regimens suggested. It would be impossible to mistake an Ezzo household, where kids quietly hand-signaled for attention during an adult conversation (the "interrupt courtesy"), for a Greenspan home front, where grownups got down on the floor and meowed. The parent-centered and the child-centered ethos had rarely been so clearly codified. Yet not too far beneath the surface, a self-conscious spirit of ever so studious, yet precarious, control prevailed in both. The engineers of these managed cultures seemed to have forgotten the impulsive, intuitive give-and-take between big and small humans, struggling to understand each other and often failing, which is what actually makes a family a moral arena like no other.

Two other experts, both of whom marketed programmatic child-rearing packages with notable success during the 1990s, aspired to restore some spontaneity—and along with it some parental pleasure, and perhaps even humility. John Rosemond's "affirmative parenting" and Dr. William Sears's "attachment parenting" aimed to get parents to go by, in Rosemond's words, "the heart and the gut," and they did it in completely different ways. A California pediatrician and the author of *Christian Parenting and Child Care* and of *Creative Parenting* (and more than twenty other books, some secular and some with a dose of Scripture), Sears blended the biblical and the bonding style to come up with his own "soft" brand of advice. His wife, Martha Sears, a registered nurse, childbirth educator, and breast-feeding consultant, was a frequent collaborator, and by the turn of the millennium, two of their eight children had joined the thriving multi-media business, with its own Web site, AskDrSears.com.

The Searses broadcast the "eight baby Bs": bonding, breast-feeding, baby-wearing, bed-sharing, believing baby's cries, building a support network, boundary building, and balance. It sounded like extreme child-focused communing—"one big give-a-thon," as Dr. Sears put it, designed to help kids "feel right." But the purpose, he emphasized, was equally parent-directed: to restore parents' instinctive, intuitive leadership and rescue them from the misconception that they are "amateur psychologists, negotiators, diplomats, rather than authority figures." Delivering a traditional message with countercultural earthiness, the Searses offered what they called "a high-touch style of parenting to balance the high-tech life of the 1990s."

They aimed to build bridges where other experts dug trenches. Attachment parenting was "God's design," Sears wrote in his Christian material (where he spoke of the "ministry of parenting" and cited Dobson with approval). But it rested on human intuition and a "finely tuned communication network" with the child, not just with God, he emphasized there and in his secular wares (invoking Brazelton, among others). America's best-known boosters of bonding were also the authors of the bluntly titled *The Discipline Book* (in which they rejected spanking on principle, yet supplied tips on the practice for those who could not resist).

With his own huge brood and his crossover clout, Dr. Bill (as his "little patients" called him) in his way resembled Covey, though when he invoked business metaphors, Sears sounded more like a foundation officer than a business manager. The process he evoked was beneficent rather than bureaucratic. "God's matching program is perfect," he announced in discussing the varieties of child temperament and parental responsiveness: "His law of supply and demand will work if people practice a style of parenting that allows the divine design for the parent-child relationship to develop." But the real secret to the Searses' success was a more Spockian appeal. Although their attachment parenting program had an acronym, AP, and its share of zealous followers, it did not run on organizational principles that must be scheduled and obeyed. It was based on those "warm fuzzy" practices of theirs. And the Searses went out of their way to acknowledge that not everybody would buy into all of them, much less all the way: How could they, given "the busy life-styles of today's parents"? Parents should help themselves to other methods, too. As one of the many Web sites that endorsed AP made sure to emphasize, "no two families practice attachment parenting in the same manner, or to the same degree."

John Rosemond, who prided himself on being the *"World's Funniest*

Psychologist" but definitely not the warmest and fuzziest, carved out his "hard" niche by supplying an irreverent management alternative. As he informed readers of his *Six-Point Plan*, he advocated the comparatively free-wheeling ethos championed by Thomas J. Peters, promoter of a "zany entrepreneur" approach to reviving corporate and workplace culture. In a line of books that began with *In Search of Excellence* (which sold a million copies when it came out in 1982), the upstart managerial guru agreed that companies should take "the process of value shaping seriously." But the ethos, Peters believed, needn't be one of studiously orchestrated cooperation favored by total quality management enthusiasts. He proselytized for a "strong culture" that did not rest on formal, bureaucratic structures and that gave employees freer rein. The secret was to "provide the opportunity to stick out, yet combine it with a philosophy and system of beliefs . . . that provide the transcending meaning—a wonderful combination." What's more, being this kind of manager is easy, Peters promised the clients crowding his schedule, whom he typically whisked out of the seminar door with exhortations to go enjoy "loud times and lots of screw-ups."

The endorsement of a rough-and-tumble ambience of independence and individualism was one that Rosemond, out on the workshop circuit in the course of the 1980s, stumbled across with a sense of recognition. He happened to find himself on a panel with the "excellence" evangelist, and he was thrilled to hear Peters and his co-author, Robert H. Waterman, Jr., extol MBWA—"management by walking around"—as the key tool of the "new manager" they championed. Rosemond realized that his own tactics fit the formula. "Instead of hovering anxiously over their children, [parents] act as consultants to their growth and development." He pursued the analogy. "Parents of this sort are authority figures, but they guide and model more than they order," Rosemond explained. "Their goal is not to make their kids subservient or dependent, but to make them independent and responsible. Toward this end, they provide a variety of opportunities for growth, but allow their kids a great deal of freedom when it comes to choosing or rejecting these opportunities." It was a managerial style, Rosemond made absolutely clear, designed not to be monopolized by Mom but to be shared: the time had long since come for her to revise her "proprietary view of herself as a parent" and make room for Dad to become more than a mere "parenting aide."

Taking a leaf from the Peters-Waterman playbook, Rosemond proceeded to market himself as the champion of child rearing made "relatively easy and enjoyable," as well as old-fashioned. Or at any rate if "not always fun, it does not have to be difficult, and it can always be rewarding"—don't believe what all the other "experts" say. "Childrearing—or *parenting*, as it's now called—has been transformed into a pseudo-intellectual 'science,' something people think they must strain their brains at in order to do properly," Rosemond complained every chance he got. "What the 'experts' haven't romanticized, sentimentalized, and idealized, they've scrutinized and analyzed."

Obfuscating the "realistic, pragmatic, and hard-headed" truths of parenting, "nouveau" experts bequeathed America all too many "demanding, disobedient, uncooperative, disrespectful, and irresponsible" children and "frustrated, anxious, guilt-ridden" parents. Listen to "the voice of grandma," Rosemond urged—and to a "heretic" expert who credited his wisdom to his "trial-and-error" experience as a parent and as a son of the sensible fifties (and of divorce), *not* to his graduate degree in child psychology. His anecdotes were derived from a feisty home sample, himself and his two kids. He freely admitted that his nononsense upbringing hadn't saved him from "pot-addled excesses" in the late 1960s, but firmly embraced them as his own decisions, not symptoms of "some family dysfunction." The escapades of his son, Eric, a wild guy, and a more tractable daughter, Amy, inspired Tom Sawyer–style humor and heartland vigor: you can't go out and play, was this dad's favorite penalty as he banished his kids to their rooms for the rest of the day.

Rosemond subscribed to the ministers' main credos—pay more attention to your marriage than to the kids, and be parents first and pals later—with a vengeance. (Forget fifteen minutes of "couch time," with the kids basking nearby in the glow of marital unity. He recommended a "30-minute" rule: parents take time off together when they get home, while the kids go off and entertain themselves.) He called child centeredness "the most invidious family dysfunction of all." But he did it all, rather incongruously, in the antic style of an overgrown adolescent—hardly the typical tone among the moral managers.

Where Rosemond truly parted ways with both camps was in his impatience with the "tendency of adults to act as though kids will botch the job of growing up unless we engineer the process for them" with intricate flowcharts, and lots of intervention; the "God Almighty Syndrome (GAS)," he called parents' presumption that they are the only force in their child's life, and that any false move by their kid is their fault—and the end of the world. Rosemond liked to say that "conservatives believe that where government is concerned, the less, the better. The same applies to the governing of children." With the right decisive—but not, to judge by his own example, stuffy or somber—figure at the top, kids could be kept in line yet given plenty of room for maneuver.

All the pre-toddlerhood fussing and fine-tuning favored by Ezzo and Greenspan were not for Rosemond. For eighteen months, he joined Dobson in saying, a baby should be "given every reason to believe that he is the One the world has been waiting for," and every occasion to explore the world, secure in the knowledge that a parent is at hand. But then life abruptly changed: henceforth, parents were to give children the attention they needed, which was "less and less as time goes on," and children were to give parents all the attention they, the parents, wanted—whenever they wanted it, and for whatever reason.

And those reasons, like the limits parents imposed, should not be dictated by "what psychologists deem best for self-esteem enhancement," Rosemond emphasized. They should be decided by parents themselves, who should not expect kids to understand or agree with them—or to have to pretend, by showing a good "attitude," that they did: "the more free they were to express their feelings about my instructions," he found of his own children, "the more likely they were to comply." But of course they often didn't. Just as Peters extolled "screw-ups," Rosemond was a firm believer in letting kids make lots of mistakes—the bigger, the better, in his view. And then parents should see to it that they bore the consequences, which he recommended should sometimes be draconian.

When Rosemond offered a "three Rs" mantra (a standard device in the era of programmatic gurus), he did not follow up the usual "respect and responsibility" with "relationship," as most mentors and ministers alike could be counted on to do. He emphasized "resourcefulness" instead, displaying a Watsonian drive to produce intrepid, independent problem solvers. Dismissive of all "the intellectual rhetoric and the flowery sentiment," Rosemond offered blunt tips to promoting autonomy—in parents and in children—and didn't bother about fine-tuning empathy ("that's a psychology word"), intimacy, and family harmony. It wasn't that love was unimportant. "The problem, as I see it," he wrote, "is that it's impossible to improve a parent's love for his or her children," and no expert should take it upon himself to try. Improving discipline is possible, and better relationships follow.

Thus he scoffed at the recipes for "active listening," offering his own tougher tenets of good communication: "Be commanding, concise, concrete." What young children need, Rosemond spelled out, is lots of unstructured time left to their own devices and no TV (certainly not before they can read, and very little after that), plenty of reading with parents and lots of chores—starting at four. That was his old-style recipe for instilling family values, and for encouraging "the many basic skills that comprise competency and creativity," which better be emerging by six or so, he said, or trouble follows. As for spanking, Rosemond was an impassioned anti–anti-spanker. He was of the view that an angry swat could sometimes—but not too often—be a useful attention-getting device, and no expert, much less policymaker, should presume to tell parents otherwise. And on toilet training, he advocated "supportive non-interference" and clear parental signals. Despite his "potty" battle with Brazelton, his position was not in fact all that different—except that Rosemond was sure that a parent who plainly meant business would get prompt results. Where Greenspan's explicit motto was "Give more, and expect more," Rosemond's implicit one was, "Expect more, get more."

By their teens, kids should be all but running the household—and running pretty free, provided that they strictly abided by the few but clear curfews and demands their parents set. A slipup, and they had to earn their privileges from scratch all over again or find themselves facing the stiffest of consequences. But he counted on them to be hardheaded when it came to upholding their end of the bargain—certainly if they had been reared in Rosemondian style. "The purpose of raising children," he liked to remind readers, "is simply to help them out of our lives and into successful lives of their own. It's called emancipation."

And mothers, too, should claim the same for themselves, he urged, for they had been "unliberated Moms" for far too long. "Women have been encouraged to buy into the falsehood that the more attention a mother pays to her child, the better a mother she is," the right-wing Rosemond complained, sounding oddly like an irate feminist—and like Bruno Bettelheim. "Female parents in our culture do not have full, unfettered permission to have lives of their own, to pursue personal or professional goals, much less say 'no' to their kids and mean it," he wrote and rendered his verdict: "You're not guilty." It was time to retool, he told them, and he had a turn-of-the-millennium video-based product at the ready, "John Rosemond's Managerial Parent Skillshop." At the end of a busy century, he was well aware of what Dr. Spock had already known at its middle, and Dr. Holt and Dr. Hall had appreciated at the start: it is the rare mother in the American middle class, however eager she may be to listen to her child, who wants to hear only from that inner (or outer) "voice of Grandma." Even, or especially, an expert who scoffed at experts could continue to count on doing a brisk business.

What to Expect from the Experts

A m I proposing an end to this age of parental enlightenment? Suggesting that parents burn their parenting books, cancel subscriptions to parenting magazines, operate on instinct and common sense alone?" The question was posed in an article in yet another *Newsweek* special on "Your Child," a 2000 rerun of the Rob Reiner–inspired best-seller of 1997. The article was written by the author of one of the most successful parenting books to appear in the closing decades of the century: Heidi E. Murkoff, part of the triumvirate of non-experts (two daughters and their mother) who produced *What to Expect When You're Expecting* in 1984, reportedly read by 93 percent of the women who consult a guidebook during their pregnancies. In that Q-and-A–style book, and its three successors—*What to Eat When You're Expecting* (1986), *What to Expect the First Year* (1989), and *What to Expect the Toddler Years* (1994)—she was the one in the trio whose specialty was coming up with the questions that Everyparent might be expected to ask. Even perusers of a *Newsweek* parenting special, Murkoff was well aware, could hardly help being of two minds about all the accumulated counsel.

A hundred years after the age of parental enlightenment had begun, where did the experts' project stand? At the National Congress of Mothers meeting, Dr. Holt had hailed the "numerous books constantly issuing from the press . . . [and] the periodicals devoted to the different phases of the child problem." Science promised eventually to reveal the secrets of children's nature and nurture, and Drs. Holt and Hall presided as complementary pioneers on the vast new terrain, very different in their approaches but united in a common cause. They basked in the adulation of their audience of elite mothers, who believed along with them that the long overlooked—and overworked—child was not the only one who would be liberated to develop his full potential. In the pursuit of "scientific motherhood," restless women "streaming outward in search of a career" would turn back and find true fulfillment.

Where "mother love [had walked] hand in hand with care and anxiety," hobbled by outmoded grandmotherly lore, scientists of the new century would guide the way to calmness and consistency. Armed with up-to-date data, the modern mother could claim new authority and autonomy: parenthood would become a prestigious profession. And social equality would dawn in America, thanks to the spread of enlightened child rearing down to the poorest and immigrant ranks. "Given one generation of children properly born and wisely trained," exclaimed an editorial in the *New York Times* extolling the National Congress of Mothers, "what a vast proportion of human ills would disappear from the earth."

By the turn of the millennium, the experts' predictions had not exactly panned out as expected. In fact, despite a century of child development research and popular parenting advice—though obviously not simply because of it—a very different America found itself caught up in concerns that echoed, in ways the pioneers could never have anticipated, some of the same fears and hopes that had helped to inspire the "movement" in the first place. Science certainly had made great inroads in exploring many mysteries of children's growth and health, from vanquishing germs down to imaging brains and mapping genes. The once physically perilous periods of pregnancy and childhood had been transformed by medical advances. But even in the physical realm, new versions of old dangers now stirred alarm. The most vulnerable mothers lacked prenatal care. Vaccines and antibiotics threatened worrisome side effects. Nutrition returned as an urgent priority with the advent of an epidemic of childhood obesity. Even the old debate over children being seen but not heard reverberated as the twentieth century drew to a close, in a national controversy over soaring rates of Ritalin prescriptions: Were children, by nature fidgety, being drugged to keep still?

After decades of psychological research into children's nature and nurture, cutting-edge cognitive scientists had been swept up again in the original "child study" spirit, curious about infants' and children's adaptive and interactive responses to their environments. And the sense shared by Holt and Hall in 1900 that they were only just beginning to discover the contours of a complex science had returned by 2000 in chastened reassessments by careful scientists. The quest to prove parents' early formative role in children's long-term social and personality development had turned out to be far more complicated, and much less definitive, than researchers had acknowledged. In the meantime, neuroscientific advances, undreamed of a hundred years before, had confirmed Holt's hunch that brains were growing inside those baby heads at a rapid rate, and revived fears of infant vulnerability. (For Holt, that meant parents should leave babies in peace, and for his successors it meant make sure to engage them—not that either had data to clinch clear-cut prescriptions.) And fumbling efforts to fathom adolescence, and to fortify characters to face a daunting world, bracketed the twentieth century at either end.

A hundred years after Holt marveled at the "numerous books constantly issuing from the press," every phase and specialized dimension of the "child problem" generated more than its share of popular advisory literature. Thousands of child-rearing Web sites had sprung up, and so had "an industry of seminars, weekend retreats and lectures designed to make us into perfect parents," as a bemused writer/father commented in one of a proliferating array of child-rearing magazines, this one called *offspring* ("the magazine of smart parenting"). Much as the pioneers had worried over the disparate counsel dispensed by too many meddling female relatives, Heidi Murkoff in *Newsweek* joined an ever louder chorus of concern that a "plethora of advice" risked leaving parents "bewildered, overwhelmed, uncertain how to proceed— paralyzed."

The male advisory mission, which had begun the twentieth century aspiring to settle the "woman question" by making motherhood an intensive "vocation" had certainly succeeded in the latter—only to confront yet more restlessness among women by the century's end, by which time the swelling ranks of experts were no longer so overwhelmingly male. "Mothers Can't Win" was the verdict on the cover of a special issue of the *New York Times Magazine* on the "joy and guilt" of motherhood, capturing the conventional wisdom of the post-feminist era that was well under way as the millennium arrived. "Work or home? Breast or bottle? Spanking or spoiling? No matter what they choose, they're made to feel bad." The summons to recognize parenthood—motherhood *and* fatherhood—as a high-status profession had never been issued with more urgency amid widespread alarm about an "assault on parenthood" and a "war against parents" (two titles from opposite ends of the political spectrum) under way in a commercial, competitive, and decadent culture that eroded family commitments.

And from the far right to the far left, Americans concurred that children, whose century the twentieth was supposed to have been, had not won, either. They had been endlessly studied, but faced the unsteadiest of lives in what one journalist called "the Age of the Imperiled Child." No longer overworked as in the dark days of factory labor, babies and children were hurried, or hovered over. Adolescents were judged dangerously adrift in a media-suffused world of their own, or precociously launched on a high-pressured path to success (or both). Poor children, as ever, were all too often overlooked. In 1900, Americans and their experts had fixed on "the figure of the child . . . [as] the key to a future which could contain both behemoth factories and nurturing hearthsides, the cold logic of Wall Street and the sentimental warmth of Christmas," as Barbara Ehrenreich and Deirdre English put it in *For Her Own Good* in 1978. Much the same fraught hopes and fears were as frequently, and as fervently, voiced a hundred years later.

But for all of these very reasons, of course, Heidi Murkoff was not about to urge a bonfire of parenting books. Hers had been a rhetorical question, and she was one for realistic answers, not extremist gestures. Abandon the experts? "Far from it," she answered herself. The trademark What to Expect response, as she once put it, "trusts a mother's instincts, but recognizes she often doesn't trust them herself": she wants counsel that acknowledges her ambivalence but rescues her (however temporarily) from bewilderment. "What I am suggesting is that parents put parenting information in perspective," Murkoff went on with the sisterly earnestness that was her style. "Use it to guide, not dictate. To augment your instincts, not supplant them. To build your confidence, not tear it down. To empower you, not paralyze you." She provided the standard guidelines for parents in quest of that calm vantage on the expert commotion. First of all, beware of dizzying "Parenting Pendulum Swings" between opposing extremes of expertise. Second, find what "fits" for you and your family—and be aware that it could change from child to child, from stage to stage.

It was sensible enough advice-about-advice spoken by a true descendant of Dr. Spock: don't embrace child-rearing expertise as dogma, or be overawed by it. And, she might have added (yet forbore to), don't expect it to save the world—or even you and your child. Murkoff made the right balance sound easy to strike, and for a "more advanced" generation of parents—"more challenging, better informed, more searching and sophisticated in their questions," as the foreword to *What to Expect the First Year* characterized the baby boomer middle class—her counsel was, if anything, too easy. They already knew, as the *Ladies' Home Journal* put it in a similar spirit, that there is no need to "look at a child-rearing expert as an absolute authority." They had surely read their share of exasperated, skeptical, outraged commentary by "mothers who think" (as the Internet magazine *Salon* called its advice-debunking department), and even by fathers. Nor did a generation long since converted from by-the-book awe to buy-the-book ways need to be told, as the *Ladies' Home Journal* also reassured readers, that it is "perfectly okay to shop around until you find someone whose overall philosophy squares with yours."

In truth, however, such a quest is all but guaranteed to be hopeless, as this story of the popular experts' family drama, from the great-grandfathers Dr. Holt and Dr. Hall on down to the progeny of Dr. Spock, has aimed to show. The advisers' own philosophies have betrayed plenty of inconsistencies. And, in any case, as Dr. Spock once observed, and every other expert has known even as he has pretended not to, "no philosophy [of child rearing] can be translated into day by day and hour by hour practical application by an inexperienced person, and no two persons will interpret a philosophy exactly the same way"— even to themselves, on the same day. Being faced with such a fickle audience has, of course, often made American experts fierce, but it has also kept them on edge and at odds with each other. That is why our advisers, avid though they have been to dispense sweeping dogmas, have been even better at exposing persistent dilemmas.

The scientific parenting crusade has certainly not wrought widespread reform in America, much less brought calm to the home front. Instead it has been a repository of the tensions—psychological and social, moral and practical—confronting middle-class families raising children in a country that has become more competitive and meritocratic, and more culturally permissive and sexually egalitarian, over a fast-changing century. What is notable about the "Parenting Pendulum

Swings" is that they have not been so dizzying after all. Two poles have defined America's child-rearing advice from the very start, and even in the cacophonous market at the close of the century they still framed an underlying debate that sounded familiar. How much power and control do, and should, parents wield over a child's journey from dependence to independence? How much freedom and intimacy do children need, or want, along the way? And, the implicit question lurking not far behind both of those over the past hundred years, when child-rearing debates have been as much about women's future and the family's plight as about children's fates: What do the answers imply about mothers' rights and responsibilities?

Widespread uncertainty is all but guaranteed to make an audience receptive to what sound like clear-cut answers. Each generation of experts has featured a pair of presiding authorities who approached those questions from opposite directions. In every period, an odd couple emerged from the growing ranks of advisers, both members of it well aware that their popularity depended in part on offering contrasting appeals in the name of science (or, more recently, against science). The "hard" believer that nurture is what counts spoke up for authority, discipline, and parental control, usually in a blunt father-knows-best tone that presumed mothers needed to be steered into line as well. The "soft" proponent of letting nature take its course urged love, bonding, and children's liberty in a solicitous style that promised mothers, too, a growth experience in the process. Even Dr. Spock, who broke the mold by aiming for the middle, found he had to scramble to become the firmer, parents-take-charge counterweight to his own original child-friendly gospel before Dr. Bettelheim stepped in.

Neither the "parent-centered" nor the "child-centered" position has ever "won," and it did not occur to the pioneers Holt and Hall that there was a contest at all. Each of their successors, however, vied for dominance in the name of more rigorous science. Dr. Watson's style was as fierce as it was in part because he was defensive in the era of the "affectionate family," and by the time his book came out, his bullying build-a-baby agenda confronted a growing Gesellian let-growth-guide-you challenge. Postwar permissiveness stands out as a rare, brief moment when the "soft" side reigned all but uncontested—and the absence of ballast caused widespread concern. It was not just conservatives worried about a collapse of authority who were alarmed, but women feeling trapped in domesticity as well, and, of course, Dr. Spock himself.

In fact, the surprising discovery that emerges from delving into the experts' own lives and labs, as well as into their advice, is the degree of ambivalence America's advisers themselves have betrayed about their own claims to scientific clarity and certainty on their end of the spectrum. In different ways, "hard" and "soft" experts have all found themselves hedging when it came down to offering day-to-day advice on the problems of parenting. For children resist easy analysis, and mothers are hard to please. Experts have been as concerned about "fit" as any parent. In fact, they are more in need of telling readers what they might want to hear than their readers have ever been in need of actually doing what any manual says; the experts' popularity has depended on it.

Thus Holt was the master of the mixed message on more than nursing. Hall's rhapsodic celebration of adolescence went hand in hand with a nostalgic vision of social order and hierarchy. Even Watson, with his "talk-it-out club," did not completely ban intimacy. With his charts and norms, Gesell hailed individuality and variety, while focusing on conformity and regularity of growth. Spock's great gift was equivocating, not least about anxiety, which he roused in aiming to soothe. Bettelheim emphasized children's need for control, along with the importance of instinctual exploration. By late century, minister-experts and mentors all rallied to the cause of "authoritative" parenting, and they blended old-style concern about character with up-to-date counsel about cognitive performance. They marketed bustling, businesslike child-rearing "systems" in the service of bolstering moral values and rescuing overstressed families.

The result has often been, despite conflicts and different conceptions of children, more convergence between the two schools in their goals and sometimes even their methods for rearing children than one might ever guess from their rhetoric. The astute Dr. Spock appreciated that "two women who in actual practice would handle a child just about the same could still argue till kingdom come about theory, because there are two sides to every theory about child-rearing." Perhaps just as notable is the converse. Two experts can prescribe very different practices—"parent-directed feeding" and attachment parenting, for example—in the name of much the same aims: stabilizing an immature metabolism and instilling security. Brazelton and Rosemond may battle over take-your-time toilet training versus the do-it-at-two strategy, but they agree that a big step toward achieving autonomy is at stake (though neither could summon definitive studies to prove that the potty is in fact such a proving ground).

The two schools never merge, of course. The attitude and the spirit informing the approaches—which are as important as actions in an enterprise like child rearing, as experts always tell parents—have always been strikingly different. Yet even here, a look back at the experts in their own contexts shakes up the usual assumptions about the tough and the gentle styles, and reveals the ongoing tensions entailed in the pursuit of those two quintessentially American goals, getting ahead and getting (which often also means going) along—autonomy and conformity. It is the "hard" advisers, busy bossing mothers around and warning about too much rather than too little bonding, who often end up leaving both mothers and children more independence and freedom to maneuver. Holt's hospital regimens were in demand among a clientele eager to be less tied down. The cold Watsonian routines of the 1920s were touted as bolstering children against the mounting pressures and allures of ever more organized society, and his anti-sentimentalism was pitched at the "advanced" Jazz Age woman. Bettelheim spoke up for mothers' need for self-fulfillment, and for children's right to self-definition.

By contrast, the "soft" experts who champion maternal engagement in children's unfolding development can turn out to be the ones scripting an emotional drama that is more controlling for all concerned. Hall and Gesell envisaged mothers raptly monitoring their children's every move, making sure no upward momentum was lost. Spock gently urged them to commune with their children's every mood as well, and keep in touch with the state of their own maternal feelings. To prescribe deep affection, abiding fascination with children, and absence of friction as the crucial ingredients for successful motherhood—and to urge that they be spontaneous and heartfelt—is not necessarily the liberation the child-centered experts advertise it to be. At the permissive end of the spectrum, the solicitous mother and the "understood" child have struggled for a sense of independence.

The basic choices on offer, in other words, have never been quite what they seem, and the chasm between them is perhaps not so deep as the ongoing debates suggest. Given that, another sort of advice-about-advice could be timely for an era in which mothers—and fathers—face more alternatives, families come in more varieties, and experts no longer command the old loyalty or scientific authority. If our advisers reflect American dilemmas more reliably than they dispense workable formulas—and if we aren't about to turn our backs on them—there is good reason to venture beyond the experts whose child-rearing philosophy, and politics, seem to "fit." The guidance that goes against the grain may prove unexpectedly enlightening. The truth is that all child-rearing advice is met with mixed feelings, as the experts themselves, from Holt to Bettelheim and beyond, have always been aware. Spock briefly thought reverence translated into obedience, but he was relieved to learn better. "We wish *someone* would tell us what to do, but on the other hand, we don't want anybody telling *us* what to do," was how the cognitive scientists who wrote *The Scientist in the Crib* summed up the typical parent's testy uncertainty.

There is an adversarial edge built into even the warmest advisory relationship—in fact, sometimes especially into the closest relationship, which is why American mothers opened the doors to the experts in the first place. The wisdom their own mothers passed on was what they felt they didn't really need, or want, to hear (not least because, as parents soon discover, they often can't help echoing the parental voices in their heads anyway): the world was changing, and maybe those scientific men were offering new options, or at any rate framing the common problems. By now it is obvious that the popular experts have no fixed or scientifically proven solutions, but are as full of contradictions as the rest of us. And what the natural constituencies of the two camps hear from their "own" advisers may turn out to be advice as useful, or more, to mothers on the other side. As women, and now men along with them, continue to wrestle with the challenges of child rearing, which have only become more complicated in the era of working parents, it is worth crossing over to find out.

In many ways, the liberal "child-centered" camp's ideology of "intensive mothering," as one scholar has called it, suits the traditionalist defenders of at-home mothering better than it fits its own often professional, "independent" family following. Surveying "a bouquet of advice books" by Brazelton, Leach, and Spock in the *New York Times Book Review*, one of their loyal working-mother readers chafed at what she found in the pages of her child-centered entourage: "The underlying message is that mothers shouldn't work while children are young." Why, she demanded, were they making people like her feel guilty? Meanwhile, the right-wing radio talk show personality Dr. Laura (Schlessinger), renowned for attacking child-centered white coats, declared herself a fan of none other than Dr. Greenspan. The author of *Parenthood by Proxy: Don't Have Them If You Won't Raise Them* (2000), a screed against "pal-parents" and "the psychologizing of our culture," claimed him as "one of my personal heroes." In Greenspan, Dr. Laura found a soul mate in her opposition to day care. If she also read further, she could find a collaborative approach to comprehensive moral guidance that went against her combative grain, yet might well surprise her with the stringency of its demands—on parent and child.

In turn, John Rosemond's parent-centered credo of less-attention-is-more sounds like what the liberal, elite believers in "nouveau parenting" whom he derides might find bracing, if disconcerting, to hear as they walk out to work. (Rosemond himself sides with Dr. Laura: stay home if you can afford to, he does not hesitate to instruct mothers.) The "most unliberated generation of women to ever inhabit this country," he lectures, should stop worrying about neglecting their kids, and quit waiting on them and micromanaging their lives. Children thrive on less interference, and parents ought to feel much freer to be "creatively selfish." More than that, supermothers need to back off and let fathers seize a domestic role and responsibilities they have long lacked (thanks in no small part to mother-centric experts), or shirked.

Coming from the right, the call to revive paternal authority and responsibility at home might well sound suspect and reactionary. But the basic insight is radical and useful, and not as prominent a theme among the "soft" advisers: women's true liberation, though it surely does entail changes and more choices at work and in day care, also requires a more fundamental rethinking of arrangements in the family than child-centered experts generally broach. The disappearance of the full-time housewife as the self-sacrificial center of the household, as one writer proposed, may well point to the need for a part-time "househusband" and "housechildren" to make the new order work. If so, it is the traditionalist "hard" proponents of serious chores, common values, and more of a group ethos who are further along the road to the future of the family. When every family member feels the tug of outside commitments and enticements ever more strongly, it is more, not less, important to emphasize authority and unity at home.

As "a liberal, a feminist, a Jew," and a parent given to "general wussiness," the reporter sent to profile Rosemond for the *New York Times* in the wake of the "potty wars" with Brazelton got an exemplary jolt from an expert who was far from her idea of a good "fit." To Susan Bolotin's ears, Rosemond barked like a harsh ideologue. And yet his message had real bite, even—or especially—for her. She came away with a fresh perspective on her own "overall philosophy" and its contradictions:

> Somewhere along the line, my female friends and I took on, unasked, a "third shift"—the job of family-happiness manager, juggling not only lessons and games and school events and nights out with adult friends, but everyone's emotional well-being, articulated or not. This is a thankless and exhausting task, particularly if it includes eradicating frustration and boredom from children's lives while simultaneously making sure they feel good about

themselves. I accepted this work, without thinking much about its consequences, until I met Rosemond.

He delivered a useful kick of wisdom: "that your kids can't grow up unless you let them do it for themselves." She had heard such counsel before, of course, since her child-centered experts all championed autonomy, too. But Rosemond made Bolotin sit up and listen. That did not mean that she had to buy his forty-five minutes a day of chores, his draconian banishment for any disobedience, or his views on spanking, much less on abortion. Nor did Bolotin have to feel guilty when she didn't obey his tactics; he was not "her" expert, and she felt no pressure to be "frantically gung-ho," as some of his disciples were. (That's the problem with a good fit: an expert who goes with the grain has far more power to goad a parent to excesses, or else to inspire guilt.) Just what "subtle Rosemond-inspired shifts in our child rearing" she and her husband made were their own decision, not done by expert prescription. And that, after all, is just the way mothers and fathers should operate, according to all the experts—especially Rosemond, who in *A Family of Value* proclaimed it his mission to rid the world of cowed parents "relying on books (like this one!) to tell 'em how to do it."

The experts' principles and their practices, though they have never worked harder to market them as tidy systems than they do now, are nothing of the sort—nor do their predictions and promises lend themselves to proof. There is a reason child-rearing advisers have always proclaimed the importance of the first three years, and it is not based on the latest brain research. Nor is it just the obvious fact that, as Brazelton puts it, "these ages . . . are almost the last ones in which parents can expect to play an undiluted role." It is that the first three years are the experts' best bet, too, to make any mark on parents. The experts, as they learned soon enough, never play an undiluted role, and they worry that whatever influence they can hope to wield will fade as the wider world (and, often, another child) intrudes. After all, it then begins to dawn on parents that no fine-tuned scheme for shaping futures lies in the experts' manuals, much less in their own homes—or even, most of the time, in their dreams. Experience conveys that lesson daily, as parents run up against the resistance and the resilience of children and the uncertainty of family, social, economic, and historical circumstances. America's conflicted experts have learned that lesson, too, not just from their labs, where studies have never been as definitive as they hoped, but also from their own lives. Their advice aims to hide the wisdom, but it can be found in reading between, and across, the experts' lines.

NOTES

Introduction

4 **"In no other country"**: Max Lerner, *America as a Civilization: Life and Thought in the United States Today* (New York: Simon & Schuster, 1957), p. 562.

4 **as Philippe Ariès argued**: Philippe Ariès, *Centuries of Childhood: A Social History of Family Life* (New York: Vintage, 1962). The French original, *L'Enfant et la vie familiale sous l'ancien régime*, appeared in 1960.

4 **"violent changes"**: Benjamin Spock, *Problems of Parents* (Boston: Houghton Mifflin, 1962), p. 21.

4 **"Advice on how to be"**: Hilde Bruch, *Don't Be Afraid of Your Child* (New York: Farrar, Straus & Giroux, 1952), p. 3.

5 **"the commonest problem"**: quoted in Ann Hulbert, "Dr. Spock's Baby," *The New Yorker* 72, no. 12 (May 20, 1996): 92.

5 **"at present a lax"**: Ellen Key, *The Century of the Child* (1909; reprint, New York: Arno, 1997), p. 130.

5 **"entirely new conception"**: ibid., p. 101.

5 **"Let mothers, fathers"**: David J. Rothman and Sheila M. Rothman, *National Congress of Mothers: The First Conventions* (New York: Garland, 1987), "The Works and Words of the National Congress of Mothers First Annual Session," Feb. 17–19, 1897 (hereafter referred to as National Congress of Mothers First Session), Mrs. Theodore W. Birney, "Address of Welcome," p. 10.

6 **"a vast proportion"**: "The Child Question," *New York Times*, Feb. 21, 1897, collected in David J. Rothman and Sheila M. Rothman, advisory eds., Gene Brown, ed., *The Family* (New York: Arno, 1979) (hereafter referred to as Rothman, *The Family*), p. 56.

6 **"I try to do"**: quoted in Paula Fass, *The Damned and the Beautiful: American Youth in the 1920s* (New York: Oxford University Press, 1977), p. 102.

6 **"Spocked when they"**: Stewart Alsop, the columnist, quoted in Thomas Maier, *Dr. Spock: An American Life* (New York: Harcourt Brace, 1998), p. 321.

6 **"the hurried child"**: David Elkind, *The Hurried Child: Growing Up Too Fast Too Soon* (Reading, MA: Addison-Wesley, 1981).

7 **"throw light on"**: Margaret Mead and Martha Wolfenstein, eds., *Childhood in Contemporary Cultures* (Chicago: University of Chicago Press, 1955), p. 17.

7 **The historians who**: See Julia Grant's very interesting *Raising Baby by the Book: The Education of American Mothers* (New Haven: Yale University Press, 1998). For a warning against reading the prescriptive literature as a window on historical reality, see Jay E. Mechling, "Advice to Historians on Advice to Mothers," *Journal of Social History* 9 (1975): 44–63.

8 **"conference on the brain":** Joe Klein, "Clintons on the Brain," *The New Yorker* 73, no. 4 (Mar. 17, 1997): 60.

8 **"raising a scientifically correct child":** Stephen S. Hall, "Test-Tube Moms," *New York Times Magazine*, Apr. 5, 1998, p. 22.

11 **"awkward, often unattractive":** G. Stanley Hall, *Adolescence: Its Psychology and Its Relations to Physiology, Anthropology, Sociology, Sex, Crime, Religion, and Education* (1904; reprint, New York: Arno, 1969), 1:315.

11 **sold 100,000 copies:** Shari L. Thurer, *The Myths of Motherhood: How Culture Reinvents the Good Mother* (Boston: Houghton Mifflin, 1994), p. 258.

12 **"Don't be overawed":** Benjamin Spock, *The Common Sense Book of Baby and Child Care* (New York: Duell, Sloan and Pearce, 1946), p. 3.

12 **"Worried Generation":** T. S. Eliot speech at Harvard in 1947, "Yesterday's News," *Harvard Magazine* 104, no. 5 (May/June 2000): 761.

12 **"the 'on-the-one-hand' ":** Benjamin Spock quoted in Maier, *Dr. Spock*, p. 250.

12 **"to an amazing degree":** Myron E. Wegman, review of *The Common Sense Book of Baby and Child Care, American Journal of Public Health* 36 (November 1946): 1329.

13 **"a major oppressor":** Benjamin Spock and Mary Morgan, *Spock on Spock: A Memoir of Growing Up with the Century* (New York: Pantheon, 1989), p. 247.

13 **"presumably more worldly":** Patricia Leigh Brown, "Magazines Remake Family, or Vice Versa," *New York Times*, Aug. 19, 1993, p. C6.

13 **"America's pediatrician":** Alan Long, "Bringing Up Baby—Online," Harvard Net News, May 30, 2000, www.researchmatters.harvard.edu/net_news2000/05.30/brazelton.5.30.html.

14 **"branding maven" to "the power of Spock":** Ilan Mochari, "Putting Stock in Dr. Spock," *Inc. Magazine*, Dec. 1, 2001, p. 41.

14 **"inimical to children":** Penelope Leach, *Children First: What Our Society Must Do—and Is Not Doing—for Our Children Today* (New York: Knopf, 1994), p. xiii.

14 **"secular humanism":** Dr. James Dobson and Gary Bauer, *Children at Risk: The Battle for the Hearts and Minds of Our Kids* (Dallas: Word Publishing, 1990), p. 29.

14 **"the prescriptions":** Dr. James Dobson, *Temper Your Child's Tantrums* (Wheaton, IL: Tyndale, 1986), p. 111.

14 **"disciples of discipline":** Susan Bolotin, "The Disciples of Discipline," *New York Times Magazine*, Feb. 14, 1999, p. 32.

14 **"nouveau parenting":** John Rosemond, *A Family of Value* (Kansas City, MO: Andrews McMeel, 1995), p. 24.

14 **"tried to make a 'science and technology' ":** John Rosemond, *John Rosemond's Six-Point Plan for Raising Happy, Healthy Children* (Kansas City, MO: Andrews McMeel, 1989), p. 3.

14 **"Age of Parenting Enlightenment":** John Rosemond, *Because I Said So!: 366 Insightful and Thought-Provoking Reflections on Parenting and Family Life* (Kansas City, MO: Andrews McMeel, 1996), p. viii.

15 **"John Rosemond's Managerial Parent Skillshop":** advertised on www.rosemond.com.

ONE: *The Century of the Child*

19 **"Nearly all trolley lines":** David J. Rothman and Sheila M. Rothman, *National Congress of Mothers: The First Conventions* (New York: Garland, 1987), "Proceedings of the Third Annual Convention of the National Congress of Mothers, Feb.

16–18, 1899" (hereafter referred to as National Congress of Mothers Third Convention), p. 193.

20 **"young enough"**: G. Stanley Hall, "Some Practical Results of Child Study," National Congress of Mothers First Session, p. 165.

20 **"strange and wonderful stories"; "Food was also scarce"**: National Congress of Mothers Third Convention, p. 194.

20 **"to educate public opinion"**: Mrs. Theodore W. Birney, "Address of Welcome," ibid., p. 199.

20 **"It is childhood's teachableness"**: Dr. W. N. Hailman, "Mission of Childhood," in David J. Rothman and Sheila M. Rothman, *National Congress of Mothers: The First Conventions* (New York: Garland, 1987), "Report of the Proceedings of the Second Annual Convention of the National Congress of Mothers, May 2–7, 1898" (hereafter referred to as National Congress of Mothers Second Convention), p. 175.

20 **"the fireside"**: Birney, "Address of Welcome," National Congress of Mothers Third Convention, p. 198.

21 **"race suicide"**: The term was a staple of anti-feminist and eugenicist rhetoric. The widely voiced fear was that the national stock would be depleted as more educated women had fewer children. See, for example, G. Stanley Hall, "The Question of Coeducation," *The Munset*, February 1906, p. 592.

21 **"illusion of *self-culture*"; "the sunlight of *service*"**: Birney, "Address of Welcome," National Congress of Mothers Third Convention, p. 201.

21 **"In a common cause"**: ibid., p. 199.

21 **"study of the little child"**: preface, National Congress of Mothers Second Convention, p. 5.

21 **"Notwithstanding the difficulties"**: National Congress of Mothers Third Convention, p. 194.

21 **"[concentrate] national attention"**: Birney, "Address of Welcome," ibid., p. 198.

22 **"the study of children"**: Hall, "Some Practical Results of Child Study," National Congress of Mothers First Session, p. 170.

22 **"at no previous time"**: L. Emmett Holt, "Physical Care of Children," National Congress of Mothers Third Convention, p. 230.

23 **"woman question"**: Birney, "Address of Welcome," National Congress of Mothers First Session, p. 7.

23 **"the family ceased to be"; "The care expended"**: Philippe Ariès, *Centuries of Childhood: A Social History of Family Life* (New York: Vintage, 1962), pp. 412–13.

23 **"Locke's educational theory"**: Jay Fliegelman, *Prodigals and Pilgrims: The American Revolution Against Patriarchal Authority, 1750–1800* (New York: Cambridge University Press, 1982), p. 13.

24 **"mother country"; "father-king"**: Philip Greven, *The Protestant Temperament: Patterns of Child-Rearing, Religious Experience, and the Self in Early America* (New York: Knopf, 1977), p. 339.

24 **"American revolution"**: Fliegelman, *Prodigals and Pilgrims*. See especially his chapter on "Educational Theory and Moral Independence."

24 *The Distresses that may attend:* ibid., p. 87. The full title of Samuel Richardson's *Clarissa* is *Clarissa or the History of a Young Lady, Comprehending the Most Important Concerns for Private Life and Particularly shewing, The Distresses that may attend the Misconduct Both of Parents and Children in Relation to Marriage.*

24 **The demographic, economic:** See T. J. Jackson Lears, *No Place of Grace: Antimodernism and the Transformation of American Culture, 1880–1920* (Chicago: University of Chicago Press, 1981), pp. 144–49.

25   **"stern exterior" to "most tender and gentle heart"**: Ann Douglas, *The Feminization of American Culture* (New York: Knopf, 1977), pp. 104, 57.

25   **"theology of the intellect" to "feminine instinct and sensitivity"**: ibid., p. 110.

25   **"weary with"**: quoted from *The Ladies' Companion* of 1838 in Barbara Welter, "The Cult of True Womanhood: 1820–1860," *American Quarterly* 18 (1966): 172.

25   **"a society given over"**: quoted in Kathryn Kish Sklar, *Catharine Beecher: A Study in American Domesticity* (New Haven: Yale University Press, 1973), p. 163.

25   **"as yet untainted"; "cult of True Womanhood"**: Welter, "The Cult of True Womanhood," pp. 172, 151.

25   **"influence"; "Like the power"**: Douglas, *The Feminization of American Culture*, p. 111.

25   **"emotions and sentiments"**: Sklar, *Catharine Beecher*, p. 162.

26   **"professionalized"**: See, for example, Mrs. Sallie S. Cotten, "A National Training School for Women" in National Congress of Mothers First Session, p. 210.

26   **"uncertain instinct"; "unhesitating insight"**: Sheila M. Rothman, *Woman's Proper Place: A History of Changing Ideals and Practices, 1870 to the Present* (New York: Basic Books, 1978), p. 103.

26   **"great brained"; "abdominal zone"**: Cynthia Eagle Russett, *Sexual Science: The Victorian Construction of Womanhood* (Cambridge, MA: Harvard University Press, 1989), pp. 44, 164.

27   **"fine and quick"**: James Sully, *Studies of Childhood* (New York: D. Appleton, 1903), p. 11.

27   **more than one child in six**: David I. Macleod, *The Age of the Child: Children in America, 1890–1920* (New York: Twayne, 1998), p. 40. See also Thomas E. Cone, *The History of American Pediatrics* (Boston: Little, Brown, 1979), p. 112.

27   **blamed on teething**: see L. Emmett Holt, *The Diseases of Infancy and Childhood* (New York: D. W. Appleton, 1897), p. 243.

28   **"an infectious disease"**: quoted in Cone, *The History of American Pediatrics*, p. 113.

28   **"germ of a human consciousness"; "Not merely to the"**: Sully, *Studies of Childhood*, pp. 7, 6.

28   **"Genetic psychology"; "We must carry"**: quoted in Michael Steven Shapiro, *Child's Garden: The Kindergarten Movement from Froebel to Dewey* (University Park: Pennsylvania State University Press, 1983), p. 129.

28   **"a perfectly cool"; "higher gift"**: Sully, *Studies of Childhood*, pp. 17, 15.

29   **When a group**: Barbara Ehrenreich and Deirdre English, *For Her Own Good: 150 Years of the Experts' Advice to Women* (New York: Anchor, 1978), p. 75. See their book for a very insightful discussion of this period, on which I draw.

29   **"is, as every one knows"**: Birney, "Address of Welcome," ibid., p. 6.

29   **The German pedagogue**: Rothman, *Woman's Proper Place*, p. 103.

29   **"the highest and holiest"**: Birney, "Address of Welcome," p. 6.

30   **"it is exceedingly interesting"**: quoted in *A Bully Father: Theodore Roosevelt's Letters to His Children* (New York: Random House, 1955), p. 49. The book was originally published in 1919 as *Letters of Theodore Roosevelt to His Children*.

30   **"Listen, I can be President"**: ibid., p. 70.

30   **"Only sentiment"**: "President Roosevelt's Address," *National Congress of Mothers Magazine* 2, no. 8 (April 1908): 175.

30   **"Sincerity, simplicity"**: quoted in Ehrenreich and English, *For Her Own Good*, p. 75.

31   **"if she looks"; "the long, slow"**: "President Roosevelt's Address," pp. 176, 173.

31 **"The successful mother"**: ibid., p. 173.

31 **"should have a right"**: ibid., p. 175.

31 **"an entirely new conception"**: Ellen Key, *The Century of the Child* (1909; reprint, New York: Arno, 1997), p. 101.

31 **"write what you will"; "Wise men have said"**: L. H. Sigourney, *Letters to Mothers* (New York: Harper & Bros., 1838), p. 10.

32 **"What, then, would we have?"**: Response to "Address of Welcome," National Congress of Mothers First Session, p. 18.

32 **85,000 were enrolled by 1900**: Rothman, *Woman's Proper Place*, p. 106.

32 **"caps and gowns"**: Mrs. Harriet Hickox Heller, "Childhood, an Interpretation," National Congress of Mothers Second Convention, p. 81; see also Ehrenreich and English's discussion in *For Her Own Good*, pp. 193–96.

32 **"turn back into the home"**: Birney, "Address of Welcome," National Congress of Mothers Third Convention, p. 198.

32 **"universal restlessness"**: Cotten, "A National Training School for Women," National Congress of Mothers First Session, p. 218.

32 **"keeping [herself]"**: Key, *The Century of the Child*, p. 114.

32 **"No boy of hers"**: quoted from "The College Woman and Motherhood" in the *National Congress of Mothers Magazine* 3 (March 1909): 211, in S. Rothman, *Woman's Proper Place*, p. 107.

32 **"every question"; "felt the drudgery"**: Heller, "Childhood, an Interpretation," National Congress of Mothers Second Convention, pp. 79, 81.

33 **The experts' role**: See the discussions in Ehrenreich and English's *For Her Own Good*, pp. 196–202, and in Richard Hofstadter's *Age of Reform: From Bryan to F.D.R.* (New York: Vintage, 1955), p. 154.

34 **"hidden mysteries"**: National Congress of Mothers First Session, p. 211.

34 **"my father's experiences of life"**: G. Stanley Hall, *Life and Confessions of a Psychologist* (New York: Appleton, 1923), p. 56.

34 **"It is a trite remark"**: Holt, "Physical Care of Children," National Congress of Mothers Third Convention, p. 230.

34 **"it is not a good thing"**: Theodore Roosevelt, "The American Woman as a Mother," *Ladies' Home Journal* 22, no. 8 (July 1905). The address was originally delivered before the National Congress of Mothers in March 1905.

34 **"the most widely read booklets"**: annual address by G. Stanley Hall to Quaboag Historical Society, reprinted in "For Man More Manly, Woman More Womanly," *Worcester Post*, June 13, 1906.

34 **"The conditions which kept"**: Holt, "Physical Care of Children," National Congress of Mothers Third Convention, p. 230.

35 **"away from Nature"**: Hall, "Some Practical Results of Child Study," National Congress of Mothers First Session, p. 167.

35 **The fertility rate**: For the statistics in this paragraph, see Macleod, *The Age of the Child*, pp. 2–3.

35 **"Profound must be"**: from a 1904 article in *Harper's Weekly*, quoted in Viviana A. Zelizer, *Pricing the Priceless Child: The Changing Social Value of Children* (New York: Basic Books, 1985), p. 5.

36 **High school attendance roughly doubled**: Macleod, *The Age of the Child*, p. 149.

36 **"its accumulated mass of cultures"**: Hall, *Adolescence*, 1: 321.

36 **"the powerful influence"**: G. Stanley Hall, "New Lights on Childhood," *Youth's Companion*, October 28, 1915.

36 **"to grapple successfully"**: Holt, "Physical Care of Children," National Congress of Mothers Third Convention, p. 249.

36 **Frederick Winslow Taylor's efficiency studies:** See Robert Kanigel, *The One Best Way: Frederick Winslow Taylor and the Enigma of Efficiency* (New York: Viking, 1997), pp. 372, 416.

37 **"delicately constructed piece of machinery"**: L. Emmett Holt, *Food, Health and Growth: A Discussion of the Nutrition of Children* (New York: Macmillan, 1922), p. 221.

37 **"immaculately dressed" to "He spoke in short, crisp"**: R. L. Duffus and L. Emmett Holt, Jr., *L. Emmett Holt: Pioneer of a Children's Century* (New York: Appleton-Century, 1940), p. vii.

37 **"he is demurring"**: Linda Mairs Holt letter to L. Emmett Holt, Jr., Oct. 30, 1910, NYU Medical Archives.

37 **"was his special combination"**: Dorothy Ross, *G. Stanley Hall: The Psychologist as Prophet* (Chicago: University of Chicago Press, 1972), p. 289.

37 **"soul of the race"**: G. Stanley Hall, "The Religious Content of the Child-Mind," an excerpt, 1901.

37 **"hates clearness"**: Ross, *G. Stanley Hall*, p. 240.

38 **"with great sincerity"**: ibid., p. 288.

38 **"miniature men and women"**: Holt, "Physical Care of Children," National Congress of Mothers Third Convention, p. 248.

38 **"a vast proportion"**: "The Child Question," *New York Times*, Feb. 21, 1897, collected in Rothman, *The Family*, p. 56.

38 **"The Supreme Peril of Modern Civilization"**: National Congress of Mothers Third Convention, p. 254.

38 **"I claim"**: Birney, "Address of Welcome," ibid., p. 197.

39 **"No man or woman"; "impressed by"**: ibid., p. 196.

39 **"sisters who are compelled to work"**: ibid., p. 199.

39 **"least likely"**: Holt, "Physical Care of Children," National Congress of Mothers Third Convention, p. 230.

39 **"The light of science"**: preface, National Congress of Mothers Second Convention, p. 5.

39 **"Our soul is to be filled"**: Key, *The Century of the Child*, p. 100.

39 **"be as entirely and simply"**: ibid., p. 109.

39 **"children [who] have been gathering"**: "Response to the Address of Welcome," National Congress of Mothers Second Convention, p. 21.

TWO: *Two Experts Grow Up*

41 **"female relatives and friends"**: L. Emmett Holt, "Physical Care of Children," National Congress of Mothers Third Convention, p. 235.

42 **"Arrested development"**: G. Stanley Hall, "Feminization in School and Home: The Undue Influence of Women Teachers—the Need of Different Training for the Sexes," *The World's Work*, May 1908, p. 10240.

42 **"superior stage of the race"**: G. Stanley Hall, *Adolescence* (1904; reprint, New York: Arno, 1969), 2: 94.

42 **"the old New England farm"**: G. Stanley Hall, *Life and Confessions of a Psychologist* (New York: Appleton, 1923), p. 177.

42 "the old home at Webster": L. Emmett Holt letter to L. Emmett Holt, Jr., Mar. 12, 1911, NYU Medical Archives.

43 "simply board" to "I have lived those times": R. L. Duffus and L. Emmett Holt, Jr., *L. Emmett Holt: Pioneer of a Children's Century* (New York: Appleton-Century, 1940), p. 23.

43 "I suppose you didn't tell them": ibid., pp. 21–22.

44 "For a time the Holt apple": ibid., p. 9.

44 "why my boys can't do big things"; "scramble for power and position": ibid., pp. 16–19.

44 "worms in the pathway"; "where those boys were raised": ibid., pp. 26–27.

45 "Holt believes in hydropathy": ibid., p. 34.

45 "sick of this writing-when-you-feel-like-it": ibid., p. 45.

45 "so large and full" to "Don't be in such hot haste": ibid., pp. 18, 60.

45 "lacked . . . the exquisite manual dexterity": ibid., p. 53.

45 "practical rather than sentimental": ibid., p. 61.

45 "museum of disease": ibid., p. 104.

46 "funny to hear": ibid., p. 90.

46 effect on children of maternal impressions: ibid., p. 96. See T. Berry Brazelton and Bertrand G. Cramer, *The Earliest Relationship: Parents, Infants, and the Drama of Early Attachment* (Reading, MA: Addison-Wesley, 1990), p. 28.

46 "required almost the equivalent": Thomas E. Cone, *The History of American Pediatrics* (Boston: Little, Brown, 1979), p. 137.

46 Europeans dismissed all the American mixing: ibid., p. 138.

46 an ideal venue: See Kathleen W. Jones, "Sentiment and Science: The Late Nineteenth Century Pediatrician as Mother's Advisor," *Journal of Social History* 17, no. 1 (Fall 1983): 81.

47 The hospital's mortality rate, and that of the "better class" and Holt's own private practice: ibid., p. 82.

48 "stewed very soft" to "without raisins": L. Emmett Holt, *The Care and Feeding of Children: A Catechism for the Use of Mothers and Children's Nurses* (New York: Appleton, 1897), p. 75.

48 "Simple instructions": "The Milk Supply of New York: Some of the Facts Brought Out by the Investigation of the Rockefeller Institute," Record Group III20, Box 45, folder 443, "Milk Supply, 1901–2," Laura Spelman Rockefeller Memorial Archives (LSRM), Rockefeller Archive Center, Tarrytown, NY.

48 "I fear I have not" to "I felt awfully sorry": L. Emmett Holt to Linda Mairs Holt, May 29, 1902, quoted in Duffus and Holt, *L. Emmett Holt*, p. 135.

48 "I realize very much more": L. Emmett Holt to Linda Mairs Holt, Jan. 10, 1892, ibid., p. 126.

49 "impulse to keep on growing": Hall, *Life and Confessions*, p. 44.

49 "I know it will seem to you frank": G. Stanley Hall letter to Julina Hall, July 20, 1923, G. Stanley Hall Papers, Clark University Archives, Worcester, MA.

49 "one of the first efforts": Hall, *Life and Confessions*, p. 46.

50 "This life-and-health book": ibid.

50 "I have regarded": ibid., p. 41.

50 "excessive domestic duties": ibid., p. 1.

50 "Perhaps she felt"; "almost brutally prone": ibid., pp. 44, 43.

50 "Perhaps she was so enamored": ibid., p. 44.

51 "bought his time"; "very successful in discipline": ibid., p. 59.

51 **"father-image"**: ibid., p. 28.

51 **"My dear son"**: Granville Hall letter to G. Stanley Hall, Aug. 4, 1850, G. Stanley Hall Papers.

52 **He recorded one severe whipping**: Hall, *Life and Confessions*, p. 74.

52 **"morbid dread of conflict"; "early and especially pubescent"**: ibid., pp. 42, 86.

53 **"harsh censure"**: ibid., p. 42.

53 **"rules of conduct"; "because *you cannot see*"**: Granville Hall letter to G. Stanley Hall, Jan. 1, 1853, G. Stanley Hall Papers.

53 **"Stanley to own the truth"**: Granville Hall letter to G. Stanley Hall, Dec. 31, 1853, G. Stanley Hall Papers.

53 **"stepped back"**: Hall, *Life and Confessions*, pp. 74–75.

53 **"the very atmosphere"; "the foundations for a certain independence"**: ibid., p. 86.

53 **"We children were incessantly"; "were always oppressed"**: ibid., p. 80.

54 **"dawn of adolescence"; "no dread was greater"**: ibid., p. 377.

54 **"Hard up against"**: ibid., p. 85.

54 **"rank lush sentiments"**: ibid., p. 162.

54 **"If ever parents lived"**: ibid., pp. 79–80.

54 **"As a youth"**: ibid., p. 176.

55 **"I do not think I have got"**: quoted in Dorothy Ross, *G. Stanley Hall: The Psychologist as Prophet* (Chicago: University of Chicago Press, 1972), p. 30.

55 **"I am twenty-five"**: G. Stanley Hall letter to his parents from Berlin, Pentecost, 1870, G. Stanley Hall Papers.

55 **"little club of Positivists"; "to make a good Christian of Hegel"**: Ross, *G. Stanley Hall*, pp. 46–47. On Hall's religious-philosophic development, see also Louis Menand, *The Metaphysical Club: The Story of an American Idea* (New York: Farrar, Straus & Giroux, 2001), p. 265.

56 **"the Geist"**: Ross, *G. Stanley Hall*, p. 36.

56 **"singularly solidified"**: quoted in ibid., p. 87.

56 **"sentiment or triviality"**: ibid., p. 94.

56 **"what love really meant"**: Hall, *Life and Confessions*, p. 221.

56 **On their way home**: See Ross, *G. Stanley Hall*, chaps. 5–7; see also Menand, *The Metaphysical Club*, p. 270.

56 **"the stages of a child's mental growth"**: G. Stanley Hall, "The Moral and Religious Training of Children," *Princeton Review* 10 (January 1882): 39.

57 **"no bigger than a small mouse"**: G. Stanley Hall, "The Contents of Children's Minds on Entering School," *Princeton Review* 2 (May 1883), reprinted in G. Stanley Hall and some of his pupils, *Aspects of Child Life and Education* (1907; reprint, New York: Arno, 1975), p. 24.

57 **"finally convinced I could"**: Hall, *Life and Confessions*, p. 253.

57 **"act of wreckage"**: ibid., p. 296.

57 **"Great Fatigue"**: Ross, *G. Stanley Hall*, p. 253.

57 **"Something of a crisis"**: Hall, *Life and Confessions*, p. 405.

57 **"a certain desiccation of the psyche"**: ibid., p. 162.

58 **"Unto you is born this day"**: G. Stanley Hall, "Child Study," in *Proceedings of the National Education Association*, 1894, p. 173.

58 **"Professor Harrington"**: manuscript by J. O. Hall, G. Stanley Hall Papers.

58 **"distant, austere"**: Ross, *G. Stanley Hall*, p. 209.

58 **Hallian questionnaires**: Hall, "Some Practical Results of Child Study," National

Congress of Mothers First Session, p. 167. And see, for example, "A Study of Dolls," *Pedagogical Seminary* 4 (December 1896); "Some Aspects of the Early Sense of Self," *American Journal of Psychology* 9 (April 1898); "A Study of Anger," *American Journal of Psychology* 10 (July 1899); "How Children and Youth Think and Feel About Clouds," *Pedagogical Seminary* 9 (December 1902).

58   "ranked among the common pests": quoted in Alexander W. Siegel and Sheldon H. White, "The Child Study Movement," in Hayne W. Reese, ed., *Advances in Child Development and Behavior* (New York: Academic Press, 1982), 17:255.

58   "lacking in stability": John Dewey, "Criticisms Wise and Otherwise on Modern Child-Study," in *The Early Works, 1882–1898*, ed. Jo Ann Boydston (Carbondale: Southern Illinois University Press, 1972), 5:209. Originally published in *Addresses and Proceedings of the National Education Association*, 1897.

59   "mere general theories": ibid.

59   "inevitable at an early stage": Hall, *Adolescence*, 2:56 fn.

59   "are themselves rejuvenated": G. Stanley Hall, "What Is a Child?" *Boston Sunday Post Magazine*, November 1907.

59   "Best of all, perhaps": G. Stanley Hall, "Child Study and Its Relations to Education," *The Forum* 29 (August 1900), reprinted in Charles E. Strickland and Charles Burgess, eds., *Health, Growth, and Heredity: G. Stanley Hall on Natural Education* (New York: Teachers College Press, 1965), p. 87.

59   "It is a nondescript": ibid., pp. 76–77.

59   "I am well aware": Ross, *G. Stanley Hall*, pp. 260–61.

59   "determination of intellectual": G. Stanley Hall, "Curiosity and Interest," *Pedagogical Seminary* 10 (1903), reprinted in Hall and some of his pupils, *Aspects of Child Life and Education*, p. 136.

60   "pour into, not onto, them": Hall, "The Contents of Children's Minds on Entering School," ibid., p. 22.

60   "into ultimate unity": ibid., p. iii.

60   "We need less sentimentality": G. Stanley Hall, "The Kindergarten," *New York Education* 3, November 1899.

60   "wide circle of readers" to "anxious mothers": Lorine Pruette, *G. Stanley Hall: A Biography of a Mind* (New York: Appleton, 1926), pp. 120–21.

60   "the book and the ideas": Edward Lee Thorndike quoted in Edward A. Krag, *The Shaping of the American High School* (New York: Harper & Row, 1964), p. 121.

60   "There is a sense": Hall, *Life and Confessions*, pp. 367–68.

60   "the best definition of genius": Hall, *Adolescence*, 2:90–91.

61   Should adults be striving: See Daniel T. Rodgers, "Socializing Middle-Class Children: Institutions, Fables, and Work Values in Nineteenth-Century America," in N. Ray Hiner and Joseph M. Hawes, *Growing Up in America: Children in Historical Perspective* (Urbana: University of Illinois Press, 1985), pp. 118–32, for a very good discussion of the contradictory aims of child-rearing literature of the time.

THREE: *Infant Regimens, Adolescent Passions*

63   as she was given to reminding: Jane Howard, *Margaret Mead: A Life* (New York: Simon & Schuster, 1984), pp. 21, 24.

63   "Not satisfied": quoted in Sheila M. Rothman, *Woman's Proper Place: A History of Changing Ideals and Practices, 1870 to the Present* (New York: Basic Books, 1978), p. 108.

64　**"When I knew" to "among other things":** Margaret Mead, *Blackberry Winter: My Earliest Years* (New York: Morrow, 1972), p. 19.

64　**"The lack of any contradiction":** ibid., p. 25.

64　**"[working] out her own solution":** L. Emmett Holt, "Physical Care of Children," National Congress of Mothers Third Convention, p. 249.

65　**"She had no gift":** Mead, *Blackberry Winter*, p. 26.

65　**"I'm not sure":** Howard, *Margaret Mead*, p. 31.

65　**study Italian immigrant children:** Phyllis Grosskurth, *Margaret Mead: A Life of Controversy* (London: Penguin, 1988), pp. 17–18.

66　**"We have no glimmer":** quoted in Ronald Clark, *The Survival of Charles Darwin: A Biography of a Man and an Idea* (New York: Random House, 1984), p. 234.

67　**"flapperdom"; "shattered old conventions":** G. Stanley Hall, "Flapper Americana Novissima," *Atlantic Monthly* 129 (June 1922): 780, 776.

67　**"the nation's bill":** L. Emmett Holt, "Diet Problems of Childhood," in Holt, editorial adviser, *The Happy Baby* (New York: Dodd, Mead, 1924), p. 85.

67　**"In the preparation"; "the style of question and answer":** L. Emmett Holt, *The Care and Feeding of Children: A Catechism for the Use of Mothers and Children's Nurses* (New York: Appleton, 1899), p. 6.

67　**"those things" to "it is thought":** ibid., p. 5.

67　**"friendless little babies":** Kathleen W. Jones, "Sentiment and Science: The Late Nineteenth Century Pediatrician as Mother's Advisor," *Journal of Social History* 17, no. 1 (Fall 1983): 82.

67　**"simplicity, brevity":** L. Emmett Holt, *The Care and Feeding of Children: A Catechism for the Use of Mothers and Children's Nurses* (New York: Appleton, 1894), p. 5.

67　**"easily [done]"; "necessary for health":** ibid., pp. 50, 53.

67　**"never until four months":** ibid., p. 57.

68　**"fuller treatment"; "Some want":** L. Emmett Holt, *The Care and Feeding of Children* (1897), p. 1.

68　**"The upper one fifth":** ibid., p. 39.

68　**"A pair of substantial mammary glands":** quoted in Thomas E. Cone, *The History of American Pediatrics* (Boston: Little, Brown, 1979), p. 138.

68　**"Mother of Level Measurements":** Laura Shapiro, *Perfection Salad: Women and Cooking at the Turn of the Century* (New York: Farrar, Straus & Giroux, 1986), p. 109.

68　**"it is well to make":** Holt, *The Care and Feeding of Children* (1897), p. 49.

69　**"What is the best":** Holt, *The Care and Feeding of Children* (1894), p. 24.

69　**"The running war":** William Kessen, ed., *The Child* (New York: Wiley, 1965), p. 1.

69　**"at least three children":** Jones, "Sentiment and Science," p. 86.

69　**"the man who has mastered":** ibid., p. 85.

70　**"more exact and definite wisdom":** Holt, "Physical Care of Children," National Congress of Mothers Third Convention, p. 232.

70　**"put herself in relation":** ibid., p. 237.

70　**turn a "deaf ear" to "the grandmother":** L. Emmett Holt, "The General Care of the Baby," in Holt, editorial adviser, *The Happy Baby*, p. 3.

70　**"manufacturers of the commercial":** Holt, "Physical Care of Children," National Congress of Mothers Third Convention, p. 236.

70　**"much that is exaggerated":** Holt, *The Happy Baby*, pp. xii–xiii.

70　**"The greatest obstacle":** L. Emmett Holt, *Food, Health and Growth: A Discussion of the Nutrition of Children* (New York: Macmillan, 1922), p. 260.

70 **"habit of close"; "work out her own solution"**: Holt, "Physical Care of Children," National Congress of Mothers Third Convention, pp. 235, 247.

70 **"deep embroidery"**: Elisabeth Robinson Scovil, *The Care of Children* (Philadelphia: Altemus, 1895), p. 88.

70 **"It is the duty"**: ibid., p. 25.

70 **"the notion of medicine"; "science in which effects"**: Holt, *The Happy Baby*, p. xii.

71 **"laws of health"**: ibid., p. xiii.

71 **"The number of feedings"**: L. Emmett Holt, "Maternal Nursing," in ibid., p. 40.

71 **"rule that"; "this is not to say"**: Mrs. Max West, *Infant Care* (Washington, DC: U.S. Government Printing Office, 1914), reprinted in David J. Rothman and Sheila M. Rothman, eds., *Child Rearing Literature of Twentieth Century America* (New York: Arno, 1972), p. 60.

71 **"parental affection"**: L. Emmett Holt, "Diet Problems of Childhood," in *The Happy Baby*, p. 78.

71 **"the natural desire of the young mother" to "as a plaything"**: Holt, "The General Care of the Baby," in ibid., pp. 3, 4.

71 **"uncontrolled emotions"**: L. Emmett Holt, *The Care and Feeding of Children: A Catechism for the Use of Mothers and Children's Nurses* (New York: Appleton, 1915), p. 48.

72 **"sphere of activity"**: Holt, "Physical Care of Children," National Congress of Mothers Third Convention, p. 232.

72 **"the care of a baby"**: quoted in Nancy Pottishman Weiss, "The Mother-Child Dyad Revisited: Perceptions of Mothers and Children in Twentieth-Century Child-Rearing Manuals," *Journal of Social Issues* 34, no. 2 (Spring 1978): 33.

72 **"nerve-excitation"; "agitation"**: Anna A. Rogers, "Why American Mothers Fail," *Atlantic Monthly* 101, no. 3 (March 1908): 291.

72 **"to secure the early bending"**: Holt, "Physical Care of Children," National Congress of Mothers Third Convention, p. 233.

72 **"no forcing, no pressure"**: ibid., p. 241.

72 **"a great deal of harm"**: Holt, "The General Care of the Baby," in *The Happy Baby*, p. 7. See West, *Infant Care*, p. 63, for an early version of by now familiar brain lore. "The first nervous impulse which passes through the baby's eyes, ears, fingers, or mouth to the tender brain makes a pathway for itself; the next time another impulse travels over the same path it deepens the impression of the first," Mrs. West wrote. She concluded that "those early stimuli [should be] sent in orderly fashion."

72 **"in these days of factory"**: Holt, "Physical Care of Children," National Congress of Mothers Third Convention, p. 241.

73 **"untrained baby"**: Holt, "The General Care of the Baby," in *The Happy Baby*, p. 2.

73 **"every child likes his own way"**: Holt, *The Care and Feeding of Children* (1915), p. 140.

73 **"period of education"**: West, *Infant Care*, p. 63.

73 **"A young baby is very easily molded"**: Holt, "The General Care of the Baby," in *The Happy Baby*, pp. 1–2.

73 **"make our nervous system"**: William James, *Talks to Teachers on Psychology and to Students on Some of Life's Ideals* (1899; reprint, Cambridge, MA: Harvard University Press, 1983), p. 48. The phrase first appears in James's *Principles of Psychology*, vol. 1, chap. 4.

73 **"The whole present tendency"** to **"If a mother would but strive"**: Rogers, "Why American Mothers Fail," p. 291.

74 **"was kept well for two years"**: Anna G. Noyes, *How I Kept My Baby Well* (Baltimore: Warwick & York, 1913), p. 11.

74 **"The problem of raising"**: ibid., p. 183.

74 **"I found it was worthwhile"; "My kind of worrying"**: ibid., p. 182.

75 **"He developed great concentration"; "He became so docile"**: Linda Mairs Holt's record of L. Emmett Holt, Jr.'s childhood, NYU Medical Archives.

75 **"a quiet, happy baby"** to **"he positively declined to conform"**: ibid.

75 **"I managed to contract"**: L. Emmett Holt, Jr., "Autobiographical Sketch," p. 4, NYU Medical Archives.

76 **"self-feeding"**: L. Emmett Holt, "Diet Problems of Childhood," in *The Happy Baby*, p. 74.

76 **"Assuming an attitude of indifference"**: ibid., p. 75.

76 **"Children who are allowed"**: Holt, *The Care and Feeding of Children* (1915), p. 14.

76 **To judge by his book:** When his son L. Emmett Holt, Jr., began revising the manual after his father's death, he did turn to behavioral issues by the 1943 edition and showed himself an eclectic, flexible adviser. He emphasized three "primary emotional needs" of children: for affection, for stability and security, and for self-expression. On his list of recommended readings was C. Anderson Aldrich's *Babies Are Human Beings* of 1938, one of the books that inspired Dr. Spock with its flexible counsel.

76 **"should be broken up"**: Holt, *The Care and Feeding of Children* (1894), p. 66.

76 **"Watch closely"** to **"medical advice should at once"**: ibid., p. 215.

76 **"diet problems"**: Holt, "Diet Problems of Childhood," p. 72.

76 **"accurate, definite knowledge"; "greatest weapon"**: Holt, *The Happy Baby*, p. xiii.

76 **"Scientific Basis"**: National Congress of Mothers Second Convention, pp. 84–86.

77 **"Take good care of yourself"**: Linda Mairs Holt letter to L. Emmett Holt, Jr., June 3, 1908, NYU Medical Archives.

77 **"How does it feel to be 13?"**: Linda Mairs Holt letter to L. Emmett Holt, Jr., Mar. 22, 1908, NYU Medical Archives.

77 **"a better climate"**: L. Emmett Holt, Jr., "Autobiography," typescript, NYU Medical Archives.

77 **"babyhood need not be"**: untitled newspaper obituary, Record Group 199.39, folder 3, L. Emmett Holt series, Laura Spelman Rockefeller Memorial Archives (LSRM), Rockefeller Archive Center, Tarrytown, NY.

77 **"I am sure from your letters"; "We are made for it"**: Linda Mairs Holt letter to L. Emmett Holt, Jr., May 3, 1911, NYU Medical Archives.

77 **"unwise and disadvantageous"; "You will lose"**: Linda Mairs Holt letter to L. Emmett Holt, Jr., Feb. 7, 1911, NYU Medical Archives.

77 **"infancy of man's higher nature"**: G. Stanley Hall, *Adolescence* (1904; reprint, New York: Arno, 1969), 2:71.

78 **"second birth"; "awkward, often unattractive"**: ibid., 1:48, 315.

78 **Criticism of contradictory kinds:** John Demos and Virginia Demos, "Adolescence in Historical Perspective," *Journal of Marriage and the Family* 31 (November 1969): 632–38.

78 **"we are today under the tyranny"**: ibid., p. 636.

78 **"an immense mass of material"; "this really great work":** review in *The Outlook* 78 (Sept. 24, 1904): 238–40.

78 **"remarkable book"; "the magnitude":** Mrs. Theodore W. Birney, "Adolescence," *The Delineator* 64 (August 1904): 272.

78 **"more fascinating"; "It is a common sight":** ibid., p. 274.

79 **Hall's idea of adolescence:** figures in this paragraph drawn from David I. Macleod, *The Age of the Child* (New York: Twayne, 1998), pp. 149, 110, 177.

79 **"useful in her development"; "our prodigy and pearl":** Kate Douglas Wiggin, *Rebecca of Sunnybrook Farm* (New York: Grosset & Dunlap, 1964), pp. 253, 292.

79 **"storm and stress period":** Hall, *Adolescence*, 2:73.

79 **"the seething age":** ibid., 1:544.

79 **"tidal wave" and "a lion in heat":** Joseph Kett, *Rites of Passage: Adolescence in America, 1790 to the Present* (New York: Basic Books, 1977), p. 134.

79 **"wild desires, restless cravings":** Demos and Demos, "Adolescence in Historical Perspective," p. 634.

79 **Hall's signal contribution:** See Dorothy Ross, *G. Stanley Hall: The Psychologist as Prophet* (Chicago: University of Chicago Press, 1972), p. 333, on his biology.

79 **"wise mentors and advisers":** Hall, *Adolescence*, 1:280.

80 **"carrying such messages":** Wiggin, *Rebecca of Sunnybrook Farm*, p. 20.

80 **"we divine how fully":** quoted in Ross, *G. Stanley Hall*, p. 336.

80 **"To rightly draw":** Hall, *Adolescence*, 1:589.

80 **"highest possible maturity of body and soul":** G. Stanley Hall, "Education in Sex-Hygiene," *Eugenics Review*, January 1910, address originally delivered at a meeting of the American Society of Sanitary and Moral Prophylaxis, Feb. 13, 1908.

80 **"and not maturity":** Hall, *Adolescence*, 2:94.

80 **"vague yearnings":** Birney, "Adolescence," p. 273.

80 **"saltatory":** Hall, *Adolescence*, 1:xiii.

80 **"without precedent in English science":** quoted in Ross, *G. Stanley Hall*, p. 385.

80 **"adolescence is the age":** Birney, "Adolescence," p. 273.

81 **"upward, creative, and not de-creative":** Hall, *Adolescence*, 2:546.

81 **"the law of transitoriness":** James, *Talks to Teachers on Psychology and to Students on Some of Life's Ideals*, p. 45.

81 **"healthy little savage":** G. Stanley Hall, "The Kindergarten," *New York Education*, 1899. In his famous article "The Story of a Sand-Pile" in *Scribner's Magazine* 3 (June 1888), Hall described the town constructed by a group of boys every summer vacation over successive years, their fascination waning "the more finished and like reality the objects became" (p. 695).

81 **"quadrennium"; "preeminently the age of drill":** G. Stanley Hall, *Educational Problems* (New York: Appleton, 1911), 2:627.

81 **"new birth":** Hall, *Adolescence*, 1:xiii.

81 **"uniformity and inflexibility":** Ross, *G. Stanley Hall*, pp. 320–21.

81 **"youth [in] . . . this larval stage":** Hall, *Adolescence*, 2:429.

81 **"whole gamut of feeling":** G. Stanley Hall, "Psychic Arrest in Adolescence," National Education Association, proceedings of the Department of Child Study, July 1903.

81 **"ardor and energy of living":** Hall, *Adolescence*, 1:405.

81 **"New zests and transforming motives":** Hall, *Educational Problems*, 2:629.

81 **"passions and desires"; "antithetic impulses":** Ross, *G. Stanley Hall*, pp. 326–27.

81 **"no age is so responsive":** Hall, *Adolescence*, 1:xviii.

81   **"parents are often shocked"**: ibid., 2:383.

82   **" 'teens' are emotionally unstable"; "youth must have excitement"**: ibid., 2:74.

82   **"occult causes"**: Demos and Demos, "Adolescence in Historical Perspective," p. 634.

82   **"hygiene of puberty"; "the curse of Eve"**: Joan Brumberg, *The Body Project: An Intimate History of American Girls* (New York: Random House, 1997), pp. 36, 40.

82   **"false and . . . morbid modesty"**: Hall, *Adolescence*, 1:465.

82   **"prudery and painstaking reticence"; "exaggerated horror"**: ibid., 1:432.

82   **"there is great reason"**: ibid., 1:280.

82   **"classes of readers"**: review in *The Outlook* 78 (Sept. 24, 1904): 240.

82   **"sex is the most potent"**: Hall, *Adolescence*, 2:109.

83   **"perhaps . . . the most perfect type"**: ibid., 1:452.

83   **"these forbidden joys of youth"; "fevered . . . pleasure"**: ibid., 1:443.

83   **"anxious urinoscopists"**: ibid., 1:459.

83   **"ever lengthening probationary period"**: ibid., 1:453.

83   **"the act . . . brutal"; "in the phylogenetic scale"**: ibid., 1:440.

83   **"The first orgasm" to "The Nemesis of depression"**: ibid., 1:438.

83   **"Abnormal acts impair self-respect"**: ibid., 1:441.

83   **"languid appetite for the larger"**: ibid., 1:443.

84   **"all the irradiations of touch"**: ibid., 1:440.

84   **"more generic and less specific"**: ibid., 1:505.

84   **"many-sided" to "in the course of the month"**: ibid., 1:503.

84   **"more sensitive, more prone to depression"**: ibid., 1:492.

85   **"She develops new sentiments" to "is less in need"**: ibid., 1:493.

85   **"have from six to fifteen times" to "the divorce between the life preferred"**: ibid., 2:391.

85   **"To millions, yes, to millions"**: *The Delineator* 81, no. 2 (February 1913): 71.

85   **"a slight sense of aimlessness"; "They wish to know"**: G. Stanley Hall, "Co-Education in the High School," National Education Association address, 1903, reprinted in Charles E. Strickland and Charles Burgess, eds., *Health, Growth, and Heredity: G. Stanley Hall on Natural Education* (New York: Teachers College Press, 1965), pp. 185–86.

86   **"the potency of good heredity"**: Hall, *Adolescence*, 1:452.

86   **"The one unpardonable thing"**: ibid., 2:384.

86   **"struggle, effort, and perhaps conflict"**: ibid., 1:467.

86   **"sissifying of the schools"**: "Dr. Hall on Sissifying of the Schools," *Worcester Evening Gazette*, Jan. 7, 1908.

87   **"the pedagogy of sex"**: Hall, *Educational Problems*, 1:388–539.

87   **"It has not yet entered"**: ibid., 1:483.

87   **"the rare combination of scientific"**: ibid., 1:484.

87   **"coital experiences are imperfect"**: ibid., 1:512.

87   **"never dreams of her passional potentialities"; "are deleterious to the conjugal relations"**: ibid., 1:513.

87   **"break away from their proper sphere"; "put forth abnormal efforts"**: ibid., 1:514.

87   **"of sexual detail"**: quoted in Ross, *G. Stanley Hall*, p. 399.

88   **"criticism that rankled like this"**: ibid., p. 400.

88   **"talked badly and endlessly"**: ibid., p. 412.

88 **"Will children reared"**: "What Is to Become of Your Baby?" *Cosmopolitan* 48, no. 5 (April 1910): 661.

88 **"special assistants and expert knowledge"**: ibid., p. 665.

88 **"precious ten"; "conscientious and rational restraint"**: Charlotte Perkins Gilman, *Concerning Children* (Boston: Small, Maynard, 1900), pp. 17, 197.

88 **"by special nurses"; "Unfortunately, we have"**: ibid., pp. 110, 71.

88 **"Never in the world"**: Hall, "What Is to Become of Your Baby?" p. 665.

88 **"we are making sure if slow progress"**: ibid., p. 662.

89 **"While we are lavishing"**: ibid., p. 665.

89 **"singularly lacking in force"**: Cornelia A. P. Comer, "Letter to the Rising Generation," *Atlantic Monthly* 107, no. 2 (February 1911): 148.

89 **"You are markedly inferior"**: ibid., p. 149.

89 **"a complete bewilderment"**: Randolph S. Bourne, *Youth and Life* (1913; reprint, New York: Books for Libraries Press, 1967), p. 33.

89 **"timorousness"; "increasingly doubtful whether"**: ibid., pp. 47, 51.

89 **"not knowing what to teach you"**: Comer, "Letter to the Rising Generation," p. 148.

89 **"What generation but the one"**: Bourne, *Youth and Life*, p. 33.

90 **"It is always hard for father and son" to "That standpoint too"**: G. Stanley Hall letter to Robert Hall, Apr. 29, 1912, G. Stanley Hall Papers, Special Collections, Robert Hutchings Goddard Library, Clark University.

91 **"Life now has many great opportunities" to "path of highest usefulness"**: L. Emmett Holt letter to L. Emmett Holt, Jr., Mar. 12, 1911, NYU Medical Archives.

91 **"We miss you"**: Linda Mairs Holt letter to L. Emmett Holt, Jr., Mar. 27, 1912, NYU Medical Archives.

91 **"To-day is my father's birthday" to "See to it that they do not"**: L. Emmett Holt letter to L. Emmett Holt, Jr., Mar. 2, 1913, quoted in R. L. Duffus and L. Emmett Holt, Jr., *L. Emmett Holt: Pioneer of a Children's Century* (New York: Appleton, 1940), p. 187.

92 **"I often wish I could bequeath"**: L. Emmett Holt letter to L. Emmett Holt, Jr., Mar. 21, 1920, quoted in ibid., p. 260.

93 **"The greatest of all pleasures"**: G. Stanley Hall letter to Arnold Gesell, Jan. 27, 1921, Arnold Gesell Papers, Library of Congress, Washington, DC.

FOUR: *The Era (and Errors) of the Parent*

97 **"was one of the freakiest days" to "Heavy overcoats"**: *New York Times*, Oct. 29, 1925, p. 1.

97 **six-day "institute"**: Steven L. Schlossman, "Philanthropy and the Gospel of Child Development," *History of Education Quarterly* 21, no. 3 (Fall 1981): 287.

98 **"The modern mother"**: "Modern Parenthood," *New York Times*, Nov. 1, 1925, collected in Rothman, *The Family*, p. 102.

98 **"lusty . . . infant"**: Hall, "Child Study," in *Proceedings of the National Education Association*, 1894, p. 173.

98 **"the primitive parental prairie" to "distinguished specialists"**: Dorothy Canfield Fisher and Sidonie Matsner Gruenberg, eds., *Our Children: A Handbook for Parents* (New York: Viking, 1932), p. 4.

98 **"hastily and cravenly"; "relentless sniping"**: ibid., p. 6.

99 **"book-l'arning"**: ibid.

99 **"organized society"**: Anna Gordin Spencer, "The Century of the Child," *Children: The Magazine for Parents* 3, no. 4 (April 1928): 9.

99 **"the great parental education movement"**: Margaret J. Quilliard, *Child Study Discussion Records: Development, Method, Techniques* (New York: CSA of America, 1928), p. 71.

99 **"the average mother"**: Mrs. Max West, *Infant Care* (Washington, DC: U.S. Government Printing Office, 1914), reprinted in David J. Rothman and Sheila M. Rothman, eds., *Child Rearing Literature of Twentieth Century America* (New York: Arno, 1972), "letter of transmittal," p. 7.

99 **As many as 125,000 letters**: Molly Ladd-Taylor, *Raising a Baby the Government Way: Mothers' Letters to the Children's Bureau, 1915–32* (New Brunswick, NJ: Rutgers University Press, 1986), p. 2.

99 **"I read in one of your leaflet"**: ibid., pp. 78–79.

99 **Sheppard-Towner Act**: See Sheila Rothman's discussion in *Woman's Proper Place: A History of Changing Ideals and Practices, 1870 to the Present* (New York: Basic Books, 1978), pp. 136–52. The Children's Bureau's lobbying on behalf of the bill and the medical establishment's mounting opposition to the act are also treated in Sydney Halpern, *American Pediatrics: The Social Dynamics of Professionalism, 1880–1980* (Berkeley: University of California Press, 1988), chap. 5; and Theda Skocpol: *Protecting Soldiers and Mothers: The Political Origins of Social Policy in the United States* (Cambridge, MA: Belknap/Harvard University Press, 1992), pp. 494–524.

99 **"the literature of child psychology"**: Nancy Pottishman Weiss, "Mother, the Invention of Necessity: Dr. Benjamin Spock's Baby and Child Care," reprinted in N. Ray Hiner and Joseph M. Hawes, eds., *Growing Up in America: Children in Historical Perspective* (Urbana: University of Illinois Press, 1985), p. 291.

99 **"the great hue and cry"**: John M. Cooper, "The Effect of Machine-Made Recreation on Family Life," in *Concerning Parents: A Symposium on Present Day Parenthood* (New York: New Republic, 1926), p. 240.

100 **"From every home"**: typescript of a radio talk by Mrs. Howard S. Gans, president of the Federation for Child Study, Box 28, folder 289, Laura Spelman Rockefeller Memorial Archives (LSRM), Rockefeller Archive Center, Tarrytown, NY.

100 **"Better Send for This Pamphlet"; "A child has a mental life"**: *New York Times*, Apr. 6, 1925, collected in Rothman, *The Family*, p. 99.

100 **"latest development"**: *New York Times*, June 29, 1924, collected in ibid.

100 **"the home is the workshop"**: Douglas A. Thom, *Child Management* (Washington, DC: U.S. Government Printing Office, 1925), reprinted in Rothman, *Child Rearing Literature of Twentieth Century America*, p. 34.

100 **"Parents and the New Psychology"**: Douglas Thom, "The Importance of the Early Years," in *Concerning Parents*, p. 99.

100 **"Hygienist Decries"**: *New York Times*, Oct. 28, 1925, collected in Rothman, *The Family*, p. 100.

100 **"Mother, when you're dummy"**: quoted in Mark Sullivan, *Our Times: America at the Birth of the Twentieth Century*, edited and with new material by Dan Rather (New York: Scribner, 1996), p. 665.

100 **"the drifting home"**: Ernest R. Groves, *The Drifting Home* (Boston: Houghton Mifflin, 1926).

100 **"in our childhood"**: Ernest R. Groves, "The Family as Coordinator of Community Forces," in *Concerning Parents*, p. 84.

101 **"The family, like a good administrator"**: Evans Clark, "Rearing of Children Becoming a Science," *New York Times*, Nov. 1, 1925, collected in Rothman, *The Family*, p. 101.

101 **"We will realize"**: Groves, "The Family as Coordinator of Community Forces," in *Concerning Parents*, p. 86.

101 **"By some strange cosmic alchemy"**: Clark, "Rearing of Children Becoming a Science," p. 100.

101 **"lay hold of every available"**: Robert S. Lynd and Helen Merrell Lynd, *Middletown* (New York: Harcourt Brace Jovanovich, 1929), p. 149.

101 **"the great crisis of parenthood"**: Dorothy Canfield Fisher, *Mothers and Children* (New York: Holt, 1914), p. 83.

101 **more private:** See Rothman, *Woman's Proper Place*, pp. 174–218. See also Weiss, "Mother, the Invention of Necessity," pp. 290–91, and Steven L. Schlossman, "The Formative Era in American Parent Education: Overview and Interpretation," in Ron Haskins and Diane Adams, eds., *Parent Education and Public Policy* (Norwood, NJ: Ablex, 1983), p. 25; and Schlossman's "Philanthropy and the Gospel of Child Development," *History of Education Quarterly* 21, no. 3 (Fall 1981).

101 **"the whole social standard"**: Spencer, "The Century of the Child," p. 9.

102 **"there was something awesome"**: Joseph Brennemann, "The Menace of Psychiatry," *American Journal of Diseases of Children* 42, no. 2 (1931): 384.

103 **"family advisers"; "the healer of disease"**: Halpern, *American Pediatrics*, pp. 14, 96.

103 **"Development, quite as much"**: Arnold Gesell, *The Guidance of Mental Growth in Infant and Child* (New York: Macmillan, 1930), p. 301.

103 **"fundamental issues of personality organization"**: Marion E. Kenworthy, "From Childhood to Youth," in *Concerning Parents*, p. 119.

103 **Like so much else:** For a useful summary of the interwar boom in research, see not only Steven Schlossman's articles but Robert Sears, *Your Ancients Revisited: A History of Child Development* (Chicago: University of Chicago Press, 1975), pp. 17–21.

103 **The child welfare reformers:** See Hamilton Cravens, *Before Head Start: The Iowa Station and America's Children* (Chapel Hill: University of North Carolina Press, 1993), p. 5. On the renaming of the Committee on Child Psychology, see pp. 68–69.

103 **"the term *child development*"; "still in its early infancy"**: Gesell, *The Guidance of Mental Growth*, pp. 271, 267.

103 **"It was felt that through the social sciences"**: quoted in Barbara Ehrenreich and Deirdre English, *For Her Own Good* (Garden City, NY: Anchor, 1978), p. 207.

104 **"systematic and intensive study"**: Milton J. E. Senn, *Insights on the Child Development Movement in the United States*, Monographs of the Society for Research in Child Development, serial no. 161, vol. 40, nos. 3–4 (August 1975): 14.

104 **"The procreative Johnny Appleseed"**: ibid., p. 22.

104 **"more or less invented"**: Schlossman, "Philanthropy and the Gospel of Child Development," p. 277.

104 **"Rearing of Children"**: *New York Times*, Nov. 1, 1925, collected in Rothman, *The Family*, p. 100.

105 **"orchestrator"**: Schlossman, "Philanthropy and the Gospel of Child Development," p. 281.

105 **"Let's have more definite formulations"; "waiting for all"**: Senn, *Insights on the Child Development Movement*, p. 23.

105 **They demurred**: Schlossman, "The Formative Era in American Parent Education: Overview and Interpretation," p. 17. For a discussion of the founding of *Children: The Magazine for Parents*, see Steven L. Schlossman, "Perils of Popularization: The Founding of *Parents' Magazine*," in Alice Boardman Smuts and John W. Hagen, eds., *History and Research in Child Development*, Monographs of the Society for Research in Child Development, serial no. 211, vol. 50, nos. 4–5 (1986): 65–77.

105 **"scientific findings"; "sugary uplift"**: *New York Times*, Sept. 23, 1926, collected in Rothman, *The Family*, p. 103.

105 **"habit of intelligent behavior"**: quoted in Schlossman, "Philanthropy and the Gospel of Child Development," p. 280.

105 **"a carefully worked out technique"**: quoted in Schlossman, "The Formative Era in American Parent Education," p. 25.

106 **"Every blow that is struck"**: Dorothy Canfield Fisher, "Freedom for the Child," in *Concerning Parents*, p. 278.

106 **"a new term . . . shows"**: Clark, "Rearing of Children Becoming a Science," p. 100.

106 **" 'no man's land' "**: Arnold Gesell, "A Decade of Progress in the Mental Hygiene of the Preschool Child," *Annals of the American Academy*, 1930, p. 143.

106 **"discharging ears"; "The child with night terrors"**: quoted in S. Rothman, *Woman's Proper Place*, p. 214.

106 **The addition of personality to the vocabulary**: See Warren Susman, "Personality and the Making of Twentieth-Century Culture," in Susman, *Culture as History: The Transformation of American Society in the Twentieth Century* (New York: Pantheon, 1973), pp. 271–85.

107 **"the gentle art of pleasing"; "the strong desire for self-improvement"**: Orison Marden, *Masterful Personality* (New York: Crowell, 1921), pp. 45, 306.

107 **"largely developed from mingling"; "poise, serenity, amiability"**: ibid., pp. 60, 337.

107 **"emotional responses"**: Ernest R. Groves and Gladys Hoagland Groves, *Parents and Children* (Philadelphia: Lippincott, 1928), p. 67.

107 **mental hygiene movement**: My discussion draws on Sol Cohen, "The Mental Hygiene Movement, the Development of Personality and the School: The Medicalization of American Education," *History of Education Quarterly*, Summer 1983, pp. 123–49; Fred Matthews, "In Defense of Common Sense: Mental Hygiene as Ideology and Mentality in Twentieth-Century America," *Prospects* 2 (Winter 1979): 459–516; Nathan Hale, *Freud and the Americans: The Beginnings of Psychoanalysis in the United States, 1876–1917* (New York: Oxford University Press, 1971).

107 **"the golden period"**: William Alanson White, "Childhood: The Golden Period for Mental Hygiene," *Mental Hygiene* 4 (April 1920).

108 **survey by the National Society for the Study of Education**: Barbara Beatty, *Preschool Education in America: The Culture of Young Children from the Colonial Era to the Present* (New Haven: Yale University Press, 1995), p. 168.

108 **"To keep a pre-school child"**: Helen T. Woolley, "The Nursery School: A Response to New Needs," in *Concerning Parents*, p. 52.

109 **By comparison, the preschool child**: See William Alanson White, *The Mental Hygiene of Childhood* (1919 ed.; reprint, New York: Arno, 1980).

109 **"a real mental life"**: Thom, *Child Management*, p. 3.

109 **"Hyper-activity, restlessness"**: Thom, "The Importance of the Early Years," in *Concerning Parents*, p. 103.

109 **"shut-in personality"**: Cohen, "The Mental Hygiene Movement," p. 129.

109 **"clinging-vine variety"**: Eunice Fuller Barnard, "Behavior of Children Is Charted and Tested," *New York Times*, Sept. 8, 1929, collected in Rothman, *The Family*, p. 107.

109 **term associated with the Freudian renegade**: See Alfred Adler and associates, *Guiding the Child: On the Principles of Individual Psychology* (New York: Gruenberg, 1930).

109 **"[build] up adequate self-reliance"**: Arnold Gesell, *The Mental Growth of the Pre-School Child: A Psychological Outline of Normal Development from Birth to the Sixth Year, Including a System of Developmental Diagnosis* (New York: Macmillan, 1925), p. 227.

110 **"The problem child has become the problems of the child"**: Cohen, "The Mental Hygiene Movement," p. 135.

110 **"The hygiene and mental hygiene"**: W. T. Root, "The Individual in the Group," in *Concerning Parents*, p. 194.

110 **"We must first have a live child"**: White, "Childhood: The Golden Period for Mental Hygiene," p. 265.

110 **"We had a little girl"**: Joseph Brennemann, "Pediatric Psychology and the Child Guidance Movement," *Journal of Pediatrics* 2, no. 1 (January 1933): 22.

111 **"turning the beam on the parents" to "If [parents] feel unable"**: "Childish Parents," *New York Times*, Nov. 24, 1928, collected in Rothman, *The Family*, p. 105.

111 **"an environment in which to live"**: Thom, "The Importance of the Early Years," in *Concerning Parents*, p. 99.

111 **"We seem to think"**: Woolley, "The Nursery School," in ibid., p. 67.

112 **"willingness to utilize"**: Kenworthy, "From Childhood to Youth," in ibid., p. 126.

112 **"Plasticity" of habit**: Thom, *Child Management*, p. 2.

112 **"liable to fall victim"**: Leta S. Hollingworth, "Getting Away from the Family," in *Concerning Parents*, p. 75.

112 **"is not an end in itself"**: Douglas A. Thom, "New Ideas About Obedience," *Parents' Magazine*, November 1929. See also Lois Hayden Meek, "Obedience and Character," *Children: The Magazine for Parents* 3, no. 1 (January 1928): 9.

112 **"it is evident that some outworn conception"**: William E. Blatz and Helen Bott, "Discipline for Parents," *Parents' Magazine*, October 1930, p. 22.

112 **"excessive worry, anxiety, and needless fear"**: Thom, "The Importance of the Early Years," in *Concerning Parents*, p. 101.

112 **"objective-minded, matter-of-fact child"**: Ernest R. Groves, "Modern Youth Needs Modern Parents," *Children: The Magazine for Parents* 3, no. 10 (October 1928): 45.

112 **"affection and serenity"**: Elton G. Mayo, "The Father in the Present-Day Home," in *Concerning Parents*, p. 42.

112 **"the spirit of mutual confidence"**: typescript of a radio talk by Mrs. Howard S. Gans. See also Thom, *Child Management*, p. 5: "To the child the parent should be companion, friend, and confidant."

112 **"a little more of a treat"**: Woolley, "The Nursery School," in *Concerning Parents*, p. 65.

112 **"too much overhead interference"**: Calvert McCay, "This Serious Business of Being a Father," *Parents' Magazine* 3, no. 10 (October 1928): 13.

112 **dad who felt generally "ostracized"**: Harry Irving Shumway, "Every Baby Needs a Father," *Parents' Magazine* 4, no. 12 (December 1929): 91.

113 **"said 'yeep' "**: ibid.

113 **"to have some life of her own"**: Woolley, "The Nursery School," in *Concerning Parents*, p. 64.

113 **"smother love"; "describe what happens"**: Sidonie Matsner Gruenberg, "Autobiography," p. 316, Sidonie Matsner Gruenberg and Benjamin Gruenberg Papers, Library of Congress, Washington, DC.

113 **"greater leisure and freedom"; "to impress herself"**: Groves, *Parents and Children*, p. 121.

113 **In postwar analyses**: Rothman, *The Family*, p. x.

113 **"the living, miraculous"; "to stalk and catch"**: Dorothy Canfield Fisher, *The Home-Maker* (1925; reprint, Chicago: Academy, 1983), pp. 77, 70.

114 **"The fact that the problems of parents"**: Kenworthy, "From Childhood to Youth," in *Concerning Parents*, p. 127.

114 **"hidden conflicts and emotional turmoils"**: quoted in Schlossman, "Formative Era in American Parent Education," p. 24.

114 **"an affliction throughout his life" to "emotional bondage"**: Groves, *Parents and Children*, pp. 40, 122, 5.

115 **Postwar adults were transfixed**: Paula Fass, *The Damned and the Beautiful: American Youth in the 1920's* (New York: Oxford University Press, 1977).

115 **"It would be interesting to read"**: Brennemann, "Pediatric Psychology and the Child Guidance Movement," p. 18.

115 **"wholesale education of the laity"**: Brennemann, "The Menace of Psychiatry," p. 383.

116 **"it is beyond the capacity"**: Rochelle Beck, "The White House Conferences on Children: An Historical Perspective," *Harvard Education Review* 43 (November 1973): 657.

116 **"would hardly dare"**: Brennemann, "Pediatric Psychology and the Child Guidance Movement," p. 18.

116 **"great child study"**: ibid., p. 16.

116 **"heartrending" account**: Brennemann, "The Menace of Psychiatry," p. 399.

116 **"well-nigh overcome"**: Quilliard, *Child Study Discussion Records*, p. 71.

117 **"increasingly frequent large sectional" to "The fruits of present research"**: Leslie Ray Marston, "Present Tendencies in Research in Child Development," unpublished paper presented at the Second Conference on Research in Child Development, Washington, DC, May 5–7, 1927, Box 106, Arnold Gesell Papers, Library of Congress, Washington, DC., p. 1.

117 **"in which popular interest" to "Notwithstanding the volume"**: ibid., p. 3.

117 **"loves science"**: Brennemann, "Pediatric Psychology and the Child Guidance Movement," p. 13.

117 **"Child Psychology between confinements"**: "The Business of Parenthood," *Harper's* 162, no. 968 (January 1931): 178.

118 **"The technique of propaganda and instruction"**: quoted in Brennemann, "Pediatric Psychology and the Child Guidance Movement," p. 25.

118 **"in a mood for magic"**: David Kennedy, *Freedom from Fear: The American People in Depression and War, 1929–1945* (New York: Oxford University Press, 1999), p. 43.

118 **"it is the business of behavioristic psychology"**: John B. Watson, *Behaviorism* (New York: Norton, 1930), p. 11.

118 **"Prediction and control"**: Arnold Gesell, handwritten notes, Box 141, Arnold Gesell Papers. See also Gesell, *The Guidance of Mental Growth in Infant and Child*, p. 146.

119 **"watches his weight"**: Kenneth Macgowan, "The Adventure of the Behaviorist," *The New Yorker* 4, no. 33 (Oct. 6, 1928): 32.

119 **"an 'enfant terrible' "**: Brennemann, "Pediatric Psychology and the Child Guidance Movement," p. 18.

119 **"the chief show piece"**: Macgowan, "The Adventure of the Behaviorist," p. 30.

119 **"Give me a dozen healthy infants"**: John B. Watson, "What the Nursery Has to Say About Instincts," in Carl Murchison, ed., *Psychologies of 1925* (Worcester, MA: Clark University Press, 1928), p. 10.

119 **"shake hands"**: John B. Watson, *The Psychological Care of Infant and Child* (New York: Norton, 1928), p. 81.

120 **"For the first time"**: advertisement in the *New York Times Book Review*, June 17, 1928, p. 23.

120 **"clear level-head"**: G. Stanley Hall recommendation for Arnold Gesell, Jan. 3, 1907, Box 28, Arnold Gesell Papers.

120 **"What if he could not verify"**: Arnold Gesell in Edwin C. Boring et al., *History of Psychology in Autobiography* (New York: Russell & Russell, 1952), 4:126–27.

120 **"an individual, after all"**: Gesell, *The Mental Growth of the Pre-School Child*, p. 226.

120 **"growth *is* lawful"**: Arnold Gesell, *Infancy and Human Growth* (New York: Macmillan, 1928), p. 21.

120 **"delightful freshness"**: Hugh Chaplin, review of *The Mental Growth of the Pre-School Child* in *Child Health Literature*, n.d., in Box 135, Arnold Gesell Papers.

120 **"wide distribution"**: Lewis Terman, review of *The Mental Growth of the Pre-School Child* in *Science* 61, no. 1582 (Apr. 24, 1925): 446.

120 **"the *first* systematic piece of work"**: Arnold Gesell letter to Beatrice Chandler Gesell, May 21, 1925, Arnold Gesell Papers.

120 **"basking in the light"**: Gesell, *Infancy and Human Growth*, p. 61.

120 **"outstanding scientific contribution"**: citation in *Parents' Magazine* 4, no. 4 (April 1929): 68.

121 **"Infants . . . already being matched"**: Brennemann, "The Menace of Psychiatry," p. 388.

FIVE: *The Misbehaviorist*

122 **"a strange orgy"; "appetite of Americans"**: quoted in William Leuchtenburg, *The Perils of Prosperity: 1924–1932* (Chicago: University of Chicago Press, 1958), p. 154.

123 **"parents today are incompetent"**: John B. Watson, "If You're a Failure—Change Your Personality," *NEA Magazine*, Nov. 3–4, 1928.

123 **"rotary plan"**: "Urges Rotary Plan to Train Children," *New York Times*, Mar. 4, 1928, collected in Rothman, *The Family*, p. 105.

123 **"Instead of leveling"**: Lillian G. Genn, interview with Dr. John B. Watson, "The Behaviorist Looks at Youth," *Independent Woman: A Magazine for Business and Professional Women* 7, no. 10 (October 1928): 479.

123 **"small hand book"**: John B. Watson, *Psychological Care of Infant and Child* (New York: Norton, 1928), p. 1.

123 **"fine well-modeled face"; "certain experiments"**: Genn, "The Behaviorist Looks at Youth," p. 439.

123 **"scientific material" as the basis of his "convictions"**: Watson, *Psychological Care of Infant and Child*, p. 1.

123 **"a common sense work"**: advertisement in the *New York Times Book Review*, June 17, 1928, p. 23.

124 **"Parents write"**: ibid.

124 **"mawkish"; "develop from within"**: Watson, *Psychological Care of Infant and Child*, pp. 82, 40.

124 **"the behaviorist does not know"; "prejudice against lab work"**: ibid., pp. 4, 16.

124 **"unquestionably unfitted"; "Even in the homes"**: ibid., pp. 6, 5.

124 **"Won't you then remember"**: ibid., p. 87.

125 **"I am sorry"**: letter from L. Emmett Holt, Jr., to Linda Mairs Holt, Sept. 20, 1926, NYU Medical Archives.

125 **"The civilized world"**: Arthur Wallace Calhoun, "The Child Mind as a Social Product," in V. F. Calverton and Samuel D. Schmalhausen, eds., *The New Generation: The Intimate Problems of Modern Parents and Children* (New York: Macauley, 1930), p. 81.

125 **"Dr. Watson's Book on Child-Nurture"**: headline of review by Dr. George A. Dorsey, *The Book Herald*, Apr. 8, 1924.

125 **"Become the Billy Sunday" to "Watsonism has become gospel"**: review of *The Ways of Behaviorism* by Mortimer Adler, *New York Evening Post*, June 16, 1928.

126 **"coarse, rude, vulgar"; "What makes you believe"**: quoted in Mark Sullivan, *Our Times: 1900–1925* (New York: Scribner's, 1936), 5:597.

126 **50,000 copies**: according to advertisement in *Parents' Magazine* 5, no. 12 (December 1930): 67.

126 **"the main emotional habits"**: John B. Watson, *The Ways of Behaviorism* (New York: Harper & Bros., 1928), p. 53.

126 **"the unverbalized"; "but the totality"**: ibid., pp. 97, 120.

127 **Watson's lineage**: Kerry W. Buckley's *Mechanical Man: John Broadus Watson and the Beginnings of Behaviorism* (New York: Guilford, 1989) is a useful biography.

127 **sent a new suit of clothes**: ibid., p. 4.

127 **"handling tools"**: John Broadus Watson autobiography, in Carl Murchison, ed., *A History of Psychology in Autobiography* (Worcester, MA: Clark University Press, 1936), 3:271.

128 **"Those years made me bitter"**: ibid., 3:272.

128 **"behaviorist self-correcting"**: Watson, *The Ways of Behaviorism*, p. 115.

128 **"better preparation"; "real university"**: quoted in Buckley, *Mechanical Man*, p. 1.

128 **"useful" institution**: ibid., p. 34.

128 **"I felt at once"; "frightfully busy years"**: Watson autobiography, p. 273.

129 **"Dewey's favorite word"; "Chicago has a School of Thought!"**: William James, "The Chicago School," *Psychological Bulletin* 1, no. 1 (Jan. 15, 1904): 1–2.

129 **"the spark was not there"; "I never knew"**: Watson autobiography, p. 274.

129 **"stream of activity"**: John Broadus Watson, "Studies in Infant Psychology," *Scientific Monthly* 13, no. 6 (December 1921): 494.

129 **Jacques Loeb**: Watson autobiography, p. 273; see also Buckley, *Mechanical Man*, pp. 46, 41; also Philip J. Pauly, *Controlling Life: Jacques Loeb and the Engineering Ideal in Biology* (Berkeley: University of California Press, 1987), p. 7.

129   **For his dissertation:** Buckley, *Mechanical Man*, pp. 42–43.

129   **"I worked night and day" to "in a way":** Watson autobiography, pp. 273, 274.

130   **"infantile carry-overs"; "one of the most":** Watson, *The Ways of Behaviorism*, p.73.

130   **"there was something in the dark" to "I carry that inferiority":** speech on advertising strategies, Apr. 18, 1934, John B. Watson Papers, Library of Congress, Washington, DC.

130   **"deep-seated inferiority"; "to save me from a little":** Watson autobiography, pp. 274, 275.

130   **"is enjoying a great 'boom' ":** quoted in Buckley, *Mechanical Man*, p. 47.

130   **"I was always uncomfortable":** Watson autobiography, p. 276.

130   **"began to perfect":** Watson autobiography, p. 277.

131   **"The whole tenor":** ibid., p. 276.

131   **"Two kids are enough":** quoted in Buckley, *Mechanical Man*, pp. 35–36.

131   **"a rising tide of discontent":** Willard Harrell and Ross Harrison, "The Rise and Fall of Behaviorism," *Journal of General Psychology* 18 (1938): 376.

131   **"an objective standard":** quoted in Buckley, *Mechanical Man*, p. 71.

131   **"Psychology as the Behaviorist Views It" to "no dividing line between":** Watson, "Psychology as the Behaviorist Views It," *Psychological Review* 20, no. 2 (March 1913): 158.

132   **"it is a far more difficult field":** John B. Watson letter to Robert Yerkes, Oct. 18, 1916, Archives of the History of American Psychology, Akron, OH.

132   **"played havoc with my work":** Watson autobiography, p. 277.

133   **"almost daily observation":** John B. Watson, "What the Nursery Has to Say About Instincts," in Carl Murchison, ed., *Psychologies of 1925* (Worcester, MA: Clark University Press, 1928), p. 17.

133   **"unlearned equipment" to "wonderfully 'good' baby":** ibid., p. 21.

133   **"stolid and phlegmatic":** John B. Watson, *Psychology from the Standpoint of a Behaviorist*, 3rd rev. ed. (Philadelphia: Lippincott, 1929), p. 241.

133   **"infants are really":** Watson, *Psychological Care of Infant and Child*, p. 17.

134   **"experimental work has been done"; "persist and modify personality":** John B. Watson and Rosalie Rayner, "Conditioned Emotional Reactions," *Journal of Experimental Psychology* 3, no. 1 (February 1920): 1, 12.

134   **"freshen the reaction":** ibid., p. 8.

134   **"When only about six inches"; "a marked fear response":** ibid., p. 9.

135   **"took hold of his left hand":** ibid., p. 11.

135   **All along, they revealed:** See Franz Samelson, "J. B. Watson's Little Albert, Cyril Burt's Twins, and the Need for a Critical Science," *American Psychologist* 35 (July 1980): 621. For another very interesting article on the many distorted accounts of Watson's experiments on Albert, see Ben Harris, "Whatever Happened to Little Albert?" *American Psychologist* 34 (February 1979): 151–59.

135   **"Our own view":** Watson and Rayner, "Conditioned Emotional Reactions," p. 12.

135   **"All of this work"; "I went to New York":** Watson autobiography, p. 279.

135   **"My total reactions":** quoted in Buckley, *Mechanical Man*, pp. 124, 128.

135   **"rub off the academic":** Watson autobiography, p. 280.

135   **"understanding counsel":** ibid., p. 279.

136   **"studying the rubber boot" to "growth of a sales curve":** ibid., pp. 279–80.

136   **"personalities . . . can be changed":** Watson, "If You're a Failure—Change Your Personality."

136   **"guts to stick"; "the zebra":** Watson, *The Ways of Behaviorism*, p. 138.

136　**"more childish than I imagined" to "his efficiency depends on these things":** William Thomas letter to Ethel Sturges Dummer, Feb. 8, 1921, quoted in Buckley, *Mechanical Man*, p. 131.

136　**"rush job"; "because I did not know enough":** Watson autobiography, p. 280.

137　**"have sold himself to the public":** ibid., p. 281.

137　**"impossible to put a grandmother":** Julia Grant, *Raising Baby by the Book: The Education of American Mothers* (New Haven: Yale University Press, 1998), p. 141.

137　**"medicine men":** Watson, *The Ways of Behaviorism*, p. 79.

137　**walking collection of the tensions of the time:** Lucille C. Birnbaum, "Behaviorism in the 1920's," *American Quarterly* 7 (1955): 20.

137　**"terrific superstructure of theory"; "position, however":** Watson, *The Ways of Behaviorism*, p. 62.

138　**"I am going beyond my facts":** Watson, "What the Nursery Has to Say About Instincts," p. 10.

138　**"There is no ideal system":** Watson, *Psychological Care of Infant and Child*, p. 184.

138　**"I believe that the internal structure":** ibid., p. 186.

138　**"iconoclast from Baltimore":** from Douglas C. Stenerson, *H. L. Mencken: Iconoclast from Baltimore* (Chicago: University of Chicago Press, 1971).

138　**In one of the more peculiar escapades:** Howard Markel and Frank A. Oski, *The H. L. Mencken Baby Book* (Philadelphia: Hanley & Belfus, 1990). In their introduction, they recount the story of Mencken and Hirshberg's collaboration, and then reprint the book.

139　**"The Slaughter of the Innocents"; "of no less than seven":** ibid., p. 27, 28.

139　**"overcoddling"; "infantile ills":** ibid., p. 33.

139　**"She loves [her child]":** ibid., p. 31.

139　**"Kissing the baby after it has been fed":** ibid., p. 33.

139　**"Is the picture overdrawn?":** ibid., p. 29.

139　**"the world's greatest specialist":** ibid., p. 21.

139　**Word was soon to leak out:** H. L. Mencken, *My Life as Author and Editor*, ed. Jonathan Yardley (New York: Knopf, 1993), p. 29.

140　**"infant farms":** Watson autobiography, p. 281.

140　**"Never make an audience":** H. A. Overstreet, *Influencing Human Behavior* (New York: People's Institute Publishing Co., 1925), p. 76.

140　**"tell [the consumer] something":** Buckley, *Mechanical Man*, p. 137.

141　**Watson raised the question:** Paula Fass, in *The Damned and the Beautiful: American Youth in the 1920's* (New York: Oxford University Press, 1977), makes a version of this point about Watson: see pp. 100–106.

141　**"The home we have with us":** Watson, *Psychological Care of Infant and Child*, p. 6.

141　**"mothers are getting modern"; "Kissing the baby to death":** ibid., p. 70.

141　**"at bottom a sex-seeking response":** ibid., p. 80.

141　**"stroking and touching its skin"; "Hard to believe?":** ibid., p. 43.

141　**"All affection":** ibid., p. 72.

142　**"Mothers just don't know":** ibid., p. 44.

142　**"child gets honeycombed":** ibid., p. 75.

142　**"nest habits":** ibid., p. 85.

142　**"conquer the difficulties":** ibid., p. 79.

142　**"Somehow I can't help wishing":** ibid., p. 84.

142　**"dull as dishwater":** John B. Watson, "The Psychology of the Consumer," speech, John B. Watson Papers.

142　**"[a] few minutes of gentle":** *Infant Care* (Washington, DC: U.S. Government

Printing Office, 1929), reprinted in David J. Rothman and Sheila M. Rothman, eds., *Child Rearing Literature of Twentieth Century America* (New York: Arno, 1972), p. 51.

142 **"developmental" variations**: under new section, "Development of the Baby," ibid., pp. 2–7.

142 **"dealing with a sensitive being"**: Mrs. Max West, *Infant Care* (Washington, DC: U.S. Government Printing Office, 1921), p. 46.

143 **"parents *slant*"; "method of handling"**: Watson, *Psychological Care of Infant and Child*, pp. 38, 39.

143 **"shape itself properly"**: John B. Watson, *Behaviorism* (New York: Norton, 1930), p. 303.

143 **"thousands of . . . things"**: Watson, *Psychological Care of Infant and Child*, p. 48.

143 **"positive method of training"**: ibid., p. 65.

143 **"rapping the fingers"; "appropriate commonsense"**: ibid., pp. 63, 64.

143 **"Fears do get built in"**: ibid., p. 65.

143 **"I swallow Watson whole"**: Grant, *Raising Baby by the Book*, p. 141.

143 **"uncensored play"**: Watson, *Psychological Care of Infant and Child*, p. 125.

143 **"*all other stimuli*"**: ibid., p. 136.

143 **"manipulation of his universe"**: ibid., p. 79.

144 **"dependent behavior"; "dawdling, loud conversation"**: ibid., p. 122.

144 **"steam roller the child"; "person in life"**: ibid., p. 150.

144 **"rough pattern"**: Watson, *Ways of Behaviorism*, p. 63.

144 **"*happy child free as air*"**: Watson, *Psychological Care of Infant and Child*, p. 150.

144 **"There is a sensible way"**: ibid., p. 81.

144 **"Never hug and kiss them"**: ibid., pp. 81–82.

145 **"the home is not so much insufficient"; "charming woman" whose "children were always treated"**: John Mason Brown and the editors of the *Ladies' Home Journal, The Ladies' Home Journal Treasury: Selected from the Complete Files* (New York: Simon & Schuster, 1956), pp. 124, 123.

145 **"a little bit queer"**: John B. Watson, introduction to G. V. Hamilton and Kenneth Macgowan, *What Is Wrong with Marriage* (New York: Boni, 1929), p. xiii.

145 **"an astonishingly frank chapter"**: Dorsey, "Dr. Watson's Book on Child-Nurture Called as Epoch-Making as Darwin's Findings," *The Book Herald*, Apr. 8, 1924. In the fall of 1928, *Children: The Magazine for Parents* was also endorsing an open parental attitude toward discussing sex: Karl de Schweinitz, "Sex Instruction— When? How?" *Children* 3, no. 10 (November 1928): 22.

145 **"talk it out club"; "a safeguard to health and sanity"**: Watson, *Psychological Care of Infant and Child*, p. 163.

145 **"golden opportunity to establish *rapport*"; "not just along sex lines"**: ibid., p. 160.

145 **"clearing house"**: ibid., p. 163.

145 **"to get [a child] *to formulate*"**: ibid., p. 162.

145 **"the danger of too strong"**: ibid., p. 163.

146 **"kiddish trick"; "time and energy"**: ibid., p. 177.

146 **"successful and skillful sex companion"; "To achieve skill in this art"**: ibid., pp. 181–82.

146 **"above all, we have tried"; "the fixed molds that our parents"**: ibid., p. 186.

146 **"boundless absorption in activity"**: ibid., p. 187.

147 **"The whole world has heard"**: Rosalie Rayner Watson, "I Am the Mother of a Behaviorist's Sons," *Parents' Magazine* 5, no. 12 (December 1930): 16.

147 **"I deprecate the onslaught"**: Bertrand Russell, "Are Parents Bad for Children?" *Parents' Magazine* 5, no. 5 (May 1930): 19.

147 **"the surprise is as great"; "behaviorist theories"**: "Are Parents Necessary?" *New York Times*, Apr. 30, 1930, collected in Rothman, *The Family*, p. 106.

148 **The same month**: Harold Laski, "The Limitations of the Expert," *Harper's Magazine* 162, no. 967 (December 1930): 101–110.

148 **"our function should be"**: quoted in Beck, "The White House Conferences on Children: An Historical Perspective," *Harvard Education Review* 43 (November 1973): 657.

148 **"If bewilderment"; "any contact"**: Ada Hart Arlitt, *The Child from One to Twelve: Psychology for Parents* (New York: Whittlesey, 1931), p. 214.

148 **"talking out all tricks of trade"**: Watson, *Behaviorism*, p. x.

149 **"Dr. John B. Watson has two young sons"**: Rosalie R. Watson, "I Am the Mother of a Behaviorist's Sons," p. 17.

149 **"homey" to "My regrets are perhaps"**: ibid., p. 18.

150 **"My most earnest wish"; "Now both my boys"**: ibid., p. 16.

150 **"to go through life"**: ibid., pp. 17–18.

150 **"youngsters have learned"**: ibid., p. 18.

151 **"I hang on to my adolescence" to "They will find love"**: ibid., p. 67.

151 **James Watson was eager:** He shared his reminiscences of his youth with me by taping answers to a series of questions early in 1999. All the quotations come from the tape.

152 **"many a reader . . . upset"**: Kenneth Macgowan, "The Adventure of the Behaviorist," *The New Yorker*, 4, no. 33 (Oct. 6, 1928): 31.

SIX: *The Anatomist of Normalcy*

154 **"cultural workshop"; "developmental philosophy"**: Arnold Gesell and Frances Ilg, in collaboration with Louise B. Ames, Janet Learned, Glenna E. Bullis, *Infant and Child in the Culture of Today* (hereafter referred to as *Infant and Child*) (Harper & Bros., 1943), pp. 4, 5.

155 **"There was this handsome Gesell" to "Everybody was either"**: interview #48 in Milton J. E. Senn Child Development Oral History Interviews, National Library of Medicine, Washington, DC.

155 **"Yale, it seems" to "the poor sprite"**: "Tom Thumb Yale Bowl," *The New Yorker* 6, no. 49 (Jan. 24, 1931): 12.

155 **"delineate what the generic individual"**: Arnold Gesell, *The Mental Growth of the Pre-School Child* (New York: Macmillan, 1925), p. 26.

155 **"Thousands of records"**: "Tom Thumb Yale Bowl," p. 12.

156 **"remarkable equanimity"**: William Kessen, ed., *The Child* (New York: Wiley, 1965), p. 209.

156 **"she knows what is happening" to "watch in a sense of security"**: Arnold Gesell's film *The Study of Infant Behavior at the Yale Psycho-Clinic* (1931).

156 **"a mild and suffused light"**: article about Gesell in the *Boston Evening Transcript*, magazine section, Jan. 31, 1931, clippings, Box 253, Arnold Gesell Papers, Library of Congress, Washington, DC.

156 **"must not peer"**: Arnold Gesell, *The Mental Growth of the Pre-School Child: A Psychological Outline of Normal Development from Birth to the Sixth Year, Including a System of Developmental Diagnosis* (New York: Macmillan, 1925), p. 401.

156 **"fine pincerlike prehension"**: Gesell's film *The Study of Infant Behavior at the Yale Psycho-Clinic* (1931).

156 **"organized by inherent inner mechanics"**: quoted from Arnold Gesell, "Maturation and Infant Behavior Pattern," *Psychological Review* 36 (1929), in Hamilton Cravens, *Before Head Start: The Iowa Station and America's Children* (Chapel Hill: University of North Carolina Press, 1993), p. 94.

157 **"infallible memory"**: Arnold Gesell, "How Science Studies the Child," *The Scientific Monthly*, 1932, p. 266.

157 **"much child guidance"; "to safeguard physical growth"**: Gesell's film *The Study of Infant Behavior at the Yale Psycho-Clinic* (1931).

157 **"quasi-primitive"; "growth is predetermined"**: Arnold Gesell, *The Guidance of Mental Growth in Infant and Child* (New York: Macmillan, 1930), p. 146. Steven L. Schlossman in "Before Home Start: Notes Toward a History of Parent Education in America, 1897–1929," *Harvard Educational Review* 36, no. 3 (August 1976): 460–61, agrees that the common portrait of Gesell as "easygoing maturationist" does not fit, certainly not between 1910 and 1930. Even during the 1930s and 1940s, the champion of intensive developmental supervision was never remotely laissez-faire in his views, as he took pains to emphasize.

157 **"plasticity"**: Gesell, *The Guidance of Mental Growth in Infant and Child*, p. 297.

157 **"Science is exploring"**: Gesell's film *The Study of Infant Behavior at the Yale Psycho-Clinic* (1931).

157 **"simplicity and beauty"; "build up attitudes"**: Arnold Gesell, "The Cinema as an Instrument for Parent Education," *Parent Education* 2, no. 4 (Nov. 15, 1935), published by the National Council of Parent Education, p. 9.

157 **"prescriptive, rule-of-thumb"**: Gesell, *The Guidance of Mental Growth in Infant and Child*, p. 134.

157 **"making over the child"; "the natural patterns"**: "The Early Years of Mental Growth," Box 141, Arnold Gesell Papers.

158 **"optimal growth"**: Gesell, *The Guidance of Mental Growth in Infant and Child*, p. 142.

158 **"wholesome attitudes"**: Arnold Gesell, typescript of paper delivered at American Academy of Pediatrics "round table on mental health," Nov. 8, 1942, "Individualization of Infant Care," p. 2, Arnold Gesell Papers.

158 **"in the most dignified" to "Although no particular kind of garment"**: department store promotional aids for the Yale University Films of Child Development, Box 136, Arnold Gesell Papers.

158 **"inborn tendency"; "suffers less"**: Gesell, *The Guidance of Mental Growth in Infant and Child*, p. 198.

158 **"almost inexhaustible"**: Arnold Gesell, "The Early Years of Mental Growth," Box 141, Arnold Gesell Papers.

158 **"growing mind"**: Gesell, *The Guidance of Mental Growth in Infant and Child*, p. 147.

159 **"parents will attune"**: ibid., p. 134.

159 **"resent . . . strenuously"**: John B. Watson, *Psychological Care of Infant and Child* (New York: Norton, 1928), p. 5.

159 **"very spontaneously"**: Arnold Gesell, 1941 notes about C. Anderson Aldrich's talk on "How to Get Parents to Think in Developmental Terms," Box 47, Arnold Gesell Papers.

159 **"Even parents should not consider themselves grownups"**: Gesell, *The Guidance of Mental Growth in Infant and Child*, p. 133.

159 **"two-street village"**: Arnold Gesell's autobiography, in Edward G. Boring et al.,

eds., *A History of Psychology in Autobiography* (New York: Russell & Russell, 1968), 4:123.

160 **"sneered at"**: obituary of Gerhard Gesell, *Buffalo County Journal*, Mar. 22, 1906. All information about Gesell's parents comes from Family Correspondence, Box 7, Arnold Gesell Papers.

160 **"photographer and proprietor"**: letterhead from Mar. 27, 1899, letter.

160 **"making his sons and daughters"; "that Americans were becoming subservient"**: funeral oration for Gerhard Gesell.

160 **"Donnerwetter"**: Christine Giesen Gesell letter to Arnold Gesell, Apr. 30, 1895.

160 **"so admirably poised"**: Christine Giesen Gesell letter to Arnold Gesell, Mar. 24, 1903.

160 **"Arnold comes to you pure"**: Christine Giesen Gesell letter to Beatrice Chandler, Feb. 17, 1909.

161 **"I have never received"**: Arnold Gesell letter to his parents, July 28, 1895, Box 1, Arnold Gesell Papers.

161 **"the state's motto"**: Walter R. Miles, "Arnold Lucius Gesell," in *Biographical Memoirs* (New York: Columbia University Press, 1964), 37:58.

161 **"the tranquil beauties of Nature"**: Gesell's autobiography, p. 124.

161 **"We made six loads hay"**: undated letter from Arnold Gesell to parents, Box 1, Arnold Gesell Papers.

161 **"I had to be perfectly assured" to "I will not go in any water"**: Arnold Gesell letter to his parents from St. Paul, 1894, ibid.

161 **"young seriousness"**: Gesell's autobiography, p. 125.

162 **"the wonders of the new electrical era"**: ibid., p. 124.

162 **"I'm glad that you're all" to "Somehow or other"**: Arnold Gesell letter to his siblings, July 15, 1894, Box 1, Arnold Gesell Papers.

162 **"I like to see you get"**: Arnold Gesell letter to his sister Bertha, Nov. 28, 1897, ibid.

162 **"He is ambitious"**: letter of recommendation for Arnold Gesell from the chairman of the Teachers Committee of the Board of Education, Chippewa Falls, WI, June 9, 1906, ibid.

163 **"ardent, exuberant"**: Gesell's autobiography, p. 127.

163 **The Stanford-Binet test**: Robert Sears, *Your Ancients Revisited: A History of Child Development* (Chicago: University of Chicago Press, 1975), p. 29.

163 **"to make a thoroughgoing study"**: Gesell's autobiography, p. 128.

163 **"the problem of exceptional school children"**: Gesell, *The Mental Growth of the Pre-School Child*, p. 39.

164 **"State Director of Child Hygiene"**: Arnold Gesell letter to Beatrice Chandler, 1915, Box 1, Arnold Gesell Papers.

164 **"personal bit of braggadocio"**: Arnold Gesell letter to Beatrice Chandler Gesell, May 21, 1925, ibid.

164 **"vast amount of descriptive material"**: Gesell, *The Mental Growth of the Pre-School Child*, p. 26.

165 **"orderly systematization" to "clinically serviceable"**: ibid., p. 42.

165 **"enable us to estimate"; "however sublime the fatuity"**: ibid., p. 419.

165 **"broader and . . . continuous"**: ibid., p. 441.

165 **"solid ground for generalization"; "danger of over-simplification"**: ibid., p. 228.

165 **"a judicious amount"**: ibid., p. 404.

165 **"confessedly preliminary"**: ibid., p. 5.

165 **"the term motor development"**: ibid., p. 210.

166 **"as a detached individual"**: ibid., p. 407.

166 **"development of personality make-up" to "so dynamic"**: ibid., p. 285.

166 **"are readily misused"**: Gesell, *The Guidance of Mental Growth in Infant and Child*, p. 141.

166 **"diffuse and prolix"**: Arnold Gesell, "The Individual in Infancy," in Carl Murchison, ed., *The Foundations of Experimental Psychology* (Worcester, MA: Clark University Press, 1929), p. 636.

166 **"sketchy state"**: Gesell, *The Mental Growth of the Pre-School Child*, p. 421.

166 **"no attempt . . . to establish"**: Lewis Terman, review of *The Mental Growth of the Pre-School Child* in *Science* 61, no. 1582 (Apr. 24, 1925): 445.

166 **"a homelike studio unit"**: Gesell's autobiography, p. 132.

166 **Louise Bates Ames and Frances Ilg**: Louise Bates Ames Papers, Library of Congress, Washington, DC; as well as Julia Grant, *Raising Baby by the Book* (New Haven: Yale University Press, 1998), pp. 213–14.

166 **"She thought"**: Louise Bates Ames Papers, Box 51, folder 7. She went on to say "I figured that he could do so much more for me; he opened so many doors, he offered such an opportunity."

167 **"He had an idea"**: Milton J. E. Senn, *Insights on the Child Development Movement in the United States*, Monographs of the Society for Research in Child Development, Serial 161, vol. 40, nos. 3–4 (August 1975): 32.

167 **fifty-eight stages of "pellet behavior"; fifty-three stages of "rattle behavior"**: Esther Thelen and Karen A. Adolph, "Arnold L. Gesell: The Paradox of Nature and Nurture," *Developmental Psychology* 28, no. 3 (1992): 376.

167 **"cinematograph"**: Senn, *Insights on the Child Development Movement in the United States*, p. 33.

168 **Berkeley Growth Study**: Cravens, *Before Head Start*, pp. 66, 99–100. See also Sears, *Your Ancients Revisited*, p. 52.

168 **"Don't worry"**: "Comments on Arnold Gesell and His Work," 1964, Box 3, Louise Bates Ames Papers.

168 **"It might be contended"**: Arnold Gesell and Helen Thompson, *Infant Behavior: Its Genesis and Growth* (New York: McGraw-Hill, 1934), p. 257.

168 **"in spite of its inexhaustible complexity"**: Gesell, "The Study and Guidance of Infant Behavior," 1931, Box 141, Arnold Gesell Papers.

168 **"vast array"; "be put to uses"**: *Time* 24 (Sept. 24, 1934): 33.

169 **"maturation plays"**: Arnold Gesell and Helen Thompson, "Learning and Growth in Identical Infant Twins: An Experimental Study by the Method of Co-Twin Control," *Genetic Psychology Monograph* 6, no. 1 (1929): 114.

169 **"the twins of Amsterdam Avenue"**: quoted in Paul M. Dennis, " 'Johnny's a Gentleman, but Jimmie's a Mug': Press Coverage During the 1930s of Myrtle McGraw's Study of Johnny and Jimmy Woods," *Journal of the History of the Behavioral Sciences* 25 (October 1989): 364. My discussion of this episode draws on Dennis's article.

169 **"incredible twins"**: Eva V. B. Hansl, "Incredible Twins," *Parents' Magazine* 10, no. 5 (May 1935): 24.

169 **" 'Conditioned' Infant Excels"**: headline in *Literary Digest* 18 (1933); see Dennis, " 'Johnny's a Gentleman, but Jimmie's a Mug,' " pp. 368 ff., 33.

170 **"Experiments Prove Value"; "shoot the chutes"**: ibid., p. 361.

170 **"negated Gesell's famous maturational theory"**: Myrtle McGraw, *Growth: A Study of Johnny and Jimmy* (1935; reprint, New York: Arno, 1975), "40 Years Reflections of the Author," 1974, n.p.

170 **"all the thwarted"; "Whatever inferiority"**: Hansl, "Incredible Twins," p. 56.

170 **" 'Just Plain' Jimmy" to "Zest of One"**: Dennis, "Johnny's a Gentleman," p. 363.

171 **"thwarted" child to "Gets All-Perfect Marks"**: ibid.

171 **"bewildering pageantry of behavior"**: Gesell et al., *Infant and Child*, p. 61.

171 **"learn to think of growth"**: ibid., p. 290.

172 **"marvellous series"; "aimless variability"**: ibid., pp. 290, 292.

172 **"innovation—integration—equilibrium" to "forward thrust"**: ibid., p. 293.

172 **"straight and narrow path"**: ibid., p. 49.

172 **"The growing organism"**: ibid., p. 292.

172 **"spirit of liberty"; "unique individuality"**: ibid., p. 10.

172 **"does not contain"**: radio broadcast about *Infant and Child*, 1947, Office of International Information and Cultural Affairs, U.S. Department of State, Box 147, Arnold Gesell Papers.

172 **"rising generation" to "necessary counterbalance"**: Arnold Gesell, "Cultural Significance of a Science of Child Development," in Lyman Bryson, L. Finkelstein, and R. M. MacIver, *Conflicts of Power in Modern Culture* (New York: Harper & Bros., 1947), p. 228.

172 **"to produce persons"; "to make of [children]"**: *Final Report on the White House Conference on Children in a Democracy*, Jan. 18–19, 1940 (Washington, DC: Children's Bureau, 1940), p. 3.

172 **"foreign to the idea"**: Arnold Gesell quoted in "Democracy Held Vital to Children," *New York Times*, Nov. 15, 1939.

172 **"fundamentally hopeful"**: quoted in Lucille C. Birnbaum, "Behaviorism in the 1920's," *American Quarterly* 7 (1955): 21.

172 **"Unity Without Uniformity"**: William Graeber, "The Unstable World of Benjamin Spock," *Journal of American History* 67, no. 3 (December 1980): 622.

173 **"clarity does not begin at home"**: Samuel D. Schmalhausen, "Family Life: A Study in Pathology," in V. F. Calverton and Samuel D. Schmalhausen, eds., *The New Generation: The Intimate Problems of Modern Parents and Children* (New York: Macauley, 1930), p. 291.

173 **"democracy, like charity"; "In some way"**: Arnold Gesell in *White House Conference on Children in a Democracy: Papers and Discussions at the Initial Session*, Apr. 26, 1939 (Washington, DC: Children's Bureau, 1939), p. 66.

173 **Ilg had urged**: Memos by Louise B. Ames on the writing of *The First Five Years* and *Infant and Child*, Box 51, Louise Bates Ames Papers.

173 **"does not mean license"**: Gesell, "Individualization of Infant Care," p. 3.

173 **"an overly moralistic"**: Arnold Gesell, 1941 notes about C. Anderson Aldrich's talk on "How to Get Parents to Think in Developmental Terms," Box 47, Arnold Gesell Papers.

174 **"behavior in a false emotional light"; "project their own personalities"**: Gesell, "The Cinema as an Instrument for Parent Education," p. 8.

174 **"Instead of striving"**: Gesell et al., *Infant and Child*, p. 57.

174 **"self-demand schedule policy"; "looking at the clock on the wall"**: ibid., p. 56.

174 **"the baby (with all his inborn wisdom)"**: ibid., p. 57.

174 **"organic sense of secureness"**: ibid., p. 56.

175 **"Words alone will not reshape"**: Gesell, "The Cinema as an Instrument for Parent Education," p. 9.

175   "loves to romp, flee and pursue": Gesell et al., *Infant and Child*, p. 161.

175   "By nature . . . is a creative": ibid., p. 65.

175   "There is much promise": ibid., p. 102.

176   "burgeoning neuro-muscular system": ibid., p. 133.

176   "the difference between himself and others": ibid., p. 125.

176   "thrustration": ibid., p. 90.

176   "Nature's favorite method": ibid., p. 179.

176   "There is something 'threeish' ": ibid., p. 203.

176   "Five is in focus": ibid., p. 246.

176   "bewildering and almost kaleidoscopic": Arnold Gesell, "How Science Studies the Child," *Scientific Monthly* 34 (1932): 266.

176   "All told": Gesell et al., *Infant and Child*, p. 248.

176   "My dear son": Arnold Gesell letter to Gerhard Gesell, June 16, 1915, Box 1, Arnold Gesell Papers.

177   "The behavior day is illustrative": Gesell et al., *Infant and Child*, p. 2.

177   "the nap follows the noon meal": ibid., p. 146.

177   "The mother is well advised": ibid., p. 88.

178   "It is very essential": ibid., p. 187.

178   "The culture must plan": ibid., pp. 45–46.

178   "a pleasing voice": ibid., p. 273.

178   "It is also well known": ibid., p. 275.

179   "most important function"; "the planning of the environmental": ibid., p. 64.

179   "The child is now both": ibid., p. 152.

179   "not only from": Gesell, *The Mental Growth of the Pre-School Child*, p. 227.

179   "self-activity": Gesell et al., *Infant and Child*, p. 166.

179   "Everything in season!": ibid., p. 117.

179   "Growth has its seasons": ibid., p. 57.

179   "development is a little like": ibid., p. 296.

179   "a sense of proportion" to "Things are not as bad": ibid., p. 90.

179   "the constant task of teacher and parent": ibid., p. 45.

179   "mental health does not take care": Arnold Gesell, "May Day and the Mental Hygiene of Children," 1932 typescript, Arnold Gesell Papers.

179   "trend toward an optimum": Gesell et al., *Infant and Child*, p. 72.

179   "democratically conceived system": ibid., p. 360.

180   "the child himself is the norm": ibid., p. 72.

180   "your boy . . . needs pressure": letter from Andover to the Gesells, Feb. 21, 1928, Box 9, Arnold Gesell Papers.

180   "I am going to keep my head up" to "The way you write": Gerhard Gesell letter to parents, n.d., Box 9, Arnold Gesell Papers.

181   "one-man show": Senn, *Insights on the Child Development Movement in the United States*, p. 32.

181   "the long, strong Freudian period": Louise B. Ames, "Evaluation of Arnold Gesell's Work," Jan. 29, 1975, Box 50, Louise Bates Ames Papers.

181   "Parents are constantly": Catherine Mackenzie, "Please Spare the Rod," *New York Times Book Review*, Aug. 8, 1943, p. 5.

181   "I keep telling you": Gerhard Gesell letter to his mother, Oct. 9, 1943, Box 1, Arnold Gesell Papers.

181   "the Mother's Point of View": Peggy Gesell letter to Arnold Gesell, n.d., ibid.

182   "self-demand routine" to "My memory was too feeble": ibid.

182   "a very simple device": Gesell et al., *Infant and Child*, p. 84.

183   **"One symbol I must"** to **"embrac[ing] moments of fussing"**: Peggy Gesell letter to Arnold Gesell, n.d., Box 1, Arnold Gesell Papers.

183   **"recording all that is pertinent"**: Anna Noyes letter to Arnold Gesell, receipt acknowledged Feb. 11, 1931, Box 34, Arnold Gesell Papers.

183   **"You will note a wide variation"** to **"That is because"**: Peggy Gesell letter to Arnold Gesell, Nov. 4, 1942, Box 1, Arnold Gesell Papers.

183   **"Popularize your literature"**: Gerhard Gesell letter to Arnold Gesell, n.d., ibid.

184   **"too little is scientifically established"**: Gesell et al., *Infant and Child*, pp. 256–57.

184   **"in spirit and technique"**: Arnold Gesell and Frances Ilg in collaboration with Louise Ames and Glenna Bullis, *The Child from Five to Ten* (New York: Harper & Bros., 1949), p. 2.

184   **"of high average or superior intelligence"**: ibid., p. 3.

184   **"expansive"** to **"a golden period"**: ibid., pp. 159, 197, 214.

184   **"a 'naughty girl'"**: ibid., p. 78.

184   **"What the mother does"**: ibid., p. 178.

185   **"convulsed, it was so true"**: Peggy Gesell letter to Arnold Gesell, Jan. 23, 1946, Box 1, Arnold Gesell Papers.

185   **"For a while"**: Peggy Gesell letter to Arnold Gesell, n.d., Box 9, Arnold Gesell Papers.

185   **"On a page"** to **"being with the less-rapid group"**: Peggy Gesell letter to Arnold Gesell, Jan. 23, 1946.

185   **Gesell's School Readiness Test**: See Patricia Kean, "Hopping to Harvard," Sept. 7, 2000, Salon.com.

185   **"I am lost"** to **"Gerry grows"**: Peggy Gesell letter to Arnold Gesell, Jan. 23, 1946.

186   **"I wish to acknowledge"**: Arnold Gesell letter to Peggy Gesell, July 10, 1947, Box 1, Arnold Gesell papers.

186   **"You have both been far more than parental"**: Gerhard Gesell letter to parents, n.d., ibid.

186   **"The children find it a bestseller"**: Peggy Gesell letter to Arnold Gesell, n.d., ibid.

186   **"I think Dr. Gesell made"**: eighth-grade comments on *Youth* in 1956, Box 45, Arnold Gesell Papers.

186   **"anatomy of normalcy"**: Helen Puner, "Gesell's Children Grow Up," *Harper's Magazine* 212, no. 1270 (March 1956): 38.

186   **"curiously non-sexy"**: ibid., p. 39.

186   **Erik Erikson**: Senn, *Insights on the Child Development Movement in the United States*, p. 31.

187   **he stuck with the "when"**: Puner, "Gesell's Children Grow Up," p. 40.

187   **"glacial public surface"**: ibid., p. 37.

SEVEN: *The Awkward Age of the Expert*

191   **"the healthy personality"; "personality in the making"**: Milton J. E. Senn, ed., *Symposium on the Healthy Personality: Transactions of Special Meetings of the Conference on Infancy and Childhood, June 8–9 and July 3–4, 1950* (New York: Josiah Macy, Jr., Foundation, 1950), and Helen Leland Witmer and Ruth Kotinsky, eds., *Personality in the Making: The Fact-Finding Report of the Midcentury White House Con-*

ference on Children and Youth (New York: Harper & Bros., 1952). (Hereafter referred to as *The Healthy Personality* and *Personality in the Making*.)

191   **"perhaps the president's"**: *New York Times*, Dec. 10, 1950, p. 2E.

192   **"We cannot insulate" to "young people"**: *New York Times*, Dec. 6, 1950, p. 19.

192   **"you'll need a new nose"**: *New York Times*, Dec. 10, 1950, p. 2E.

192   **"our democratic"; "I do not claim"**: *New York Times*, Dec. 6, 1950, p. 19.

192   **"the ability to face life"**: quoted in Betty Friedan, *The Feminine Mystique* (New York: Norton, 1983), p. 191.

192   **"coddled"**: See David Halberstam, *The Fifties* (New York: Villard, 1993), p. 72.

192   **"build up those inner resources"**: *New York Times*, Dec. 6, 1950, p. 19.

192   **"This White House Conference"**: Edward A. Richards, ed., *Proceedings of the Midcentury White House Conference on Children and Youth: Report of the Conference Sessions, Dec. 3–7, 1950* (Raleigh, NC: Health Publications Institute, 1951), p. 16.

193   **"synthesize the relevant findings"**: *The Healthy Personality*, p. 38.

193   **"broad-scale citizens' "**: ibid., p. 15.

193   **"the major strength of the conference"**: ibid., p. 16.

193   **"How can we rear"**: ibid., p. 13.

193   **"artificially fragmented"**: ibid., p. 10.

193   **"great chasms of ignorance"; "Our nation at midcentury"**: *Personality in the Making*, pp. x, 444.

193   **"very difficult problem"**: *The Healthy Personality*, p. 13.

193   **"the best now known"**: *Personality in the Making*, p. x.

193   **"to build their self-confidence"; "Dr. Spock's gift"**: *The Healthy Personality*, p. 13.

194   **"I was too polite"**: Benjamin Spock Papers, Syracuse University Library, Department of Special Collections.

194   **"remarkable ease"**: *The Healthy Personality*, p. 110.

194   **"reports on the complexity"**: Spock's talk at the White House Conference, Benjamin Spock Papers.

194   **"In such a world"**: Richards, *Proceedings of the Midcentury White House Conference on Children and Youth*, p. 55.

195   **"precious inheritance"; "quickly subdues"**: *The Healthy Personality*, p. 94.

195   **"His paper relieves me"**: ibid., p. 38.

195   **a version of "Eight Ages of Man"**: Lawrence J. Friedman, *Identity's Architect: A Biography of Erik Erikson* (New York: Scribner, 1999), p. 228. See also H. Stuart Hughes, *The Sea Changes: The Migration of Social Thought, 1930–65* (New York: Harper & Row, 1975), pp. 222–27.

196   **"charts, to paraphrase Lincoln"**: Erik H. Erikson, *Childhood and Society* (New York: Norton, 1963), p. 70.

196   **His own map**: Friedman, *Identity's Architect*, p. 221.

196   **The boom in child development studies**: Robert R. Sears, *Your Ancients Revisited: A History of Child Development* (Chicago: University of Chicago Press, 1975), pp. 21–22.

196   **In a speech at Clark University**: Anna Freud, "The Contribution of Psychoanalysis to Genetic Psychology," *American Journal of Orthopsychiatry* 21, no. 3 (July 1951): 476–97.

197   **"gentleness and reassurance"; "the required conduct"**: ibid., p. 489.

197   **"the process of socialization"**: Lawrence Frank, "Freud's Influence on Western Thinking and Culture," *American Journal of Orthopsychiatry* 10, no. 4 (October 1940): 881.

198 **"not, strictly speaking, derived"; "what [a child's] upbringing":** Sigmund Freud, "Analysis of a Phobia in a Five-Year-Old Boy," *The Standard Edition of the Complete Psychological Works of Sigmund Freud*, translated from the German under the general editorship of James Strachey, in collaboration with Anna Freud, assisted by Alix Strachey and Alan Tyson (London: Hogarth Press and the Institute of Psycho-Analysis, 1959), 10:5, 146.

198 **"right proportion":** Anna Freud, *Psychoanalysis for Teachers and Parents*, translated by Barbara Low (New York: Emmerson Books, 1935), pp. 104–105.

198 **"Freud was much too smart":** "A Talk with Dr. Spock: In Praise of the Young Generation," *Newsweek* 72, no. 13 (Sept. 23, 1968): 71.

199 **"What is the cause"; "this powerful tendency":** Hilde Bruch, *Don't Be Afraid of Your Child* (New York: Farrar, Straus & Giroux, 1952), pp. 4, 11.

199 **"the average citizen" to "solid, demonstrable fact":** *Life*, June 6, 1950, p. 117.

199 **"Conflict arose"; "pediatricians were confounded":** Milton J. E. Senn, "Peregrinations of a Pediatrician," Milton J. E. Senn Child Development Oral History Interviews, National Library of Medicine, Washington, DC.

199 **"*known* about the 'healthy personality' ":** *The Healthy Personality*, p. 92.

200 **"honorable but very uninspiring" to "I am concerned":** ibid., pp. 92–94.

200 **"much of this knowledge"; "great need for tested knowledge":** *Personality in the Making*, p. ix.

200 **"Probably there will be":** ibid., p. 91.

201 **"normal run-of-the-mill" to "when we look":** Jean W. Macfarlane, Lucile Allen, and Marjorie P. Honzik, *A Developmental Study of the Behavior Problems of Normal Children Between Twenty-one Months and Fourteen Years* (Berkeley: University of California Press, Publications in Child Development, 1954), pp. 1, 220–21.

201 **"mental hygiene sensitized group":** Jean Walker Macfarlane, "Studies in Child Guidance, I: Methodology of Data Collection and Organization," Monographs of the Society for Research in Child Development 3, Serial 19, no. 6 (Washington, DC: Society for Research in Child Development, National Research Council, 1938), p. 2. See also Robert Sears, *Your Ancients Revisited*, pp. 52–53.

201 **"social learning" theories:** Eleanor E. Maccoby, "The Role of Parents in the Socialization of Children: An Historical Overview," *Developmental Psychology* 28, no. 6 (November 1992): 1008.

201 **"forbidding atmosphere":** John Dollard, Leonard W. Doob, Neal E. Miller, D. H. Mowrer, and Robert R. Sears, *Frustration and Aggression* (New Haven: Yale University Press, 1967), p. 78.

202 **An article in the *Psychological Bulletin*:** Harold Orlansky, "Infant Care and Personality," *Psychological Bulletin* 46 (1949): 1–48.

202 **"the problem of tracing":** *Personality in the Making*, p. 444.

202 **Along with several colleagues:** See Robert R. Sears, Eleanor E. Maccoby, and Harry Levin, *Patterns of Child Rearing* (Evanston, IL: Row, Peterson, 1957).

202 **"few connections were found":** Maccoby, "The Role of Parents," p. 1008.

202 **And as Margaret Mead:** Sears, *Your Ancients Revisited*, pp. 39–41. For one of the most ambitious cross-cultural studies, see John W. M. Whiting and Irvin L. Child, *Child Training and Personality: A Cross-Cultural Study* (1953; reprint, Westport, CT: Greenwood, 1989). Whiting and his wife, Beatrice Whiting, went on to do further studies, which resulted in their well-known *Children of Six Cultures: A Psycho-Cultural Analysis* (Cambridge, MA: Harvard University Press, 1975).

202   **"overeager interpretations"; "diaperology":** Bruch, *Don't Be Afraid of Your Child*, p. 44.

203   **Lewin and several colleagues:** Kurt Lewin, Ronald Lippitt, and Ralph K. White, "Patterns of the Aggressive Behavior in Experimentally Created 'Social Climates,' " *Journal of Social Psychology* 10, no. 2 (May 1939): 271–99. See also Alfred J. Marrow, *The Practical Theorist: The Life and Works of Kurt Lewin* (New York: Teachers College Press, 1977), pp. 123–28.

203   **Alfred Baldwin of the Fels Institute:** Alfred L. Baldwin, "Socialization and the Parent-Child Relationship," *Child Development* 19, no. 3 (September 1948): 129.

203   **finding clear-cut extremes:** Goodwin Watson, "Some Personality Differences in Children Related to Strict or Permissive Parental Discipline," *Journal of Psychology* 44 (1957): 231.

203   **"upper-middle-class Westchester":** ibid., p. 233.

203   **And parental approaches:** Evelyn Millis Duvall, "Conceptions of Parenthood," *American Journal of Sociology* 52 (1946): 193–203.

203   **"a correlational study cannot":** Watson, "Some Personality Differences," p. 239.

203   **"no more than a schematic outline":** T. W. Adorno et al., *The Authoritarian Personality* (New York: Harper & Bros., 1950), p. 384.

203   **"The social and economic situation"; "low family income":** *Personality in the Making*, pp. 195, 116.

203   **Surveys back in 1930:** See John E. Anderson, *The Young Child in the Home: A Survey of Three Thousand American Families, Report of the Committee on the Infant and Preschool Child*, White House Conference on Child Health and Protection (New York: Appleton-Century, 1936), pp. 20, 220–21.

204   **A Chicago study:** Allison Davis, "Socio-Economic Influences upon Children's Learning," in Richards, ed., *Proceedings of the Midcentury White House Conference on Children and Youth*, pp. 79–80.

204   **Maternal overprotection:** See Philip Wylie, *Generation of Vipers* (New York: Holt, Rinehart and Winston, 1955); David Levy, *Maternal Overprotection* (New York: Norton, 1966).

204   **With Dorothy Burlingham:** Dorothy Burlingham and Anna Freud, *Infants Without Families: The Case For and Against Residential Nurseries* (London: George Allen & Unwin, 1943), pp. 43–52.

204   **René Spitz:** See Robert Karen, *Becoming Attached: Unfolding the Mystery of the Infant-Mother Bond and Its Impact on Later Life* (New York: Warner, 1994), p. 21.

205   **"mother-love"; "is at many points":** John Bowlby, *Maternal Care and Mental Health* (Geneva: World Health Organization, 1951), p. 158.

205   **"constant attention"; "warm, intimate, and continuous":** ibid., p. 67.

205   **"brings in its train":** ibid., p. 12.

205   **"There is much too much talk":** editorial in *Parents' Magazine* 25, no. 9 (February 1950): 26.

205   **"studies of the effects"; "has not been subjected":** *Personality in the Making*, p. 97.

205   **"the idea of rejection":** Anna Freud, "The Concept of the Rejecting Mother," reprinted in E. James Anthony and Therese Benedek, eds., *Parenthood: Its Psychology and Psychopathology* (Northvale, NJ: Aronsons, 1976), p. 378.

205   **It was also a sign of new assurance:** Clark E. Vincent, "Trends in Infant Care Ideas," *Child Development* 22, no. 3 (September 1951): 207.

205   **"here to stay":** Bruch, *Don't Be Afraid of Your Child*, p. 13.

206 **A wave of surveys:** See Vincent, "Trends in Infant Care Ideas"; Martha Wolfenstein, "Trends in Infant Care," *American Journal of Orthopsychiatry* 23, no. 1 (January 1953); Celia Stendler, "Sixty Years of Child Training Practices," *Journal of Pediatrics* 36 (1950); Sibylle Escalona, "A Commentary upon Some Recent Changes in Child Rearing Practices," *Child Development* 20, no. 3 (September 1949); Ralph H. Ojemann et al., "A Functional Analysis of Child Development Material in Current Newspapers and Magazines," *Child Development* 19, nos. 1 and 2 (March–June 1948); Christine Olden, "Notes on Child Rearing in America," *Psychoanalytic Study of the Child*, vol. 7, symposium held at the Seventeenth Congress of the International Psycho-Analytical Association, Amsterdam, Holland, Aug. 8, 1951.

206 **"with a conscience":** Erikson, *Childhood and Society*, p. 95.

206 **"This dynamic country":** ibid., p. 285.

207 **"American children are growing up"; "So longstanding":** quoted in *The Story of the White House Conferences on Children and Youth* (Washington, DC: U.S. Department of Health, Education and Welfare Social and Rehabilitative Service, Children's Bureau, 1967), p. 18.

207 **"tell parents what to do":** *Personality in the Making*, p. 206.

207 **"parents sometimes feel threatened":** ibid., p. 207.

207 **"to help parents"; "mutual study began to replace":** ibid., p. 206.

208 **The term "nuclear family":** *New York Times*, May 18, 2001.

208 **"source of emotional security" to "one of the few places":** *Personality in the Making*, p. 178.

209 **"middle-class U.S.A.":** ibid., p. 196.

209 **"vain in her appearance":** Erikson, *Childhood and Society*, p. 290.

209 **"middle-class American married women":** *Personality in the Making*, p. 196.

209 **"in one form or another"; "part of the process":** Bruch, *Don't Be Afraid of Your Child*, p. 58.

209 **The birthrate:** Steven Mintz and Susan Kellogg, *Domestic Revolutions: A Social History of American Family Life* (New York: Free Press, 1988), pp. 180, 179.

209 **the start of a "Children's Decade":** editorial, *Parents' Magazine* 25, no. 1 (January 1950): 18.

209 **"being a real father":** quoted in Elaine Tyler May, *Homeward Bound: American Families in the Cold War* (New York: Basic Books, 1988), p. 146.

209 **"third-generation American":** Margaret Mead, *And Keep Your Powder Dry: An Anthropologist Looks at America* (New York: Morrow, 1942), p. 37.

210 **"worried version of life"; "outdistanced and outmoded":** ibid., pp. 87, 52.

210 **"become a very special thing"; "their children final status":** ibid., p. 41.

210 **"an unknown chart called 'happiness' "; "achievements, upon the way":** ibid., pp. 87, 90.

210 **"foster and sustain":** *Personality in the Making*, p. 178.

210 **"Conflicts between mother's ways"; "All the mass transformations":** *The Healthy Personality*, p. 108.

210 **"a sort of final examination":** Dr. Spock quoted in Dorothy Barclay, "Changing Ideals in Homemaking," *New York Times*, July 19, 1953, collected in Rothman, *The Family*, p. 183.

210 **"an antidote to the critical":** *The Healthy Personality*, p. 71.

210 **" 'naturalism,' ":** *Personality in the Making*, p. 102.

211 **"artificial, 'scientific' methods":** ibid.

211 **"the absolute answers"; "children's sound development":** ibid., p. 205.

211 **"for a generation or more":** ibid., p. 201.

211 **"It has been discovered":** ibid., p. 5.

211 **"natural, intuitive" to "libidinal" mother:** Barbara Ehrenreich and Deirdre English, *For Her Own Good: 150 Years of the Experts' Advice to Women* (Garden City, NY: Anchor, 1978), pp. 221–25.

211 **"There is some danger":** *Personality in the Making*, p. xvi.

212 **"As for parents":** quoted from *The New Republic*, Oct. 6, 1952, in Nathan G. Hale, Jr., *The Rise and Crisis of Psychoanalysis in the United States: Freud and the Americans, 1917–1985* (New York: Oxford University Press, 1995), p. 284.

212 **"Mothers are not ready":** quoted in *The Story of the White House Conferences on Children and Youth*, p. 17.

212 **"When he publishes his findings"; "I know Gesell's work":** Mary McCarthy, *The Group* (New York: Harcourt Brace Jovanovich, 1982), p. 442.

212 **"Most of Freud's out of date":** ibid., p. 443.

212 **"toidey-seat":** ibid., p. 436.

212 **"give up his anal pleasures":** ibid., p. 440.

213 **"Have you read Margaret Mead?":** ibid.

213 **"the American identity"; "The functioning American":** Erikson, *Childhood and Society*, p. 286.

213 **"be a genuine person":** *The Healthy Personality*, p. 145.

213 **"unable to take the responsibility":** "When and How to Say No," *Parents' Magazine* 25, no. 1 (January 1950): 74.

213 **"hard to know":** *The Healthy Personality*, p. 145.

214 **"suddenly and for no plain reason":** quoted in Mintz and Kellogg, *Domestic Revolutions*, p. 195.

214 **"stampede to the suburbs":** See Anne Kelley, "Suburbia—Is It a Child's Utopia?" *New York Times*, Feb. 2, 1958, collected in Rothman, *The Family*, p. 187.

214 **"Femininity Begins at Home":** Friedan, *The Feminine Mystique*, p. 44.

214 **"the best adjusted people":** William H. Whyte, Jr., *The Organization Man* (New York: Simon & Schuster, 1956), p. 297.

214 **"adaptability" to "geared to change":** *Personality in the Making*, p. 186.

214 **"increasingly complex and centralized systems"; "autonomy in the form of independence":** *The Healthy Personality*, p. 139.

214 **"an increasing number of social and economic activities" to "On this point":** *Personality in the Making*, p. 200.

214 **David Riesman suggested:** David Riesman with Nathan Glazer and Reuel Denny, *The Lonely Crowd: A Study of the Changing American Character* (New Haven: Yale University Press, 1950).

215 **"a document of American life":** *"Cheaper by the Dozen* Goes to Hollywood," *Parents' Magazine* 25, no. 5 (May 1950): 126.

215 **"All in all, then":** *Personality in the Making*, p. 202.

215 **"reflecting changing cultural prototypes":** Erikson, *Childhood and Society*, p. 312.

215 **"This new conception"; "would provide a firmer basis":** *Personality in the Making*, p. 202.

215 **"plan the education":** Bruch, *Don't Be Afraid of Your Child*, p. 31.

216 **" 'boredom' . . . with household tasks":** *Personality in the Making*, p. 195.

216 **"These new attitudes" to "the rules of the new child-rearing scheme":** ibid., p. 201.

216 **"demi-professionals"**: Bruch, *Don't Be Afraid of Your Child*, p. 46.

216 **"they have always been the ones"; "intuitive, nonverbal knowledge"**: *Personality in the Making*, pp. 207–208.

217 **"At present there is a tendency" to "It has to do with their own past"**: *The Healthy Personality*, pp. 208–209.

217 **"technical mastery"**: Escalona, "A Commentary upon Some Recent Changes in Child Rearing Practices," p. 160.

217 **"to make many of the recommended"; "burden[ing] children"**: ibid., p. 162.

218 **"those who have come to recognize"; "one is purblind"**: *Personality in the Making*, p. 246.

218 **"the strivings characteristic of each"; "have, to some greater extent"**: ibid., p. 247.

218 **"Human childhood is long"**: *The Healthy Personality*, p. 145.

219 **"The reproach raised"**: Bruch, *Don't Be Afraid of Your Child*, p. 205.

219 **"began to be conceived"**: *Personality in the Making*, p. 232.

219 **"interacting with a different cultural environment"; "experiencing, learning, acquiring"**: ibid., p. 234.

219 **"one big hunger"**: James L. Hynes, *A Healthy Personality for Your Child* (Washington, DC: Federal Security Agency, Social Security Administration, Children's Bureau—Publication no. 337, 1957), p. 3.

220 **"a feeling that his world is O.K."; "good, strong, firm feeling"**: ibid., pp. 4, 6.

220 **"He is the one"**: ibid., p. 2.

220 **"to handle and investigate everything"**: Wolfenstein, "Trends in Infant Care," p. 122.

220 **"Don't Be Afraid of Strong Feelings" to "even we grownups"**: *Parents' Magazine* 25, no. 5 (May 1950): 44, 38.

220 **Bowel training was an opportunity**: Wolfenstein, "Trends in Infant Care," p. 128.

220 **"chocolate cake"**: McCarthy, *The Group*, p. 456.

221 **"on the quiet side"**: Margaret Mead, *Blackberry Winter: My Earlier Years* (New York: Morrow, 1972), p. 259.

221 **"poked and tickled"**: Mary Catherine Bateson, *With a Daughter's Eye: A Memoir of Margaret Mead and Gregory Bateson* (New York: HarperPerennial, 1994), p. 22.

221 **As for Mead's insistence**: anecdote in Myrtle McGraw interview, #48, Milton J. E. Senn Child Development Oral History Interviews, National Library of Medicine, Washington, DC.

221 **"a complex household"**: Bateson, *With a Daughter's Eye*, p. 34.

221 **"avoid the tightness"**: ibid., p. 35.

221 **"great households"**: Margaret Mead, "South Sea Hints on Bringing Up Children," *Parents' Magazine* 4, no. 9 (September 1929): 22.

221 **"most important characteristic"**: Bateson, *With a Daughter's Eye*, p. 29.

222 **"Daddy is good with nature"**: ibid., p. 43.

222 **"Fear and rage"**: Mead, *Blackberry Winter*, p. 266.

222 **"Cathy was chosen"**: ibid., p. 268.

222 **"Behavior grows"**: Box 3, Louise Bates Ames Papers, Library of Congress, Washington, DC.

222 **"persons strategic"**: *Personality in the Making*, pp. 254–55.

223 **"children always impress me"**: Bruch, *Don't Be Afraid of Your Child*, p. 214.

223 **"How much was temperament?"**: Mead, *Blackberry Winter*, p. 268.

223 **"you cannot fool children"**: *The Healthy Personality*, p. 145.

223 **"does not have the time"**: ibid., p. 108.

EIGHT: *The Therapist*

226 **"He's as sympathetic"**: Benjamin Spock Papers, Syracuse University Library, Department of Special Collections.

226 **Scan the classic:** I owe this insight to Louis Menand. See also Louis Menand, "Cat People," *The New Yorker*, Dec. 23 and 30, 2002, pp. 148–54.

227 **"typify the present-day departure"**: Myron E. Wegman, review of *The Common Sense Book of Baby and Child Care*, *American Journal of Public Health* 36 (November 1946): 1329.

227 **"There is an indication"**: *The Healthy Personality*, p. 110.

228 **"Don't you realize"**: Benjamin Spock, *Problems of Parents* (Boston: Houghton Mifflin, 1962), p. v.

228 **"I never looked at my records"**: Benjamin Spock Papers.

229 **Benjamin McLane Spock:** Thomas Maier's *Dr. Spock: An American Life* (New York: Harcourt Brace, 1998) has been a very useful resource.

230 **"Sandor Rado gave the impression"**: ibid., p. 116.

231 **"She tormented the child"**: Sandor Rado, "An Anxious Mother: A Contribution to the Analysis of the Ego," in *Psychology of Behavior: Collected Papers* (New York: Grune & Stratton, 1956), p. 41.

231 **"ego [to wallow] in its hyper-morality"; "her secret pleasure in aggression"**: ibid., pp. 43, 41.

231 **"refused to play bridge"**: Benjamin Spock, "How My Ideas Have Changed," *Redbook* 121, no. 6 (October 1963): 51.

232 **"South Wind"; "hot-air kids"**: Maier, *Dr. Spock*, pp. 22–23.

232 **"We would have just loved"**: Benjamin Spock Papers.

233 **"very attractive"; "You just have a pleasant smile"**: Benjamin Spock and Mary Morgan, *Spock on Spock: A Memoir of Growing Up with the Century* (New York: Pantheon, 1989), p. 66.

233 **"By the way, this is very private"**: Benjamin Spock letter to Mildred Spock, Box 91, Benjamin Spock Papers.

233 **"when you come back to New Haven"**: Maier, *Dr. Spock*, p. 33.

233 **"my immaturity"**: ibid., p. 26.

234 **"The inferiority complex"**: ibid., p. 41.

234 **"Think of all the creatures"**: ibid., p. 64.

235 **"In the stern family"**: Benjamin Spock, *Dr. Spock on Parenting: Sensible Advice from America's Most Trusted Child-Care Expert* (New York: Simon & Schuster, 1988), p. 186.

235 **"too sensitive"**: Maier, *Dr. Spock*, p. 80.

236 **"nonsense"**: ibid., p. 78.

236 **"negative kind of knowledge"; "positive, practical advice"**: Spock, "How My Ideas Have Changed," p. 124.

236 **"lacked the strength of character"**: Maier, *Dr. Spock*, p. 113.

237 **"rebelliousness and uneasiness" to "My picture of myself"**: Benjamin Spock Papers.

237 **"I worried a lot"**: Spock, "How My Ideas Have Changed," p. 124.

238 **"Though I knew I was wrong"**: *Dr. Spock Talks with Mothers: Growth and Guidance* (Boston: Houghton Mifflin, 1961), p. 153.

238 **"The man with the gentle face"**: Maier, *Dr. Spock*, p. 103.

238 **"very concerned"**: Benjamin Spock Papers.

238 **"Don't let yourself be *seen*"; "the fancy job"**: ibid.

238 **"pillar of strength and wisdom"**: Spock, "How My Ideas Have Changed," p. 122.

239 **key texts**: Nathan G. Hale, Jr., *The Rise and Crisis of Psychoanalysis in the United States: Freud and the Americans, 1917–1985* (New York: Oxford University Press, 1995), pp. 47–51.

239 **"a person who's learned"**: Dr. Spock interview #67a, Milton J. E. Senn Child Development Oral History Interviews, National Library of Medicine, Washington, DC.

239 **The 1942 and 1945 editions**: See Martha Wolfenstein, "Trends in Infant Care," *American Journal of Orthopsychiatry* 23, no. 1 (January 1953): 121.

239 **"the child who has strong drives"**: quoted in Rita Kramer, "A Look Back in Wonder," *New York Times Magazine*, June 8, 1969, p. 93.

240 **Mead's daughter . . . chided**: Bateson, *With a Daughter's Eye: A Memoir of Margaret Mead and Gregory Bateson* (New York: HarperPerennial, 1994), p. 23.

240 **"tremendous disappointment"**: Maier, *Dr. Spock*, p. 68.

241 **"it is well for doctors"**: Nina Ridenour, "Keystones in Psychological Thinking About Young Children," *New York State Journal of Medicine* 47 (February 1947): 281. Address delivered May 1946.

241 **"All parents do their best job"**: Benjamin Spock, *The Common Sense Book of Baby and Child Care* (New York: Duell, Sloan & Pearce, 1946), p. 4.

241 **"Our ideas about how to treat"**: ibid., p. 2.

241 **"I feel as if you were talking"**: Ann Hulbert, "Dr. Spock's Baby," *The New Yorker* 72, no. 12 (May 20, 1996): 82.

241 **"go along pleasantly"**: C. Anderson Aldrich review in *Parents' Magazine* 21, no. 2 (February 1946): 140.

241 **"quite sensible"**: Spock and Morgan, *Spock on Spock*, p. 136.

242 **"free, warm, life-loving"**: Benjamin Spock Papers.

242 **"He just gives this [impression]" to "First I seem"**: ibid.

243 **his proceeds**: Katharine Davis Fishman, "The Less Permissive Dr. Spock," *New York Times Book Review*, Feb. 16, 1969, p. 32.

243 **"judged, criticized, scared"**: Hulbert, "Dr. Spock's Baby," p. 89, based on my interview with John Spock.

243 **"pontifical" to "he turned absolutely scarlet"**: Benjamin Spock Papers.

243 **"It's a revelation"**: quoted in Martha Weinman, "Now 'Dr. Spock' Goes to the White House," *New York Times Magazine*, Dec. 4, 1960, p. 121.

243 **"authoritative preachment"**: Hulbert, "Dr. Spock's Baby," p. 87.

244 **"getting into trouble"**: Benjamin Spock, *Baby and Child Care* (New York: Pocket Books, 1957), p. 1.

244 **"new and strategic significance" to "intelligent middle-of-the-road viewpoint"**: Ethel Kawin, *Parenthood in a Free Nation*, vol. 1: *Basic Concepts for Parents* (New York: Macmillan, 1954), p. 148.

244 **"Baby in a Box"**: Daniel W. Bjork, *B. F. Skinner: A Life* (New York: Basic Books, 1993), pp. 137, 141.

244 **"camouflaged in such palatable form"**: Weinman, "Now 'Dr. Spock' Goes to the White House," p. 121.

244 **"fascinating, stimulating"**: Dr. Spock interview, Milton J. E. Senn Child Development Oral History Interviews.

244 **" 'child psychiatrist' "**: Hilde Bruch, *Don't Be Afraid of Your Child* (New York: Farrar, Straus & Giroux, 1952), p. 15.

245 **one of the ten "unknockables"**: Maier, *Dr. Spock*, p. 211.

245 **"was not too shaken"**: ibid., p. 185.

245 **"the eyes water"**: Benjamin Spock Papers.

245 **"the need for greater understanding"**: Spock, *Baby and Child Care* (1957), p. 1.

245 **"foolish enough to say"**: Benjamin Spock, typescript of "Self-Regulation, Spoiling and Sleep Problems," paper read at a meeting of the American Academy of Pediatrics, Milwaukee, WI, June 1948, p. 3, Benjamin Spock Papers.

245 **"need to monkey around"**: Maier, *Dr. Spock*, p. 208.

245 **"there is a big difference"; "How Far Permissive Attitudes?"**: Kramer, "A Look Back in Wonder," p. 105.

246 **"especially about discipline"**: Spock, *Baby and Child Care* (1957), p. 1.

246 **"tried to give a more balanced view"**: ibid.

246 **"a sort of Get-Even-with-Mothers"**: Herschel Alt, "In Defense of Mothers," *Parents' Magazine* 25, no. 2 (February 1950): 26.

246 **"He says to himself"**: Benjamin Spock, *Baby and Child Care* (New York: Pocket Books, 1992), p. 388.

247 **"non-critical, sympathetic listener"**: Benjamin Spock, typescript of "Values and Limits of Parent Education," delivered at the Ninth Annual Institute for Workers in Parent Education, New York, March 1955, published by the Child Study Association, p. 12, Benjamin Spock Papers.

247 **"scolders of parents"**: Dr. Spock interview, Milton J. E. Senn Child Development Oral History Interviews.

247 **"Mother's Big Helper"**: Barbara Land, "Mother's Big Helper," *New York Times*, Sept. 25, 1955, sect. 2, p. 11.

247 **"It's almost a form of group therapy"**: Weinman, "Now 'Dr. Spock' Goes to the White House," p. 121.

247 **"modern mother . . . paddling frantically"**: ibid., p. 26.

247 **"It might well be entitled"; "a weepy and anxious mother"**: Rollene Waterman, "A Mother's Guide to Spockmanship," *Saturday Review* 40, no. 36 (Sept. 7, 1957): 31.

247 **"I can hardly bear"**: Spock, *Problems of Parents*, pp. 41–42.

247 **"anticipatory guidance"**: Spock, "Values and Limits of Parent Education," p. 9.

248 **"how unattractive"**: ibid.

248 **"we all learn to be parents"**: ibid., p. 11.

248 **"gospel according to Spock"**: J. D. Ratcliff, "Gospel According to Spock," *Reader's Digest* 72, no. 433 (May 1958): 182.

248 **"Different parents seem to find"**: ibid., p. 186.

248 **more of an "organization man"**: See William Graebner, "The Unstable World of Benjamin Spock: Social Engineering in a Democratic Culture, 1917–1950," *Journal of American History* 67, no. 3 (December 1980): 612–29. For an interesting analysis of Spock as "neither savior nor saboteur of the rising generation," but America's "universal nanny," see Michael Zuckerman, "Dr. Spock: The Confidence Man," in Charles E. Rosenberg, *The Family in History* (Philadelphia: University of Pennsylvania Press, 1975), pp. 179–207.

248 **"wanting to be like"**: Spock, *Common Sense Book of Baby and Child Care* (1946), p. 294.

248 **"reasonable, friendly"**: ibid., p. 19.

248 **"parents of girls"**: ibid., p. 2.

248 **"wants to do the right thing"**: ibid., p. 270.

248 **"back to nature"**: ibid., p. 30.

248 **"leave bowel training"**: ibid., p. 196.

248 **"a nice age"**: ibid., p. 294.

248 **"I heard of a little girl"**: ibid., p. 300.

249 **fathers, who had at last acquired**: Barbara Ehrenreich and Deirdre English, *For Her Own Good: 150 Years of the Experts' Advice to Women* (Garden City, NY: Anchor, 1978), pp. 247–48.

249 **"give him the feeling"; "little things like approving"**: Spock, *Common Sense Book of Baby and Child Care* (1946), p. 255.

249 **"take his place"**: ibid., p. 312.

249 **"discipline, good behavior"; "part of the unfolding"**: ibid., p. 20.

249 **"natural . . . comfortable, affectionate"; "what . . . they instinctively"**: ibid., pp. 21, 4.

249 **"if the cause and the cure"**: ibid., p. 253.

249 **"When in doubt"**: Maier, *Dr. Spock*, p. 154.

249 **"At its worst"**: Benjamin Spock, typescript of "Preventing Early Problems," *American Journal of Orthopsychiatry* 18, no. 4 (October 1947): 3.

249 **"a balky, suspicious attitude"**: Spock, *Common Sense Book of Baby and Child Care* (1946), p. 81.

249 **"may last for years"; "other behavior problems, too"**: ibid., p. 220.

249 **"are resilient"**: Dorothy Barclay, "Educated Mother Subject to Panic," *New York Times*, Apr. 24, 1953, in Rothman, *The Family*, p. 197.

250 **"anxious deference"**: Spock, *Problems of Parents*, p. 283.

250 **"the more they submit"**: Spock, *Baby and Child Care* (1957), p. 185.

250 **"Don't be afraid to love [your baby]"**: Spock, *Common Sense Book of Baby and Child Care* (1946), p. 19.

250 **"Don't be afraid to love him and enjoy him"**: Spock, *Baby and Child Care* (1957), p. 43.

251 **the academics who were busy blending**: Christopher Lasch, *Haven in a Heartless World: The Family Besieged* (New York: Norton, 1995), pp. 111–13.

251 *McCall's* **magazine launched**: Betty Friedan, *The Feminine Mystique* (New York: Norton, 1982), p. 48.

251 **"quest for a utopian equilibrium"; "development as a co-operative social person"**: William H. Whyte, Jr., *The Organization Man* (New York: Simon & Schuster, 1956), p. 391.

251 **"The concepts of the responsible worker"**: Peter Drucker, *The Concept of the Corporation*, with a new introduction by the author (New Brunswick, NJ: Transaction, 1993), pp. 303–304.

251 **"commonest problem in child rearing"**: Hulbert, "Dr. Spock's Baby," p. 87.

251 **"child-care experts"**: Spock, "Self-Regulation, Spoiling and Sleep Patterns," p. 18.

251 **"air of cheerful certainty"**: Spock, *Common Sense Book of Baby and Child Care* (1946), p. 258.

251 **"can be quite impressed"**: Spock, "Self-Regulation, Spoiling and Sleep Problems," p. 23.

252 **"steered . . . in a friendly, automatic way"**: Spock, *Common Sense Book of Baby and Child Care* (1946), p. 267.

252 "to feel that his mother and father": ibid., pp. 268–69.

252 "firming effect on the mother"; "I mean business": Spock, "Self-Regulation, Spoiling and Sleep Problems," p. 23.

252 "reasonable amount of consistency"; "really feel like": Spock, *Dr. Spock Talks with Mothers*, p. 108.

252 "judgment and decisiveness": Spock, "Self-Regulation, Spoiling and Sleep Problems," p. 18.

252 "as fanatical in their devotion": ibid., p. 3.

252 "he doesn't know what's good for him": Spock, *Baby and Child Care* (1957), p. 185.

252 "bullied into a jam": Barclay, "Educated Mother Subject to Panic," p. 197.

252 "advancing on the baby": Spock, *Baby and Child Care* (1957), p. 342.

253 "continuing need for parental control": Spock, *Dr. Spock Talks with Mothers*, p. 216.

253 "instrumental" to "personnel manager": Lasch, *Haven in a Heartless World*, p. 122.

253 "the grittiness" to "firmly but cordially": Spock, *Dr. Spock Talks with Mothers*, pp. 218, 220, 219.

253 "uncompromising goals and standards": Drucker, *The Concept of the Corporation*, p. 303.

253 "relaxation of standards": Spock, *Dr. Spock Talks with Mothers*, p. 269.

253 "it's difficult to bring up": *The Healthy Personality*, p. 78.

253 "We are uncertain" to "Russian moral superiority": Spock, *Problems of Parents*, pp. 290, 296, 297.

254 "belongingness": Whyte, *The Organization Man*, p. 32.

254 "unworthy, they just don't serve": Spock, *Problems of Parents*, p. 298.

254 "tradition against traditions": Spock, "Self-Regulation, Spoiling and Sleep Problems," p. 1.

254 "hard to settle"; "the flood of unsettling": Spock, *Problems of Parents*, pp. 298, 285.

254 "the self-assurance and firmness": Spock, *Dr. Spock Talks with Mothers*, p. 268.

254 "basic convictions that parents have" to "And it comes": Spock, "Values and Limits of Parent Education," pp. 11–12.

254 "work by will power alone": Spock, *Dr. Spock Talks with Mothers*, p. 110.

254 "This is nothing to be ashamed of": Spock, *Baby and Child Care* (1957), p. 47.

254 "I would suggest as a heading": quoted in Sydney Halpern, *American Pediatrics: The Social Dynamics of Professionalism, 1880–1980* (Berkeley: University of California Press, 1988), p. 13.

255 "In summary, I am making": Spock, *Problems of Parents*, p. 291.

NINE: *The Moralists*

256 "officially retiring to a boat": Richard Reeves, "Peace, Man, Says Baby Doctor Spock," *New York Times Magazine*, July 16, 1967, p. 49.

256 "to not being loved by everyone": Benjamin Spock, "The Professional Man's Muzzle," *American Journal of Orthopsychiatry* 35, no. 1 (January 1965): 40.

257 "I guess I've said" to "Some people say I'm preaching": Roland Weisz, "The Brave New World of Dr. Spock," *Woman*, Aug. 26, 1967, p. 8.

257 **"a fizzle"**: Thomas Maier, *Dr. Spock: An American Life* (New York: Harcourt Brace, 1998), p. 313.

257 **"a spectacle of nit-picking"**: Donald Jackson, "The U.S. versus Coffin and Spock," *Life*, May 17, 1968, p. 69.

257 **"I say to the American people"**: quoted in David Lyle, "Dr. Spock Misbehaves," *Esquire*, February 1969, p. 132.

258 **"It is clearly a terrible burden"**: Betty Friedan, *The Feminine Mystique* (New York: Norton, 1983). pp. 197–98.

258 **"Spocklash"**: Philip E. Slater, "Spocklash: Age, Sex, Revolution," *Washington Monthly*, February 1970, p. 30.

258 **"Many people expected that the arrest"**: Philip E. Slater, *The Pursuit of Loneliness: American Culture at the Breaking Point* (Boston: Beacon, 1970), p. 62.

258 **"respect for authority"**: Christopher Jencks, "Is It All Dr. Spock's Fault?" *New York Times Magazine*, Mar. 3, 1968, p. 27.

258 **"Is Dr. Spock to Blame?"**: *Newsweek* 72, no. 13 (Sept. 23, 1968): 68.

258 **"the most undisciplined"**: quoted in Benjamin Spock, "The Fuss over 'Baby and Child Care,' " *Redbook* 131, no. 6 (October 1968): 48.

258 **"thinks it can get"; "Feed 'em whatever"**: quoted in "Is Dr. Spock to Blame?" *Newsweek*, p. 68.

258 **"Spocked when they should have been"**: Maier, *Dr. Spock*, p. 321.

258 **"charming group of little children"**: "Is Dr. Spock to Blame?" *Newsweek*, p. 68.

258 **"spoiled brats who never had"**: quoted in Barbara Ehrenreich and Deirdre English, *For Her Own Good: 150 Years of the Experts' Advice to Women* (Garden City, NY: Anchor, 1978), p. 261.

258 **"fog of permissiveness"**: Maier, *Dr. Spock*, p. 323.

258 **"Dick . . . never said a harsh word"; "didn't try to dominate"**: "How Mrs. Nixon Brought Up Tricia and Julie," *McCall's* 96, no. 6 (March 1969): 176, 75.

259 **"always stressed"**: ibid., p. 75.

259 **"a catchall code for moral breakdown"**: Barbara Ehrenreich, *Fear of Falling: The Inner Life of the Middle Class* (New York: Pantheon, 1989), p. 169.

259 **"turned out a generation of infants"**: quoted in Ehrenreich and English, *For Her Own Good*, p. 261.

259 **The absence of "Spock-marked"**: Louis Menand, "You Say It's Your Birthday," *The New Republic* 198, no. 16 (Apr. 18, 1988): 36.

259 **"emotionally disturbed"; "parents who failed to give them"**: Bruno Bettelheim, "The Anatomy of Academic Discontent," in Sidney Hook, ed., *In Defense of Academic Freedom* (Pegasus, NY: Bobbs-Merrill, 1971), p. 70.

259 **"Although often very bright"; "Nor should the symbolic"**: ibid., pp. 68, 65.

260 **"suffer from both"**: Bruno Bettelheim, "Education and the Reality Principle," in *Surviving and Other Essays* (New York: Knopf, 1979), p. 133.

260 **"strong-father-figures"**: Bettelheim, "The Anatomy of Academic Discontent," p. 70.

260 **"In an age of confrontation politics"**: David Dempsey, "Bruno Bettelheim Is Dr. No," *New York Times Magazine*, Jan. 11, 1970, p. 22.

260 **"with an accent not unlike Dr. Strangelove's"**: ibid., p. 107.

260 **"Dr. Brutalheim"**: Richard Pollak, *The Creation of Dr. B: A Biography of Bruno Bettelheim* (New York: Simon & Schuster, 1997), p. 317.

261 **"Dr. Spock is for my husband"**: Maier, *Dr. Spock*, p. 219.

261 **"an upsurge of purpose"**: Bruno Bettelheim, "The Problem of Generations," *Daedalus* 91, no. 1 (Winter 1962): 92.

261 **"intelligent and fairly cultured"; "swamped with literature"**: Bruno Bettelheim, *Dialogues with Mothers* (Glencoe, IL.: Free Press, 1962), pp. 9, 2.

261 **"The Holy Work of Bruno Bettelheim"**: William Ryan, review of *The Empty Fortress, Commonweal,* May 26, 1967, p. 283.

261 **"A Hero of Our Time"**: Robert Coles, review of *The Empty Fortress, The New Republic* 156, no. 9 (Mar. 4, 1967): p. 23.

261 **"spectacular successes"**: Pollak, *The Creation of Dr. B,* p. 271.

261 **"the precipitating factor"**: Bruno Bettelheim, *The Empty Fortress: Infantile Autism and the Birth of the Self* (New York: Free Press, 1967), pp. 125–26.

262 **Leo Kanner**: Pollak, *The Creation of Dr. B,* p. 275.

262 **"Chicago's 'Dr. Yes' "**: *Time,* July 5, 1968, p. 49.

262 **"Dr. Spock as a Father"; "No Mollycoddler"**: *New York Times,* Nov. 8, 1968, p. 54.

262 **"The Less Permissive Dr. Spock"**: Katharine Davis Fishman, *New York Times Book Review,* Feb. 16, 1969, p. 4.

262 **"This whole house"**: Alison Lurie, *The War Between the Tates* (New York: Random House, 1974), p. 231.

262 **"worshiped [as] gods"**: ibid., p. 78.

262 **"You always give us"**: ibid., p. 190; ellipses in the original.

262 **"secretly abandoned the adult side"**: ibid., p. 55.

262 **"How has it all come about?"**: ibid., p. 5.

263 **"I have come smack back"**: "Dr. Spock as a Father—No Mollycoddler," *New York Times,* Nov. 8, 1968, p. 55.

263 **"What I'm really being"**: "Dr. Spock Misbehaves," p. 113.

263 **"stern, puritanical"**: "Dr. Spock as a Father—No Mollycoddler," p. 55.

263 **"to be a warmonger"**: "Dr. Spock Misbehaves," p. 113.

264 **Anna Freud, the original inspiration**: Diane E. Eyer, *Mother-Infant Bonding: A Scientific Fiction* (New Haven: Yale University Press, 1992), p. 69.

264 **"Despite the fact"**: Benjamin Spock letter to Anna Freud, Sept. 28, 1964, Benjamin Spock Papers, Syracuse University Library, Department of Special Collections. All the information on the Child Rearing Study comes from his papers.

265 **"Professional counselors" to "it was a healthy phenomenon"**: typescript of Mary Bergen's reflections on the Child Rearing Study, Benjamin Spock Papers.

265 **"robbing educated parents" to "I keep saying"**: Benjamin Spock letter to Urie Bronfenbrenner, Dec. 10, 1957, Benjamin Spock Papers.

266 **"I sometimes think"**: Spock, "How My Ideas Have Changed," *Redbook* 121, no. 6 (October 1963): 123.

266 **"recourse to clinics"; "monstrous middle-classness"**: Paul Goodman, "For Post-Infancy, a New Companion," *New York Herald Tribune,* Oct. 28, 1962, p. 3.

266 **"sturdy New England grandfather"**: Fishman, "The Less Permissive Dr. Spock," p. 4.

266 **"today's child-centered viewpoint"**: Benjamin Spock, *Baby and Child Care* (New York: Pocket Books, 1968), p. xvi.

267 **"needs from them"**: ibid.

267 **"Fortunate are the parents"; "in a disenchanted"**: ibid., p. 13.

267 **"basic principles" to "We've lost a lot"**: ibid., p. 10.

267 **"God's Salesman"**: Carol V. R. George, *God's Salesman: Norman Vincent Peale and the Power of Positive Thinking* (New York: Oxford University Press, 1993).

267 **"Progress in human relations"**: Spock, *Baby and Child Care* (1968), p. 16.

268 **"parental hesitancy":** Benjamin Spock, "Kinds of Rebellion in Adolescence," *Redbook* 127, no. 3 (July 1966): 24.

268 **"The parent's experience"; "In the end":** Spock, *Baby and Child Care* (1968), p. 427.

268 **"adolescents, like adults"; "serious obligations":** ibid., p. 428.

268 **"cultivate dishevelment":** ibid., p. 13.

268 **"the most socially conscious youth":** Slater, *The Pursuit of Loneliness*, pp. 63–64.

268 **"I'd be proud to be responsible":** Spock, "The Fuss over 'Baby and Child Care,'" p. 52.

269 **"Dr. Spock," Gloria Steinem:** Benjamin Spock and Mary Morgan, *Spock on Spock* (New York: Pantheon, 1989), p. 247.

269 **children's freedom; women's oppression:** In *The Pursuit of Loneliness*, Philip Slater usefully discusses both trends—"the postwar ultradomestication of the American female" and more freedom for children—and Spock's relation to them, pp. 64–65.

269 **"opinions about other areas" to "an extreme conservative":** Box 1, Benjamin Spock Papers.

270 **"I'm counting my chickens":** ibid.

270 **"have more serious consequences":** John Gagnon and William Simon, "Is a Women's Revolution Really Possible?" *McCall's* 97, no. 1 (October 1969): 76.

270 **"from the very beginning Spock's book":** Slater, *The Pursuit of Loneliness*, p. 64.

270 **"It was motherhood":** Friedan, *The Feminine Mystique*, p. 197.

271 **"not as apt as a boy":** Benjamin Spock, *Decent and Indecent: Our Personal and Political Behavior* (New York: McCall, 1970), p. 12.

271 **"a strong urge to satisfy"; "when women are encouraged":** ibid., pp. 34, 47.

271 **"in working at unexciting"; "indispensable as wives":** ibid., pp. 32, 34.

271 **"My prime concern is that":** quoted in Maier, *Dr. Spock*, p. 355.

271 **"idealistic, spiritual, and creative" to "dominate over greed":** Spock, *Decent and Indecent*, pp. 6, 131, xi.

271 **"very reasonable and charming":** quoted in Maier, *Dr. Spock*, p. 359.

271 **"I always listen to criticism":** ibid., p. 360.

271 **"Well, I'm just back of him":** ibid., p. 369.

272 **"What's most interesting":** Nancy McGrath, "By the Book," *New York Times*, June 27, 1976, collected in Rothman, *The Family*, p. 299.

272 **"I'm a writer":** Patti Hagan, "Dr. Spock Tells Why He No Longer Sings in Praise of Hims," *New York Times*, Oct. 13, 1973, collected in ibid., p. 286.

272 **"The Family Is Changing" to "feel that the care of children":** Spock, *Baby and Child Care* (New York: Hawthorn, 1976), p. 30.

273 **"I might have been more of a somebody" to "[taken] up with a 38-year-old":** "The Spocks: Bittersweet Recognition in a Revised Classic," *New York Times*, Mar. 19, 1976, p. 28.

274 **"the deterioration of the environment"; "the influence of giant corporate interests":** Benjamin Spock and Steven J. Parker, *Dr. Spock's Baby and Child Care* (New York: Pocket Books, 1998), p. xxx.

274 **"would make a new life":** quoted in Pollak, *The Creation of Dr. B*, p. 93.

274 **"I see exactly":** ibid., pp. 307–309.

275 **"achieve a unified personality":** Bruno Bettelheim, *The Uses of Enchantment: The Meaning and Importance of Fairy Tales* (New York: Vintage, 1989), p. 90.

275 **"We must live by fictions":** quoted in Pollak, *The Creation of Dr. B*, p. 15.

275 **two biographers:** Both Richard Pollak's biography and Nina Sutton's *Bettel-*

heim: A Life and a Legacy (New York: Basic Books, 1996) have been valuable resources.

275 **"children nobody else did"**: quoted in Sutton, *Bettelheim*, p. 229.

276 **"magical years"**: ibid., p. 256.

276 **"superego" to the children's "id"; Big Bad Wolf role**: ibid., p. 382.

276 **"total therapeutic environment"**: Bruno Bettelheim, "Mental Health and Current Mores," *American Journal of Orthopsychiatry* 22, no. 1 (January 1952): 76.

277 **Drugs and delinquency**: Bruno Bettelheim, *The Children of the Dream* (London: Collier-Macmillan, 1969), p. 4.

277 **"self-identity"; "a place in society"**: Bettelheim, "The Problem of Generations," p. 77.

277 **"did a good job"**: ibid., pp. 83–84.

277 **"absurd" set of "strangely"**: Bruno Bettelheim, "Growing Up Female," in *Surviving and Other Essays*, p. 223.

277 **"the kind of work"; "(of necessity) a drudge"**: Bettelheim, "The Problem of Generations," pp. 86, 76.

278 **"being a full-time wife and mother"; "overly about her infant"**: Bruno Bettelheim, "Women: Emancipation Is Still to Come," *The New Republic* 151, no. 10 (Nov. 7, 1964): 55, 49.

278 **"Some of our psychologists"**: ibid., p. 58.

278 **"an emotional flatness"**: Bettelheim, *The Children of the Dream*, p. 287.

278 **"experiment"; "restless dissatisfaction of youth"**: ibid., pp. 1, 4.

279 **"Scientific rigor"**: quoted in Pollak, *The Creation of Dr. B*, p. 252.

279 **Bettelheim claimed "good" results**: Bettelheim, *The Empty Fortress*, p. 413. See also Sutton, *Bettelheim*, pp. 424–25, and Pollak, *The Creation of Dr. B*, pp. 261–72. By 1973, Bettelheim had inflated his success rate to 85 percent of the autistic children who arrived before they were seven or eight. See Edward Dolnick, *Madness on the Couch: Blaming the Victim in the Heyday of Psychoanalysis* (New York: Simon & Schuster, 1998), p. 212.

280 **"leisure, the absence"; "The affluent middle-class American"**: Bruno Bettelheim, "The Roots of Radicalism," *Playboy* 18, no. 3 (March 1971): 208.

280 **"to stand up"**: quoted in Sutton, *Bettelheim*, p. 269.

280 **"nothing to push against"**: quoted in Dempsey, "Bruno Bettelheim Is Dr. No," p. 107.

280 **"What I would really like to do"**: quoted in Sutton, *Bettelheim*, p. 448.

280 **The birthrate dropped**: David Frum, *How We Got Here: The 70's, the Decade That Brought You Modern Life (for Better or Worse)* (New York: Basic Books, 2000), p. 106.

281 **the *Times* announced**: Keith Love, "For First Time in U.S., Divorces Pass 1 Million," *New York Times*, Feb. 18, 1976, collected in Rothman, *The Family*, p. 250.

281 **a bumper crop**: Frum, *How We Got Here*, p. 106.

281 **"there are many more books"**: McGrath, "By the Book," p. 295.

281 **"lying snugly against"**: James Dobson, *Dare to Discipline* (Wheaton, IL: Tyndale., 1986), p. 38.

281 **the book that coined the verb**: Fitzhugh Dodson, *How to Parent* (Los Angeles: Nash, 1970), p. 1.

281 **"Thou shalt NOT"**: quoted in McGrath, "By the Book," p. 296.

281 **"the intellectual development"; "particularly deficient"**: Dodson, *How to Parent*, p. 394; see also pp. 8–9.

281 **"the inferiority complex"**: See Alfred Adler, *The Education of Children* (New

York: Greenberg, 1930), p. 77; Phyllis Bottome, *Alfred Adler: A Portrait from Life* (New York: Vanguard, 1957).

281 **"unrestricted freedom"**: Rudolf Dreikurs, with Vicki Stolz, *Children: The Challenge* (New York: Plume, 1964), p. 10.

282 **family council**: ibid., p. 287.

282 **"logical consequences" to "Homework not done"**: ibid., pp. 76–85.

282 **"insight is insufficient"**: Haim Ginott, "Between Parent and Teenager," *McCalls'* 96, no. 9 (1969): 122.

282 **"forbidding sound"**: Richard Flaste, "Learning to Solve Family Conflicts Without Fights," *New York Times*, Mar. 14, 1975, collected in Rothman, *The Family*, p. 293.

282 **"The raising of a child"**: Dodson, *How to Parent*, pp. 1–2.

282 **Dr. Burton L. White**: See Burton L. White, *The First Three Years of Life* (New York: Prentice-Hall, 1990).

283 **"Very frightening"**: Benjamin Spock Papers.

283 **"Why Working Mothers Have Happier Children"**: Bruno Bettelheim column, *Ladies' Home Journal* 87, no. 6 (June 1970): 24.

283 **"unsatisfying existence"**: Bruno Bettelheim, "What's Happening to the Family," *Ladies' Home Journal* 88, no. 5 (May 1971): 37.

284 **"one family member"; "a life of bondage"**: ibid., pp. 37, 39.

284 **"resentment that her life" to "She works doubly hard"**: Bettelheim, *The Children of the Dream*, p. 57.

284 **"adult responsibility"; "in their minds"**: Bruno Bettelheim, "It Wasn't Me Who Wet," *Ladies' Home Journal* 87, no. 3 (March 1970): 62.

284 **"psychoanalysis tends to see"**: Bruno Bettelheim, "Alienation and Autonomy," in *Surviving*, p. 337.

284 **"raw emotions"**: Bruno Bettelheim, "Expressing Anger," *Ladies' Home Journal* 88, no. 2 (February 1971): 26.

285 **"act on the basis"**: Bruno Bettelheim, "Teaching Self-Control to a Screaming Two-Year-Old," *Ladies' Home Journal* 89, no. 12 (December 1972): 29.

285 **"efforts are monumental"**: Bettelheim, "Alienation and Autonomy," in *Surviving*, p. 338.

285 **"What was wrong"**: Bruno Bettelheim, "Children Must Learn to Fear," *New York Times*, Apr. 13, 1969, p. 135.

285 **"the debilitating fear"**: Bettelheim, "Teaching Self-Control to a Screaming Two-Year-Old," p. 29.

285 **"the crippling price of inhibition"**: Bettelheim, "Education and the Reality Principle," in *Surviving*, p. 133.

285 **"What was wrong with"**: Bettelheim, "Children Must Learn to Fear," p. 135.

285 **"accept themselves as imperfect beings"**: Bettelheim, "Expressing Anger," p. 26.

285 **"much greater autonomy"**: Bettelheim, "Alienation and Autonomy," in *Surviving*, p. 349.

285 **"instinctual experience"; "decisions on what to repress"**: Bettelheim, "Children Must Learn to Fear," p. 140.

285 **"Didn't I let you hang onto"**: ibid., p. 141.

285 **"a desire that our children"**: Bruno Bettelheim, "What Does Independence Really Mean?" *Ladies' Home Journal* 88, no. 1 (January 1971): 26.

286 **"the most important thing of all"**: Bruno Bettelheim, "About Summerhill," in *Surviving*, p. 179.

286 **"free of serious difficulties"**: Bruno Bettelheim, "Recreating Family Life: The Means Are in Our Hands," *Parents' Magazine* 51, no. 10 (October 1976): 64.

286 **"the prime task of psychoanalytic"**: Bettelheim, "About Summerhill," in *Surviving*, p. 181.

286 **"feeling of belonging"; "If the correct view"**: ibid., pp. 72, 64.

286 **"God-given . . . but"**: Bettelheim, "What's Happening to the Family," p. 184.

287 **"So long as the working mother"**: Bettelheim, "Why Working Mothers Have Happier Children," p. 87.

287 **"Another change in inner attitude" to "Children must not be isolated"**: Bettelheim, "What's Happening to the Family," p. 184.

287 **"New York Public Library's list"**: Pollak, *The Creation of Dr. B*, p. 351.

287 **"only to the sunny side"**: Bettelheim, *The Uses of Enchantment*, p. 7.

287 **"a magic mirror which reflects"**: ibid., p. 309.

288 **" 'explain' to the child"**: ibid., p. 155; see also pp. 18–19.

288 **"nameless anxieties"; "chaotic, angry"**: ibid., p. 7.

288 **"As the stories unfold" to "a great deal to overcome"**: ibid., p. 6.

288 **"moral education which subtly"**: ibid., p. 5.

288 **"warmth, humane and urgent"**: John Updike, review of *The Uses of Enchantment*, in *Hugging the Shore: Essays and Criticism* (New York: Knopf, 1983), p. 651.

289 **"vexed" him**: ibid., pp. 653–54.

289 **"At its end"**: Bettelheim, *The Uses of Enchantment*, p. 215.

289 **"The story's ambiguity" to "running away"**: ibid., p. 224.

289 **"unsolvable predicament"; "more and more persons"**: ibid., p. 218.

290 **"as much as [children] identify"**: Bruno Bettelheim, *A Good Enough Parent: A Book on Child-Rearing* (New York: Viking, 1987), p. 25.

290 **"the depth of our commitment"**: ibid., p. 34.

290 **If only, Bettelheim**: Pollak, *The Creation of Dr. B*, p. 404.

TEN: *All in the Family*

293 **At the Baltimore meeting**: Ann Hulbert, "The Baltimore Bust," *The New Republic* 182, no. 26 (June 28, 1980): 20–21.

294 **"the learning of childhood"**: quoted in Hillary Clinton, *It Takes a Village: And Other Lessons Children Teach Us* (New York: Simon & Schuster, 1996), p. 101.

294 **"a unique process of listening"**: *Listening to America's Families*, White House Conference on Families pamphlet, May 1980, opening page.

294 **"ordinary" Americans**: ibid., p. 2.

294 **"racial and ethnic groups"**: Diane Ravitch, "In the Family's Way," *The New Republic* 182, no. 26 (June 28, 1980): 20.

294 **"reach out to all Americans"**: *Listening to America's Families*, p. 3.

294 **"national family policy"**: Jonathan Alter, "Stand By for the Non-Event of the Year," *Washington Monthly* 12, no. 4 (June 1980): 22.

294 **"speak-outs"; "flashpoint issues"**: Hulbert, "The Baltimore Bust," p. 21, and Ravitch, "In the Family's Way," p. 19.

294 **"Jobless Rate Soars"**: *New York Times*, June 7, 1980, p. 1.

294 **"contaminated by the liberal Carter machine"**: Hulbert, "The Baltimore Bust," p. 21.

295 **"there are no neat norms"**: Ravitch, "In the Family's Way," p. 19.

295 **"urgent priority"**: Alter, "Stand By for the Non-Event of the Year," p. 22.

295   **"What *is* new"**: Kenneth Keniston and the Carnegie Council on Children, *All Our Children: The American Family Under Pressure* (New York: Harcourt Brace Jovanovich, 1977), p. 4.

295   **"speak out on what they think"**: *Listening to America's Families*, p. 5.

295   **"to articulate their needs"**: Hulbert, "The Baltimore Bust," p. 20.

295   **"tide of femininity"; "sisters who are compelled to work"**: Mrs. Theodore W. Birney, "Address of Welcome," National Congress of Mothers Third Convention, pp. 198, 199.

295   **more than half:** Census Bureau report cited in Marie Winn, *Children Without Childhood* (New York: Pantheon, 1983), p. 121; also Keniston, *All Our Children*, p. 4.

296   **up to 45 percent:** Steven Mintz and Susan Kellogg, *Domestic Revolutions: A Social History of American Family Life* (New York: Free Press, 1988), p. 218.

296   **"The Superwoman Squeeze"**: *Newsweek* 95, no. 20 (May 19, 1980): 72.

296   **slightly more than 60 percent:** Jack P. Shonkoff and Deborah A. Phillips, eds., *From Neurons to Neighborhoods: The Science of Early Childhood Development* (Washington, DC: National Academy Press, 2000), p. 269.

296   **"to make home"**: Robert S. Lynd and Helen Merrell Lynd, *Middletown: A Study in Contemporary American Culture* (New York: Harcourt Brace, 1929), p. 136.

296   **"breakdown of the family"**: Keniston, *All Our Children*, p. 22.

296   **Forty percent of American marriages** to **one in eight:** Ravitch, "In the Family's Way," p. 24.

296   **more than double:** Keniston, *All Our Children*, p. 5.

296   **By 1997, the proportion** to **The racial differences:** Shonkoff and Phillips, *From Neurons to Neighborhoods*, p. 283.

296   **By eighteen, the average American youth:** Keniston, *All Our Children*, p. 7.

296   **"early sophistication"**: Lynd and Lynd, *Middletown*, p. 135. "Precocity" had already unnerved the Progressive Era experts, who worried about the "miniature men and women" who were the casualties of too little fresh air and free play.

297   **" 'adultification' of children"**: Neil Postman, *The Disappearance of Childhood* (New York: Vintage, 1994), p. 124.

297   **"increasingly complex"**: Winn, *Children Without Childhood*, p. 5.

297   **"childified"**: Postman, *The Disappearance of Childhood*, p. 126.

297   **"in a pressure-cooker"**: David Elkind, *The Hurried Child: Growing Up Too Fast Too Soon* (Reading, MA: Addison-Wesley, 1981), p. 3.

297   **"competence"**: Benjamin S. Bloom, ed., *Developing Talent in Young People* (New York: Ballantine, 1985), p. 486. He was quoting from Robert W. White. See also M. Brewster Smith, "Competence and Socialization," in John A. Claysin, ed., *Socialization and Society* (Boston: Little, Brown, 1908), pp. 273–74.

297   **"that sap their self-esteem"; "In addition to being in charge"**: Keniston, *All Our Children*, pp. 23, 214.

298   **"We don't think"**: "All in the Family," *Newsweek* 115, no. 24 (June 16, 1980): 31.

298   **"laundry list of hopes and intentions"**: Ravitch, "In the Family's Way," p. 24.

298   **"[translated] . . . into reality"**: *Listening to America's Families*, p. 3.

298   **"another study to gather dust"**: Alter, "Stand By for the Non-Event of the Year," p. 24.

298   **"beautifully prepared"**: T. Berry Brazelton, *Infants and Mothers: Differences in Development*, rev. ed. (New York: Delta/Seymour Lawrence, 1983), p. xxiii.

298   **"competence will call up competence"**: "The New Dr. Spock: 'A Great Dad,' " *Time* 122, no. 7 (Aug. 15, 1983): 54.

298   **"In nurturing a small baby"**: Brazelton, *Infants and Mothers*, p. xxiii.

298   **"We used to see"**: "The New Dr. Spock," p. 54.

298   **"an 'interactive pediatrician' "**: T. Berry Brazelton, "Assessment as a Method for Enhancing Development," *Zero to Three* (bulletin of the National Center for Clinical Infant Programs) 2, no. 1 (September 1981): 1.

299   **the first woman elder**: Peter Worstman, "T. Berry Brazelton: Babies' Best Friend," *P and S Journal* 16, no. 2, cpmcnet.columbia.edu.

299   **"the most widely quoted"**: Andrew T. Weil, "Harvard's Bruner and His Yeasty Ideas," *Harper's* 229, no. 1375 (December 1964): 81.

299   **"Accumulated evidence"**: Jerome Kagan, Richard B. Kearsley, and Philip R. Zelazo, *Infancy: Its Place in Human Development* (Cambridge, MA: Harvard University Press, 1978), p. 46. The publication of John H. Flavell's *The Developmental Psychology of Jean Piaget* in 1963 made his enormous opus more accessible to American psychologists. For a sense of Piaget's spreading influence, see both the 1970 and the 1983 editions of the *Handbook of Child Psychology*, where he reappeared after an absence since the 1931 edition. Popular interest and understanding were spurred by Jean Piaget and Barbel Inhelder, *The Psychology of the Child*, trans. Helen Weaver (New York: Basic Books, 1969), an accessible "synthesis, or summing up," as they put it in their preface. See also Mary Ann Spencer Pulaski, *Understanding Piaget: An Introduction to Children's Cognitive Development* (New York: Harper & Row, 1980; originally published in 1978 as *Your Baby's Mind and How It Grows: Piaget's Theory for Parents*).

300   **"It just turned Jerry on"**: T. Berry Brazelton interview #13 with Milton J. E. Senn in Senn Child Development Oral History Interviews, National Library of Medicine, Washington, DC. See also Jerome S. Bruner, *In Search of Mind: Essays in Autobiography* (Cambridge, MA: Harvard University Press, 1983), pp. 145–48.

300   **"Possibly the first conscious"**: G. Stanley Hall, "Notes on the Study of Infants," *Pedagogical Seminary* 1 (June 1891): 134.

300   **a powerful analogy**: Alison Gopnik, Andrew N. Meltzoff, and Patricia K. Kuhl, *The Scientist in the Crib: Minds, Brains, and How Children Learn* (New York: Morrow, 1999), p. 21. See also their very good description of experimental methods and habituation, pp. 26–28.

301   **"two-way circuit"**: Stella Chess, Alexander Thomas, and Herbert G. Birch, *Your Child Is a Person: A Psychological Approach to Parenthood Without Guilt* (New York: Penguin, 1985), p. 75.

301   **"goodness of fit"**: Robert Karen, *Becoming Attached: Unfolding the Mystery of the Infant-Mother Bond and Its Impact on Later Life* (New York: Warner, 1994), p. 272.

301   **"complex of nesting"; "growing capacity"**: Urie Bronfenbrenner: *The Ecology of Human Development: Experiments by Nature and Design* (Cambridge, MA: Harvard University Press, 1979), p. 8.

301   **"the tallest two-year-old"**: Worstman, "T. Berry Brazelton."

301   **much-filmed Mary Catherine Bateson**: Bateson, *With a Daughter's Eye* (New York: HarperPerennial, 1994), p. 215.

301   **"What Do Babies Know?"; "Much more"**: cover story in *Time* 122, no. 7 (Aug. 15, 1983): 52.

302   **"began cutting"; "Most of the pictures"**: Joyce Maynard, *Baby Love* (New York: Viking, 1981), pp. 22–23.

302   **"deepest principle is mutuality"; "the first time"**: Brazelton, *Infants and Mothers*, pp. xviii, xvii.

302 **"tell whether a baby"**: T. Berry Brazelton, *What Every Baby Knows* (Reading, MA: Addison-Wesley, 1987), p. 226.

303 **"his or her repertoire"**: T. Berry Brazelton, "Introduction," in Arnold J. Samiroff, ed., *Organization and Stability in Newborn Behavior: A Commentary on the Brazelton Neonatal Behavior Assessment Scale*, Monographs of the Society for Research in Child Development 43, nos. 5–6, serial no. 177 (1976): 3.

303 **"newborn, even under stress" to "active, eager interactant"**: Brazelton, "Assessment as a Method," p. 1.

303 **"adaptive and coping strategies"; "caring mother and father"**: Brazelton, "Introduction," p. 3.

303 **"window into"; "from each new level"**: Brazelton, "Assessment as a Method," pp. 6, 4.

303 **"Babies are competent"**: Brazelton, *Infants and Mothers*, p. xxiv.

304 **"Don't frighten parents!"**: "What Do Babies Know?" p. 53.

304 **"rich and abstract representations"**: Alison Gopnik, "The Post-Piaget Era," *Psychological Science* 7, no. 4 (July 1996): 221. Her article is a very useful overview of Piagetian revisionism, in which she surveys the various "theory fragments, almost-theories, and pseudotheories bobbing around us" and points toward "a kind of developmental pluralism." Different theories, she proposes, may prove to explain different developmental phenomena.

304 **"I think that's very rude"**: "What Do Babies Know?" p. 55.

304 **"gold standard"**: Margaret Talbot, "Attachment Theory: The Ultimate Experiment," *New York Times Magazine*, May 24, 1998, p. 98.

304 **"still-face situation"**: T. Berry Brazelton and Bertrand G. Cramer, *The Earliest Relationship* (Reading, MA: Addison-Wesley, 1990), pp. 107–109.

305 **an academic industry**: See Karen, *Becoming Attached*, pp. 217–20.

305 **"the wizard act of 'intersubjective' sharing"**: Jerome Bruner, "Tot Thought," *New York Review of Books* 47, no. 4 (Mar. 9, 2000): 27.

305 **"theory theory"**: Gopnik, "The Post-Piaget Era," p. 221.

305 **"top-down conceptions"**: Eleanor E. Maccoby, "The Role of Parents in the Socialization of Children: An Historical Overview," *Developmental Psychology* 28 (1992): 1006.

306 **"socialize adults or anybody else"**: Urie Bronfenbrenner interview #12, Milton J. E. Senn Child Development Oral History Interviews, National Library of Medicine, Washington, DC.

306 **"Indeed, the implications"**: Eleanor E. Maccoby and John A. Martin, "Socialization in the Context of the Family: Parent-Child Interaction," in Paul H. Mussen (series ed.) and E. Mavis Hetherington (vol. ed.), *Handbook of Child Psychology*, vol. 4, *Socialization, Personality, and Social Development*, 4th ed., 1983, p. 82. See the whole article for a subtle overview of the state of socialization research, its theories and methods of study. The work of behavioral geneticists became more widely known over the rest of the decade.

307 **"America's pediatrician"**: Alan Long, "Bringing Up Baby Online," Harvard Net News, May 30, 2000, www.researchmatters.harvard.edu/net_news2000/05.30/brazelton.5.30.html.

307 **"social pressure to be"**: T. Berry Brazelton, *Working and Caring* (Reading, MA: Addison-Wesley, 1985), p. xvii.

307 **"cocksure 'cog sci' "**: Bruner, "Tot Thought," p. 27.

307 **"Parents need as much care"; "the great energy"**: T. Berry Brazelton, *Touch-*

points: *Your Child's Emotional and Behavioral Development* (Reading, MA: Addison-Wesley, 1992), pp. 37, xviii.

307 **"powerful confirmation of well-being" to "Oooh, aren't you amazing!":** Brazelton, *Infants and Mothers*, p. xxiv.

308 **"Wow! I've done it":** ibid.

308 **"hunger for professional support":** Brazelton, *What Every Baby Knows*, p. 264.

308 **"an active part of each family":** Brazelton, *Touchpoints*, p. xxi.

308 **"touched and excited" to "too tired":** Jack Westman, ed., *Parenthood in America: Undervalued, Underpaid, Under Siege* (Madison: University of Wisconsin Press, 2001), p. viii.

309 **"man who really likes children":** "Somersaults and Sympathy," *Newsweek*, Feb. 11, 1989, p. 72.

309 **"breakthroughs in brain research"; "potential to revolutionize":** *Newsweek*, special edition on "Your Child: From Birth to Three," Spring/Summer 1997, pp. 4, 63.

309 **"the leading experts":** transcript of proceedings of the White House Conference on Early Childhood Development and Learning (hereafter referred to as the Clinton conference), p. 3.

309 **"powerful institutions of society":** Carnegie Task Force on Meeting the Needs of Young Children, *Starting Points: Meeting the Needs of Our Youngest Children* (New York: Carnegie Corporation of New York, 1994), p. viii.

310 *Beyond Rhetoric:* Ann Hulbert, "Animal Dreams," *The New Republic* 210, no. 23 (June 6, 1994): 42.

310 **"the wide gap between":** David Hamburg, transcript of the proceedings of the Clinton conference, p. 24.

311 **"Researchers say that neurobiologists":** Carnegie Task Force, *Starting Points*, p. 8.

311 **"new techniques in brain imaging":** William Greenough et al., "The Impact of the Caregiving Environment on Young Children's Development: Different Ways of Knowing," *Zero to Three* 21, no. 5 (April/May 2001): 20.

311 **PET scans:** John T. Bruer, *The Myth of the First Three Years: A New Understanding of Early Brain Development and Lifelong Learning* (New York: Free Press, 1999), p. 78. Bruer's book is a thorough account of the Reiner campaign and the Clinton conference, and provides a nonspecialist's guide to the state of neurobiological research in 1999.

312 **interactive, resilient "plasticity":** See also Gopnik, Meltzoff, and Kuhl, *The Scientist in the Crib*, p. 179.

312 **in their brief turns:** transcript of the proceedings of the Clinton conference, pp. 38–41, 45–49. See also Bruer's summaries in *The Myth of the First Three Years*, pp. 6–8.

313 **it appeared to be the pattern:** Bruer, *The Myth of the First Three Years*, p. 122.

313 **"The question of how to rear":** Kagan quoted in Stephen P. Hirsh and Karen Livin, "How Love Begins Between Parent and Child," in Paul Henry Mussen, John Janeway Conger, and Jerome Kagan, eds., *Readings in Child and Adolescent Psychology: Contemporary Perspectives* (New York: Harper & Row, 1980), p. 39.

313 **"either at the small scale":** Gopnik, Meltzoff, and Kuhl, *The Scientist in the Crib*, p. 199.

314 **"Babies understand":** transcript of proceedings of the Clinton conference, p. 20.

314 **"Science, as we will hear"** to **"anxious or imprison"**: ibid., pp. 3, 7, 6.

314 **"Only 20 to 30 percent"**: quoted in "Teach Your Parents Well," *Newsweek*, Apr. 28, 1997, p. 72.

314 **"research can't tell"**: transcript of proceedings of the Clinton conference, p. 51.

314 **"could tell by a child's behavior"**: T. Berry Brazelton, "Building a Better Self-Image," *Newsweek*, special edition, Spring/Summer 1997, p. 77.

314 **Nor had research**: Erica Goode, "Mozart for Baby? Some Say, Maybe Not," *New York Times*, Aug. 3, 1999, p. D1.

314 **"affects the spatial-temporal reasoning"**: quoted in Bruer, *The Myth of the First Three Years*, p. 62.

315 **"some minimum threshold"** to **"very, very clever"**: transcript of proceedings of the Clinton conference, pp. 53–54.

315 **"new insights into early development"**: Rima Shore, *Rethinking the Brain: New Insights into Early Development* (New York: Families and Work Institute, 1997), p. 65.

315 **"the policy implications are absolutely clear"; "I hadn't thought of that"**: Joe Klein, "Clintons on the Brain," *The New Yorker* 73, no. 4 (Mar. 17, 1997): 60, 62.

315 **"But to an uncertain end"**: *Newsweek*, special edition, Spring/Summer 1997, p. 63.

316 **It was an analysis**: See also Malcolm Gladwell, "Baby Steps," *The New Yorker*, Jan. 10, 2000, p. 87.

316 **"Goodnight mush"**: Rob Reiner's ABC TV special "I Am Your Child," Apr. 28, 1997.

316 **"fragile, elfin"**: Malcolm Gladwell, "Do Parents Matter?" *The New Yorker* 74, no. 12 (August 17, 1998): 55.

316 **"Kicked out of"**: Judith Rich Harris, *The Nurture Assumption: Why Children Turn Out the Way They Do* (New York: Free Press, 1998), p. xvi.

317 **"cherished cultural myth"**: ibid., p. 4.

317 **"notion that parents are the most important"**: ibid., p. 15.

317 **"would come to be seen"**: ibid., p. xiii.

317 **"Do Parents Matter?"**: *Newsweek* 132, no. 10 (Sept. 7, 1998).

317 **"some nerves in this age"**: Robert Wright, "The Power of Their Peers," *Time* 152, no. 8 (Aug. 24, 1998): 67.

317 **"self-absorbed parents"**: John Leo, "Parenting Without a Care," *U.S. News & World Report* 125, no. 11 (Sept. 21, 1998): 14.

318 **"English garden"**: William Damon, ed., *Handbook of Child Psychology*, 5th ed. (New York: Wiley, 1998), p. xv.

318 **"artificial experimental set-up"** to **"the slamming of a door"**: Leslie Ray Marston, "Present Tendencies in Research in Child Development," unpublished paper presented at the Second Conference on Research in Child Development, Washington, DC, May 5–7, 1927, Box 106, Arnold Gesell Papers, Library of Congress, Washington, DC.

319 **"parents have no predictable effects"**: Harris, *The Nurture Assumption*, p. 37.

319 **"correlations come"**: ibid., p. 322.

319 **"It is indeed true"** to **"we do not really know"**: Howard Gardner, "Do Parents Count?" *New York Review of Books* 45, no. 17 (Nov. 5, 1998): 20.

319 **"no present concept"**: Jerome Kagan, *Three Seductive Ideas* (Cambridge, MA: Harvard University Press, 1998), p. 198.

320 **"the allure of infant determinism"**: ibid., p. 83.

320   **telling mothers to kiss:** ibid., p. 91.

320   **"well-meaning advocates"; "under the anxious":** Jack P. Shonkoff and Deborah A. Phillips, eds., *From Neurons to Neighborhoods: The Science of Early Childhood Development—An Introduction*, Zero to Three bulletin, vol. 21, no. 5 (April/May 2001): 5, 1.

321   **"false self-reassurance" to "Faint Praise!":** Emily Fenichel, "From Neurons to Neighborhoods: What's in It for You?," *Zero to Three* bulletin, vol. 21, no. 5 (April/May 2001): 14.

321   **"core concepts of development":** Shonkoff and Phillips, eds., *From Neurons to Neighborhoods*, pp. 22–32.

321   **"science . . . based largely on"; "guides responsible policy"** ibid., pp. 23, 22.

321   **"the recent focus on 'zero to three' ":** ibid., p. 7.

321   **"growth of self-regulation [that] is a cornerstone":** ibid., p. 3, and chap. 5, "Acquiring Self-Regulation," pp. 93–123.

321   **"become a very complex endeavor":** ibid., p. 228.

322   **"one of the most consistent":** ibid., p. 275.

322   **"enhancement of parenting skills":** ibid., p. 263.

322   **"Shifting parental behavior":** ibid., p. 226.

322   **"child-focused" programs:** ibid., p. 344.

322   **"family-centered, community-based":** ibid., pp. 366–67.

323   **"The key is to blend":** William Greenough et al., "The Impact of the Caregiving Environment on Young Children's Development," *Zero to Three* bulletin, vol. 21, no. 5 (April/May 2001): 23.

323   **"a new national dialogue":** ibid., p. 7.

323   **"typically viewed":** ibid., p. 6.

323   **"nurture, protect, and ensure" to "ethical and moral values":** Shonkoff and Phillips, eds., *From Neurons to Neighborhoods*, p. 3.

323   **"well-being and 'well-becoming' ":** ibid., p. 413.

324   **"the foundation of morality":** T. Berry Brazelton and Stanley Greenspan, "Our Window to the Future," *Newsweek* 131, no. 17A (Fall/Winter 2000): 36.

324   **"a moral person": "What Matters Most,"** in ibid., p. 6.

ELEVEN: *Ministers, Mentors, and Managers*

325   **"It shall be the glorious":** Reverend William H. Milburn, "Opening Prayer," National Congress of Mothers First Session, p. 5.

326   **"disciples of discipline":** Susan Bolotin, "The Disciples of Discipline," *New York Times Magazine*, Feb. 14, 1999, p. 32.

326   **" 'helping' professionals":** John Rosemond, *A Family of Value* (Kansas City, MO: Andrews McMeel, 1995), p. 30.

326   **"Eastern establishment":** James Dobson quoted in Gil Alexander-Moegerle, *James Dobson's War on America* (Amherst, NY: Prometheus Books, 1997), p. 40.

326   **"the last defense against":** Rosemond, *A Family of Value*, p. 7.

326   **"competitive mastery"; "nurturing care":** T. Berry Brazelton and Stanley I. Greenspan, *The Irreducible Needs of Children: What Every Child Must Have to Grow, Learn, and Flourish* (Cambridge, MA: Perseus, 2000), p. xix.

326   **"professionals and parents are embracing":** ibid., p. xviii.

327   **"children of character":** Dan Kindlon, *Too Much of a Good Thing: Raising Children of Character in an Indulgent Age* (New York: Hyperion, 2001).

327   **"conscience is as important"**: William Damon, *The Moral Child: Nurturing Children's Natural Moral Growth* (New York: Free Press, 1988), p. x.

327   **"one of developmental"**: ibid., p. xiii.

327   **"however much"**: James Q. Wilson, *The Moral Sense* (New York: Free Press, 1993), p. xii.

327   **"surprisingly, we do not know"; "what anyone can reasonably"**: James Q. Wilson, *On Character: Essays* (Washington DC: AEI Press, 1995), pp. 50, 5.

328   **Even as busy researchers:** For useful summaries of the state of research on children's morality, see Elliot Turiel, "The Development of Morality" in William Damon, ed., *Handbook of Child Psychology*, 5th ed., vol. 3: *Social, Emotional, and Personality Development*, vol. ed. Nancy Eisenberg (New York: Wiley, 1998). See also Jerome Kagan and Sharon Lamb, *The Emergence of Morality in Young Children* (Chicago: University of Chicago Press, 1987). For an overview of research on parenting implications, see Nancy Eisenberg and Bridget Murphy, "Parenting and Children's Moral Development," in Marc Bornstein, ed., *Handbook of Parenting*, vol. 4: *Applied and Practical Parenting* (Mahwah, NJ: Erlbaum, 1995).

328   **"catalysts for the growth"**: Jack P. Shonkoff and Deborah A. Phillips, eds., *From Neurons to Neighborhoods: The Science of Early Child Development* (Washington, DC: National Academy Press, 2000), p. 24.

328   **"the voice of Grandma"**: Rosemond, *A Family of Value*, p. 11.

328   **"hearts and minds"**: Gary and Anne Marie Ezzo, *Growing Kids God's Way: Biblical Ethics for Parenting* (Chatsworth, CA: Micah 6:8, 1997), p. 10.

329   **"Nothing short of"**: Dobson and Bauer, *Children at Risk*, p. 19.

329   **"the issue of child care"**: ibid., p. 21.

330   **"biblical ethics"**: Ezzo, *Growing Kids God's Way*, subtitle.

330   **"capture the hearts"**: ibid., p. 10.

330   **a million parents:** Hanna Rosin, "A Tough Plan for Raising Children Draws Fire," *Washington Post*, Feb. 27, 1999, p. 1.

330   **"minds of today's parents"; "rightly applying"**: Growing Families International Web site, www.gfi.org.

330   **"loose cannon"**: John Rosemond, *Because I Said So!: 366 Insightful and Thought-Provoking Reflections on Parenting and Family Life* (Kansas City, MO: Andrews McMeel, 1996), p. vii.

330   **"antipsychologist's psychologist"**: Beth Brophy, "Because I Said So!" *U.S. News & World Report* 123, no. 18 (Nov. 10, 1997): 69.

330   **"recovering liberal"; "possible to separate"**: Rosemond, *A Family of Value*, p. 101.

330   **"ultraliberals, leftists"**: Bolotin, "The Disciples of Discipline," p. 34.

330   **"big government"**: Rosemond, *A Family of Value*, p. 118.

330   **Book sales:** Bolotin, "The Disciples of Discipline," p. 32.

331   **Her book; Brazelton's:** Sharon Hays, *The Cultural Contradictions of Motherhood* (New Haven: Yale University Press, 1996), p. 51.

331   **"What is needed now"; "an adult world whose values"**: Penelope Leach, *Children First: What Our Society Must Do—and Is Not Doing for Our Children Today* (New York: Knopf, 1994), pp. xv, 23.

331   **"one hell of a pamphleteer"**: Gwen Kinkead, "Penelope Leach," *New York Times Magazine*, Apr. 10, 1994, p. 34.

331   **"more caring, seamless system"**: Brazelton and Greenspan, *The Irreducible Needs of Children*, p. 186.

331   **"the least child-oriented society"**: Kinkead, "Penelope Leach," p. 34.

331   **"give them back"**: Brazelton and Greenspan, *The Irreducible Needs of Children*, p. 65.

332   **"cause-related" public relations**: Alan Long, "Bringing up Baby Online," Harvard Net News, May 30, 2000, www.researchmatters.harvard.edu/net_news2000/05.30/brazelton.5.30.html.

332   **"floor time"**: Stanley I. Greenspan with Jacqueline Salmon, *Playground Politics: Understanding the Emotional Life of Your School-Age Child* (Reading, MA: Addison-Wesley, 1993), p. 271.

332   **"foundation for any lasting sense"**: Brazelton and Greenspan, *The Irreducible Needs of Children*, p. 148.

332   **"what specific types of experiences"; "optimal structure"**: ibid., pp. x, 39.

332   **"Two Experts Do Battle"**: Erica Goode, "Two Experts Do Battle over Potty Training," *New York Times*, Jan. 12, 1999, p. 1.

332   **"A Tough Plan"**: Rosin, "A Tough Plan for Raising Children Draws Fire."

333   **"no debate is more contentious"**: Erica Goode, "Findings Give Some Support to Advocates of Spanking: Adding Fuel to Bitter Debate on Child Care," *New York Times*, Aug. 25, 2001.

333   **"abstinence-only" message:** Jeffrey P. Moran, *Teaching Sex: The Shaping of Adolescence in the 20th Century* (Cambridge, MA: Harvard University Press, 2000), pp. 209, 213.

333   **save-their-souls-and-self-esteem counsel:** See Nicholas Lemann, "The Battle over Boys," *The New Yorker*, July 10, 2000, p. 79.

334   **Five times as many:** Anne Cassidy, *Parents Who Think Too Much: Why We Do It, How to Stop* (New York: Dell, 1998), p. 11.

334   **"out-of-control parents"**: Marie Winn, *Children Without Childhood* (New York: Pantheon, 1983), p. 11.

334   **"counsel, if not outright insistence"**: Alvin Rosenfeld and Nicole Wise, *Hyper-Parenting: Are You Hurting Your Child by Trying Too Hard?* (New York: St. Martin's, 2000), pp. xi, xxv.

334   **"puffy eyes"; "answer mecca"**: Gary Ezzo and Robert Bucknam, *On Becoming Preteen Wise: Parenting Your Child from Eight to Twelve Years Old* (Sisters, OR: Multnomah, 2000), p. 11.

335   **"authoritative parenting" to "permissive parenting"**: See Diana Baumrind, "Rearing Competent Children," in William Damon, ed., *Child Development Today and Tomorrow* (San Francisco: Jossey-Bass, 1989), pp. 349–78. This typology of parenthood became popular in child development circles—and beyond—thanks to Baumrind's studies dating back to the mid-1960s, which linked high levels of parental "responsiveness" *and* "demandingness" to measures of "optimal competence" in children.

335   **"Disciplinary activity"; "One must *dare to discipline*"**: Dr. James Dobson, *The New Dare to Discipline* (Wheaton, IL: Tyndale, 1992), pp. 6, 7.

335   **"May all doubts"**: ibid., p. 12.

335   **"The principles in this book"**: ibid., p. 34.

335   **"epidemic of inferiority"**: Dr. James Dobson, *Hide or Seek* (Old Tappan, NJ: Revell, 1979), p. 173.

335   **"authoritarian household" to "child who is bitter"**: Ezzo, *Growing Kids God's Way*, pp. 180, 45, 312.

335   **"benevolent dictatorship" to "encourage discussion"**: Rosemond, *John Rose-*

mond's Six-Point Plan for Raising Happy, Healthy Children (Kansas City, MO: Andrews McMeel, 1989), p. 48.

335 **"goal is not to make the child"**: Rosemond, *A Family of Value*, p. 171.

336 **feeling good is not the precursor**: Gary Ezzo and Robert Bucknam, *On Becoming Teenwise* (Sisters, OR: Multnomah, 2000), p. 34.

336 **"a nightmare"**: T. Berry Brazelton, *What Every Baby Knows* (Reading, MA: Addison-Wesley, 1987), p. 63.

336 **"abdication of parental responsibility"**: T. Berry Brazelton, *To Listen to a Child: Understanding the Normal Problems of Growing Up* (Reading, MA: Addison-Wesley, 1984), p. 82.

336 **"frightened of themselves"**: Brazelton, *What Every Baby Knows*, pp. 63–64.

336 **"the enormous power of frustration"**: T. Berry Brazelton, *Touchpoints: Your Child's Emotional and Behavioral Development* (Reading, MA: Addison-Wesley, 1992), p. 364.

336 **"won't be easy," to "Understand that your children"**: Stanley I. Greenspan with Nancy Thorndike Greenspan, *The Essential Partnership: How Parents and Children Can Meet the Emotional Challenges of Infancy and Childhood* (New York: Viking, 1989), pp. 146, 57, 171.

336 **"morally responsible child"**: Gary Ezzo and Robert Bucknam, *On Becoming Babywise, Book Two* (Sisters, OR: Multnomah, 1995), p. 10.

336 **"respectful, responsible young citizens"; "honesty, truthfulness, and unselfishness"**: Dobson, *The New Dare to Discipline*, p. 15.

336 **"human beings . . . able to work cooperatively"**: Brazelton and Greenspan, *The Irreducible Needs of Children*, p. xix.

337 **"healthy minds"**: Stanley I. Greenspan with Nancy Breslau Lewis, *Building Healthy Minds: The Six Experiences That Create Intelligence and Emotional Growth in Babies and Young Children* (Cambridge, MA: Perseus, 1999).

337 **"Oh yes"**: Dr. James Dobson, *Temper Your Child's Tantrums* (Wheaton, IL: Tyndale, 1986), p. 6.

337 **"well-designed model or 'game plan' "**: ibid., p. 7.

337 **total quality management:** John Micklethwait and Adrian Wooldridge, *The Witch Doctors: Making Sense of the Management Gurus* (New York: Times Books, 1996), pp. 247, 280. See also Leon Wieseltier, "Total Quality Meaning," *The New Republic* 209, nos. 3 and 4 (July 19 and 26, 1993): 16–26.

337 **"strong culture"**: Gideon Kunda, *Engineering Culture: Control and Commitment in a High-Tech Corporation* (Philadelphia: Temple University Press, 1992), p. 9.

337 **"world's most influential management thinker"**: "Confessor to the Boardroom," *The Economist*, Feb. 24, 1996, p. 74.

338 **" 'motherly' work culture"**: Arlie Russell Hochschild, *The Time Bind: When Work Becomes Home and Home Becomes Work* (New York: Metropolitan, 1997), p. 20.

338 **"managed values"; "common vision"**: ibid., pp. 17–18.

338 **"an absolute natural. It fits"**: Stephen R. Covey, *The 7 Habits of Highly Effective Families* (New York: Golden Books, 1997), p. 2.

338 **"7 Habits material"**: ibid.

338 **"total quality management for the character"**: "Confessor to the Boardroom," p. 74.

339 **sold two million copies:** Adele Faber and Elaine Mazlish, *How to Talk So Kids Will Listen & Listen So Kids Will Talk* (New York: Avon, 20th anniversary edition, 1999), cover.

339 **"learning organization"**: Micklethwait and Wooldridge, *The Witch Doctors*, p. 124.

339 **"family flight plan"; "principles of mutual respect"**: Covey, *The 7 Habits of Highly Effective Families*, pp. 9, 171.

339 **"empathic listening"**: Covey, *The 7 Habits of Highly Effective Families*, p. 223.

339 **"turbulent world"**: ibid., subtitle.

339 **"spiritual renewal"; "worshiping together"**: ibid., pp. 279, 299.

339 **"from 'me' to 'we' "**: ibid., p. 20.

339 **"You are your children's"**: ibid., p. 335.

340 **"you care about them"**: ibid., p. 329.

340 **"without any moral evaluation"**: ibid., p. 13.

340 **"the feeling, the 'vibes' "**: ibid., p. 20.

340 **"Every family problem"**: ibid., p. 64.

340 **"four 'cancers' "**: ibid., p. 261.

340 **"like developing a muscle"**: ibid., p. 36.

340 **"creative force"; "an agent of change"**: ibid., pp. 18 ff., 15.

341 **"turbulent, family-unfriendly"**: ibid., p. 16.

341 **"Run, share"**: Stephen R. Covey, *Loving Reminders for Kids: 60 Nurturing Notes and 60 Stickers* (Salt Lake City: Franklin Covey Company, 1998).

341 **sales of *The 7 Habits***: telephone calls to Franklin Covey Company, April 2002 and January 2003.

341 **soon passing the quarter-million mark**: Rosin, "A Tough Plan for Raising Children Draws Fire," p. 1.

341 **"moral training"**: Ezzo and Bucknam, *On Becoming Babywise, Book Two*, p. 85.

341 **"healthy intellectual,"**: Greenspan, *Building Healthy Minds*, p. 7.

342 **"enabling all the members"**: ibid.

342 **"can't sit back"**: Gary Ezzo and Robert Bucknam, *On Becoming Childwise* (Sisters, OR: Multnomah, 1999), p. 63.

342 **"facilitating a child's nature"**: Ezzo, *Growing Kids God's Way*, pp. 307–308.

342 **"willful defiance"**: Dobson, *Hide or Seek*, p. 93.

342 **How 100,000 New Parents**: Gary Ezzo and Robert Bucknam, *On Becoming Babywise* (Sisters, OR: Multnomah, 1995), subtitle.

343 **"an infant-management strategy" to "hunger cues"**: ibid., pp. 32–39.

343 **"love, caring"; "legalistic"**: ibid., pp. 41, 104.

343 **"role in the family"**: ibid., p. 23.

343 **"metabolic confusion" to "negatively impact"**: ibid., pp. 43–53.

344 **"religiously insist"**: Growing Families International Web site, www.gfi.org/java/art_CL_PDF.jsp.

344 **"I've never attacked it"**: Dr. James Dobson, transcript of brief remarks, www.ezzo.info.

344 **"moral model"**: Ezzo and Bucknam, *On Becoming Babywise, Book Two*, p. 9.

344 **"self-control training"; "delivers the whole package"**: ibid., pp. 56, 68.

344 **"Highchair manners" to "light swats"**: ibid., pp. 55–60.

345 **"stage-acquired activities"; "moral developmental skills"**: ibid., p. 31.

345 **"a better way"**: Ezzo, *Growing Kids God's Way*, p. 27.

345 **"playpen time" to "free playtime"**: ibid., pp. 71–79.

345 **"nestling"**: ibid., p. 78.

345 **"flirting with your baby"; "your baby does not need"**: Ezzo and Bucknam, *On Becoming Babywise*, pp. 116–17.

345 **"reaching the heart"**: Gary and Anne Marie Ezzo, *Reaching the Heart of Your*

Teen: Basics of Communication Between Parent and Teenager (Sisters, OR: Multnomah, 1997).

345 "relational goal": Ezzo, Growing Kids God's Way, p. 131.

345 "ultimate responsibility": ibid., p. 11.

346 "heart training" to "otherness appreciation": Ezzo and Bucknam, On Becoming
Childwise, pp. 114, 64.

346 "when willful defiance": Dobson, Hide or Seek, p. 93.

346 "Childwise will not address": Ezzo and Bucknam, On Becoming Childwise, p. 214.

346 "from authority to influence": Ezzo and Bucknam, On Becoming Preteen Wise,
p. 63.

346 "pre-loaded": ibid., p. 119.

346 "willful desire to overthrow": ibid., p. 26.

346 "family think"; "power of groupthink": ibid., p. 149.

346 "active part of the management team"; "encourager of the family": Ezzo,
Growing Kids God's Way, pp. 90, 95.

346 "healthy, proactive communication": Ezzo, Reaching the Heart of Your Teen,
p. 149.

346 "communication has become": ibid., p. 140.

346 "couch time": Ezzo and Bucknam, On Becoming Preteen Wise, p. 169.

346 "primary love languages": Ezzo and Bucknam, On Becoming Teenwise, p. 137.

346 "the sex talk": Ezzo and Bucknam, On Becoming Preteen Wise, p. 197.

347 "aggressive sex-ed": Dobson and Bauer, Children at Risk, p. 61.

347 "keep your son's sexuality"; "the awkward stiffness": Ezzo and Bucknam, On
Becoming Preteen Wise, p. 201.

347 "self-control with purpose": ibid., p. 203.

347 "Adolescence is a time": Ezzo and Bucknam, On Becoming Teenwise, p. 32.

347 "heartburn and indigestion"; "Christian parents": Dobson, Hide or Seek, pp.
118, 111.

347 "moral community": Ezzo and Bucknam, On Becoming Teenwise, p. 44.

347 too "radical"; "courtship" concept: ibid., p. 171.

347 "Bounding" rather than "bridging": Karen Springen, "Raising a Moral Child,"
Newsweek 136, no. 17A (Fall/Winter 2000): 73.

347 "invested in the stock"; "consult the state": Ezzo and Bucknam, Reaching the
Heart of Your Teen, p. 98.

347 "the essential partnership": Greenspan, The Essential Partnership.

348 "a good play partner": Greenspan, Building Healthy Minds, p. 281.

348 "A playful exchange of meows": ibid., p. 154.

348 "rich, ongoing interaction"; "loving compassion and caring": ibid., p. 57.

348 "child's sense of morality": ibid., p. 56.

348 "intellectual, social, and emotional": ibid., p. 64.

348 "the beginning of character": ibid., p. 176.

348 "help your child learn": Greenspan, The Essential Partnership, p. 1.

348 "meant to be a rigid": Greenspan, Playground Politics, p. 299.

348 Greenspan had embarked: See Natalie Wexler, "Beyond Quality Time," Washington Post Magazine, March 24, 1996, pp. 18–34.

349 "theory-building": Stanley I. Greenspan, Intelligence and Adaptation: An Integration of Psychoanalytic and Piagetian Developmental Psychology (New York: International Universities Press, 1979), p. 134.

349 "road map"; "emotional thinking": Greenspan, Playground Politics, pp. xiii, 23.

349 "reason about feelings": Greenspan, The Essential Partnership, p. 32.

349 **"build bridges"**: Greenspan, *Playground Politics*, p. 23.

349 **"ability to reflect"**: Greenspan, *Building Healthy Minds*, p. 273.

349 **"five principles of healthy parenting"**: Greenspan, *Playground Politics*, p. 25.

350 **"one-on-one bonding time"**: Covey, *The 7 Habits of Highly Effective Families*, p. 18.

350 **"secular therapists"; "facilitating a child's nature"**: Ezzo, *Growing Kids God's Way*, p. 302.

350 **"regulate her impulses"**: Stanley I. Greenspan and Nancy Thorndike Greenspan, *First Feelings: Milestones in the Emotional Development of Your Baby and Child* (New York: Viking, 1985), p. 181.

350 **"Functional Developmental Growth Chart"**: Greenspan, *Building Healthy Minds*, p. 374.

350 **"ability to look, listen"**: Greenspan, *Playground Politics*, p. 17.

350 **"falling in love"**: Greenspan, *Building Healthy Minds*, chap. 2, pp. 49–82.

350 **"two-way communicator"**: ibid., chap. 3, pp. 85–129.

351 **"solving problems"**: ibid., chap. 4, pp. 131–98.

351 **"She is not just sitting"**: Greenspan, *The Essential Partnership*, p. 25.

351 **"your job is to let" to "complicated social, emotional"**: Greenspan, *Building Healthy Minds*, p. 169.

351 **"circle of communication"**: ibid., p. 333.

351 **"being a creative and logical thinker"; "become empathic"**: ibid., p. 96.

351 **"command voice"**: Ezzo and Bucknam, *On Becoming Babywise, Book Two*, p. 92.

351 **"to think of yourself"**: Greenspan, *Building Healthy Minds*, p. 160.

351 **"collaborator in exploring the world"**: ibid., p. 256.

352 **"your child . . . gradually"**: Greenspan, *Playground Politics*, p. 44.

352 **"find out what is going on"; "open-window moments"**: Ezzo and Bucknam, *On Becoming Preteen Wise*, pp. 187, 168.

352 **"a stable sense of self"**: Greenspan, *Playground Politics*, p. 270.

352 **"*Give more, and expect more*"**: Greenspan, *Building Healthy Minds*, p. 364.

352 **"four-thirds solution"**: ibid., p. 365. And see Stanley I. Greenspan with Jacqueline Salmon, *The Four-Thirds Solution: Solving the Child-Care Crisis in America Today* (Cambridge, MA: Perseus, 2001).

353 **"If parents try"**: Brazelton and Greenspan, *The Irreducible Needs of Children*, p. 13.

353 **"the fact is"**: Benjamin Spock, *Dr. Spock Talks with Mothers: Growth and Guidance* (Boston: Houghton Mifflin, 1961), pp. 121–22.

353 **"at a minimum . . . four 20-minute"; "breaks for facilitating"**: Brazelton and Greenspan, *The Irreducible Needs of Children*, p. 41.

353 **"the completely independent time"; "seamless back-and-forth manner"**: ibid., pp. 41, 43.

353 **"key interaction and attention"**: Greenspan, *Building Healthy Minds*, p. 365.

353 **"too much time in the independent mode"**: Brazelton and Greenspan, *The Irreducible Needs of Children*, p. 45.

353 **"the capabilities necessary"**: Stanley I. Greenspan with Beryl Lieff Benderly, *The Growth of the Mind and the Endangered Origins of Intelligence* (Reading, MA: Addison-Wesley, 1997), pp. 193–95.

354 **"interrupt courtesy"**: Ezzo and Bucknam, *On Becoming Childwise*, p. 99.

354 **"the heart and the gut"**: Rosemond, *John Rosemond's Six-Point Plan*, p. 2.

355 **"eight baby Bs"**: William Sears and Martha Sears, *The Growing Years* (Nashville: Nelson, 1998), p. ix.

355 **"one big give-a-thon"; "feel right"**: ibid., pp. xi, 42.

355 **"amateur psychologists"**: ibid., p. 57.

355 **"a high-touch style of parenting"**: William Sears and Martha Sears, *The Baby Book: Everything You Need to Know About Your Baby—from Birth to Age Two* (Boston: Little, Brown, 1993), p. xiii.

355 **"God's design"**: Sears, *The Growing Years*, preface, p. xx.

355 **"ministry of parenting"**: William Sears and Martha Sears, *The Ministry of Parenting Your Baby* (Elgin, IL: LifeJourney Books, 1990).

355 **"finely tuned communication network"**: Sears, *The Growing Years*, p. 46.

355 bluntly titled *The Discipline Book*: William Sears and Martha Sears, *The Discipline Book: Everything You Need to Know to Have a Better-Behaved Child—from Birth to Age Ten* (Boston: Little, Brown, 1995).

355 **"little patients"**: www.askdrsears.com/aboutdrsears.asp.

355 **"God's matching program"; "His law of supply and demand"**: Sears, *The Growing Years*, p. ix.

355 **"warm fuzzy"**: William Sears, *Nighttime Parenting: How to Get Your Baby and Child to Sleep* (Schaumburg, IL: La Leche League International, 1999), p. 128.

355 **"the busy life-styles"**: Sears, *The Baby Book*, p. xiii.

355 **"no two families"**: "Welcome to Attachment Parenting Answers!" on the Web, www.ivillage.com.

355 *"World's Funniest Psychologist"*: Rosemond, *Because I Said So!*, p. vii.

356 **"zany entrepreneur"**: Micklethwait and Wooldridge, *The Witch Doctors*, p. 90.

356 **"the process of value shaping"**: Thomas Peters and Robert Waterman, *In Search of Excellence* (New York: Harper & Row, 1982), p. 280.

356 **"provide the opportunity to stick out"**: ibid., p. 81.

356 **"loud times and lots of screw-ups"**: Micklethwait and Wooldridge, *The Witch Doctors*, p. 80.

356 **"management by walking around" to "Parents of this sort"**: Rosemond, *John Rosemond's Six-Point Plan*, p. 95.

356 **"proprietary view of herself as a parent"; "parenting aide"**: Rosemond, *A Family of Value*, p. 34.

356 **"relatively easy and enjoyable"**: Rosemond, *John Rosemond's Six-Point Plan*, p. 2.

357 **"not always fun"**: ibid., p. 4.

357 **"Childrearing—or *parenting*"**: ibid., p. 2.

357 **"realistic, pragmatic, and hard-headed"**: ibid., p. 3.

357 **"demanding, disobedient"; "frustrated, anxious"**: Rosemond, *A Family of Value*, p. 39.

357 **"trial-and-error"**: Rosemond, *John Rosemond's Six-Point Plan*, p. 2.

357 **"pot-addled excesses"; "some family dysfunction"**: John Rosemond, *Teen-Proofing: A Revolutionary Approach to Fostering Responsible Decision Making in Your Teenager* (Kansas City, MO: Andrews McMeel, 1998), p. 14.

357 **"the most invidious family dysfunction"**: Rosemond, *A Family of Value*, p. 71.

357 **"tendency of adults"**: ibid., p. 150.

357 **"God Almighty Syndrome"**: Rosemond, *Teen-Proofing*, p. 9.

357 **"conservatives believe"**: Rosemond, *A Family of Value*, p. 181.

358 **"given every reason to believe"**: ibid., p. 133.

358 **"less and less as time goes on"**: ibid., p. 125.

358 **"what psychologists deem best"**: ibid., p. 141.

358 **"the more free they were"**: ibid., p. 146.

358 **"three Rs"; "resourcefulness"**: ibid., p. 18.

358 **"the intellectual rhetoric"**: Rosemond, *John Rosemond's Six-Point Plan*, p. 12.

358 **"that's a psychology word"**: Rosemond, *A Family of Value*, p. 272.

358 **"The problem, as I see it"**: ibid., p. 162.

358 **"Be commanding"**: Rosemond, *John Rosemond's Six-Point Plan*, p. 49ff.

359 **"the many basic skills"**: ibid., p. 166.

359 **"supportive non-interference"**: ibid., p. 8.

359 **"The purpose of raising children"**: ibid., p. 12.

359 **"unliberated Moms"**: Rosemond, *A Family of Value*, p. 30.

359 **"Women have been encouraged"; "Female parents in our culture"**: ibid., p. 285.

EPILOGUE: *What to Expect from the Experts*

360 **"Am I proposing"**: Heidi Murkoff, "The Real Parenting Expert Is . . . You," *Newsweek* 136, no. 17A (Fall/Winter 2000): 21.

361 **"mother love [had walked]"**: Mrs. W. H. Felton, "Heredity," National Congress of Mothers First Session, Feb. 17–19, 1897, p. 184.

361 **"Given one generation"**: *New York Times*, Feb. 21, 1897, collected in Rothman, *The Family*, p. 56.

362 **"an industry of seminars"**: George Kalogerakis, "The 60-Day Plan to Perfect Parenting," *offspring*, June/July 2000, p. 5.

362 **"plethora of advice"**: Murkoff, "The Real Parenting Expert," p. 20.

363 **"Mothers Can't Win"**: *New York Times Magazine*, Apr. 5, 1998.

363 **"assault on parenthood"; "war against parents"**: See Dana Mack, *The Assault on Parenthood: How Our Culture Undermines the Family* (New York: Simon & Schuster, 1997), and Sylvia Ann Hewlett and Cornel West, *The War Against Parents: What We Can Do for America's Beleaguered Moms and Dads* (Boston: Houghton Mifflin, 1998).

363 **"the Age of the Imperiled Child"**: Michael Chabon in "Breakfast Table" discussion in *Slate*, Jan. 28, 2001.

363 **"the figure of the child"**: Barbara Ehrenreich and Deirdre English, *For Her Own Good: 150 Years of the Experts' Advice to Women* (Garden City, NY: Anchor, 1978), p. 189.

363 **"Far from it"**: Murkoff, "The Real Parenting Expert," p. 21.

363 **"trusts a mother's instincts"**: Arlene Eisenberg, Heidi E. Murkoff, and Sandee Eisenberg Hathaway, *What to Expect the First Year* (New York: Workman, 1989), p. xxiv.

363 **"Parenting Pendulum Swings"**: Murkoff, "The Real Parenting Expert," p. 21.

364 **"more advanced" generation**: Eisenberg et al., *What to Expect the First Year*, p. xxi.

364 **"look at a child-rearing expert"; "perfectly okay"**: Marge Kennedy, "Should You Spank? And Nine Other Really Tough Questions," *Ladies' Home Journal* 114, no. 2 (February 1997): 84.

364 **"no philosophy"**: Benjamin Spock, typescript of "Self-Regulation, Spoiling and Sleep Problems," paper read at a meeting of the American Academy of Pediatrics, Milwaukee, WI, June 1948, pp. 25–26, Benjamin Spock Papers.

366 **"two women who in actual practice"**: Benjamin Spock, *Problems of Parents* (Boston: Houghton Mifflin, 1962), p. 22.

368 **"We wish *someone*"**: Alison Gopnik, Andrew N. Meltzoff, and Patricia K. Kuhl, *The Scientist in the Crib: Minds, Brains, and How Children Learn* (New York: Morrow, 1999), p. 200.

368 **"a bouquet of advice books"; "The underlying message"**: Susan Chira, "Still Guilty After All These Years: A Bouquet of Advice Books for the Working Mom," *New York Times Book Review*, May 8, 1994, p. 11.

368 **"pal-parents" to "one of my personal heroes"**: Dr. Laura Schlessinger, *Parenthood by Proxy: Don't Have Them If You Won't Raise Them* (New York: Cliff Street Books, 2000), pp. 159, 160, 94.

369 **"most unliberated generation"**: Beth Brophy, "Because I Said So!" *U.S. News & World Report* 123, no. 18 (Nov. 10, 1997): 70.

369 **"creatively selfish"**: John Rosemond, *John Rosemond's Six-Point Plan for Raising Happy, Healthy Children* (Kansas City, MO: Andrews McMeel, 1989), p. 24.

369 **"househusband" and "housechildren"**: Viviana A. Zelizer, *Pricing the Priceless Child: The Changing Social Value of Children* (Princeton: Princeton University Press, 1999), p. 223.

369 **"a liberal, a feminist"**: Susan Bolotin, "The Disciples of Discipline," *New York Times Magazine*, Feb. 14, 1999, pp. 35–36.

369 **"Somewhere along the line"**: ibid., p. 37.

370 **"that your kids"**: ibid.

370 **"frantically gung-ho"; "subtle Rosemond-inspired shifts"**: ibid., p. 36.

370 **"relying on books"**: John Rosemond, *A Family of Value* (Kansas City, MO: Andrews McMeel, 1995), p. 172.

370 **"these ages . . . are almost the last"**: T. Berry Brazelton, *Toddlers and Parents: A Declaration of Independence* (New York: Delacorte, 1974), p. xii.

ACKNOWLEDGMENTS

Books entail even more labor than children do, and authors require even more support and guidance than parents do, or so at least I have discovered. I owe many thanks to many people and institutions for their help over the years I worked on this project.

I could not have begun it without the good luck of receiving a fellowship from the John Simon Guggenheim Foundation. A year spent in a room in a high tower of the Smithsonian castle as a fellow at the Woodrow Wilson Center for International Scholars helped me get my bearings.

I went on to do a good deal of burrowing, and I'm grateful to various libraries and archives for making their collections of fascinating papers available. I have quoted from the G. Stanley Hall Papers by permission of the Clark University Archives of the Robert Hutchings Goddard Library. I would like to thank Eleanor Rutledge Holt for permission to use the L. Emmett Holt material housed in the New York University Medical Archives. The Rockefeller Archive Center granted me permission to cite documents from its collection of Holt material and records of the Laura Spelman Rockefeller Memorial Foundation.

The Library of Congress was a mainstay in my research. Thanks to Bruce Martin, I had office space there as long as I needed it. I also spent time in the library's manuscript division. Katherine Walden kindly granted permission to consult the Arnold L. Gesell Papers, and I owe thanks to Rex Walden in her stead for letting me quote from them, as well as to Peggy Gesell for permission to cite her wonderful letters in the collection.

I consulted the much smaller collection of John B. Watson material at the Library of Congress, too, and quoted from some of it by permission of his grandson, James S. Watson. I'm grateful to Dr. Charles Brewer for directing me to letters from the Cedric Larson/John Watson Papers in the Archives of the History of American Psychology. The reminiscences of Watson's son James B. Watson were especially helpful. I'm sorry I didn't have a chance to thank him adequately before he died.

I hope Dr. Spock was aware of how invaluable the time and help that he gave me before his death were for my work. His wife Mary Morgan shared her memories, and was ready with whatever assistance I needed. She warmly granted me access to all the material housed in the Benjamin Spock Papers at the Syracuse University Library and gave me permission to quote from it.

Dr. Milton J. E. Senn's Oral History of the Child Development Movement in the United States, at the National Library of Medicine at the National Institutes of Health, has been an important resource. I'm grateful to Steven L. Schlossman for calling it to my attention early on in my research.

I owe the original inspiration for this book to Nick Lemann, who also read an early version of early chapters. Mike Kinsley invited me to be a contributor to *Slate* as I launched the project; Judith Shulevitz was the ideal editor there, and saw to it that much of the writing I did also helped me in thinking about the book. Dorothy Wickenden signed me up to do an essay for *The New Yorker* about Dr. Spock that set me on my way. Jay Tolson not only published a version of the first chapter in *The Wilson Quarterly*, but urged me onward and read through a later draft of the whole, offering incisive guidance as I revised. Alan Wolfe read several of my later chapters toward the end of my work. Luke Menand went through the entire manuscript and was the honest and clear-eyed critic no writer can afford to be without. Margaret Talbot gave me just what I needed when I needed it most: fruitful conversation about children and experts, and about chapters as they were gelling, and then a close and enthusiastic reading of the whole. Without Mary Jo Salter, I would not have been able to write this book. She was once again the friend and loyal reader whose acute thoughts and comments every step of the way helped to steer me and, more than once, rescue me. Many thanks also to my patient agent Rafe Sagalyn. And to Ann Close, an editor who never made me feel like a burdensome writer even when I was one, I owe great gratitude. I could not have written this the way I have without her as a guide and a guardian, making sure I had the time and counsel I needed. Ilana Kurshan supplied welcome assistance at the end.

I owe the hugest of debts to my husband, Steve Sestanovich. This book turned out to be one I could not gestate and rear without him by my side offering encouragement and insight. My astute and tireless in-house editor, he was ready morning, noon, and night to help, especially at the end. Our children, Ben and Clare, have grown far more rapidly than these pages did and have been a constant source of inspiration. I could not have asked for more than the awe and pleasure of watching the two of them become who they are.

PHOTO CREDITS

*Grateful acknowledgment is made to the following for
permission to reprint the photographs that appear in this book.*

Bettman/CORBIS
    p. 256: Dr. Bruno Bettelheim, © Bettmann/CORBIS

Charles A. Nelson Lab, Univeristy of Minnesota
    p. 293: Studying the infant brain

Frederick Gutekunst, U.S. National Library of Medicine
    p. 41: Dr. G. Stanley Hall

Harris & Ewing, U.S. National Library of Medicine
    p. 154: Dr. Arnold Gesell

Library of Congress, Prints & Photographs Division
    p. 19: Our Baby Congress, 1898, © A. W. McCausland and A. T.
        Reynolds
    p. 63: Lesson in the care of children, c. 1910
    p. 97: The Better Babies Contest, 1931
    p. 191: High school class in family living, 1950, Carl Iwasaki/TIMEPIX
    p. 256: Dr. Benjamin Spock, *U.S. News & World Report* Magazine
        Collection

Mary Morgan
    p. 225: Dr. Benjamin Spock with his son Michael

Sam Ogden Photography
    p. 325: Dr. T. Berry Brazelton and a young patient

Underwood & Underwood/CORBIS
    p. 122: Dr. John B. Watson, © Underwood & Underwood/CORBIS

PERMISSIONS ACKNOWLEDGMENTS

*Grateful acknowledgment is made to the following
for permission to reprint previously published material:*

HarperCollins Publishers Inc.: Excerpts from *Infant and Child in the Culture of Today* by Arnold Gesell and Frances L. Ilg. Copyright © 1943 by Arnold Gesell and Frances L. Ilg; renewed © 1971 by Frances L. Ilg, Gerhard Gesell, and Katherine Gesell Walden. Excerpts from *Personality in the Making* edited by Helen Leland Witmer and Ruth Kotinsky. Copyright © 1952 by Harper & Brothers; renewed © 1980 by T. Richard Witmer. Reprinted by permission of HarperCollins Publishers Inc.

Josiah Macy, Jr. Foundation: Excerpts from *Symposium on the Healthy Personality: Transactions for Special Meeting of the Conference on Infancy and Childhood* edited by Milton J. E. Senn. Reprinted by permission of the Josiah Macy, Jr. Foundation.

Ladies' Home Journal: Excerpt from "What's Happening to the Family" by Bruno Bettelheim (*Ladies' Home Journal*, May 1971). Copyright © May 1971 by Meredith Corporation. All rights reserved. Reprinted by permission of the *Ladies' Home Journal*.

Lescher & Lescher and Pocket Books: Excerpts from *Dr. Spock's Baby and Child Care* by Benjamin Spock, M.D., and Steven J. Parker, M.D. Copyright © 1945, 1946, 1957, 1968, 1976, 1985, 1992 by Benjamin Spock, M.D. Copyright renewed © 1973, 1974, 1985, 1996 by Benjamin Spock, M.D. Revised and updated material copyright © 1998 by The Benjamin Spock Trust. Reprinted by permission of Lescher & Lescher and Pocket Books, an imprint of Simon & Schuster Adult Publishing Group.

The New York Times: Excerpts from "Modern Parenthood" an editorial (*The New York Times*, November 1, 1925). Copyright © 1925 by The New York Times Agency. Excerpts from "Rearing of Children Becoming a Silence" by Evans Clark (*The New York Times*, November 1, 1925). Copyright © 1925 by The New York Times Agency. Reprinted by permission of The New York Times.

W. W. Norton & Company, Inc.: Excerpts from *Psychological Care of Infant and Child* by John B. Watson. Copyright 1928 by W. W. Norton & Company, Inc. Reprinted by permission of W. W. Norton & Company, Inc.

William Morris Agency, Inc.: Excerpt from "Fathers" by Alice Munro. Copyright © 2002 by Alice Munro. Reprinted by permission of William Morris Agency, Inc. on behalf of the author.

INDEX

Page numbers in *italics* indicate photographs.